SOCIAL STATISTICS

SOCIAL STATISTICS

An Introduction Using SPSS® for Windows®

J. Richard Kendrick, Jr.
State University of New York College at Cortland

Mayfield Publishing Company
Mountain View, California
London • Toronto

Library of Congress Cataloging-in-Publication Data

Kendrick, J. Richard.
   Social statistics : an introduction using SPSS for Windows / J. Richard Kendrick.
     p. cm.
   Includes index.
   ISBN 0-7674-1001-7
   1. SPSS for Windows. 2. Social sciences--Statistical methods. I. Title.

  HA32 .K46 2000
  300'.285'5369--dc21   99-054594

Manufactured in the United States of America
10   9   8   7   6   5   4   3   2   1

Mayfield Publishing Company
1280 Villa Street
Mountain View, California 94041

Sponsoring editor, Serina Beauparlant; *production editor,* Linda Ward; *manuscript
editor,* Helen Walden; *design manager,* Susan Breitbard; *art editor,* Robin Mouat;
text designer, Richard Kharibian; *cover designer,* Laurie Anderson; *illustrator,*
Lotus Art; *photo researcher,* Brian Pecko; *manufacturing manager,* Randy Hurst.
The text was set in 11/13 Times by Carlisle Communications and printed on 45#
Highland Plus by R. R. Donnelley & Sons Company.

Cover photo: © 1997 Associated Press AP/Richard Drew.

Text credits appear on page 631, which constitutes an extension of the copyright
page.

 This book is printed on acid-free, recycled paper.

To Marcia, Ben, Hope, and Tim

Preface

As you begin looking over this text, you are probably wondering why someone would undertake to write yet another statistics book. I have asked myself
this question often, but the answer is simple. I have been teaching an Introduction to Statistics course to sociology and anthropology undergraduates for
the past eight years, and I am always looking for—but not often finding—
ways to help students master course material they approach with a great deal
of trepidation. Many are fearful of the mathematical content and uncertain
about their ability to do the computer work that is a part of the course. On the
other hand, most students have at least an inkling that the skills learned *might*
be useful in their daily lives and careers, if only they knew how to apply them
and make sense of the results.

With these considerations in mind, I thought that the ideal statistics text
for reaching the students in my classes would meet four goals:

- Make the mathematical content clear and accessible
- Build confidence in the manual computations of statistics and the
  computer skills for performing the same functions
- Help students understand how to apply statistics
- Develop skills for the interpretation of statistics

At the same time, the book would not sacrifice conceptual understanding—
there would be as much "why" as "how to." Does this text "walk the walk"?
I think it does, by incorporating a number of unique features.

INTERACTIVE PEDAGOGY

The text includes built-in opportunities for students to test their conceptual
understanding and practice the mathematical skills as they are introduced. In

addition, I show students how to evaluate their own work and I try to clear up common misconceptions.

- Concepts and computations are introduced in manageable segments. Each segment is followed by relevant examples to work in "Skills Practices" sections. Students can check their answers against the answers to the "Skills Practices" found at the end of each chapter. The answers to the "Skills Practices" are followed by additional problem sets, and the answers to the odd-numbered problems in these additional practice sets are included at the back of the text.

- Students are shown how to evaluate their work in the "Checking Your Work" sections.

- I try to anticipate the ways students often get stuck or confused—and offer tips about how to get unstuck—in the "Avoiding Common Pitfalls" sections.

STRONGER INTEGRATION OF SPSS

The text integrates learning statistical concepts with learning about the General Social Survey (GSS) and an up-to-date version of the Statistical Product and Service Solutions (SPSS) computer software program for the analysis of quantitative data. Explanations of statistical concepts are woven into the examples students use to perform the SPSS functions with a subset of variables from the 1996 General Social Survey.

- There are many opportunities to practice the computational skills for statistics, both manually and using the computer. The book integrates manual computations with instructions for using SPSS to do statistical computations.

- The text shows students how to set up data in SPSS. Most texts assume the existence of databases. These databases are helpful for showing students how to apply and interpret statistics, but students should also know how the data got there to begin with.

- There is greater consistency in this text between manual computations of statistics and SPSS computations. Whereas some texts already attempt to integrate manual and computer computations, their formulas for manual computations are not always consistent with the formulas SPSS uses for the same statistic. As a result, these texts don't take advantage of the ability to create practice problems using SPSS.

- SPSS basics are highlighted in each chapter as clearly delineated "SPSS Guides." Advanced SPSS features are covered in an appendix, "Bells and Whistles," so students can learn some of the ins and outs of the program.

Although the text is based in SPSS version 9.0, the differences (at least for the statistics students learn in a first course) from previous versions are minimal. For example, the main differences between versions 8.0 and 9.0 are that the Statistics menu item has been replaced by the Analyze menu item, and the Summarize drop-down menu item has been replaced by Descriptive Statistics. As a result, the command path for finding many of the most commonly used descriptive and inferential statistics is different. In version 8.0, to obtain a frequency distribution and related statistics you followed the command path Statistics ➡ Summarize ➡ Frequencies. In version 9.0, the command path is Analyze ➡ Descriptive Statistics ➡ Frequencies. Similarly, contingency tables were found previously with the command path Statistics ➡ Summarize ➡ Crosstabs. Now you use Analyze ➡ Descriptive Statistics ➡ Crosstabs. Whereas version 8.0 placed the reporting features of SPSS under the Summarize drop-down menu item, version 9.0 places them directly under Analyze as the drop-down item Reports. The output you receive as a result of executing these commands is substantially the same.

INCREASED EMPHASIS ON THE APPLICATION AND INTERPRETATION OF STATISTICS

I find that most students can do the relatively simple mathematics and execute the computer commands necessary for the computation of introductory statistics. Students experience more difficulty with explaining what their results mean. As a result, I give more attention to the interpretation and analysis of statistics.

- There are a number of "News to Use" sections—examples of research from newspapers, magazines, and the Internet. These sections demonstrate how statistics are used in everyday life and, at the same time, provide models for the analysis and interpretation of data. The models are then applied to relevant variables extracted from the General Social Survey for 1996.

- Each chapter is oriented to a question or set of questions that the statistics help answer.

- Examples show students how statistics are interpreted. They are followed by opportunities for students to practice their own analytical skills.

- A codebook for the GSS variables is included as an appendix so students can better understand the data they will be interpreting.

INSTRUCTOR'S MANUAL AND DATA DISK

Along with the text, instructors receive a Data Disk containing a subset of the 1996 GSS variables. This data disk can be made available through your computer labs to students or you can copy it for students. An Instructor's Manual is also available that contains answers to the even-numbered problems at the end of each chapter, shows instructors how to create practice problems with answers using SPSS, and explains how to download GSS data from the Internet.

ACKNOWLEDGMENTS

The composition of any text is a daunting task. This text would not have been possible without the support of the many people who helped out along the way. First and foremost, I would never have undertaken to write this text or seen it through to its completion were it not for the support and vision of Serina Beauparlant, Senior Editor. I would also like to thank the following people for their help.

- The reviewers: Peter Brandon, University of Massachusetts; John R. Dugan, Central Washington University; Susan Eve, University of North Texas; Marilyn Fernandez, Santa Clara University; Lisa M. Frehill, New Mexico State University; A. Leigh Ingram, University of Colorado at Denver; Max Kashefi, Eastern Illinois University; Debra S. Kelley, Longwood College; Rhoda Estep Macdonald, California State University at Stanislaus; Randall MacIntosh, California State University at Sacramento; David Mitchell, University of North Carolina at Greensboro; Melanie Moore, University of North Colorado; Pam Rosenberg, Gettysburg College; Robert Tillman, St. John's University; John Tinker, California State University at Fresno; and Roger Wojtkiewicz, Louisiana State University, whose detailed attention to the manuscript improved it in countless ways. Although I benefited from their many ideas and suggestions, ultimately I am the one responsible for the text and any errors—sins of commission or omission.

- SUNY Cortland—in particular, Craig Little, Department Chair for Sociology–Anthropology, and John Ryder, Dean of Arts and Sciences—for the sabbatical leave that made it possible for me to get most of the writing done.

- Kristina Wolff, Syracuse University, for double-checking all the problem sets.

- The staff at Mayfield Publishing, including Linda Ward, the production editor, who meticulously attended to every facet of the preparation of this text for publication; Helen Walden, the copy editor; and Susan Shook, who supervised the preparation of the Instructor's Manual. In addition, I would like to acknowledge the contributions of Michelle Rodgerson, Jay Bauer, Susan Breitbard, Robin Mouat, Marty Granahan, Rennie Evans, April Wells-Hayes, Mary Johnson, and Brian Pecko. Thanks for your hard work and dedication to this project.

- Gilda Haines, Kim Collins, and the work–study students in the Sociology–Anthropology Department at SUNY Cortland who stepped in to provide secretarial assistance at critical moments.

- My students, especially those who gave this text its trial run in the Spring semester of 1999.

- My family—my wife, Marcia, and my children, Ben, Hope, and Tim—who encouraged me and, most important, simply made time for me to get it done. This book is dedicated to them.

Contents

Getting Started: Fundamentals of Research Design

INTRODUCTION

There is no getting around statistics. **Statistics**—numbers that help us find patterns in data, such as averages and medians—are in use nearly every day on TV and in magazines and newspapers, including the sports pages. For example, if you log on to *USA Today* online at <http://www.usatoday.com> you will be treated to a daily "USA Snapshot: A Look at the Statistics That Shape Our Lives," like the one in Figure 1.1.[1]

Most of us are entertained by illustrations like this one, because we already know enough about statistics to understand them. We also probably take this knowledge for granted.

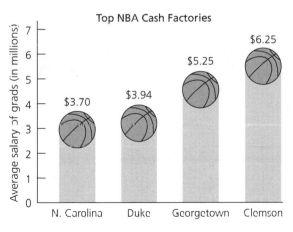

Top NBA Cash Factories

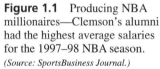

Figure 1.1 Producing NBA millionaires—Clemson's alumni had the highest average salaries for the 1997–98 NBA season.
(Source: SportsBusiness Journal.)

---

[1]*USA Today Desktop News,* 11 August 1998, <http://www.usatoday.com>. The Internet addresses cited in footnotes are for documenting the sources of information you see in the text. What is available on the Internet changes rapidly, and the information you see here may no longer be available online.

It is because you already know something about statistics that you can interpret charts like the one in Figure 1.1. The better we are at understanding statistics, the better we will be at assessing what is going on in the world around us. What do the numbers mean that we see in use every day? How have they been generated? Should we change our behavior on the basis of the statistics we are reading or hearing about, or are they suspect?

Today, as I write this chapter, there are two stories in the news debating the interpretations and applications of research to social policy. (You will find them in the section entitled "News to Use: Statistics in the 'Real' World.") The first article examines the impact of raising the price of cigarettes on teenage smoking. Although this seems to be a popular approach, some research suggests there has not been a significant reduction in the number of teenagers who start smoking in those states that have raised cigarette prices compared to those that haven't.[2] The second article reports the result of an experiment evaluating various methods of sex education among African American middle school students in Philadelphia. The researchers conclude that students who receive abstinence education engage in more sexual activity than those who receive sex education that includes information about condom use, and, not surprisingly, they are less likely to use birth control. As the article points out, though, we are spending a good deal of our sex education money on abstinence education.[3] Understanding the social policy research on issues like these helps us to make more informed decisions—as citizens and as social science professionals.

---

[2]"Disputed Statistics Fuel Politics in Youth Smoking," by Barry Meier, *The New York Times on the Web*, 20 May 1998, <http://www.nytimes.com/yr/mo/day/news/washpol/tobacco-forecasts.htm>.
[3]"Condom Emphasis Works Over Abstinence," Associated Press, *USA Today*, 20 May 1998, <http://www.usatoday.com/life/health/sexualit/lhsex005.htm>.

NEWS TO USE: Statistics in the "Real" World

Disputed Statistics Fuel Politics in Youth Smoking[4]

BARRY MEIER

It is the mantra of the nation's opponents of smoking: that sweeping changes in the way cigarettes are marketed and sold over the next decade will stop thousands of teenagers each day from starting the habit and spare a million youngsters from untimely deaths.

President Clinton recently warned, for example, that 1 million people would die prematurely if Congress did not pass tobacco legislation this year. Sen. John McCain, R-Ariz., and the author of a $516 billion

---

[4]*The New York Times on the Web*, <http://www.nytimes.com>, 20 May 1998.

tobacco bill, has urged lawmakers to stop "3,000 kids a day from starting this life-threatening addiction."

But with the Senate beginning debate on Monday on tobacco legislation, many experts warn that such predictions are little more than wild estimates that are raising what may be unreasonable expectations for change in rates of youth smoking.

After the $368.5 billion settlement proposal between tobacco producers and state officials was reached last year, for example, the American Cancer Society said a 60% decrease in youth smoking in coming years could reduce early deaths from diseases like lung cancer by a million. But while many politicians say the legislation would most likely produce a 60% drop in youth smoking, that figure appears to have come from projections and targets.

Social issues often spark unfounded claims cloaked in the reason of science. But the debate over smoking, politically packaged around the emotional subject of the health of children, is charged with hyperbole, some experts say. Politicians and policy makers have tossed out dozens of estimates about the impact of various strategies on youth smoking, figures that turn out to be based on projections rather than fact.

"I think this whole business of trying to prevent kids from smoking being the impetus behind legislation is great politics," said Richard Kluger, the author of *Ashes to Ashes* (Knopf, 1996), a history of the United States' battle over smoking and health. "But it is nonsense in terms of anything that you can put numbers next to."

Everyone in the tobacco debate agrees that reducing youth smoking would have major benefits because nearly all long-term smokers start as teenagers. But few studies have analyzed how steps like price increases and advertising bans affect youth smoking. And those have often produced contradictory results.

Consider the issue of cigarette pricing. In recent Congressional testimony, Lawrence H. Summers, the Deputy Treasury Secretary, cited studies saying that every 10% increase in the price of a pack of cigarettes would produce up to a 7% reduction in the number of children who smoke. Those studies argue that such a drop would occur because children are far more sensitive to price increases than adults.

"The best way to combat youth smoking is to raise the price," Mr. Summers said. But a recent study by researchers at Cornell University came to a far different conclusion, including a finding that the types of studies cited by Mr. Summers may be based on a faulty assumption.

Donald Kenkel, an associate professor of policy analysis and management at Cornell, said earlier studies tried to draw national patterns by correlating youth smoking rates and cigarette prices in various states at a given time.

But in the Cornell study, which looked at youth smoking rates and cigarette prices over a period of years, researchers found that price had little effect. For example, the study found that states that increased tobacco taxes did not have significantly fewer children who started smoking compared with states that raised taxes at a slower rate or not at all.

Mr. Kenkel added that he had no idea how the price increase being considered by Congress—$1.10 per pack or more—would affect smoking rates because the price of cigarettes, now about $2 a pack, has never jumped so much. And he added that there were so few studies on youth smoking rates and price that any estimate was a guess.

"It is very difficult to do good policy analysis when the research basis is as thin and variable as this," Mr. Kenkel said.

Jonathan Gruber, a Treasury Department official, said that the Cornell study had its own methodological flaws and that the earlier findings about prices supported the department's position. He also pointed out that Canada doubled cigarette prices from 1981 to 1991 and saw youth smoking rates fall by half.

Under the tobacco legislation being considered in the United States, cigarette prices would increase by about 50%. And while advocates of the legislation say that the increase would reduce youth smoking by 30% over the next decade, they say that an additional 30% reduction would come through companion measures like advertising restrictions and more penalties for store owners who sold cigarettes to under-age smokers and for youngsters who bought them. . . .

In California, for example, youth smoking began to decline in the early 1990s, soon after the state began one of the most aggressive anti-smoking campaigns in the country. But it has begun to rise again in recent years.

Dr. John Pierce, a professor of cancer prevention at the University of California at San Diego, said he thought that reversal might reflect the ability of cigarette makers to alter their promotional strategies to keep tobacco attractive to teenagers even as regulators try to block them. . . .

Experts agree that unless significant changes are made in areas like price and advertising, youth smoking rates will not decline. But unlike politicians, many of them are unwilling to make predictions. Instead, they say that the passage of tobacco legislation would guarantee only one thing: the start of a vast social experiment whose outcome is by no means clear.

Condom Emphasis Works Over Abstinence[5]

THE ASSOCIATED PRESS

CHICAGO—Safe-sex lessons for children are more effective if condom use instead of abstinence is emphasized, researchers found in a study of inner-city Blacks.

A separate finding underscored the compelling need for the grown-up subject matter: Although the youngsters' average age was just 11, 25% of them said they were no longer virgins.

"We have to begin earlier to give children the kind of information they need to protect themselves," said Princeton University psychologist John B. Jemmott III, the lead author. The study of 659 sixth- and seventh-graders at three inner-city Philadelphia schools sought ways to stem the high rate of sexually transmitted diseases among Black adolescents.

Among 13-to-19-year-olds with AIDS, Blacks represented 57% and Whites just 23% in 1996, federal statistics show, while the gonorrhea rate among 15-to-19-year-olds was about 24 times higher among Blacks than Whites.

The researchers in the Philadelphia study divided the youngsters into three groups, each receiving 8 hours of health education. One focused on abstinence, one concentrated on condom use and a control group addressed avoiding nonsexual diseases.

Three months later, 12.5% of the abstinence-group students reported having recent sex, compared with 16.6% among the condom group and 21.5% in the control group.

At 6 months, slightly more of the abstinence-group students were having sex than the condom-group students. By 12 months, 20% of the abstinence group had recent sex, compared with 16.5% of the condom group and 23.1% of the control group.

The abstinence group also reported having engaged in more unprotected sex than the condom group.

"If the goal is reduction of unprotected sexual intercourse, the safer-sex strategy may hold the most promise, particularly with those adolescents who are already sexually experienced," the researchers wrote in Wednesday's Journal of the American Medical Association.

Conservative groups such as the Family Research Council have pushed the abstinence approach, and the federal government has mandated that states use $50 million in sex education money for abstinence-only programs.

But in a JAMA editorial, Emory University psychologist Ralph DiClemente said the findings "indicate a need to reconsider the role of abstinence programs" in safe-sex education.

Gracie Hsu, a Family Research Council policy analyst, said the abstinence program probably would have had more success if the class lasted longer.

---

[5]*USA Today Desktop News,* 20 May 1998, <http://www.usatoday.com/life/health/sexualit/lhsex005/htm>.

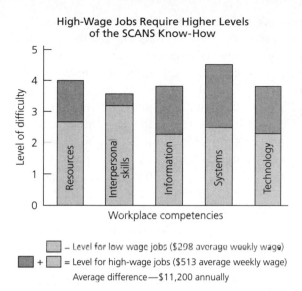

Figure 1.2 SCANS report's "Workplace Competencies." See the complete SCANS report, "Principles and Recommendations" from *Learning a Living: A Blueprint for High Performance* at <http://infinia.wpmc.jhu.edu/principles.html>.

Another indication that statistics play an important part in our lives is that it *pays* to understand statistics! The Secretary of Labor established a commission (called SCANS—Secretary's Commission on Achieving Necessary Skills) to come up with a list of the skills needed to succeed in the job market of the year 2000 and beyond. Their list is grouped into five "Workplace Competencies." One of the competency categories is "Information," which includes the ability to "acquire and evaluate data, organize and maintain files, interpret and communicate, and use computers to process information." The commission estimates that people with superior skills in the five listed areas will make, on average, over $11,000 a year more than people who don't have superior skills in these five areas. (See Figure 1.2.)

Many organizations are creating specific jobs that use information skills. The *New York Times* reported on a new workplace trend—the development of knowledge managers, "a growing number of employees whose job it is to take the overwhelming mass of information in our lives and make it tangible, accessible and useful."[6]

We can make information "tangible, accessible and useful" by finding the patterns in it—and statistics help us do that. They are invaluable tools, from very simple statistics that simply describe data, like percentages, to more complex ones that assess the accuracy with which we can make generalizations from relatively small numbers of people to much larger groups.

The goal of this text is to teach you how to understand and use these important tools. We begin with a review of the concepts that form the foundation

---

[6]"New Breed of Worker Transforms Raw Information Into Knowledge," by Matt Richtel, *The New York Times on the Web,* 15 October 1997, <http://www.nytimes.com>.

for understanding statistics, starting with how researchers conduct their projects. As the concepts are introduced, they will be illustrated with examples from newspapers, magazines, online news sources, and scholarly journals. You will be doing your own analysis of variables, like the ones in the examples, using a set of data included with this text. The data set is drawn from the 1996 General Social Survey (GSS) of the National Opinion Research Center (NORC) at the University of Chicago and is designed to represent the population of American adults, 18 years of age or older, who are English-speaking and noninstitutionalized. (We will see more on this in a little while.) Finally, you will be learning to do your analysis two ways: with pencil, paper, and calculator; and using a software program on a computer, the Statistical Product and Service Solutions (**SPSS**) for Windows.

The text is divided into two sets of statistical skills: skills for computing and interpreting descriptive statistics and skills for computing and interpreting inferential statistics. **Descriptive statistics** are numbers that summarize sets of data. They help us to *describe* patterns in sets of data like the General Social Survey, which is a sample drawn from a larger population. Some statistics simply describe the prevalence of a characteristic (sex, age, race), whereas other statistics describe relationships between characteristics (sex and education, or sex and income). Descriptive statistics don't tell us anything about whether the samples are actually representative of the populations from which they are drawn. **Inferential statistics,** on the other hand, help us to assess whether generalizations, or *inferences,* from samples to populations are appropriate. Inferential statistics let us see whether what we are learning about a sample, like the General Social Survey, is also likely to be true of the larger population from which the sample was drawn.

Let's get started on understanding descriptive and inferential statistics by going over the process of doing research, reviewing some of the fundamental concepts for social research design, and seeing how these concepts are applied in the General Social Survey.

THE PROCESS OF SOCIAL RESEARCH

Some students come to a statistics course after taking a course on research design or research methodology. In these courses you learn that research in the social sciences follows a process, and adherence to the process is what makes the research scientific. Typically, the **research process** involves the following steps.[7]

---

[7]From *Finding Out* (2nd ed., pp. 35–36), by Jane Audrey True, 1989, Belmont, CA: Wadsworth. You will find a description of a process similar to this one in the first few chapters of most textbooks on social science research methods.

1. **Specify research goals**
   - Decide what it is you want to study and come up with a research question to guide your investigation.

2. **Review the literature**
   - Place your question in the context of what is already known—relevant theory and the research-to-date.

3. **Formulate hypotheses**
   - Come up with one or more hypotheses from which variables of interest are identified.

4. **Measure and record**
   - Decide how to make observations of your variables—for example, using surveys, direct observations, or experiments—and how to record your observations as data.
   - Make systematic observations and collect data.

5. **Analyze the data**
   - Extract patterns from the data you collect.
   - Test hypotheses.
   - Draw conclusions.

6. **Invite scrutiny**
   - Make your research and analysis available to others.
   - Open yourself up for review of the processes you followed, data you collected, and the conclusions you reached.

Let's go through these steps, using as an example a research project I completed examining the impact of service learning on student achievement in an Introduction to Sociology course.[8] Service learning is an approach to teaching in which community service assignments are incorporated into a course. In the Introduction to Sociology course I teach, students have a choice of assignments. Some work with the group on campus doing education and advocacy to reduce hunger and homelessness in the Cortland community. Others work in day care centers, serve as teaching assistants in the public schools, or volunteer in an adult literacy program. My *research goal* was to find out whether these service learning assignments improve student achievement compared to a more traditional, classroom-based approach to teaching an Introduction to Sociology course.

Before I decided how to conduct my research project (or even whether it was worth it to do research in this area at all), I had to find out what researchers had

---

[8]"Outcomes of Service Learning in an Introduction to Sociology Course," by J. R. Kendrick, Jr., 1996, *Michigan Journal of Community Service Learning, 3,* pp. 72–81.

already learned about service learning and its effect on student achievement. I began by *reviewing the literature* already published on this topic. I found that little research had been done that attempted to isolate the effects of service learning on college students. The few studies in this area involved students in journalism, psychology, and political science, but not sociology. There was more about the effects of service learning on high school students, but not very much.

Reviewing the literature in light of my research goals helped me to *formulate a hypothesis:* students in service learning courses show higher levels of achievement than students in non–service learning courses. More specifically, I hypothesized that students in the section of my Introduction to Sociology course that included service learning would show higher levels of achievement than students in the section that did not involve service learning.

The question remained: How could I find out whether students in my service learning course do better than students in my non–service learning course? What counts as "achievement," and how can it be measured? I had to come up with a plan for *measuring and recording* data related to the variables of interest in my project. I decided to use the students' grades, along with other measures like course attendance, to measure achievement. In addition, I asked students to respond to a questionnaire designed to measure attitudes in a variety of areas, such as concern for social justice, responsibility for addressing social issues, and ability to make changes in society. However, I couldn't limit my observations to just two variables, the independent variable (type of course: service learning or not) and dependent variable (student achievement). I had to collect some background data on the students in the course, like age, sex, race, high school GPA, and SAT scores. All of the data I collected were entered into an SPSS data file by a student assistant.

The process of *analyzing the data and drawing conclusions* started by simply describing the students in the two sections of my Introduction to Sociology course to establish that the students in the two sections were, for all practical purposes, comparable. Then I began testing my hypothesis. Did students in the service learning course achieve more than students in the non–service learning course? I concluded that students in the service learning course did, in fact, do better than the other group in some areas but not others. Students in the service learning section showed greater growth in the areas of developing a sense of social responsibility and personal efficacy. Even though there wasn't a significant difference in grades between the two courses, the students in the service learning section believed that they had learned more as compared with students in the other section of the course.

Finally, I subjected my results to the *scrutiny of others.* First, I asked colleagues in my college to read my conclusions in a paper I wrote about the project. Then I submitted the paper for publication to a journal. Before publishing the paper, the editor of the journal asked a set of reviewers to critique it. After I revised the paper, the editor agreed to publish it. The act of publishing the paper subjected it to scrutiny by the larger community of scholars interested in service learning in general and service learning as an approach to teaching sociology in particular.

As I started thinking about how to gather data to answer the question of interest to me, I had to decide whom (or what) to study, how the individuals (or other entities of interest) would be selected, what information to collect about each of them, and how to collect it. The next section covers the concepts associated with these tasks—population, sample, hypothesis, variables (including independent, dependent, and control variables)—and ties them to the two articles in "News to Use" and the General Social Survey, the set of data you will be working with throughout the text.

FUNDAMENTALS OF RESEARCH DESIGN

Populations, Elements of Populations, and Units of Analysis

As researchers identify research questions, they think about whom (or what) they must study to answer their questions. Researchers have to collect information (data) about the characteristics of those individuals, groups, organizations, or other units they want to study. A **population** is the set of those elements a researcher wants to know something about. An **element** is a single entity of the population.

The set of elements may be large, as in the population represented by the **General Social Survey (GSS),** which is designed to represent all English-speaking Americans 18 years old or older who live in households (as opposed to group quarters, like college dormitories or other institutional settings).[9] The set may also be relatively small, as in the population of students in your college or university.

The single elements that make up a set may be individuals, groups, organizations, or institutions, or any other socially organized unit (like a city, state, or nation), formal or informal. Some populations consist of sets of individuals, in which case a single element of the population is an individual. Used this way, the term *population* means about the same as it does generally—to denote a set of individuals. Other populations may consist of sets of cities, states, or nations, of which a single element is a specific city, state, or nation. A researcher interested in crime rates in large cities may study the population (or set) of all large cities in the United States, of which a single element would be a specific large city like Los Angeles, New York, Dallas, or Chicago. A researcher interested in the level of support for public education may study the population of all states

---

[9]*The NORC General Social Survey,* by James A. Davis and Tom W. Smith, 1992, Newbury Park, CA: Sage. You can learn more about the General Social Survey at the Web site <http://www.norc.uchicago.edu>.

in the United States, of which a single element would be a single state like California, New York, Texas, or Illinois. A researcher interested in poverty at the global level could study the population of all nations, of which a single element would be one nation like the United States, Brazil, or Zimbabwe.

Avoiding Common Pitfalls   The meaning of the term *population* is sometimes confusing, because it has a more specific meaning for researchers than it does in general usage. When most people talk about a population, they are referring to a group of individuals who make up a community, state, or nation. When researchers use the term, it can refer to any set of elements about which researchers gather information: individuals, groups, organizations, cities, states, or nations.

Researchers collect information from the elements in a population to discover the patterns in one or more characteristics of the population as a whole. What are those characteristics of the population in which the researcher is interested? The answer to this question leads us to the unit of analysis. A **unit of analysis** is the specific entity the researcher wants to know something about. Usually, the elements of a population and the units of analysis are the same. For most questions in the General Social Survey, the unit of analysis is the individual. General Social Survey researchers gather information in face-to-face interviews from individuals about characteristics of the individuals themselves, like sex, race, religion, and the respondent's income. However, there are also questions in the GSS about other units of analysis. For example, there are a number of questions about households, like household income and the number of wage earners in the household. For these variables, the unit of analysis is the household.

Avoiding Common Pitfalls   Identifying the units of analysis in a study involves separating who is being asked to participate in a survey from what they are being asked about. It is an important point, because researchers often use individuals in a population to gather information about other entities. For example, researchers may ask one person in a household to answer questions *about* the entire household (total income of everyone in the household; number of people in the household). In this case, the household is the unit of analysis. Researchers may also ask a representative of an organization to answer questions *about* the entire organization (total budget, number of employees). In this case, the organization is the unit of analysis. To correctly identify the units of analysis, it is important to distinguish between the entity *from* which a researcher is collecting information and the entity *about* which he or she is collecting information.

Samples and Sampling Frames

Researchers can rarely study entire populations—they are simply too large. Think about trying to gauge the attitudes of American adults on an issue like abortion. It would be an impossible task to interview everyone in the United States. To deal with this problem, researchers have devised ways to draw samples from populations. A **sample** is a smaller, more manageable set of elements—a subset of a population—selected to represent the population from which it is drawn. To maximize the likelihood that a sample will be representative of a population, researchers draw samples according to the rules of probability. A **probability sample** is selected in such a way that each element in the population has the same chance of being drawn into the sample as every other element in the population.

Before any sample can be drawn, however, researchers have to come up with a **sampling frame,** or a list of the elements in the population. A population, remember, is the set of elements that researchers want to learn about. In order to sample, researchers have to know which elements, specifically, make up the population. If the elements of a population are individuals, then the researchers need a list of the people in the population. If the elements of a population are states, then they need a list of all of the states in the population. With a frame or list in hand, researchers can draw samples. Some common methods of drawing probability samples include simple random sampling and systematic sampling.

Simple random sampling Simple random sampling is like drawing names out of a hat: listing each element in a sampling frame on separate slips of paper, mixing them up, and then drawing out a certain number of them. This same procedure can be done electronically using computer programs for creating random samples, or it can be done by hand using a random number table. The researcher numbers each element on a list and then uses a random number table to select the elements from the list for the sample.

Systematic sampling with a random start Systematic sampling with a random start is like simple random sampling, except that only the first element is selected using a random number table. After identifying the first participant in the sample that way, the researcher simply selects every nth—second, third, fourth, fifth—element after that (depending on how large the population is and how large the sample needs to be).

Multistage sampling processes   Some sampling procedures are more complex in design, involving a number of different steps (or stages). Researchers may first *stratify* the frames from which they draw their samples. **Stratification** involves grouping the elements on a list by a characteristic like ethnicity or sex. Researchers stratify sampling frames to ensure that their samples will be representative of one or more important characteristics in a population. For example, researchers may divide a frame into categories by sex, creating separate lists of males and females. Then they may draw either a simple random sample or a systematic sample from each list. Stratification allows the researchers to make sure their sample includes males and females in proportion to their representation in the entire population.

Another sampling strategy involves **clustering.** Clusters are used when researchers can't come up with a good frame, or list, of the elements in a population. As a result, they create a list of the clusters, or socially organized entities, in which the elements of interest can be found. For example, researchers who want to survey the population of American adults won't be able to find a list of all American adults. However, they can find a frame for all of the geographic units in which American adults can be found, whether the units are rural areas or city blocks. With this frame, they can draw a random sample of clusters, using simple random sampling or systematic sampling. Then they can randomly select individuals within each cluster to respond to their survey.

The General Social Survey is an example of a research project that uses clustering extensively. Beginning in 1994, GSS researchers started taking a probability sample of nearly 3,000 adults every 2 years to represent the population of noninstitutionalized, English-speaking American adults (at least 18 years old). The sample is selected using a multistage process that involves dividing the United States into geographic areas or units, sampling from those units to ensure representation of the population by certain characteristics (such as ethnicity), selecting blocks or districts from each geographic unit, selecting households within each block, and then selecting respondents from the households.[10]

Variables

Researchers sample to select the specific elements in a population from which data will be collected—but what does the researcher want to know? If we can answer this question, we are on our way to understanding the concept of variables—those characteristics about which data are collected. A **variable** is any aspect of a unit of analysis that can vary from one unit to the next. If the unit of analysis is an individual, variables can include characteristics like age, sex, race, years of education, and religion.

---

[10]See Footnote 9.

Researchers who administer the General Social Survey are interested in a large number of variables. They collect quite a bit of information on the demographic or background characteristics of the individuals who are selected for participation. In addition to the variables mentioned, they collect data on variables like marital status, class identification (lower-, working-, middle-, or upper-class), political affiliation (Democrat, Independent, Republican), and political views (liberal, moderate, conservative). They also collect information on the attitudes of GSS respondents toward a variety of issues, like abortion, and GSS researchers ask about behaviors like church attendance and voting. Each GSS includes some special topics about which researchers ask questions. In 1996 these topics included gender issues, mental health, and volunteering. Appendix E is a guide to the GSS variables we will be using in this text.

Skills Practice 2 Identify the variables discussed in each of the two articles, "Disputed Statistics Fuel Politics in Youth Smoking" (the Cornell study) and "Condom Emphasis Works Over Abstinence" (the Philadelphia study). List the variables (characteristics of each of the units of analysis) that are mentioned in the articles.

Categories, Values, and Data

For each variable, researchers gather data (specific pieces of information about the variables) in categories. If you ever answered a survey, you are familiar with the **categories of a variable**—they are the response categories the researcher asked you to check off. Typically, surveys ask respondents to check off whether they are male or female (categories of the variable *sex*), or they may ask how old you are. The number you give in response forms a category of the variable *age*. Variables must have at least two categories. (If a variable has only one category, there is nothing to vary from one respondent to another. When a characteristic does not vary from one respondent to another, it is called a **constant.**)

Sometimes researchers assign numbers to the categories of variables. For example, they may assign the number 1 to everyone who answers "male" in response to a sex variable. Everyone who answers "female" becomes a 2. The numbers that researchers assign to variable categories are called **values.**

The **data** for each variable consist of the specific responses obtained for each question. For example, the data for the variable *sex* are the specific responses given by a set of respondents to the question about sex. The data for the variable *age* are the exact answers given by everyone who answered the question about age. In Appendix E you can see the response categories and values for each of the GSS variables.

At this point, the concepts of population, elements (and units of analysis), samples, and variables and their categories should be sounding familiar. In

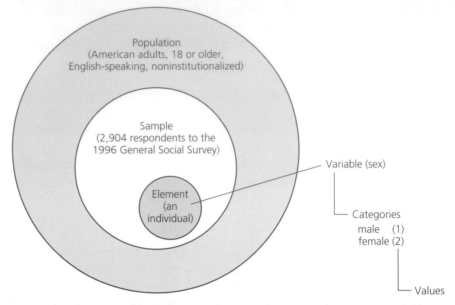

Figure 1.3 Diagram of relationship between population, sample, elements, variables, categories of variables, and values for the 1996 General Social Survey.

addition, you should be developing an understanding of how these concepts are related to one another. The diagram in Figure 1.3 shows how these concepts can be applied to the General Social Survey.

Hypotheses

Sometimes researchers gather data about variables simply to describe their respondents. The variables in the GSS can be used for this purpose. What is the proportion of males to females? What percentage of respondents is married? How educated are they? Are they employed? More often, researchers are trying to learn about associations between variables. Do men have more education, on average, than women? Are men more likely to have full-time jobs than women? Who is more likely to be working in the home as opposed to outside of the home?

Usually researchers embark on a research project with one or more guesses or hunches about an association in mind. These guesses or hunches may be based on knowledge of the theory and research already developed in a specific area of study, or they may be based on the personal experiences or observations a researcher has made of some phenomenon. When researchers express these guesses or associations as statements that describe a relationship between at least two variables, they have developed a **hypothesis** about an association. Take the following hypothesis as an example:

Men are more educated, on average, than women.

This statement expresses an association between the variables *sex* (male or female) and *education*. It is also specific about the nature of the association, how the variables are related to one another (men are more educated than women). To assess whether the hypothesis is valid or not, we could gather data from a group of men and women and ask how many years of education they have completed. Then we could compare how many years of education men have as compared to women.

Hypotheses can go further, though, and express relationships that involve third variables. For example, we may hypothesize that men are more educated than women because they are more likely to have to support themselves than are women. If our hypothesis has merit, we would expect to find proportionately more men than women as the primary breadwinners in their families. We would also expect to see that, among those who are the primary breadwinners, women are no less educated than men. If so, we could conclude that how much education one has achieved has less to do with one's sex and more to do with whether or not one has to earn one's own living.

Skills Practice 3   Write possible hypotheses for the Cornell ("Disputed Statistics Fuel Politics in Youth Smoking") and Philadelphia ("Condom Emphasis Works Over Abstinence") studies in "News to Use," one for each study.

Independent and Dependent Variables

From the relationship specified in a hypothesis, we can tell how the variables are related to one another—which variable is assumed to be affecting the other. The variable that is producing or creating the effect is the **independent variable,** whereas the variable being affected is the **dependent variable.** Another way to think about it is that a variable that is assumed to be having an impact on some other variable is the independent variable; the variable assumed to be changed or influenced in some way is the dependent variable. In the preceding hypothesis, the independent variable is sex, male or female. It is the variable that we assume is influencing how much education someone has (the dependent variable). The relationship can be diagrammed this way:

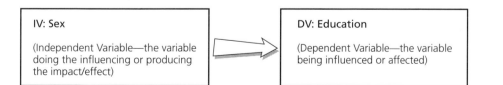

IV: Sex	DV: Education
(Independent Variable—the variable doing the influencing or producing the impact/effect)	(Dependent Variable—the variable being influenced or affected)

Note that I avoided using the word *cause* to describe this relationship. Whereas the variable *sex* is assumed to be having some influence on the variable *education,* we cannot assume that one's sex *causes* one to have (or prevents one from having) a certain level of education. Although we often think of independent–dependent variable relationships in terms of cause and effect, the most we can do is establish an association between two variables. When the characteristic of one variable is found (sex is male), then we tend to find a particular characteristic of a second variable to be present as well (educational achievement is high).

Independent–dependent variable relationships can have a *predictive* quality to them, though. When the characteristic of one variable is present, then we can predict, with varying degrees of accuracy, the presence of a second characteristic. In a later chapter we will be applying techniques for prediction to examine the association between variables like parents' educational levels and their offsprings' educational levels. Do the educational achievements of one's parents allow us to predict the educational achievements of their children?

Skills Practice 4   Identify the independent and dependent variables in each of the hypotheses you constructed for Skills Practice 3.

Control Variables

Control variables are any variables (other than the independent or dependent variables) that can have an influence on an independent–dependent variable relationship. For example, when we hypothesized that men are more educated than women *because* they are more likely to have to support themselves, we introduced a control variable—employment status. We speculated that the reason men might have more education than women has more to do with whether they support themselves than with any difference based on gender alone.

As another example, let's go back to the chart at the beginning of the chapter that shows an association between where athletes go to college and their NBA salaries. Can you think of other variables that might affect an NBA player's salary besides where he went to school? You could probably quickly list several. Take talent, for instance. Maybe you broke talent down into more measurable characteristics like average points scored per game, rebounds per game, and assists per game. All of these variables could be control variables. If you ranked players based on points scored per game, for example, you would expect salaries to be highest for players with the highest point averages, regardless of where they went to school.

As we explore the General Social Survey, we will be analyzing variables one at a time, associations between variables, and the effects of third variables on relationships between independent and dependent variables. First, however, we have to become familiar with the program we will be using to help with the analysis, SPSS,[11] and we have to become familiar with the set of GSS variables with which we'll be working. Let's begin by having a look at the General Social Survey using SPSS.

INTRODUCING SPSS 9.0 FOR WINDOWS

SPSS is a widely available computer software program (SPSS says it has over 250,000 customer sites) for analyzing quantitative data used by researchers in colleges and universities, public institutions, and private companies.[12] Consequently, it is likely that over the course of your career—whether in an applied setting (like criminal justice, social work, policy analysis, or law) or an academic environment—you will encounter SPSS or a program like it. (There are a variety of other software programs that perform similar functions, such as MicroCase, SAS, and Minitab. The skills you learn doing SPSS are easily transferred to these other programs.)

Getting Familiar With the Program

SPSS is a complex program. You will be learning about selected features of the program to gain a fundamental understanding of the software. Throughout the course, you may very well find yourself exploring some features of the program on your own, and learning more about it than can be covered in one introductory-level text. You may even learn things about the program your instructor doesn't know.

I will be taking you through each of the functions in the program step by step, using a series of "SPSS Guides."

---

[11]When it was first created, SPSS stood for "Statistical Package for the Social Sciences." SPSS is now the registered trademark of SPSS, Inc., and it stands for "Statistical Product and Service Solutions."

[12]To learn more about SPSS, Inc., the company that markets the software program, visit its Web site at <http://www.spss.com>.

To start, let's open the program and get familiar with how it works. Your instructor may have to give you directions on how to open the SPSS program on your campus computers. Generally, however, computers operating with Windows will display a menu of icons (symbols) when you boot (start) them up. To begin, look for an icon for SPSS 9.0 on your computer screen. It will look like the illustration on the left.

Then use the SPSS Guide that follows to open your SPSS program.

SPSS Guide: Opening the SPSS Program

Use your mouse to place your cursor on the SPSS icon and double-click. You will see a set of windows like the ones here.

❶ Click on the ○ (called a radio button) next to Type in Data.

❷ Then click on OK.

SPSS Guide: Exploring the SPSS Program

The menu

After opening the program, you will be at the SPSS Data Editor window. Begin by looking at the menu items across the top of the screen: File, Edit, View, Data, and so on. Point at the first item, File, and click once. A list of options for each item will open up, like the one shown. This list is called a pull-down menu. Get used to moving the cursor from menu item to menu item, holding it on each one for a second, to see the options under each one. (We will explore how to use many of these features later in the book.)

The toolbar

Move your cursor to the next row, a row of icons (symbols) called the *toolbar*. A toolbar provides easy access to many of the most frequently used features of a program. Hold your cursor on each item until a box appears describing the item, starting with the first icon, which looks like a file folder. The words Open File appear when you hold your cursor on the icon. You will see labels for each of the icons as you move your cursor across the toolbar.

SPSS Guide: Opening SPSS Data Files

With your SPSS program open, click on the Open File icon on your toolbar.

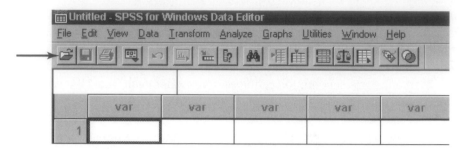

The Open File window appears. You will see a list of data files that come with the SPSS software. You may want to explore them later on. For now, we will assume you are working with a set of data on a diskette.

The Open File window shows:

Open File

Look in: spss90

- Acrobat
- Looks
- Odbc
- Scripts
- Setup
- AML survival
- Anxiety 2
- Anxiety
- Breast cancer survival
- Cars
- Coronary artery data
- Employee data
- Fat surfactant
- Glass strain

File name:

Files of type: SPSS (*.sav)

Open

Paste

Cancel

To open a data file on your diskette, insert your diskette into the appropriate slot in the computer. Then click on the down arrow ▼ you see next to the Look in box. A list of options will appear. These are different locations in the computer for retrieving files. Among the options is the drive for your diskette. Click on 3½ Floppy [A:].

A list of the files on your diskette will appear. The one we will use is called gss96subset (for General Social Survey, 1996).

❶ Click on gss96subset.

❷ Click on Open.

Your data file will appear in the SPSS Data Editor window. This window may look familiar if you have had any experience with spreadsheet programs like Excel, Dbase, or Lotus. Each *row* in the window contains the responses of a single respondent to the variables in the 1996 General Social Survey. Each *column* lists all responses to a single variable. The first variable, *id,* is the identification number of each of the respondents to the GSS.

	id	age	relig	marital	sibs	childs	agekdbrn	educ	paeduc	maeduc	speduc	degree
1	1	79	3	1	2	0	0	12	98	97	12	1
2	2	32	2	5	1	0	0	17	16	14	97	3
3	3	55	5	3	2	3	24	18	97	12	97	4
4	4	50	2	1	98	4	16	6	97	97	14	0
5	5	56	4	4	7	4	20	8	98	98	97	0
6	6	51	2	4	4	4	20	17	98	12	97	3
7	7	48	1	4	1	3	20	12	97	3	97	1
8	8	29	1	5	4	1	24	13	97	12	97	1
9	9	40	4	4	6	0	0	13	97	98	97	1
10	10	46	1	4	3	4	16	13	12	12	97	1
11	11	37	5	5	0	0	0	19	97	16	97	4
12	12	43	3	3	1	0	0	16	16	14	97	4
13	13	45	3	5	1	0	0	16	12	12	97	3
14	14	44	2	3	3	0	0	13	10	12	97	1
15	15	53	5	3	2	1	22	16	12	12	97	3

Having opened a file, let's have a look at some of the variables in our data. Follow the directions in the next SPSS Guide to explore the variables in your file.

SPSS Guide: Exploring Variables

With your gss96subset file open, look at the Data Editor to see the variables that are listed across the columns of the table and the cases that are listed down the side. Not all of the data fit on one screen. You have to use your cursor to *scroll*—move up and down, and side to side—to see all of your cases and all of your variables.

① Place your cursor on the arrows at the side of the screen to scroll up and down.

② Or place it on the arrows at the bottom of the screen to move side to side.

With your cursor on the arrow, hold down the left-most click key on your mouse, and you will see the data start to move.

	id	age	relig	marital	sibs	childs	agekdbrn	educ	paeduc	maeduc	speduc	degree
1	1	79	3	1	2	0	0	12	98	97	12	1
2	2	32	2	5	1	0	0	17	16	14	97	3
3	3	55	5	3	2	3	24	18	97	12	97	4
4	4	50	2	1	98	4	16	6	97	97	14	0
5	5	58	4	4	7	4	20	0	90	98	97	0
6	6	51	2	4	4	4	20	17	98	12	97	3
7	7	48	1	4	1	3	20	12	97	3	97	1
8	8	29	1	5	4	1	24	13	97	12	97	1
9	9	40	4	4	6	0	0	13	97	98	97	1
10	10	46	1	4	3	4	16	13	12	12	97	1
11	11	37	5	5	0	0	0	19	97	16	97	4
12	12	43	3	3	1	0	0	16	16	14	97	4
13	13	45	3	5	1	0	0	16	12	12	97	3
14	14	44	2	3	3	0	0	13	10	12	97	1
15	15	53	5	3	2	1	22	16	12	12	97	3

gss96subset - SPSS for Windows Data Editor

File Edit View Data Transform Analyze Graphs Utilities Window Help

1:id   1

SPSS for Windows Processor is ready

Now look at the SPSS variable names. You will notice that SPSS variable names are no more than 8 characters long, and they look strange because they are shortened versions of much longer variable labels (which we will look at in a minute). These shortened variable names are called **mnemonics.** They are labels designed to jog our memories about what the variables represent. Some of them—like *age, sex,* and *race*—are easy to figure out, and you can probably guess what *marital* and *relig* stand for (marital status and religion). It's harder to guess what variables like *polviews, partyid,* and *hompop* are about. To get more information about each of the variables, simply hold your cursor on a variable name, like *id.* A variable label (a lengthier variable description) will appear to give you an idea of what each variable is about. (See the next illustration.) Refer to the codebook in Appendix E to become more familiar with each of the variables.

For the variable *age,* the variable label is AGE OF RESPONDENT.

When you get to the variable *relig,* you encounter a commonly used abbreviation in the variable label RS, which stands for respondent's, so *relig* is respondent's religious preference.

Now let's take a look at the General Social Survey variables along with the categories of the variables (called **value labels** in the SPSS program) and their values, using the Variables window. Note that the terms *categories* and *value labels* will be used interchangeably as you use "SPSS Guide: The Variables Window" to tour the SPSS variables, their values, and their value labels.

SPSS Guide: The Variables Window—Variables, Values, and Value Labels

To see a description of each of the GSS variables along with their values and value labels, click on the toolbar Variables icon (the one with the blue question mark on it).

A window called Variables opens up. You will see an alphabetical list of each variable in the gss96subset file. The first variable, *abany,* is highlighted. To the right of the variable, there is a box labeled Variable Information.

You will see the variable name *abany* along with the longer variable label ABORTION IF WOMAN WANTS FOR ANY REASON. Following the variable label, you will see the level of measurement listed—ordinal for *abany*—and the value labels for the variable. The value labels represent the categories of the variable—YES and NO in this case. You will also see some other categories listed, like NAP, DK, and NA. These are categories for people who did not answer or were not asked this particular question. NAP means the question is not applicable (wasn't asked for one reason or another), DK means the respondent answered "don't know," and NA means no answer. Categories like these—NAP, DK, and NA—are generally treated as **missing values** of the variable, responses that are not meaningful for describing characteristics of the respondents. Missing values are generally excluded from the analysis of a variable's categories.

Click on some of the other variables to see the information about them. As you do so, you will notice that the only value labels some variables have are the ones for the people who didn't respond to the question. Let's look at the variable *age* as an example. The only two categories listed are DK (don't know) and NA (no answer). This doesn't mean that those variables have no categories. What it means is that these variables are being measured at the numerical level, as indicated by the absence of any values or value labels (other than missing values codes). The researcher doesn't need to provide value labels for the categories, because the numerical values for the variable are meaningful. You will learn more about levels of measurement and these kinds of variables in the next chapter.

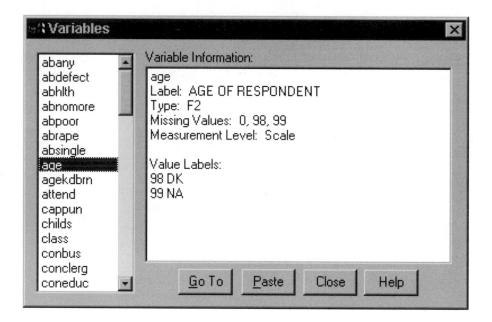

Some variables, like *childs,* look like they might be numerical, but they still have category labels—one called EIGHT OR MORE and one for NA. For some number variables, researchers combine some of the higher, less frequently found categories into a single category. Relatively few respondents have 8 or more children (25 in 1996, or less than 1% of all respondents). There is not much to be gained by keeping track of the exact numbers, so the decision is made to simplify the data-gathering and coding process by grouping everyone who has 8 or more children into one category.

When you are finished looking at the variables, click on the X—the exit button—in the top right-hand corner of the window to exit.

To see the General Social Survey data, you have to look no further than the SPSS Data Editor window. The Data Editor window is one of several output screens you will learn to use. Others will be introduced as we come to them. Follow the "SPSS Guide: Exploring Data" to take a look at the data for each of the variables in your file.

SPSS Guide: Exploring Data

Look at the SPSS Data Editor window and read down the column of numbers under each variable. The first variable, *id,* is simply the identification number for each respondent in the survey. Under *age* you see the ages of each GSS respondent: the first respondent is 79 years old, the second respondent is 32 years old, and so on.

gss96subset - SPSS for Windows Data Editor

File Edit View Data Transform Analyze Graphs Utilities Window Help

1:id   1

	id	age	relig	marital	sibs	childs	agekdbrn	educ	paeduc	maeduc	speduc	degree
1	1	79	3	1	2	0	0	12	98	97	12	1
2	2	32	2	5	1	0	0	17	16	14	97	3
3	3	55	5	3	2	3	24	18	97	12	97	4
4	4	50	2	1	98	4	16	6	97	97	14	0
5	5	56	4	4	7	4	20	8	98	98	97	0
6	6	51	2	4	4	4	20	17	98	12	97	3

The data under the variable *relig* (respondent's religious preference) make a little less sense. What does the piece of data for the first respondent, the value 3, mean? What about the value 2 for the second respondent? There are a couple of ways to find out. To see the value labels for the variable, open up the Variables window (using the Variables toolbar icon—the one with the blue question mark). Then click on the variable *relig*. You can quickly see that the value 3 stands for JEWISH and the value 2 stands for CATHOLIC.

Finally, let's look at how to exit from the SPSS program when we are finished with our work each day. Use "SPSS Guide: Exiting From the SPSS Program."

SPSS Guide: Exiting From the SPSS Program

There are two options for exiting.

❶ Click on the X box in the upper right-hand corner of the screen (as you would to exit from any Windows program).

❷ Or click on the menu item, File, then click on Exit.

If this window opens up, click on No. You will go back to your main Windows menu.

SUMMARY

In this chapter we examined the steps in the research process: specifying research goals, reviewing the research literature, formulating hypotheses, measuring and recording observations, analyzing data, and inviting scrutiny. I illustrated the steps with examples from a research project about the impact of service learning on student achievement in the classroom.

You were introduced to some of the fundamental concepts for research design and the analysis of quantitative data: a population, a sample from the population, elements and units of populations and samples, variables, categories of variables, values of variables, hypotheses, independent and dependent variables, and control variables. These concepts were applied to the set of data you will be using throughout this text, the General Social Survey (GSS) for 1996. The population for the GSS consists of all English-speaking, American, noninstitutionalized adults 18 years old or older. The sample is a multistage probability sample of nearly 3,000 adults. Variables include many demographic characteristics, like sex, age, race, and education. There are also variables designed to measure attitudes toward various issues, like support for abortion and confidence in government, and variables that measure behaviors, like church attendance and voting.

Before moving on to the next chapter, be sure you can open the data set you will use with this text, a subset of the 1996 GSS variables called gss96subset. You should also be able to move around in the file to view the variables and their labels.

In the next chapter you will learn to assess the levels at which variables are being measured, including the GSS variables we will be working with.

KEY CONCEPTS

SPSS
Statistics
Descriptive statistics
Inferential statistics
Research process
Population
Element
General Social Survey (GSS)
Unit of analysis
Sample

Probability sample
Sampling frame
Simple random sampling
Systematic sampling with a random start
Multistage sampling process
Stratification
Clustering
Variable

Categories of a variable
Constant
Values of a variable
Data
Hypothesis
Independent variable
Dependent variable
Control variable
Value label
Mnemonics
Missing values

ANSWERS TO SKILLS PRACTICES

1. The population of the Cornell study consists of states in the United States—those that have raised prices for cigarettes and those that haven't. The elements and the units of analysis are the same—the states. The population of the Philadelphia study consists of sixth and seventh graders in three inner-city schools in Philadelphia, Pennsylvania. The elements and the units of analysis are individuals or the sixth and seventh graders about which the researchers are collecting data.

2. Cornell study variables include cigarette prices, smoking rates among children, enforcement of laws against tobacco sales to children, enforcement of laws prohibiting children from buying cigarettes, restrictions on advertising tobacco products to children, investment in health education (like antismoking campaigns). Philadelphia study variables include health education class, sexual activity, safe-sex practices, age, grade in school, sexual experience, school attended.

3. Answers to this Skills Practice may vary. However, they should be along the lines of the following:
Cornell study: States with higher tobacco prices will show lower rates of smoking among children than states with lower tobacco prices; or the higher a state's tobacco prices, the lower the rate of youth smoking. Philadelphia study: Sex education programs that emphasize abstinence are less effective at preventing teenage pregnancy than programs that include information about safe-sex practices; or sex education programs that include information on condom use are more likely to result in safe-sex behaviors than sex education programs that emphasize abstinence.

4. Cornell study independent variable: tobacco prices; dependent variable: smoking rates among children or youth. Philadelphia study independent variable: health education class (type of health education to which the study participants were exposed); dependent variable: safe-sex practices.

5. Cornell study control variables (characteristics of states that could affect the association between tobacco price and the smoking rate among children): enforcement of laws against tobacco sales to children, enforcement of laws prohibiting children from buying cigarettes, restrictions on advertising tobacco products to children, investment in health education (like antismoking campaigns), activities by tobacco companies to promote smoking. Philadelphia study control variables (characteristics of middle school students that could affect the association between health education and safe-sex practices): age, grade in school, sexual experience, school attended.

GENERAL EXERCISES

1. In the "Process of Social Research" section of this chapter, I described a research project to evaluate the effects of service learning on students in an Introduction to Sociology course at the college at which I work, the State University of New York College at Cortland.

   a. What is the population for the research project?

   b. What are the elements of the population?

   c. What is the unit of analysis?

   d. Identify the independent and dependent variables in the hypothesis I constructed for the study.

   e. List possible control variables.

2. Read the newspaper article in Box 1.1, then answer the following:

   a. What is the population?

   b. What are the elements of the population?

   c. What is the unit of analysis of interest to the researcher?

   d. Write a hypothesis relevant to the study.

   e. Identify the independent and dependent variables in the hypothesis.

   f. List possible control variables.

3. Write a hypothesis for the relationship between sex and support for making birth control pills available to teenagers (the *pillok* variable in Appendix E). Identify the independent and dependent variables in the hypothesis. Suggest a control variable and explain how it could affect the association between the independent and dependent variables.

4. Write a hypothesis for the relationship between support for sex education in the public schools and level of educational achievement (the *degree* variable in Appendix E). Identify the independent and dependent variables in the hypothesis. Suggest a control variable and explain how it could affect the association between the independent and dependent variables.

5. Write a hypothesis for the relationship between age and attitudes toward teenagers having sex (the *teensex* variable in Appendix E). Identify the independent and dependent variables in the hypothesis. Suggest a control variable and explain how it could affect the association between the independent and dependent variables.

BOX 1.1 Black Gains Found Meager in Old Segregated States[13]

Ethan Bronner

The first comprehensive study of public higher education in the 19 states that once operated racially separate colleges presents a picture of continuing segregation fueled by political fatigue, court rulings, and admissions and financial-aid policies.

Historically Black colleges in those states are still overwhelmingly Black, the study finds, while Whites dominate flagship state institutions in numbers disproportionate to their share of the population.

And while the number of Black freshmen in the 19 states has grown since the 1970s, the percentage of Blacks among freshmen has barely inched up, to 17% in 1996 from 15% in 1976— small numbers, given that in all but four of those states, the percentage of Blacks among freshmen is significantly lower than the percentage of Blacks among all 18- to 24-year-olds. Nine states, in fact, reported a decline from 1991 to 1996 in the proportion of Blacks in their freshman classes.

The report, "Miles to Go," was issued Tuesday by the Southern Education Foundation, an Atlanta advocacy group that works to improve educational opportunities for Black and poor Southerners.

---

[13]*The New York Times on the Web*, 26 August 1998, <http://www.nytimes.com>.

KEEPING TRACK

Student Diversity   A new report charges that in the 19 states ordered by the Supreme Court to dismantle vestiges of segregation in higher education, Blacks' access is still limited.

	Percentage of first-time, full-time freshmen who are Black students	
	1976	1996
Alabama	20.2%	25.1%
Arkansas	19.6	19.9
Delaware	12.1	16.2
Florida	15.9	17.6
Georgia	19.6	23.9
Kentucky	8.8	9.9
Louisiana	28.1	31.6
Maryland	18.2	28.8
Mississippi	40.5	40.8
Missouri	6.8	6.8
North Carolina	22.9	23.5
Ohio	10.2	9.1
Oklahoma	7.6	10.1
Pennsylvania	7.4	9.1
South Carolina	15.9	20.2
Tennessee	22.3	17.7
Texas	10.6	13.8
Virginia	17.4	17.3
West Virginia	4.5	5.4

Source: Southern Education Foundation

6. Look through Appendix E and write three hypotheses for variables you find in the General Social Survey (other than the ones I used in Exercises 3–5).

   a. Identify the independent and dependent variables in each hypothesis.

   b. For each hypothesis, suggest a control variable, and explain how it could affect the association between the independent and dependent variables in your hypothesis.

2 Levels of Measurement

INTRODUCTION

As an instructor, I often clip articles to use in my classes. One that caught my eye had the headline "Parental Supervision, Strong Values Reduce Likelihood of Teen Sex."[1] The article led me to the home page for the National Campaign to Prevent Teen Pregnancy <http://www.teenpregnancy.org> on which there was, in its entirety, the report about their survey. Some excerpts from the survey are included in the "News to Use" section. Read them over now, because I will refer to them throughout the next several chapters as we learn to assess the levels at which variables are measured, use that skill to create data sets of our own, and then begin to analyze variables.

Apart from my own personal interest in it, the National Campaign to Prevent Teen Pregnancy (NCPTP) survey makes an interesting case study for several reasons. First, it illustrates uses of statistics covered in this text. Second, the researchers asked questions that are similar to many of the questions in the GSS. For example, they gathered data about demographic variables for each of the respondents, like sex, age, marital status, and political affiliation. In addition, they gathered data about attitude variables pertinent to the topic of their study—attitudes toward teenagers having sex, access to birth control, and the availability of information about sex, topics about which General Social Survey researchers also collected data. Third, and most important for the skills we will be learning in this chapter, it includes information about how the researchers measured their variables.

---

[1] *The Washington Post,* "Parental Supervision, Strong Values Reduce Likelihood of Teen Sex." Syracuse *Post-Standard,* 6 June 1998, p. C-2.

Parents of Teens and Teens Discuss Sex, Love, and Relationships: Polling Data[2]
INTERNATIONAL COMMUNICATIONS RESEARCH

What's the biggest barrier to effective communication between parents and teens about sex?

Well over half of parents and teens agree that the biggest barrier is that teens and parents are not comfortable discussing sex with each other.

- Almost one-fourth of parents (24%) say the biggest barrier is that parents are not comfortable talking to their kids about sex. Interestingly, only 17% of teens feel that is the biggest barrier.

- Almost four in ten teens (39%)—and three in ten parents of teens (30%)—said the biggest barrier is that teens are not comfortable hearing from their parents about sex.

- Close to one-third of parents of teens (32%) said the biggest barrier to effective communication is that most teens "think they know it all already." However, only 6% of teens said it's because teens "know as much as or more than parents about sex and relationships."

- Fourteen percent of teens said the biggest barrier is that parents are "too judgmental."

---

[2]A summary of findings from National Omnibus Survey questions conducted for the National Campaign to Prevent Teen Pregnancy, <http://www.teenpregnancy.org>. This nationally representative survey of parents of teens and teens age 12 to 17 was conducted by International Communications Research—on behalf of the National Campaign—in early April 1998. The teen survey was conducted April 1–5, and the parent survey was conducted April 1–12. The goal of the survey was to ascertain perceptions and attitudes about communications between parents and teens on sex, love, and relationships. The survey questioned 294 parents of teens and 507 teens. Adult responses have a margin of error of plus or minus 5.72 percentage points. Teen responses have a margin of error of plus or minus 4.35 percentage points.

When should teens start steady, one-on-one, dating?

Parents and teens disagree about when parents should allow teens to begin steady, one-on-one dating.

- Eighty-seven percent of parents of teens said teens should be at least 16 before they begin steady, one-on-one dating.

- Fifty-five percent of teens, however, said that 15 or younger is when kids should be allowed to begin steady dating.

- Fifteen percent of teens said that steady, one-on-one dating should be allowed for those between the ages of 10 and 13.

So what do teens say they most want to hear their parents talk more about?

Teens say they want their parents to talk more about a wide variety of important issues—from contraception to dating, from sexually transmitted diseases to knowing how and when to say "no" to sex.

- Nearly one in four (23%) said they want to hear more about sexually transmitted diseases, contraception, and pregnancy prevention.

- One in five (21%) said they want to hear more about how to manage dating, relationships, and sex.

- Another one in five (22%) would like to hear more about knowing when and how to say "no" to sex.

- Sixteen percent said they want to hear more about what to do if they or their partner gets pregnant.

- Eleven percent said they want to hear their parents talk more about values relating to sex.

What do parents say they tell their teens about sex?

Nine in ten parents of teens (90%) who answered the question directly (that is, those who did not reply "none of the above") said that they have told their kids that they should not have sex until they're at least out of high school. Nearly four in ten of these parents (39%) say they have also told their kids that school-age teens who are having sex should have easy access to contraceptives.

- This finding agrees with a poll released last May by the National Campaign that said a clear majority of both teens and adults feel that high school-age teenagers should not be sexually active but those teens who are engaged in sexual activity should have access to contraception.

This concept, measurement, is fundamental to understanding how to use the statistical tools to which you'll be exposed. Just like the tools in a toolbox, statistics have specific uses. Which statistics are used depends on how variables are measured. In this chapter you will learn to identify the levels of measurement—categorical and numerical, ordinal and nominal—and to distinguish between discrete and continuous variables as a first step toward the application of statistics.

CLASSIFYING VARIABLES BY LEVELS OF MEASUREMENT

Levels of measurement refers to the way researchers collect data about variables. To learn about the characteristics of the elements of a population, researchers have to make observations. Although there are many techniques for making observations, researchers who employ quantitative methods often use survey instruments. The survey instrument may be administered through the mail, over the phone, face-to-face, or even on the Internet. As a researcher develops an instrument, decisions have to be made about how to collect data and what data to collect—the specific pieces of information about each characteristic or variable of interest.

Skills Practice 1 What are the variables of interest to the researchers in the excerpts from the NCPTP study in the "News to Use" section? Make a list of the variables mentioned in the article.

Data for a single variable, such as *age,* can be gathered in a variety of ways. For the adults in the study, the researchers for the National Campaign to Prevent Teen Pregnancy seemed to be collecting data about age in categories (based on how they reported their results). The ages of the participants in the survey were summarized as follows:

Age of respondent

18–20	30–34	45–49	60–64
21–24	35–39	50–54	65–70
25–29	40–44	55–59	

Presumably, a respondent checked off the age category to which he or she belonged.

On the other hand, researchers for the General Social Survey ask this question: "What is your date of birth?" The answer is then converted to the actual age of the respondent.

Researchers decide how to gather data based on what they want to know, how likely people are to respond, and how researchers want to use the data. For some projects, researchers need to know the exact ages of their respondents. For other projects, age categories are sufficient. There are variables, like income, to which people are more likely to respond if the data are being collected in categories. People are less likely to answer if they are asked to write down their annual income to the nearest dollar. Finally, how the data will be used by researchers in their analysis influences how the data are collected. As we will see later, some statistics require us to use data that have been gathered as numbers (a respondent's exact age) rather than categories.

The different ways of gathering data can be classified into levels. Let's begin by understanding the differences between categorical and numerical levels of measurement. In my experience, this is one of the easiest distinctions to make. When you can tell the difference between categorical and numerical variables, it is much easier to make the other distinctions necessary to apply statistics correctly.

The Differences Between Categorical and Numerical Variables

To decide whether variables are categorical or numerical, you have to look at how the researcher is collecting the data about the variables. Just about any given variable can be measured at more than one level. For example, the variable *age* in the survey by the National Campaign to Prevent Teen Pregnancy is categorical. The same variable, *age,* in the General Social Survey is numerical, because the data are gathered as a date from which a respondent's age is computed. How can we tell which is which?

Categorical variables Categorical variables are those variables for which data are gathered in response categories that have been set up or predetermined by the researcher. Examples of variables for which data are often collected at the categorical level are illustrated in Box 2.1.

BOX 2.1   Examples of Categorical Variables

Demographic variables   The following are examples from the NCPTP survey and the GSS:

Sex—male and female

Race—Black, White, and Other

Marital status—married, widowed, divorced, separated, never married

Attitude variables   Data are almost always gathered in categories, like these examples from the NCPTP survey and the GSS:

- How important do you think it is for teens to be given a strong message from society that they should abstain from sex until they are at least out of high school?

    1   Very important
    2   Somewhat important
    3   Not too important
    4   Not at all important

- There's been a lot of discussion about the way morals and attitudes about sex are changing in this country. [If a man and a woman] are in their early teens, say 14 to 16 years old . . . , do you think sex relations before marriage are

    1   Always wrong
    2   Almost always wrong
    3   Wrong only sometimes
    4   Not wrong at all

Behaviors   Data are often collected in categories, as in this question from the General Social Survey:

- Have you ever had sex with someone other than your husband or wife while you were married?

    1   Yes
    2   No
    3   Never married

Numerical (or scale) variables   Numerical variables (also called *scale variables* in the SPSS program) are those variables for which data are gathered as numbers with no attempt by the researcher to precategorize the answers (Box 2.2).

The following two questions from the GSS illustrate how variables can be measured numerically.

1.   How many brothers and sisters do you have? Please count those born alive but no longer living, as well as those alive now. Also include step-brothers and stepsisters, and children adopted by your parents.
2.   How many children have you ever had? Please count all that were born alive at any time (including any you had from a previous marriage).

There are two types of numerical variables: **ratio** and **interval** variables. Although you should be aware of the differences between the two, for statistical purposes all numerical (scale) variables—whether ratio or interval—are usually treated the same way.

Ratio variables   Ratio-level measures are first and foremost numerical, but the numbers being gathered have some unique characteristics.

- Any response of zero collected at the ratio level means the absence of the characteristic being measured. For example, if you entered a zero in answer to the question "How many brothers and sisters do you have?" we could assume that you don't have any.

- The distances between each of the units on a ratio scale of measurement are the same. Take *age,* for example. When the variable is measured numerically, there is the same "distance" between someone who is 18 years old and someone who is 19 years old—365 days.

- The distances between each of the units on a ratio scale are proportional. The proportionality of distance allows us to make meaningful comparisons among units on the scale. Someone who is 36 is twice as old as someone who is 18, and a 20-year-old is half as old as a 40-year-old.

For the measurement of a variable to be considered ratio, all three of these characteristics must be present: zero must be meaningful and represent the absence of the characteristic being measured, the distance between each unit on the scale must be the same or constant, and the distances between each of the units must be proportional.

Interval variables   Interval-level measures are also numerical, but they do not share the characteristics of ratio-level measures. For one thing, interval-level scales either do not use zero or, if they do, zero doesn't mean the absence of the characteristic. In the social sciences, the interval-level measure most of us have read about is the IQ scale. It is designed to measure levels of intelligence, but the scale has no true zero. In the natural sciences, the thermometer is an example of an interval-level measure. Zero is on the thermometer, but it doesn't mean absence of the characteristic (temperature). The zero indicates a certain level of the characteristic. On the Celsius thermometer, zero is the freezing point of water. By way of contrast, the Kelvin thermometer measures temperature on a ratio scale. Zero on the Kelvin thermometer represents the absence of heat.

Second, the distances between units of measurement on an interval scale are not proportional. Consequently, we can't make statements like, "someone who scores 120 on an IQ scale is 20% more intelligent than someone who scores 100," or "someone who scores 50 is half as intelligent as someone who scores 100." It isn't twice as hot at 100 degrees as at 50 degrees, and it isn't half as cold at 10 degrees as it is at 20 degrees.

Avoiding Common Pitfalls   There are several ways of getting confused about making the distinction between categorical and numerical variables.

Categorical data can be gathered as numbers   We often see categorical data gathered using numbers, because researchers attach numbers to categories (variable values) to help with data entry and analysis. For example, an attitude variable may be gathered by asking respondents to enter a number from a scale like this one:

1 = Always wrong
2 = Almost always wrong
3 = Wrong only sometimes
4 = Not wrong at all

In this case, even though a number is being collected as the response, it has no meaning apart from the word category it represents, and it is simply a shorthand representation of a word category. Consequently, data collected this way are categorical, not numerical.

(continued)

Avoiding Common Pitfalls (*continued*)

Data that could be collected numerically are often collected categorically
A fairly common example is how researchers gather data about the variable *income*. Rather than asking people how much money they make (and collect data about income at the numerical level), researchers often set up response categories for the variable. Here's how the researchers working for the NCPTP measure income in categories.

> *Total annual household income*
> Under $10,000
> $10,000–14,999
> $15,000–19,999
> $20,000–24,999
> $25,000–29,999
> $30,000–39,999
> $40,000–49,999
> $50,000–74,999
> $75,000–99,999
> $100,000 or more

Even though variables like income could be measured at the numerical-ratio level, we have to pay attention to how the researcher is actually gathering the data to determine the level of measurement.

Categories can be numbers   The previous example about income illustrates another common pitfall—the categories themselves can be numbers. When you have categories as numbers, how do you tell the difference between categorical-level and numerical-level variables? Look to see whether the numbers have been grouped into intervals or ranges of values, as in the previous example. If they have, then you are dealing with categorical-level measures. If not, then you are probably looking at a variable that is being measured numerically.

Numerical variables can look categorical   Some numerical variables have only a few categories, so researchers list them all when they collect data about the variable. Think about the research involving sex education among middle school students summarized in Chapter 1. The students involved were in grades 6 and 7, so the ages of the participants were probably limited to only a few possibilities. Consequently, researchers *could* gather age in categories, like this:

> How old are you? (Circle one)   10   11   12   13   14

However, the categories cover the entire range of possibilities for the variable. Consequently, there is no difference between the question asked this way and the question asked as simply, "How old are you?"

Categorical Variables: The Differences Between Nominal and Ordinal Variables

Learning how to tell the difference between categorical and numerical level variables is half the battle. The other half is learning to distinguish between types of categorical variables—**nominal** and **ordinal.**

Nominal variables   Nominal variables are those being measured in such a way that the categories simply indicate differences among respondents, with no hierarchy or rank order implied in those differences. One very common example of a nominal-level variable is *sex,* when it is measured in the categories of male and female. Male and female are categories of difference, with no rank order or hierarchy inherent in the categories. Another common example is the variable *race,* measured in the NCPTP survey this way:

White non-Hispanic	Black Hispanic
White Hispanic	Hispanic
Black non-Hispanic	Other race

The categories are categories of difference, not rank.

Ordinal variables   Ordinally measured variables, by comparison, have categories in which there is some inherent rank, hierarchy, or order to the categories. By hierarchy or rank it is not implied that individuals who respond in one category are necessarily better than (or higher than) individuals who respond in another category. Instead, hierarchy or rank means that the categories enable us to arrange individuals along some dimension or in some order. These dimensions may be ones in which individuals in one category express stronger or weaker feelings toward something or feel more or less favorable toward it. Likewise, categories can measure how often something happens or someone does something; how long someone has been doing something; or how much of something (like money) someone has.

   Some examples of categories that have this quality of rank or order to them include these two sets of commonly used answer scales for measuring attitudes:

Very important	Always wrong
Somewhat important	Almost always wrong
Not too important	Wrong only sometimes
Not at all important	Not wrong at all

In addition, the categories of variables like *total household income* are ordinal, because they have an inherent rank or order to them.

Avoiding Common Pitfalls

Dichotomous variables Students are sometimes confused about how to handle **dichotomous variables,** variables with only two categories. Dichotomous variables can be nominal, like

Sex: male or female
Race: White or non-White
Religion: Christian or non-Christian

They may also be ordinal, such as

Attitude: agree or disagree
Behavior: yes or no

What's the difference between nominal and ordinal dichotomies? The same as the difference between any other nominal- and ordinal-level variables. In nominal dichotomies there is no inherent rank or order to the categories of the variable. In ordinal dichotomies the categories of the dichotomy can be ranked or ordered. For example, when people are asked to agree or disagree with a particular statement they are ranking the extent of their support for the statement. People who agree support the statement more than those who disagree. If people are asked to respond "yes" or "no" to a particular behavior, we can conclude that people who respond "yes" engage in the behavior more frequently than those who say "no."

As you move on in the study of statistics, you will find that dichotomous variables may be treated differently from nondichotomous variables. You will also be exposed to a particular type of dichotomous variable called a **dummy variable.** Dummy variables are special kinds of dichotomies with their own properties. Generally, a dummy variable has two categories: one to indicate the absence of a characteristic and the other to indicate its presence. For example, *sex* could be constructed as a dummy variable by treating one category as the absence of a characteristic (not male) and the other as its presence (male). You will learn more about constructing dummy variables when you get to Chapter 11.

Although it is beyond the scope of the skills introduced in this chapter, you should be aware that sometimes nominal dichotomies are treated as ordinal or numerical-level variables, and ordinal dichotomies and dummy variables are sometimes treated as though they are numerical. At this point it is sufficient to make the nominal/ordinal distinction and to recognize when nominal and ordinal variables are also dichotomies.

The Hierarchy of Measurement

In addition to correctly classifying variables according to their level of measurement, we should understand that there is a **hierarchy** to the levels. Numerical variables are treated as the highest level of measurement, followed by variables that are categorical and ordinal. Variables that are categorical and

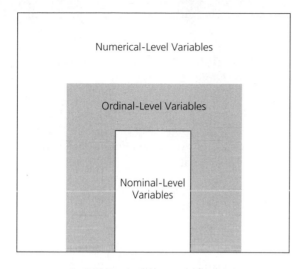

Figure 2.1 The hierarchy of levels of measurement.

nominal are at the bottom of the hierarchy. Figure 2.1 is a diagram of the relationship among the levels of measurement.

Statistics that are appropriate for the lowest level of measurement, nominal variables, can also be applied to variables at the higher levels—ordinal and numerical. Statistics appropriate for ordinal variables can be applied to numerical variables. However, statistics appropriate for numerical variables can be applied only to that level and not to ordinal and nominal variables. Consequently, there are many tools for the analysis of numerical-level variables, somewhat fewer tools available for ordinal variables, and even fewer for nominal variables.

Skills Practice 2 Classify the following General Social Survey variables. First decide whether they are categorical or numerical. Then, decide whether the categorical variables are nominal or ordinal.

A. MARITAL STATUS: Are you currently married, widowed, divorced, separated, or have you never been married?

1   Married   4   Separated
2   Widowed   5   Never married
3   Divorced

B. SUBJECTIVE CLASS IDENTIFICATION: If you were asked to use one of four names for your social class, which would you say you belong in: the lower class, the working class, the middle class, or the upper class?

1   Lower class   3   Middle class
2   Working class   4   Upper class

(continued)

Skills Practice 2 *(continued)*

C. DOES RESPONDENT OR SPOUSE BELONG TO UNION: Do you (or your spouse) belong to a labor union? (Who belongs?)

  1 Respondent belongs
  2 Spouse belongs
  3 Respondent and spouse belong
  4 Neither belongs

D. LABOR FORCE STATUS: Last week were you working full-time, part-time, going to school, keeping house, or what?

  1 Working full-time
  2 Working part-time
  3 Temporarily not working
  4 Unemployed, laid off
  5 Retired
  6 In school
  7 Keeping house
  8 Other

E. RS RELIGIOUS PREFERENCE: What is your religious preference? Is it Protestant, Catholic, Jewish, some other religion, or no religion?

  1 Protestant
  2 Catholic
  3 Jewish
  4 None
  5 Other

F. WEEKS R. WORKED LAST YEAR: Now I'd like to ask you about last year. In 1993 how many weeks did you work either full-time or part-time not counting work around the house—including paid vacations and sick leave? _____

G. RS HIGHEST DEGREE: If finished 9th through 12th grade: Did you ever get a high school diploma or a GED certificate? Did you complete one or more years of college for credit—not including schooling such as business college, technical or vocational school? If yes: How many years did you complete? Do you have any college degrees? (If yes, what degree or degrees?) Circle the highest degree earned.

  0 Less than high school
  1 High school
  2 Junior college
  3 Bachelor
  4 Graduate

H. NUMBER OF HOURS R. WORKED LAST WEEK: If working full- or part-time, how many hours did you work last week, at all jobs? _____

I. NUMBER OF HOURS SPOUSE WORKED LAST WEEK: If working full- or part-time, how many hours did your spouse work last week, at all jobs? _____

CLASSIFYING VARIABLES AS DISCRETE OR CONTINUOUS

In addition to classifying the measurement of variables as categorical (and nominal or ordinal) or numerical, we should be able to determine whether the variables being measured are discrete or continuous. Knowing whether variables are continuous or discrete, like the assessment of levels of measurement, helps us apply statistics correctly. Unlike making the categorical–numerical distinction, whether or not variables are discrete or continuous has less to do with how researchers are gathering data about the variables than it does with the nature of the characteristic being measured. Different statistical tools may be used depending on the nature of the variables being analyzed.

Discrete Variables

Variables or characteristics that are **discrete** can be counted. In addition, they are countable in discrete quantities, or quantities that cannot be reduced to ever smaller units or numbers. For example, if you are asking people about how many brothers and sisters they have, you are measuring a discrete variable. People come in discrete quantities—units of 1. We do not report having 1½ brothers or sisters. Income is another discrete variable. If you ask someone exactly how much they earn before taxes each week, they will not report anything less than dollars and cents.

Continuous Variables

Continuous variables, on the other hand, are variables for which the characteristic being measured is infinitely reducible. For example, variables that have a time dimension—like age, length of time spent doing something, number of years involved in some activity—are continuous, because time is infinitely reducible, to years, hours, minutes, seconds, fractions of seconds. (However, if you are asked about your age or how many years you have been involved in some activity, like getting an education or working in a particular job, you respond with the nearest year and you don't reduce the variable to its most precise measurement.)

Variables that measure attitudes are also continuous, because attitudes come in an infinite array of perspectives (even though it is more convenient to treat attitudes as if they do not). Whereas you may be asked if you think something is always wrong, almost always wrong, wrong only sometimes, or not wrong at all, your actual attitude may fall at a given category or anywhere in between—between always wrong and almost always wrong, for instance. You usually check off the attitude *closest* to the one that represents your point of view. If you have ever been involved with doing a survey of attitudes, this phenomenon is readily apparent. Invariably, at least a few respondents will refuse to check off one of the appropriate boxes, choosing instead to indicate that their attitude falls somewhere in between the boxes. They will resist treating a continuous variable as if it were discrete!

You can get a sense of the continuous nature of many characteristics by looking at the different approaches to measuring them. Compare, for example, the way that researchers for the General Social Survey ask about race (in three categories: White, Black, and Other) with the way the researchers for the NCPTP subdivided the categories of a similar variable (using seven categories: White non-Hispanic, White Hispanic, Black non-Hispanic, Black Hispanic, Hispanic unspecified, Other). Do you think the categories of a variable like race are infinitely reducible?

Figure 2.2 summarizes the important difference between continuous and discrete variables. Between any two response categories of a continuous variable, there are an unlimited or infinite number of other possible responses. For example, between the ages 0 and 1, there are an unlimited number of other possible ages, although we don't tend to think in those terms. Between any two response categories of a discrete variable, there are either no other possibilities (between one child and two children) or the possibilities are limited (finite)—between $1 and $2 there *are* other possibilities, but not more than 99 of them.

Avoiding Common Pitfalls

Discrete variables can be turned into continuous variables   Sometimes, researchers take variables that are, by nature, discrete and turn them into variables that are continuous. For example, researchers may ask how much money you earned last year, a discrete variable; or they may ask how much money you earned, on average, for the last 3 years, a continuous variable. The amount you earned last year is discrete because your earnings for a single year is a number that is not infinitely reducible. Then why are earnings averaged over a 3-year period continuous? Because an average can be carried out to an unlimited number of decimal places. If someone earns $100,000 over a 3-year period, the average ($100,000 ÷ 3) equals $33,333.333$\overline{3}$.

Continuous variables can be treated as if they are discrete   Researchers often treat continuous variables as if they are discrete. For example, when asked about our age, we don't write 21 years 6 months 5 days 3 hours 18 minutes and 7.12359 seconds. Instead, we round off to our last birthday. Similarly, when someone asks us what time it is, it is common to round it off to the nearest hour and minute. Even variables like attitudes, which are by nature continuous, are often treated as if they are discrete. We either agree or disagree, nothing in between.

One way to determine whether a variable is truly discrete or is simply being treated as if it is discrete is to ask yourself, "Are there an infinite number of other possible categories between any two given categories of this variable?" If you have two attitude categories, Agree and Disagree, are there an infinite variety of other possible attitudes between those two answer categories? The answer is yes. What about the income categories $1,000 and $2,000? The answer is no. Although there are a number of other possible categories, the number is not infinite. The smallest possible category between the two would be increments of a penny. Thus you could have categories $1,000.01, $1,000.02, $1,000.03, and so on between $1,000 and $2,000, but you couldn't have anything smaller than that (such as $1,000.001 or $1,000.0001).

Figure 2.2   The difference between discrete and continuous variables.

Skills Practice 3   Classify variables F through J in Skills Practice 2 as either continuous or discrete.

SUMMARY

We began this chapter by learning to distinguish between categorical and numerical variables. Generally speaking, categorical variables are those for which researchers gather data in predetermined categories. Numerical variables are those for which researchers gather data as numbers. Categorical variables can be further subdivided into two levels: nominal and ordinal. Nominal variables are those for which there is no rank or order among the categories—the categories indicate difference, nothing more. Ordinal variables are those for which the categories have a rank or order.

We learned that many variables (age and level of education are examples) can be measured in different ways, depending on what researchers want to know and how they want to analyze the variables. Consequently, classifying a variable's level of measurement requires us to look at the way a researcher gathers information about it.

On the other hand, deciding whether variables are continuous (have infinitely divisible categories) or discrete (do not have infinitely divisible categories) requires us to think about the nature of the variable itself. If we are measuring numbers of people, we are dealing with a discrete variable—something that cannot be subdivided past a unit of one. If we are measuring age, we are dealing with a continuous variable—something that can be infinitely subdivided.

In the next chapter, you will learn how to organize data once they have been collected by setting up data files in SPSS, and you will be applying the concept of levels of measurement as you create an SPSS data file.

KEY CONCEPTS

Levels of measurement	Ratio variable	Dummy variable
Categorical variable	Interval variable	Hierarchy of measurement
Numerical (scale) variable	Nominal variable	Discrete variable
	Ordinal variable	Continuous variable
	Dichotomous variable	

ANSWERS TO SKILLS PRACTICES

1. The variables in the survey include whether the respondent is a parent or teen, age, barriers to communication about sex, attitudes toward dating, topics teens would like to hear their parents discuss, and what parents say they tell teens about sex.

2. For categorical vs. numerical (scale) variables: categorical variables are A–E, G, and J; numerical variables are F, H, and I. For nominal vs. ordinal variables: nominal variables are A, C, D, and E; ordinal variables are B, G, and J.

3. Variables F–J are all continuous.

GENERAL EXERCISES

1. Here is a set of variables with their categories drawn from the National Campaign to Prevent Teen Pregnancy survey of teenagers and parents "to ascertain perceptions and attitudes about communications between parents and teens on sex, love, and relationships."[3] Classify each of the variables as categorical or numerical. Then decide whether the categorical variables are nominal or ordinal.

Adult Demographic Variables

1. **Own or rent home?**

   Own

   Rent

   Don't know

   Refused [to answer]

2. **Marital status**

   Single

   Single, living with a partner

   Married

   Separated

   Widowed

   Divorced

3. **Are you the head of the household?**

   Yes

   No

4. **Employment status**

   Full-time

   Part-time

   Retired

   Housewife

   Student

   Temporarily unemployed

   Disabled/handicapped

   Other

---

[3]International Communications Research, 1998, "Parents of Teens and Teens Discuss Sex, Love, and Relationships: Polling Data," <http://www.teenpregnancy.org/98poll.htm>.

5. **Political party affiliation**

Republican   Independent

Democrat   Other

6. **Total number of adults 18 or older living in household**

One   Four

Two   Five

Three   Six

7. **Level of education**

Less than high school graduate

High school graduate

Some college

College graduate

Postgraduate school or more

Technical school/other (unspecified)

8. **Total number living in household**

Two   Six

Three   Seven

Four   Eight or more

Five

Teen Demographics

9. **Age of respondent**

Age 12   Age 15

Age 13   Age 16

Age 14   Age 17

Teen and Adult Attitude Variables

10. Some people think it is basically acceptable for high school teenagers to be sexually active, as long as they take steps to prevent pregnancy and sexually transmitted diseases including AIDS. Others do not think it is acceptable for high school teenagers to be sexually active whether they take precautions or not. Which comes closer to your view, the first statement or the second one?

    a. Teen sexual activity acceptable as long as teens take precautions; OR

    b. Teen sexual activity not acceptable even if they take precautions.

11. I'm going to read you three statements about teens and sex. Please tell me which one comes closest to your view:

    a. Teens should NOT be sexually active and should not have access to birth control;

    b. Teens should NOT be sexually active, but teens who ARE should have access to birth control; OR

    c. It's OKAY for teens to be sexually active, AS LONG AS they have access to birth control.

2. Classify each of the variables in Appendix E as categorical (and nominal or ordinal) or numerical. (Some of them will be familiar from Skills Practice 2.)

3. Classify variables 8 through 11 in General Exercise 1 as continuous or discrete.

4. Find a survey—perhaps one you got in the mail or found in a newspaper or magazine. You may even come across them online if you are an Internet surfer. Classify the variables in the survey: Are they categorical or numerical? If categorical, are they nominal or ordinal? Which variables are continuous and which are discrete?

SPSS EXERCISES

1. Check your work for General Exercise 2 using the SPSS program. (Use the SPSS Guides in Chapter 1 to open the program and the Variables window. In the Variables window, you can see the level of measurement for each of the variables in the gss96subset file.)

Creating an SPSS Data File

INTRODUCTION

As you begin working with the General Social Survey, you may wonder how all these data got set up in the computer in the first place. Also, although there are many sets of data like the General Social Survey—already formatted for SPSS and waiting to be analyzed—it is very likely you will be asked at some point in your career to do research that will require you to create your own data set.

In this chapter you will learn how to set up a data file in SPSS using a small set of responses randomly selected from the GSS. You will be working with many of the same variables with which you became familiar in Chapters 1 and 2—variables similar to those used in the GSS and the National Campaign to Prevent Teen Pregnancy (NCPTP) study—along with some new ones. To demonstrate the process of creating a data set, let's assume that you have collected data from 20 people using the survey instrument in Box 3.1, and now you want to get it ready for analysis.

The process of setting up data in SPSS has five steps:

Step 1. Prepare the survey questions to be defined in the SPSS program.

Step 2. Use SPSS to set up, or define, each of the variables in the survey.

Step 3. Enter the data.

Step 4. Check the data to be sure it has been entered accurately.

Step 5. Save the data file.

BOX 3.1 Survey of 10 Questions Adapted from the General Social Survey

1. What is your age (as of your last birthday)? _____
   Check here if you don't know or you're not sure: _____

2. Are you

   _____ male   _____ female

3. Are you currently

   _____ married
   _____ widowed
   _____ divorced
   _____ separated
   _____ never married

4. Think about the people who live in your household. Please include any persons who usually live here but are away temporarily—on business, on vacation, or in a general hospital—and include all babies and small children. Do not include college students who are living away at college, persons stationed away from here in the Armed Forces, or persons away in institutions. How many people live in your household? _____
   Check here if you don't know or you're not sure: _____

5. Last week were you

   _____ working full-time   _____ retired
   _____ working part-time   _____ in school
   _____ temporarily not working   _____ keeping house
   _____ unemployed, laid off   _____ other

6. In which of these groups did your total family income fall, from all sources, last year before taxes?

   _____ Less than $1,000   _____ $17,500–19,999
   _____ $1,000–2,999   _____ $20,000–22,499
   _____ $3,000–3,999   _____ $22,500–24,999
   _____ $4,000–4,999   _____ $25,000–29,999
   _____ $5,000–5,999   _____ $30,000–34,999
   _____ $6,000–6,999   _____ $35,000–39,999
   _____ $7,000–7,999   _____ $40,000–49,999
   _____ $8,000–9,999   _____ $50,000–59,999
   _____ $10,000–12,499   _____ $60,000–74,999
   _____ $12,500–14,999   _____ $75,000+
   _____ $15,000–17,499   (continued)

7. There's been a lot of discussion about the way morals and attitudes about sex are changing in this country. If a man and woman have sex relations before marriage, do you think it is

_____ always wrong

_____ almost always wrong

_____ sometimes wrong

_____ not wrong at all

8. What if they are in their early teens, say, 14 to 16 years old? In that case, do you think sex relations before marriage are

_____ always wrong

_____ almost always wrong

_____ sometimes wrong

_____ not wrong at all

9. What is your opinion about a married person having sexual relations with someone other than the marriage partner?

_____ always wrong

_____ almost always wrong

_____ sometimes wrong

_____ not wrong at all

10. Have you ever had sex with someone other than your husband or wife while you were married?

_____ yes   _____ no   _____ never married

PREPARING THE SURVEY QUESTIONS

We will begin the process of setting up our data by deciding how to treat the variables in our survey.

Naming the Variables

Each variable has to be named, and we have to decide what to name it. Remember each **variable name** is a mnemonic, which means that it is an abbreviated version of the lengthier variable label. The name we assign to a variable should remind us of what it stands for. Box 3.2 gives a few rules to follow for assigning names to make them compatible with the SPSS program.

If you make a mistake, SPSS will let you know. If you try to put in a name longer than 8 characters, SPSS will accept only the first 8 characters entered. If you try to start with a number, SPSS will tell you about your mistake when you try to enter the variable name. Later in this chapter you will learn how to see a list of the rules for variable names as you are setting up your data with SPSS.

> **Skills Practice 1**   Give each of the variables in Box 3.1 an 8-character name. Write the name next to the variable it describes. There is no right or wrong answer as long as the name means something to you and it conforms to the rules listed in Box 3.2. If you get stuck, see how similar variables are named in the General Social Survey (using the codes in Appendix E).

Specifying Levels of Measurement

SPSS will want to know how the variables are being measured. How the variables are measured affects the process of assigning values to variable categories (the next step), so it's important to get this right.

> **Skills Practice 2**   Classify each variable in Box 3.1 as categorical or numerical (scale). If the variable is categorical, classify it as nominal or ordinal. Write the level of measurement next to each variable.

Coding the Variable Categories

Coding **variable categories** involves assigning **category values,** or numbers, to the categories of each of the variables. For numerical (scale) variables this task is easy, because the responses to numerical variables are meaningful and can be entered as they were written by the respondent. The only problem you might encounter is how to treat missing values.[1] For categorical variables, the variable categories have to be turned into numbers, and, as with numerical variables, you have to decide how to treat any missing data.

Start the process by taking the variables in Box 3.1 one at a time, beginning with the first (and the easiest), the respondent's age. This variable is a numerical variable; no codes are necessary except for missing value codes. In the next section we will discuss how researchers deal with missing data and assign codes to keep track of it.

Move on to the second variable, the respondent's sex. There is a little more for us to do with this one. Begin by assigning values (numbers) to the meaningful variable categories, those categories that are responses to the question being asked. (Disregard, for the time being, any categories that are not responsive to the question, like Don't Know.) The simplest way to do that is to number the categories consecutively, starting with the first one. The categories for the variable *sex* would be numbered as follows:

1 male

2 female

Skills Practice 3   Assign category values to the rest of the variables in Box 3.1. Write your category values next to the categories of each of the variables.

Assigning Missing Values

The term **missing values** is a little misleading, because the values themselves aren't missing. What *is* missing is a respondent's answer to a particular question. The missing values are the category codes or numbers assigned to keep track of the missing answers. Specifying missing values is important, because we are deciding which values of our variables will be regarded as meaningful and which ones we are going to treat, in effect, as a failure to respond (regardless of the reason). Treating a response as missing excludes it from any statistical analysis we might do with the variable.

There are several reasons why data could be missing. Sometimes, respondents are not asked a question. Some respondents may simply overlook one or more questions. Others refuse to answer certain questions. Although missing data are usually excluded from the statistical analysis of the responses to variables, it is important to keep track of them. Researchers need to be sure that there aren't a lot

---

[1]You may recall from Chapter 1 that missing values are those categories of response that are not meaningful answers to a question. They are assigned when individuals simply don't answer a question (skip over it, perhaps), say they don't know, refuse to answer, or aren't asked a particular question for one reason or another.

of missing data as a result of respondents overlooking or refusing to answer their questions, and they need to be sure that there isn't any *systematic* overlooking of or refusal to answer certain questions. To make sure this isn't happening, researchers need to be able to see how many data are missing. If there are a lot of missing data, they have to examine the characteristics of those who don't answer the questions and compare them with those who do. If those who don't answer are different in important ways (for example, male vs. female, young vs. old, high income vs. low income), then the ability to generalize from the results of a survey can be affected by missing data and researchers have to point that out.

Missing values categories are only sometimes listed as response categories on survey forms. For example, a researcher might list Refuse to Answer or Don't Know as one of the response options for a question and then treat everyone who chose that option as "missing" for that variable. However, sometimes people skip over a question entirely and give no answer, or they give an answer that has nothing to do with the question. Think about how you would code these nonresponses. Box 3.3 is a list of the guidelines to use for assigning values to missing data.

Skills Practice 4   Assign missing values to each of the variables in Box 3.1. Write your missing values next to their respective variables.

BOX 3.3   Guidelines for Assigning Missing Values

- Use numbers that aren't already category values and cannot be category values. Generally, use no more digits for the missing value than there are digits in the category values. If your category values are all single-digit values, then use a single-digit missing value code. If your category values can take up to three digits, then use a 3-digit missing value code. For example, if you are assigning a missing value to the variable *sex,* which can be assigned the value categories 1 and 2, you can use 9 as the missing value code. However, if you are assigning a missing value to the variable *age,* use 99 or 999.

- Be as consistent as possible. The numbers 9, 99, 999, 9999, and so on, are often used as missing values because they usually (but not always) fall outside the range of all possible values for variables. In the General Social Survey, you will also see negative 1 (-1) and zero (0) used as missing values along with variations of 8 (like 8, 98, and 998). Decide in advance which response categories will be used for which kinds of missing data. The GSS uses -1 or 0 whenever a question isn't applicable to a particular respondent, 8 (or a variation) for respondents who don't know the answer to a particular question, and 9 (or a variation) for respondents who don't answer a question. We will follow these practices and use 9, 99, or 999 whenever an answer is missing (simply skipped over), and use 8, 98, or 998 for all "don't know" answers.

Creating a Respondent ID Number

As questionnaires are completed or survey forms are returned, it is customary to assign each respondent an identification number. This identification number can be very useful if you need to go back and check to be sure the responses from a particular survey form have been entered accurately. Also, this number is usually used as a code for filing surveys once the data have been entered from them. Add the number to the bottom right corner of the survey form. Treat it like any other variable. Name it, label it, and specify its level of measurement. (It is a nominal-level variable because the identification number is simply a substitute for naming each respondent.)

At this point, you should have a name for each variable, the level of measurement for each variable, and a numbering scheme for the categories of each variable, including missing values. Compare what you have with Box 3.4. The variable labels, levels of measurement, category values, and missing values are in a different typeface. With this information in hand, we can start to create our data set in SPSS.

BOX 3.4 Variable Names, Levels of Measurement, Category Values, and Missing Values for the Survey of 10 Questions Adapted from the General Social Survey

1. What is your age (as of your last birthday)? _____

   98 Check here if you don't know or you're not sure:

   _____

   age
   Numerical
   No answer = 99

2. Are you

   1 _____ male   2 _____ female

   sex
   Categorical—nominal
   No answer = 9

3. Are you currently

   1 _____ married   4 _____ separated

   2 _____ widowed   5 _____ never married

   3 _____ divorced

   marital
   Categorical—nominal
   No answer = 9

4. Think about the people who live in your household. Please include any persons who usually live here but are away temporarily—on business, on vacation, or in a general hospital—and include all babies and small children. Do not include college students who are living away at college, persons stationed away from here in the Armed Forces, or persons away in institutions. How many people live in your household? _____

   98 Check here if you don't know or you're not sure:

   _____

   hompop
   Numerical
   No answer = 99

---

5. Last week were you

1	_____	working full-time
2	_____	working part-time
3	_____	temporarily not working
4	_____	unemployed, laid off
5	_____	retired
6	_____	in school
7	_____	keeping house
8	_____	other

wrkstat
Categorical—nominal
No answer = 9

6. In which of these groups did your total family income fall, from all sources, last year before taxes?

income
Categorical—ordinal
No answer = 99

1	_____	Less than $1,000		13	_____	$20,000–22,499
2	_____	$1,000–2,999		14	_____	$22,500–24,999
3	_____	$3,000–3,999		15	_____	$25,000–29,999
4	_____	$4,000–4,999		16	_____	$30,000–34,999
5	_____	$5,000–5,999		17	_____	$35,000–39,999
6	_____	$6,000–6,999		18	_____	$40,000–49,999
7	_____	$7,000–7,999		19	_____	$50,000–59,999
8	_____	$8,000–9,999		20	_____	$60,000–74,999
9	_____	$10,000–12,499		21	_____	$75,000+
10	_____	$12,500–14,999				
11	_____	$15,000–17,499				
12	_____	$17,500–19,999				

7. There's been a lot of discussion about the way morals and attitudes about sex are changing in this country. If a man and woman have sex relations before marriage, do you think it is

1	_____	always wrong
2	_____	almost always wrong
3	_____	sometimes wrong
4	_____	not wrong at all

premarsx
Categorical—ordinal
No answer = 9

8. What if they are in their early teens, say, 14 to 16 years old? In that case, do you think sex relations before marriage are

1	_____	always wrong
2	_____	almost always wrong
3	_____	sometimes wrong
4	_____	not wrong at all

teensex
Categorical—ordinal
No answer = 9

(continued)

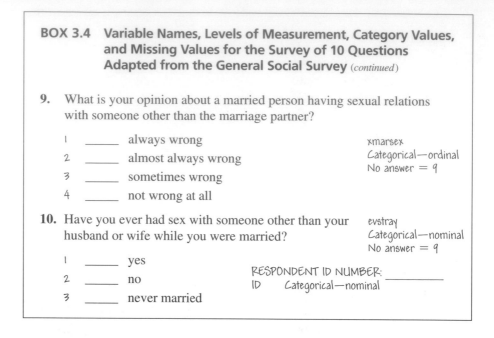

9. What is your opinion about a married person having sexual relations with someone other than the marriage partner?

   1 _____ always wrong
   2 _____ almost always wrong
   3 _____ sometimes wrong
   4 _____ not wrong at all

   xmarsex
   Categorical—ordinal
   No answer = 9

10. Have you ever had sex with someone other than your husband or wife while you were married?

   1 _____ yes
   2 _____ no
   3 _____ never married

   evstray
   Categorical—nominal
   No answer = 9

   RESPONDENT ID NUMBER: _____
   ID   Categorical—nominal

SETTING UP (DEFINING) DATA IN THE SPSS PROGRAM

Defining and Naming Variables

The first step for setting up data in SPSS is telling the program about the variables. The process, called defining variables, has six steps:

Step 1. Name each variable.

Step 2. Specify the variable type.

Step 3. Assign labels to each variable and its values.

Step 4. Designate missing values.

Step 5. Format the columns for each variable.

Step 6. Identify the level of measurement of each variable.

All six steps are completed in one window, called Define Variable. As you go through the process, have your survey with the variable names, levels of measurement, and category and missing value codes (Box 3.4) in front of you.

Start by opening the SPSS program and moving to the SPSS Data Editor screen. (Use the SPSS Guide in Chapter 1, "Opening the SPSS Program," if you need help.) The Data Editor is ready to receive data, but before it can make sense of any numbers you might give it, you have to tell it something about the data. Use the SPSS Guide, "Defining Variables in SPSS," to open the Define Variable window and begin the process of naming your variables.

SPSS Guide: Defining Variables in SPSS

To start, put your cursor on the first variable box (labeled VAR) in the SPSS Data Editor and double-click (click two times in rapid succession). A window called Define Variable will open up. Everything you need to do to define your variables is in this window. Here are the steps:

1. Name the variable.
2. Specify the variable type.
3. Label the variable.
4. Identify missing values.
5. Set the column format.
6. Identify the level of measurement.

Step 1: Name the variable Type in the name of your first variable, *age* (directly from your answer to Skills Practice 1). As you begin to type, the default variable name, VAR0001, will be replaced by your new variable name. When you're done, click on Type to move to Step 2.

Define Variable	×

Variable Name: age

Variable Description
Type: Numeric8.2
Variable Label:
Missing Values: None
Alignment: Right

Change Settings

Type...	Missing Values...
Labels..	Column Format...

Measurement

⦿ Scale   ○ Ordinal   ○ Nominal

[OK]   [Cancel]   [Help]

You can check the rules for naming variables by putting your cursor on the words, Variable Name, and using your right-most mouse key. A box will appear explaining the naming rules. To close the box, click again with the left-most click key.

> A name assigned to a variable. The name can be up to 8 characters in length. It must begin with a letter (A-Z) or the @ character. The remaining characters in the name can be any letter, any digit, or any of the five characters _.@#$.

Step 2: Define variable type   This feature tells SPSS about the format of the variables.

```
Define Variable Type:                                    [X]
  (•) Numeric                                      ┌─────────────┐
  ( ) Comma                          Width: [8]    │  Continue   │
  ( ) Dot                    Decimal Places: [2]   └─────────────┘
  ( ) Scientific notation                          ┌─────────────┐
  ( ) Date                                         │   Cancel    │
  ( ) Dollar                                       └─────────────┘
  ( ) Custom currency                              ┌─────────────┐
  ( ) String                                       │    Help     │
                                                   └─────────────┘
```

You will see a number of choices, some of which already have black circles next to them. For example, the choice Numeric already has a dark dot next to it, which means that Numeric is the **default position** or default setting—the choice that SPSS will make in the absence of any other directions or instructions from you. The default positions can usually be changed and often have to be changed.

Even though you see a lot of options here, there are really only two choices. SPSS variables are formatted as numeric variables (or some variation thereof) or string variables. In SPSS, **numeric variables** are any variables that will be entered as numbers. **String variables** are any variables that will be entered as letters, like someone's name or initials. It is important to note that in SPSS numeric variables are not the same as numerical- (or scale-) level variables. All of the variables we are working with are numeric variables, but only some are numerical (scale). Most of the choices you see—such as Comma, Dot, Scientific Notation, and so on—are options for formatting numeric variables. For example, if you want commas to appear in your numbers, you can select the Comma option, and if you want dollar signs to appear, use the Dollar option.

❶ Select one of the Variable Type choices by clicking on the circle next to it. If you forget what the options mean, remember that a very helpful feature of SPSS 9.0 allows you to point your cursor at almost any of the choices you see on the screen and click your right-most click key to make a brief explanation of the choice appear. Try it: Put your cursor on the choice Numeric and right-click. A box will open:

> A variable whose values are numbers. Values are displayed in standard numeric format, using the decimal delimiter specified in the Regional Setting control panel. The Data Editor accepts numeric values in standard format; or in scientific notation.

To close the box, click again with the left click key.

2 Check the variable Width. To change the width, put your cursor in the box next to Width, click, and type in the desired width. The default setting is 8. This means that you can enter up to 8 digits (or characters) for the variable.

3 Check Decimal Places. Unless the data contain decimals, change the decimal place setting to zero. Put your cursor in the box next to Decimal Places, click, and type in 0. The default position is 2 decimals, but usually we don't need any.

4 Click on Continue to return to the Define Variable window. At the Define Variable window, click on Labels to move to Step 3.

Step 3: Define labels   This feature allows us to assign variable and value labels to describe our variables to the SPSS program. We can give our variables labels (phrases that explain what each variable means), and we can tell SPSS what each of the values and value labels (categories) of the variable will be. Begin by entering a longer description of the variable in the Variable Label box. The **variable label** is a descriptive phrase, usually only a few words long, that captures the essence of what the variable is about. There is no right or wrong answer for making up variable labels—use whatever will help you make sense of your data. Variable labels can have up to 20 characters (although SPSS will not always display labels that long), and you can use spaces, numbers, or other symbols in your label. If you need help, use your right-most click key to display information about making up variable labels. For the variable *age,* let's enter RESPONDENT'S AGE to see how this works.

Specify the values and create value labels for categorical variables. The values and value labels come directly from your survey form. Because the variable *age* is numerical there are only two categories: one for "don't know" and one for those who didn't answer the question. Both are missing values categories. (When you are working with categorical variables, nominal or ordinal, there will be more values and value labels to enter.)

① Click on the box next to Value and type in the first value, 98, for the variable *age*.

② Hit the tab key to move to the Value Label box and type in the category label, DON'T KNOW, that goes with the value.

③ Click on Add to create your first value and value label.

Your Define Labels window should look like this:

Repeat Steps 1 through 3 for the next category of the variable *age*—NO ANSWER. Add the value, 99, and value label, NO ANSWER. Then, click on Add. The Define Labels window should now look like this:

Define Labels:

Variable Label: Respondent's Age

Value Labels

Value: 99

Value Label: No Answer

[Add] [Change] [Remove]

98 = "Don't Know"
99 = "No Answer"

[Continue] [Cancel] [Help]

Review your values and labels and correct any mistakes. If you find an error, click on the value and its label in the window to highlight it. Click on Remove to delete the incorrect value and value label. Type in your corrected value and label, using the Value and Value Label boxes. Then click on Add. When you are satisfied with your values and labels, click on Continue. You will go back to the Define Variable window. At the Define Variable window, click on Missing Values to move to Step 4.

Step 4: Define missing values   The missing values feature allows us to tell SPSS which values are to be disregarded as meaningful values of a variable. Values designated as missing are not included in the statistical calculations that SPSS runs. The Define Missing Values window opens, and four choices appear.

Define Missing Values:

⦿ No missing values
○ Discrete missing values

[   ] [   ] [   ]

○ Range of missing values

Low: [   ]   High: [   ]

○ Range plus one discrete missing value

Low: [   ]   High: [   ]

Discrete value: [   ]

[Continue] [Cancel] [Help]

The default setting is No Missing Values. However, the variable *age* has the missing values of 98 and 99, so we have to pick another option. In most cases, the Discrete Missing Values option allows us enough room to list each of our missing values.

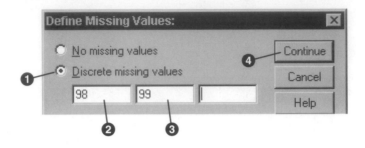

We follow these steps to define our missing values:

❶ Click on Discrete Missing Values.

❷ Type the first missing value, 98, in the first box.

❸ Tab over to the second box, and type in the second missing value, 99.

❹ When you're finished, click on Continue to return to the Define Variable window. At the Define Variable window, click on Column Format to move to Step 5.

Step 5: Define column format With the column format feature we can tell the SPSS program how we want each column to look. Usually, the column format is set automatically, depending on the type of variable we have (numeric or string) and the width we specified under Type. Sometimes we need to correct one or more of the column format settings.

Generally, the default settings will be acceptable. However, if you changed the variable width in the Type box, make sure the change also appears in the

Column Width box. For numeric variables, the values will be right-justified (aligned with the right margin of each column in which they're displayed) when you type them in; for string variables, the words you type in will be left-justified (aligned with the left margin). There is usually no need to change these settings, but if you should need to change them, here's what you do:

- **Width:** Put your cursor on the box next to width and type in how many characters wide you would like the column to be.

- **Text alignment:** Click on the circle next to your choice.

Click on Continue to go back to the Define Variable window.

Step 6: Specify level of measurement   SPSS version 9.0 allows us to tell the program at what level each of our variables is being measured. Choose the Measurement level from the list of options. The Scale (numerical) level is the default value. The variable *age* is numerical, so we don't need to change the level of measurement. (Note that you can right-click to see definitions of each level of measurement.)

We are finished defining our first variable, *age*. Click on OK to add your variable definition to your Data Editor. The name of your variable appears in the Data Editor window.

To check the variable and its definition, click on the Variable (blue question mark) icon on the toolbar. You will have only one variable on your list at this point.

Make sure everything is OK. After checking your variable, click on Close. If you need to correct errors, return to the Define Variable window by double-clicking on the name of the variable—*age,* in this case.

At this point, you now have one variable set up and ready to receive data. You could enter the ages of each of the respondents to your survey. However, researchers usually don't begin entering data until all of their variables are set up, so let's finish defining our variables. We will try another example, this time with a categorical variable, *sex*.

Another Example: Categorical Variables

Let's run through one more example, using the second variable in our survey (Box 3.4), *sex*. Look at how you numbered the categories of the variable, assigned missing values, and specified the level of measurement. Now open the Define Variable window by double-clicking on the variable immediately to the right of *age*.

Step 1. Name the variable At the Define Variable window, enter a variable name: *sex*. Then click on Type.

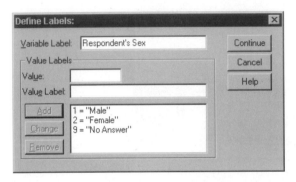

Step 2. Define variable type The default settings, Numeric and Width, are correct and don't need to be changed. The values of this variable have no decimal places, so set Decimal Places to zero (delete the 2 and replace it with a 0). Click on Continue.

Step 3. Define labels At the Define Variable window, click on Labels to open the Define Labels window. Enter a variable label: RESPONDENT'S SEX. Then enter the values and value labels for each category, using the three-step process:

1. Type in the Value, hit Tab.

2. Type in the Value Label.

3. Click on Add.

Don't forget to enter a value for the Missing Values category, No Answer. Click on Continue when you're done.

Step 4. Define missing values At the Define Variable window, click on Missing Values to open the Define Missing Values window. Specify the discrete missing value, 9, for the variable *sex*. Then click on Continue.

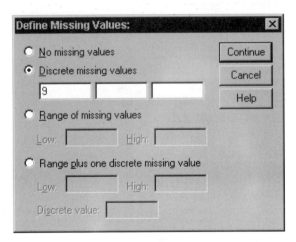

Step 5. Define column format At the Define Variable window, click on Column Format to open the Define Column Format window. As is usually the case, the default settings for the column format are fine. Click on Continue.

Step 6. Specify level of measurement
Finally, click on the appropriate level of measurement. The variable *sex* is nominal.

Define Variable	☒
Variable Name: sex	

Variable Description
Type: Numeric8.0
Variable Label: Respondent's Sex
Missing Values: 9
Alignment: Right

Change Settings

Type...	Missing Values...
Labels..	Column Format...

Measurement
○ Scale   ○ Ordinal   ⦿ Nominal

| OK | Cancel | Help |

To conclude the process, click on OK. The variable *sex* will now appear in your SPSS Data Editor, and you can check it using the Variables icon.

Untitled - SPSS for Windows Data Editor

File Edit View Data Transform Analyze Graphs Utilities Window Help

age	sex	var	var	var

Skills Practice 5   Define the rest of the variables in Box 3.4. Don't forget the identification variable. Check your work using the Variables icon (the one with the blue question mark). Compare what you have with the answers at the end of the chapter. If you need to fix anything, just double-click on the variable name in the Data Editor window to return to the Define Variable window.

ENTERING AND CHECKING DATA

Now we are ready to enter the data. As a practical matter, data are usually entered directly from the survey forms that respondents (or interviewers) fill out. Sometimes data are entered directly into computer programs as people

TABLE 3.1 Code Sheet for Responses to Survey Questions in Box 3.1

	AGE	SEX	MARITAL	HOMPOP	WRKSTAT	INCOME	PREMARSX	TEENSEX	XMARSEX	EVSTRAY	ID
1	79	1	1	2	5	17	4	1	1	2	1
2	81	1	5	1	1	17	9	9	1	3	2
3	63	1	4	2	1	18	3	1	9	1	3
4	53	1	4	1	5	1	4	2	9	9	4
5	76	1	1	2	5	12	3	1	1	2	5
6	43	1	1	2	7	99	4	1	1	2	6
7	41	1	2	1	7	99	4	1	9	9	7
8	77	2	5	1	1	10	3	1	9	3	8
9	70	2	1	2	1	15	9	9	1	2	9
10	68	2	1	1	1	19	1	1	9	1	10
11	53	2	5	2	1	15	9	9	1	3	11
12	39	2	1	4	7	99	1	1	9	2	12
13	42	2	5	2	2	21	4	2	9	3	13
14	43	2	1	4	2	21	9	9	2	1	14
15	47	2	5	2	1	15	3	1	1	3	15
16	48	2	3	3	1	19	3	1	9	1	16
17	38	2	5	2	7	17	9	9	1	3	17
18	36	2	1	4	2	17	4	3	1	2	18
19	46	2	1	4	1	18	1	1	1	2	19
20	40	2	1	3	1	16	3	2	1	2	20

answer. However, to save space and simplify the process of data entry, we will be working with data that a researcher has already transferred from survey forms onto a **code sheet** (Table 3.1). A code sheet lists each of the variables across the top (the columns of the sheet) and each of the responses in the rows. For example, Table 3.1 tells us the first respondent said that he is 79 years old, male (1), married (1), has two people in his household, and so on.

Setting your data up on a code sheet eases the transfer from paper to computer, because it matches the format of the SPSS Data Editor. You should note that the Data Editor window lists the variables across the top of the screen (in columns), and it assumes that the responses of each of your cases (the elements of your sample) will be listed across the rows. To enter data, begin with the first respondent and the first variable on the code sheet (Table 3.1).

SPSS Guide: Entering Data

To begin, place your cursor in the first cell of the first variable and click. The cell is highlighted with a black border.

Type in the value of the first respondent to the first variable, *age*—79. The value won't appear in the cell as you type it; it shows up in a box at the top of the screen instead. To make the value appear in the cell, do one of the following:

press the Tab key,

press the right cursor key on the keyboard (the cursor key pointing to the right), or

simply click on the first cell under the next variable, *sex*.

Then your screen will look like this:

Continue across the row entering the data for the first respondent. The first several variables will look like these:

> **Skills Practice 6**   Finish entering the data in Table 3.1 in the Data Editor window. *Check your work* against Table 3.1 to make sure all of the data have been entered correctly. If you make a mistake, put your cursor on the cell that contains the error, then replace the wrong value with the correct one. Press the Tab key to enter the correction.

Checking your data is an important part of the process of setting up a data file. You should always verify that the data you entered matches their original source. One way to do that is to check the numbers on the screen against the data source (a survey form or code sheet, for example). Another way to do it is to create a list of the cases with the values entered for each variable. The Statistics ➡ Summary ➡ Case Summaries command path in SPSS allows you to do that. For more information on this procedure, see "Using Case Summaries to Check Data" in Appendix F.

SAVING YOUR DATA

Once you are satisfied that your data are just as you want, you can save your data as an SPSS data file. (Actually, you can save your file any time you want to save your work, whether you have finished checking your data or not.)

SPSS Guide: Saving an SPSS Data File

With your Data Editor window open, click on the Save File icon (the diskette) on the toolbar.

The Save Data As window opens. Next,

❶ Click on the down arrow in the box next to Save In.

❷ Click on 3½ Floppy [A]:

❸ Type in a file name next to the File Name box. You can name a file anything you want, but be sure it's a name that will remind you of what's in the file. Let's use attsurv (for attitude survey) so everyone who is doing this exercise will use the same file name.

❹ Click on Save.

If you want to be sure you have saved your file, click on the Open File icon.

You should now see a list of all files on your 3½ inch disk, including the file you just created.

Close this window by clicking on the X in the upper right-hand corner of the Open File screen.

SUMMARY

In this chapter you learned how to set up a data file in SPSS. The process assumes that you are entering data from a survey instrument. The first step is to prepare your survey form by defining each of the variables on it and adding an identification variable. This step involves naming each variable, classifying its level of measurement, coding the response categories of the variable (if the variable is a categorical one), deciding how to code missing values, and creating an identification code.

The second step is to set up the variables in the SPSS program by using the Define Variable feature. The Define Variable window is where you can type in a variable name, a variable label, values and value labels, and missing values. You can specify the column format for the variable and its level of measurement.

The third step involves entering your data. Often data are entered directly from the survey forms as they are completed. Sometimes, data are coded for entry (as in Table 3.1).

The fourth step, checking your data, is an extremely important part of the process. Unless you can be confident that you have entered your data accurately, you cannot be confident in the results you obtain.

The fifth step is to save your data file. This step is one of the easiest, involving nothing more than using the Save File As command and naming your data file.

In the next chapter we will begin the process of analyzing data. You will use the gss96subset file to produce frequency distributions and describe the respondents to the General Social Survey for 1996.

KEY CONCEPTS

Variable name	Missing values	String variable
Variable category	Code sheet	Variable label
Category (variable) value	Default position	Value label
	Numeric variable	

ANSWERS TO SKILLS PRACTICES

1. Notice that the variable names are either identical or similar to the ones used in the General Social Survey.

1	*age*	6	*income*
2	*sex*	7	*premarsx*
3	*marital*	8	*teensex*
4	*hompop*	9	*xmarsex*
5	*wrkstat*	10	*evstray*

2. Type of variable and levels of measurement are as follows:

   1 and 4: numerical (scale)

   2 and 3, 5, 10: categorical and nominal

   6 through 9: categorical and ordinal

3. Category values for the variables are as follows:

marital

1	married	4	separated
2	widowed	5	never married
3	divorced		

hompop

No category numbers are necessary because *hompop* is a numerical variable.

wrkstat

1	working full-time	5	retired
2	working part-time	6	in school
3	temporarily not working	7	keeping house
4	unemployed, laid off	8	other

income

1	Less than $1,000	12	$17,500–19,999
2	$1,000–2,999	13	$20,000–22,499
3	$3,000–3,999	14	$22,500–24,999
4	$4,000–4,999	15	$25,000–29,999
5	$5,000–5,999	16	$30,000–34,999
6	$6,000–6,999	17	$35,000–39,999
7	$7,000–7,999	18	$40,000–49,999
8	$8,000–9,999	19	$50,000–59,999
9	$10,000–12,499	20	$60,000–74,999
10	$12,500–14,999	21	$75,000+
11	$15,000–17,499		

premarsx, teensex, and xmarsex

1	always wrong	3	sometimes wrong
2	almost always wrong	4	not wrong at all

evstray

1   yes

2   no

3   never married

4. Missing values are as follows:

age		*sex*	
98	Don't know	9	No answer
99	No answer		

marital		*hompop*	
9	No answer	98	Don't know
		99	No answer

wrkstat		*income*	
9	No answer	99	No answer

premarsx, teensex, xmarsex, and evstray

9   No answer

5. Your SPSS Data Editor screen should now show these additional variables:

	marital	hompop	wrkstat	income	premarsx	teensex	xmarsex	evstray
1								

Check each of your new variables using the Variables icon. They should look like these:

Variables

age
evstray
hompop
id
income
marital
premarsx
sex
teensex
wrkstat
xmarsex

Variable Information:

marital
Label: Marital Status
Type: F7
Missing Values: 9
Measurement Level: Nominal

Value Labels:
1 Married
2 Widowed
3 Divorced
4 Separated
5 Never Married
9 No Answer

Go To   Paste   Close   Help

Variables

age
evstray
hompop
id
income
marital
premarsx
sex
teensex
wrkstat
xmarsex

Variable Information:

hompop
Label: Number in household
Type: F8
Missing Values: 98, 99
Measurement Level: Scale

Value Labels:
98 Don't Know
99 No Answer

Go To   Paste   Close   Help

For some variables with a lot of categories, like *wrkstat* and *income,* you need to use the scroll bar to see all of the categories of the variable. Next you see only the first six categories of each variable, but this should be enough to see whether you are on the right track.

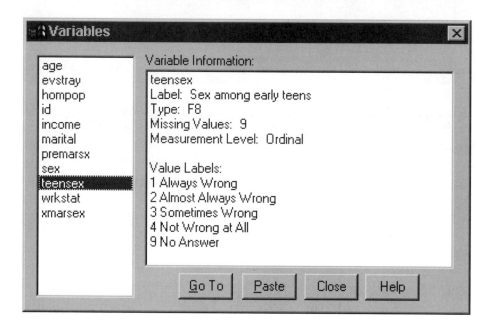

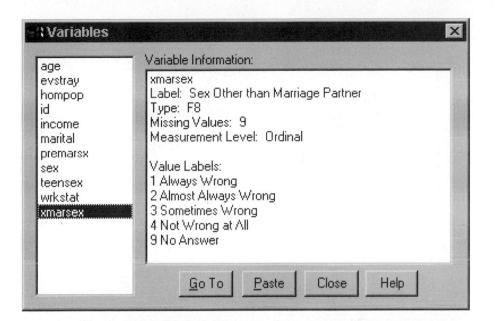

```
┌─────────────────────────────────────────────────────────────────┐
│ ╦╣Variables                                                [X]   │
├─────────────────────────────────────────────────────────────────┤
│ ┌──────────┐   Variable Information:                             │
│ │ age      │   ┌───────────────────────────────────────────┐    │
│ │ evstray  │   │ id                                        │    │
│ │ hompop   │   │ Label:  Respondent's id number            │    │
│ │ id       │   │ Type:  F8                                  │    │
│ │ income   │   │ Missing Values:  none                     │    │
│ │ marital  │   │ Measurement Level:  Nominal               │    │
│ │ premarsx │   │                                           │    │
│ │ sex      │   │ Value Labels:                             │    │
│ │ teensex  │   │                                           │    │
│ │ wrkstat  │   │                                           │    │
│ │ xmarsex  │   │                                           │    │
│ │          │   └───────────────────────────────────────────┘    │
│ └──────────┘                                                     │
│              [Go To]  [Paste]  [Close]  [Help]                   │
└─────────────────────────────────────────────────────────────────┘
```

GENERAL EXERCISES

1. Use the variables from the survey about teen pregnancy in General Exercise 1 in Chapter 2 to name each variable, specify its level of measurement, and decide on a coding scheme for each variable (including a code for missing data). Be sure to add a variable for an identification code for each respondent.

2. Using the survey you found for General Exercise 4 in Chapter 2, name each variable in the survey, and decide on a coding scheme for each variable (including a code for missing data). You should have already specified its level of measurement. Be sure to add a variable to identify each respondent.

SPSS EXERCISES

1. Set up a new SPSS data file in the SPSS Data Editor for the survey you coded in General Exercise 1. Use the Define Variable window to name each variable and specify variable type, labels, missing values, column format (if necessary), and level of measurement; then save your new data file to your A: drive with the filename teenpreg.

2. Set up a new SPSS data file in the SPSS Data Editor for the survey you coded in General Exercise 2. Use the Define Variable window to name each variable and specify variable type, labels, missing values, column format (if necessary), and level of measurement; then save your new data file to your A: drive.

4 Analyzing Frequency Distributions

INTRODUCTION

I am writing this text against the backdrop of the impeachment and trial of President Bill Clinton. He is alleged to have committed perjury and obstruction of justice in covering up his sexual involvement with a White House intern, Monica Lewinsky. Ultimately, President Clinton was acquitted of these charges by the Senate, but the allegations of his marital infidelity prompted a national examination of the state of marriage in America. Are most Americans faithful to their spouses, or do they stray, as President Clinton was accused of doing? The "News to Use" article that follows is an excerpt from a report on this subject based on 1994 General Social Survey data. Notice the contrast between what the author finds to be the case and the popular perception of infidelity among American adults. In addition to the relevance of the subject matter, what interests me about this article is its reliance on frequency distributions to assess the behavior of GSS respondents. You will see several examples of frequency distributions in the tables that support the text of the article.

Later in this chapter, you will have the opportunity to compare the responses of 1996 GSS participants to the responses of the 1994 survey participants. When you make these comparisons you will be using frequency distributions, which are fairly simple but very powerful tools for analyzing data. With frequency distributions, you will be analyzing variables one at a time. This type of analysis is called **univariate** (uni = one; variate = variable) analysis. Let's begin by looking at the characteristics of frequency distributions.

American Sexual Behavior: Trends, Socio-Demographic Differences, and Risk Behavior[1]

Tom W. Smith

INTRODUCTION

Sexual behavior is not only of basic biological importance, but of central social importance. Not only

[1]Report from the National Opinion Research Center, University of Chicago, GSS Topical Report No. 25 (updated December 1994). General Social Survey Data Retrieval and Information System, 18 June, 1996 release, <http://www.icpsr.umich.edu/gss/report/t-report/topic25.htm>.

does it perpetuate the human species, but it is the central behavior around which families are formed and defined, a vital aspect of the psychological well-being of individuals, and a component of a variety of social problems. Among current concerns tied in part to sexual behavior are the familial problems of marital harmony and divorce; criminal problems of rape, incest, child molestation, and prostitution; reproductive problems of infertility, sterility, unwanted and mistimed pregnancies, and abortion; and health problems related to transmitted diseases (STDs).

TABLES **Extramarital Sexual Relations by Socio-Demographic Groups**

	% Having Sexual Relations With Person Other Than Spouse During Last 12 Months (Currently Married)	% Ever Having Sexual Relations With Person Other Than Spouse While Married (Ever Married)
Gender		
Men	4.7	21.2
Women	2.1	11.3
Race		
Whites	2.8	14.5
Blacks	8.9	23.9
Age		
18–29	5.4	11.7
30–39	2.9	14.6
40–49	4.2	20.3
50–59	3.6	18.0
60–69	1.2	16.3
70+	1.1	6.3
Marital Status		
Married	2.8	9.9
Widowed	—	9.6
Divorced	—	30.7
Separated	—	40.2
Never married	—	—
Remarried	4.9	20.8

	% Having Sexual Relations With Person Other Than Spouse During Last 12 Months (Currently Married)	% Ever Having Sexual Relations With Person Other Than Spouse While Married (Ever Married)
Education		
Less than high school	4.5	12.8
High school graduate	3.1	16.8
Associate college degree	3.6	16.9
Bachelor's degree	1.9	11.8
Graduate degree	4.4	17.1
Household Income		
Less than $10,000	5.9	19.7
$10,000–19,999	5.6	16.2
$20,000–29,999	3.4	17.2
$30,000–39,999	2.3	16.2
$40,000–59,999	2.9	13.1
$60,000+	3.0	16.5
Church Attendance		
Rarely	3.9	20.6
Occasionally	3.7	15.3
Regularly	2.3	9.7
Marital Satisfaction		
Very happy	2.4	9.9
Pretty happy	3.9	16.2
Not too happy	14.8	23.9

ADULT AND GENERAL SEXUAL BEHAVIOR

Compared to the amount of information available on premarital and adolescent sexual behavior, until recently there has been little scientifically reliable data on the sexual behavior of adults or of the population in general. Moreover, the dearth of representative and credible studies has created a vacuum that has been filled by unrepresentative and incredible misinformation from popular magazines, sex gurus, and others. In this section we review what is known about extramarital relations. . . .

There are probably more scientifically worthless "facts" on extramarital relations than on any other facet of human behavior. Popular magazines (e.g., *Redbook, Psychology Today, Cosmopolitan*), advice columnists (Dear Abby and Dr. Joyce Brothers), pop-sexologists (e.g., Morton Hunt and Shere Hite) have all conducted or reported on "studies" of extramarital relations. These studies typically find extremely high levels of extramarital activity. Hite for example reported that 70% of women married 5 or more years "are having sex outside of their marriage (Smith, 1988)." They also often claim that extramarital relations have become much more common over time. Dr. Brothers (1990), for example, claims that 50% of married women now have sex outside of marriage, double the level of a generation ago.

But representative, scientific surveys (Greeley, 1994; Greeley, Michael & Smith, 1990; Laumann, Gagnon, Michael & Michaels, 1994; Leigh, Temple & Trocki, 1993; Tanfer, 1994) indicate that extramarital relations are less prevalent than pop and pseudoscientific accounts contend [see the tables in this excerpt]. The best estimates are that about 3–4% of currently married people have a sexual partner besides their spouse in a given year and about 15% of ever-married people have had a sexual partner other than their spouse while married (Michael, Laumann & Gagnon, 1993).

There is little direct and reliable trend information on extramarital relations before 1988. Since then, levels have not changed. Prior to then there is indirect evidence that extramarital relations may have increased across recent generations. The figure of ever having extramarital relations rises from 12% among those 18–29 to 20% among those 40–49 [see the Age table]. It then falls to 6% among those 70 and older. Since these are lifetime rates, one would normally expect them either to increase across age groups or to increase until a plateau is reached (this would be the case if few first-time, extramarital relations were started among older adults). The drop among those 50 and older suggests that members of birth cohorts before about 1940 were less likely to engage in extramarital relations than are spouses from more recent generations (Laumann, Gagnon, Michael & Michaels, 1994; Greeley, 1994).

In terms of current extramarital relations [the Age table] indicates that they are more common among younger adults. This is largely a function of younger adults having been married a shorter period of time. Some recently married people have difficulty adjusting from a premarital pattern of multiple sexual partners to a monogamous partnership and in general recent marriages are more likely to end in divorce than long-term marriages. The rates of extramarital relations are about twice as high among husbands as among wives [see table labeled Gender]. Extramarital relations are also more common among Blacks, those with less education and lower incomes, those who attend church less frequently, those who have been divorced (including those who have remarried), and those who are unhappy with their marriage. . . .

WHAT IS A FREQUENCY DISTRIBUTION?

When researchers first collect data, all they have is a set of **raw data** and **raw scores**—data that have not been processed and scores that have not been summarized in any way. Raw data are unprocessed. They may consist of a collection of survey forms that people have filled out or a set of questionnaires to which a researcher has gathered responses in face-to-face interviews. These survey forms or questionnaires may be sitting in a stack on the researcher's desk awaiting processing. If the researcher created an SPSS data file as the data came in, the raw data would become raw scores. Raw scores are a list of the responses of each participant in a study to each variable. If you open an SPSS file and look down the columns of each variable, you are looking at raw scores. When there are nearly 3,000 cases, as there are in the gss96subset file, having raw scores isn't very useful for seeing patterns in the data. Tools are needed to help sift out the general characteristics from all the specific details.

A very useful tool for seeing patterns in single variables is the frequency distribution. A **frequency distribution** is a summary of the responses to the categories of a variable. In its simplest form, it lists the frequencies of response (number of responses) to each category of a variable—but frequency distributions take many forms. Some display the percentages of response to each category of a variable in addition to (or instead of) the frequencies of response. Frequency distributions in SPSS are even more elaborate, as you will see.

The frequency distribution is such an important tool that you can scarcely pick up a newspaper or magazine without reading the results of frequency distribution analysis. Sometimes you're not even aware that what you're reading is a description of a frequency distribution. In Chapter 2, I described a survey conducted for the National Campaign to Prevent Teen Pregnancy (NCPTP), which explored the attitudes of parents and teenagers toward sex education. The summary of the findings (excerpted in Chapter 2) is basically an analysis of frequency distributions like the ones in Table 4.1.[2] There are more examples of frequency distributions in the tables in the "News to Use" article for this chapter.

In many of these frequency distributions, the researchers report all of the categories of the variable along with the frequency of response for each category. However, in some cases the researchers report only a few of the categories. Notice that in the "News to Use" tables only two of three GSS categories of the variable *race* are used. Similarly, in the table that analyzes fidelity (*evstray*) by categories of the variable, church attendance (*attend* in SPSS), several of the categories of *attend* were combined to create an abbreviated version of the variable. The process of creating new variables from old ones is called *recoding*. In this chapter you will learn to produce frequency distributions—using SPSS and by hand—and to recode variables.

Characteristics of a Frequency Distribution

As you can see from these examples, frequency distributions are used for all kinds of variables, numerical and categorical, continuous and discrete. Researchers use them to summarize demographic characteristics—like age, sex, race, marital status, religion, and political identity—and they use them to analyze the attitudes and behaviors of those they study (such as their attitudes toward extramarital sex and whether or not they actually engage in extramarital affairs). The specific form a frequency distribution takes can vary. However, the previous examples illustrate some of the essential features of a frequency distribution.

---

[2]International Communications Research, 1998, "Parents of Teens and Teens Discuss Sex, Love, and Relationships: Polling Data," <http://www.teenpregnancy.org/98poll.htm>.

TABLE 4.1   Frequency Distributions From the Report "Parents of Teens and Teens Discuss Sex, Love, and Relationships: Polling Data"

Question: Which one of the following do you think is the biggest barrier to effective communication between parents and teens on sex and relationships?

All Teens

16.9%	Parents are not comfortable talking to their kids [about] sex
38.7	Teens are not comfortable hearing from their parents about [sex]
19.1	Teens don't want to hear from their parents about sex
6.3	Teens know as much [as] or more than parents about sex and relationships
14.0	Parents are too judgmental
4.8	Don't know
0.2	Refused [to answer]

Question: Which one of the following topics would you most like your parents to talk with you more about?

All Teens

21.4%	How to manage dating, relationships, and sex
23.3	Sexually transmitted diseases, contraception, and pregnancy prevention
21.5	Knowing how and when to say "no" to sex
16.0	What to do if you or your partner gets pregnant
11.3	Values about sex
3.7	None
2.4	Don't know
0.3	Refused [to answer]

They each describe a variable of interest   The first variable in Table 4.1 might be labeled "barriers to effective communication," whereas the second variable in Table 4.1 might be called "topics teens want to know more about."

They list the categories of a variable   The categories of the first variable, *barriers to effective communication,* include "Parents are not comfortable talking to their kids about sex," "Teens are not comfortable hearing from their parents about sex," and so on. The categories of the second variable, *topics teens want to know more about,* include "How to manage dating, relationships, and sex" and "Sexually transmitted diseases, contraception, and pregnancy prevention."

They list the distribution of responses for the categories of the variable   In these two examples, the response frequencies are expressed as percentages. We can see what percentage of the respondents answered in each of the categories, but we can't tell how many respondents answered in a particular category.

As we will see in the next section, SPSS frequency distributions look a little different from these illustrations. Nevertheless, they share the essential characteristics of these examples while telling us more about the distribution of responses to each of our variables. Let's look at some examples from the General Social Survey.

OBTAINING A FREQUENCY DISTRIBUTION USING SPSS

Using SPSS to Produce a Frequency Distribution

Frequency distributions are fairly easy to obtain using SPSS. We will begin by obtaining a frequency distribution for one of the variables in the General Social Survey examining the issue of fidelity among American adults—*evstray*. Use "SPSS Guide: Obtaining a Frequency Distribution" to produce a frequency distribution for the variable.

SPSS Guide: Obtaining a Frequency Distribution

Open the SPSS program and your gss96subset file (see the SPSS Guides in Chapter 1, "Opening the SPSS Program" and "Opening SPSS Data Files," if you need help). Then, click on the Analyze menu item. A list of options will open in a drop-down menu.

Click on Descriptive Statistics. A second list of options appears in another drop-down menu. Click on Frequencies.

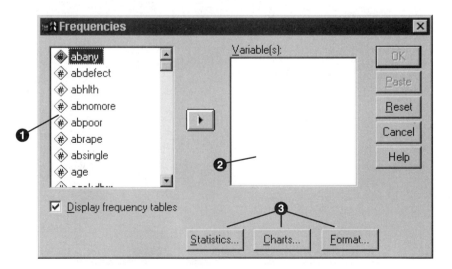

A Frequencies window opens. This window is called a **dialog box.** Each statistical procedure you use in SPSS has its own dialog box. These boxes have several features in common:

❶ A source variable list of all of the variables in a file; the gss96subset variables in this case

❷ A target variable list in which to place the variables you want to use—the box labeled Variable(s)

❸ Several command buttons, which cause SPSS to run various functions

To use these features, the steps are similar from one dialog box to another.

 Find the source variable you want. (Scroll down to the variable *evstray,* and click). The variable will be highlighted.

 Put the source variable in the target list. Click on the arrow ▶ pointing at the Variables box. The variable will appear in the Variables box.

If you make a mistake, click on the variable in the Variable(s) window, then click on the arrow pointing at the list of variables. Your variable moves from the Variable(s) window to the variables list.

❸ Use one of the command buttons to produce a frequency distribution for the variable *evstray.* Click on OK.

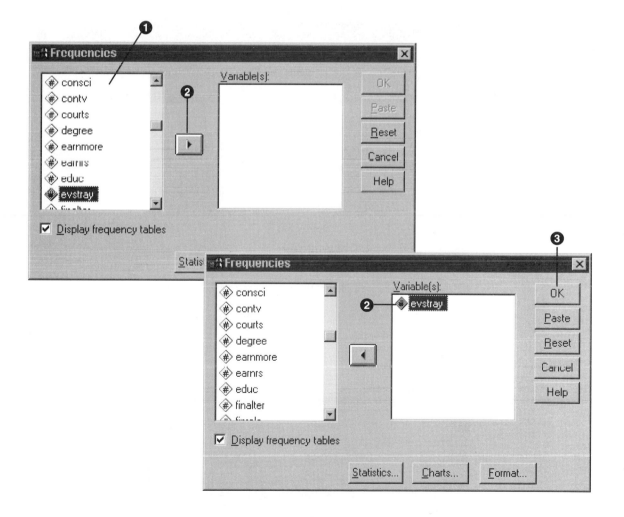

SPSS Guide: Using the Output Window

Your frequency distribution and a few summary statistics will appear in a separate Output window. As the frequency distribution opens, an Output—SPSS Viewer window appears. This Output window keeps track of your work during each of your SPSS sessions. All of the work you do is temporarily stored in the Output window, and you can go back to it at any time. (When you exit from the SPSS program, your session is ended. The work in your Output window is automatically deleted unless you save it to a specific output file.)

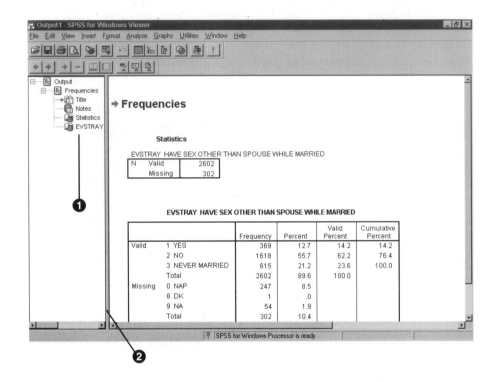

You may also see an Output outline ❶. You can hide this Output outline by putting your cursor on the bar between the outline and the rest of the screen ❷. Hold the left click key down while you move your mouse to the left to close the outline.

Several advanced features of SPSS are available in the Output window. For example, you can learn how to use the outline to move around in the Output window, and you can save output to its own file for later use. The section in Appendix F called "Using the Outline Feature in the Output Window" shows you how to use some of these features. You can switch from the Output window to the SPSS Data Editor window by pointing and clicking on the appropriate buttons at the bottom of the screen, as shown on the next page.

❶   ❷

There is a button ❶ for the Data Editor (it has your file name, gss96subset, on it), and there is a button ❷ for the Output—SPSS Viewer (it has Output on it). Try clicking on each of the buttons to see what happens.

Another way to move between screens in any Windows program is to use the Alt–Tab key combination on the keyboard. Press the Alt key and hold it down while pressing the Tab key. You will see a box open up on your screen. Continue to hold down the Alt key, and tap the Tab key until the icon for the SPSS Data Editor is highlighted. Then release the Alt and Tab keys. You will go to the Data Editor screen.

Understanding the SPSS Output for a Frequency Distribution

The output you get for the variable *evstray* will look like Table 4.2. Let's look at how to read it.

TABLE 4.2   **Frequency Distribution for the gss96subset Variable** *evstray*

Frequencies

Statistics

EVSTRAY HAVE SEX OTHER THAN SPOUSE WHILE MARRIED

N	Valid	2602
	Missing	302

EVSTRAY HAVE SEX OTHER THAN SPOUSE WHILE MARRIED

		Frequency	Percent	Valid Percent	Cumulative Percent
Valid	1 YES	369	12.7	14.2	14.2
	2 NO	1618	55.7	62.2	76.4
	3 NEVER MARRIED	615	21.2	23.6	100.0
	Total	2602	89.6	100.0	
Missing	0 NAP	247	8.5		
	8 DK	1	.0		
	9 NA	54	1.9		
	Total	302	10.4		
Total		2904	100.0		

Statistics The Statistics box—the small box at the top of Table 4.2—tells us the number of valid cases there are for a variable. **Valid cases** are the number of meaningful responses to a question. You will also see the number of **missing cases**—the number of cases for which respondents did not know the answer to a question, did not answer a question, or were not asked the question for a variable.

One of the most important pieces of information in the Statistics output is *N*. *N* represents the number of responses we have to a particular variable. *N* can be viewed a couple of ways: as the number of all valid responses we have or as the total number of all responses, both meaningful and missing. In most of its computations, SPSS regards *N* as the number of valid cases. For the variable *evstray*, there are 2,602 valid cases or 2,602 people who gave a meaningful response to the variable. 302 respondents were not asked, didn't know the answer to, or did not answer the question about marital fidelity. The number of both valid and missing cases is 2,904 (the 2,602 valid cases plus the 302 missing cases).

Frequency distribution The frequency distribution produced by SPSS includes all of the information in our example in Table 4.1 plus a lot more. Figure 4.1 breaks it down.

SPSS lists meaningful categories of a variable separately from categories that represent missing values. The meaningful response categories—like Yes, No, and Never Married—are listed first.

The number of responses to each of the categories of the variables are listed in the Frequency column.

EVSTRAY HAVE SEX OTHER THAN SPOUSE WHILE MARRIED

		Frequency	Percent	Valid Percent	Cumulative Percent
Valid	1 YES	369	12.7	14.2	14.2
	2 NO	1618	55.7	62.2	76.4
	3 NEVER MARRIED	615	21.2	23.6	100.0
	Total	2602	89.6	100.0	
Missing	0 NAP	247	8.5		
	8 DK	1	.0		
	9 NA	54	1.9		
	Total	302	10.4		
Total		2904	100.0		

Missing values categories—like NAP, DK, and NA are listed separately.

There are two separate calculations of percentage—one that uses all cases (valid and missing) in its computation of percentage, labeled Percent, and one that includes only valid cases, labeled Valid Percent.

The Cumulative Percent column is a running total of the Valid Percent column.

Figure 4.1 Understanding an SPSS frequency distribution.

A discussion of the most important features of the frequency distribution follows.

Values and frequencies   One of the first distinctions to make is between the values of a variable and the frequencies of response to a particular value and its category. The values and categories of a variable are listed in the first column of the frequency distribution. If we want to know the **frequency of response**—how many respondents answered with a particular value or in a particular category—we have to use the Frequency column. For the variable *evstray,* we can see that 369 respondents (the frequency) said yes (the category), they have had sex with someone other than their spouse while married (the value, 1).

Percent and Valid Percent   The Percent and Valid Percent columns are very helpful for finding patterns in data. They allow us to get a sense of where the respondents fall in relation to the categories of a variable, and they standardize the responses to a variable so that we can make comparisons between distributions with different numbers of responses. We will make use of this standardizing feature a little later on as we look at how different groups of respondents respond to the same variable.

For computing **Percent,** SPSS divides the frequency of response to a particular category by the sum of all cases, valid and missing. For example, to find the Percent for the category Yes, divide 369 by 2,904 and multiply your answer by 100. To compute **Valid Percent,** SPSS divides the frequency of response to a particular category by the sum of valid cases only. To find Valid Percent for Yes, divide 369 by 2,602 (the total number of valid cases) and multiply the result by 100. For Table 4.2, the results are fairly close, because the total number of all cases (2,904) is only 302 more than the number of valid cases only (2,602). In other tables, you will see larger differences between the Percent and the Valid Percent columns, because not all questions were asked of all 2,904 GSS respondents. There is a set of core questions that are asked of all respondents, but there are also questions on specific topics that are asked of only a portion of the respondents. GSS researchers do this to reduce the number of questions GSS respondents have to answer.

Cumulative Percent   The **Cumulative Percent** column uses only valid cases in its computation of cumulative percentage. It is a running total of all responses, and it is computed by adding the number of respondents to a particular category to those of all preceding categories, dividing by the number of valid cases, and multiplying by 100. For example, the cumulative percentage for the No category is computed by adding the number of people who answered "No" to those who answered "Yes": 369 (yes) + 1,618 (no) = 1,987. To get the cumulative percentage, divide 1,987 by the number of valid cases (2,602) and multiply by 100. Round to the first decimal.

Interpreting the Frequency Distribution

What does the frequency distribution for the variable *evstray* tell us about the General Social Survey respondents? One way to answer this question is to ask yourself, "If I were to carry away one impression from the frequency distribution, what would it be?" You could also put yourself in the position of a newswriter who has to come up with a headline to describe the state of marriage among the GSS respondents. What would you write?

To decide how to interpret the data, start by noticing the percentage of respondents who actually answered the question related to the variable. Look down the Percent column until you get to the Total percentage for valid cases. Second, draw out the general characteristics of those who responded, using the Valid Percent and Cumulative Percent columns. For the variable *evstray,* you could point out that

> most Americans are faithful to their marriages. Nearly all respondents
> answered the question about sex outside of marriage (nearly 90%). Of those
> who responded (valid cases), nearly two thirds said they have never had
> sex with anyone other than their spouse (62.2%), whereas 14.2% said they
> have had sex outside of their marriages. About one quarter (23.6%) of those
> who answered the question said they have never been married.

Heterogeneous and homogeneous distributions   In addition to helping us see the general patterns in data, frequency distributions help us to evaluate the **dispersion** (or distributions) of responses to a variable to determine whether these distributions are **heterogeneous** or **homogeneous.** Heterogeneous distributions are those in which the respondents are fairly evenly distributed, dispersed, or spread out across all of the categories of a variable. In perfectly heterogeneous distributions, each category of a variable has the same number (and percentage) of respondents. For example, for the variable *sex,* a perfectly heterogeneous distribution is one in which 50% of the respondents are male and 50% are female. For the variable *race*—a three-category variable in the General Social Survey—a heterogeneous distribution is one in which 33.3% of the respondents identify themselves as White, 33.3% as Black, and 33.3% as Other. The more a distribution deviates from an even dispersion of respondents across the categories of a variable, the less heterogeneous it is.

Homogeneous distributions, on the other hand, are those in which the respondents are clustered or grouped into only a few categories of a variable. A perfectly homogeneous distribution is one in which all respondents are in a single category of a variable, as follows.

Sex	Percentage	Race	Percentage
Male	100	White	0
Female	0	Black	100
		Other	0

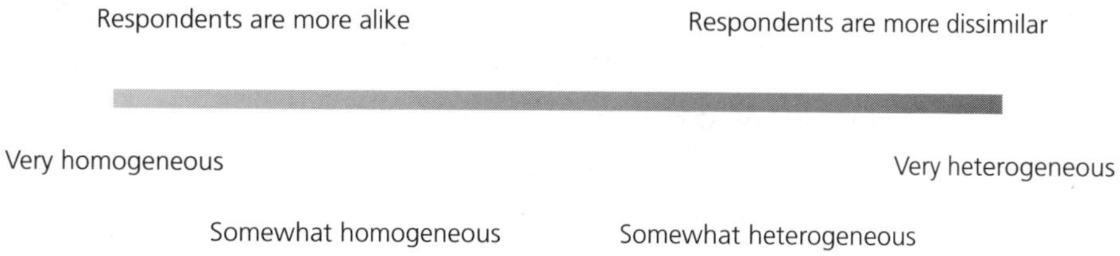

Respondents are more alike   Respondents are more dissimilar

Very homogeneous   Very heterogeneous

Somewhat homogeneous   Somewhat heterogeneous

Figure 4.2 Continuum for describing extent to which frequency distributions are homogeneous or heterogeneous.

We rarely see perfectly heterogeneous or perfectly homogeneous distributions, so we have to describe distributions on a continuum from very heterogeneous to somewhat heterogeneous or fairly heterogeneous on one end to fairly homogeneous or somewhat homogeneous to very homogeneous on the other, depending on how far the distribution deviates from perfectly heterogeneous or homogeneous. Figure 4.2 illustrates this continuum for describing a distribution of responses to a variable.

Avoiding Common Pitfalls   A confusing aspect of frequency distributions is that distributions are most *hetero*geneous when the frequencies and percentages of response are *alike*, because the more alike the frequencies and percentages are, the more dissimilar the respondents are from one another. Conversely, distributions are most *homo*geneous when the frequencies and percentages of response are *dissimilar*, because the more dissimilar the frequencies and percentages of response are from one another, the more alike the respondents are in relation to one another. Compare the frequency distribution for the variable *evstray* with the one for the variable *partyid* (in Table 4.3). Which distribution is more heterogeneous, and which one is more homogeneous?

The answer: The distribution of responses to the variable *partyid* is more heterogeneous; the distribution of responses to the variable *evstray* is more homogeneous. How do we know? Notice that the response frequencies and the percentages (using Valid Percents) for the variable *evstray* are fairly *dissimilar*, ranging from a high of 62.2% down to 14.2%. This tells us that the respondents are somewhat alike—the distribution is more homogeneous—with nearly three quarters saying they haven't had sex outside of their marriages. Now look at the frequency distribution for the variable *partyid* (party identification) in Table 4.3.

In this distribution, the response frequencies look more alike (hovering around 400 or 500 respondents in many categories), and the percentages (using Valid Percents) are somewhat alike, too, at around 15%. One category, Other Party, has very few respondents, with only 1.5% of those who answered the question. Even though the frequencies and the percentages are somewhat alike, what this means is that the respondents are more dissimilar from one another,

(*continued*)

TABLE 4.3   **Frequency Distribution for the gss96subset Variable *partyid***

PARTYID POLITICAL PARTY AFFILIATION

		Frequency	Percent	Valid Percent	Cumulative Percent
Valid	0 STRONG DEMOCRAT	400	13.8	13.8	13.8
	1 NOT STR DEMOCRAT	577	19.9	19.9	33.7
	2 IND,NEAR DEM	356	12.3	12.3	46.0
	3 INDEPENDENT	457	15.7	15.8	61.8
	4 IND,NEAR REP	258	8.9	8.9	70.7
	5 NOT STR REPUBLICAN	500	17.2	17.3	87.9
	6 STRONG REPUBLICAN	307	10.6	10.6	98.5
	7 OTHER PARTY	43	1.5	1.5	100.0
	Total	2898	99.8	100.0	
Missing	9 NA	6	.2		
Total		2904	100.0		

or more dispersed, across the categories of the variable. They are very heterogeneously distributed across the categories of the variable *party identification.*

Another common pitfall is that it is easy to confuse heterogeneity or homogeneity of a distribution across the categories of a variable with whether or not the categories of a variable are themselves homogeneously or heterogeneously distributed. For example, think about a demographic variable like *age.* The categories of the variable can vary widely. In the General Social Survey, the categories for the variable *age* range from 18 to 89. The categories of the variable are widely distributed. However, in other populations, the categories may not be as widely distributed. Suppose we survey students in a high school. Chances are the age categories will range from 14 to 18, give or take a couple of years. The categories of the variable *age* in a high school population are not very spread out or dispersed.

When analyzing data, it is worth noting the range of categories for a variable. However, in assessing whether or not the responses are homogeneously or heterogeneously distributed, look at the dispersion of responses across the categories of the variable. It is possible to have a very homogeneous distribution of responses to an age variable even when the range of ages is 18 to 89, and a very heterogeneous distribution of responses when the range of ages is only 14 to 18. In Chapter 6, you will learn some statistical techniques for assessing whether distributions of responses are homogeneous or heterogeneous.

> **Skills Practice 1**   Use SPSS to produce and interpret frequency distributions for the following variables: *marital, degree, wrkstat,* and *xmarsex.* Use the command path Analyze ➡ Descriptive Statistics ➡ Frequencies. When the Frequencies window opens, click on the Reset button to clear your previous work. Then select your first variable for analysis, *marital.*
>
> **Hints for writing your interpretations of the variables:** Start out with a newspaper-style headline—how would you summarize each of the tables? Support your headline using information from the table (as we did when we analyzed the frequency distribution for the variable *evstray*). Is the distribution of responses homogeneous or heterogeneous?

In addition to assessing the characteristics of all respondents to a survey on a particular variable, it is very useful to be able to construct frequency distributions for subgroups within a survey. For example, the "News to Use" article, "American Sexual Behavior," discusses the behavior of the general adult population with regard to sex outside of marriage. Then it divides the GSS respondents into groups—by sex, race, age, church attendance, and so on—to report on differences in behavior. Let's see how you can separate a data file by the categories of a variable for the purpose of comparing the responses of different groups to a particular variable.

SPLITTING A DATA FILE

The technique for dividing a set of data into groups according to the categories of one of its variables is called *split file,* because you are literally splitting the data file—dividing it up—by the characteristics of the respondents. For example, if you want to know how males and females compare on attitudes toward extramarital sex, you can split the file by the variable *sex.* Splitting the file divides the data set into two groups: one of male respondents and one of female respondents. Use the SPSS Guide, "The Split File Command," to learn the split file procedure.

SPSS Guide: The Split File Command

With the gss96subset file open (see the SPSS Guides in Chapter 1, "Opening the SPSS Program" and "Opening SPSS Data Files," if you need help), click on Data from the menu, then click on Split File.

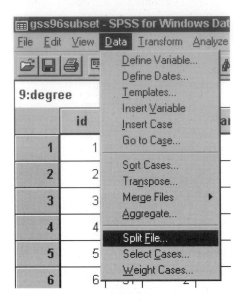

❶ When the Split File window opens, click on Organize Output by Groups.

❷ Scroll down to the variable *sex*. Click on it to highlight it, and then click on the ▶ pointing at the Groups Based On box to select it.

❸ Click on OK to return to the SPSS Data Editor window.

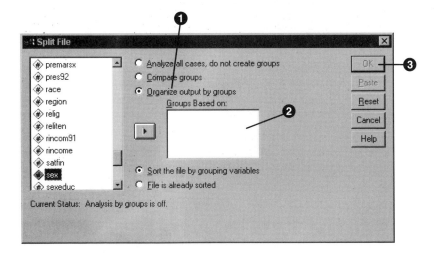

When you return to the SPSS Data Editor, notice that the Split File On message appears in the bottom right corner of the screen.

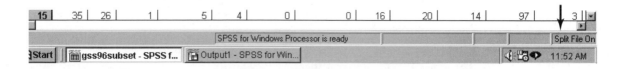

You won't see any "output" just by turning on the Split File. However, notice what happens when you run a frequency distribution. Let's use the variable *evstray,* which asks GSS respondents whether they have ever had sex outside of their marriages. Click on Analyze ➡ Descriptive Statistics ➡ Frequencies to open the Frequencies window, and click on Reset to clear any previous work. Select the variable *evstray.* (Highlight the variable, move it to the Variable(s) box by clicking on the ▶ pointing at the Variable(s) box.) Then click on OK. You will get two frequency distributions—one for male respondents, one for female respondents—like the ones in Table 4.4.

Compare the respondents. Which group—males or females—is more likely to say they have had sex outside of their marriages? How do these responses compare with the ones in the "News to Use" article?

To make your comparisons, focus on the second column of frequency distributions, "% Ever Having Sexual Relations With Person Other Than Spouse While Married," in the tables at the end of the "News to Use" article. Remember that the percentages standardize the responses. Focusing on the frequencies can be misleading. Notice that in Table 4.4 there are more female respondents than male respondents to this variable.

If you pay attention to the larger number of responses to a category of a variable, you can be misled into thinking that one group is more likely than the other to have a particular characteristic simply because there are more respondents in that group as compared to the other. To standardize the responses to a variable, look at the percentages of response to the categories of the variable. More specifically, pay attention to the percentage of meaningful (valid) responses. When you use the valid percentages to compare male and female respondents, you should come to conclusions like these:

> A larger percentage of males (17.8%) than females (11.3%) say they've had sex outside of their marriages. These percentages are down for males from the 1994 GSS, but are the same for females. According to the "News to Use" article, 21.2% of male respondents and 11.3% of female respondents said they had sex outside of their marriages.

TABLE 4.4 Frequency Distributions for the Variable *evstray*, with the gss96subset File Split by *sex*

SEX = 1 MALE

Statistics[a]

EVSTRAY HAVE SEX OTHER THAN SPOUSE WHILE MARRIED

N	Valid	1150
	Missing	135

a. SEX RESPONDENTS SEX = 1 MALE

EVSTRAY HAVE SEX OTHER THAN SPOUSE WHILE MARRIED[a]

		Frequency	Percent	Valid Percent	Cumulative Percent
Valid	1 YES	205	16.0	17.8	17.8
	2 NO	643	50.0	55.9	73.7
	3 NEVER MARRIED	302	23.5	26.3	100.0
	Total	1150	89.5	100.0	
Missing	0 NAP	111	8.6		
	8 DK	1	.1		
	9 NA	23	1.8		
	Total	135	10.5		
Total		1285	100.0		

a. SEX RESPONDENTS SEX = 1 MALE

SEX = 2 FEMALE

Statistics[a]

EVSTRAY HAVE SEX OTHER THAN SPOUSE WHILE MARRIED

N	Valid	1452
	Missing	167

a. SEX RESPONDENTS SEX = 2 FEMALE

EVSTRAY HAVE SEX OTHER THAN SPOUSE WHILE MARRIED[a]

		Frequency	Percent	Valid Percent	Cumulative Percent
Valid	1 YES	164	10.1	11.3	11.3
	2 NO	975	60.2	67.1	78.4
	3 NEVER MARRIED	313	19.3	21.6	100.0
	Total	1452	89.7	100.0	
Missing	0 NAP	136	8.4		
	9 NA	31	1.9		
	Total	167	10.3		
Total		1619	100.0		

a. SEX RESPONDENTS SEX = 2 FEMALE

When you are through with your analysis, turn the Split File off by going back to the SPSS Data Editor (using the gss96subset button at the bottom of your screen). Use the command path Data ➥ Split File to return to the Split File window. At the Split File window, click on Reset and OK, in that order. You will return to the SPSS Data Editor, but now there will be no Split File On message in the bottom left corner of the screen.

Skills Practice 2   Split the file by the variable *sex.* Produce a frequency distribution for the variable *xmarsex,* which asks about attitudes toward sex outside of marriage. (Remember to use the Reset button in the Frequencies window to clear your previous work.) Which group—males or females—is more likely to say that extramarital sex is always wrong? Which group is more likely to say it's not wrong at all?

Let's turn our attention next to looking at data pictorially—using graphs to display frequency distributions for the purpose of analyzing our variables.

USING CHARTS AND GRAPHS TO ANALYZE DISTRIBUTIONS

To help us analyze distributions of variables, SPSS has a number of options for producing charts and graphs that give us visual representations of frequency distributions like the one in Figure 1.1 at the beginning of this text. Take a look at some of the choices.

SPSS Guide: Exploring Graph Options

With your gss96subset file open, at the SPSS Data Editor click on Graphs in the SPSS menu. A list of options appears. Click on Gallery. A screen opens illustrating the different types of graphs available.

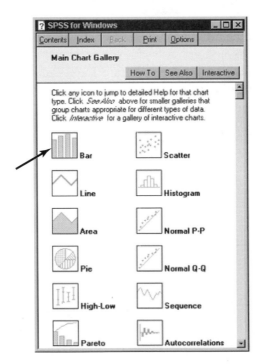

Put the cursor on one of the graphs. The cursor turns into a hand with a pointed finger. Now click. (Try the chart labeled Bar to begin with.)

A window with a description of the graph appears. Across the top of the window are several options. Click on How To. Instructions appear for creating the graph you have selected. Look them over. Then click on the X button to exit.

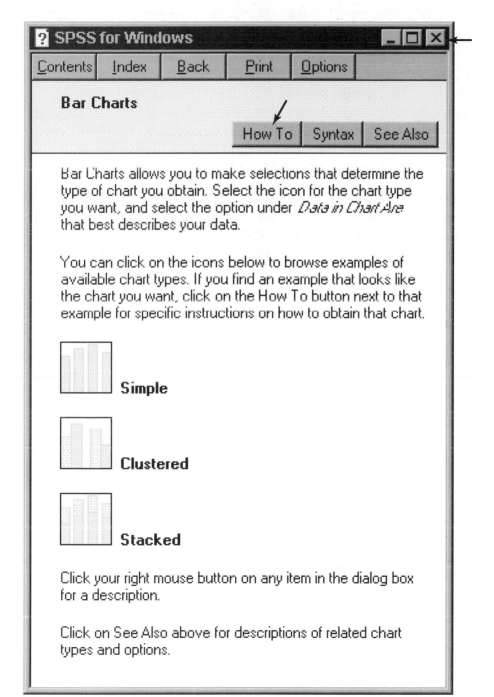

Click on any icon to get detailed Help for any of the other chart types. Click on the X button when you're through.

There are many graphs to choose from, and I'm not going to cover them all, so let's narrow the field down a little by looking at a few of the most commonly used ones for displaying frequency distributions.

Bar Charts and Histograms

Use the command path Graphs ➡ Gallery. Look at the charts labeled Bar and Histogram. You will see that they look very much alike. **Bar charts** and **histograms** are bar graph-type representations of data, with the size of the bar depending on the number or percentage of respondents in a particular category of a variable. The difference between the two is that bar chart bars don't touch each other but histogram bars do. For this reason, bar charts are often used to represent discrete variables, whereas histograms are reserved for continuous variables. However, the features that SPSS includes with each of these options assume that the decision to use a bar chart or histogram will be based on the categorical–numerical distinction. In SPSS, bar charts are set up to handle categorical variables and histograms are for numerical variables. (Refer to Chapter 2 if you need to refresh your memory about levels of measurement.)

Creating a bar chart   Use the SPSS Guide "Creating a Bar Chart" with the categorical variable *evstray* to produce a bar chart.

SPSS Guide: Creating a Bar Chart

Click on the Graphs menu item. A list of options appears. Then click on Bar.

When the Bar Charts window opens, click on Define.

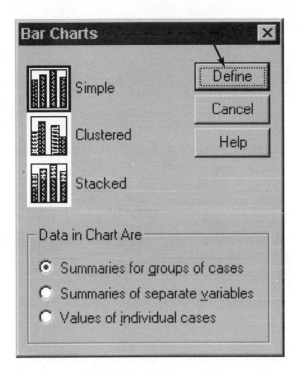

The Define Simple Bar: Summaries for Groups of Cases window opens. For univariate analysis of frequency distributions, most of the default settings in the Bar Charts window are fine—they describe a simple bar chart with summaries for groups of cases, which means that each bar will represent all of the cases for a particular category of a given variable. There are a couple of settings to change, though.

❶ Under Bars Represent, click on the ○ next to % of Cases.

❷ Select a variable by highlighting it. Scroll down to *evstray* and click. Move it to the Category Axis box by clicking on ▶ pointing at Category Axis. The variable appears in the Category Axis box.

❸ Turn off the default settings to prevent missing values from appearing in the bar graph. Click on the Options button.

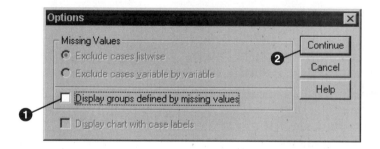

The Options window will open next.

① When the Options window opens, click on the box next to Display Groups Defined by Missing Values to make the √ disappear.

② Click on Continue.

When you return to the Define Simple Bar: Summaries for Groups of Cases window, click on OK.

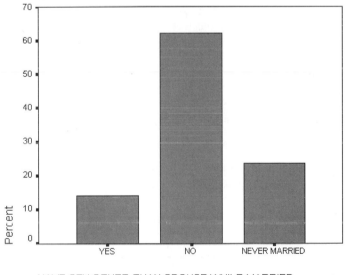

A graph like the one in Figure 4.3 appears in the SPSS Output window.

HAVE SEX OTHER THAN SPOUSE WHILE MARRIED

Figure 4.3 Bar chart for the variable *evstray* in the gss96subset file.

Interpreting a bar chart　The bar chart contains information much like a frequency distribution. The variable label HAVE SEX OTHER THAN SPOUSE WHILE MARRIED is displayed across the bottom of the chart and the categories of the variable (Yes, No, and Never Married) are displayed on the horizontal axis, the *x*-axis, of the graph. The valid percentages (remember we excluded missing cases from our graph) are displayed along the vertical axis, the *y*-axis, of the graph.

We interpret the bar chart in much the same way as a frequency distribution. We want to know what the general characteristics of the respondents for the variable are. In addition, charts help us answer the question "Does the distribution appear to be homogeneous or heterogeneous?" Bar charts in which the distribution of responses is more homogeneous will have large differences in the sizes of the bars, as in the previous bar chart for the variable *evstray*. Bar charts in which the distribution of responses is more heterogeneous will have bars that are more equal in height. To see an example, let's look at the attitudes of GSS respondents toward premarital sex using the variable *premarsx*.

Skills Practice 3　Obtain a bar chart for the variable *premarsx*.

Use the command path Graphs ➡ Bar ➡ Define. When the Define Simple Bar: Summaries for Groups of Cases window opens, click on the Reset button to clear the window of all previous work. Then

- Select the variable *premarsx*.
- Click on % of Cases.
- Click on Options.
- Turn off Display Groups Defined by Missing Values.
- Click on Continue.
- At the Define Simple Bar window, click on OK.

Does this distribution look more homogeneous or heterogeneous in comparison to the distribution of responses to the variable *evstray*? Why do you think so?

Creating a histogram　Use the next SPSS Guide to create a histogram. Histograms assume that you are using numerical variables, so we will examine one of the demographic variables, *age,* which is numerical.

SPSS Guide: Creating a Histogram

Look for the Graphs menu item—it appears at the top of the Output window. You can also return to the SPSS Data Editor to find it. (Use the gss96subset button at the bottom of the screen to go back to the Data Editor.) When the list of options appears, click on Histogram.

At the Histogram window, scroll down to the variable *age,* and click on it to highlight it. Click on the ▶ pointing at the Variable box to select it; then click on OK.

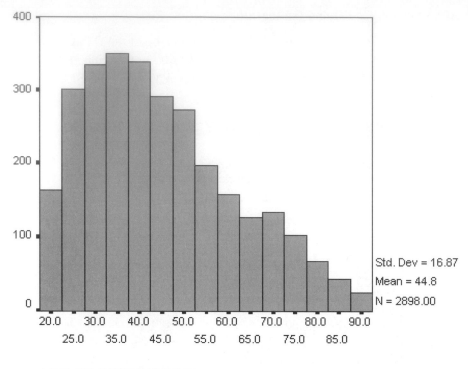

Std. Dev = 16.87
Mean = 44.8
N = 2898.00

AGE OF RESPONDENT

Figure 4.4 Histogram for the variable *age* in the gss96subset file.

A graph appears like the one in Figure 4.4.

Interpreting a histogram   Notice that, like in the bar chart, the *x*- (horizontal) axis is the variable axis, showing the categories of the variable *age.* On the *y*- (vertical) axis, you see the frequencies for the variable *age,* not the percentages. Only valid cases are counted.

SPSS automatically grouped the respondents into age intervals, with each bar representing 5 years. How can you tell how many years are represented by each histogram bar? Simply subtract the midpoint of the first bar (20) from the midpoint of the second bar (25): $25 - 20 = 5$. Each bar represents 5 years. Where do you find the midpoint for each bar? The midpoints are displayed along the horizontal (*x*-axis) of the histogram. The first bar shows how many respondents are in the age interval from 18 (the youngest person in the survey) to 22. SPSS displays the midpoint of the interval, age 20, under the first bar. The second bar shows how many respondents are in the interval 23 through 27. The midpoint of the interval is age 25.

Without percentages, histograms are a little more difficult to interpret. (There are some unique features of histograms that allow us to draw conclusions about distributions of numerical variables, which we will discuss in

Chapter 5.) However, we can at least tell how homogeneous or heterogeneous a distribution is by looking at the relationships among the bars, just like for a bar chart. Does this distribution look more homogeneous or heterogeneous? The answer is that it is somewhat on the homogeneous side of the continuum, because most of the respondents seem to be clustered around age 40. The respondents could be characterized as mostly middle-aged or close to it.

> **Skills Practice 4**   Obtain a histogram for the variable *educ*. Evaluate the distribution: Is it more homogeneous or heterogeneous?
>
> Use the command path Graphs ➡ Histogram. When the Histogram window opens, click on the Reset button to clear any previous work. Then select the variable *educ* and click on OK.

Pie Charts

Pie charts are a very popular way to present data graphically. They can be used with variables measured at any level—categorical or numerical. As a practical matter, pie charts are harder to read the more categories a variable has. If a variable has many categories, you would be better off illustrating it with a bar chart or histogram. We'll use the variable *evstray* to create a pie chart.

SPSS Guide: Creating a Pie Chart

In the Output window or at the SPSS Data Editor window, click on the Graphs menu item. When the list of options appears, click on Pie.

The Pie Charts window opens. There is no need to change the default setting, Summaries for Groups of Cases, in the Pie Charts window. Now click on Define.

The Define Pie: Summaries for Groups of Cases window opens. It looks much like the Define Bar window and works the same way.

❶ Select % of Cases.

❷ Select a variable (click on the variable *evstray*, then click on the ▶ pointing at the Define Slices By box).

❸ Click on Options. When the Options window opens, turn off Display Groups Defined by Missing Values. (Remove the √ from the box next to it.) Click on Continue. When you return to the Define Pie window, click on OK.

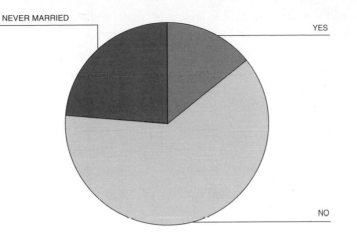

NEVER MARRIED

YES

NO

Figure 4.5 Pie chart for the variable *evstray* in the gss96subset file.

A pie chart like the one in Figure 4.5 appears in your Output window.

Interpreting a pie chart As with bar charts and histograms, we want to know the general characteristics of the respondents to the variable represented by the chart. We also want to know about the dispersion of responses across the categories of the variable. Pie charts show us the distribution of meaningful responses by valid percentages (remember we excluded missing data). Unfortunately, the default settings in SPSS do not cause the percentages to be displayed. However, the sizes of the pie slices give a pretty good picture of the data. More heterogeneous distributions will have slices of roughly equal size, whereas more homogeneous distributions will have some slices that are much larger than others.

Skills Practice 5 Produce a pie chart for the variable *xmarsx*. Does it look more homogeneous or heterogeneous? Use the command path Graphs ➡ Pie ➡ Define. When the Define Pie window opens, click on the Reset button to clear your previous work. Remember to select % of Cases and click on the Options button to turn off the Display Groups Defined by Missing Values.

In the next section, we will begin learning to construct a frequency distribution by hand. This is the first section of several in the text that will show you how to compute statistics with a pencil, paper, and a calculator. Learning to compute statistics manually is useful for a couple of reasons.

- It will improve your understanding of what the statistics mean. If we know how statistics are calculated, our ability to interpret them is enhanced.

- It provides you with a set of simple techniques for organizing and making sense of data, which can be very helpful if you are working with fairly small sets of data or when you don't have immediate access to a computer for processing data.

However, even as we learn how to calculate statistics by hand, we won't be leaving the computer, SPSS, or our GSS variables behind, as you will see in the next section. We will use some of the demographic variables in SPSS, like the ones the researcher used in the "News to Use" article, to practice the skills for building frequency distributions by hand.

CONSTRUCTING A FREQUENCY DISTRIBUTION BY HAND

Suppose a researcher has collected data from 20 respondents, asking the same kinds of questions that GSS researchers asked. Among the variables for which data have been collected is *marital.* Table 4.5 shows the raw scores collected from each of the respondents, which are numbered 1 through 20 to keep track of how many scores have been gathered. Let's construct a frequency distribution to analyze the data by following these steps.

Step 1: Listing Each of the Categories of Response

The categories of a variable should be listed in some logical sequence. For ordinal and numerical variables, we will follow the practice of arranging the categories in order from low to high. For a nominal variable like *marital,* your list of categories might look like this:

Marital Status

Married

Widowed

Divorced

Separated

Never married

Step 2: Counting the Responses

Count how many responses fall into each of the categories of the variable. You can either cross off each of the responses as you count them, or you might want to make a tick mark next to the categories on your frequency distribution as you count each response. Either way, the result is the frequency of response for each

TABLE 4.5   Summary of Responses to the Variable *marital*

Case Summaries

	Marital Status		Marital Status
1	Divorced	12	Never married
2	Never married	13	Divorced
3	Married	14	Married
4	Married	15	Never married
5	Married	16	Married
6	Divorced	17	Separated
7	Widowed	18	Divorced
8	Never married	19	Widowed
9	Widowed	20	Married
10	Divorced	Total *N*	20
11	Married		

TABLE 4.6   Step 2, Counting Frequencies, for Constructing a Frequency Distribution by Hand

Marital Status	Frequency
Married	7
Widowed	3
Divorced	5
Separated	1
Never married	4

category of the variable. List it next to each of the categories in a column labeled Frequency. Your frequency distribution for the variable *marital* should now have two columns: one for the categories of the variable and one for the frequency count for each category, like the frequency distribution in Table 4.6.

Step 3: Totaling the Responses to Find *N*

Find *N*, the number of respondents we have for a particular variable. If we add up the frequencies—sum the frequency column—we can easily see how many people answered the question about the variable *marital*.

Expressed as a formula,

FORMULA 4.1: $N = \Sigma f$

where Σ means "add up (or sum) the following," and f stands for frequencies of the categories of a variable.

Marital Status	Frequency
Married	7
Widowed	3
Divorced	5
Separated	1
Never married	4
	$N = 20$

Example: To find *N* for the frequency distribution for the table we are constructing, add up the frequencies using Formula 4.1 as follows:

$$N = \Sigma f = 7 + 3 + 5 + 1 + 4 = 20$$

Enter the result, *N,* in your table in the frequencies column as illustrated in Table 4.7.

 Checking Your Work   You can make sure you have included all of your scores on the frequency distribution by counting your raw scores and confirming that *N* is the same number.

Step 4: Computing the Percentages of Response

Calculate the percentage of response for each category of your variable, and then total the percentage column. A **percentage** is simply the proportion of respondents in a particular category of a variable multiplied by 100. A **proportion** is computed by dividing the frequency for a given category by the total number of respondents to a variable. The formula for a proportion is

FORMULA 4.2: $\text{Proportion} = \dfrac{f}{N}$

where *f* stands for the frequency for a given category, and *N* is the total number of respondents for a given variable.

To turn the proportion into a percentage, multiply the result by 100. Expressed as a formula,

**TABLE 4.8   Step 4, Finding Percentages, for Constructing a
Frequency Distribution by Hand**

Marital Status	Frequency	Percent
Married	7	35.0
Widowed	3	15.0
Divorced	5	25.0
Separated	1	5.0
Never married	4	20.0
	$N = 20$	100.0

FORMULA 4.3:   Category percentage $= \left(\dfrac{f}{N}\right) \times 100$

where f stands for the frequency for a given category, and N is the total
number of respondents for a given variable.

Example: We can find out what percentage of respondents are married by
doing the following calculation, using Formula 4.3.

$$\left(\frac{f}{N}\right) \times 100 = \left(\frac{7}{20}\right) \times 100 = .35 \times 100 = 35\%$$

As we compute the category percentage, we enter the result in our frequency distribution under a third column heading, Percent. See Table 4.8 for an illustration.

✓ **Checking Your Work**   You can make sure you have computed the percentages
correctly by adding them up. They should total 100%. (Later on, you will be rounding the percentages you compute to the nearest whole percent. When you do that, the
total percentage may add up to a little less than or a little more than 100%.)

With the percentages in place, it is easy to see that about a third (35%) of the
respondents are married, another 45% were married at some point, and 20%
have never been married.

Step 5: Calculating the Cumulative Percentages

Calculate the cumulative percentage for each category of your variable. Cumulative percentages are running totals of the percentages for each category
of a variable. They are computed most accurately by adding the frequency for

a particular category to the frequencies of all preceding categories, dividing by *N*, and multiplying by 100.

Expressed as a formula,

FORMULA 4.4: Cumulative percentage $= \left(\dfrac{\text{cum} f}{N}\right) \times 100$

where cum *f* is the sum of the frequency for a given category and the frequencies of all preceding categories, and *N* is the total number of respondents for a given variable.

Example 1: To find the cumulative percentage for the category widowed, first find the cumulative frequency (cum *f*). The cumulative frequency for the category widowed is the frequency for that category (3) plus the frequencies for all preceding categories (7), or 10. Divide the cumulative frequency by *N* (20), and multiply the result by 100. Using Formula 4.4, our computations for the cumulative percentage of the category widowed are as follows:

$$\left(\frac{\text{cum} f}{N}\right) \times 100 = \left(\frac{10}{20}\right) \times 100 = .50 \times 100 = 50\%$$

Cumulative percentages are entered into a fourth column of the frequency distribution, Cumulative Percent.

Example 2: To compute the cumulative percentage for the category divorced, you first find cum *f:*

$$\text{cum} f = 5 + 3 + 7 = 15$$

Then apply Formula 4.4:

$$\left(\frac{\text{cum} f}{N}\right) \times 100 = \left(\frac{15}{20}\right) \times 100 = .75 \times 100 = 75\%$$

Now finish the table by finding the cumulative percentage for the categories married, separated, and never married. Your frequency distribution should look like Table 4.9.

 Checking Your Work For the first category, the cumulative percentage will always be the same as the percentage for that category, and the cumulative percentage for the last category will always be at or near 100%. If it isn't, then it is likely there is a mistake, so go back and check your work.

There is another pattern here. The cumulative percentage for each of the categories is the same as the percentage for that category plus the percentages for all preceding categories. Therefore, another way to get cumulative percentages is to add them up using the Percent column. For example, if you add the percentage of widowed respondents to the percentage of married respondents, you get 50%, the cumulative percentage for the category widowed. This is a less accurate way of computing cumulative percentage, but you will come close to the correct answer, and it is another way to check your work.

TABLE 4.9 Step 5, Finding Cumulative Percentages, for Constructing a Frequency Distribution by Hand

Marital Status	Frequency	Percent	Cumulative Percent
Married	7	35.0	35.0
Widowed	3	15.0	50.0
Divorced	5	25.0	75.0
Separated	1	5.0	80.0
Never married	4	20.0	100.0
	$N = 20$	100.0	

What does the cumulative percentage tell us? It lets us know the percentage of respondents who fall at or below a particular category. For example, we can tell that 80% of the respondents in our survey have been married at some point (the cumulative percentage at the category separated). We can characterize the distribution of responses by saying something like, "Most respondents are currently or have been married—80%. One fifth (20%) have not married."

Percentages and Percentiles Another way to interpret percentages and cumulative percentages is by viewing them as response percentiles. A **percentile** is simply the point at or below which a specified percentage of responses fall. You are probably somewhat familiar with this term if you have ever taken a standardized test. Your scores are usually reported along with their corresponding percentiles. If you score a 90 on a reading test, for example, you may also learn that your score was at the 93rd percentile. This means that 93% of the people who took the test scored a 90 or lower. Only 7% of the people who took the test scored higher than 90.

Using Table 4.9, we can use the Percent column to say, as we did earlier, that 35% of the respondents are married—or we can say that the response Married falls at the 35th percentile because it includes the first 35 percent of the respondents. Likewise, we can use the Cumulative Percent column to say that 80% of the respondents have been married at some point—or we can say that the category Separated falls at the 80th percentile. The category Separated, along with the preceding categories, includes the first 80% of the responses. We will use this concept in Chapters 5 and 6 to find values or categories at specified intervals, or percentiles, of responses.

Before moving on, take a minute to review what you have learned. The steps for constructing a frequency distribution are summarized next. Use these steps as a guide for completing Skills Practice 6.

1. List the categories of the variable.

2. Count the frequencies of response for each category.

3. Add up the frequencies of response to find N.

$$N = \Sigma f$$

4. Calculate the percentages of response for each category:

$$\left(\frac{f}{N}\right) \times 100$$

5. Calculate the cumulative percentages of response for each category:

$$\left(\frac{\text{cum} f}{N}\right) \times 100$$

Skills Practice 6 Construct a frequency distribution for the randomly selected set of raw scores in the following table gathered in response to the variable *degree*—Respondent's Highest Degree. (Hint: LT high school = less than high school, graduate = graduate degree.) Notice that this is an ordinal-level variable. As you construct your frequency distribution, arrange the categories of the variable in order, from low to high. After you finish the frequency distribution, write a few sentences describing the respondents.

Raw Scores for the Variable *degree* for a Randomly Selected Set of 20 Cases from the gss96subset File

Case Summaries

	RS Highest Degree			RS Highest Degree
1	High school		11	High school
2	LT high school		12	LT high school
3	High school		13	High school
4	High school		14	LT high school
5	Graduate		15	High school
6	High school		16	High school
7	LT high school		17	LT high school
8	High school		18	High school
9	LT high school		19	LT high school
10	High school		20	LT high school

In the next section you will be learning to produce and analyze frequency distributions for variables that you create out of existing GSS variables. The process is called *recoding,* and it is used to simplify the analysis of variables that have a lot of categories.

RECODING

What Is Recoding?

Recoding is a technique for data analysis that allows us to change how the respondents to a variable are classified by recombining category values—grouping two or more categories of a variable together to simplify the process of analysis. For example, if you look at the variable *church attendance* in the "News to Use" article at the beginning of this chapter, you will see that it has only three categories: rarely, occasionally, and regularly. Compare this variable with the variable *attend* as it is set up in the General Social Survey. Notice that it has nine categories. How did the researcher writing about marital infidelity change a nine-category variable into a three-category variable? Through the process of recoding.

Why make this change? As you may have noticed, the more values a variable has, the harder it is to see the patterns in the responses. The task becomes easier if we can recombine the values into variables with fewer categories. You will see how important this is as we analyze recoded variables in this section.

The process of recoding has six steps:

Step 1. Prepare to recode a variable.

Step 2. Use the SPSS Recode command to create a new variable.

Step 3. Use the SPSS Define Variable command to label the new variable.

Step 4. Check the new variable to be sure the recoding is correct.

Step 5. Save the new variable in your data file (the gss96subset file, in this case).

Step 6. Analyze your recoded variable.

The first step in the process of recoding a variable involves looking at a frequency distribution for an existing variable and deciding how to change it.

Step 1: Preparing to Recode

Use a frequency distribution to see current coding   If you want to recode a variable, you have to begin by looking at how the variable is currently coded. Produce a frequency distribution to see the original values and categories of the variable to be recoded, which we will call the **old variable.** Figure out which values and categories you want to combine to create a **new variable** with new categories.

Skills Practice 7   Produce a frequency distribution for the variable *attend* using the gss96subset file. Use the command path Analyze ➡ Descriptive Statistics ➡ Frequencies. (See the SPSS Guide, "Obtaining a Frequency Distribution," if you need help.)

Prepare a diagram of current and new values and categories   After you produce a frequency distribution, use it to list the values and value labels of the old variable on paper. Then decide how you want to change your variable. How you change it will depend on several considerations: the research question you are trying to answer, the statistics you want to apply to the variable, and how much sense it makes to combine specific categories of a variable. For example, you can change the variable *attend* in a number of ways depending on what you are interested in. You can put the variable into the same three categories as the "News to Use" researcher did. You can also change the variable into four categories: never, once a year or less, at least once a month, and at least once a week. It makes sense to combine the categories indicating infrequent attendance, and it makes sense to combine the categories indicating frequent attendance. It wouldn't make sense to combine those who say they never attend with those who say they attend more than once a week.

For this exercise, assume we're interested in looking at the variable this way, in four categories. Having decided how we want to change our variable, *attend,* the next step is to complete the **recode diagram** you started on paper—like the one in Figure 4.6—showing how the variable is to be changed.

Name and label the new (recoded) variable   Decide on a name for the new variable you are creating. (Review the rules for naming variables in Chapter 3.) For consistency in the examples that follow, name the new variable *rcattend* and use the label RECODED CHURCH ATTENDANCE. Write your new variable name and variable label on your recode diagram.

Identify the level of measurement of the new variable   Sometimes recoding a variable changes its level of measurement. Numerical variables may become categorical ones. Ordinal variables can become nominal ones. Sometimes we can even turn nominal variables into ordinal variables by changing the order of the categories. (See Chapter 2 if you need to review these concepts.) When you prepare to do a recode, take a look at the new categories you have created and ask yourself, "At what level is this variable being measured now that I have recoded it?" In this case, what is the level of measurement of the *rcattend* variable? Write it down on the recode diagram.

Old Values of *attend*	Old Labels of *attend*	New Labels	New Values
0	Never	Never	0
1	Less than once a year		
2	Once a year	Once a year or less	1
3	Several times a year		
4	Once a month		
5	2–3 times a month	At least once a month	2
6	Nearly every week		
7	Every week	At least once a week	3
8	More than once a week		
9	DK/NA	DK/NA	9

The **old labels and values** come from the frequency distribution for the variable *attend*.

You make up the **new labels and values** based on how you want your new, recoded variable to look.

New variable name: *rcattend*
New variable label: RECODED CHURCH ATTENDANCE
Level of measurement: Ordinal

Figure 4.6   Recode diagram for the variable *attend*.

Step 2: Using the SPSS Recode Command to Create a New Variable

SPSS Guide: Recoding Variables

Follow these steps to recode variables:

 Click on the Transform menu item in the SPSS Data Editor window.

❷ Then hold your cursor on Recode.

❸ Two choices appear: Click on Into Different Variables, because choosing Into Same Variables will actually replace your original variable with a recoded new variable.

The Recode Into Different Variables window opens. At this window, there are five functions to perform. I will take you through the process step by step.

❶ Select the variable to be recoded from the variable list (click on Attend, then click on the ▶ pointing at the Input Variable → Output Variable box). The variable will appear in the Input Variable → Output Variable box.

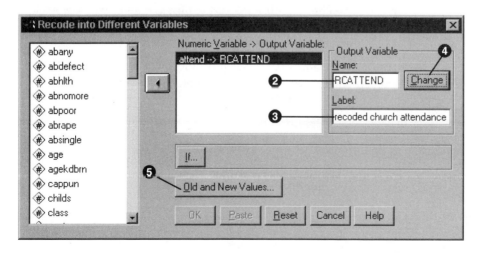

Name the new variable. Put your cursor on the box under Output Variable—Name. Click and type in the mnemonic, *rcattend,* for your new, recoded variable in the box. The mnemonic will appear in the Output Variable—Name box. (Be sure you do not use the same name as the original variable, *attend.)*

Label the new variable. Put your cursor on the box under Output Variable—Label. You can type in a longer variable name. Click and type in Recoded Church Attendance as the label for your new, recoded variable. The label will appear in the Output Variable—Label box.

Click on Change.

Click on Old and New Values.

When you click on Old and New Values, the Recode Into Different Variables: Old and New Values window opens. This window lets us tell SPSS which old values of the variable, *attend,* are to be grouped into which new values of the new variable, *rcattend.* An overview of the process follows, with step-by-step instructions. You will need to refer to the recode diagram (Figure 4.6) as you go through this process.

1. For *each category* of your new variable, enter the old value or range of old values to be combined to make the new category. Take these values directly from the recode diagram.

2. Enter the new value.

3. Click on Add.

4. After you have entered all of the old values and new values for your variable, click on Continue.

❶ Start by giving SPSS the Old Value for the first set of values to be recoded, which involves making old value 0 (Never) into the new value 0 (Never). To do this, click on Value, then type in the first value, 0.

❷ Move your cursor to New Value and type 0.

Recode into Different Variables: Old and New Values

Old Value
- ⦿ Value: [0] ❶
- ○ System-missing
- ○ System- or user-missing
- ○ Range:
  [   ] through [   ]
- ○ Range:
  Lowest through [   ]
- ○ Range:
  [   ] through highest
- ○ All other values

New Value
- ⦿ Value: [0] ❷   ○ System-missing
- ○ Copy old value(s)

❸ → [Add]

Old --> New:

[Change]
[Remove]

☐ Output variables are strings Width: [8]
☐ Convert numeric strings to numbers ('5'->5)

[Continue] [Cancel] [Help]

❸ Now click on Add. Your window will look like this:

Recode into Different Variables: Old and New Values

Old Value
- ⦿ Value: [   ]
- ○ System-missing
- ○ System- or user-missing
- ○ Range:
  [   ] through [   ]
- ○ Range:
  Lowest through [   ]
- ○ Range:
  [   ] through highest
- ○ All other values

New Value
- ⦿ Value: [   ]   ○ System-missing
- ○ Copy old value(s)

Old --> New:

[Add]   0 --> 0
[Change]
[Remove]

☐ Output variables are strings Width: [8]
☐ Convert numeric strings to numbers ('5'->5)

[Continue] [Cancel] [Help]

If you make a mistake: Click on the error in the Old → New box. The values to be fixed will be highlighted. Go back to the Old Value or New Value boxes and make corrections. Then click on Change.

Repeat steps 1–3 for each category of your new variable Give SPSS the next set of changes from your recode chart (Figure 4.6)—the Old Values 1 through 3, which will be recoded into the New Value 1. Because you are taking a range of values and transforming them into a single new value, use the Range feature under Old Value.

1 Click on Range. Enter the Old Value 1, and tab over to the next box. Type in the Old Value 3.

2 Put your cursor in the New Value box and type in 1.

3 Click on Add.

The Recode Into Different Values window will look like this:

Move to the next set of values to be recoded:

At Range, enter 4 through 6; at New Value, enter 2; then click on Add.

At Range, enter 7 through 8; at New Value, enter 3; then click on Add.

At Value, enter 9; at New Value, enter 9; then click on Add.

(For more information about when to use Value and when to use Range, see "Avoiding Common Pitfalls" at the end of this section.)

✓ Checking Your Work   All of your old and new values should appear in the Old → New box, and they should look like the ones that follow. If they don't, see the previous directions for making changes. When your changes are correct, click on Continue.

Complete the recode   When you return to the Recode Into Different Variables window, your window should look like this:

Click on OK to execute the recode and return to the SPSS Data Editor window.

Find your new variable At the SPSS Data Editor window, check to see whether your new variable is now part of your data set. Scroll (to the right, using the scroll arrow, ▶, in the bottom right-hand corner of the screen) to go to the end of your variables. Your new variable, *rcattend,* should be the last variable on your list.

	conmedic	contv	conjudge	consci	conlegis	tvhours	rcattend
1	1	8	1	2	1	-1	1.00
2	1	2	3	8	2	2	1.00

Avoiding Common Pitfalls When to use Value and when to use Range in the Recode Into Different Variables: Old and New Values window is often a source of confusion. You have several options for specifying Old Values, depending on how many old values are being regrouped into a new value. When you are recoding a single value of an old variable into a single value of a new variable, use the Value button (as when value 0, Never, remains value 0, Never). When you are recoding several values of an old variable into a single value of a new variable, use the Range button (as when values 1 through 3, Less Than Once a Year through Several Times a Year, become value 1, Once a Year or Less).

Step 3: Labeling the New Variable and Its Values

The next step is to **define the recoded variable**—label the values of your variable (if your new variable is categorical—nominal or ordinal), label any missing values, and specify the level of measurement of your new variable. The skills involved are not new. They are the same ones you used in Chapter 3 to define new variables.

To define your new, recoded variable *rcattend,* place your cursor on the variable name itself and double-click. The Define Variable window opens, with the name of your new variable in the Variable Name box. As you did when you were setting up your own data set, follow the six steps to check the variable name; specify variable Type, Labels, Missing Values, and Column Format; and identify the level of measurement.

Check the variable name When you open the Define Variable window, it should look like the one you see here.

Define the variable type Click on the Type button in the Define Variable window. Change the decimal places to zero. Click on Continue.

```
┌─────────────────────────────────────────────────────────┐
│ Define Variable Type: rcattend                      [X]  │
├─────────────────────────────────────────────────────────┤
│  ⊙ Numeric                                 ┌──────────┐  │
│  ○ Comma                      Width: [8]   │ Continue │  │
│  ○ Dot                                     └──────────┘  │
│  ○ Scientific notation    Decimal Places: [0]  ┌────────┐│
│  ○ Date                                        │ Cancel ││
│  ○ Dollar                                      └────────┘│
│  ○ Custom currency                         ┌──────────┐  │
│  ○ String                                  │   Help   │  │
│                                            └──────────┘  │
└─────────────────────────────────────────────────────────┘
```

Define the labels Click on the Labels button in the Define Variable window. Type in a value and a value label for each category of your new variable. Use the values and value labels on your recode diagram (Figure 4.6). Define Labels should look like the following illustration when you are finished. Click on Continue.

```
┌──────────────────────────────────────────────────────────┐
│ Define Labels: rcattend                              [X]  │
├──────────────────────────────────────────────────────────┤
│ Variable Label: [recoded church attendance]  ┌──────────┐ │
│ ┌Value Labels───────────────────────┐        │ Continue │ │
│ │ Value: [        ]                  │        └──────────┘ │
│ │                                    │        ┌──────────┐ │
│ │ Value Label: [                   ] │        │  Cancel  │ │
│ │                                    │        └──────────┘ │
│ │ ┌─────┐  ┌──────────────────────┐ │        ┌──────────┐ │
│ │ │ Add │  │0 = "Never"          ▲│ │        │   Help   │ │
│ │ └─────┘  │1 = "Once a year or less" │     └──────────┘ │
│ │ ┌───────┐│2 = "At least once a month"│                  │
│ │ │Change ││3 = "At least once a week" │                  │
│ │ └───────┘│9 = "DK, NA"         ▼│ │                     │
│ │ ┌───────┐└──────────────────────┘ │                     │
│ │ │Remove │                          │                     │
│ │ └───────┘                          │                     │
│ └───────────────────────────────────┘                     │
└──────────────────────────────────────────────────────────┘
```

Specify missing values Click on the Missing Values button in the Define Variable window. Click on Discrete Missing Values, and type in the missing value, 9, in the first box. Then click on Continue.

Define the column format Click on the Column Format button in the Define Variable window. You should see a Column Width of 8 and Text Alignment of Right. (If not, make the necessary changes.) Click on Continue.

Specify the level of measurement At the Define Variable window, look under Measurement and click on Ordinal. Now you're ready to check your new variable. Click on OK.

Step 4: Checking the Recoded Variable

To check your recoding, produce a frequency distribution for your new, recoded variable, *rcattend,* and compare it to a frequency distribution for the old variable, *attend.* Use the command path Analyze ➡ Descriptive Statistics ➡ Frequencies. Select the variables *attend* and *rcattend.* Click on OK. You should be looking at frequency distributions like the ones in Tables 4.10 and 4.11.

TABLE 4.10 **Frequency Distribution for the Variable *attend* in the gss96subset File**

ATTEND HOW OFTEN R ATTENDS RELIGIOUS SERVICES

		Frequency	Percent	Valid Percent	Cumulative Percent
Valid	0 NEVER	438	15.1	15.5	15.5
	1 LT ONCE A YEAR	253	8.7	9.0	24.5
	2 ONCE A YEAR	400	13.8	14.2	38.6
	3 SEVRL TIMES A YR	416	14.3	14.7	53.4
	4 ONCE A MONTH	190	6.5	6.7	60.1
	5 2-3X A MONTH	271	9.3	9.6	69.7
	6 NRLY EVERY WEEK	160	5.5	5.7	75.4
	7 EVERY WEEK	486	16.7	17.2	92.6
	8 MORE THN ONCE WK	209	7.2	7.4	100.0
	Total	2823	97.2	100.0	
Missing	9 DK,NA	81	2.8		
Total		2904	100.0		

TABLE 4.11 **Frequency Distribution for the Recoded *attend* Variable in the gss96subset File**

RCATTEND recoded church attendance

		Frequency	Percent	Valid Percent	Cumulative Percent
Valid	0 Never	438	15.1	15.5	15.5
	1 Once a year or less	1069	36.8	37.9	53.4
	2 At least once a month	621	21.4	22.0	75.4
	3 At least once a week	695	23.9	24.6	100.0
	Total	2823	97.2	100.0	
Missing	9 DK, NA	81	2.8		
Total		2904	100.0		

✅ Checking Your Work How do you know whether your recoding is correct? Make sure that

- The variable name and label show up on the table exactly as you entered them.
- The values and their labels appear on the table.

If the variable name, label, or value labels are incorrect, go back to the Define Variable window to correct them.

Compare your frequency distribution for *rcattend* with the frequency distribution for *attend:*

- *N* for the recoded variable should be the same as *N* for the original variable.
- The number of valid cases and missing cases for the new variable should be the same as they were for the old variable.
- If you made a mistake, follow the command path Transform ➡ Recode ➡ Into Different Variables and correct your error(s).

Step 5: Saving the Variable

When you are satisfied that your recoded variable is correct, you can save it by clicking on the Save File icon.

Step 6: Analyzing the Recoded Variable

Recoding a variable is an aid to the analysis of data, not an end in itself. What does recoding a variable help us to do? Let's use our recoded variable *rcattend* to do the same thing that the "News to Use" researcher did: look to see whether people who attend church regularly are more or less likely to have sex outside of marriage. To separate our GSS file by the categories of the variable *rcattend,* we have to use the Split File command. Go to the SPSS Data Editor window.

- Follow the command path Data ➡ Split File ➡ Organize Output by Groups.
- Select the variable *rcattend,* and click on OK.

Look at frequency distributions for the variable *evstray.*

- Follow the command path Analyze ➡ Descriptive Statistics ➡ Frequencies.
- Select the variable *evstray,* and click on OK.

Skills Practice 8 What conclusion can you draw? Are those who attend church at least once a week more or less likely to have had sex outside of their marriages than those who never attend church?

Skills Practice 9 Recode the variable *age* into the same categories as the "News to Use" researcher. Follow these steps:

- Produce a frequency distribution for the variable *age*.
- Create a recode diagram on a piece of paper showing how you will recode *age* into the following categories:

  Group the respondents who are ages 18–29 into category 1, Age 18–29.

  Group the respondents who are ages 30–39 into category 2, Age 30–39.

  Group the respondents who are ages 40–49 into category 3, Age 40–49.

  Group the respondents who are ages 50–59 into category 4, Age 50–59.

  Group the respondents who are ages 60–69 into category 5, Age 60–69.

  Group the respondents who are ages 70–89 into category 6, Age 70 and up.

  Category 99 (DK) will be new category 99, and it will be classified as a missing data value.

- Give your variable an 8-character name (call it *rcage*) and a label, and decide at what level it is being measured.
- Create a new, recoded variable. Use the command path Transform ➡ Recode ➡ Into Different Variables. Define it.
- Produce and check the frequency distribution for your new variable.
- When your new variable checks out, save your data file to add the new variable.

SUMMARY

The emphasis in this chapter has been on producing and analyzing frequency distributions. Frequency distributions summarize data for single variables, and they help us to see the patterns in the responses to variables so that we can describe or characterize the respondents.

Frequency distributions usually list the categories of a variable, the frequencies—or number of responses—for each category, and the percentage of the responses to each category. Frequency distributions in SPSS list percentages two ways: one percentage distribution for all cases and one for valid cases only. In addition, SPSS frequency distributions show cumulative percentages for the response categories of a variable.

You learned how to produce and analyze frequency distributions for 1996 General Social Survey variables using the command path Analyze ➥ Descriptive Statistics ➥ Frequencies in SPSS, and you learned how to produce frequency distributions by hand. Producing frequency distributions by hand is a five-step process of listing the categories of a variable, counting the frequencies of response to each category, summing the frequencies of response to find the total number of responses, calculating the percentages of response to each category, and calculating the cumulative percentages of response.

More important is that you practiced writing about what you learned from frequency distributions—describing the general characteristics of the respondents to a variable using a headline or topic sentence and then elaborating on your general conclusions with details from the frequency distribution.

We went over the process of splitting a data file by one variable (using the Data ➥ Split File command path) and then comparing frequency distributions for a second variable. For example, we split the file by the variable *sex* to compare frequency distributions for the variable *evstray* for male and female respondents. This procedure allows us to see whether there are differences between males and females in their responses to the variable on ever having had sex outside of their marriages.

We supplemented our analysis of frequency distributions with various graphs—bar charts, histograms, or pie charts—that help us to analyze visually the distributions of responses to variables. Such graphs are particularly helpful aids for assessing the extent to which a distribution of responses to a variable is homogeneous or heterogeneous.

Finally, you learned to recode—combine categories of variables—to create new variables. The process of recoding involves preparing a diagram showing how we are going to combine categories of an existing variable to create a new one; using the SPSS Recode command to create a new variable; using the Define Variable window to label the new variable, its values, and its categories; and checking the new variable to be sure our recoding is correct. The goal of recoding is to help us analyze responses to variables. Consequently, the final step in the recoding process is to produce a frequency distribution for the variable we create through the recoding process and to analyze it.

In the next chapter you will learn to supplement the analysis of frequency distributions with a set of statistics called measures of central tendency.

KEY CONCEPTS

Univariate analysis
Raw data
Raw scores
Frequency distribution
Dialog box
Valid cases
Missing cases
N
Frequency of response
Percent column
Valid Percent column

Cumulative Percent
 column
Dispersion of response
Heterogeneous
 distribution
Homogeneous
 distribution
Bar chart
Histogram
x-axis and y-axis
Pie chart

Percentage
Proportion
Percentile
Recoding
Old variable
New variable
Recode diagram
Old label and value
New label and value
Define a recoded
 variable

ANSWERS TO SKILLS PRACTICES

1. *marital*   Over three quarters (77.3%) of the respondents to the 1996 General Social Survey have at least tried marriage (are married, separated, divorced, or widowed), whereas less than one quarter have never been married. Almost half of the respondents (47.9%) were married at the time of the survey, and almost one fifth (19.8%) were either divorced or separated.

   degree   Most of the respondents to the General Social Survey for 1996—nearly 85%—have at least completed high school. Only 15.5% haven't obtained high school diplomas. Nearly one quarter have bachelor's or graduate degrees.

   wrkstat   Almost exactly two thirds (66.9%) of the GSS respondents are working full-time or part-time. Only a little more than half (56.5%) are working full-time, although the percentage who are keeping house (11.6%) should probably be added to that number. Almost 5% are either temporarily not working, unemployed, or laid off.

   xmarsex   Nearly all respondents to the General Social Survey for 1996 (93%) believe sex outside of marriage is either always wrong (77.9%) or almost always wrong (15.1%). Less than 2% think it's not wrong at all, whereas 5.2% think it's sometimes wrong.

   Homogeneous vs. heterogeneous: All of these variables are examples of more homogeneous distributions of responses.

2. A somewhat higher percentage of females say that sex outside of marriage is always wrong (80.0%) as compared to males (75.2%). Whereas relatively few respondents say that sex outside of marriage is not wrong at all, a larger percentage of males express that view (2.3%) than females (1.5%).

3. Bar chart for the variable *premarsx*. It is a somewhat heterogeneous distribution because the bars are more even in height, indicating more dispersion of responses across the categories of the variable in comparison to the distribution of responses to the *evstray* variable.

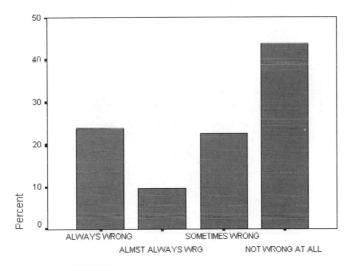

SEX BEFORE MARRIAGE

4. Histogram for the variable *educ*. Notice that each bar represents 2.5 years of education. (Subtract the midpoint of the first bar [0] from the midpoint of the second bar [2.5]. 2.5 − 0 = 2.5.) The histogram shows a relatively homogeneous distribution of responses to the variable, with most respondents having completed at least some high school or college training.

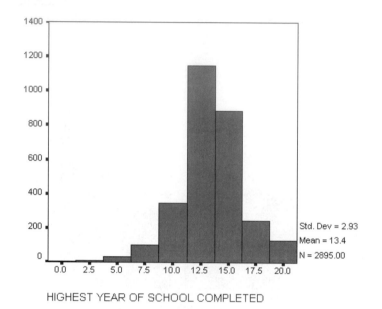

HIGHEST YEAR OF SCHOOL COMPLETED

5. Pie chart for *xmarsx*. The distribution of responses to this variable is more homogeneous, because it is clear that over three quarters of the respondents believe extramarital sex is always wrong.

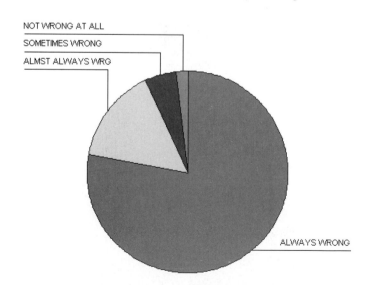

6. Your frequency distribution should look like this one:

Respondent's Highest Degree

	Frequency	Percent	Cumulative Percent
LT high school	8	40.0	40.0
High school	11	55.0	95.0
Graduate	1	5.0	100.0
Total	$N = 20$	100.0	

Nearly two thirds of the respondents (60%) finished high school or obtained a graduate degree. Whereas a majority of the respondents finished high school, 40% left school before getting their high school diplomas.

7. Your frequency distribution for *attend* should look like this one:

ATTEND HOW OFTEN R ATTENDS RELIGIOUS SERVICES

		Frequency	Percent	Valid Percent	Cumulative Percent
Valid	0 NEVER	430	15.1	15.5	15.5
	1 LT ONCE A YEAR	253	8.7	9.0	24.5
	2 ONCE A YEAR	400	13.8	14.2	38.6
	3 SEVRL TIMES A YR	416	14.3	14.7	53.4
	4 ONCE A MONTH	190	6.5	6.7	60.1
	5 2-3X A MONTH	271	9.3	9.6	69.7
	6 NRLY EVERY WEEK	160	5.5	5.7	75.4
	7 EVERY WEEK	486	16.7	17.2	92.6
	8 MORE THN ONCE WK	209	7.2	7.4	100.0
	Total	2823	97.2	100.0	
Missing	9 DK,NA	81	2.8		
Total		2904	100.0		

8. Those who attend church at least once a week are less likely than those who never attend church to have sex with someone other than their spouse while married. 16.2% of those who never attend church say they have had sex with someone other than their spouse, whereas only 9.9% of those who attend church at least once a week say they have had sex outside of their marriages. 50.6% of those who never attend church say that they have not had sex with someone other than their spouse while married, whereas 75% of those who attend church at least once a week say that they have not had sex outside of their marriages. 15.1% of those who attend church at least once a week have never married, whereas 33.2% of those who never attend church have never married.

9. Your recode diagram for transforming *age* into *rcage* should look like the following:

Current Values	Labels[3]	New Labels	New Values
18–29		Age 18–29	1
30–39		Age 30–39	2
40–49		Age 40–49	3
50–59		Age 50–59	4
60–69		Age 60–69	5
70–89		Age 70 and up	6
99	NA	99	NA

Variable name: *rcage*

Variable label: RECODED AGE

Level of measurement (*rcage*): Ordinal

Your frequency distribution for the recoded variable, *rcage,* should look like this one:

rcage recoded age

		Frequency	Percent	Valid Percent	Cumulative Percent
Valid	1 Age 18–29	591	20.4	20.4	20.4
	2 Age 30–39	696	24.0	24.0	44.4
	3 Age 40–49	623	21.5	21.5	65.9
	4 Age 50–59	394	13.6	13.6	79.5
	5 Age 60–69	278	9.6	9.6	89.1
	6 Age 70 and up	316	10.9	10.9	100.0
	Total	2898	99.8	100.0	
Missing	99 NA	6	.2		
Total		2904	100.0		

---

[3]Age is numerical, so there are no value labels for the *age* variable.

GENERAL EXERCISES

Construct and analyze frequency distributions for the given variables using the following sets of data, randomly selected from the 1996 General Social Survey.

1. *sex*

Case Summaries

	Respondent's Sex			Respondent's Sex
1	Female		12	Male
2	Female		13	Male
3	Female		14	Female
4	Female		15	Male
5	Male		16	Female
6	Female		17	Female
7	Male		18	Female
8	Male		19	Male
9	Male		20	Male
10	Male		Total N = 20	
11	Female			

2. *earnrs* (number of people in a family who earned money)

Case Summaries

	How Many in Family Earned Money			How Many in Family Earned Money
1	1		12	1
2	1		13	2
3	1		14	1
4	1		15	1
5	1		16	1
6	1		17	3
7	3		18	1
8	1		19	0
9	1		20	0
10	0		Total N = 20	
11	3			

3. *educ* (highest year of school completed)

Case Summaries

	Highest Year of School Completed		Highest Year of School Completed
1	12	16	15
2	18	17	16
3	8	18	13
4	12	19	18
5	18	20	13
6	14	21	13
7	10	22	16
8	14	23	14
9	14	24	10
10	8	25	12
11	10	26	14
12	10	27	16
13	12	28	13
14	18	Total $N = 28$	
15	17		

4. *teensex* (attitudes toward sex before marriage for teens ages 14 through 16)

Case Summaries

	Sex Before Marriage— Teens 14–16		Sex Before Marriage— Teens 14–16
1	Always wrong	9	Not wrong at all
2	Always wrong	10	Always wrong
3	Always wrong	11	Always wrong
4	Always wrong	12	Always wrong
5	Always wrong	13	Always wrong
6	Always wrong	14	Almost always wrong
7	Sometimes wrong	Total $N = 14$	
8	Always wrong		

5. *premarsx* (attitudes toward premarital sex)

Case Summaries

	Sex Before Marriage			Sex Before Marriage
1	Not wrong at all		8	Not wrong at all
2	Sometimes wrong		9	Sometimes wrong
3	Not wrong at all		10	Not wrong at all
4	Not wrong at all		11	Not wrong at all
5	Always wrong		12	Not wrong at all
6	Sometimes wrong		13	Sometimes wrong
7	Always wrong		Total $N = 13$	

6. *race*

Case Summaries

	Race of Respondent			Race of Respondent
1	White		16	White
2	White		17	White
3	White		18	Black
4	White		19	White
5	White		20	Black
6	White		21	White
7	White		22	White
8	Black		23	White
9	Black		24	Black
10	White		25	White
11	White		26	White
12	White		27	White
13	White		28	Black
14	White		Total $N = 28$	
15	Black			

SPSS EXERCISES

For Exercises 1–5, produce and write an analysis of the frequency distribution for the GSS variable listed.

1. *sex*
2. *childs*
3. *race*
4. *sexeduc*
5. *pillok*
6. Write your own article, similar to the one in the "News to Use" section of this chapter, summarizing your analysis of the variables *sex, childs, race, pillok,* and *sexeduc* from Exercises 1–5.
7. Are there differences between males and females in their attitudes toward providing birth control pills to teenagers? (Split your gss96subset file using the variable *sex,* then produce and analyze frequency distributions for *pillok.*)
8. Are there differences between males and females in their attitudes toward sex education in the schools? (Split your gss96subset file using the variable *sex,* then produce and analyze frequency distributions for *sexeduc.*)
9. Are there differences between those who identify themselves as White, Black, and Other on the issue of providing birth control to teenagers? (Split your gss96subset file using the variable *race,* then produce and analyze frequency distributions for *pillok.*)
10. Are there differences between those who identify themselves as White, Black, and Other on the issue of sex education in the public schools? (Split your gss96subset file using the variable *race,* then produce and analyze frequency distributions for *sexeduc.*)

For Exercises 11–14, produce an appropriate graph (depending on the level of measurement) for the GSS variables listed. Is the distribution of responses homogeneous or heterogeneous? Why do you think so?

11. *sex*

12. *childs*

13. *pillok*

14. *sexeduc*

For Exercises 15 and 16, do the recode. Then analyze your new variable. If you had to write a headline, what would it be? Use the frequency distribution for your new variable to characterize the respondents. Produce an appropriate graph. Does the distribution appear to be homogeneous or heterogeneous?

15. Recode the GSS variable *teensex* into two categories, acceptable and not acceptable. Save it as the variable *rcteensx*. Compare the frequency distribution for your recoded variable with the following frequency distribution from the NCPTP study.

Question: Some people think it is basically acceptable for high school teenagers to be sexually active, as long as they take steps to prevent pregnancy and sexually transmitted diseases including AIDS. Others do not think it is acceptable for high school teenagers to be sexually active whether they take precautions or not. Which comes closer to your view, the first statement or the second one?

Percentages

35%	Teen sexual activity acceptable as long as teens take precautions
63%	Teen sexual activity not acceptable even if they take precautions
2%	Don't know/refused to answer
100%	

---

16. Recode the GSS variable *pillok* into two categories, agree and disagree. Save it as the variable *rcpillok.* Compare the frequency distribution for your recoded variable with the following table from the NCPTP study.

Question: I'm going to read you three statements about teens and sex. Please tell me which one comes closest to your view:

1. Teens should NOT be sexually active and should not have access to birth control;
2. Teens should NOT be sexually active, but teens who ARE should have access to birth control; OR
3. It's OKAY for teens to be sexually active, AS LONG AS they have access to birth control.
4. Don't know/refused to answer

Percentages

22%   Teens should NOT be sexually active and should not have access to birth control

59%   Teens should NOT be sexually active, but teens who ARE should have access to birth control

14%   It's OKAY for teens to be sexually active, AS LONG AS they have access to birth control

 5%   Don't know/refused to answer
_____
100%

Do the recodes in Exercises 17–19 to create variables for use in the next several chapters of the text.

17. Recode the GSS variable *age* into the following categories:

18–25

26–39

40–64

65–89

Save your new variable as *agecat.*

18. Recode the GSS variable *partyid* as follows:

Strong Democrat and Not Strong Democrat into the category Democrat

Independent—Near Democrat, Independent, and Independent—Near Republican, into the category Independent

Strong Republican and Not Strong Republican into the category Republican

Other remains Other

Save your new variable as *partyaf.*

19. Recode the GSS variable *polviews* as follows:

Extremely Liberal, Liberal, and Slightly Liberal into the category Liberal

Moderate remains Moderate

Extremely Conservative, Conservative, and Slightly Conservative into the category Conservative

Save your new variable as *polaf.*

5 Measures of Central Tendency

INTRODUCTION

Like all statistics, measures of central tendency—the mode, median, and mean—help us find patterns in data. Like frequency distributions, these measures are in use every day—in news reports about what is happening in our economy and how it is affecting the lives of American families, for example. In the "News to Use" sections are articles illustrating how the median and the mean are often used. The first article is about changes in household incomes, and the second article (which is introduced later on in this chapter) describes what it takes to be a millionaire.

NEWS TO USE: Statistics in the "Real" World

Household Incomes Rise[1]

RANDOLPH E. SCHMID

WASHINGTON (AP)—The contribution of America's working wives and mothers has accounted for the bulk of the increase in household income in recent decades.

A new Census Bureau analysis shows the incomes of married couples with children increased by 25.3% between 1969 and 1996.

But women have increasingly joined the work force. If their income is not counted, the increase in household income is just 1.5%, according to the report.

[1]*The Wire*—News From the AP, 1 September 1998, <http://www.ap.org>.

The Census statisticians sought to determine why median household income rose a modest 6.3%—from $33,072 to $35,172—while per capita income leaped 51%—from $11,975 to $18,136. They used constant 1996 dollars, which removes the effect of inflation.

They found major changes in household composition, including increases in the number of single-person households and both men and women raising children without a spouse present.

Among the changes was the increase in the proportion of wives working full-time, year-round. That climbed from 17% to 39% in households with children.

Married-couple households with no children and working wives increased from 42% to 60% when a householder was under 40 years old, and from 31% to 46% when a householder was 40 to 64 years old.

Looking at such households' earnings, married-couple households without children also had substantial gains in median income between 1969 and 1996. Again, the increased importance of the income of the wife was evident, the report noted.

Among such households with someone under 65 years old, median income increased by 34% over the period, but only by about 16% when the earnings of wives were excluded. The median is the midpoint figure, meaning half made more and half less.

Among other findings:

- The average income of households at or below the median grew by only 3.9%

between 1969 and 1996, while the average income of households above the median grew by 30%.

- In households with incomes above the median, the proportion of people 25 years old and over with a college degree grew from 16% to 33%. In households with incomes below the median, the proportion of those 25 years old and over with a college degree grew from 5% to 11%.

- There was a decline in the number of married-couple households with children (from 41% to 26% of households), an increase in the number of households with children but no spouse present (from 6% to 11%) and an increase in one-person households (from 17% to 25%).

- The median income of households with a female householder with children and no spouse rose by 10% between 1969 and 1996, but the median income of households with a male householder with children and no spouse fell by 8%.

- Married-couple households with a householder 65 years old or over had substantial gains in median income, increasing 57% (34% when the income of wives was excluded).

- Among one-person households with a householder 65 years old or over, the median income of both men and women rose 63%.

Measures of central tendency are univariate statistics, applied to one variable at a time. They help us find out, for example, whether the respondents to surveys—like the ones described in the "News to Use" sections—tend to be young or old, male or female, employed or unemployed, rich or poor, optimistic or pessimistic about their financial futures. In short, they tell us what the respondents to a survey are generally like.

Throughout this chapter and the next you'll be learning to describe survey respondents, first with measures of central tendency and then with measures of dispersion. The measures of central tendency we will be working with are the mode, the median, and the mean. I will show you what each measure means, how to compute it by hand, and how to find it using SPSS. More important, I will be showing you how each measure tells us something new and interesting about the respondents to a survey.

THE MODE

The **mode** tells us which category of a variable is the one most frequently chosen by respondents. Another way to describe the mode is that it is the category chosen by *the most* respondents. The mode is not the same as the category or categories that contain *most of* the respondents. We will look at this again in the next "Avoiding Common Pitfalls."

When to Use the Mode

The mode can be used with variables at any level of measurement, categorical or numerical; it is the *only* measure of association for nominal variables.

Finding the Mode

Use a frequency distribution to find the mode. If you are trying to find the mode by hand, you must first put your data into that form. Then you simply read down the Frequency column and locate the highest number(s). The mode is the category or categories associated with the largest frequency (or frequencies, if there is a tie for the mode—more than one frequency with the same number).

It is important to remember that the mode is the *category* associated with the highest frequency, and not the highest frequency itself. For example, if we want to know the mode—the most commonly occurring response—for the GSS respondents to the variable asking about their work status, we could produce a frequency distribution for *wrkstat*. Do that now; you will get a frequency distribution like the one in Table 5.1.

TABLE 5.1 Frequency Distribution for the Variable *wrkstat*

WRKSTAT LABOR FORCE STATUS

		Frequency	Percent	Valid Percent	Cumulative Percent
Valid	1 WORKING FULLTIME	1641	56.5	56.5	56.5
	2 WORKING PARTTIME	302	10.4	10.4	66.9
	3 TEMP NOT WORKING	60	2.1	2.1	69.0
	4 UNEMPL, LAID OFF	75	2.6	2.6	71.6
	5 RETIRED	350	12.1	12.1	83.6
	6 SCHOOL	84	2.9	2.9	86.5
	7 KEEPING HOUSE	338	11.6	11.6	98.1
	8 OTHER	54	1.9	1.9	100.0
	Total	2904	100.0	100.0	

To find the mode, read down the Frequency column and find the largest number. In this case it is 1641. Now look across the frequency distribution table to find the category of the *work status* variable associated with the largest frequency. It is Working Full Time. We now know that the most commonly occurring response to the variable asking about work status is "working full time."

When there is more than one modal category, then the distribution of responses is called multimodal (bimodal, if there are two modes; trimodal, if there are three), and we report each of the modes we find.

Finding the Mode Using SPSS

Finding the measures of central tendency (mode, median, and mean) with SPSS is a fairly simple task, as described in the following SPSS Guide.

SPSS Guide: Finding Measures of Central Tendency

Use the command path Analyze ➡ Descriptive Statistics ➡ Frequencies to open the Frequencies dialog box (see the SPSS Guide, "Obtaining a Frequency Distribution," in Chapter 4 if you need help).

❶ Scroll down to *wrkstat* and click on it to highlight it.

❷ Click on the ▶ pointing at the Variable(s) box to put the variable in the box.

❸ Then click on the Statistics button.

At the Frequencies: Statistics dialog box, find the box labeled Central Tendency.

❶ Click on the measure(s) you want SPSS to compute. (You can select one or more than one.)

❷ Click on Continue to return to the Frequencies dialog box, and click on OK at the Frequencies dialog box.

TABLE 5.2 Statistics Table for the Variable *wrkstat*

Statistics

WRKSTAT LABOR FORCE STATUS

N	Valid	2904
	Missing	0
Mode		1

In the Output window, you will see a frequency distribution for the variable *wrkstat* along with a report like the one in Table 5.2. The report tells you how many valid cases (responses to the variable) and how many missing cases there are (individuals who did not respond). You will also see that it reports the mode as a value (not as a value label). If you look back at the frequency distribution for *wrkstat* in Table 5.1, you can look up the value label associated with value 1, WORKING FULL TIME.

Interpreting the Mode

Measures of central tendency—including the mode—can be used to back up or elaborate on the descriptions of GSS respondents we might come up with by analyzing a frequency distribution. For example, in discussing the frequency distribution for the variable *labor force status,* we might point out that

> respondents to the 1996 GSS tend to be employed. The most commonly occurring response to the question about labor force status is "working full time," with a little over half of the respondents answering in that category.

Keep in mind that you may have more than one mode. If so, your interpretation will be along the lines of, "The most commonly occurring responses are . . ."

Avoiding Common Pitfalls   The most frequently occurring response is not necessarily the same thing as the category or categories to which most respondents answered. When the word *most* is used to describe some characteristic of the respondents, it should refer to at least a majority of them. A little more than half of the respondents to the variable *labor force status* say that they are working full-time. In this case, we *can* say that a majority of the respondents—most of them—are working full-time (56.5%). When we use the mode, it is important to check the Percent column to see whether, in addition to being the most frequently chosen response category, it is also the one to which most respondents answered.

Let's practice the skills covered so far. In this chapter, you will begin integrating the manual (pencil, paper, calculator) skills for computation with computer skills. For each of the Skills Practices, first obtain a frequency distribution from SPSS (without the associated measure of central tendency). Find the appropriate measure of central tendency (starting with the mode) on your own. Then use SPSS to get the measure of central tendency you need to answer the Skills Practice questions. Check the measure of central tendency you came up with against the one produced by SPSS.

Skills Practice 1   It is a little surprising to me that only a little more than half of the GSS96 respondents are working full-time. What's going on? Could it be that there is more employment among some groups of respondents and less among others? What if we looked at the sample divided by the categories of the variable *sex*. Is a larger percentage of men working full-time as compared to women? Let's split the sample into groups based on sex. Remember the split file procedure from Chapter 4? Let's try it.

Click on Data, then Split File. When the Split File window opens,

- Click on Organize Output by Groups.
- Click on the variable *sex* from the variable list.
- Click on the ▶ to put the variable in the Groups Based On box. Click on OK.

Your split file is on (as indicated by the Split File On message in the lower left-hand corner of the screen). Now let's get a frequency distribution for labor force status again (*wrkstat*). This time you will get two frequency distributions—one for each group, males and females. Find the mode, then check your work by finding the mode with SPSS. Did you get the right answer? Write a few sentences describing what you found—use the frequency distributions and the modes to compare the two groups.

THE MEDIAN

Whereas the mode is the value that occurs most often for a particular variable, the **median** tells us which value divides the respondents in half, such that half of the respondents to a variable fall at or below the median value and half of the respondents are at or above it. Probably the most common use of the median in the popular press is in reporting economic news. In the first "News to Use" article, you see the median used to compare changes in household incomes between 1969 and 1996.

When to Use the Median

The median is used with variables that are ordinal or numerical. It cannot be used with variables that are nominal, because interpretation of the median assumes that variables have categories that can be ranked or ordered.

An advantage of the median is that, unlike the mean (the number commonly called *the average*), it is not affected by extreme scores in a set of data. I will illustrate how this works later on in this chapter.

Finding the Median by Hand

The process of finding the median involves three steps:

Step 1. Arrange the respondents to a variable in order, low to high (or high to low), based on their categories of response.

Step 2. Find the respondent in the middle (the **median case**).

Step 3. Find the category or value associated with the respondent in the middle (the **median value**).

To illustrate, suppose there is a college class of nine traditional-age students for which we want to know the median age. The first thing to do is arrange the students in order by age, youngest to oldest (or oldest to youngest, it doesn't matter). One way to do this is have the students line up by age, youngest on the left to the oldest on the right. Our line might look like the one in Figure 5.1.

Next, we have to find the student in the middle of the line. That's fairly easy—it's the fifth student from the beginning (or the end) of the line, student number 5. However, the number, 5, isn't the median; it is simply the rank assigned to the person in the middle of the line or the number assigned to the person who is the median case.

Student:	1	2	3	4	5	6	7	8	9
Age:	19	20	20	20	21	22	22	23	24

Figure 5.1 Ages of nine students in a class.

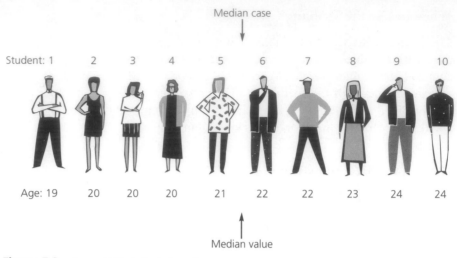

Figure 5.2 Ages of 10 students in a class.

To find the median value, we need to know the age of the person in the middle of the line. The age of the fifth student is 21, so we learn the median age of the students in the class is 21.

Half of the students are 21 or younger, and half are 21 or older.

What happens when there are 10 students instead of 9? We follow the same process. We line them up by age. With 10 traditional-age college students our line might look like Figure 5.2.

The question is, which student is in the middle: student #5 or student #6? The answer is neither. The student in the middle falls between student #5 and student #6. If we add 5 and 6 together (to get 11) and divide by 2, we regard the result, 5.5, as the middle student, or the middle case, in the line of respondents to the variable *age*.

What is the median value, the age associated with student 5.5? As you may have guessed, the median age is found by adding the ages associated with student #5 and student #6 together (21 + 22 = 43) and dividing by 2 to get 21.5, the median value.

Half of the students are younger than 21.5, and half are older.

When we are dealing with only a few cases in response to a particular variable, it is a fairly simple task to find the median by lining up the respondents, locating the one in the middle, and then identifying the value associated with that respondent. However, when we have a large number of cases—think about the nearly 3,000 respondents to the GSS—we need shortcuts. We need a way to (1) arrange the respondents in order (without having to line them all up), (2) find the median case, and (3) find the median value.

TABLE 5.3   Ages of 25 Respondents Selected at Random From the gss96subset File

CASE	AGE
1	49
2	37
3	41
4	34
5	37
6	35
7	49
8	33
9	37
10	43
11	45
12	38
13	45
14	40
15	33
16	42
17	37
18	43
19	44
20	39
21	34
22	46
23	32
24	49
25	36

Frequency distributions provide us with the shortcut. They can be used to arrange the respondents in order by response category or value, and formulas can be used to find the median case and locate the median value associated with it.

Follow this process with another example using a set of 25 raw scores for the variable *age* that were drawn at random from the 1996 GSS. The data in the form of raw scores are displayed in Table 5.3.

Our first task is to arrange the respondents in order. We will follow the practice of listing variable values in order from low to high. With the categories of the variable arranged in this order, a frequency distribution for the data in Table 5.3 would look like Table 5.4.

Now we need to find the respondent in the middle of the distribution—the median case. A formula helps us do that. To find the median case, we add 1 to the total number of responses, N. Then we divide the result by 2. (Remember

TABLE 5.4 Frequency Distribution for a Random Sample of Scores From the 1996 GSS for the Variable *age*

				AGE AGE OF RESPONDENT			
Reading the frequency distribution as an index to the cases:			Frequency	Percent	Valid Percent	Cumulative Percent
respondent 1	Valid	32	1	4.0	4.0	4.0
respondents 2–3		33	2	8.0	8.0	12.0
respondents 4–5		34	2	8.0	8.0	20.0
respondent 6		35	1	4.0	4.0	24.0
respondent 7		36	1	4.0	4.0	28.0
respondent 8–11		37	4	16.0	16.0	44.0
respondent 12		38	1	4.0	4.0	48.0
respondent 13		39	1	4.0	4.0	52.0
		40	1	4.0	4.0	56.0
		41	1	4.0	4.0	60.0
		42	1	4.0	4.0	64.0
		43	2	8.0	8.0	72.0
		44	1	4.0	4.0	76.0
		45	2	8.0	8.0	84.0
		46	1	4.0	4.0	88.0
		49	3	12.0	12.0	100.0
		Total	25	100.0	100.0	

that SPSS uses only valid responses in its statistical computations.) The formula for finding the median case can be expressed as follows.

FORMULA 5.1: Median case $= (N + 1) \times .50$

Note: Multiplying a value by ½ (or .50) is the same mathematically as dividing it in half, by 2.

Example: The median case for the preceding distribution would be

median case $= (N + 1) \times .50 = (25 + 1) \times .50 = 26 \times .50 = 13.$

The next step is to find the median value associated with the median case by reading down the Frequencies column. For example, if we look at the first category of the variable *age,* we see that the frequency for that category is 1. We already know that this number tells us that 1 respondent answered, "32," in response to the variable *age.*

If we now understand that the frequency distribution has, in essence, lined up our respondents, low to high, according to their answers to the variable *age,* we can use the frequency distribution as an index to the order of the cases. Reading down the Frequencies column, we can see that respondent number 1 answered "32" to the variable *age;* respondents 2 and 3 answered "33"; respondents 4 and 5 answered "35;" and so on.

Where is respondent 13? He or she is in the frequency associated with the median value, 39.

Half of the respondents are 32 to 39 years old, and the other half are 39 to 49 years old.

Finding the Median Using the Cumulative Percentage on a Frequency Distribution

An alternative to finding the median computationally is to use the Cumulative Percent column on a frequency distribution. Remember the median is the value that divides a set of data in half. This means that 50% of the respondents will fall at or below the median and 50% at or above it. Consequently, you can read down the Cumulative Percent column on a frequency distribution until you find the halfway point in the data, also known as the 50th percentile. Then read across the frequency distribution to find the value associated with the halfway point in the data.

Example: Look down the Cumulative Percent column for Table 5.4. Notice that 4% of the respondents are 32 years old, 12% are 32 or 33 years old, and so on. If you keep on reading down the Cumulative Percent column, you come to the cumulative percentage that includes the halfway point in the data (the 50th percentile) at 52%. Reading across the frequency distribution, you can find the value associated with the 50th percentile, 39.

Half of the respondents are 39 years old or younger (down to age 32), and half are 39 years old or older (up to age 49).

Note that when you are using the Cumulative Percent column to find the median, you will rarely find the data divided evenly at the median. This means that you will normally find the 50th percentile included in a range of percentiles. In this example, the 50th percentile is included in the range of percentiles at age 39.

What to Do When the Median Falls Between Two Values

What happens when the median case falls between two values? Sometimes this happens with a frequency distribution just like it did when we lined up our 10 students in the previous example. Calculate the median case for the frequency distribution in Table 5.5 to see how this might occur.

Follow the same process as you did in the example of the 10 college students. Find the median case using the formula

median case $= (N + 1) \times .50 = (20 + 1) \times .50 = 21 \times .50 = 10.5.$

Next, find the value associated with case 10.5. However, there is no case 10.5. What do you do? Locate the case immediately before the median case (case 10) and after the median case (case 11), then identify the values associated with

TABLE 5.5 Frequency Distribution for a Random Sample from the 1996 GSS for the Variable *age*

AGE AGE OF RESPONDENT

		Frequency	Percent	Valid Percent	Cumulative Percent
Valid	35	2	10.0	10.0	10.0
	36	1	5.0	5.0	15.0
	37	3	15.0	15.0	30.0
	39	1	5.0	5.0	35.0
	40	2	10.0	10.0	45.0
	44	1	5.0	5.0	50.0
	45	2	10.0	10.0	60.0
	46	1	5.0	5.0	65.0
	48	3	15.0	15.0	80.0
	49	4	20.0	20.0	100.0
	Total	20	100.0	100.0	

Median value between values 44 and 45 (value 44.5) ——

Median case between cases 10 and 11 (case 10.5)

each of those cases. The corresponding values are 44 and 45. Add the two values (44 and 45) to get 89, and divide by 2. The median value is 44.5.

> Half of the respondents are 35 to 44 years old, and the other half are 45 to 49 years old.

Using the frequency distribution Even if you locate the median using the Cumulative Percent column on a frequency distribution, you should be aware that sometimes the median can fall between two values. It would be tempting to look down the Cumulative Percent column of Table 5.5, find the 50th percentile, and identify the median as age 44. As we learned in the previous section, though, the median for the distribution of ages in Table 5.5 is 44.5, and not age 44. You need to be aware that when the number of valid cases in a distribution is even *and* one of the values in a frequency distribution is located exactly at the 50th percentile, the median has to be located between two values: the value at the 50th percentile and the value immediately above it.

Example: The frequency distribution in Table 5.5 illustrates this point. Notice that the number of valid cases in the distribution is even. The 50th percentile is at value 44 (44 years of age). Value 44 is the value associated with case 10. However, case 10 is not the median case. The median case is actually case 10.5. We determine this by using our formula for the median case: $(N + 1)(.50)$. Consequently, we have to locate the median value halfway between case 10 and case 11, or halfway between values 44 and 45. The median value, then, is 44.5.

Checking Your Work To make sure you have located the median value and have not stopped at finding the median case, ask yourself, "Does the number I am treating as the median value fall within the range of values for the variable?" Usually (but not always), the median case doesn't make sense as a value of the variable. (This is especially true when you are finding the median for ordinal-level variables and when you are dealing with a large number of cases.) For example, when you found the median case 10.5 for the preceding frequency distribution, you couldn't assume it was the median value because there are no values of 10.5 among the categories of the variable *age*. It wouldn't make sense to say half the respondents are less than 10.5 years old and half the respondents are more than 10.5 years old.

Finding the Median Using SPSS

Finding the median with SPSS is similar to finding the mode. Use the SPSS Guide, "Finding Measures of Central Tendency," but when you open the Frequencies: Statistics dialog box, click on Median in addition to (or instead of) Mode.

With an SPSS file open, follow the command path Analyze ➡ Descriptive Statistics ➡ Frequencies.

- At the Frequencies dialog box, click on the Statistics button.
- At the Frequencies: Statistics dialog box, select Median, then click on Continue.
- At the Frequencies dialog box, click on OK.

Try this with the variable *income91*. (Remember to turn Split File off. Follow the command path Data ➡ Split File, then click on Reset and OK, in that order.)

In the Output window, you will get a frequency distribution for *income91* and a Statistics report like the one in Table 5.6. The median and mode are listed as values of the variable. To find the value labels, look them up on the frequency distribution for *income91*.

TABLE 5.6 Statistics for the Variable *income91* From the gss96subset File

Statistics

INCOME91 TOTAL FAMILY INCOME

N	Valid	2561
	Missing	343
Median		16.00
Mode		21

Interpreting the Median

The median, like the mode, should supplement our description of a frequency distribution. For example, look at the frequency distribution for *income91* and think about how you would characterize the respondents to the variable. Then use the median (and the mode) to elaborate on your description. You might write something like,

> Most respondents (87.2%) are living on family incomes of $60,000 to $74,999 or less. Relatively few respondents (12.8%) have family incomes of over $75,000, even though the "$75,000+" category is the most frequently occurring category of response. Half have family incomes in the $30,000 to $34,999 range or less. The median for the GSS respondents falls a little lower than the median for household incomes as reported in the article, "Household Incomes Rise"—$35,712.

Skills Practice 2   Use Split File to divide your gss96subset file into the categories of the variable *sex*. Obtain frequency distributions for the variable *income91*. Locate the mode and the median for each group. Then check your work by asking SPSS to find the modes and the medians for the two groups. Write an analysis comparing the two groups, males and females.

THE MEAN

The **mean** is commonly referred to as the average. It is the measure with which you have probably had the most experience, as most students are interested in their grade point averages or their average grades for a course. You probably already know how to find the mean—add up all the grades you have and divide by how many grades there are. You may be less familiar with knowing when the mean is supposed to be used.

When to Use the Mean

In the second of the "News to Use" articles—an excerpt from the book *The Millionaire Next Door*—you will find several examples of how the mean, or average, is used to summarize data. In each case, notice that the mean is being used only with numerical variables. Although researchers sometimes use it with any type of continuous, ordinal variable, and you may also see it used with dichotomous variables, this text follows the practice of using the mean only with numerical variables.

NEWS TO USE: Statistics in the "Real" World

The Never-Before Unearthed Secrets of America's Wealthy[2]

THOMAS J. STANLEY   WILLIAM D. DANKO

Who is the prototypical American millionaire? What would he tell you about himself?

- I am a 57-year-old male, married with three children. About 70% of us earn 80% or more of our household's income.

- About one in five of us is retired. About two-thirds of us who are working are self-employed. Interestingly, self-employed people make up less than 20% of the workers in America but account for two-thirds of the millionaires.

- Our household's total annual realized (taxable) income is $131,000 (median, or 50th percentile), while our average income is $247,000. Note that those of us who have incomes in the $500,000 to $999,999 category (8%) and the $1 million or more category (5%) skew the average upward.

- We have an average household net worth of $3.7 million. Of course, some of our cohorts have accumulated much more. Nearly 6% have a net worth of over $10 million. Again,

these people skew our average upward. The typical (median, or 50th percentile) millionaire household has a net worth of $1.6 million.

- On average, our total annual realized income is less than 7% of our wealth. In other words, we live on less than 7% of our wealth.

- We have more than 6½ times the level of wealth of our non-millionaire neighbors but, in our neighborhood, these nonmillionaires outnumber us better than 3 to 1. Could it be that they have chosen to trade wealth for acquiring high-status material possessions?

- As a group, we are fairly well educated. Only about one in five are not college graduates. Many of us hold advanced degrees. Eighteen percent have master's degrees, 8% law degrees, 6% medical degrees and 6% Ph.D.s.

- What would be the ideal occupations for our sons and daughters? . . . Our kids should consider providing affluent people with some valuable service . . . So we recommend accounting and law to our children. Tax advisers and estate-planning experts will be in demand over the next 15 years.

---

[2]*The Millionaire Next Door*, by Thomas J. Stanley and William D. Danko, 1996, Marietta, GA: Longstreet Press, pp. 8–11.

- I am a tightwad. That's one of the main reasons I completed a long questionnaire for a crispy $1 bill. Why else would I spend two or three hours being personally interviewed by these authors? They paid me $100, $200 or $250. Oh, they made me another offer—to donate in my name some money I earned for my interview to my favorite charity. But I told them, "I am my favorite charity."

Computing the Mean by Hand

Mean: raw scores formula   The simplest way to find the mean is to add up a set of values and divide by the number of values you have. This process of finding the mean is called the *raw scores formula*. The scores are "raw" in that you haven't tried to condense them or process them in any way (by putting them into a frequency distribution, for example). The formula for the mean computed with raw scores is

FORMULA 5.2(A):   Mean (raw scores)

$$\overline{X} = \frac{\Sigma X}{N}$$

where $\overline{X}$ is the symbol for the mean; Σ means "add up the following"—in this formula, X, or scores; and N stands for the number of scores you have.

Thus, the equation can be read as follows:

Add up the scores you have, then divide by the number of scores.

Example: If you want to know the average of the ages of the students in a class, you would add up the ages of the students to get ΣX:

Student:	1	2	3	4	5	6	7	8	9
Age:	19 +	20 +	20	+ 20	+ 21	+ 22	+ 22	+ 23	+ 24 = 191

Then divide the sum of their ages by the number of students (N):

$$\frac{191}{9} = 21.22$$

You could then say,

The average of the ages of the students is 21.22.

Mean: ungrouped frequency distribution formula   Computing the mean scores for large numbers of cases becomes much easier if you first put them into a frequency distribution. The formula for the mean for an ungrouped frequency distribution is simply a variation on the formula for the mean—raw scores, with the exception that we must multiply each score (X) by its frequency of occurrence, f. When you multiply each score by its frequency, you are performing the same mathematical function as adding up the scores one by one.

FORMULA 5.2(B):   Mean (ungrouped frequency distribution)

$$\overline{X} = \frac{\Sigma(fX)}{N}$$

where Σ tells us to "add up the following"—in this formula, each frequency multiplied by each associated score or value, and N represents the number of cases (the sum of the Frequency column).

Order of operations   As formulas become more complex, it is important to understand the process for doing the computations within a formula. For any formula:

1. Do any computations within parentheses first, followed by computations within brackets (if any), working from left to right.
2. Within parentheses do the computations in this order:
   - Complete all of the computations in a numerator or denominator before dividing the numerator by the denominator.
   - Find any squares or square roots.
   - Next do the multiplication, followed by the division.
   - Then do the addition or subtraction.
3. Within brackets follow the same order of computations.
4. Follow the same order of computations for any computations outside of parentheses or brackets, working from left to right.

For this formula then:

1. Find each fX by multiplying each frequency by each of its associated scores or values.

2. Add up each of the results (each fX) to get the sum of fX.

3. Divide the sum of fX by N.

Understanding the order of operations allows us to read the formula as follows:

> To find the mean, multiply each frequency by its associated score or value, and then add up the results. Divide the total, the sum of fX, by N.

Example: Let's apply this formula to the data in Figure 5.1, the ages of nine traditional-age college students. Begin by constructing a frequency distribution for the data.

Age

(X)	f
19	1
20	3
21	1
22	2
23	1
24	1
	$N = 9$

Once you have constructed the frequency distribution, multiply each frequency by its corresponding value or score to get fX. Then add up the results (each fX) to get the sum of fX (ΣfX). Now your frequency distribution should look like this:

Age

(X)	f	f · X
19	1	19
20	3	60
21	1	21
22	2	44
23	1	23
24	1	24
	$N = 9$	$\Sigma fX = 191$

With this table, you have everything you need to work the formula

$$\frac{\Sigma(fX)}{N} = \frac{191}{9} = 21.22.$$

The average of the ages of the students is 21.22 years old.

Does the answer look familiar? It's the same one you got with the raw scores formula for the mean. Simply putting the data into a frequency distribution doesn't change the mean, but it does make the computation a little easier.

✅ **Checking Your Work**   The mean will always fall within the range of values of the variable for which the mean is computed. For example, in the preceding set of data, the range of values is ages 19 to 24. You cannot have a mean less than 19 or greater than 24.

Skills Practice 4   Find the mean using the formula for an ungrouped frequency distribution, first using the data in Figure 5.2 and then using the data in Table 5.3.

Finding the Mean Using SPSS

Finding the mean with SPSS is like finding the median and mode. With an SPSS file open, the command path to follow is Analyze ➡ Descriptive Statistics ➡ Frequencies.

- At the Frequencies dialog box, click on the Statistics button.
- At the Frequencies: Statistics dialog box, select Mean (in addition to or instead of Median and Mode—you may need more than one), then click on Continue.
- At the Frequencies dialog box, click on OK.

If you need help following this series of steps, refer to the SPSS Guide, "Finding Measures of Central Tendency."

Interpreting the Mean

The mean, like the mode and median, is used to elaborate on our analysis of frequency distributions. It is simply the average of a set of scores, so its interpretation is along the lines of

The average age of the students in the class was 21.22.

Let's use the measures of central tendency to analyze the GSS question about the number of wage earners in a household, *earnrs*. (Remember to make sure the Split File is turned off. Use the command path Data ➥ Split File; then click on Reset and click on OK.)

Follow the command path Analyze ➥ Descriptive Statistics ➥ Frequencies.

- Select the variable *earnrs*.

- Click on the Statistics button.

- Click on Mean, Median, and Mode.

- Click on Continue.

- Click on OK.

You should see a table like Table 5.7.

What does this tell us? Nearly half (42.7%) of all families are one-wage-earner families, the most commonly occurring category. Most families (nearly

TABLE 5.7 Frequency Distribution With Measures of Central Tendency for the Variable *earnrs* in the gss96subset File

Statistics

EARNRS HOW MANY IN FAMILY EARNED MONEY

N	Valid	2841
	Missing	63
Mean		1.41
Median		1.00
Mode		1

EARNRS HOW MANY IN FAMILY EARNED MONEY

		Frequency	Percent	Valid Percent	Cumulative Percent
Valid	0	432	14.9	15.2	15.2
	1	1213	41.8	42.7	57.9
	2	920	31.7	32.4	90.3
	3	186	6.4	6.5	96.8
	4	70	2.4	2.5	99.3
	5	15	.5	.5	99.8
	6	5	.2	.2	100.0
	Total	2841	97.8	100.0	
Missing	9 NA	63	2.2		
Total		2904	100.0		

85%) have *at least* one wage earner, and 42.1% of them have two or more wage earners. Nearly 10% of all families rely on three or more wage earners, whereas 15.2% of all families have no wage earners. The average of the wage earners per household is 1.41. It is interesting that the percentage of two-wage-earner families (32.4%) is fairly close to the percentage of families with children whose mothers work (39%), as reported in the article, "Household Incomes Rise."

Skills Practice 5 Let's have a look at the number of wage earners per family in families with children as compared to families without children. Recode the variable *childs* into two categories: respondents with no children and those who have children. Call your new variable *rchilds* and save it in your gss96subset file. (Refer to the SPSS Guide, "Recoding Variables," in Chapter 4 if you need help with the process.) Then use *rchilds* to split your file (using the command path Data ➥ Split File) to compare the number of wage earners (*earnrs*) between the two groups—those with children and those without. Analyze each of the frequency distributions. Compute the mean, median, and mode for each group by hand. Then have SPSS obtain the measures of central tendency. Check your work, and write an analysis comparing the two groups. (Note: Because the variable *childs* has missing cases, you will get three frequency distributions when you split your file—one for respondents with no children, one for those with children, and one for the respondents who didn't answer the question about number of children but did answer the question about the number of wage earners in their families. Use the frequency distributions for those with no children and those who have children for this Skills Practice, and ignore the frequency distribution of missing values.)

CHARACTERISTICS OF THE MEAN, MEDIAN, AND MODE

Having an understanding of the characteristics of the mode, median, and mean is important for two reasons. First, it helps us interpret the measures of central tendency. Second, it helps us make sense of how we can make inferences or generalizations from samples, like the General Social Survey, to the populations (like the one the GSS is designed to represent) from which they're drawn.

Characteristics Affecting Interpretation: Susceptibility to Extreme Scores

The mode and the median are the measures of central tendency least changed or altered by unusually high or low (extreme) scores in a set of data. The mean, on the other hand, is the measure of central tendency most susceptible to (changed by) the presence of unusually high or low scores. For example, if we take the age data we used in Figure 5.1 and change the age of the 9th student from 24 to 42, we can see that the mode and median don't change, but the mean gets much larger. Compute the mode, median, and the mean for the following data:

Student:	1	2	3	4	5	6	7	8	9
Age:	19	20	20	20	21	22	22	23	42

The mode for this group of students remains 20 and the median is still 21, but the mean becomes 23.22. The age, 42, pulls the mean further from the center of the distribution of scores (the median). Consequently, when we report the mean for a distribution, we should look at the range of values to see whether the mean is being affected by extreme scores, at either the low end or the high end of the distribution.

Characteristics Affecting Inferences

These characteristics of the mean, median, and mode are important because they form the foundation for statistics you will be learning later. When you get to Chapter 10 you will be introduced to inferential statistics—statistics for making generalizations about populations from samples. The concepts covered in this section help you understand the conceptual fundamentals of inferential statistics.

Stability in randomly drawn samples The mean is the most stable measure of central tendency for randomly drawn samples. If you were to draw a series of samples from the same population, there would be less variability in the means than in either the medians or the modes.

Let's see how this works. Suppose the respondents to the 1996 General Social Survey are treated as a population. Using the command path Data ➡ Select Cases ➡ Select Random Sample of cases, a series of random samples can be drawn from the gss96subset file. For each sample, the mean, median, and mode can be obtained and recorded.

	Mean	Median	Mode
Sample 1	44.68	40.00	29
Sample 2	51.17	49.00	49
Sample 3	37.46	35.00	22
Sample 4	50.39	46.50	25
Sample 5	43.69	43.00	43

Notice the range of values you get for each of the three measures of central tendency. The means range from a low of 37.46 years to a high of 51.17

years—a difference of 13.71 years. The medians range from a low of 35 years to a high of 49 years—a difference of 14 years. The modes range from 22 years to 49 years, a difference of 27 years. The samples of the means show the least variation as measured by the range of values.

By making some simple calculations, you can see that the means obtained from the sample are close to the actual mean of the population. In fact, the sample means are closer to the population mean than the sample medians or modes in relation to the population median and mode. The average of the ages of the individuals in the population is 44.78. (This number comes from the mean for the variable *age* in the gss96subset file.) Now look at this number in relation to each of the sample means.

	Sample Mean	Population Mean	Difference
Sample 1	44.68	44.78	−.10
Sample 2	51.17	44.78	6.39
Sample 3	37.46	44.78	−7.32
Sample 4	50.39	44.78	5.61
Sample 5	43.69	44.78	−1.09

If we add up the differences between each of the sample means and the population mean, but ignore the signs (treating negative numbers as if they were positive), the sum of the differences is 20.51. If we divide the sum of the differences by 5 (the number of sample means we have), we can see that the average of the differences is 4.10 years; the average of the differences between our sample means and the population mean is about 4 years.

Now let's do the same sort of computation with our sample medians and our sample modes. Do we get similar results? If you add up the differences between each of the sample medians and the population median, you would get the following:

	Sample Median	Population Median	Difference
Sample 1	40.00	42.00	−2.00
Sample 2	49.00	42.00	7.00
Sample 3	35.00	42.00	−7.00
Sample 4	46.50	42.00	4.50
Sample 5	43.00	42.00	1.00

Total the differences (ignoring the signs). The sum of the differences between the sample medians and the population median equals 21.5. Dividing this total by 5 (the number of samples) shows us that the average of the differences between the sample medians and the population median is 4.3 years.

You can do the same set of computations for the mode. The population mode is 37. If you add up the differences between each of the sample modes and the population mode (again ignoring the signs), you would get a difference

TABLE 5.8 Ages of Nine Students, With an Average Age of 21, Illustrating How the Sum of the Deviations From the Mean Equals Zero

Age		Mean	Deviations From the Mean
19	−	21	= −2
20	−	21	= −1
20	−	21	= −1
21	−	21	= 0
21	−	21	= 0
21	−	21	= 0
22	−	21	= 1
22	−	21	= 1
23	−	21	= 2
Σ of the deviations from the mean =			0

of 53. If we divide 53 by the number of samples (5), we can see that the average of the differences between the sample modes and the population mode is 10.6 years.

In these examples, sample means were drawn from a population for which we know the population characteristics, like the mean, median, and mode. Later in the book, this characteristic of the mean—its stability across randomly drawn samples from populations—will be used to make estimates about populations, even when nothing is known about the population itself.

The sum of the deviations from the mean equals zero   Another property of the mean is that the sum of the deviations from the mean always equals zero. This means that if you subtract each score in a set of data from the average of all scores, you will always get zero. Let's try it for the set of data in Table 5.8. The mean—the average of the ages of the students—is 21. Subtract the mean from each of the ages in the distribution. If you add up the results (don't ignore the signs!) you will get zero.

In the next chapter you will see how we can use the deviations from the mean to compute measures that assess the dispersion of distributions.

USING MEAN, MEDIAN, AND MODE TO ANALYZE DISTRIBUTIONS: ARE THEY NORMAL OR NOT?

Every graphic distribution of responses to a variable has a shape. If we produced a histogram for a variable and drew a line around the bars on the histogram, we could look at the shape of the distribution. For example, if we

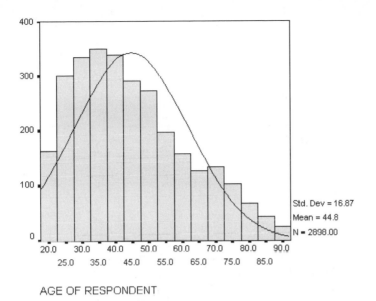

AGE OF RESPONDENT

Figure 5.3 Histogram for the variable *age* in the gss96subset file.

produced a histogram for the variable *age* in the gss96subset file, it would look like Figure 5.3.

When the shape of a distribution is perfectly bell-shaped (the curved line in Figure 5.3), the distribution is said to be **normal.** When we say a distribution is perfectly bell-shaped, we don't mean that it has to look exactly like the Liberty Bell, but it does have to be unimodal and symmetrical. A **unimodal** distribution has a single mode, and a **symmetrical distribution** has as many cases above the mean as below it (so the mean and median are equal). Moreover, if you draw a line through the middle of a symmetrical distribution, the shape of the distribution to the right of the line will mirror the shape of the distribution to the left.

A symmetrical distribution can have many possible shapes, from fairly flat-looking bells (like Figure 5.4) to bells that look like the Liberty Bell (Figure 5.5) to bells that are more peaked (Figure 5.6). In a symmetrical distribution, the mean, median, and mode have the same value. For each of the distributions in Figures 5.4 through 5.6, the mean, median, and mode are the same.

We rarely encounter distributions that are perfectly normal. We are more likely to find distributions that are **skewed**—distributions in which there are more cases below the mean than above it (Figure 5.7), or distributions with more cases above the mean than below it (Figure 5.8). These distributions may look somewhat bell-shaped, but they are not symmetrical. Instead, the distributions of responses to the variables tend to be clustered to one side of the mean or the other.

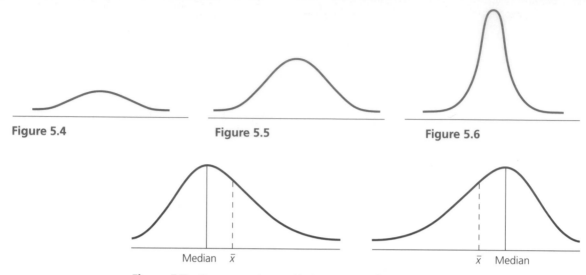

Figure 5.4

Figure 5.5

Figure 5.6

Figure 5.7 Responses clustered below the mean: positively skewed.

Figure 5.8 Responses clustered above the mean: negatively skewed.

The mean in its relation to the median helps evaluate the shape of a distribution. When the mean and median are different, the distribution is skewed. (Keep in mind, however, that just because distributions have identical means and medians, they are not necessarily normal. In addition to having the same values for the mean, median, and mode, normal distributions must be unimodal and symmetrical.) When the mean is below the median, we know there are more cases clustered above the mean than below it. These distributions are described as **negatively skewed.** There are some unusually low values in a set of data pulling the mean down from the median. However, when the mean falls above the median, we know there are more cases clustered below the mean than above it. These distributions are described as **positively skewed;** there are some unusually high values in a set of data pulling the mean up from the median.

Avoiding Common Pitfalls Students tend to treat the mean as the point of comparison, and they try to evaluate skew by looking at whether the median falls above or below the mean. Although skew can be looked at this way, it is more confusing. It is less confusing if you can remember that the median should be the statistic for comparison, and always evaluate the mean in its relation to (whether it is above or below) the median. Even then, students have a hard time remembering how to evaluate skew—which is negative and which is positive? It is helpful to treat the median as the zero point on a number line. When the mean is below (less than) the median, it falls on the negative side of the mean, and we label the distribution *negatively skewed;* when it is above (more than) the median, it falls on the positive side, and we label the distribution *positively skewed.* The following figure may help you to visualize this:

Evaluating Skew

– (Negative side)	Median	(Positive side) +
Mean less than median		Mean more than median

Why is it important to evaluate skew? First, the relationship between the mean, median, and mode helps us assess whether the mean is an accurate representation of the distribution of the responses to a variable. For example, the article "The Never-Before Unearthed Secrets of America's Wealthy" points out that "[millionaires] have an average household net worth of $3.7 million." However, it goes on to say that "nearly 6% have a net worth of over $10 million." Consequently, the average may not be a very accurate indicator of the central value around which the true wealth of millionaires tends to gather. The article concludes, "These people [the 6% with incomes over $10 million] skew our average upward." We would expect a distribution of net worth, then, to be positively skewed, with some extremely high net worths pulling the mean away from the median toward the high end of the scale. In highly skewed distributions of responses to a variable, the median may be a better measure of central tendency than the mean.

The second reason it is important to evaluate skew is because the assumption that a set of responses to a variable is normally distributed underlies the computation of many statistics. Consequently, having the ability to evaluate this assumption is important for the correct applications of some of the statistics we will learn later on in this text and those you may learn about in advanced courses.

> **Skills Practice 6**   Look at the measures of central tendency for the five samples I selected from the gss96subset file for the variable *age* (see p. 180). Use the mean, median, and mode for each sample to answer these questions: Are the distributions skewed? If so, in which direction? How can you tell?

USING MEASURES OF CENTRAL TENDENCY

Use the following chart as a guide to the correct application of the mode, median, and mean. The use of these statistics depends on the level of measurement of the variable to which the statistics are being applied. This chart should help you decide when and how to use each of the measures of central tendency.

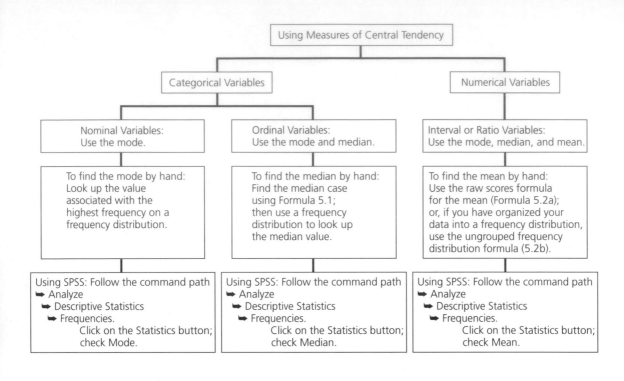

SUMMARY

At this point you should understand the differences between the mode, median, and mean. The median is the most frequently selected or chosen value or category in a distribution of responses to a variable. The median is the category that divides a distribution of responses in half. The mean is the arithmetical average of a distribution of responses to a variable.

The mode is the only measure of association appropriate for nominal variables, although it also can be used with ordinal and numerical variables. The median is used with ordinal and numerical variables, and the mean can be used only with numerical variables.

You should be able to calculate the mode, median, and mean by hand, and you should be able to use the SPSS command path Analyze ➡ Descriptive Statistics ➡ Frequencies to find them. More important, you should understand what they mean, and you should be able to interpret them. In addition, you should be able to use them together to evaluate the extent to which a set of responses to a variable is skewed.

Finally, you should have an understanding of some of the properties of the mean, median, and mode. The mean is more susceptible to extreme scores in a distribution, unlike the mode and the median. The mean is more stable (it is subject to less variation than the mode or the median) in random samples drawn from a population. An important property of the mean is that the sum of the deviations from the mean equals zero.

In the next chapter we will be using these concepts, along with statistics that assess dispersion, to evaluate variability.

KEY CONCEPTS

Measures of central
  tendency
Mode
Median
Median case
Median value
Mean

Susceptibility of mean
  to extreme scores
Stability of mean in
  randomly drawn
  samples
Sum of deviations from
  the mean equals zero

Normal distribution
Unimodal distribution
Symmetrical
  distribution
Skew
Negative skew
Positive skew

ANSWERS TO SKILLS PRACTICES

1. Over two thirds of the male respondents (69%) work full-time, and the most frequently occurring response is "working full-time." On the other hand, just under half of the female respondents work full-time (46.6%), the most commonly occurring response to the labor force status question. One fifth, 20%, say they keep house. Although the mode for both groups is the same—working full-time—a larger percentage of males than females say they work full time.

2. For males: The mode is income category 21 ($75,000 and up). The median is income category 17. To find the median,

   a. Find the median case.
      Use the formula $(N + 1) \times .50$.
      $N = 1,154$ (valid cases only), and
      $N + 1 = 1,155$. $1,155 \times .50 = 577.5$.

   b. Use the median case to find the median value.
      Read down the frequency column, adding up the frequencies as you go, until you find the category that contains the median value. (Category 1, less than $1,000, contains cases 1–8; category 2, $1,000 to $2,999, contains cases 9–19, and so on.) The median case, 577.5, is in category 17 ($35,000–39,999). You can double-check your work by noticing that the 50th percentile is at category 17.

   For females: The mode is category 21 ($75,000 or more), the category associated with the largest number in the Frequency Distribution column. The median is category 15.

$N + 1 = 1,408$ (1,407, the number of valid responses, plus 1). $1,408 \times .50 = 704$.

Category 15 ($25,000–29,999) contains the median case, 704.

Comparing males and females: The income category most frequently reported by males is the same as that reported by females for their families. However, the median family income for males is higher than that of females. Half of the male respondents have family incomes of $35,000 to $39,999 or less, whereas half of the female respondents have family incomes of $25,000 to $29,999 or less.

3. Use the formula for the mean—raw scores: $\overline{X} = \dfrac{\Sigma X}{N}$

   a. Add up the ages ($\Sigma X = 215$). Divide by $N(10)$. $\overline{X} = 21.50$.
   b. Add up the ages ($\Sigma X = 998$). Divide by $N(25)$. $\overline{X} = 39.92$.
4. Use the formula for the mean—ungrouped frequency distribution:

$$\overline{X} = \frac{\Sigma(fX)}{N}$$

   a. Put the scores into a frequency distribution. Multiply each score by its frequency, then add them up to get $\Sigma fX = 215$. Divide by $N(10)$. $\overline{X} = 21.50$.
   b. Put the scores into a frequency distribution. Multiply each score by its frequency, then add them up to get $\Sigma fX = 998$. Divide by $N(25)$. $\overline{X} = 39.92$.
5. The Statistics summaries you will get for the two groups, those with no children and those with children, are shown in Table 5.9. There is a difference in the number of earners in the households of respondents who have children compared to those who don't. The most commonly occurring category for both groups is one wage earner. However, a larger percentage of respondents with no children (53.6%) have only one wage earner in their households, compared to 38.5% of respondents with children. The median for both groups is the same, too—half have one wage earner or less, half have one or more. However, 26% of the respondents who have no children say they have two wage earners in their families, compared with 34.8% of those who have children. The average of the number of wage earners per household among respondents is the same for both groups, 1.41.

6. The distribution of ages in all five samples is positively skewed—the mean is higher than the median in each one. This is probably because the distribution of responses to the variable *age* in the gss96subset file is positively skewed. Check it out.

TABLE 5.9 Statistics for the Variable *earnrs* With the gss96subset File Split by the Recoded *childs* Variable *rchilds*

Statistics[a]

EARNRS HOW MANY IN FAMILY EARNED MONEY

N	Valid	796
	Missing	26
Mean		1.41
Median		1.00
Mode		1

a. RCHILDS Recoded childs
variable = 0 Has no children

Statistics[a]

EARNRS HOW MANY IN FAMILY EARNED MONEY

N	Valid	2033
	Missing	34
Mean		1.41
Median		1.00
Mode		1

a. RCHILDS Recoded childs variable = 1 Has children

GENERAL EXERCISES

What are the characteristics of 1996 GSS respondents in the age group 18–21 years old? How are they doing financially? Next you will find a set of frequency distributions for variables you can use to answer these questions. Complete the following exercises for calculating measures of central tendency by hand.

1. Find and interpret the mode for the frequency distribution shown here.

MARITAL MARITAL STATUS

		Frequency	Percent	Valid Percent	Cumulative Percent
Valid	1 MARRIED	16	13.6	13.6	13.6
	3 DIVORCED	1	.8	.8	14.4
	5 NEVER MARRIED	101	85.6	85.6	100.0
	Total	118	100.0	100.0	

2. Find and interpret the mode for the frequency distribution shown here.

WRKSTAT LABOR FORCE STATUS

		Frequency	Percent	Valid Percent	Cumulative Percent
Valid	1 WORKING FULLTIME	44	37.3	37.3	37.3
	2 WORKING PARTTIME	25	21.2	21.2	58.5
	3 TEMP NOT WORKING	3	2.5	2.5	61.0
	4 UNEMPL, LAID OFF	3	2.5	2.5	63.6
	6 SCHOOL	30	25.4	25.4	89.0
	7 KEEPING HOUSE	12	10.2	10.2	99.2
	8 OTHER	1	.8	.8	100.0
	Total	118	100.0	100.0	

3. Find and interpret the mode for the frequency distribution in General Exercise 5.

4. Find and interpret the mode for the frequency distribution in General Exercise 6.

5. Find and interpret the median for the frequency distribution shown here.

DEGREE RS HIGHEST DEGREE

		Frequency	Percent	Valid Percent	Cumulative Percent
Valid	0 LT HIGH SCHOOL	34	28.8	29.3	29.3
	1 HIGH SCHOOL	78	66.1	67.2	96.6
	2 JUNIOR COLLEGE	4	3.4	3.4	100.0
	Total	116	98.3	100.0	
Missing	9 NA	2	1.7		
Total		118	100.0		

6. Find and interpret the median for the frequency distribution shown here.

RINCOM91 RESPONDENTS INCOME

		Frequency	Percent	Valid Percent	Cumulative Percent
Valid	1 LT $1000	8	6.8	10.0	10.0
	2 $1000-2999	17	14.4	21.3	31.3
	3 $3000-3999	11	9.3	13.8	45.0
	4 $4000-4999	4	3.4	5.0	50.0
	5 $5000-5999	7	5.9	8.8	58.8
	6 $6000-6999	4	3.4	5.0	63.8
	7 $7000-7999	3	2.5	3.8	67.5
	8 $8000-9999	4	3.4	5.0	72.5
	9 $10000-12499	3	2.5	3.8	76.3
	10 $12500-14999	8	6.8	10.0	86.3
	11 $15000-17499	3	2.5	3.8	90.0
	12 $17500-19999	2	1.7	2.5	92.5
	13 $20000-22499	1	.8	1.3	93.8
	14 $22500-24999	4	3.4	5.0	98.8
	16 $30000-34999	1	.8	1.3	100.0
	Total	80	67.8	100.0	
Missing	0 NAP	33	28.0		
	99 DK/NA	5	4.2		
	Total	38	32.2		
Total		118	100.0		

7. Find and interpret the median for the frequency distribution shown here.

SATFIN SATISFACTION WITH FINANCIAL SITUATION

		Frequency	Percent	Valid Percent	Cumulative Percent
Valid	1 NOT AT ALL SAT	34	28.8	28.8	28.8
	2 MORE OR LESS	48	40.7	40.7	69.5
	3 SATISFIED	36	30.5	30.5	100.0
	Total	118	100.0	100.0	

8. Find and interpret the median for the frequency distribution shown here.

FINRELA OPINION OF FAMILY INCOME

		Frequency	Percent	Valid Percent	Cumulative Percent
Valid	1 FAR BELOW AVERAGE	6	5.1	5.1	5.1
	2 BELOW AVERAGE	28	23.7	23.9	29.1
	3 AVERAGE	62	52.5	53.0	82.1
	4 ABOVE AVERAGE	20	16.9	17.1	99.1
	5 FAR ABOVE AVERAGE	1	.8	.9	100.0
	Total	117	99.2	100.0	
Missing	8 DK	1	.8		
Total		118	100.0		

9. Find and interpret the median for the frequency distribution in General Exercise 11.

10. Find and interpret the median for the frequency distribution in General Exercise 12.

11. Find and interpret the mean for the frequency distribution shown here.

EARNRS HOW MANY IN FAMILY EARNED MONEY

		Frequency	Percent	Valid Percent	Cumulative Percent
Valid	0	7	5.9	6.1	6.1
	1	35	29.7	30.4	36.5
	2	26	22.0	22.6	59.1
	3	31	26.3	27.0	86.1
	4	12	10.2	10.4	96.5
	5	3	2.5	2.6	99.1
	6	1	.8	.9	100.0
	Total	115	97.5	100.0	
Missing	9 NA	3	2.5		
Total		118	100.0		

12. Find and interpret the mean for the frequency distribution shown here.

AGEKDBRN R'S AGE WHEN 1ST CHILD BORN

		Frequency	Percent	Valid Percent	Cumulative Percent
Valid	13	2	1.7	7.1	7.1
	15	1	.8	3.6	10.7
	16	3	2.5	10.7	21.4
	17	8	6.8	20.6	50.0
	18	9	7.6	32.1	82.1
	19	2	1.7	7.1	89.3
	20	3	2.5	10.7	100.0
	Total	28	23.7	100.0	
Missing	0 NAP	89	75.4		
	99 NA	1	.8		
	Total	90	76.3		
Total		118	100.0		

13. Find and interpret the mean for the frequency distribution shown here.

EDUC HIGHEST YEAR OF SCHOOL COMPLETED

		Frequency	Percent	Valid Percent	Cumulative Percent
Valid	7	2	1.7	1.7	1.7
	9	3	2.5	2.5	4.2
	10	8	6.8	6.8	11.0
	11	25	21.2	21.2	32.2
	12	51	43.2	43.2	75.4
	13	17	14.4	14.4	89.8
	14	10	8.5	8.5	98.3
	15	2	1.7	1.7	100.0
	Total	118	100.0	100.0	

14. Find and interpret the mean for the frequency distribution shown here.

SIBS NUMBER OF BROTHERS AND SISTERS

		Frequency	Percent	Valid Percent	Cumulative Percent
Valid	1	33	28.0	28.0	28.0
	2	31	26.3	26.3	54.2
	3	19	16.1	16.1	70.3
	4	14	11.9	11.9	82.2
	5	7	5.9	5.9	88.1
	6	5	4.2	4.2	92.4
	7	6	5.1	5.1	97.5
	8	1	.8	.8	98.3
	9	2	1.7	1.7	100.0
	Total	118	100.0	100.0	

15. Is the distribution in General Exercise 11 skewed? Is it positively or negatively skewed? How do you know?

16. Is the distribution in General Exercise 12 skewed? Is it positively or negatively skewed? How do you know?

17. Is the distribution in General Exercise 13 skewed? Is it positively or negatively skewed? How do you know?

18. Is the distribution in General Exercise 14 skewed? Is it positively or negatively skewed? How do you know?

SPSS EXERCISES

Obtain and analyze frequency distributions along with the appropriate measures of central tendency to answer the following questions:

1. How long do GSS respondents say they work each week? Use the variable *hrs1*.

2. How much do GSS respondents make? Use *rincome91*.

3. How large are the households of the GSS respondents? Use *hompop*.

4. Which families have the highest incomes—those with respondents who have children or those whose respondents do not? Use *income91* and split your file using your recoded variable *rchilds*.

5. Which respondents work the longest hours—those with children or those without? Use *hrs1* and split your file using your recoded variable *rchilds*.

6. Are the GSS respondents satisfied with their financial situations? Use frequency distributions and appropriate measures of central tendency for the variables *satfin, finalter,* and *finrela* to answer this question.

7. Are there any differences in satisfaction with one's financial situation by (*satfin*) by sex? Split your gss96subset file using the variable *sex* to find out.

8. Are there any differences in satisfaction with one's financial situation (*satfin*) by race? Split your gss96subset file using the variable *race* to find out.

9. Are there any differences in perceptions of one's financial situation in relation to others (*finrela*) by sex? Split your gss96subset file using the variable *sex* to find out.

10. Are there any differences in perceptions of one's financial situation in relation to others (*finrela*) by race? Split your gss96subset file using the variable *race* to find out.

6 Measures of Dispersion

INTRODUCTION

In Chapter 5 we analyzed a number of variables bearing on the financial well-being of those who responded to the General Social Survey. In this chapter we add a related question: How much are Americans working to secure their financial futures? From soccer moms to workaholic dads, there seems to be at least an article a week devoted to our stressed-out schedules. "How to work smarter instead of harder." "How to balance work and family." "How to simplify our lives." Thus I was struck when the article in the "News to Use" section of this chapter appeared, because it discusses the research of two sociologists interested in the issues of how hard Americans are working and what effect work schedules are having on families—issues that are related to some of the variables in the General Social Survey. For example, when you analyzed the GSS variable *hrs1* for an exercise at the end of Chapter 5, you learned that the average number of hours worked in a week by the respondents to the 1996 General Social Survey is 42.35.

What does this mean? Do most of the respondents work 42 hours, or is the range of responses to the variable *hrs1* more spread out, with some respondents closer to 8 and others closer to 80? The answer tells us how accurate our measure of central tendency really is for describing the general characteristics of the respondents. Without knowing about the *dispersion* of responses, we may come away with an incomplete—or even misleading—picture of the patterns in our data.

Consequently, to form a more complete picture of the responses to a variable, we have to add measures of dispersion to the list of tools at our disposal. Whereas measures of central tendency reveal one set of patterns in data—the values around which distributions of responses tend to cluster—measures of dispersion reveal another—the extent to which distributions are dispersed or spread out. Measures of central tendency and dispersion work together. Measures of central tendency are statistics that give us an indication of the values around which respondents "gather." **Measures of dispersion** are statistics that show us show how tightly packed—or spread out—the respondents are in relation to one or more measures of central tendency.

Analysis of dispersion is closely connected to the analysis of frequency distributions. Frequency distributions help us evaluate the extent of homogeneity (similarity) and heterogeneity (difference) in the distribution of responses to variables. Measures of dispersion provide us with statistics for assessing how homogeneous or heterogeneous a distribution is.

NEWS TO USE: Statistics in the "Real" World

Study: Work Conventions Squeeze Women, Families
Both working parents and stay-at-home parents long for scarce part-time jobs[1]

LILLIAN ABBOTT PFOHL

About one-third of American women in two-income couples want to work less, but can't because their employers don't offer that option.

At the same time, 25% of married women who are not employed outside the home want to join the work force, but can't because there aren't enough part-time opportunities.

And married couples who feel burdened by their hours at work report the lowest quality of life among working couples.

Those are some of the findings from studies done by Cornell University sociologists Phyllis Moen and Marin Clarkberg. Both studies are being presented at the American Association for the Advancement of Science's annual meeting in Anaheim, Calif.

While some two-income couples want to work less and some stay-at-home spouses want to work more, the lack of part-time opportunities keeps both groups from achieving their goals, said Clarkberg.

"Women who do enter the job market are shoehorned into men's templates of 40-plus-hour jobs, which works against women and cheats family life," Clarkberg said.

Her research indicates that while one in six couples wishes both partners could work part-time, only one in 50 do.

"Although about two-fifths of men work more than they would prefer, the adjustment is a small one, and men tend to slip relatively painlessly into the standard role of full-time employment," Clarkberg said.

"Women, on the other hand, tend to want a more middling number of work hours and are caught between a rock and a hard place and must choose either to stay home full time or work the very long hours that many jobs demand."

When both spouses work long hours, they experience more conflict between work and personal life, more stress and more feelings of overload than other working couples, Moen said.

"Married working couples who are launching young families are the ones who tend to work the longest hours and, therefore, report the lowest quality of life among working couples," Moen said.

Parents often report feeling squeezed between work and family responsibilities, said Terry Wisnieski, an associate with Syracuse-based Success by 6, a community group devoted to improving the quality of life for children.

[1] *Syracuse Online,* 22 January 1999, <http://www.syracuse.com>.

"We want to encourage employers to offer more choices to help employees better manage that balance between work and family," she said. "For example, maybe offer a compressed work week. Or allow parents to work earlier shifts so they can get their kids from day care without worry."

That kind of flexibility pays off for Textwise, a software development company in Syracuse.

"A good employee is a good employee, and to have good people sometimes you need to be flexible about their work," said John Liddy, finance and operations manager. "For us, that sometimes means part-time work, although more often it means flexible hours or telecommuting arrangements."

Why is understanding the dispersion of responses important? There are a couple of reasons. First, as mentioned already, we can make a more accurate characterization of the respondents—are they all alike on a certain variable, or are they different? Second, it helps us to understand the concept of variability. **Variability** refers to the degree of variation in the responses to a variable. The more homogeneous a distribution of responses, the less variability (or variation) there is in the responses to the variable. The more heterogeneous a distribution, the more variability (or variation) there is in the responses to the variable. As we will see later, the concept of variability plays an important role in our ability to use what we learn from random samples so we can generalize to the populations from which those samples were drawn.

In this chapter, we will be learning to calculate—by hand and with SPSS— several of the more common measures of dispersion: the index of qualitative variation, range, interquartile range, and standard deviation. Let's start with the index of qualitative variation to see whether General Social Survey respondents in the 18-to-21-year age bracket tend to be working full-time or not.

THE INDEX OF QUALITATIVE VARIATION

The index of qualitative variation (IQV) is a statistic that tells us how much variability there is in a variable with nominal categories. The IQV ranges in value from 0 to 1.0. The closer the IQV is to 0, the less variability there is in the distribution of responses to a variable; the closer to 1, the more variability. In other words, the closer to 0 the index is, the more homogeneous a set of responses; the closer to 1, the more heterogeneous. In a distribution in which the respondents are evenly divided among all of the categories of response, the IQV is 1, because the distribution is perfectly heterogeneous. In distributions like the ones of sex and race in Chapter 4, in which the respondents are all concentrated in a single category of the variable, the IQV is zero, because the distribution is perfectly homogeneous. The number line in Figure 6.1 will help in interpreting the index.

| 0 | .10 | .20 | .30 | .40 | .50 | .60 | .70 | .80 | .90 | 1.0 |

Homogeneous
(no variability)

Heterogeneous
(maximum possible
variability)

Figure 6.1   Interpreting the index of qualitative variation.

Calculations of the IQV assume that you have constructed a frequency distribution for a set of responses to a variable. Let's use the frequency distribution in Figure 6.1, responses to a recoded *wrkstat* (labor force status) variable for the male GSS respondents who are between 18 and 21 years old, as an illustration. Start by examining the frequency distribution in Table 6.1. What's your analysis? Does this appear to be a distribution with a lot of variability (more heterogeneous) or a little (more homogeneous)?

The IQV itself is a proportion—a statistical statement of the relationship between the *observed* differences among respondents to the categories of a variable and the maximum number of *possible* differences among respondents to the categories of a variable.

The idea of "differences among respondents" is a fairly abstract one. How do we figure out how many differences there are among the respondents? One way would be to ask ourselves: If one of the respondents is employed full-time, how many differences are there between that respondent and every other respondent? The answer resides in multiplying the full-time respondent by all of the other respondents who aren't working full-time. From the preceding distribution, we can see that there are 33 respondents who are working part-time, not working, or not in the labor force. Therefore, in relation to the respondent who is working full-time, there are 33 differences—33 other respondents different from the respondent working full-time.

However, there isn't only one respondent working full-time, there are 26 of them. As a result, to find the total number of differences that exist between all 26 respondents who are working full-time and the 33 respondents who aren't, we have to multiply 26 by 33. The product, 858, tells us there are 858 differences between the 26 respondents who are working full-time and all the 33 respondents who aren't.

If we multiply the number of those who are working part-time (15) by the total of those who are not working or who are not in the market (18), we can find out how many differences there are between those respondents. $15 \times 18 = 270$, so there are 270 differences between those who are working part-time and those who either are not working or are not in the market. (Remember that the differences between those who are working full-time and those who are working part-time are included in the figure 858, which is the total number of differences between the full-timers and everyone else.)

The IQV expresses a relationship between the differences among the respondents and the number of *possible* differences among the respondents, or

TABLE 6.1   **Frequency Distribution for Male Respondents Ages 18 to 21 to a Recoded** *wrkstat* **Variable From the gss96subset File**

RCWRKSTA recoded work status

		Frequency	Percent	Valid Percent	Cumulative Percent
Valid	1 Working fulltime	26	44.1	44.1	44.1
	2 Working parttime	15	25.4	25.4	69.5
	3 Not working	4	6.8	6.8	76.3
	4 Not in the market	14	23.7	23.7	100.0
	Total	59	100.0	100.0	

the number of differences there would be in a perfectly heterogeneous distribution of responses to a variable. What if the 59 respondents in the frequency distribution in Figure 6.1 were evenly divided among all four categories of the variable? How many differences between the respondents would there be then?

Fortunately, we don't have to answer that question by actually dividing the 59 respondents among the four categories and then multiplying to get an answer. The good news is that there is a formula to simplify this process of figuring out the total differences for us—the formula for the index of qualitative variation.

FORMULA 6.1: The **index of qualitative variation (IQV)**

$$IQV = \frac{\text{total observed differences}}{\text{maximum possible differences}}$$

There are separate formulas to help us with the numerator (the total number of observed differences in the frequency distribution) and the denominator (the number of maximum possible differences in a set of data).

Let's get started by finding the total number of observed differences, the numerator.

FORMULA 6.1(A): Total observed differences—the numerator of the IQV

$$\text{Observed differences} = \Sigma f_i f_j$$

where Σ means to add up or sum the following, and $f_i f_j$ means to multiply the frequency of a given category by the frequencies of the succeeding categories.

Taken as a whole, the equation asks you to sum the products you obtain when you multiply each frequency in a frequency distribution by the sum of the frequencies that follow it in the distribution. This isn't as complicated as it sounds.

Example: For Table 6.1,

Step 1. Multiply the first frequency, 26, by the sum of the succeeding frequencies:

$$f_i f_j = (26)(15 + 4 + 14)$$
$$= (26)(33)$$
$$= 858$$

Step 2. Multiply the second frequency, 15, by the frequencies below it, like this:

$$f_i f_j = (15)(4 + 14)$$
$$= (15)(18)$$
$$= 270$$

Step 3. Multiply the third frequency, 4, by the frequency just below it, 14:

$$f_i f_j = 4 \times 14$$
$$= 56$$

Step 4. Add up all of the $f_i f_j$s to get their sum (Σ):

$$\Sigma f_i f_j = 858 + 270 + 56$$
$$= 1,184$$

The process can be diagrammed as in Table 6.2.

TABLE 6.2

RCWRKSTA recoded work status

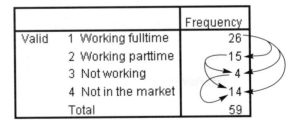

		Frequency
Valid	1 Working fulltime	26
	2 Working parttime	15
	3 Not working	4
	4 Not in the market	14
	Total	59

Avoiding Common Pitfalls   You have to find the $f_i f_j$ for as many categories as there are for a given variable. You may have four categories, as in the previous example, or you can have fewer or a lot more categories. The trick is to begin at the first category, multiplying the frequency for that category by the sum of the succeeding frequencies. Move to the second category and repeat the process. Continue until you reach the next-to-the-last category. Then add up the products of each $f_i f_j$.

Now let's find the denominator.

FORMULA 6.1(B): Maximum possible differences—the denominator of the IQV

$$\text{Possible differences} = \frac{K(K-1)}{2}\left(\frac{N}{K}\right)^2$$

where K is the number of (nonmissing data) categories for a variable, and N is the number of valid cases for a variable.

Example: If we apply this formula to the frequency distribution in Table 6.1, we would work the formula as follows:

$K = 4$, the number of categories for the variable (excluding missing value categories)

$N = 59$, the number of valid cases

$$\text{Possible differences} = \frac{K(K-1)}{2}\left(\frac{N}{K}\right)^2$$

$$= \frac{4(4-1)}{2}\left(\frac{59}{4}\right)^2 = \frac{4(3)}{2}(14.75)^2$$

$$= \frac{12}{2}(217.5625) = 6(217.5625)$$

$$\text{Possible differences} = 1{,}305.375$$

Finding the IQV

Remember that what we have so far are the numerator and the denominator for the formula for the IQV. Let's plug our values for the numerator and the denominator into the formula (6.1):

$$\text{IQV} = \frac{\text{total observed differences}}{\text{maximum possible differences}}$$

$$= \frac{1{,}184}{1{,}305.375}$$

$$\text{IQV} = .91$$

Interpreting the IQV

The IQV is much closer to 1.0 than to 0, indicating that the distribution is fairly heterogeneous. When we are working with statistics, we always have to ask ourselves whether our answers make sense. Are they supported by other ways of looking at a variable? In this case, does the frequency distribution support this claim? The answers are yes and no. Although the responses of males age 18 to 21 are somewhat dispersed across the categories of the labor force status variable, 44% of the respondents are concentrated in the working full-time category. A little over one quarter of the respondents said they are working part-time, and nearly one quarter said they are not in the market. Responses to the labor force status variable are more homogeneous than the IQV indicates.

Skills Practice 1 Find the IQV for the following frequency distribution for female respondents between the ages of 18 and 21 to a recoded *wrkstat* variable for the gss96subset file. What does it tell you about the distribution of the responses to the variable? Is the IQV consistent with your analysis of the frequency distribution?

RCWRKSTA recoded work status

		Frequency	Percent	Valid Percent	Cumulative Percent
Valid	1 Working fulltime	18	30.5	30.5	30.5
	2 Working parttime	10	16.9	16.9	47.5
	3 Not working	2	3.4	3.4	50.8
	4 Not in the market	29	49.2	49.2	100.0
	Total	59	100.0	100.0	

SPSS does not include a statistic like the index of qualitative variation for the analysis of variability in nominal-level variables.[2] There are several statistics for the analysis of variability among ordinal and numerical variables, like the range and the interquartile range.

THE RANGE AND THE INTERQUARTILE RANGE

Calculating the Range and the Interquartile Range by Hand

The range and interquartile range tell us about the distributions of responses to variables that are categorical and ordinal, or numerical.

The range The range is one of the simplest statistics to compute. It is found by subtracting the lowest value in a set of data from the highest. Let's use the range to look at how many wage earners there are in the households of the GSS respondents. First, get the frequency distribution for *earnrs*. (Open your gss96subset data file, and use the command path

---

[2]It is possible to write equations for SPSS so that it can do the computations for the IQV; however, these skills are beyond the scope of this text.

TABLE 6.3   Finding the Quartile Values and Interquartile Range for a Frequency Distribution

EARNRS HOW MANY IN FAMILY EARNED MONEY

			Frequency	Percent	Valid Percent	Cumulative Percent
Cases 1–432	Valid	0	432	14.9	15.2	15.2
Cases 433–1645		1	1213	41.8	42.7	57.9
Cases 1646–2565		2	920	31.7	32.4	90.3
Cases 2566–2751		3	186	6.4	6.5	96.8
		4	70	2.4	2.5	99.3
		5	15	.5	.5	99.8
		6	5	.2	.2	100.0
		Total	2841	97.8	100.0	
	Missing	9 NA	63	2.2		
	Total		2904	100.0		

Analyze ➡ Descriptive Statistics ➡ Frequencies to obtain the frequency distribution for *earnrs* shown in Table 6.3.)

To find the range, subtract the lowest value—using only valid response categories—from the highest value. The lowest value is 0, and the highest value is 6. The range is simply $6 - 0 = 6$.

Interpreting the range   What does the range tell us? Using the lowest value in the range (0) and the highest (6), we can say that

the responses to the question about wage earners ranged from 0 (no earners) up to six earners per household.

In addition, the range gives us some idea of how much variation there is in the *categories* of a variable. Some variables have more response categories than others. Sometimes the number of response categories depends on the number of possible responses there are to a particular variable (like wage earners), and sometimes it is determined by the researchers who collect the data (as with variables that measure attitudes in categories, like strongly agree, agree, neutral, disagree, strongly disagree). Generally, the higher the range, the more variation in the categories of response; the smaller the range, the less variation in the categories of response.

In addition to its inherent meaning, the range provides us with a context in which to interpret other measures of dispersion, like the interquartile range and standard deviation. These statistics help us evaluate the dispersion of responses to a variable (as opposed to the variability in response categories). These dispersions may be homogeneous or heterogeneous in relation to the number of response categories for a variable. We will discuss this further in the next section.

Interquartile range   The interquartile range (IQR) is a measure of dispersion that tells us about the distribution of responses to a variable in relation to the median. It is used with variables that are ordinal or numerical, and it tells us the range of values that encompass the middle 50% of the respondents to a variable. Conceptually, it is a lot like the median. Whereas the median divides a set of data into two parts by splitting the data in half, the IQR is computed by dividing the responses to a variable into four parts, or quarters, with each part having the same number of cases.

Each quarter has a value associated with it, called a **quartile.** The value at the first quartile, Q_1, is the value at or below which the first 25% of the respondents to a variable fall. The value at the second quartile, Q_2, is the value at or below which 50% of the respondents fall—the median. The value at the third quartile, Q_3, is the value at or below which 75% of the respondents fall. The formula for the IQR is

FORMULA 6.2:   The interquartile range (IQR)

$$IQR = Q_3 - Q_1$$

where Q_3 is the value at the third quartile, and Q_1 is the value at the first quartile.

Let's illustrate the concept of the interquartile range by going back to our example of lining up students by some characteristic or variable. This time, we'll line up the students according to how many wage earners are in each of their households.

Student	1	2	3	4	5	6	7	8
Earners	1	1	2	2	2	2	3	3

Given that we have only eight cases (students), it's easy to see that if we divide the respondents into four equal parts (quarters), there will be two students in each part.

Student	1	2		3	4		5	6		7	8
Earners	1	1		2	2		2	2		3	3
			Q_1			Q_2			Q_3		

Simply dividing the students into four parts doesn't tell us much. We need to know the values associated with each of the quarters so we can describe the distribution of responses. In this example, we can see that the first one quarter of the students includes one wage earner. The second one quarter includes two wage earners. The third one quarter of the students includes two wage earners, and the last one quarter of the students includes three wage earners in their households.

Is this distribution homogeneous or heterogeneous? Let's look at it in the context of the range. For this set of responses to the variable *wage earners,* the range is $3 - 1 = 2$. We can see from the preceding diagram that half of the respondents, the respondents between Q_1 and Q_3, are clustered into only one of the response categories (two wage earners). Thus, half of the respondents are grouped into half of the categories in the range. This distribution is fairly homogeneous—respondents are more alike than different. Half of the respondents' households have two wage earners, while the other half are split between one wage earner and three wage earners.

As with the median, it's rarely practical to find quartile values by lining up respondents. Instead, we put our data into a frequency distribution and use formulas to find the *case*—or respondent—at each quartile and the *value* at each quartile. The process of finding the interquartile range is like the one for finding the median but it involves a few more steps.

Step 1. Find the case at the first quartile, using Formula 6.2(a).

> **FORMULA 6.2(A):** Case at the first quartile $= (N + 1) \times .25$
>
> Note: Notice the similarity to the formula for the case at the median. To find the median case, we multiplied $N + 1$ by .50 to divide the data in half. To find the case at the first quartile, we multiply $N + 1$ by .25 to divide the data into quarters. Multiplying $N + 1$ by .25 is the same mathematically as dividing $N + 1$ by 4.

Step 2. Find the value at the first quartile. Look up the case on a frequency distribution using the cumulative frequency column, as you did to find the median value. Then identify the value associated with the case at the first quartile.

Step 3. Find the case at the third quartile, using Formula 6.2b.

> **FORMULA 6.2(B):** Case at the third quartile $= (N + 1) \times .75$

Step 4. Find the value at the third quartile. Look up the case at the third quartile using a frequency distribution, and then find the value associated with the case at the third quartile.

Step 5. Insert the values for Q_3 and Q_1 in the formula for the IQR (Formula 6.2).

Example: Let's follow this process using the frequency distribution for the wage earners variable, *earnrs,* in Table 6.3.

Step 1. The case at the first quartile is $(N + 1) \times .25$, where N is the number of valid cases only.

$$2,842 \times .25 = 710.5$$

Step 2. The value at the first quartile is the category (number of wage earners) associated with case 710.5. How do we find it? By reading down the frequency column, as we did for the median. At value 0, no wage earners, we have cases 1 through 432. At value 1, 1 wage earner, we have cases 433 through 1,645.[3] Case 710.5 is in the range of cases between 433 and 1,645, so the value associated with the case at the first quartile is 1. One quarter of the respondents to the 1996 General Social Survey have one wage earner or less in their households.

Step 3. The case at the third quartile is:

$$(N + 1) \times .75 = 2,842 \times .75 = 2,131.5$$

Step 4. The value of the case at the third quartile is the value associated with case 2,131.5. Read down the frequencies column until you come to the category that includes case 2,131.5. From finding the value at the first quartile, we know that cases 1 through 432 are at value 0 (no wage earners in the household) and cases 433 through 1,645 are at the second value (1 wage earner). Cases 1,646 through 2,565 are at value 2 (2 wage earners). The case at the third quartile, case 2,131.5, is in the range of cases from 1,646 through 2,565, so the value at the third quartile is 2.

✔ **Checking Your Work**   It is easy to confuse the case at quartile 1 or 3 with the value at each quartile, as it's easy to confuse the median case with the median value. To check your work,

(1) Make sure that the number you are calling the quartile value falls within the range of values for the variable you are analyzing. You won't have a quartile value lower than the lowest value or higher than the highest value for your variable.

(2) Use the Cumulative Percent column on your frequency distribution to make sure that the quartile values you find are associated with the 25th percentile (for the value at quartile 1) and the 75th percentile (for the value at quartile 3). Notice that the 25th percentile is contained within the range of percentiles at value 1. Value 1 is at percentile 57.9. This means that 57.9% of the respondents have one wage earner or less in their households. However, we can also say that value 1 encompasses percentiles 15.3 through 57.9. This range of percentiles includes the 25th percentile. Likewise, the 75th percentile is in the range of percentiles associated with value 2. Using the Cumulative Percent column we can see that 90.3% of the respondents have 2 or less wage earners in their households. Value 2 encompasses percentiles 58 through 90.3, a range that includes the 75th percentile.

---

[3]Find the upper limit of the range of cases at the second value (1 wage earner) by adding the frequency at the second value, 1,213, to the frequency at the first value, 432. Find the upper limit of the range of cases at the third value, 2 wage earners, by adding the frequency at the third value, 920, to the combined frequencies for the first and second values, 432 and 1,213.

Step 5. The IQR (interquartile range) is found by subtracting the value at Q_1 from the value at Q_3. Use formula 6.2. IQR $= Q_3 - Q_1$. In this case, the IQR $= 2 - 1 = 1$.

Interpreting the interquartile range As in the preceding example, the IQR, in the context of the range for this variable, 6, tells us we have a very homogeneous distribution. A diagram of the dispersion of responses to the variable might help us to see this.

Range	0	1	2	3	4	5	6
Quartiles		Q_1------Q_3					

Notice the relationship of the interquartile range (Q_1 and Q_3) to the full range of values in the variable. Fifty percent of the cases (the cases between Q_1 and Q_3) are concentrated in the interquartile range, and this 50% of the cases is distributed among only two values of the variable. Generally, the smaller the IQR is in relation to the range, the more homogeneous is a distribution of responses to a variable (and the less variability there is in the distribution). The larger the IQR is in relation to the range, the more heterogeneous is a distribution of responses (and the more variability there is).

Skills Practice 2 Let's contrast our analysis of the variable *wage earners* with a distribution that is more heterogeneous. Use the variable *earnmore*, which looks at who earns more in a household—the respondent or the respondent's spouse or partner. Using SPSS, obtain a frequency distribution for *earnmore*. Find the range, the values at the first and third quartiles, and the interquartile range by hand.

What happens when the cases at the first or third quartiles fall between two values? As with the median, the cases for quartiles 1 and 3 can fall between two values. Let's look at an example to see how this is possible. Find the cases at the first and third quartiles for the frequency distribution in Table 6.4 (created by taking a random sample of 10 cases from the 1996 GSS).

Let's do the computations to find the interquartile range.

First, find the case at Q_1.

$$(N + 1) \times .25 = (10 + 1) \times .25 = 11 \times .25 = 2.75$$

Next, look up case 2.75 in the frequency distribution in Table 6.4.

You will notice that it doesn't fall at one of the values, because case 2.75 is between value 0, which contains cases 1 and 2, and value 1, which has cases 3 through 5. Thus case 2.75 (2¾) falls between values 1 and 2—but where, exactly, does it fall? The answer is three quarters of the way between value 1 and value 2.

TABLE 6.4   Frequency Distribution for a Randomly Selected Sample of Cases From the gss96subset File for the Variable *earnrs*

EARNRS

		Frequency	Percent	Valid Percent	Cumulative Percent
Valid	0	2	20.0	20.0	20.0
	1	5	50.0	50.0	70.0
	2	2	20.0	20.0	90.0
	4	1	10.0	10.0	100.0
	Total	10	100.0	100.0	

We know this by once again thinking of the case as an index to the value. If you think of the case at quartile 1 as case 2 and 3/4—three quarters of the way between case 2 and 3—then the value has to correspond and be three quarters of the distance between the values 0 and 1. This would make the value at quartile 1 equal to .75, three quarters of the way between 0 and 1.

Now find the case and value at quartile 3.

The case at $Q_3 = (N + 1) \times .75 = 11 \times .75 = 8.25$

The value at $Q_3 = 2$ (the value with cases 8 through 9)

Finally, compute the IQR and interpret it. The IQR $= 2 - .75 = 1.25$. The range for this distribution is 4 ($4 - 0$). The distribution is fairly homogeneous because the IQR, 1.25, is small in relation to the range, 4.

Skills Practice 3   Find and interpret the range and the IQR for the following frequency distribution.

EARNRS

		Frequency	Percent	Valid Percent	Cumulative Percent
Valid	0	1	11.1	11.1	11.1
	1	6	66.7	66.7	77.8
	2	2	22.2	22.2	100.0
	Total	9	100.0	100.0	

Finding the Range and Interquartile Range Using SPSS

With our analysis of range and interquartile range, you have been learning about the dispersion of responses to the GSS variable about the number of earners in a household. Now let's look at household earnings. How much are these earners bringing in? In the examples that follow, we will use SPSS to find the range and interquartile range for the variable *income91*.

Like the measures of central tendency, the measures of dispersion are found at the Frequencies dialog box.

SPSS Guide: Finding the Range and Interquartile Range

Start at the SPSS Data Editor window. Follow the command path Analyze ➡ Descriptive Statistics ➡ Frequencies. At the Frequencies dialog box, select the variable *income91*. Then click on Statistics.

At the Frequencies: Statistics window, do the following:

❶ Select your measures of dispersion: Click on Quartiles, then click on Range.

❷ Select your measures of central tendency.

❸ Click on Continue.

When you return to the Frequencies dialog box, click on OK. Your statistics and your frequency distribution appear in the Output window. They should look like the ones in Table 6.5.

Interpreting the interquartile range using SPSS   In Chapter 5, by using measures of central tendency appropriate for the *income91* variable—the mode and the median—you found that the most commonly occurring income category is category 21, $75,000 and up. The median category is 16 ($30,000–$34,999). Half of the respondents have family incomes in the $30,000 to $34,999 range or less, and half have family incomes in the $30,000 to $34,999 range or more.

What do measures of dispersion add to our analysis? Notice the value at the first quartile (Percentile 25 on the table of Statistics) is 11, while the value at the third quartile (Percentile 75 on the table of Statistics) is 19. By locating the value labels associated with these values, we can see that

> half of the respondents have family incomes from $15,000 up to $59,999.

The range of values is 20, whereas the interquartile range is 8. (Note that SPSS doesn't actually compute the IQR from the Frequencies dialog box, but it is easy to calculate from the values at percentiles 25 and 75. The IQR = 19 − 11.)

> The interquartile range is fairly small in relation to the range, suggesting a more homogeneous than heterogeneous distribution of responses to the variable.

If you picture the distribution on a graph, it is easier to see how the distribution of responses to the variable is concentrated.

Income Categories   1 2 3 4 5 6 7 8 9 10 11 12 13 14 15 16 17 18 19 20 21
Q_1---------------------- Q_2----------- Q_3

Although there is some concentration of responses in the higher income categories, it is not a highly concentrated distribution. Thus the distribution, while more homogeneous than heterogeneous, is not a very homogeneous one.

Skills Practice 4   Analyze the incomes of the individual respondents to the 1996 GSS using *rincome91*. Use appropriate measures of central tendency and dispersion. (Note: For additional practice with the computation of the range and the IQR, first obtain the frequency distribution. Use the frequency distribution to do all of the computations by hand. Then check your work by getting the range and IQR using SPSS.)

TABLE 6.5 Statistics and Frequency Distribution for the Variable *income91*

Statistics

INCOME91 TOTAL FAMILY INCOME

N	Valid	2561	
	Missing	343	
Median		16.00	
Mode		21	
Range		20	
Percentiles	25	11.00	—— Value at Quartile 1
	50	16.00	—— Value at Quartile 2 (the median)
	75	19.00	—— Value at Quartile 3

INCOME91 TOTAL FAMILY INCOME

		Frequency	Percent	Valid Percent	Cumulative Percent
Valid	1 LT $1000	26	.9	1.0	1.0
	2 $1000-2999	35	1.2	1.4	2.4
	3 $3000-3999	18	.6	.7	3.1
	4 $4000-4999	31	1.1	1.2	4.3
	5 $5000-5999	43	1.5	1.7	6.0
	6 $6000-6999	42	1.4	1.6	7.6
	7 $7000-7999	31	1.1	1.2	8.8
	8 $8000-9999	77	2.7	3.0	11.8
	9 $10000-12499	119	4.1	4.6	16.5
	10 $12500-14999	124	4.3	4.8	21.3
	11 $15000-17499	104	3.6	4.1	25.4
	12 $17500-19999	82	2.8	3.2	28.6
	13 $20000-22499	100	3.4	3.9	32.5
	14 $22500-24999	120	4.1	4.7	37.2
	15 $25000-29999	187	6.4	7.3	44.5
	16 $30000-34999	218	7.5	8.5	53.0
	17 $35000-39999	185	6.4	7.2	60.2
	18 $40000-49999	259	8.9	10.1	70.3
	19 $50000-59999	231	8.0	9.0	79.3
	20 $60000-74999	200	6.9	7.8	87.2
	21 $75000+	329	11.3	12.8	100.0
	Total	2561	88.2	100.0	
Missing	22 REFUSED	187	6.4		
	98 DK	117	4.0		
	99 NA	39	1.3		
	Total	343	11.8		
Total		2904	100.0		

Graphing the Interquartile Range

SPSS has a feature called boxplot that allows us to see the interquartile range pictorially. A **boxplot** is a graphic representation of the distribution of responses to a variable focusing on the responses in the interquartile range. Let's use the command path Graphs ➡ Boxplot to obtain a boxplot.

SPSS Guide: Creating Boxplots for the Interquartile Range

Start at the SPSS Data Editor window. With a data file open, click on the Graphs menu item and then on Boxplot.

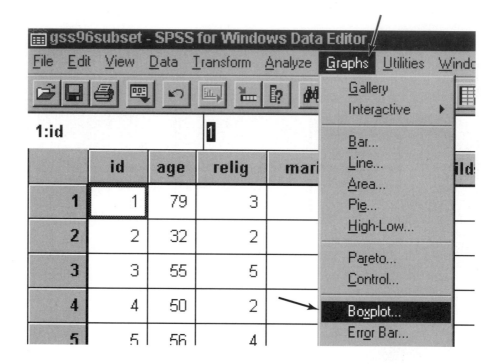

When the Boxplot window opens, click on Summaries of Separate Variables, then on Define.

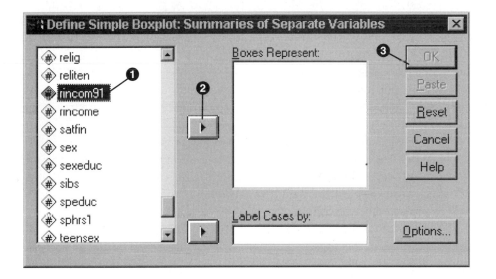

At the Define Simple Boxplot dialog box, scroll down to the variable *rincome91.*

❶ Click on your variable to highlight it.

❷ Click on the ▶ to move your variable into the Boxes Represent: area.

❸ Click on OK.

In your Output window, you will get a boxplot like this one:

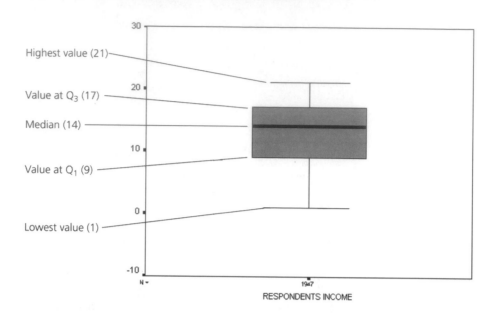

RESPONDENTS INCOME

To interpret the diagram, notice that the boxplot is constructed so that the values of the variable are on the y- (vertical) axis. The box itself represents the cases in the interquartile range—the cases between Q_1 and Q_3. The heavy black line across the box is the median value. The lines that extend beyond the box are called *whiskers* (and boxplots are sometimes referred to as *box and whiskers* diagrams.) Boxplots may also show you which values are **outliers,** unusually high or low values of a variable, and **extreme values,** exceptionally high or low values, in relation to the interquartile range. SPSS uses specific formulas for assessing whether a particular value is an outlier or an extreme value.

The whisker at the bottom of the boxplot represents either the smallest value in the range of category values or the smallest value that is not an *outlier.* An **outlier in the bottom range** of a variable's values is a value that is equal to or less than the value at Q_1 minus the interquartile range (IQR) times 1.5, as indicated by the formula $Q_1 - (IQR \times 1.5)$.

The whisker at the top represents either the highest value in the range of category values or the largest value that is not an outlier. An **outlier in the upper range** of a variable's values is a value that is equal to or greater than the value at Q_3 plus the interquartile range times 1.5, as indicated by the formula $Q_3 + (IQR \times 1.5)$.

For the preceding example, the bottom whisker represents the lowest value in the range and the top whisker represents the highest value in the range.

Interpretation   The larger the box is in relation to the range of values in the diagram, the more heterogeneous is the distribution (the more variability in the responses). The smaller the box is in relation to the range of values, the more homogeneous is the distribution (the less variability in the responses).

> For the variable *rincome91,* the distribution appears to be somewhat homogeneous, because the interquartile range appears relatively small in relation to the range of values for the variable.

Let's look at another example: Find a boxplot for the variable *educ.* To help interpret the boxplot, find the median, mode, and quartile values for the variable. (Use the command path Graphs ➡ Boxplot to get the chart you need, and use the path Analyze ➡ Descriptive Statistics ➡ Frequencies ➡ Statistics to get the frequency distribution and related measures of central tendency and dispersion.)

The boxplot for the variable *educ* should look like the one in Figure 6.2. Like the boxplot for *rincome91,* the box represents the interquartile range for the variable. The line at the bottom of the box is the value at the first quartile, 12 years of education. The line at the top of the box represents the value at the third quartile, 16 years of education. The heavy line through the box is the median,13 years of education. The whisker at the top of the box represents the highest value for the variable, 20 years of education. However, the whisker at the bottom of the box is the smallest value for the variable that is not an outlier.

Recall that an outlier is any value of a variable equal to or less than the value at quartile 1 minus the IQR times 1.5, or the value at quartile 3 plus the IQR times 1.5. To find the values of outliers in relation to the first quartile, multiply the IQR by 1.5. The IQR for *educ* is 4 (16 years of education − 12 years = 4 years): 4 × 1.5 = 6. Subtract the result from the value at the first quartile (12): 12 − 6 = 6. Thus outliers are any values of the variable *educ* equal to or less than 6. Consequently, the bottom whisker represents the value 7—the smallest value of the variable *educ* that is not an outlier. The circles represent the values of the outliers—all values of the variables that are equal to or less than 6.

Outliers in relation to the third quartile can be found by adding the IQR (4) × 1.5 to the value at quartile 3, which is 16. 4 × 1.5 = 6. Then 16 + 6 = 22. There are no values of the variable that go that high, so the whisker at the top of the boxplot represents the highest value for the variable, 20.

The asterisk at the bottom of the chart represents a value that is not only an outlier but an extreme value. **Extreme values** of a variable are values that are equal to or less than the value at the first quartile minus the IQR times 3, or equal to or greater than the value at the third quartile plus the IQR times 3. An extreme value in the bottom of the range for the variable *educ* would be equal to 12 (the value at the first quartile) minus the IQR (4) times 3. Because

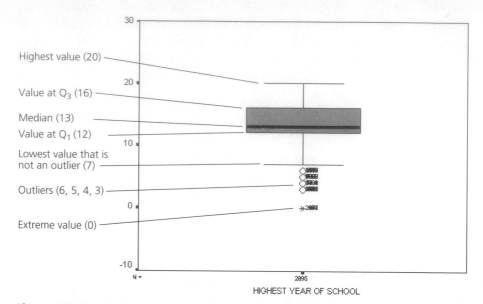

Figure 6.2 Boxplot for the variable *educ* in the gss96subset file.

$4 \times 3 = 12$, and the value at the first quartile is 12, an extreme value is equal to or less than 0.

If there are no outliers in relation to either the first or third quartiles, there can be no extreme values either. Consequently, there are no extreme values in relation to quartile 3.

MEAN DEVIATION, VARIANCE, AND STANDARD DEVIATION

Mean deviation, variance, and standard deviation are conceptually similar to the interquartile range in that they provide us with measures of how similar or dissimilar, homogeneous or heterogeneous, respondents are to a particular variable. Because the mean is part of the formulas for these measures, they are used only with numerical variables.

Mean Deviation

Deviations can be computed in relation to any of the measures of central tendency. To find a deviation simply means to figure out how much a set of scores deviates from one of the measures of central tendency—the mode, the median, or the mean.

The **mean deviation** is the average of the deviations from the mean. It is a fairly simple but little-used measure of dispersion. SPSS doesn't compute it, but I am presenting it here because understanding it helps us make sense of measures like variance and standard deviation. The mean deviation draws on the property of the mean discussed in Chapter 5—the sum of the deviations from the mean equals 0. However, instead of adding up the differences, we will average them.

The process involves the following:

Step 1. Subtract the mean for a set of data from each score in the set to find its deviation from the mean.

Step 2. Find the absolute value of each of the deviations from the mean.[4]

Step 3. Add up the results to get the sum of the deviations from the mean.

Step 4. Divide the sum of the deviations from the mean by N, to get the average of the deviations from the mean.

The following illustrates the process.

Age		Mean		Deviations from the Mean	Absolute Values of the Deviations From the Mean
19	−	21	=	−2	2
20	−	21	=	−1	1
20	−	21	=	−1	1
21	−	21	=	0	0
21	−	21	=	0	0
21	−	21	−	0	0
22	−	21	=	1	1
22	−	21	=	1	1
23	−	21	=	2	2

Σ of the deviations from the mean $= 0$ Σ of absolute values $= 8$

The mean deviation is computed by dividing the sum of the absolute values of the deviations from the mean by N: $8 \div 9 = .89$. The average of the deviations from the mean is .89 year.

As a very broad rule of thumb, smaller mean deviations indicate dispersions with less variability than larger mean deviations, but the mean deviation has to be interpreted in the context of the range of values for a variable. Mean deviation can also be used to compare distributions of a variable across different samples or subsets of data. For example, we can use the mean deviation to compare the variability of ages in the GSS for 1996 with the variability of ages in another

---

[4]Taking an absolute value means to remove the positive or negative sign from a number. In essence, when we use absolute values we are treating all numbers as positive values.

set of data. We can also use mean deviation to compare groups. For example, we can analyze the variable *age* for males and females. We can use mean deviation to see whether the distribution of male respondents to *age* is more homogeneous or heterogeneous than the distribution of female respondents.

Variance

Variance is a measure computed somewhat like the mean deviation. The difference is that instead of taking the absolute values of each of the deviations from the mean, we square each one. The squares of the deviations from the mean are totaled. Then the squares of the deviations are averaged by dividing the sum of the squares by $N - 1$:

Age		Mean		Deviations From the Mean	Squaring the Deviations From the Mean
19	−	21	=	−2	4
20	−	21	=	−1	1
20	−	21	=	−1	1
21	−	21	=	0	0
21	−	21	=	0	0
21	−	21	=	0	0
22	−	21	=	1	1
22	−	21	=	1	1
23	−	21	=	2	4

Σ of the deviations from the mean = 0 Σ of the squares = 12

The variance is computed by dividing the sum of the squares of the deviations from the mean by $N - 1$: $12 \div 8 = 1.50$. Thus the variance equals 1.50.[5]

As with mean deviation, the variance can be used to compare the distribution of responses to a variable in one set of data with the distribution of responses in another. In addition, it can be used to compare groups, like males and females. What is the advantage of the variance over the mean deviation? The variance has a property that mean deviation doesn't have—it can be used to find the standard deviation, which is simply the square root of the variance. Standard deviation also has some unique characteristics that make it a very powerful tool for analyzing distributions.

---

[5]You may be guessing that, although the computation of the variance seems relatively straightforward for small sets of data, it is more complicated for larger sets. As there is for the mean, there is a raw scores method (the process in the preceding illustration) and a method for use with ungrouped frequency distributions. Because variance and standard deviation are so closely related, I will show you how to find both in the next section.

Standard Deviation

Standard deviation is a measure of dispersion that, like the interquartile range, uses a measure of central tendency—the mean—as a point of comparison and, like variance, gives us an indication of the dispersion of responses to a variable. The standard deviation helps us to assess variability by using what is "standard" about standard deviation.

What *is* "standard" about standard deviation? To answer this question, I need to explain one of the properties of a normal distribution. (Remember the normal distribution from the previous chapter? It is a symmetrical and unimodal distribution of responses to a variable in which the mean, median, and mode are the same.) You may recall from previous math experience that we can compute the area of any object, whether it's a square, a rectangle, a circle, or even a curve. A normal distribution is a curve, and we can picture the area under a curve as follows:

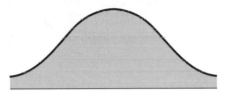

When a distribution is normal, the area under a curve is divided into two equal portions at the mean (which has the same value as the median in a normal distribution). In effect, the mean divides the area under the curve in half. Half of the area under the curve falls below the mean and half falls above it.

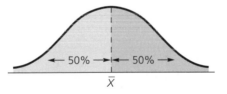

Even more important is that we can use the area under the curve of a normal distribution to make more precise measurements of the dispersion of responses in relation to the mean. The "standard" in the standard deviation is the mathematical "given" that 34.13% of the area under a normal curve always falls between the mean and one standard deviation above the mean, while another 34.13% of the area falls between the mean and one standard deviation below it. Because the area under a normal curve represents the responses to a variable, this "given" allows us to assume that 34.13% of all respondents to a variable will fall between the mean and one standard deviation above the mean. By the same token, 34.13% of all respondents will fall between the mean and one standard deviation below the mean. If you add these percentages together, then we can see that 68.26% (34.13 + 34.13) of all respondents will fall between one standard deviation below the mean and one standard deviation above it. The following shows this distribution.

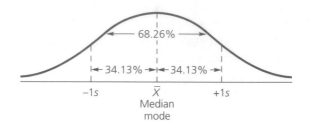

How do we find the standard deviation? Two of the methods, the raw scores method and the ungrouped frequencies distribution method, are demonstrated in the next two sections.

Raw scores method   The raw scores method of finding the standard deviation is used whenever we have a set of scores that have not been organized into a frequency distribution and every score or category for a variable is listed for each one of the respondents, like the set of raw scores in Table 6.6. Conceptually, the raw scores formula finds the standard deviation (symbolized by the letter s) by taking the square root of the variance. The variance is computed by summing the squared deviations from the mean and dividing them by $N - 1$. This method is expressed in the following formula, often called the conceptual formula:

$$s = \sqrt{\frac{\Sigma(X - \bar{X})^2}{N - 1}}$$

However, this formula can be cumbersome to compute, even for small sets of data. Therefore, we will use Formula 6.3(a) for finding the standard deviation from raw scores, sometimes called the computational formula.[6]

FORMULA 6.3(A):   Standard deviation—raw scores

$$s = \sqrt{\left(\frac{\Sigma X^2}{N - 1}\right) - \left[\left(\frac{N}{N - 1}\right)(\bar{X})^2\right]}$$

where s stands for standard deviation, ΣX^2 means to sum (add up) each of the scores in a distribution after they have each been squared,[7] $N - 1$

---

[6]Standard deviation can be computed in a number of ways using a variety of formulas. For the sake of consistency with SPSS, the formulas in the text follow the SPSS methods of computation.
[7]To "square" a score or value means to multiply the score or value against itself. For example, to square the score or value 2 means to multiply 2 × 2. The score or value 2 squared equals 4.

TABLE 6.6   A Random Sample of GSS 1996 Respondents for the Variable *earnrs*

Cases	*earnrs*	Cases	*earnrs*
1	2	11	1
2	0	12	2
3	1	13	1
4	3	14	1
5	1	15	1
6	1	16	2
7	3	17	2
8	0	18	2
9	2	19	2
10	2		

is equal to the number of scores you have minus 1, and $(\overline{X})^2$ means to square the mean.

A look at the formula tells us we need to do a few computations before we can begin finding the standard deviation. First, we need to know the mean. Second, we need to have the sum of the scores squared (we need to square each score and then add up the results). Once we have this information, we can find the standard deviation by filling in the information required by the formula.

Example: Find the standard deviation for the set of scores in Table 6.6 for the variable *number of wage earners in a household* (drawn from a random sample of GSS respondents).

Step 1.   Find the mean for the distribution. Use the raw scores formula to find the mean.

$$\overline{X} = \frac{\Sigma X}{N} = \frac{29}{19} = 1.5263$$

Step 2.   Square the mean ($1.5263 \times 1.5263 = 2.3296$).

Step 3.   Square each of the scores in the distribution. You can create a table like Table 6.7 to keep track of each of the scores and the result.

Step 4.   Add up each of the *squared* scores. The sum of the squared scores is 57.

Step 5.   Now, plug the results into the formula for standard deviation, as illustrated in Box 6.1.

Interpreting variance and standard deviation   What do we learn from computing the standard deviation? First, notice the variance, which we computed on our way to finding the standard deviation. The variance for the random sample of cases in Table 6.7 for the variable *earnrs* is .7076, the number we find before taking its square root to get standard deviation. We can use the variance to compare distributions.

Second, knowledge of the standard deviation, combined with the assumptions we are allowed to make about normal distributions, allows us to estimate the dispersion of values in relation to the mean. In this case we know the mean is 1.53 (rounded to the second decimal). One standard deviation from the mean is .84. If we add one standard deviation to the mean (1.53 + .84), the score at $+1s$ (one standard deviation) from the mean is 2.37. If we

TABLE 6.7 **Squaring Raw Scores for a Random Sample of Cases From the 1996 GSS for the Variable *earnrs***

Cases	*earnrs*	X^2	Cases	*earnrs*	X^2
1	2	4	11	1	1
2	0	0	12	2	4
3	1	1	13	1	1
4	3	9	14	1	1
5	1	1	15	1	1
6	1	1	16	2	4
7	3	9	17	2	4
8	0	0	18	2	4
9	2	4	19	2	4
10	2	4		$N = 19$	$\Sigma X^2 = 57$

subtract one standard deviation from the mean (1.53 − .84), we find the score at −1*s* from the mean, .69. We can diagram this relationship as follows:

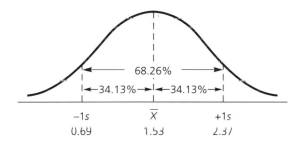

We can assume that, in a normally distributed set of responses to a variable, about 68.26% of the responses will fall within one standard deviation of the mean. 34.13% of the responses will fall between the mean and one standard deviation above it (the score at +1*s*, or 2.37 in this example). 34.13% of the responses will fall between the mean and one standard deviation below it (the score at −1*s*, or .69 in this example).

Finally, note that the standard deviation is expressed in units of the original variable. A standard deviation of .84 for wage earners tells us that 34.13% of the respondents lie .84 wage earner from the mean of 1.53. When we say that a given score is one standard deviation above the mean, we are saying that 34.13% of the respondents have between 1.53 (the mean) and 2.37 wage earners (the mean plus one standard deviation) in their families. Similarly, a score that is one standard deviation below the mean tells us that 34.13% of the respondents have between .69 and 1.53 wage earners.

Consequently, we can claim that, in a normally distributed set of responses to the variable *wage earners,* with a mean of 1.53 and a variance of .7076, about 68% of the responses will fall between .69 (nearly one wage earner per family) and 2.37 (a little more than two wage earners per family). But is our set of responses normally distributed? Look at the relationship between the mean, median, and mode to see how safe it is to make this assumption.

Is this a homogeneous distribution (one with little variability) or a heterogeneous distribution (one with a lot of variability)? To answer this question we have to look at the standard deviation *in relation to the range.* Like the interquartile range, the standard deviation has no absolute interpretation. The same standard deviation in two different distributions could have entirely different meanings.

Let's assume we have two different sets of responses to an age variable. In one set, the range of ages in a sample of the adult population in the United States is 18–89. In another distribution, the range of ages in a sample of students at a college is 18–23. Both distributions have standard deviations of 2. Which distribution is more homogeneous than the other: the one with the larger range or the one with the smaller range? I hope you answered the one with the larger range. Why? Because in the distribution with ages ranging from 18 to 89, about 68% of the respondents are clustered into relatively few values of the variable (a total of 4 years, 2 years—or standard deviations—below the mean and 2 above it). The range of values is 71, and 68% of the respondents are "crammed" into only 4 of them. However, with the smaller range, the distribution of ages 18 to 23 has a range of 5, and 68% of the respondents are spread across four of the six categories of the variable, a heterogeneous distribution.

In the example with which we've been working, a distribution of responses to the wage earners variable, the range of scores is 3 (3 – 0). One standard deviation above the mean plus one standard deviation below the mean is 1.68 (.84 + .84). Approximately 68%—over two thirds—of the responses fall within an interval that encompasses a little more than 1½ of the range of three categories. More than half of the responses are within an interval of about half the response categories. The data are more concentrated (homogeneous) than spread out (heterogeneous).

Skills Practice 5 Find and interpret the standard deviation for the following set of data for the variable *hrs1* (number of hours worked last week). Is this a normally distributed set of responses? How do you know?

Case Summaries

	HRS1 NUMBER OF HOURS WORKED LAST WEEK
1	46
2	40
3	40
4	50
5	20
6	40
7	15
8	40
9	35
10	50
11	40
12	40
13	40
Total N	13

Ungrouped frequency distribution method As with the mean, we can use a variation on the raw scores technique to compute standard deviation from an ungrouped frequency distribution.

FORMULA 6.3(B): Standard deviation—ungrouped frequency distribution

$$s = \sqrt{\left(\frac{\Sigma f X^2}{N - 1}\right) - \left[\left(\frac{N}{N - 1}\right)(\overline{X})^2\right]}$$

where $\Sigma f X^2$ means to square each score, multiply the squared score by its associated frequency, and then add up all of the $f X^2$; $N - 1$ is the number of valid responses minus one; and $\overline{X}^2$ is the mean squared.

Like the raw scores formula for standard deviation, the formula for computing standard deviation from an ungrouped frequency distribution tells us we need to do a few computations before we can begin finding the standard deviation. Unlike the raw scores method, the first task is to put our data into a frequency distribution. Let's do this, using the data in Table 6.6 as an example. You should have a frequency distribution like this one to work with.

Earners (X)	f	fX
0	2	0
1	7	7
2	8	16
3	2	6
	N = 19	Σ(fX) = 29

The next step is to find the mean. Because we are working with an ungrouped frequency distribution, we need to use the ungrouped frequency distribution formula for finding the mean:

$$\overline{X} = \frac{\Sigma(fX)}{N} = \frac{29}{19}$$

You should come up with the same answer as for the raw scores mean, 1.5263.

Now we need to square each score and multiply it against its corresponding frequency. As with standard deviation for raw scores, the easiest way to keep track of the steps in the process is by simply adding the relevant computations to our frequency distribution. We can add a column for each of the scores squared. Then we can add a column that shows each squared score multiplied by its associated frequency.

Earners (X)	f	Square each score to get X^2	Multiply each squared score by its frequency to get fX^2
0	2	0	0
1	7	1	7
2	8	4	32
3	2	9	18

Finally, we can add up the results to get ΣfX^2: $\Sigma fX^2 = 57$

By filling in the information required by the formula for standard deviation from an ungrouped frequency distribution, you should be able to set up the problem this way:

$$\bar{X} = 1.5263 \qquad \Sigma fX^2 = 37 \qquad N - 19$$

$$s = \sqrt{\left(\frac{\Sigma fX^2}{N - 1}\right) - \left[\left(\frac{N}{N - 1}\right)(\bar{X})^2\right]}$$

$$= \sqrt{\left(\frac{57}{19 - 1}\right) - \left[\left(\frac{19}{19 - 1}\right)(1.5263)^2\right]}$$

As you do the computations required by the formula, remember to follow the rules for order of operations.

Step 1. Work within the brackets and square the mean first.

Step 2. Do the subtraction within the denominators of each portion of the formula in parentheses.

Step 3. Do the division for each portion of the formula in parentheses.

Step 4. Do the multiplication required by the portion of the formula in the brackets.

Step 5. Do the subtraction.

Step 6. Find the square root of the result.

Your answer should be identical to the one you obtained using the raw scores method, $s = .84$.

Skills Practice 6   Put the data in Skills Practice 5 into an ungrouped frequency distribution, and calculate standard deviation using the formula for an ungrouped frequency distribution. Identify the variance in your computations.

Finding Variance and Standard Deviation Using SPSS

Finding the variance and standard deviation with SPSS follows the same process as finding the interquartile range. Let's look at the variable *hrs1*, number of hours worked in the last week. Follow the procedures in the next SPSS Guide to find the standard deviation for *hrs1*.

SPSS Guide: Finding the Standard Deviation

Start by opening your gss96subset file. Then open the Frequencies dialog box using the command path Analyze ➡ Descriptive Statistics ➡ Frequencies. At the Frequencies dialog box, select your variable, *hrs1*.

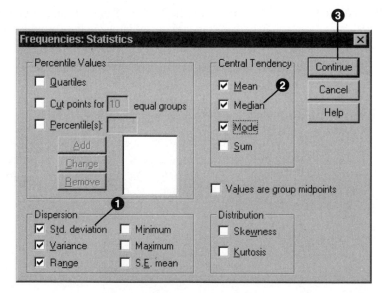

Next click on Statistics to open the Frequencies: Statistics window.

❶ Select your measures of dispersion: Click on Std. Deviation, Variance and Range.

❷ Select your measures of central tendency.

❸ Click on Continue. When the Frequencies dialog box returns, click on OK.

TABLE 6.8 Statistics for the Variable *hrs1* in the gss96subset File

Statistics

HRS1 NUMBER OF HOURS WORKED LAST WEEK

N	Valid	1935
	Missing	969
Mean		42.35
Median		40.00
Mode		40
Std. Deviation		14.14
Variance		199.95
Range		87

A set of statistics like the one in Table 6.8, along with the frequency distribution for *hrs1,* appears in the Output window.

What do measures of dispersion add to what you learned about *hrs1* using measures of central tendency? We already know that the average number of hours worked is 42.35—a full-time work week. Half of the respondents worked 40 hours a week or less, and half worked 40 hours a week or more, and the most commonly occurring work schedule is 40 hours. The distribution is nearly normal, but the mean is higher than the median, so we know the dispersion is positively skewed. When a distribution is positively skewed, there are values at the high end of the distribution pulling the mean away from the median. Some people worked a lot of hours and skewed the distribution—pulled it away from normal.

Now let's add measures of dispersion to the analysis. Are the respondents grouped fairly closely around the mean, or are they spread out around it? The standard deviation tells the story. The range of values is 87—quite a large range. One standard deviation from the mean is 14.14. In a normal distribution with a mean of 14.14 (and, by extension, a mode and median of 14.14) and a variance of 199.95, we could assume about 34% of the respondents worked between 28.21 hours per week (the mean minus one standard deviation, or 42.35 minus 14.14) and 42.35 hours (the mean), whereas another 34% worked between 42.35 hours per week (the mean) and 56.49 hours per week (the mean plus one standard deviation, or 42.35 plus 14.14). Sixty-eight percent of the respondents are dispersed across about 28 (two standard deviations) of the 87 values in the range. Over two thirds of the respondents are spread across about one quarter of the values in the range of values, suggesting a more homogeneous than heterogeneous distribution. Assuming a normal distribution of responses, over two thirds of the respondents to the GSS worked at least 28 hours up to about 56 hours.

Although the standard deviation helps us analyze dispersions for single variables, it can also be used, along with variance, as a basis of comparison between two groups of respondents for the same variable. For example, we can use variance and standard deviation to compare males and females. Which group is more homogeneous (has less variability) than the other in their responses to a particular variable? The answer is: the group with the lower of the two standard deviations for that variable.

Skills Practice 7   Split the gss96subset file by *sex*. Analyze the dispersion of *hrs1* for each of the two groups—using the mean, median, mode, range, variance, and standard deviation. Then answer these questions: Which group worked the most hours? Which group is the most homogeneous? Are either of the distributions, for males or females, normal? If not, in which direction are they skewed? How do you know?

Now let's look at another use of standard deviation—to evaluate the dispersion of responses in two groups with similar means. Ordinarily, we might be tempted to believe that in two groups with similar means, the dispersion of responses is also similar. However, this is not always the case, and analyzing the dispersion of responses allows us to test our assumption that groups with similar means have similar distributions of responses to a variable.

Skills Practice 8   Split the gss96subset file with your recoded *childs* variable, and obtain the standard deviation for the variable *earnrs*. You should be looking at a set of statistics like the following:

Statistics[a]

EARNRS HOW MANY IN FAMILY EARNED MONEY

N	Valid	796
	Missing	26
Mean		1.41
Median		1.00
Mode		1
Std. Deviation		.93
Range		6

a. RCHILDS recoded childs variable = 0 Has no children

Statistics[a]

EARNRS HOW MANY IN FAMILY EARNED MONEY

N	Valid	2033
	Missing	34
Mean		1.41
Median		1.00
Mode		1
Std. Deviation		.97
Range		6

a. RCHILDS recoded childs variable = 1 Has children

You already learned that the means for these two groups—those with children and those without—for the variable *earnrs* are the same. Does this mean that the dispersions for each of the two groups are the same? Which group is more homogeneous than the other? How do you know? The answers follow.

You should see that the distribution of responses to the variable *earnrs* is slightly more homogeneous among those with no children as compared to those with children. The standard deviation is a little lower (.93) for the distribution of those with no children as compared to the distribution of the respondents with children (.97).

Graphing the Normal Distribution: Creating Histograms With the Normal Curve

To assist us with our evaluation of the dispersion of numerical variables, we can obtain a **histogram with a normal curve**—a histogram that has a normal curve superimposed on it. From the shape of the curves and the relationship between the distribution of responses and the normal curve, we can assess the degree of variability and the skew.

SPSS Guide: Histograms With the Normal Curve

At the SPSS Data Editor window, use Split File with the variable *sex* to divide your gss96subset file into two groups, males and females. Next, click on Graphs, then Histogram.

❶ When the Histogram dialog box opens, scroll down to the variable *educ*. Click on it to highlight it, and click on the arrow to move it into the Variable box.

❷ Click on Display Normal Curve.

❸ Click on OK.

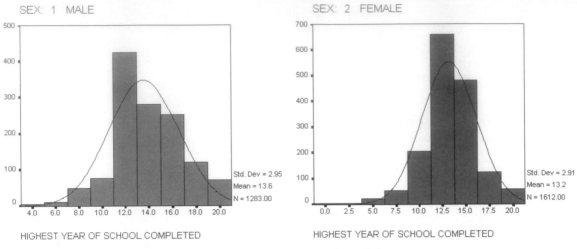

Figure 6.3   Histograms for the variable *educ* with the gss96subset file split by *sex*.

You should get two charts—one for males and one for females—like the ones in Figure 6.3.

Notice the shape of the normal curve in the charts you created. The normal curve shows you what a distribution would look like for a set of data having the same mean and variance as the data you see in the histogram but having a unimodal and symmetrical distribution of values in relation to the mean. The more peaked is the normal curve, the more homogeneous is the distribution; the less peaked, or the flatter, is the normal curve, the more heterogeneous is the distribution. See the following illustrations, which show you how to compare the shapes of normal distributions.

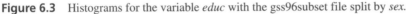

More heterogeneous   More homogeneous

Compare the normal curves of the years of education for males and females, and notice that the curve for male respondents looks a little less pointed than the curve for female respondents. This tells us that the distribution of scores for years of education is more heterogeneous for males than females. This conclusion is borne out by the standard deviations—notice that the standard deviation for the distribution of male respondents is higher than the standard deviation for the female respondents, indicating more heterogeneity or variability in the dispersion of years of education. You may also notice that males report having, on average, more years of education than females.

USING MEASURES OF DISPERSION

Use the following chart as a guide to the correct applications of measures of dispersion. Different statistics are appropriate depending on the level of measurement of the variable being evaluated. This chart will help you decide when and how to apply these statistics.

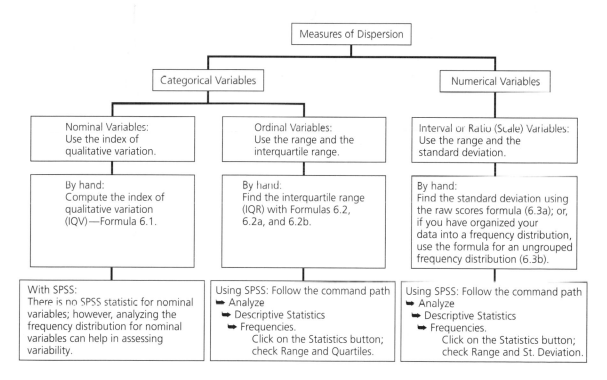

SUMMARY

After finishing this chapter you should be able to apply measures of dispersion appropriately. They include the index of qualitative variation, range, interquartile range, variance, and standard deviation, and they help us to determine how homogeneous or heterogeneous a distribution is, or how much variation there is in the responses to a variable. The index of qualitative variation is used with nominal variables, whereas the range and interquartile range can be applied to ordinal or numerical variables. The standard deviation (interpreted in the context of the range) is used only with numerical variables.

You should be able to compute the index of qualitative variation, range, interquartile range, and standard deviation by hand, and you should know how to obtain the range, interquartile range, variance, and standard deviation, along with either a boxplot or a histogram with a normal curve, using SPSS. The range, interquartile range, and standard deviation can all be found using the Statistics button in the Frequencies dialog box.

As in previous chapters, emphasis has been placed on the interpretation of the measures, starting with the index of qualitative variation (the IQV). The IQV is a guide to the dispersion of responses across the categories of a variable based on a scale of 0 (more homogeneous) to 1.00 (more heterogeneous).

The range assesses the degree of variability in response categories (but not necessarily the dispersion of responses across those categories), and it provides the context for the interpretation of the interquartile range and standard deviation. The interquartile range (IQR) allows us to focus on the middle 50% of the responses to a variable. Analyzing the IQR in relation to the range lets us assess the homogeneity or heterogeneity of these responses without the influence of outliers or extreme values. The standard deviation, on the other hand, allows us to focus on the middle 68% of the responses. Like the IQR, it has to be interpreted in relation to the range. Unlike the IQR, the interpretation of the standard deviation assumes a normal distribution of responses to a variable.

In the next chapter we will move from univariate analysis to analysis that involves two or more variables. We will begin by looking at associations between variables using contingency tables.

KEY CONCEPTS

Measures of dispersion	Interquartile range	Standard deviation
Variability	Quartile	Mean deviation
Index of qualitative variation	Boxplot	Variance
Range	Outlier	Histogram with a normal curve
	Extreme values	

ANSWERS TO SKILLS PRACTICES

1. The formula for the IQV is

$$IQV = \frac{\text{total observed differences}}{\text{maximum possible differences}}$$

Begin by finding the numerator, using Formula 6.1(a):

$$\text{observed differences} = \Sigma f_i f_j$$

1. Multiply the first frequency, 18, by the sum of the succeeding frequencies:

$$f_i f_j = (18)(10 + 2 + 24) - (18)(41) = 738$$

2. Multiply the second frequency, 3, by the frequencies below it, like this:

$$f_i f_j = (10)(2 + 29) = (10)(31) = 310$$

3. Multiply the third frequency, 1, by the frequency below it, 2:

$$f_i f_j = 2 \times 29 = 58$$

4. Add up all of the $f_i f_j$s to get their sum (Σ):

$$\Sigma f_i f_j = 738 + 310 + 58 = 1,106$$

Find the denominator, using Formula 6.1(b):

$$\text{possible differences} = \frac{K(K-1)}{2}\left(\frac{N}{K}\right)^2$$

$$= \frac{4(4-1)}{2}\left(\frac{59}{4}\right)^2 = \frac{4(3)}{2}(14.75)^2$$

$$= \frac{12}{2}(217.5625) = 6(217.5625)$$

$$\text{possible differences} = 1,305.375$$

Finally, insert the values for the total differences (the numerator) and the maximum differences (the denominator) into the formula for the IQV:

$$IQV = \frac{\text{total observed differences}}{\text{maximum possible differences}}$$

$$= \frac{1,106}{1,305.375}$$

$$IQV = .85$$

Interpretation: The distribution of response among GSS female respondents in the 18 to 21 age bracket appears more heterogeneous. At .85, the IQV is closer to 1.0 than to 0. Although the female respondents age 18 to 21 are fairly well distributed across the categories of the variable, nearly half the respondents (49.2%) are concentrated in the Not in the Market category. Nearly one third said they are working full-time and almost 17% said they are working part-time. Only about 3% of the respondents said they are not working. The distribution appears to be a little more homogeneous than the IQV by itself would lead us to believe.

2. The frequency distribution for *earnmore* should look like this:

EARNMORE Who earns more money?

		Frequency	Percent	Valid Percent	Cumulative Percent
Valid	1 I earn much more than my spouse	278	9.6	36.8	36.8
	2 I earn somewhat more than my spouse	66	2.3	8.7	45.6
	3 We earn about the same amount	81	2.8	10.7	56.3
	4 My spouse-partner earns somewhat more	130	4.5	17.2	73.5
	5 My spouse-partner earns much more	200	6.9	26.5	100.0
	Total	755	26.0	100.0	
Missing	0 NAP	2124	73.1		
	9 NA	25	.9		
	Total	2149	74.0		
Total		2904	100.0		

Start by finding the values at quartile 1 and quartile 3.

Step 1. The case at quartile 1 = $(N + 1) \times .25 = 756$ (valid cases only) $\times .25 = 189$.

Step 2. The value at quartile 1 is the value associated with case 189. Reading down the Frequency column, we see that the first value (1, I earn much more than my spouse) consists of cases 1 through 278. Case 189 is included in that range of cases, so the value of quartile 1 is 1 (I earn much more than my spouse).

Step 3. The case at quartile 3 = $(N + 1) \times .75 = 756 \times .75 = 567$.

Step 4. The value at quartile 3 is the value associated with case 567. Reading down the Frequency column, we find case 567 in the range of cases, 556–755, associated with the last value, 5 (my spouse–partner earns much more than I do).

Step 5. Find the interquartile range IQR $= Q_3 - Q_1 = 5 - 1 = 4$.

If we plot these values on a graph, it helps us to analyze the distribution of responses to the variable.

Range   1   2   3   4   5

Quartiles Q_1 ---------------------------------- Q_3

The range is equal to $5 - 1 = 4$, and the interquartile range is equal to $5 - 1 = 4$. In this case, the dispersion of responses is very heterogeneous. The interquartile range is the same as the range.

3. The case at $Q_1 = (N + 1) \times .25 = (9 + 1) \times .25 = 10 \times .25 = 2.5$.

The value at $Q_1 = 1$ (the value that contains cases 2 through 6).

The case at $Q_3 = (N + 1) \times .75 = (9 + 1) \times .75 = 10 \times .75 = 7.5$.

The value at $Q_3 = 1.50$ (halfway between value 1 and value 2, because case 7.5 is halfway between case 7 and case 8).

The IQR $= 1.5 - 1 = .5$. The range $= 2 (2 - 0)$. The distribution is fairly homogeneous because the IQR (.5) is small in relation to the range (2).

4. You should get the following statistics using SPSS. You can use them to check your computations.

Statistics

RINCOM91 RESPONDENTS INCOME

N	Valid	1947
	Missing	957
Median		14.00
Mode		16
Range		20
Percentiles	25	9.00
	50	14.00
	75	17.00

To find the mode by hand, simply look down the Frequency column of the frequency distribution for *rincome91* until you find the largest frequency. Then identify the category or value associated with it, category 16 ($30,000 to $34,999).

To find the median by hand, first find the median case using the formula $(N + 1) \times .50$. Remember that N includes valid cases only.

$$(1,947 + 1) \times .50 = 1,948 \times .50 = 974$$

Then find the median value. Look down the Frequency column, adding the frequencies up as you go along. Cases 1–28 are associated with category 1 (LT $1,000), cases 29–116 are associated with category 2 ($1,000–2,999), and so on. Cases 954–1058 are associated with category 14 ($22,500–24,999). The median case is in that range, so the median value is 14.

To find the range by hand, note that the range is simply the highest value, 21, minus the lowest value, 1. The range is 20.

To find the interquartile range by hand, find the case and value at quartile 1 (Q_1).

The case at $Q_1 = (N + 1) \times .25 = (1{,}947 + 1) \times .25 = 487$.

The value at Q_1 is found by counting down the Frequency column of the frequency distribution for *rincome91* until you get to the category that contains case 487, category 9. (Category 9, $10,000–12,499, contains cases 381–498.)

Find the case and value at quartile 3 (Q_3).

The case at $Q_3 = (N + 1) \times .75 = (1{,}947 + 1) \times .75 = 1{,}461$.

The value at Q_3 is found by counting down the Frequency column of the frequency distribution for *rincome91* until you get to the category that contains case 1,461, category 17. (Category 17, $35,000–39,999, contains cases 1,416–1,521.)

Compute the interquartile range (IQR):

$$IQR = Q_3 - Q_1 = 17 - 9 = 8$$

Interpretation: The median income for 1996 GSS respondents is in the $22,500–24,999 category, with half of the GSS respondents having incomes in that range or less. Relatively few, 4.5%, have incomes over $75,000. The most frequently occurring response to the income question is $30,000–34,999, although only about 9% of the respondents earn that much. Over two thirds have incomes in that range or less. Half of the respondents have earnings in the $10,000 to 39,999 range. The distribution of responses seems fairly homogeneous, with a range of 20 and an IQR of 8.

You can picture the relationship between the categories of the variable and the interquartile range like this:

Income Categories 1 2 3 4 5 6 7 8 9 10 11 12 13 14 15 16 17 18 19 20 21
Quartiles Q_1 -------------- Q_2 -------- Q_3

5. The formula requires that we have the mean for the distribution. Using the formula for the mean for raw scores, the mean is computed as follows:

$$\bar{X} = \frac{\Sigma X}{N} = \frac{496}{13} = 38.1538$$

The next step is to find the sum of the scores squared. We can add a column to our set of data for the squared scores, square each score, and add up the results as follows:

	HRS1	X^2
1	46	2,116
2	40	1,600
3	40	1,600
4	50	2,500
5	20	400
6	40	1,600
7	15	225
8	40	1,600
9	35	1,225
10	50	2,500
11	40	1,600
12	40	1,600
13	40	1,600
Total		$\Sigma X^2 = 20{,}166$

Finally, we can plug the relevant computations into our formula for standard deviation from raw scores as follows:

$$\overline{X} - 38.1538 \qquad \Sigma X^2 = 20{,}166 \qquad N = 13$$

$$s = \sqrt{\left(\frac{\Sigma X^2}{N-1}\right) - \left[\left(\frac{N}{N-1}\right)(\overline{X})^2\right]} = \sqrt{\left(\frac{20{,}166}{13-1}\right) - \left[\left(\frac{13}{13-1}\right)(38.1538)^2\right]}$$

$$= \sqrt{\left(\frac{20{,}166}{12}\right) - \left[\left(\frac{13}{12}\right)(1{,}455.7124)\right]}$$

$$= \sqrt{1{,}680.5 - [(1.0833)(1{,}455.7124)]}$$

Now we can interpret our results. Assuming a normal distribution, about 34% of the responses to the number of hours worked fall between the mean (38.15) and one standard deviation above the mean (38.15 + 10.17 = 48.32), while another 34% of the responses fall between the mean and one standard deviation below the mean (38.15 − 10.17 = 27.98). In a normally distributed set of responses, about 68% of the responses would fall between 27.98 and 48.32, suggesting a more homogeneous set of responses. Sixty-eight percent of the responses fall across an interval of about 20 hours out of the range of 35 hours (range = 50 − 15 = 35). Nearly two thirds of the responses fall within a range encompassing a little over half of the values of the variable. In plainer English, nearly two thirds of the respondents work a little less than a full-time (40-hour) work week up to a little more than a full-time work week. It is a fairly homogeneous distribution.

Is this a normally distributed set of data? Almost, but not quite. The mean is 38.15, nearly the same as the mode (40) and the median (40). The mean is lower than the median, indicating a negatively skewed distribution.

6. Your frequency distribution for the data should look like this:

Hours Worked (X)	Frequency
15	1
20	1
35	1
40	7
46	1
50	2
Total	$N = 13$

Once the frequency distribution is complete, you can find the mean (using the formula for an ungrouped frequency distribution).

$$\overline{X} = \frac{\Sigma fX}{N} = \frac{496}{13} = 38.1538$$

Now, complete the frequency distribution for the squared scores. Multiply each squared score by its frequency (to get fX^2) and then sum the results (to get ΣfX^2).

Hours Worked (X)	Frequency	X^2	fX^2
15	1	225	225
20	1	400	400
35	1	1,225	1,225
40	7	1,600	11,200
46	1	2,116	2,116
50	2	2,500	5,000
Total	$N = 13$		$\Sigma fX^2 = 20,166$

Plug the results into your formula for standard deviation using an ungrouped frequency distribution.

$$\overline{X} = 38.1538 \qquad \Sigma fX^2 = 20,166 \qquad N = 13$$

$$s = \sqrt{\left(\frac{\Sigma fX^2}{N-1}\right) - \left[\left(\frac{N}{N-1}\right)(\overline{X})^2\right]} = \sqrt{\left(\frac{20,166}{13-1}\right) - \left[\left(\frac{13}{13-1}\right)(38.1538)^2\right]}$$

Follow the order of operations for solving the formula for standard deviation. You should get the same result, $s = 10.17$, as you did for the raw scores computation. The variance is 103.5268 (the standard deviation squared).

7. Here are the Statistics boxes you should get for the variable *hrs1,* split by categories of the variable *sex.*

Statistics[a]

HRS1 NUMBER OF HOURS WORKED LAST WEEK

N	Valid	972
	Missing	313
Mean		45.63
Median		43.00
Mode		40
Std. Deviation		14.01
Variance		196.40
Range		87

a. SEX RESPONDENTS SEX = 1 MALE

Statistics[a]

HRS1 NUMBER OF HOURS WORKED LAST WEEK

N	Valid	963
	Missing	656
Mean		39.04
Median		40.00
Mode		40
Std. Deviation		13.49
Variance		181.91
Range		87

a. SEX RESPONDENTS SEX = 2 FEMALE

The 40-hour work week seems to be alive and well for both men and women. Sixty-six percent of the female respondents and about 82% of the male respondents report working 40 hours or more per week. The most commonly occurring response to the question about the number of hours worked last week is 40, with over one quarter (29%) of the male respondents and over one third (37.2%) of the female respondents answering in that category. Women are more likely than men to work 40 hours, but men are more likely than women to work more than 40 hours. Men worked a few more hours on average (45.63 hours per week) than women (39.04 hours per week). Half of the male respondents worked 43 hours or less per week, and half worked 43 hours or more. Half of the female respondents reported working 40 hours or more in one week, and half reported working 40 hours or less.

The distribution of responses for males is more heterogeneous than the distribution for females, based on both the variance (larger for males than females) and standard deviation (also larger for males than females). Neither distribution is normal. The distribution for males is positively skewed. The distribution for females is negatively skewed. However, the distribution for females is closer to normal than the one for males.

Assuming normal distributions for both sets of data, we can estimate that 68% of male respondents worked between 31.62 hours per week (the mean minus one standard deviation) and 59.64 hours per week (the mean plus one standard deviation). Sixty-eight percent of the female respondents worked between 25.55 and 52.53 hours per week.

GENERAL EXERCISES

1. Compute and interpret the index of qualitative variation for the table in General Exercise 1 in Chapter 5.

2. Compute and interpret the index of qualitative variation for the table in General Exercise 2 on page 190 in Chapter 5.

3. Compute and interpret an appropriate measure of central tendency and the index of qualitative variation for the following frequency distribution (for 1996 GSS respondents who earn $75,000 a year or more).

WRKSTAT LABOR FORCE STATUS

		Frequency	Percent	Valid Percent	Cumulative Percent
Valid	1 WORKING FULLTIME	79	90.8	90.8	90.8
	2 WORKING PARTTIME	3	3.4	3.4	94.3
	3 TEMP NOT WORKING	3	3.4	3.4	97.7
	7 KEEPING HOUSE	2	2.3	2.3	100.0
	Total	87	100.0	100.0	

4. Compute and interpret an appropriate measure of central tendency and the index of qualitative variation for the frequency distribution below (for 1996 GSS respondents who earn $75,000 a year or more).

SEX RESPONDENTS SEX

		Frequency	Percent	Valid Percent	Cumulative Percent
Valid	1 MALE	69	79.3	79.3	79.3
	2 FEMALE	18	20.7	20.7	100.0
	Total	87	100.0	100.0	

In Exercises 5–8, for the given tables in Chapter 5, compute and interpret the interquartile range.

5. The table in General Exercise 5.

6. The table in General Exercise 6.

7. The table in General Exercise 7.

8. The table in General Exercise 8.

9. Compute and interpret appropriate measures of central tendency and the interquartile range for the following frequency distribution (for 1996 GSS respondents who earn $75,000 a year or more).

EARNMORE Who earns more money?

		Frequency	Percent	Valid Percent	Cumulative Percent
Valid	1 I earn much more than my spouse	34	39.1	82.9	82.9
	2 I earn somewhat more than my spouse	1	1.1	2.4	85.4
	3 We earn about the same amount	4	4.6	9.8	95.1
	4 My spouse-partner earns somewhat more	2	2.3	4.9	100.0
	Total	41	47.1	100.0	
Missing	0 NAP	46	52.9		
Total		87	100.0		

10. Compute and interpret appropriate measures of central tendency and the interquartile range for the following frequency distribution (for 1996 GSS respondents who earn $75,000 a year or more).

FINRELA OPINION OF FAMILY INCOME

		Frequency	Percent	Valid Percent	Cumulative Percent
Valid	1 FAR BELOW AVERAGE	6	6.9	7.0	7.0
	2 BELOW AVERAGE	1	1.1	1.2	8.1
	3 AVERAGE	8	9.2	9.3	17.4
	4 ABOVE AVERAGE	55	63.2	64.0	81.4
	5 FAR ABOVE AVERAGE	16	18.4	18.6	100.0
	Total	86	98.9	100.0	
Missing	8 DK	1	1.1		
Total		87	100.0		

In Exercises 11–14, for the given tables in Chapter 5, pages 192–193, compute and interpret the standard deviation.

11. The table in General Exercise 11.

12. The table in General Exercise 12.

13. The table in General Exercise 13.

14. The table in General Exercise 14.

15. Compute and interpret appropriate measures of central tendency and the standard deviation for the following frequency distribution (for 1996 GSS respondents who earn $75,000 a year or more).

EDUC HIGHEST YEAR OF SCHOOL COMPLETED

		Frequency	Percent	Valid Percent	Cumulative Percent
Valid	11	1	1.1	1.1	1.1
	12	12	13.8	13.8	14.9
	13	1	1.1	1.1	16.1
	14	2	2.3	2.3	18.4
	15	6	6.9	6.9	25.3
	16	26	29.9	29.9	55.2
	17	7	8.0	8.0	63.2
	18	8	9.2	9.2	72.4
	19	4	4.6	4.6	77.0
	20	20	23.0	23.0	100.0
	Total	87	100.0	100.0	

16. Compute and interpret an appropriate measure of central tendency and the standard deviation for the following frequency distribution (for 1996 GSS respondents who earn $75,000 a year or more).

HOMPOP NUMBER OF PERSONS IN HOUSEHOLD

		Frequency	Percent	Valid Percent	Cumulative Percent
Valid	1	9	10.3	10.3	10.3
	2	38	43.7	43.7	54.0
	3	16	18.4	18.4	72.4
	4	13	14.9	14.9	87.4
	5	5	5.7	5.7	93.1
	6	3	3.4	3.4	96.6
	7	3	3.4	3.4	100.0
	Total	87	100.0	100.0	

SPSS EXERCISES

1. Use the appropriate measures of dispersion to add to your analysis of the variable *rincome91* in SPSS Exercise 2 in Chapter 5.

2. Use the appropriate measures of dispersion to add to your analysis of the variable *hompop* in SPSS Exercise 3 in Chapter 5.

3. Use the appropriate measures of dispersion to add to your analysis of the variable *income91* split by the recoded variable *rchilds* in SPSS Exercise 4 in Chapter 5. Compare the boxplots for each of the two groups, those with no children and those with children.

4. Use the appropriate measures of dispersion to add to your analysis of the variable *hrs1* split by the recoded variable *rchilds* in SPSS Exercise 5 in Chapter 5. Compare the histograms for each of the two groups, those with no children and those with children.

5. Use appropriate measures of dispersion to compare the answers to the variable *satfin* (satisfaction with one's financial situation) for males and females.

6. Use appropriate measures of dispersion to compare the answers to the variable *finrela* (perceptions of one's financial situation in relation to others) for males and females.

Analyzing Contingency Tables

INTRODUCTION

In this chapter, you will begin learning techniques for analyzing two variables together, **bivariate** (two variable) analysis. Bivariate analysis allows us to examine relationships between variables to answer questions such as, What is the effect of one variable on another? and, Which characteristics of one variable are generally associated with which characteristics of a second variable? We have already started thinking about relationships among variables while working with the General Social Survey data. In the previous chapters we used the Split File command to separate the data into groups to answer questions like the following:

- Do households with children have more wage earners than households without children?

- Who works more hours—males or females?

- Are White Americans more likely to be satisfied with their financial situations than Black Americans?

As with the statistical techniques we have used so far, we can see applications of bivariate analysis around us every day. During the presidential elections of 1996, in which Bill Clinton (Democrat) ran against Bob Dole (Republican), the media paid a great deal of attention to a so-called gender gap in politics. Women were widely believed to be more sympathetic than men to Democratic candidates and issues, whereas men were regarded as being more sympathetic to Republican ones. In an interview on the *McNeil-Lehrer News Hour,* Loleta Didrickson, Illinois delegate to the Republican national convention, commented,

> Well, I do believe that there is a gender gap. Polls are showing us that that's true. White males are attracted to the Republican Party. So now we have to

roll up our sleeves and make certain that our message is pointed to women and minorities.

In effect, Ms. Didrickson was hypothesizing a relationship between two variables, sex and political affiliation, in which men are more likely than women to be Republicans. The "News to Use" article in this chapter explores the gender gap further using bivariate analysis to see whether it is true that women were more likely than men to support Bill Clinton in his campaign for the Presidency. Bivariate analysis could also answer questions such as, Are Black Americans more likely to be Democrats than White Americans? and, If there is a difference, is it large or small?

To answer these questions, we can turn to one of the most useful techniques of statistical analysis, the construction of contingency tables. A contingency table is a very simple yet very powerful tool for examining the associations between the values or categories of variables like *sex* and *political affiliation*. To see an example of what a contingency table looks like, go to Table 7.2 and look at the chart at the bottom, which is a contingency table drawn from the 1996 General Social Survey showing the relationship between sex and party affiliation.

As a general rule, we can do contingency table analysis with any combination of nominal, ordinal, or numerical variables. As a practical matter, however, contingency tables are more difficult to interpret when you work with variables that have large numbers of categories. To begin with, we will keep our tables simple by working with variables that have only a few categories each.

Skills Practice 1   Write three questions that you could answer using General Social Survey variables. Identify the independent and dependent variables in each of your questions.

NEWS TO USE: Statistics in the "Real" World

Portrait of the Electorate: The Vote Under a Microscope[1]

MARJORIE CONNELLY

As in 1992, Bill Clinton won re-election [in 1996] without a majority of the popular vote. He was able to hold on to the support of many of the demo-graphic groups who elected him President in the first place and, in some cases, increase his share of their votes. Women, blacks, young voters, Democrats and liberals all gave Mr. Clinton a majority of their votes. He did well with swing groups, like independents and suburbanites. Bob Dole's best showing was with conservatives, Republicans and

[1]*The New York Times on the Web,*
<http://www.nytimes.com/library/politics/elect-port.html>.

white Protestants. Ross Perot received only 7%, down from 19% in 1992. . . .

The exit polls used to draw this portrait of voters are based on large numbers of respondents, making it possible to measure the preferences of some groups, like Jewish and Asian voters, or young women or conservative Democrats, whose portion of the voting population makes them too small to examine in typical telephone surveys.

THE GENDER GAP

The gender gap, the difference between a candidate's votes from men and his votes from women, was first noted in 1980, when men were 8 percentage points more likely to support Ronald Reagan than women were. Since then, the gender gap has ranged from 4 to 7 points in magnitude. This year there is an 11-point gap among Mr. Clinton's voters. A gender gap is seen in all age groups, from 17 points between men and women under 30, to 8 points for those aged 45 to 59. The gender gap persists even among black voters, who supported Mr. Clinton very strongly over all.

PARTY IDENTIFICATION AND IDEOLOGY

In the 1996 election, Mr. Clinton was more successful at holding the votes of self-described Democrats than he was the last time around. In the end Mr. Dole was supported by most Republicans. But while Democrats who described themselves as conservative strongly supported their party's ticket, Republicans who characterized their political ideology as liberal were closely divided between Mr. Clinton and Mr. Dole.

Independent voters in 1992 split their votes evenly among the three candidates, but this year only 17% of them supported Mr. Perot, while Mr. Clinton's share of their vote increased to 43%. Mr. Clinton did particularly well with liberal and moderate independents, while Mr. Dole was favored by independents who described themselves as conservative.

POCKETBOOK CONCERNS

Incumbents usually win the support of voters who say their own finances have improved during a President's tenure. Four years ago, for example, George Bush was backed by voters who said their family's finances were better than four years earlier, and Mr. Clinton won the support of those who characterized their situation as declining. This year, the reverse was true. Mr. Clinton, the incumbent, got two-thirds of the votes from those who said their personal economics had improved, while Bob Dole won the support of people whose economic condition had deteriorated.

Over all, the number of people who see their economic situation as worsening dropped from a third of all voters to a fifth, and those who perceive their finances in a positive fashion increased from a quarter to a third of all voters.

HOW THE DATA WERE COLLECTED

Data for 1996 were collected by Voter News Service based on questionnaires completed by 16,627 voters leaving 300 polling places around the nation on Election Day. Data for 1992 were collected by Voter Research and Surveys based on questionnaires completed by 15,490 voters.

UNDERSTANDING A CONTINGENCY TABLE

Contingency tables, or crosstabs (short for crosstabulations) in SPSS lingo, display data in such a way that we can look at whether or not one variable (referred to as the **independent variable**) *seems to be* having an effect or influence on a second variable (the **dependent variable**). Does one's sex (an independent variable) have any effect on one's political affiliation (the dependent variable)? The difference between saying that one variable *seems to be having an effect* on another and saying that one variable *causes* changes in another was discussed in the first chapter. It bears repeating, because it is important to understand that we are not usually able to conclude from single contingency tables whether one variable is causing changes in a second variable. We can only tell whether there is an association or relationship between the two variables. More precisely, we can tell whether the differences in response to the categories (or values) of one variable are associated with or related to differences of response to the categories (or values) of a second variable.

In Chapter 4, we learned to approach questions like these using the Split File feature in SPSS and then finding frequency distributions.

Skills Practice 2 Split your file (click on Data then Split File) using the variable *sex,* then find frequency distributions (using the command path Analyze ➡ Descriptive Statistics ➡ Frequencies) for the variable you created in Chapter 4, *partyaf.* You should get distributions like the ones in Table 7.1. Do you see a difference between males and females in their political party affiliations? How can you tell? (The answers follow.)

By focusing on the differences in the valid percentages between males and females for the categories of the variable *partyaf,* you probably noticed that a larger percentage of women than men say they are Democrats (38.8% compared to 27.3%), and a larger percentage of men (31.2% for men vs. 25.2% for women) say they're Republicans. A higher percentage of men than women (40.1% vs. 34.5%) say they're Independents. There are no differences between men and women reporting affiliation with some "Other" party.

Another, more efficient, way to explore the same relationship is by using a single table, like the one in Table 7.2, that shows us the categories of the variable *partyaf* broken down by the variable *sex* in one chart.

Notice the similarities between Table 7.2 and the frequency distributions in Table 7.1. The contingency table for the variables *sex* and *partyaf* is simply a combined display of information from the frequency distributions in Table 7.1. For the variable *sex,* the information in the first column of Table 7.2, Male, is identical to the information in the frequency distribution (Frequency and Valid Percent columns) for males; the information in the second column, Female, is identical to the information in the Frequency and Valid Percent columns for females.

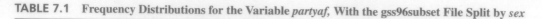

TABLE 7.1 Frequency Distributions for the Variable *partyaf,* With the gss96subset File Split by *sex*

PARTYAF recoded party identification[a]

		Frequency	Percent	Valid Percent	Cumulative Percent
Valid	1 Democrat	(350)	27.2	(27.3)	27.3
	2 Independent	514	40.0	40.1	67.3
	3 Republican	400	31.1	31.2	98.5
	4 Other	19	1.5	1.5	100.0
	Total	1283	99.8	100.0	
Missing	9 DK	2	.2		
Total		1285	100.0		

a. SEX RESPONDENTS SEX = 1 MALE

PARTYAF recoded party identification[a]

		Frequency	Percent	Valid Percent	Cumulative Percent
Valid	1 Democrat	(627)	38.7	(38.8)	38.8
	2 Independent	557	34.4	34.5	73.3
	3 Republican	407	25.1	25.2	98.5
	4 Other	24	1.5	1.5	100.0
	Total	1615	99.8	100.0	
Missing	9 DK	4	.2		
Total		1619	100.0		

a. SEX RESPONDENTS SEX = 2 FEMALE

PARTYAF recoded party identification * SEX RESPONDENTS SEX Crosstabulation

			SEX RESPONDENTS SEX		Total
			1 MALE	2 FEMALE	
PARTYAF recoded party identification	1 Democrat	Count	350	627	977
		% within SEX RESPONDENTS SEX	27.3%	38.8%	33.7%
	2 Independent	Count	514	557	1071
		% within SEX RESPONDENTS SEX	40.1%	34.5%	37.0%
	3 Republican	Count	400	407	807
		% within SEX RESPONDENTS SEX	31.2%	25.2%	27.8%
	4 Other	Count	19	24	43
		% within SEX RESPONDENTS SEX	1.5%	1.5%	1.5%
Total		Count	1283	1615	2898
		% within SEX RESPONDENTS SEX	100.0%	100.0%	100.0%

TABLE 7.2 Contingency Table for the Variables *partyaf* and *sex* in the gss96subset File

Let's look at Table 7.2 in a little more detail. In each of the squares or **cells** under the column headings Male and Female, you see a **cell frequency.** In the first cell, the number 350 is the number of respondents who are both male and Democrats. In addition, there is a column percentage. The percentage, 27.3%, in the first cell is identical to the valid percent for the category Democrat, in the frequency distribution for males in Table 7.1. Now let's turn our attention to the format of the contingency table.

The Independent and Dependent Variables

Notice how the two variables, *sex* and *party affiliation,* are displayed. The independent variable, *sex,* is displayed across the top of the table, and its categories—male and female—form the columns of the table. The categories of the dependent variable, *party affiliation,* are displayed down the left side of the table and its categories—Democrat, Independent, Republican, and so on—form the rows of the table. Generally, contingency tables are set up in this fashion (although you will undoubtedly see many exceptions in newspapers, magazines, and other publications).[2] Deciding how one variable stands in relation to another (as an independent or dependent variable) is discussed in the next "Avoiding Common Pitfalls."

Cell Frequencies and Column Percentages

Look at the numbers in each of the table's squares (or cells). There are two of them in each cell, a cell frequency and a column percentage.

Frequencies   A cell frequency (called the cell count) is simply the number of respondents who belong in each cell. When we look at the first cell, the cell frequency tells us there are 350 males who identify themselves as Democrats.

Column percentages   The percentage you see in each cell is called a **column percentage.** (You may also see these percentages referred to as "percentages on the independent variable" or "percentages down.") They are computed by dividing the cell frequency by the number of responses in the column (the column total) and multiplying by 100. The column percentage (350 divided by the column total, 1283, and multiplied by 100) is 27.3%. This means that 27.3% of the male respondents identify themselves as Democrats.

---

[2]It is possible to set up a contingency table with the categories of the dependent variable across the top of the table and the categories of the independent variable down the side. When a table is set up this way, the cell percentages have to be calculated differently than when the table is set up with the categories of the independent variable in the columns.

Reading down the column labeled Male is like reading a frequency distribution. We can see that more males identify themselves as Independents than as Democrats, Republicans, or Other. 40.1% of the male respondents identify themselves as Independents, whereas 27.3% identify themselves as Democrats, 31.2% as Republicans, and 1.5% as Other. Men are a little more likely to say they are Independents than Democrats, Republicans, or members of some other party.

Unlike males, females are a little more likely to say they are Democrats than Independents, Republicans, or Other. Looking down the column for females, we can see that 38.8% of the female respondents identify themselves as Democrats, whereas 34.5% identify themselves as Independents, 25.2% as Republicans, and 1.5% as Other.

So far we have emphasized reading contingency tables down the columns like frequency distributions. It is even more important for assessing associations between variables to read across the rows of a contingency table. Reading across the rows allows us to look for variations in responses to a dependent variable by categories of the independent variable. What we are looking for are differences in percentages across the rows. For example, reading across the top row of the table for the association between sex and political affiliation, we learn that larger percentages of women identify themselves as Democrats as compared to men. Consequently, we learn there is a relationship between the categories of the independent and dependent variables: women are more likely than men to say they are Democrats. We will be working on reading across the rows of contingency tables throughout this chapter.

Column Marginals and Column Marginal Percentages

The summary statistics labeled Total at the bottom of each column tell us how many of the respondents are male (1283) and female (1615). These totals of the number of respondents in each column are called **column marginals.** In addition, there is a column marginal percentage, 100% for each column. If you add up the column percentages in each cell, you should get at or close to 100%. (You may not get exactly 100% due to the rounding that occurs in each cell.)

Row Marginals and Row Marginal Percentages

The totals at the end of each horizontal row tell us how many (and what percentage) of the respondents fall into each of the categories of the dependent variable. In essence, these row totals—called **row marginals**—are a frequency distribution of the dependent variable *party affiliation.* We can tell how many respondents (ignoring whether they are male or female) call themselves Democrats (977), Independents (1071), Republicans (807), or Other (43), and what percentage of all respondents say they are Democrats (33.7%), Independents (37.0 %), Republicans (27.8%), or Other (1.5%).

The Table Total (N)

The number in the bottom right corner of the table, 2,898, tells us that there were 2,898 respondents who answered both the sex question *and* the party affiliation question. This number can be found by adding up the row marginals *or* the column marginals (but not both together), and it constitutes *N* for a contingency table (total number of respondents).

At the conclusion of the next section, you can test your ability to analyze a contingency table on your own.

PRODUCING CONTINGENCY TABLES USING SPSS

To create your own contingency table using SPSS, use the Crosstabs command, which can be found by using the command path Analyze ➡ Descriptive Statistics. To illustrate the process, let's see whether there is a gap in party affiliation by region of the country in which one resides.

Skills Practice 3 Recode the variable *region* into four new categories: Northeast (New England and Middle Atlantic), Midwest (E. Nor. Central and W. Nor. Central), Southeast (South Atlantic, E. Sou. Central, and W. Sou. Central), and West (Mountain and Pacific). Call the new variable *rcregion*. Remember the recoding process:

- Prepare a recode diagram for your variable. Use the command path Analyze ➡ Descriptive Statistics ➡ Frequencies to produce a frequencies distribution for the variable *region* and use the frequency distribution to prepare a recode diagram.
- Use the command path Transform ➡ Recode ➡ Into Different Variables to create your new variable. Call it *rcregion*. (See the SPSS Guide, "Recoding Variables," in Chapter 4 for help with the Recode Into Different Variables command.)
- Use Define Variable to assign new value labels and to set the variable type, column format, missing values, and level of measurement. (See the SPSS Guide in Chapter 3 for help with the Define Variables command.)
- Use the command path Analyze ➡ Descriptive Statistics ➡ Frequencies to produce a frequency distribution for your new variable, *rcregion*. Check it against the frequency distribution for *region* to make sure your recoding is correct. (You can also check it against the answer for Skills Practice 3 at the end of this chapter.)
- Save your new variable in your gss96subset file (by clicking on the Save File icon).

SPSS Guide: Producing a Contingency Table

Open the gss96subset data file. Then click on Analyze and Descriptive Statistics. From the list of options that appears, click on Crosstabs.

The Crosstabs dialog box opens.

❶ Select your dependent variable (*partyaf*): scroll down to *partyaf*, highlight it with your mouse, and click on the arrow key, ▶, which points at the box labeled Row.

❷ Select your independent variable (*rcregion*): scroll down to *rcregion*, highlight it with your mouse, and click on the arrow key, ▶, which points at the box labeled Column.

❸ Click on Cells.

❹ In the Crosstabs: Cell Display window, look under Percentages and click on Column.

❺ Click on Continue to return to the Crosstabs dialog box.

❻ At the Crosstabs dialog box, click on OK.

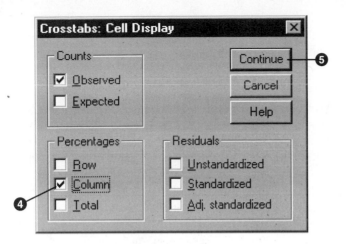

A table like the one in Table 7.3 should appear in your Output window.

TABLE 7.3   Contingency Table for *partyaf* and *rcregion* Using the gss96 Subset File

PARTYAF recoded party identification * RCREGION recoded region variable Crosstabulation

| | | | \multicolumn{4}{c}{RCREGION recoded region variable} | |
			1 Northeast	2 Midwest	3 Southeast	4 West	Total
PARTYAF recoded party identification	1 Democrat	Count	202	227	345	203	977
		% within RCREGION recoded region variable	35.3%	32.6%	34.1%	32.9%	33.7%
	2 Independent	Count	231	278	339	223	1071
		% within RCREGION recoded region variable	40.4%	39.9%	33.5%	36.1%	37.0%
	3 Republican	Count	131	182	316	178	807
		% within RCREGION recoded region variable	22.9%	26.1%	31.2%	28.8%	27.8%
	4 Other	Count	8	10	12	13	43
		% within RCREGION recoded region variable	1.4%	1.4%	1.2%	2.1%	1.5%
Total		Count	572	697	1012	617	2898
		% within RCREGION recoded region variable	100.0%	100.0%	100.0%	100.0%	100.0%

Skills Practice 4   See if you understand Table 7.3 by answering the following questions:

A.   How many of the respondents who live in the Northeast are Democrats? How many call themselves Independents, Republicans, Other? Continue your analysis for each category of the independent variable (Midwest, Southeast, and West).

B.   What percentage of the respondents who live in the Northeast say they are Democrats? What percentage identify themselves as Independents, Republicans, Other? Continue your analysis for each category of the independent variable (Midwest, Southeast, and West).

C.   What percentage of all respondents (those who answered both the question about party affiliation and the question about region) say they are Democrats, Independents, Republicans, or Other?

D.   What is the total number of respondents for the table (*N*)?

E.   How many of the respondents say they are from the Northeast, the Midwest, the Southeast, and the West?

F.   If you were a Republican and wanted to live in an area where you would be likely to meet other like-minded people, where should you live?

G.   On the other hand, if you were more interested in living in a politically heterogeneous part of the country, where should you go?

Avoiding Common Pitfalls: Deciding Which Variable Is Independent in Relation to the Other   Sometimes it's hard to figure out how to set up contingency tables using SPSS, because it isn't always clear which variable in a relationship should be the dependent variable and which one should be the independent variable. For some sets of variables, it appears that neither variable is independent or dependent in relation to the other. How can you tell what to do? There are several rules of thumb you can use to decide how to treat variables:

Logic of the relationship between the variables   There has to be a logical reason to think that the independent variable can influence the dependent variable. Can you think of *how* one variable influences the other? For instance, with the example we used at the beginning of the chapter, the relationship between sex and party affiliation, can you think of reasons why one's gender might have an influence on one's political affiliations? One explanation may be that Democrats are perceived to be more likely to support issues of concern to women, like education or child care. On the other hand, Republicans may be perceived to be more likely to support issues of concern to men, like defense and balancing the federal budget. One way to check yourself is to look at the relationship between two variables in reverse. Does it make any sense to say that one's political affiliation has an effect on one's sex? No, so we are left with treating the variable *sex* as the independent variable.

Time   Independent variables must happen in time before dependent variables. In our example, one's sex is assigned (one's sexual identity develops) before one's party affiliation.

Ascribed vs. achieved characteristics   **Ascribed characteristics** (characteristics one inherits or over which one has little or no control) are almost always independent variables. Ascribed variables are variables such as *sex, ethnicity,* and *age.* Some variables may be treated as ascribed (or inherited traits) even though they can be changed, such as the socioeconomic status of one's family of origin (the family a person was born into and grew up in) or the religion of one's family of origin.[3] **Achieved characteristics** are often (but not always) treated as dependent variables. Achieved characteristics are those attributes that one develops or earns as one grows up, "acquired through some combination of choice, effort, and ability" (Ferrante, 1995, p. 303).[4] The attitudes one develops or behaviors one engages in are achieved characteristics, as are the years of education one completes and the socioeconomic status one attains as an adult.

What if neither variable seems to be independent in relation to the other? Sometimes two variables in a relationship are neither independent nor dependent in relation to the other, although they may be associated with one another. For example, researchers are often interested in the attitudes of those they study. However, one attitude does not necessarily cause or have an effect on another attitude. If one is liberal, for example, one may be pro-choice on the issue of abortion and also more likely to favor affirmative action. However, it doesn't make much sense to say that one's attitude toward abortion causes one to be more or less supportive of affirmative action. These attitudes are associated with one another, though. Among those who are pro-choice, it is more likely that you will find attitudes favorable to affirmative action. Relationships in which the two variables being analyzed are neither independent nor dependent in relation to one another are called **symmetrical** relationships or associations. (The importance of this concept will be clearer when we start looking at statistical measures of association.) In these cases, it usually doesn't matter which variable you treat as independent. Either variable could be the column variable for a contingency table. However, you may decide to treat one variable as independent in relation to another based on the specific research question you are trying to answer.

_____

[3]Most introductory sociology texts discuss these concepts.
[4]*Sociology: A Global Perspective* by Joan Ferrante, 1995, Belmont, CA: Wadsworth.

Skills Practice 5   Using the gss96subset file, produce two more contingency tables to see whether there are other "gaps" in political affiliations besides the ones for gender and region.

A. Produce a contingency table for the relationship between religion (the variable *relig*) and party affiliation (the variable *partyaf*).

B. Produce a contingency table to examine the relationship between age (using *agecat*) and party affiliation.

SETTING UP A CONTINGENCY TABLE BY HAND

To practice setting up a contingency table by hand, we will use the randomly selected set of 25 responses to the General Social Survey for the variables *sex* and *political affiliation* in Table 7.4. Even though you will be using the same variables we have been analyzing with SPSS, you may get a somewhat different outcome because these examples draw on a very small subset of the GSS sample.

Before you begin constructing a table, notice the total number of cases you will be dealing with. This number, *N* for the contingency table, allows us to check our work when we are finished and make sure we have counted all of our respondents. There are 25 cases in the random sample in Table 7.4.

To set up a contingency table, assign the categories of one of the two variables to the columns of the table, and assign the categories of the other to the rows, depending on which variable is to be regarded as independent and which variable is to be regarded as dependent. In this example, *sex* is the independent variable and *party affiliation* is the dependent variable. Your table should be set up as the one following, with *sex* as the column variable and *party affiliation* as the row variable.

Party Affiliation	Sex	
	Male	Female
Democrat		
Independent		
Republican		
Other		

Then fill in each of the cells (squares) of the table with the number of respondents who meet the criteria for each cell. For example, in the first cell

TABLE 7.4 Randomly Selected Sample of 25 Cases From the gss96subset File for the Variables *sex* and *partyaf*

Case Summaries

	SEX RESPONDENTS SEX	PARTYAF Party Affiliation
1	FEMALE	Republican
2	MALE	Republican
3	FEMALE	Democrat
4	FEMALE	Democrat
5	FEMALE	Democrat
6	MALE	Democrat
7	MALE	Independent
8	MALE	Other
9	FEMALE	Democrat
10	FEMALE	Democrat
11	MALE	Independent
12	FEMALE	Democrat
13	FEMALE	Independent
14	FEMALE	Democrat
15	MALE	Independent
16	FEMALE	Republican
17	MALE	Republican
18	FEMALE	Independent
19	FEMALE	Republican
20	MALE	Democrat
21	MALE	Independent
22	FEMALE	Republican
23	MALE	Independent
24	FEMALE	Democrat
25	MALE	Republican
Total N	25	25

(the cell in the upper left corner), we would enter the number of respondents who are both male and Democrat. If we count down our table of data in Table 7.4, we see that there are 2. Moving over one cell to the right, we count the number of respondents who are female and Democrat. There are 8. Going on to the next row, we count the number of respondents who are male and Independent (5). We continue with this process until all of the cells of the table are filled in. (If there are no respondents who meet the criteria for a particular cell, we enter 0. (SPSS leaves these cells blank, indicating no respondents for a particular cell.) Now your table should look like the one here.

Party Affiliation	Sex	
	Male	Female
Democrat	2	8
Independent	5	2
Republican	3	4
Other	1	0

The last step in the process of completing the table involves finding the column and row marginals, computing the table total, figuring the column percentages, and computing the row marginal percentages. The steps for completing the table are compiled in the following list:

To find the	Do the following:	Use the formula
Column marginals	Add up the number of respondents in each column.	
Row marginals	Add up the number of respondents in each row.	
Table total	Add up the row marginals; check your answer by adding up the column marginals (you should get the same answer either way).	
Row marginal percentages	Divide the total number of respondents in each row by N (the table total) and multiply by 100.	(Row f/N) $\times$ 100, where f is the row marginal frequency
Column percentages	Divide each cell frequency (the number of respondents in each cell) by its column total, then multiply by 100.	(Cell f/column total) $\times$ 100, where cell f is the cell frequency
Column marginal percentages	Add up the column percentages for each column.	

Now your table should look like the following:

Political Affiliation	Sex		Row Marginals
	Male	Female	
Democrat	2 (18.2%)	8 (57.1%)	10 (40.0%)
Independent	5 (45.5%)	2 (14.3%)	7 (28.0%)
Republican	3 (27.3%)	4 (28.6%)	7 (28.0%)
Other	1 (9.1%)	0 (0.0%)	1 (4.0%)
Totals	11 (100.1%)	14 (100.0%)	$N = 25$ (100.0%)

✓ **Checking Your Work** How can you make sure the table you've created is correct? There are several ways to check your work.

- Make sure the N for the table matches the number of cases you have in your list of raw scores. If it doesn't, check your cell frequencies and your row and column totals.

- Your column marginal percentages should be at or near 100%. If they aren't, check the work you did to calculate your column percentages.

- Your row marginal percentages should add up to or be near 100%. If not, check your computations.

Skills Practice 6   Use the set of data in the following table to construct a contingency table. The data are a randomly selected sample of 25 cases from the gss96subset file for the variables *sex* and *partyaf*.

Case Summaries

	SEX RESPONDENTS SEX	PARTYAF Party Affiliation
1	FEMALE	Independent
2	MALE	Democrat
3	FEMALE	Democrat
4	MALE	Independent
5	MALE	Democrat
6	FEMALE	Democrat
7	FEMALE	Republican
8	FEMALE	Republican
9	FEMALE	Independent
10	MALE	Republican
11	MALE	Democrat
12	MALE	Independent
13	FEMALE	Republican
14	MALE	Republican
15	MALE	Democrat
16	MALE	Independent
17	MALE	Republican
18	FEMALE	Republican
19	MALE	Independent
20	MALE	Independent
21	MALE	Democrat
22	FEMALE	Independent
23	FEMALE	Democrat
24	FEMALE	Independent
25	FEMALE	Independent
Total N	25	25

INTERPRETING CONTINGENCY TABLES

As we have already seen, contingency tables help us find the patterns of association between variables in sets of data. They are a very commonly used and powerful tool. Academic researchers are not the only ones who use them; you will undoubtedly find examples in nearly every daily newspaper or weekly magazine.

Finding the Patterns in a Contingency Table

The most important part of interpreting a contingency table is understanding what it is telling us about the association between two variables. Interpreting a table can be divided into two parts: understanding the nature of an association and assessing its strength.

Understanding the nature of the association   When researchers construct contingency tables, it is usually with some question in mind, like the one we have been working with. Is there a gender gap in politics? You probably already have a sense of the answer from previous exercises. No doubt you have concluded that women are more likely than men to be Democrats than Republicans, Independents, or Other, whereas men are more likely than women to be Independents than Democrats, Republicans, or Other. It is obvious that there is a gender gap.

By reading *across* the rows of the dependent variable, we noticed the differences in the column percentages to assess the association between the variables. One way to focus on the differences in column percentages across the rows of a contingency table is to look across each row (each category of the dependent variable), and circle the highest percentage (not counting the row marginals column). See the example in Table 7.5.

Let's begin our analysis by looking at the first category of the dependent variable, Democrat. We can see that women are more likely to be Democrats than are men. How can we tell that? Because the percentage of women who are Democrats is higher than the percentage of men who are Democrats. By the same token, if we look at the third category of the dependent variable, Republican, we can see that men are more likely to say they are Republicans than are women, because the percentage of men who say they are Republicans is higher than the percentage of women who say they are Republicans. On the other hand, reading across the row labeled Independent, we can see that men are more likely than women to say they are Independents, because the percentage of men who say they are Independent is larger than the percentage of women who say that. What about the category Other? Men are as likely as women to identify with some other party.

TABLE 7.5   Contingency Table for the Association Between Sex and Party Affiliation for the gss96subset File

PARTYAF recoded party identification * SEX RESPONDENTS SEX Crosstabulation

			SEX RESPONDENTS SEX		Total
			1 MALE	2 FEMALE	
PARTYAF recoded party identification	1 Democrat	Count	350	627	977
		% within SEX RESPONDENTS SEX	27.3%	38.8%	33.7%
	2 Independent	Count	514	557	1071
		% within SEX RESPONDENTS SEX	40.1%	34.5%	37.0%
	3 Republican	Count	400	407	807
		% within SEX RESPONDENTS SEX	31.2%	25.2%	27.8%
	4 Other	Count	19	24	43
		% within SEX RESPONDENTS SEX	1.5%	1.5%	1.5%
Total		Count	1283	1615	2898
		% within SEX RESPONDENTS SEX	100.0%	100.0%	100.0%

You may be noticing that contingency tables are generally interpreted in sentences that describe relationships between variables. Generally, one interprets contingency tables in statements that link the independent and dependent variables, much like a hypothesis statement. These statements can take several forms, as illustrated in Box 7.1.

Understanding the strength of the association   A question that remains is: How large is the gender gap? Using Table 7.5, we have already determined that female respondents are more likely to say they are Democrats than are male respondents, whereas male respondents are more likely to say that they are Independents. How big is the gender gap? *How much* more likely is it that women will say they are Democrats? *How much* more likely is it that men will say they are Independents? The answer resides in the size of the differences in the percentages when you read across the rows of the contingency table. If the size of the difference is large, then the gap is large and the association is strong. If the size of the difference is small, then the gap is small and the association is weak. The differences in the percentages across the rows in Table 7.5 are fairly small, so we would describe the relationship between the two variables as somewhat weak.

To get at the implications of this statement, we can make an analogy to gambling. If there was a way to maximize our likelihood of winning a bet, we would use it, wouldn't we? In one sense, that is exactly what a contingency table can help us do. Contingency tables help us determine how likely it is that, if we know something about one variable (*sex*, in this example), we can correctly guess a second variable (i.e., *political affiliation*). The larger are the differences in the percentages across the rows, the better are the odds of predicting the dependent variable if one knows the independent variable.

Suppose I show you the table in Table 7.5, and then I select at random one female respondent and one male respondent from the General Social Survey. Next I ask you to bet $100 on the person most likely to be a Democrat. Knowing what you know now, you would probably (and correctly) bet on the woman. There are 38.8 chances in 100 that the woman is, in fact, a Democrat. (How do we know? Because 38.8% of the female respondents said they are Democrats.) Likewise, there are 27.3 chances in 100 that the male is a Democrat. If you bet on the woman the odds of winning are better, but far from perfect. How much better are the odds, in your opinion? If they aren't much better, then we can conclude that the gap, although it exists, is small. If the odds are a lot better, then we can conclude that the gap is large.

Is this an important difference? That depends on the context in which one is interpreting the data. If I am a politician in a close race, the difference may be important to me, because whether I win or lose could hinge on only a few percentage points of the vote. If I am a strategist for one of the parties, trying to decide whether it is worth my time and money to convince more men that they should become Democrats, I may decide that the difference isn't very large and that I can better use my resources.

Skills Practice 8   Use SPSS to produce a contingency table with the variables *race* and *partyaf* to analyze a different kind of gap—the race gap, differences in party affiliation by race. Describe the nature and the strength of the relationship between race and party affiliation.

Interpreting Tables With Ordinal or Numerical Variables

Contingency tables in which you are examining the relationships between ordinal variables, numerical variables, or some combination of the two can be interpreted a little differently than tables in which one or both variables are nominal. In these cases, we can look for **linear** (straight line) **associations** between the variables, associations that can be interpreted along the lines of the models in Box 7.2.

Generally, a linear association can be detected by circling the highest percentage in each row of a contingency table. If the values line up diagonally—top left to bottom right or bottom left to top right—then you have a linear association. In linear associations, increases in the values of one variable are associated with increases or decreases in the values of a second variable. Two illustrations follow that use hypothetical variables, which I have simply labeled as an Independent Variable and a Dependent Variable. In each row, I have marked with an X the cell with the highest percentage.

Positive associations   Figure 7.1 shows you what a linear association might look like in which the diagonal runs top left to bottom right—a **positive association** between the variables. Positive associations are ones in which increases in the values of one variable are associated with increases in the values of a second variable, like the association between education and income I used previously. The more education respondents have, the more money they are likely to earn. Conversely, the less education respondents have, the less money they are likely to earn.

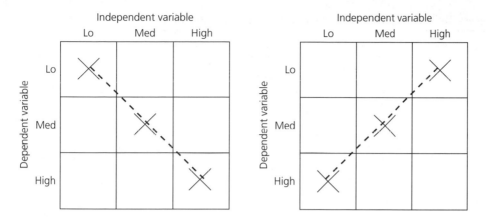

Figure 7.1 Positive association.

Figure 7.2 Negative association.

Negative associations   Figure 7.2 shows you what a linear association might look like in which the diagonal runs bottom left to top right—a **negative association.** Negative associations are ones in which increases in the values of one variable are associated with decreases in the values of a second variable, or vice versa. A negative association would be interpreted as follows: The more education respondents have, the fewer the children they are likely to have. Conversely, the less education respondents have, the more children they are likely to have.

To illustrate what a linear (and in this case, positive) association might look like, examine the contingency table for the variables *degree* and *life* to answer the question: Does level of education have an effect on perceptions of life as exciting or dull? (See Table 7.6.) Notice that by circling the highest percentage in each row (excluding the row marginal percentage), a diagonal line can be drawn through the circled boxes, running from the upper left corner to the lower right corner. The diagonal line tells us we have a positive association that can be interpreted as follows:

> The more education respondents have, the more likely they are to think their lives are exciting (and, conversely, the less education respondents have, the less likely they are to think their lives are exciting).

Skills Practice 9   Look at the relationships between the respondents' educational achievements (*degree*) and their fathers' and mothers' educational achievements (*padeg* and *madeg*). Are the associations you find positive or negative? How can you tell? Write a sentence for each table to describe the association.

TABLE 7.6   Contingency Table for the Variables *degree* and *life* From the gss96subset File

LIFE IS LIFE EXCITING OR DULL * DEGREE RS HIGHEST DEGREE Crosstabulation

| | | | DEGREE RS HIGHEST DEGREE | | | | | |
			0 LT HIGH SCHOOL	1 HIGH SCHOOL	2 JUNIOR COLLEGE	3 BACHELOR	4 GRADUATE	Total
LIFE IS LIFE EXCITING OR DULL	1 DULL	Count	34	43	1	2		80
		% within DEGREE RS HIGHEST DEGREE	11.2%	4.2%	.8%	.7%		4.2%
	2 ROUTINE	Count	162	502	55	101	47	867
		% within DEGREE RS HIGHEST DEGREE	53.3%	49.6%	46.8%	33.0%	30.3%	45.7%
	3 EXCITING	Count	108	467	64	203	108	950
		% within DEGREE RS HIGHEST DEGREE	35.5%	46.1%	53.3%	66.3%	69.7%	50.1%
Total		Count	304	1012	120	306	155	1897
		% within DEGREE RS HIGHEST DEGREE	100.0%	100.0%	100.0%	100.0%	100.0%	100.0%

Interpreting tables with nonlinear associations   Not all associations involving ordinal or numerical variables will be linear. In fact, most won't be. You will find any number of other patterns in data, and you have to be open to the possibility of nonlinear associations, too. It is important to interpret a set of data as it presents itself, not as you would like it to be, expect it to be, or wish it were. For example, you may have tables that show associations in any of a number of patterns or different combinations. (When you are working with real data, the possibilities are limitless.) Figures 7.3–7.6 illustrate some of the possible "shapes" that associations can take.

As an illustration of a nonlinear association, let's look at a contingency table for the variables *political affiliation* (using *polaf,* a variable you created with the recode procedure in Chapter 5) and *degree* (Table 7.7). Note that if you circle the highest column percentage in each row (excluding the row marginal percentage), the line that best fits the data is a curved one—a **curvilinear relationship** or association. The data appear linear up to a point (the dotted line), but a curved line (the solid one) is the one that best fits through all of the circled boxes.

How do you interpret a table like this? First, you can draw out the general pattern in the data:

> The more education the respondents have, the more likely they are to identify themselves as either liberal or conservative, whereas those respondents with less education are more likely to call themselves moderates.

Next, look to see how consistent the general pattern seems to be. The consistency of the pattern tells us how strong the association is: The more consistent is the pattern, the stronger is the association; the less consistent is the pattern, the weaker is the association. Looking across the row of the first category of the dependent variable, Liberal, you can see that,

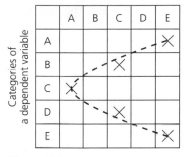

Figure 7.3 Categories of an independent variable.

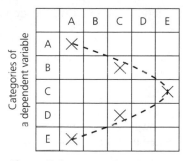

Figure 7.4 Categories of an independent variable.

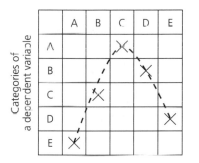

Figure 7.5 Categories of an independent variable.

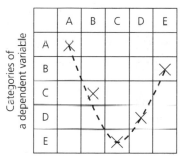

Figure 7.6 Categories of an independent variable.

TABLE 7.7 Contingency Table for the Variables *polaf* and *degree* in the gss96subset File

POLAF recoded political views * DEGREE RS HIGHEST DEGREE Crosstabulation

			DEGREE RS HIGHEST DEGREE					
			0 LT HIGH SCHOOL	1 HIGH SCHOOL	2 JUNIOR COLLEGE	3 BACHELOR	4 GRADUATE	Total
POLAF recoded political views	1 Liberal	Count	89	326	43	163	75	696
		% within DEGREE RS HIGHEST DEGREE	23.1%	21.9%	23.9%	35.3%	33.8%	25.4%
	2 Moderate	Count	164	631	67	119	62	1043
		% within DEGREE RS HIGHEST DEGREE	42.5%	42.4%	37.2%	25.8%	27.9%	38.1%
	3 Conservative	Count	133	531	70	180	85	999
		% within DEGREE RS HIGHEST DEGREE	34.5%	35.7%	38.9%	39.0%	38.3%	36.5%
Total		Count	386	1488	180	462	222	2738
		% within DEGREE RS HIGHEST DEGREE	100.0%	100.0%	100.0%	100.0%	100.0%	100.0%

in general, the more education respondents have, the more liberal they tend to be.

However, you should note the exception:

Respondents with less than high school educations are as likely to say they are liberal as those with junior college educations.

In the second category of the dependent variable, Moderate, the opposite trend is evident.

> As the respondents' education rises, the likelihood that the respondents are moderate decreases.

What are the exceptions to this general trend?

> Those respondents with graduate-level educations are more likely to be moderate than those with bachelor-level educations.

Skills Practice 10   What is the general trend of association in the third category of the dependent variable in Table 7.7, Conservative? Are there any exceptions to the general pattern? If so, what are they?

What conclusion can we now draw about the strength of the association? Given that we see a curvilinear relationship in the data, does it appear to be a very strong relationship?

> The fact that most rows of the dependent variable follow a pattern—as education goes up, political outlook is more polarized—suggests a fairly strong association. On the other hand, the trend isn't completely consistent across each of the rows of the dependent variable, suggesting that the relationship overall might be weak.

Later on, we will look at measures of association that are designed to help determine how strong these associations are likely to be.

Skills Practice 11   Analyze the associations between political affiliation (*polaf*) as a dependent variable and the following independent variables: *agecat, satfin,* and *pillok.* Write a paragraph for each table you create, describing the nature of the association and its direction and strength.

CONTROLLING FOR A THIRD VARIABLE

What Does "Control for a Third Variable" Mean?

Sometimes it is useful to examine relationships between two variables in the light of a third variable through a process of analysis called **elaboration.**

TABLE 7.8 Frequency Distribution for the Variable *vote92* in the gss96subset File

VOTE92 DID R VOTE IN 1992 ELECTION

		Frequency	Percent	Valid Percent	Cumulative Percent
Valid	1 VOTED	1907	65.7	66.8	66.8
	2 DID NOT VOTE	763	26.3	26.7	93.6
	3 NOT ELIGIBLE	184	6.3	6.4	100.0
	Total	2854	98.3	100.0	
Missing	4 REFUSED	10	.3		
	8 DK	38	1.3		
	9 NA	2	.1		
	Total	50	1.7		
Total		2904	100.0		

For example, in addition to looking at the association between gender and party affiliation, we may want to know whether the gender gap is likely to affect the outcome of an election. There may very well be a gender gap among those who identify themselves as Democrats, Republicans, or Independents, but now we want to know if the gap means anything as far as elections are concerned. Are women who vote more likely to be Democrats than men who vote? What about those who do not vote? If the gender gap is a factor in elections, then we would expect to find that, among those who vote, there are important differences between males and females. On the other hand, if the gender gap isn't a factor, then we would expect to find that, among those who vote, there are no real differences between men and women. To explore these associations, we can separate our sample into the categories of this third, or control, variable to examine voting behavior in the 1992 election (*vote92*).

To get an idea of what is happening to the data set when we control for a third variable, let's look at a frequency distribution for *vote92* (Table 7.8). Notice that the categories of the variable are Voted, Did Not Vote, and Not Eligible. The two categories of most interest to us are the first ones, Voted and Did Not Vote. When we control for a variable like *vote92,* we are, in effect, dividing our data set by the categories of the control variable, creating as many subsets of our data as there are categories of the control variable. In this case, using *vote92,* we are creating three subsets of data: one for Voted, one for Did Not Vote, and one for Not Eligible. Dividing the data this way allows us to examine the association between gender and party affiliation for each of our subsets, two of which are the voters and the nonvoters. We can now see whether there is a gender gap among those who voted in 1992 and whether there is a gender gap among nonvoters.

Creating Contingency Tables Using a Control Variable

To control for third variables (subdivide our data set by the categories of a variable), we return to the Crosstabs command in SPSS.

SPSS Guide: Producing Contingency Tables Using a Control Variable

At the SPSS Data Editor window, follow the command path Analyze ➡ Descriptive Statistics ➡ Crosstabs. At the Crosstabs dialog box, follow these steps:

① Select your dependent variable, *partyaf,* from the variables list. Put it in the Row box.

② Select your independent variable, *sex,* and put it in the Column box.

③ Select your control variable, *vote92.* Scroll down to it with your mouse, click on it, and then click on the arrow pointing at the Layer 1 of 1 box.

④ Click on Cells. When the Crosstabs: Cell Display window opens, look under Percentages, and click on Column. Then, click on Continue to return to the Crosstabs dialog box.

⑤ Click on OK.

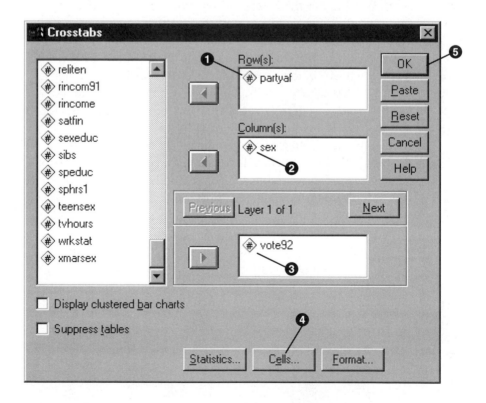

TABLE 7.9   Partial Tables for the Variables *sex* and *partyaf* With the Control Variable, *vote92,* for the gss96subset File

PARTYAF recoded party identification * SEX RESPONDENTS SEX * VOTE92 DID R VOTE IN 1992 ELECTION Crosstabulation

VOTE92 DID R VOTE IN 1992 ELECTION					SEX RESPONDENTS SEX		Total
					1 MALE	2 FEMALE	
1 VOTED	PARTYAF recoded party identification	1 Democrat		Count	245	479	724
				% within SEX RESPONDENTS SEX	29.9%	44.1%	38.0%
		2 Independent		Count	267	200	547
				% within SEX RESPONDENTS SEX	32.6%	25.8%	28.7%
		3 Republican		Count	299	310	609
				% within SEX RESPONDENTS SEX	36.5%	28.6%	32.0%
		4 Other		Count	9	16	25
				% within SEX RESPONDENTS SEX	1.1%	1.5%	1.3%
	Total			Count	820	1085	1905
				% within SEX RESPONDENTS SEX	100.0%	100.0%	100.0%
2 DID NOT VOTE	PARTYAF recoded party identification	1 Democrat		Count	82	111	193
				% within SEX RESPONDENTS SEX	23.6%	26.9%	25.4%
		2 Independent		Count	179	217	396
				% within SEX RESPONDENTS SEX	51.4%	52.5%	52.0%
		3 Republican		Count	77	79	156
				% within SEX RESPONDENTS SEX	22.1%	19.1%	20.5%
		4 Other		Count	10	6	16
				% within SEX RESPONDENTS SEX	2.9%	1.5%	2.1%
	Total			Count	348	413	761
				% within SEX RESPONDENTS SEX	100.0%	100.0%	100.0%
3 NOT ELIGIBLE	PARTYAF recoded party identification	1 Democrat		Count	19	28	47
				% within SEX RESPONDENTS SEX	20.0%	31.8%	25.7%
		2 Independent		Count	55	44	99
				% within SEX RESPONDENTS SEX	57.9%	50.0%	54.1%
		3 Republican		Count	21	15	36
				% within SEX RESPONDENTS SEX	22.1%	17.0%	19.7%
		4 Other		Count		1	1
				% within SEX RESPONDENTS SEX		1.1%	.5%
	Total			Count	95	88	183
				% within SEX RESPONDENTS SEX	100.0%	100.0%	100.0%

You should now be looking at a set of three tables—one table for each category of the control variable. They should look like Table 7.9. (The output looks like one large table, but note that it is really made up of several smaller tables—one for each of the categories of the control variable.) These smaller tables are also known as **partial tables** or simply "partials."

Interpreting contingency tables using a control variable   How do we make sense of all this information? What are we looking for? There are a couple of general patterns we should explore. First, we should look to see whether any association we saw between our variables of interest (without the influence of the control variable) is changed in any way across the categories of the control variable. Second, we should look to see in what way the association changes.

If the association weakens considerably, to the point where there is almost no association at all between the variables of interest across the categories of a third variable, we can conclude that the association between our variables of interest is a **spurious** one. This means that something else accounts for the dependent variable other than the independent variable. For example, if we were to find that the association between sex and party affiliation disappears when we control for voting behavior, then we can conclude that we are going down the wrong road in trying to explain differences in party affiliation on the basis of gender. We ought to be looking at participation in the political process as an alternative explanation of party affiliation.

On the other hand, we may see that an association between the two variables still exists, but the nature and/or strength of the association changes across the categories of the control variable. Situations in which the strength or nature of an association between two variables changes across the categories of the control variable are called **conditional associations.** The strength of an association is conditional upon the category of the third variable. We can expect to find many associations that are at least conditional.

To begin the process of elaboration, we can analyze the association between sex and party affiliation for *each category* of the control variable, starting with the voters and the nonvoters. Circle the highest percentage in each row of each table (not including the row marginal percentages or column marginal percentages). Commenting on the nature and the strength of the association in each table, we can make statements like the following:

Among those who voted, it appears that the gender gap is wider. Women are still more likely than men to say they are Democrats (44.1% vs. 29.9%). Male respondents remain more likely to be Independents (32.6%) and Republicans (36.5%) than are female respondents (25.8% and 28.6%, respectively).

Among those who did not vote, the gender gap is smaller. Females are only a little more likely to say they are Democrats (26.9%) than are males (23.6%). 51.4% of the male respondents identify themselves as Independents as compared to 52.5% of female respondents. Males are only slightly more likely to be Republicans (22.1%) than are females (19.1%). Males are a little more likely to identify with some "Other" party (2.9%) as compared to females (1.5%). Overall, what we are seeing is that the gender gap is strongest among those who voted in 1992, and much weaker among those who did not vote.

Now we can compare the association we see for these two categories of the control variable with the association we observed at the beginning of this chapter for all respondents.

> Is the gap among voters larger or smaller than that for all respondents together? It appears that, when the control variable is introduced, the gap gets larger for voters and smaller for nonvoters. Moreover, the nature of the gap changes somewhat among nonvoters. Consequently, the association between sex and party affiliation is conditional. Among those who said they participated in the 1992 presidential election, the gap between the percentages of males who identify as Democrats and females who so identify is much wider. Among those who did not participate, the gap is smaller. It is interesting that this gap among voters is much like the gender gap we might have expected to see based on the comments of the politician quoted at the beginning of the chapter.

Skills Practice 12 Use the variables *sex* and *partyaf* to look at the association between sex and party affiliation, and control for the variable *race*. Answer the following questions:

A. Is the nature of the gender gap the same across racial categories?

B. For which category of the control variable is the gap the strongest? For which is it the weakest?

C. What general conclusions can you draw about the effect of the control variable, *race,* on the association between sex and party affiliation?

WRITING UP YOUR CONTINGENCY TABLE ANALYSIS

So far, we have learned about analyzing contingency tables in order to extract the general patterns in the data. Now we need to look at ways to write about what we are seeing in the data. How can we describe what we are learning to others?

First, an analysis of a contingency table should begin with a description of the general pattern—the nature of the association between variables—you see in the table. You may start off by commenting on the distribution of the respondents among the categories of the variables. Using the example of the association between *sex* and *partyaf,* you can write about the percentage of all respondents who say they are Democrats, Independents, Republicans, or Other. You can say something like,

> Respondents to the General Social Survey for 1996 are split fairly evenly among three broad categories of party affiliation: Democrat, Independent, and Republican. The distribution is fairly heterogeneous.

Then describe the general pattern found in the data. Is there a gender gap, and what is its nature? You can make a statement along the lines of,

> Female respondents are more likely to say they are Democrats than are male respondents, who are more likely than females to identify themselves as Independents or Republicans.

After that, what do we do? To offer a complete analysis, we should go beyond the general pattern and look at the rest of the story. For example, we can comment on the category Other.

> Female respondents are as likely as male respondents to say they belong to some "Other" party.

Your analysis should point out the exceptions to the general pattern. For example, in our discussion of the relationship between education (*degree*) and political orientation (*polaf*), we saw a general pattern—the more education respondents have, the more likely they are to be polarized politically as liberals or conservatives. The less education respondents have, the more likely they are to classify themselves as moderates. However, there are some exceptions, as we noted previously, and they should be included as you write up your analysis.

To lend credence to your conclusions and to describe the *size* of the association, support your conclusions with relevant statistics from your table. In addition to saying that female respondents are more likely to identify themselves as Democrats than are male respondents, mention that

> 38.8% of the female respondents say they are Democrats as opposed to 27.3% of male respondents, whereas 31.2% of the male respondents call themselves Republicans compared to 25.2% of the female respondents. By the same token, 40.1% of the male respondents said they are Independents, compared to 34.5% of the female respondents.

A complete analysis for Table 7.2, the association between *sex* and *partyaf,* would look like the following:

> Data from the General Social Survey for 1996 support the claim that there is a gender gap in politics. Whereas respondents were fairly evenly divided among three general political categories, Democrat, Independent, and Republican, females were more likely than males to identify themselves as Democrats and male respondents were more likely than females to call themselves Independents or Republicans.
>
> Overall, about a third of the respondents fell into the three major groupings for party registration: 34% called themselves Democrats, 37% said they are Independents, and 28% referred to themselves as Republicans. However, when this distribution is analyzed by sex, it is clear that women are more likely to say they are Democrats (39%) as compared to men

(27%). Men are more likely than women to say that they are Independents (40% for males vs. 35% for females) or Republicans (31% for males vs. 25% for females).

We can further develop our analysis by introducing the breakdown of the general association by the categories of a control variable, like *voting behavior* (*vote92*). For example, we may add the following:

It is noteworthy that the gender gap is larger among those respondents who claim to have voted in the 1992 elections compared to those who said they did not vote. For example, among those who voted in 1992, 44% of female respondents identify themselves as Democrats, whereas 30% of the male respondents call themselves Democrats. On the other hand, 37% of male respondents call themselves Republicans compared to 29% of the female respondents who voted.

Among nonvoters, the gender gap narrows 27% of the female respondents identify themselves as Democrats compared to 24% of male respondents, a gap of 3%. The gap is about the same for those who claim to affiliate with the Republican party; 22% of male nonvoters say they are Republicans versus 19% of female nonvoters. The gap is smaller between female respondents who say they are Independents (53%) and males who call themselves Independents (51%).

This raises the question: Which group of respondents is most likely to have voted, males or females? Looking at the association between *sex* and *vote92* might shed light on whether the "gap" issue is really one of gender or one of who votes. In addition, it would be interesting to know whether any association between one's sex and one's voting behavior is affected by one's party affiliation.

Skills Practice 13 Examine the association between voting (*vote92*) and *sex*. (Be sure to correctly identify the independent and dependent variable relationship.) Then look to see what happens to this relationship when you control for *partyaf*. Use the models previously discussed to write an analysis. Be sure to describe the general association between *vote92* and *sex*. Then write an analysis of the association for Democrats, an analysis of the association for Independents, and an analysis for Republicans. Finally, discuss the differences between the general association and the associations you found for the categories of the control variable *partyaf*.

At this point, you should be able to use a number of tools for data analysis: frequency distributions, measures of central tendency, measures of distribution, and now contingency table analysis. The goal of learning all of these skills is to combine them in different ways to analyze data. In the next chapter we will be building on these skills by learning to add measures of association to our analysis of contingency tables.

SUMMARY

This chapter has introduced you to the process of bivariate, or two-variable, analysis using contingency tables. A contingency table is a display of the categories of one variable by the categories of a second variable. Generally, they are set up in such a way that the independent variable forms the columns of the table and the dependent variable forms the rows. Consequently, it is important to be able to tell which variable in an association ought to be treated as the independent variable and which variable ought to be treated as the dependent variable.

Two techniques for producing contingency tables were described: producing contingency tables using SPSS and the Analyze ➥ Descriptive Statistics ➥ Crosstabs command path, and producing contingency tables by hand.

The process of analyzing a contingency table is much like the process of examining frequency distributions when a data file has been split by some other variable. Contingency tables are more efficient means to the same end—understanding associations between variables. To analyze an association between two variables, you have to first obtain the column percentages—the percentages of response in each category of the independent variable. Then these percentages are analyzed by reading across each row or category of the dependent variable and looking for variations in the percentages across the rows.

Interpreting contingency tables involves using the column percentages, but analyze them across the rows, to describe the nature of an association—what the association is, exactly, between an independent and dependent variable. In addition, the strength of the association should be assessed. Finally, when you are dealing with two ordinal variables or higher, the direction of the association has to be evaluated.

To assess the impact of third variables on an independent–dependent variable relationship, we can use the process of elaboration. This process involves analyzing a series of partial tables—mini-contingency tables for the categories of the control variable. The goal is to identify whether or not a relationship between independent and dependent variables is spurious or conditional.

A great deal of attention is given to the interpretation of contingency tables and partial tables in this chapter. There are models of interpretation throughout the chapter, and you should come away with a fairly good idea of how you can write about bivariate relationships with and without control variables.

In the next chapter we will extend our analysis of bivariate associations with statistics for measuring associations, beginning with statistics based on contingency tables.

KEY CONCEPTS

Bivariate analysis	Ascribed characteristic	Linear association
Contingency table	Achieved characteristic	Positive association
Independent variable	Symmetrical	Negative association
Dependent variable	association	Curvilinear association
Cell	Nature of an	Control (third) variable
Cell frequency	association	Elaboration
Cell percentage	Strength of an	Partial table
Column percentage	association	Spurious association
Column marginals	Direction of an	Conditional association
Row marginals	association	

ANSWERS TO SKILLS PRACTICES

3. See the frequency distribution for the recoded *region* variable, *rcregion,* in the following table. (You may have a different variable label. The level of measurement is nominal.)

RCREGION recoded region variable

		Frequency	Percent	Valid Percent	Cumulative Percent
Valid	1 Northeast	572	19.7	19.7	19.7
	2 Midwest	699	24.1	24.1	43.8
	3 Southeast	1013	34.9	34.9	78.7
	4 West	620	21.3	21.3	100.0
	Total	2904	100.0	100.0	

4. A. Reading the cell frequencies down the columns (the categories of the variable *rcregion*), we can see there are 202 respondents from the Northeast who are Democrats, 231 are Independents, 131 are Republicans, and 8 are Other. 227 of the respondents from the Midwest are Democrats, 278 are Independents, 182 are Republicans, and 10 are Other. 345 of the respondents from the Southeast are Democrats, 339 are Independents, 316 are Republicans, and

12 are Other. 203 of the respondents from the West are Democrats, 223 are Independents, 178 are Republicans, and 13 are Other.

B. Reading the cell percentages down the columns, we can see that 35.5% of the respondents who live in the Northeast are Democrats, 40.4% are Independents, 22.9% are Republicans, and 1.4% are Other. 32.6% of the respondents who live in the Midwest are Democrats, 39.9% are Independents, 26.1% are Republicans, and 1.4% are Other. 34.1% of the respondents who live in the Southeast are Democrats, 33.5% are Independents, 31.2% are Republicans, and 1.2% are Other. 32.9% of the respondents who live in the West are Democrats, 36.1% are Independents, 28.8% are Republicans, and 2.1% are Other.

C. Reading down the row marginals, we see that 33.7% of the respondents to both variables, *partyaf* and *rcregion,* are Democrats, 37% are Independents, 27.8% are Republicans, and 1.5% are Other.

D. The total number of respondents, *N,* is 2,898.

E. Reading across the column marginals, we see that 572 of the respondents are from the Northeast, 697 are from the Midwest, 1,012 are from the Southeast, and 617 are from the West.

F. If I were a Republican, I would want to live in the Southeast because a larger percentage of respondents say they are Republicans compared with the percentage of respondents who identify themselves as Republicans in other regions. (Read across the row of the category Republican of the dependent variable.)

G. The most politically heterogeneous region is the Southeast. Read down the column of the independent variable Southeast. Note that there is more variation in the political affiliations of those in the Southeast than in any other region.

5. A. In the relationship between religion and party affiliation, *religion* should be treated as the independent variable, and you should get a contingency table like the following:

PARTYAF recoded party identification * RELIG RS RELIGIOUS PREFERENCE Crosstabulation

			RELIG RS RELIGIOUS PREFERENCE					
			1 PROTESTANT	2 CATHOLIC	3 JEWISH	4 NONE	5 OTHER	Total
PARTYAF recoded party identification	1 Democrat	Count	559	248	38	92	38	975
		% within RELIG RS RELIGIOUS PREFERENCE	33.6%	36.4%	55.9%	27.3%	26.6%	33.7%
	2 Independent	Count	535	252	19	180	82	1068
		% within RELIG RS RELIGIOUS PREFERENCE	32.2%	37.0%	27.9%	53.4%	57.3%	36.9%
	3 Republican	Count	548	172	7	60	20	807
		% within RELIG RS RELIGIOUS PREFERENCE	33.0%	25.2%	10.3%	17.8%	14.0%	27.9%
	4 Other	Count	21	10	4	5	3	43
		% within RELIG RS RELIGIOUS PREFERENCE	1.3%	1.5%	5.9%	1.5%	2.1%	1.5%
Total		Count	1663	682	68	337	143	2893
		% within RELIG RS RELIGIOUS PREFERENCE	100.0%	100.0%	100.0%	100.0%	100.0%	100.0%

B. In the relationship between age and party affiliation, the *agecat* variable should be treated as independent, and you should produce a table like this one:

PARTYAF recoded party identification * AGECAT recoded age - four categories Crosstabulation

			AGECAT recoded age - four categories				
			1 18 thru 25	2 26 thru 39	3 40 thru 64	4 65 thru 89	Total
PARTYAF recoded party identification	1 Democrat	Count	96	272	408	198	974
		% within AGECAT recoded age - four categories	27.3%	29.2%	35.0%	44.7%	33.7%
	2 Independent	Count	176	367	417	108	1068
		% within AGECAT recoded age - four categories	50.0%	39.4%	35.8%	24.4%	36.9%
	3 Republican	Count	77	272	329	129	807
		% within AGECAT recoded age - four categories	21.9%	29.2%	28.2%	29.1%	27.9%
	4 Other	Count	3	21	11	8	43
		% within AGECAT recoded age - four categories	.9%	2.3%	.9%	1.8%	1.5%
Total		Count	352	932	1165	443	2892
		% within AGECAT recoded age - four categories	100.0%	100.0%	100.0%	100.0%	100.0%

6. Your contingency table should look like the following:

Party Affiliation	Sex		Row Marginals
	Male	Female	
Democrat	5 (38.5%)	3 (25.0%)	8 (32.0%)
Independent	5 (38.5%)	5 (41.7%)	10 (40.0%)
Republican	3 (23.1%)	4 (33.3%)	7 (28.0%)
Totals	13 (100.1%)	12 (100.0%)	N = 25 (100.0%)

8. Your contingency table should look like this:

PARTYAF recoded party identification * RACE RACE OF RESPONDENT Crosstabulation

			RACE RACE OF RESPONDENT			Total
			1 WHITE	2 BLACK	3 OTHER	
PARTYAF recoded party identification	1 Democrat	Count	648	259	70	977
		% within RACE RACE OF RESPONDENT	27.6%	64.6%	45.8%	33.7%
	2 Independent	Count	891	121	59	1071
		% within RACE RACE OF RESPONDENT	38.0%	30.2%	38.6%	37.0%
	3 Republican	Count	767	17	23	807
		% within RACE RACE OF RESPONDENT	32.7%	4.2%	15.0%	27.8%
	4 Other	Count	38	4	1	43
		% within RACE RACE OF RESPONDENT	1.6%	1.0%	.7%	1.5%
Total		Count	2344	401	153	2898
		% within RACE RACE OF RESPONDENT	100.0%	100.0%	100.0%	100.0%

There appears to be a very large race gap in the party affiliations of 1996 GSS respondents. Blacks are more likely to say they are Democrats (64.6%) than are Whites (27.6%) or those who say their race is Other (45.8%). On the other hand, Whites are more likely to be Republicans (32.7%) than are Blacks (4.2%) or those who say their race is Other (15.0%). Blacks are less likely to say they are Independents (30.2%) than are Whites (38.0%) or those who say their race is Other (38.6%), and they are less likely to identify themselves with some Other party (1%) than are Whites (1.6%), but more likely to do so than those who say their race is Other (.7%).

The gap appears to be large between White respondents and Black respondents, particularly when it comes to affiliations with one of the two major parties. There is a difference of 37% in the percentage of White and Black respondents who say they are Democrats, and there is a difference of over 28% in the percentage of White and Black respondents who say they are Republicans.

9. Your contingency tables should look like the following ones. (*padeg* and *madeg* are the independent variables and *degree* is the dependent variable.)

DEGREE RS HIGHEST DEGREE * PADEG FATHERS HIGHEST DEGREE Crosstabulation

			PADEG FATHERS HIGHEST DEGREE					
			0 LT HIGH SCHOOL	1 HIGH SCHOOL	2 JUNIOR COLLEGE	3 BACHELOR	4 GRADUATE	Total
DEGREE RS HIGHEST DEGREE	0 LT HIGH SCHOOL	Count	200	56	3	6	1	266
		% within PADEG FATHERS HIGHEST DEGREE	23.0%	6.4%	6.3%	2.6%	.6%	12.2%
	1 HIGH SCHOOL	Count	501	506	21	76	57	1161
		% within PADEG FATHERS HIGHEST DEGREE	57.5%	58.1%	43.8%	33.5%	35.6%	53.3%
	2 JUNIOR COLLEGE	Count	40	72	11	21	6	150
		% within PADEG FATHERS HIGHEST DEGREE	4.6%	8.3%	22.9%	9.3%	3.8%	6.9%
	3 BACHELOR	Count	72	173	10	86	62	403
		% within PADEG FATHERS HIGHEST DEGREE	8.3%	19.9%	20.8%	37.9%	38.8%	18.5%
	4 GRADUATE	Count	58	64	3	38	34	197
		% within PADEG FATHERS HIGHEST DEGREE	6.7%	7.3%	6.3%	16.7%	21.3%	9.0%
Total		Count	871	871	48	227	160	2177
		% within PADEG FATHERS HIGHEST DEGREE	100.0%	100.0%	100.0%	100.0%	100.0%	100.0%

			MADEG MOTHERS HIGHEST DEGREE					
			0 LT HIGH SCHOOL	1 HIGH SCHOOL	2 JUNIOR COLLEGE	3 BACHELOR	4 GRADUATE	Total
DEGREE RS HIGHEST DEGREE	0 LT HIGH SCHOOL	Count	244	95	2	3	3	347
		% within MADEG MOTHERS HIGHEST DEGREE	28.2%	7.3%	2.1%	1.4%	3.6%	13.5%
	1 HIGH SCHOOL	Count	470	756	39	90	26	1381
		% within MADEG MOTHERS HIGHEST DEGREE	54.3%	57.8%	41.5%	42.3%	31.0%	53.9%
	2 JUNIOR COLLEGE	Count	30	106	13	12	7	168
		% within MADEG MOTHERS HIGHEST DEGREE	3.5%	8.1%	13.8%	5.6%	8.3%	6.6%
	3 BACHELOR	Count	71	239	30	84	29	453
		% within MADEG MOTHERS HIGHEST DEGREE	8.2%	18.3%	31.9%	39.4%	34.5%	17.7%
	4 GRADUATE	Count	50	111	10	24	19	214
		% within MADEG MOTHERS HIGHEST DEGREE	5.8%	8.5%	10.6%	11.3%	22.6%	8.3%
Total		Count	865	1307	94	213	84	2563
		% within MADEG MOTHERS HIGHEST DEGREE	100.0%	100.0%	100.0%	100.0%	100.0%	100.0%

The association in each of the tables is positive. We can see the pattern of the association by circling the highest percentage in each of the rows of the dependent variable. The more education a respondent's father has, the more education the respondent has. Likewise, the more education a respondent's mother has, the more education the respondent has.

10. The trend in the category Conservative is that as the respondents' level of education rises, they tend to be more conservative. However, there is one exception—those with graduate degrees are *less* likely than those with bachelor's degrees to be conservative.

11. *agecat* and *polaf:* Generally, the older the respondents, the more likely they are to say they are conservative. The association is positive. The association is a weak one, because it is not very linear. Respondents of retirement age are more likely to say they are moderate than are younger adults.

   satfin and *polaf:* The less satisfied respondents are with their financial situations, the more likely they are to be liberal. Conversely, the more satisfied respondents are, the more likely they are to be conservative. The association is positive, and it looks fairly strong.

   pillok and *polaf:* The more that respondents agree that giving birth control pills to teenagers is OK, the more likely they are to be liberals;

the more that respondents disagree, the more likely it is that they are conservatives. The association is a positive one, and it appears to be fairly strong.

12. A. The nature of the association is about the same for White respondents and Black respondents as it is for the respondents as a whole. (Men are more likely than women to be Independents or Republicans, whereas women are more likely than men to say they are Democrats.) Among Black respondents, men are slightly more likely to say they belong to some other party than are women. Among White respondents, there is almost no difference in the percentage of men and women who belong to some other party. The nature of the association changes for those who are in the "Other" category. Men are more likely than women to be Republicans or in some other party, whereas women are more likely than men to be Democrats or Independents.

   B. The gap is the strongest among Black respondents, and weakest among those who say they are White.

   C. Race has an effect on the gender gap. The nature of the gap changes among those who say they are of some other race. It gets larger (and therefore stronger) for the respondents who are Black, and smaller (and therefore weaker) among those who identify themselves as White.

13. Women are more likely than men to have voted in the 1992 elections. Men are more likely than women to say they did not vote or were not eligible to vote. The association doesn't appear to be very strong, because the gap between male and female voters is only about 3%, whereas the gap between male and female nonvoters is about 1%. The gap between males and females not eligible to vote is less than 2%.

   Among Democrats, the gap is larger. The nature of the gap doesn't change, but it is much wider (and therefore the association is stronger). For Independents, the nature of the gap changes. Men are more likely than women to say they voted or weren't eligible in 1992, whereas women are more likely than men to say they did not vote. Among Republicans, the nature of the gap is almost the same, but it is much weaker than it is among respondents as a whole.

   The variable *partyaf* seems to be influencing the association between *sex* and whether or not respondents voted in 1992. Of the three major party affiliations, the gap is largest among Democrats and smallest among Republicans, which tells us that the strength of the association is affected by the respondents' political party affiliations. The nature of the gap changes most for those who say they are Independents.

GENERAL EXERCISES

For Exercises 1–4, construct and analyze a contingency table for the given set of data (a set of randomly selected cases from the 1996 General Social Survey).

1.

Case Summaries

	SEX RESPONDENTS SEX	PARTAF Party Affiliation
1	FEMALE	Republican
2	MALE	Republican
3	FEMALE	Democrat
4	FEMALE	Democrat
5	FEMALE	Democrat
6	MALE	Democrat
7	MALE	Independent
8	MALE	Other
9	FEMALE	Democrat
10	FEMALE	Democrat
11	MALE	Independent
12	FEMALE	Democrat
13	FEMALE	Independent
14	FEMALE	Democrat
15	FEMALE	Republican
16	MALE	Republican
17	FEMALE	Independent
18	FEMALE	Republican
19	MALE	Democrat
20	MALE	Independent
21	FEMALE	Republican
22	MALE	Independent
23	FEMALE	Democrat
24	MALE	Republican
Total N	24	24

2.

Case Summaries

	RCREGION Recoded region variable	PARTAF Party Affiliation
1	Northeast	Republican
2	Northeast	Republican
3	Midwest	Democrat
4	Midwest	Democrat
5	West	Democrat
6	Northeast	Democrat
7	Southeast	Independent
8	Southeast	Other
9	West	Democrat
10	West	Democrat
11	Midwest	Independent
12	Midwest	Democrat
13	Midwest	Independent
14	Southeast	Democrat
15	West	Republican
16	Midwest	Republican
17	Midwest	Independent
18	Midwest	Republican
19	Midwest	Democrat
20	Midwest	Independent
21	Southeast	Republican
22	West	Independent
23	West	Democrat
24	West	Republican
Total N	24	24

3.

Case Summaries

	SATFIN SATISFACTION WITH FINANCIAL SITUATION	VOTE92 DID R VOTE IN 1992 ELECTION
1	MORE OR LESS SATISFIED	VOTED
2	NOT AT ALL SATISFIED	VOTED
3	SATISFIED	VOTED
4	NOT AT ALL SATISFIED	VOTED
5	MORE OR LESS SATISFIED	VOTED
6	SATISFIED	VOTED
7	MORE OR LESS SATISFIED	DID NOT VOTE
8	MORE OR LESS SATISFIED	VOTED
9	SATISFIED	VOTED
10	NOT AT ALL SATISFIED	DID NOT VOTE
11	MORE OR LESS SATISFIED	VOTED
12	NOT AT ALL SATISFIED	VOTED
13	SATISFIED	VOTED
14	NOT AT ALL SATISFIED	VOTED
15	MORE OR LESS SATISFIED	VOTED
16	SATISFIED	VOTED
17	NOT AT ALL SATISFIED	VOTED
18	MORE OR LESS SATISFIED	VOTED
19	SATISFIED	VOTED
20	MORE OR LESS SATISFIED	VOTED
21	MORE OR LESS SATISFIED	VOTED
22	NOT AT ALL SATISFIED	DID NOT VOTE
23	SATISFIED	VOTED
24	NOT AT ALL SATISFIED	VOTED
25	MORE OR LESS SATISFIED	VOTED
26	SATISFIED	VOTED
27	NOT AT ALL SATISFIED	VOTED
28	NOT AT ALL SATISFIED	VOTED
29	NOT AT ALL SATISFIED	VOTED
Total N	29	29

4.

Case Summaries

	RELIG RS RELIGIOUS PREFERENCE	PRES92 VOTE FOR CLINTON, BUSH, PEROT
1	NONE	CLINTON
2	PROTESTANT	PEROT
3	PROTESTANT	CLINTON
4	CATHOLIC	CLINTON
5	PROTESTANT	BUSH
6	PROTESTANT	PEROT
7	NONE	CLINTON
8	PROTESTANT	CLINTON
9	CATHOLIC	CLINTON
10	PROTESTANT	PEROT
11	PROTESTANT	BUSH
12	PROTESTANT	BUSH
13	CATHOLIC	CLINTON
14	PROTESTANT	BUSH
15	NONE	BUSH
16	PROTESTANT	CLINTON
17	CATHOLIC	BUSH
18	PROTESTANT	CLINTON
19	CATHOLIC	CLINTON
20	PROTESTANT	BUSH
21	PROTESTANT	CLINTON
22	CATHOLIC	BUSH
23	PROTESTANT	CLINTON
24	OTHER	BUSH
25	PROTESTANT	PEROT
26	PROTESTANT	BUSH
Total N	26	26

SPSS EXERCISES

1. Produce a contingency table for the association between *rcregion* and *vote92*. Make sure that the independent variable is the column variable and the dependent variable is the row variable in your table. Check to see that you have obtained column percentages for the table.

   a. Which region had the highest number of respondents who voted in the 1992 elections? Which region had the highest number who did not vote?

   b. Which region had the highest percentage of respondents who voted in the 1992 elections? Which region had the highest percentage of respondents who did not vote? Which region had the highest percentage of respondents who were not eligible to vote?

   c. What percentage of all respondents voted? What percentage did not vote?

   d. How many respondents answered both the questions about region and 1992 voting?

2. Produce a contingency table for the association between *race* and *vote92*. Make sure that the independent variable is the column variable and the dependent variable is the row variable in your table. Check to see that you have obtained column percentages for the table.

   a. Which group—Blacks, Whites, or Other—had the highest number of voters in 1992?

   b. Which group had the highest percentage of voters? nonvoters? those who were not eligible to vote?

   c. What percentage of all respondents voted? What percentage did not vote?

   d. How many respondents answered both the questions about race and 1992 voting?

3. Produce a contingency table for the association between *relig* and *vote92*. Make sure that the independent variable is the column variable and the dependent variable is the row variable in your table. Check to see that you have obtained column percentages for the table.

   a. Which religion had the highest number of respondents who voted in the 1992 elections? Which religion had the highest number who did not vote?

   b. Which religion had the highest percentage of respondents who voted in the 1992 elections? Which religion had the highest percentage of respondents who did not vote? Which religion had the highest percentage of respondents who were not eligible to vote?

c. What percentage of all respondents voted? What percentage did not vote?

d. How many respondents answered both the questions about religion and 1992 voting?

4. Produce a contingency table for the association between *agecat* and *vote92*. Make sure that the independent variable is the column variable and the dependent variable is the row variable in your table. Check to see that you have obtained column percentages for the table.

   a. Which age category had the highest number of respondents who voted in the 1992 elections? Which age category had the highest number who did not vote?

   b. Which age category had the highest percentage of respondents who voted in the 1992 elections? Which age category had the highest percentage of respondents who did not vote? Which age category had the highest percentage of respondents who were not eligible to vote?

   c. What percentage of all respondents voted? What percentage did not vote?

   d. How many respondents answered both the questions about age and 1992 voting?

5. Write a few sentences analyzing the nature and strength of the association between *rcregion* and *vote92*.

6. Write a few sentences analyzing the nature and strength of the association between *race* and *vote92*.

7. Write a few sentences analyzing the nature and strength of the association between *relig* and *vote92*.

8. Write a few sentences analyzing the nature and strength of the association between *agecat* and *vote92*.

9. Interpret (analyze the nature, strength, and direction, if appropriate) of the association between *rcattend* (recoded church attendance variable) and *polaf* (recoded political affiliation variable).

10. Interpret (analyze the nature, strength, and direction, if appropriate) of the association between *sex* and *if92who* (who respondents would have voted for in 1992, had they voted).

11. Control the association between *rcregion* and *vote92* for the variable *sex*. Answer the following questions.

    a. Is the nature of the association between the variables the same across the categories of the control variable *sex*?

b. For which category of the variable *sex* is the association the strongest? For which category is it the weakest?

c. What general conclusions can you draw about the effect of the control variable *sex* on the association?

12. Control the association between *relig* and *vote92* for the variable *sex*. Answer the following questions.

a. Is the nature of the association between the variables the same across the categories of the control variable *sex*?

b. For which category of the variable *sex* is the association the strongest? For which category is it the weakest?

c. What general conclusions can you draw about the effect of the control variable *sex* on the association?

13. Control the association between *agecat* and *vote92* for the variable *sex*. Answer the following questions.

a. Is the nature of the association between the variables the same across the categories of the control variable *sex*?

b. For which category of the variable *sex* is the association the strongest? For which category is it the weakest?

c. What general conclusions can you draw about the effect of the control variable *sex* on the association?

14. In Exercise 10 you examined the association between *sex* and *if92who*. Now control the association for *agecat* to see whether any gender gap among those who voted was consistent across age categories. Write an analysis of the association between *sex* and *if92who* and assess the impact of the control variable on the association.

8

Measures of Association
for Contingency Tables

INTRODUCTION

In the last chapter, you learned how to analyze contingency tables and evaluate the nature and strength of associations between variables. In this chapter and the next, you will be introduced to **measures of association**—statistics that help us evaluate these relationships. It may help to begin with a brief review of what we mean by "association." When two variables are associated, variations in the responses to the values or categories of one variable are associated with variations in the responses to the values or categories of a second variable. For example, if we say that the variables *sex* and *party affiliation* are associated, we are saying that variations in the responses to the categories of the variable *sex* are associated with variations in the responses to the categories of the variable *party affiliation*. Measures of association allow us to assess the degree to which variations in the responses to the categories of one variable are associated with the variations in the responses to the categories of a second variable.

Measures of association function as indexes, somewhat like the index of qualitative variation you learned to calculate in Chapter 6. Whereas the index of qualitative variation provided you with an indication of the degree of variability in a frequency distribution, measures of association act as a guide to the degree of association between two variables. The measure or statistic itself ranges in value between -1 and $+1$, and it gives us information about the strength of an association. The closer to $+1$ or -1 the value is, the stronger is the association between two variables, and the closer to 0 the value is, the weaker is the association between two variables. The sign on the value—positive or negative—gives us information about the nature of an association (Figure 8.1).

-1	0	+1
Strong negative association	No association	Strong positive association

Figure 8.1

To demonstrate how a measure of association works, let's go back to the example with which we began the last chapter, the relationship between the variables *sex* and *party affiliation* (Table 8.1). We found that there is a gender gap between males and females in their political affiliations. The nature of the gap is that women are more likely to be Democrats than are men, whereas men are more likely than women to say they are Independents or Republicans. The size of the gap didn't appear to be large—ranging from 6% to 12%.

Other than just "eyeballing" a contingency table, is there another way to assess the strength of an association? The answer is yes, with measures of association. Let's take one measure, called lambda. It is a measure appropriate for the variables *sex* and *party affiliation,* and, for the table in Figure 8.1, it has a value of .04.

The advantage of a measure like lambda is that it can be read as an index to the strength of an association, with 0 indicating no association and 1.0 indicating a perfect association. When there is no association between two variables, variations in the responses to the categories of one variable have no relationship to variations in responses to the categories of the second. Whether a respondent is male or female would have nothing to do with, or no association with, how respondents answered the question about political affiliation. On the other hand, in perfect associations, the variations in the responses to the categories of one variable are tied to variations in the responses to the categories of a second variable. In a perfect association, every male would be a Republican and every female a Democrat (or vice versa). Whether one is male or female guarantees one's response to a variable measuring party affiliation.

Very few measures of association will produce values indicating no association whatsoever or a perfect association. Most will fall somewhere in between. A value of .04, because it's much closer to 0 (no association) than 1 (perfect association) confirms that the association between the variables *sex* and *party affiliation* is a weak one. We will explore exactly what this means in this chapter.

In addition, you will learn how to apply measures of association: which measures can be used with which levels of measurement, how some of the measures are computed, and how they can be interpreted. We will start with interpretation, because many of these measures have common characteristics:

TABLE 8.1 Contingency Table for the Variables *sex* and *partyaf* in the gss96subset File

PARTYAF recoded party identification * SEX RESPONDENTS SEX Crosstabulation

			SEX RESPONDENTS SEX		Total
			1 MALE	2 FEMALE	
PARTYAF recoded party identification	1 Democrat	Count	350	627	977
		% within SEX RESPONDENTS SEX	27.3%	38.8%	33.7%
	2 Independent	Count	514	557	1071
		% within SEX RESPONDENTS SEX	40.1%	34.5%	37.0%
	3 Republican	Count	400	407	807
		% within SEX RESPONDENTS SEX	31.2%	25.2%	27.8%
	4 Other	Count	19	24	43
		% within SEX RESPONDENTS SEX	1.5%	1.5%	1.5%
Total		Count	1283	1615	2898
		% within SEX RESPONDENTS SEX	100.0%	100.0%	100.0%

they give us information about the strength and, in some cases, the nature of an association. Some of them tell us even more, because they have a proportional reduction in error interpretation that allows us to be more precise in our assessment of how much an independent variable is associated with a dependent variable. I will be illustrating the use of measures of association by returning to many of the variables we analyzed in Chapter 7. In this way, I can show you how the analysis of contingency tables is supplemented with (but not replaced by) measures of association.

Measures of Association and the Number Line

For interpreting measures of association it is helpful to have an understanding of the relationship between the numbers on a number line, because we rarely get measures of association that are at 0 or close to +1 or −1. It is more likely that we will get measures that are somewhere in between, and you have to know how to describe them. For example, in the association between sex and party affiliation, a measure of association we might use equals .04. Where on the number line does that fall—closer to 0 or closer to 1? Let's break down the number line to find out (Figure 8.2).

The value .04 falls between 0 and .10, suggesting a very weak association between sex and party affiliation.

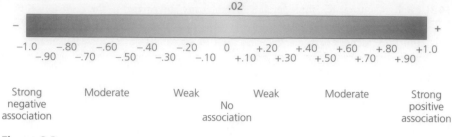

Figure 8.2

Proportional Reduction in Error Interpretation

What does "weak association" mean exactly? In addition to their interpretation in the context of the number line, some measures of association have an interpretation called **proportional reduction in error** (or PRE). To understand this concept, let's remember back to when we were trying to assess the strength of the association between sex and party affiliation. I asked you to think of the situation in terms of gambling. Imagine that I pick a man and a woman at random from the respondents to the General Social Survey. Then I ask you to bet on the one most likely to be the Democrat. If you know something about the association between the variables *sex* and *party affiliation,* you can make a better guess than if you don't know anything about the association. The extent to which you can make a better guess is what proportional reduction in error assesses.

How much does knowing the nature of an independent–dependent variable relationship improve our ability to guess (or, more precisely, to reduce our errors in guessing) the dependent variable? In this case, the PRE statistic tells us the proportion (.04) by which errors at guessing someone's party affiliation would be reduced if we knew the association between sex and party affiliation. By multiplying the PRE statistic times 100, we can compute the percentage of the reduction in errors, or 4%. Knowing that women are more likely than men to be Democrats, whereas men are more likely than women to be Independents or Republicans, reduces our errors at predicting, or guessing, party affiliation by 4%. This is a very small reduction, suggesting a very weak association between the variables *sex* and *party affiliation.*

Nature of an Association

Measures of association for ordinal and numerical variables have signs, positive and negative. (Some measures of association for nominal variables have signs, too, but they don't mean the same thing as the signs on associations between ordinal and numerical variables—more about that later on in this chapter.) A negative association is indicated by the minus sign $(-)$ attached to the measure. A positive association is indicated by the absence of any sign at all.

What does the sign tell us? If you remember the discussion in Chapter 7 about positive and negative associations (see "Interpreting Tables With Ordinal or Numerical Variables"), you may guess that a positive association means that as the value of one variable increases, the value of the second variable increases as well. The larger is the value of an independent variable, the larger is the value of a dependent variable. If you looked at the association between education and income, you would get a measure of association with a positive value, suggesting that the more education a respondent has, the higher the person's earnings are likely to be.

A negative sign on an association indicates that as the value of one variable goes up, the value of the other variable goes down. As the value of an independent variable rises, for example, the value of a dependent variable may fall (or as the value on an independent variable falls, the value of a dependent variable goes up). For example, the sign on an appropriate measure of association for the relationship between education and the number of children a respondent has would be negative, suggesting that the more education respondents have, the fewer children they are likely to have (or, conversely, the less education respondents have, the more children they are likely to have).

These concepts may become clearer as we turn our attention to some of the specific measures we can use, their applications, and their interpretations.

MEASURES OF ASSOCIATION FOR NOMINAL VARIABLES

Measures of association, like all other statistics, have to be applied correctly. Each measure of association is more (or less) appropriate depending on the level at which variables are being measured. In addition, they each make certain assumptions about relationships between variables, assumptions that may be more (or less) accurate, depending on the nature of the variable (such as whether it is continuous or discrete) and the distribution of responses to the variable (such as whether the distributions are linear or not, normal or not).

Measures of association for nominal variables are used whenever one or both variables in a bivariate association are nominal. For example, in the association between sex and party affiliation, we are working with two nominal variables, but in the association between degree and party affiliation we are working with one ordinal variable and one nominal variable. In either case, measures of association for nominal variables are applied.

What are some of the measures of association we can use with nominal variables? We will look at SPSS to find out.

SPSS Guide: Measures of Association

To see the various measures of association available for use with contingency tables in SPSS, open the Crosstabs dialog box. (Use the command path Analyze ➥ Descriptive Statistics ➥ Crosstabs.)

❶ Click on the Statistics button to open the Crosstabs: Statistics window.

❷ Notice the list of measures for nominal variables and the list for ordinal variables. Put the cursor on any of the measures and click with the right-most key on your mouse to see a description of it. Try it. Click again to close the description.

❸ Click on Cancel to return to the Crosstabs dialog box. At the Crosstabs window, click on Cancel again.

Of these measures, we will look at one, lambda, in detail. You will be introduced to a few more later on.

Lambda

Lambda is a measure of association for use with nominal variables, which means that it is used whenever both of the variables in a pair are nominal, or when one of the variables is nominal and the other is ordinal.

Interpreting lambda   Lambda can range in value from 0 to 1.0. The closer the value of lambda is to 0, the weaker is the association; the closer it is to 1, the stronger is the association. Associations involving nominal variables have no direction. (It doesn't make any sense to say that the more male you are the more likely you are to be a Republican, for example.) Consequently, lambda has no direction; it can never be a negative number, but the fact that it is positive doesn't tell us anything about the nature of an association.

Lambda has a proportional reduction in error interpretation, however. To get a better handle on this concept, let's go through the logic of the computation of lambda. Suppose you had to place a bet on the political affiliations of someone picked at random from the respondents to the General Social Survey, knowing only that people in general are more likely to be Independents than Democrats, Republicans, or Other. You would have to guess that the person is an Independent. Now imagine you do this for each and every respondent to the General Social Survey. Assume they are Independent. How many mistakes or errors would you make in trying to guess their party affiliation?

To find out, you have to compare the number of respondents who really are Independents to the number that you guessed might be Independents (all of them). How can you do that? Just look back at the contingency table for the variables *sex* and *partyaf* in Table 8.1. You guessed that all 2,898 respondents are Independents, but it turns out that only 1,071 of them are Independents. (How do you know how many are Independents? Look at the row marginal for the category Independent.) Thus, 1,071 of your guesses were right, but 1,827 of your guesses (2,898 minus 1,071) were wrong. If you divide the number of wrong guesses, 1,827, by the total number of guesses you made, 2,898, you will find your proportion of error, .630. If you multiply your proportion of error by 100, you will obtain your percentage of error, 63%. This means that 63% of your guesses were wrong.

Now, assume you know something about the association between the independent and dependent variables—that women are more likely to be Democrats than Independents, Republicans, or Other, and that men are more likely to be Independents than Democrats, Republicans, or Other. What happens to your ability to guess? If you are presented with a respondent to the GSS, told that the respondent is female, and then asked to place a bet on her party affiliation, you will bet that she is a Democrat. On the other hand, if you are presented with a male respondent, you will bet that he is an Independent.

How many male respondents and female respondents will be correctly classified if you do this for each person in the GSS? Again, the answer can be found in the contingency table. You can see that 514 male respondents are Independents. This means that you will get 514 of your guesses right for males, but you will get 769 wrong (1,283, the total number of male respondents, minus 514). For females, you will get 627 of your guesses right (the number of female Democrats), but you will get 988 wrong (1,615, the total number of female respondents, minus 627). You will get a total of 1,141 guesses right (514 plus 627), and will make 1,757 mistakes (769 + 988). By dividing your mistakes, 1,757, by 2,898 (the total number of respondents), you can figure your proportion of error, .606. If you multiply the proportion of error by 100, you can compute the percentage of error, 61%.

Are your guesses better if you know something about the association between the independent and dependent variables? Yes, but not much. If you try to guess party affiliation without knowing anything about the association between the variables, *sex* and *party affiliation,* you will guess correctly 1,071 times, and if you know the association between the variables, you will guess correctly 1,141 times, for a total of 70 *more* correct guesses (1,141 minus 1,071).

The *proportion* of the reduction in error is found by dividing this difference, 70, by the number of mistakes you would make if you knew nothing about the association between the variables, 1,827. The PRE = 70 ÷ 1,827 = .04. If you multiply this result by 100, you have the PRE as a percentage, 4%. How is this interpreted?

First, very roughly, this tells us that knowing the nature of the association between the variables (females are more likely to be Democrats, whereas males are more likely to be Independents) improves our ability to guess the dependent variable (their party affiliation) by about 4%. More specifically, what this number tells us is that we make 4% fewer errors at guessing the dependent variable if we know the association between the independent and dependent variables than if we don't know what it is.

We can look at this number another way using the proportions of error we computed. We found that

the proportion of errors you would make if you try to guess the dependent variable not knowing anything about the association between the independent and dependent variables is .630, and

the proportion of errors you would make if you do know the association is .606.

We can subtract .606 from .630 to find the *difference* between the proportions of errors we would make based on whether or not we know what the association is between the independent and dependent variables. To find the proportional *reduction* in error, we divide the amount of the difference, .024, by the proportion of errors we would make if we don't know what the association is between the independent and dependent variables: .024 ÷ .630 = .04. Hence, the proportion reduction in error is .04, or 4%.

Computing lambda   Fortunately, the process described at length in the preceding section can be reduced to a fairly simple formula:

FORMULA 8.1:   Lambda

$$\lambda = \frac{E_1 - E_2}{E_1}$$

where E_1 is the number of errors you would make guessing the dependent variable if you did not know the independent variable, and E_2 is the number of errors you would make guessing the dependent variable if you knew the categories of the independent variable.

To find E_1, simply subtract the largest row marginal total from N. To find E_2, add up the highest frequencies of each category of the independent variable and subtract the sum from N.

Example: Let's look at the association between the respondents' region of residence and their party affiliation and find lambda for the association between the recoded region variable (*rcregion*) and party affiliation (*partyaf*).

Skills Practice 1   Produce a contingency table for the association between *rcregion* and *partyaf*, using SPSS (the command path Analyze ➡ Descriptive Statistics ➡ Crosstabs). The row variable is *partyaf* and *rcregion* is the column variable. Don't forget to click on the Cells button to get column percentages. (See the SPSS Guide, "Producing a Contingency Table," in Chapter 7 if you need help.) Analyze the nature of the association and the strength of the association.

Let's see whether lambda confirms our analysis of the strength of the association. Start the process of computing lambda by finding E_1.

Step 1.   Look down the row marginal totals until you find the highest frequency of the dependent variable *partyaf*. The highest frequency is associated with the category Independent, so circle the frequency for that category, 1,071. Find E_1 by subtracting 1,071 from N. $E_1 = 2{,}898 - 1{,}071 = 1{,}827$.

Step 2. Find E_2 by looking down each column of the independent variable and circling the highest frequency in each column (excluding the column marginal totals). In the column Northeast, the highest frequency is 231. Circle it. In the next column, Midwest, the highest frequency is 278, so circle it. Circle 345 in the Southeast column and 223 in the West column. Now add the circled frequencies. $231 + 278 + 345 + 223 = 1,077$. Subtract 1,077 from N to get E_2. $E_2 = 2,898 - 1,077 = 1,821$.

Step 3. Apply Formula 8.1.

$$E_1 = 1,827 \qquad\qquad E_2 = 1,821$$

$$\lambda = \frac{E_1 - E_2}{E_1} = \frac{1,827 - 1,821}{1,827} = \frac{6}{1,827} = .003$$

Interpretation   Read the value .003 as a guide to the strength of the association between one's region of residence and party affiliation.

Our conclusion that the relationship is very weak is confirmed. Knowing the nature of the association between the independent and dependent variables improves our ability to predict the dependent variable very little. In relation to the errors we might make in predicting party affiliation *without* knowing the independent variable, we can reduce our mistakes (or improve our guesses) only by about .3% (.003 $\times$ 100).

✔ **Checking Your Work**   Lambda will always result in a positive number with a value between 0 and 1.0. If you get a negative number, or a number greater than 1.0, you have done something wrong. Make sure you have

- Subtracted the *single* highest row marginal frequency from N.

- Circled and added up each of the highest frequencies for *each* of the categories of the independent variable (you will have as many frequencies as there are categories), and subtracted the result from N.

Skills Practice 2   Use SPSS to produce a contingency table for the variables *relig* and *partyaf.* Compute and interpret lambda.

Finding lambda using SPSS   All of the measures of association for contingency tables, including lambda, are found using the Crosstabs command.

SPSS Guide: Measures of Association for Nominal and Ordinal Variables

To begin, open the Crosstabs dialog box (use the command path Analyze ➡ Descriptive Statistics ➡ Crosstabs). At the Crosstabs dialog box, let's find lambda for the variables *sex* and *partyaf*.

❶ Enter the dependent variable, *partyaf*, as the row variable.

❷ Enter the independent variable, *sex*, as the column variable.

❸ Click on Cells. At the Crosstabs: Cell Display window, look under Percentages and click on Column. Then click on Continue.

❹ Click on Statistics.

The Crosstabs: Statistics window opens. Look for the measure of association you would like SPSS to compute. There are two sets of statistics, one labeled Nominal and one labeled Ordinal. Lambda is under the heading Nominal.

➊ Click on the box next to the measure you want to use, Lambda in this case, to make the √ appear in it.

➋ Then click on Continue to return to the Crosstabs dialog box. At the Crosstabs dialog box, click on OK.

If you want to see a description of the statistic, put your cursor on the word Lambda. Use the right-most click key on your mouse and click. A description like this one will appear:

A measure of association which reflects the proportional reduction in error when values of the independent variable are used to predict values of the dependent variable. A value of 1 means that the independent variable perfectly predicts the dependent variable. A value of 0 means that the independent variable is no help in predicting the dependent variable.

To close the description, click again with the right-most key.

TABLE 8.2   Lambda Statistics Obtained Using the Crosstabs Command

❶ Symmetric lambda

❷ Asymmetric lambda as you set up the table (consistent with the manual computation of lambda)

Directional Measures

			Value	Asymp. Std. Error[a]	Approx. T[b]	Approx. Sig.
Nominal by Nominal	Lambda	Symmetric	.023	.011	2.036	.042
		PARTYAF recoded party identification Dependent	.038	.018	2.036	.042
		SEX RESPONDENTS SEX Dependent	.000	.000	c	c
	Goodman and Kruskal tau	PARTYAF recoded party identification Dependent	.007	.002		.000[d]
		SEX RESPONDENTS SEX Dependent	.015	.004		.000[d]

a. Not assuming the null hypothesis.

b. Using the asymptotic standard error assuming the null hypothesis.

c. Cannot be computed because the asymptotic standard error equals zero.

d. Based on chi-square approximation

❸ Asymmetric lambda, looking at the independent–dependent relationship opposite from the way the table is set up, treating the column variable as dependent

In addition to the contingency table for *sex* and *partyaf,* you will get a set of statistics like the ones in Table 8.2.

There is quite a bit of output, but we will focus on just a few of the statistics, the lambda statistics. (If you do advanced work in this area, more of these results will make sense.) Lambda is the first set of statistics you come to in the table labeled Directional Measures, and there are three values of lambda in the column labeled Value.

The first value is a **symmetric value** of lambda, followed by two asymmetric measures. The symmetric computation of lambda is useful for pairs of variables in which there is no clear independent–dependent variable relationship. When lambda is figured this way, neither variable is treated as independent in relation to the other. Instead, it is assumed that the variables are *associated,* without one variable necessarily *causing* an effect on the other. (See the Avoiding Common Pitfalls section in Chapter 7, "Deciding Which Variable Is Independent in Relation to the Other," if you need to review this concept.)

The next values are **asymmetric values** of lambda. These computations treat one of the variables in the pair as independent in relation to the other. The first asymmetric value treats the row variable in the contingency table as the dependent variable, as you did when you set up the table in SPSS. It is the value for which you learned the manual computation. The second value treats

TABLE 8.3 Contingency Table for the Variables *partyaf* and *sex,* Treating *sex* as the Dependent Variable, in the gss96subset File

SEX RESPONDENTS SEX * PARTYAF recoded party identification Crosstabulation

| | | | | PARTYAF recoded party identification | | | | |
				1 Democrat	2 Independent	3 Republican	4 Other	Total
SEX RESPONDENTS SEX	1 MALE	Count		350	514	400	19	1283
		% within PARTYAF recoded party identification		35.8%	48.0%	49.6%	44.2%	44.3%
	2 FEMALE	Count		627	557	407	24	1615
		% within PARTYAF recoded party identification		64.2%	52.0%	50.4%	55.8%	55.7%
Total		Count		977	1071	807	43	2898
		% within PARTYAF recoded party identification		100.0%	100.0%	100.0%	100.0%	100.0%

the column variable as the dependent variable, and it allows you to look at the relationship differently from the way you set it up in SPSS.

Even though these values make different assumptions about which variable is independent and which is dependent, they all arrive at about the same number. In using lambda as an index, none of the values indicate a very strong association—and none of them suggest that knowing the association between the variables helps to predict the dependent variable very much.

A limitation of lambda   All statistics have their limits—patterns they are good at finding and not so good at finding. For lambda, one limitation is that it treats as "no association" (with a value of 0) those patterns in which all of the highest frequencies for each category of the independent variable line up in the same row. To see how this can happen, find lambda for Table 8.3.

Your computations should look like these:

$$\lambda = \frac{E_1 - E_2}{E_1} = \frac{1,283 - 1,283}{1,283} = \frac{0}{1,283} = 0$$

When you get a lambda equal to zero, does that necessarily mean there is no association between these two variables? No. If you read across the rows—the categories of the dependent variable—it is clear that there is an association. Even though it may not make sense to analyze the table this way, it is clear that Independents and Republicans are more likely than Democrats and those who identify with some other party to be men, whereas Democrats and those who identify with some other party are more likely than Independents and Republicans to be women. Thus, there is an association between the variables.

For a contingency table like this one, lambda is misleading. Even though lambda is zero, it doesn't mean that there is no association between the variables. The table shows us that there is an association. The fact that we get a computation of zero is simply a limitation of the statistic.

Other Measures for Nominal Variables

Goodman and Kruskal's tau   When lambda doesn't help us out, what can we use instead? Look at the output chart in Table 8.2. There is another statistic that accompanies lambda—Goodman and Kruskal's tau. It has a similar (although not identical) PRE interpretation. It is an index to the strength of an association as well as an indicator of how much knowing the independent–dependent variable relationship improves our ability to predict the dependent variable. Moreover, tau doesn't have the limitation that lambda does; it won't show you a zero when there is an association between two variables.

Like lambda, you get more than one computation of tau, but both are asymmetric computations. The first one is for the association between *sex* and *partyaf* with *partyaf* as the dependent variable. The second one treats *sex* as the dependent variable. What does it mean? First, like lambda, tau indicates that the association between sex and party affiliation is pretty weak. Second, it tells us that knowing the association between the independent and dependent variables reduces the proportion of errors we might make in predicting the dependent variable by about .7%.

Phi and Cramer's V   There is another set of measures in SPSS for nominal variables that you may find helpful—phi and Cramer's V. Phi can be used with contingency tables with no more than four cells (which means that each variable can have only two categories). Like lambda, the value of phi ranges from 0 to 1, and the value allows us to estimate the strength of an association. Unlike lambda, it does *not* have a proportional reduction in error interpretation.

Cramer's V is for contingency tables with more than four cells. Like phi, the value of Cramer's V ranges from 0 to 1, and it measures the strength of an association. Like phi, it does *not* have a proportional reduction in error interpretation.

Both of these measures can be found in the Crosstabs: Statistics window under the list of Nominal measures (follow the command path Analyze ➡ Descriptive Statistics ➡ Crosstabs, and at Crosstabs click on Statistics).

MEASURES OF ASSOCIATION FOR ORDINAL VARIABLES

In addition to measures of association for nominal variables, there are separate measures for pairs of variables in which *both* variables are ordinal. The most meaningful difference between measures for nominal variables and measures for ordinal variables is that the sign—positive or negative—of the measures is important. Begin by having a look at the list of the measures for ordinal variables. (Use the command path Analyze ➡ Descriptive Statistics ➡ Crosstabs, then click on the Statistics button in the Crosstabs dialog box.) There are several measures listed, starting with gamma.

Gamma

Gamma is a measure of association that, like lambda, has a proportional reduction in error interpretation. Conceptually, though, gamma is a little different. To explain it, let's assume we are interested in the relationship between a respondent's satisfaction with his or her finances and the person's political affiliation as a liberal, moderate, or conservative. You may recall from the previous chapter that the general pattern among the 1996 GSS respondents is that the more satisfied the respondents, the more likely they are to identify themselves as Republicans. How can we assess the strength of the association? The answer is relatively simple—by comparing each of the respondents on their answers to each of the variables.

It will help to follow this example if you recall that the values of the variable, satisfaction with one's finances, are scored from 1 (not at all satisfied) to 3 (satisfied). The *lower* the value of the variable is, the less satisfied is the respondent. (Look at the frequency distribution—follow the command path Analyze ➡ Descriptive Statistics ➡ Frequencies—for the variable *satfin,* if you need to refresh your memory about the categories of the variable). The values of the variable *political affiliation* run from 1 (liberal) to 3 (conservative). The higher the value is, the more conservative is the respondent.

To illustrate the process of comparing respondents on their answers to pairs of variables, let's take the answers given by four respondents to the two variables *satisfaction with one's finances* and *political affiliation.*

	Satisfaction with finances		Political affiliation	
Respondent A	More or less satisfied	(value 2)	Moderate	(value 2)
Respondent B	Satisfied	(value 3)	Conservative	(value 3)
Respondent C	Satisfied	(value 3)	Liberal	(value 1)
Respondent D	More or less satisfied	(value 2)	Conservative	(value 3)

If we start by comparing the answers of respondent A to those given by respondent B, we see that respondent B is more satisfied and also more conservative than respondent A. Respondent B scores higher (when looking at the values) on both categories of each variable. Based on just these two respondents, this suggests a positive association between the categories of the variables. The more satisfied one is, the more conservative one is likely to be; the less satisfied, the less conservative. We call these relationships between cases **concordant pairs.** One respondent is lower (or higher) than the other on both categories of the variables being compared.

Now let's compare respondent A to respondent C. In this case, we see that respondent C is more satisfied than respondent A, but also less conservative than respondent A. Based on the comparison between these two cases—A and C—we can assume a negative association between these two variables. Respondent C scores *higher* on the satisfaction scale than respondent A, but *lower* on the political affiliation variable (based on the values of the categories). This is called a **discordant pair**—one respondent scores higher (or lower) than the other on one category of the variable being compared, but lower (or higher) on the second category.

Finally, let's compare respondent A to respondent D. Respondent D is tied with respondent A on the satisfaction variable (they each have the same value), but respondent D is higher than respondent A on the political affiliation category. This is called a **tied pair.** Pairs for which the respondents are the same on either or both values of the categories being compared are tied.

Although you have compared only a few cases to get a handle on the concept of concordant, discordant, and tied pairs, the computation of gamma, in essence, involves comparing every case (every respondent) in a set of data against every other respondent in the data. Can you imagine doing this for 2,904 cases? Luckily for us, it isn't necessary to do these one by one to compute gamma.

The gamma statistic is figured by dividing the difference between the number of concordant and discordant pairs by the sum of all concordant and discordant pairs. The formula for gamma is

FORMULA 8.2: Gamma

$$\text{Gamma} = \frac{C - D}{C + D}$$

where C stands for the number of concordant pairs, and D represents the number of discordant pairs.[1]

To find gamma, subtract the number of discordant pairs from the number of concordant pairs, then divide the result by the sum of concordant and discordant pairs. As you can probably tell, if there are more concordant than discordant pairs, the gamma value will be positive. If there are more discordant than concordant pairs, the gamma value will be negative. The larger the difference is between the number of concordant and discordant pairs, the larger the gamma value will be. Because gamma can be positive or negative, the

---

[1]Note that tied pairs are excluded from the computation of gamma. Excluding tied pairs has consequences for the interpretation of gamma that will be discussed later in this chapter.

TABLE 8.4 Contingency Table for *satfin* and *polaf* for a Randomly Selected Sample of 24 Respondents From the gss96subset File

POLAF Political Affiliation * SATFIN SATISFACTION WITH FINANCIAL SITUATION Crosstabulation

			SATFIN SATISFACTION WITH FINANCIAL SITUATION			
			1 NOT AT ALL SAT	2 MORE OR LESS	3 SATISFIED	Total
POLAF Political Affiliation	1 Liberal	Count	1	6		7
		% within SATFIN SATISFACTION WITH FINANCIAL SITUATION	16.7%	42.9%		29.2%
	2 Moderate	Count	2	7	1	10
		% within SATFIN SATISFACTION WITH FINANCIAL SITUATION	33.3%	50.0%	25.0%	41.7%
	3 Conservative	Count	3	1	3	7
		% within SATFIN SATISFACTION WITH FINANCIAL SITUATION	50.0%	7.1%	75.0%	29.2%
Total		Count	6	14	4	24
		% within SATFIN SATISFACTION WITH FINANCIAL SITUATION	100.0%	100.0%	100.0%	100.0%

possible values of gamma range from -1.0 to $+1.0$. The closer gamma is to either -1 or $+1$, the stronger is the association; the closer to 0, the weaker the association.

To show you how to find the number of concordant and discordant pairs, let's use a table constructed from a random sample of 24 respondents to the 1996 GSS for the variables *satisfaction with finances* and *political affiliation* (Table 8.4).

As with all measures of association, begin your analysis with an understanding of the association in the contingency table. The general pattern in this subsample of 1996 GSS respondents is like the one we saw among all respondents. It appears that the more satisfied respondents are with their financial situations, the more conservative they are likely to be. The relationship doesn't appear to be very strong, however.

Finding concordant pairs How can we assess the strength and nature of the association with gamma? First, we find the number of concordant pairs in the table. To do so we start with the cell in the top left corner of the table as our point of comparison—equivalent to our respondent A in the previous illustration. Let's call this cell A. In cell A there is one respondent who said he is not at all satisfied with his financial situation and identified himself as a liberal—scoring a 1 on the satisfaction variable as well as on the political affiliation variable. Where do we find the respondents who scored higher on

Cell A 1	Cell B 6	Cell C 0
Cell D 2	Cell E 7	Cell F 1
Cell G 3	Cell H 1	Cell I 3

Figure 8.3 Concordant pairs in relation to cell A.

Cell A 1	Cell B 6	Cell C 0
Cell D 2	Cell E 7	Cell F 1
Cell G 3	Cell H 1	Cell I 3

Figure 8.4 Concordant pairs for cell B.

both variables in relation to the respondent in cell A? They are below and to the right of cell A, in cells E, F, H, and I. (Figure 8.3 illustrates the relationship.) Why? Think about it a second. The respondents in cell E all said they are more or less satisfied (value 2 on the satisfaction variable) *and* moderate (value 2) on political affiliation—higher on both categories of the variables being compared to the respondent in cell A. The respondents in cell F are satisfied (value 3) and moderate (value 2)—also higher on both categories in comparison to the respondent in cell A.

To find the number of concordant pairs in relation to cell A, we add the number of respondents in all of the cells below and to the right of cell A together, and we multiply the result by the number of respondents in cell A. We call the number of respondents in a cell the cell frequency, so we can find the number of concordant pairs in relation to cell A by multiplying the frequency for cell A by the sum of the cell frequencies for cells E, F, H, and I. The concordant pairs in relation to cell A are 1 (7 + 1 + 1 + 3) = 1 (12) = 12.

This isn't the end of the process, because we have to find the number of concordant pairs for all of the cells in the table. Having found the number of concordant pairs in relation to cell A, we move to the right across the table to cell B. The concordant pairs in relation to cell B can be found in the cells below and to the right of cell B—cells F and I. The concordant pairs in relation to cell B are 6(1 + 3) = 6(4) = 24. See Figure 8.4.

Let's move one more cell to the right, to cell C. What are the concordant pairs in relation to cell C? This is a trick question, because there aren't any. There are no cells below and to the right (except for the row and column marginals, which don't count for the purpose of finding concordant pairs).

We do have to move down to the next row, though, starting on the left side, at cell D. Are there any concordant pairs for cell D? Yes, cells H and I. Can

Cell A 1	Cell B 6	Cell C 0
Cell D 2	Cell E 7	Cell F 1
Cell G 3	Cell H 1	Cell I 3

Figure 8.5   Concordant pairs for cell D.

Cell A 1	Cell B 6	Cell C 0
Cell D 2	Cell E 7	Cell F 1
Cell G 3	Cell H 1	Cell I 3

Figure 8.6   Concordant pairs for cell E.

you calculate the total of concordant pairs in relation to cell D? The answer is $2(1 + 3) = 2(4) = 8$. See Figure 8.5.

Move one cell to the right to cell E. Are there concordant pairs in relation to cell E? Yes, there are, but only in one cell, cell I. Thus, finding the number of concordant pairs in relation to cell E is easy: $7(3) = 21$. See Figure 8.6.

Note that there are no concordant cells for cells F, G, H, or I, because there are no cells below and to the right of those cells.

To get the total number of concordant pairs for all cells, we have to add up the number of concordant pairs we found in relation to cells A, B, D, and E.

Concordant pairs in relation to cell A = 12
Concordant pairs in relation to cell B = 24
Concordant pairs in relation to cell D = 8
Concordant pairs in relation to cell E = 21
Total number of concordant pairs = 65

Finding discordant pairs   The next step is to find the discordant pairs—the pairs that would be higher on the values of one variable but lower on the values of the other. Start the process of finding discordant pairs in the upper right corner of the contingency table, with cell C. This is a little tricky, because there are no respondents in cell C. Consequently, there are no discordant pairs in relation to that cell. When you encounter empty cells or cells with no respondents in them, the value of the concordant or discordant pairs in relation to the empty cell is zero.

Had there been respondents in cell C, which cells would have been discordant in relation to cell C? The answer is all cells below and to the left of cell C. Respondents in cell C would have been satisfied (at value 3 of the satisfaction

Cell A 1	Cell B 6	Cell C 0
Cell D 2	Cell E 7	Cell F 1
Cell G 3	Cell H 1	Cell I 3

Figure 8.7 Discordant pairs for cell C.

Cell A 1	Cell B 6	Cell C 0
Cell D 2	Cell E 7	Cell F 1
Cell G 3	Cell H 1	Cell I 3

Figure 8.8 Discordant pairs for cell B.

variable) and liberal (at value 1 of the political affiliation variable). Respondents below and to the left are all lower on the values of the independent variable but higher on the values of the dependent variable. Take for example the respondents in cell E, who are more or less satisfied (value 2, lower than any respondents who might have been in cell C) and moderate (value 2, higher than any respondents who might have been in cell C). See Figure 8.7.

Now we move one cell to the left, to cell B. The cells that are discordant in relation to cell B are below and to the left: cells D and G. To find the number of discordant pairs in relation to cell B, multiply the cell frequency of cell B by the sum of the cell frequencies of cells D and G: 6(2 + 3) = 6(5) = 30. See Figure 8.8.

There are no cells that are discordant in relation to cell A (because there are no cells below and to the left), so we move down one row and all the way to the right, to cell F. The cells that are discordant in relation to cell F are cells G and H. The number of pairs that are discordant in relation to cell F are 1(3 + 1) = 1(4) = 4. See Figure 8.9.

Now move to cell E. There is only one discordant cell in relation to cell E, cell G. The number of pairs discordant in relation to cell E are 7(3) = 21.

To find the total number of discordant pairs, total the discordant pairs we found in relation to cells C, B, F, and E:

Discordant pairs in relation to cell C =   0
Discordant pairs in relation to cell B = 30
Discordant pairs in relation to cell F =   4
Discordant pairs in relation to cell E = 21
Total number of discordant pairs   = 55

Cell A 1	Cell B 6	Cell C 0
Cell D 2	Cell E 7	Cell F 1
Cell G 3	Cell H 1	Cell I 3

Figure 8.9 Discordant pairs for cell F.

Finding gamma   We have all the information we need to work our formula for gamma. C is the number of concordant pairs (65) and D is the number of discordant pairs (55).

$$\text{Gamma} = \frac{C - D}{C + D}$$

$$= \frac{65 - 55}{65 + 55} = \frac{10}{120}$$

$$\text{Gamma} = .083$$

✔ **Checking Your Work**   The result of your computation of gamma will always be a number between -1 and $+1$. You should not get a value of gamma less than -1 or greater than $+1$. If you do, you have made a mistake and you need to go back and check your work.

In reading gamma as a guide to the strength of the association, it is clear that the association in our table of 24 GSS respondents is weak. The sign on gamma is important. In this case it is positive, which tells us that a high value on the independent variable is associated with a high value on the dependent variable. The more satisfied respondents are with their finances, the more conservative they are likely to be. Conversely, the less satisfied they are, the more liberal they are likely to be. Finally, the PRE interpretation of gamma suggests that knowing the association between the independent and dependent variables improves our ability to predict the dependent variable by about 8%.

Avoiding Common Pitfalls   There are two aspects of computing gamma that students find a little tricky. First, it's easy to include row and column totals in the computations, especially when you are working with SPSS tables to practice your skills. Be sure you are clear about the difference between cell frequencies and the row and column marginals so that you only work with cell frequencies in your computations.

Second, the number of computations you have to do expands and contracts depending on the size of the table you are working with. The more cells a table has, the more computations you have to do; the fewer cells, the fewer computations. The number of computations is determined by how many concordant pairs (the cells below and to the right) and the number of discordant pairs (the cells below and to the left). Be sure when you do your computations that you are picking up all possible concordant and discordant pairs (without including row totals and column totals).

Another example of gamma   Let's try another example. This time, use the contingency table in Table 8.5.

Skills Practice 5   Write an analysis of the contingency table in Table 8.5. For this random sample of GSS respondents, what's the nature of the association between the level of education achieved by the respondents (*degree*) and their political affiliation (*polaf*)? Is it positive or negative; strong or weak?

Now let's find gamma, using Formula 8.2.

$$\text{Gamma} = \frac{C - D}{C + D}$$

Find the concordant pairs   As you did in the preceding example, begin in the upper left corner of the table with cell A to find the number of pairs concordant in relation to cell A. Multiply the frequency in cell A by the sum of the frequencies in all cells below and to the right of cell A. You probably notice that you are working with more cells in this example than in the previous example, because the table is bigger. Remember that the number of computations you have to do depends on the size of (the number of cells in) the table. The concordant pairs in relation to cell A are 4(8 + 2 + 0 + 1 + 8 + 0 + 2 + 1) = 4(22) = 88. See Figure 8.10.

TABLE 8.5   Contingency Table for _degree_ and _polaf_ for a Subset of 47 Cases From the gss96subset File

POLAF recoded political views * DEGREE RS HIGHEST DEGREE Crosstabulation

			DEGREE RS HIGHEST DEGREE					
			0 LT HIGH SCHOOL	1 HIGH SCHOOL	2 JUNIOR COLLEGE	3 BACHELOR	4 GRADUATE	Total
POLAF recoded political views	1 Liberal	Count	4	6		2	2	14
		% within DEGREE RS HIGHEST DEGREE	26.7%	27.3%		50.0%	50.0%	29.8%
	2 Moderate	Count	2	8	2		1	13
		% within DEGREE RS HIGHEST DEGREE	13.3%	36.4%	100.0%		25.0%	27.7%
	3 Conservative	Count	9	8		2	1	20
		% within DEGREE RS HIGHEST DEGREE	60.0%	36.4%		50.0%	25.0%	42.6%
Total		Count	15	22	2	4	4	47
		% within DEGREE RS HIGHEST DEGREE	100.0%	100.0%	100.0%	100.0%	100.0%	100.0%

Figure 8.10   Concordant pairs for cell A.

Skills Practice 6   Find the rest of the concordant pairs in Table 8.5. (Hint: Move to the right, to cell B. Find the concordant pairs in relation to cell B. Then move to the right again, to cell C, and find the concordant pairs in relation to cell C. When you have found all of the concordant pairs for the first row, move down to the second row. Begin on the far left with cell F. Find all of the concordant pairs for the cells on the second row.) When you have finished, add up all of the concordant pairs to get the total number of concordant pairs for the table.

Cell A 4	Cell B 6	Cell C 0	Cell D 2	Cell E 2
Cell F 2	Cell G 8	Cell H 2	Cell I 0	Cell J 1
Cell K 9	Cell L 8	Cell M 0	Cell N 2	Cell O 1

Figure 8.11 Discordant pairs for cell E.

Find the discordant pairs Starting with the cell in the upper right corner of the table, cell E, find the discordant pairs. The discordant pairs in relation to cell E are those below and to the left of cell E. Multiply the cell frequency for cell E by the sum of the frequencies of the cells that are discordant in relation to cell E. The discordant pairs in relation to cell E are $2(2 + 8 + 2 + 0 + 9 + 8 + 0 + 2) = 2(31) = 62$. See Figure 8.11.

> **Skills Practice 7** Find the rest of the discordant pairs in Table 8.5. (Hint: Move to the left, to cell D. Find the discordant pairs in relation to cell D. Then move to the left again, to cell C, and find the discordant pairs in relation to cell C. When you have found all of the discordant pairs for the first row, move down to the second row. Begin on the far right with cell J. Find all of the discordant pairs for the cells on the second row.) When you have finished, add up all of the discordant pairs to get the total number of discordant pairs for the table.

Finding gamma Plug the total numbers of concordant pairs and discordant pairs into your formula for gamma.

$$\text{Gamma} = \frac{C - D}{C + D}$$

$$= \frac{180 - 311}{180 + 311} = -\frac{131}{491}$$

$$\text{Gamma} = -.267$$

Interpreting gamma The gamma statistic confirms the negative association we observed in the contingency table. The more education respondents have (the higher the values on the *degree* variable), the more liberal respondents are (the lower the values on the political affiliation variable). The less education respondents have, the more conservative they are. The association is fairly consistent across the Liberal and Moderate categories of the political affiliation variable, but less consistent across the Conservative category. The gamma statistic is closer to 0 than to -1, indicating an association that is on the weaker side. Nevertheless, the PRE interpretation tells us that knowing the independent–dependent variable relationship improves our ability to predict the dependent variable by about 27%, and that's relatively good.

Skills Practice 8 Use the contingency table shown here to analyze the association between a respondent's religious views (fundamentalist to liberal), *fund,* and their political views (conservative to liberal), *polaf.* The table consists of a randomly selected sample of 85 respondents from the 1996 GSS.

A. What is the nature of the association between the variables? How strong is it? What is its direction?

B. Calculate and interpret gamma. Does gamma support your analysis of the table?

POLAF Political Affiliation * FUND HOW FUNDAMENTALIST IS R CURRENTLY Crosstabulation

			FUND HOW FUNDAMENTALIST IS R CURRENTLY			
			1 LIBERAL	2 MODERATE	3 FUNDAMENTALIST	Total
POLAF Political Affiliation	1 Liberal	Count	7	2	9	18
		% within FUND HOW FUNDAMENTALIST IS R CURRENTLY	29.2%	5.4%	37.5%	21.2%
	2 Moderate	Count	9	20	10	39
		% within FUND HOW FUNDAMENTALIST IS R CURRENTLY	37.5%	54.1%	41.7%	45.9%
	3 Conservative	Count	8	15	5	28
		% within FUND HOW FUNDAMENTALIST IS R CURRENTLY	33.3%	40.5%	20.8%	32.9%
Total		Count	24	37	24	85
		% within FUND HOW FUNDAMENTALIST IS R CURRENTLY	100.0%	100.0%	100.0%	100.0%

Finding Gamma Using SPSS

Finding gamma is just like finding lambda. Follow the command path Analyze ➡ Descriptive Statistics ➡ Crosstabs. At the Crosstabs dialog box, click on the Statistics button. Look for gamma in the Crosstabs: Statistics window in the column labeled Ordinal. (See the SPSS Guide "Measures of Association" if you need help with this.)

Let's try finding gamma using the variables *fund* (how religiously fundamentalist a respondent is) and *polaf* (a respondent's political affiliation).

- Use the command path Analyze ➡ Descriptive Statistics ➡ Crosstabs to get to the Crosstabs dialog box.

- At the Crosstabs window, scroll down the variable list to select your independent and dependent variables.

- Click on the Cells button to select Percentages for the Column. Then click on Continue.

- Click on the Statistics button to select Gamma from the list of Ordinal measures. Click on Continue.

- At the Crosstabs dialog box, click on OK.

Your output should include a contingency table and a set of statistics like the ones in Table 8.6.

Interpretation   First, remember that you should begin your analysis with the contingency table. What does it tell us about the nature of the association, its strength and direction? Second, what does gamma add to the analysis?

> The more liberal in terms of religion respondents are, the more politically liberal they are. The relationship appears to be fairly strong, because it is very consistent across the categories (rows) of the dependent variable. Moreover, the differences in the percentages across the rows are fairly large. The biggest difference is about 16 percentage points—the gap between those religious liberals who are politically liberal and the religious fundamentalists who are politically liberal. The association is positive. The more liberal respondents are in terms of religion (the low value on the independent variable), the more liberal they are politically (the low value on the dependent variable).

What does gamma add? The gamma statistic, .200, is found in the column headed Value. It confirms our analysis of the association from the contingency table. The association is positive, meaning that the more liberal respondents are in terms of religion, the more politically liberal they are likely to be.

> The relationship is somewhat weak, with gamma closer to 0 than to 1. However, knowing the association between the respondents' religious beliefs and their political affiliation allows us to improve our ability to predict the respondents' religious affiliation by 20%.

TABLE 8.6   Contingency Table for the Variables *fund* and *polaf* From the gss96subset File

POLAF recoded political views * FUND HOW FUNDAMENTALIST IS R CURRENTLY Crosstabulation

| | | | FUND HOW FUNDAMENTALIST IS R CURRENTLY | | | |
			1 LIBERAL	2 MODERATE	3 FUNDAMENTALIST	Total
POLAF recoded political views	1 Liberal	Count	266	229	157	652
		% within FUND HOW FUNDAMENTALIST IS R CURRENTLY	35.0%	23.0%	18.8%	25.2%
	2 Moderate	Count	266	396	311	973
		% within FUND HOW FUNDAMENTALIST IS R CURRENTLY	35.0%	39.8%	37.3%	37.6%
	3 Conservative	Count	227	369	365	961
		% within FUND HOW FUNDAMENTALIST IS R CURRENTLY	29.9%	37.1%	43.8%	37.2%
Total		Count	759	994	833	2586
		% within FUND HOW FUNDAMENTALIST IS R CURRENTLY	100.0%	100.0%	100.0%	100.0%

Symmetric Measures

		Value	Asymp. Std. Error[a]	Approx. T[b]	Approx. Sig.
Ordinal by Ordinal	Gamma	.200	.026	7.553	.000
N of Valid Cases		2586			

a. Not assuming the null hypothesis.

b. Using the asymptotic standard error assuming the null hypothesis.

Skills Practice 9   In the previous skills practices, you looked at the association between satisfaction with one's finances, *satfin,* and one's political affiliation, *polaf,* for a random sample of GSS respondents. Now look at the association for all respondents. Produce a contingency table for the association between *satfin* and *polaf,* and use SPSS to find and interpret gamma.

Limitations of Gamma

Like lambda, gamma is better at picking up on some kinds of patterns than others. First, gamma is a measure of association most appropriately used with symmetric associations—relationships between variables in which there is no clear independent–dependent association or causal relationship.

Second, gamma is best at finding linear relationships between variables—associations in which the highest percentages across the rows of the table line up on the diagonal (as in Table 7.6 in Chapter 7). Gamma is not as effective at describing associations that may have a curved pattern to them. For example, let's look at the association between one's level of education using the variable *degree* and one's political views using the variable *polaf.* You may recall from Chapter 7 that it seemed that the association was one in which the more education respondents have, the more extreme politically they are likely to be. Highly educated respondents were likely to be more conservative and more liberal than less well educated respondents. What does gamma lead us to believe?

Skills Practice 10 Find and interpret gamma for the association between *degree* and *polviews.* Check your answer against the interpretation that follows.

You should see a gamma statistic of $-.04$, suggesting a very weak, negative association (the more education respondents have, the more liberal they are likely to be). However, taking gamma at face value, without complementing its interpretation with an analysis of the contingency table, would be misleading. To supplement (or replace) gamma in certain situations, you could use one or more of the measures described in the next section.

Additional Measures of Association for Ordinal Variables

Somer's *d* Unlike gamma (and like lambda), Somer's *d* has both a symmetric and an asymmetric computation. It doesn't ignore tied pairs, as does gamma. Consequently, it usually indicates weaker associations than does gamma. Somer's *d* is normally used instead of gamma when the association between two variables is clearly asymmetric.

Kendall's tau-*b* and Kendall's tau-*c* Kendall's tau-*b* and tau-*c* are symmetric measures of association. They are similar in interpretation to gamma in that they function as indexes of association to help assess the strength of an association. The values of tau-*b* and tau-*c* range from -1 to $+1$. Tau-*b* can be used only with square contingency tables (tables in which the independent variable has the same number of categories as the dependent variable). Tau-*c* can be used with tables of any size. Tau-*b* and tau-*c* are different from gamma in that they do not ignore tied pairs. As a result, they normally indicate weaker associations than does gamma.

CONTROLLING FOR THIRD VARIABLES

Just as contingency tables can help us assess the effect of third variables on associations between independent and dependent variables, measures of association can provide us with information about their impact. Let's look at an example. Recall that we started this chapter with an analysis of the relationship between sex and party affiliation. Look back at Figures 8.1 and 8.2 to refresh your memory about the nature and strength of the association as indicated by the contingency table and lambda. Then use SPSS to produce contingency tables for the sex and party affiliation (*partyaf*) variables controlled for age (using *agecat*). In addition to the percentages on the column, ask for the statistic, lambda.

- Use the command path Analyze ➥ Descriptive Statistics ➥ Crosstabs.
- Enter the independent, dependent, and control variables.
- Click on Cells, then Column, and Continue.
- Click on Statistics, then Lambda, and Continue.
- At the Crosstabs dialog box, click on OK.

You should get a set of contingency tables and statistics like the ones in Tables 8.7 and 8.8. What do we do with all of this information? Start by analyzing the association between sex and party affiliation for each of the categories of the control variable, *agecat*.

Skills Practice 11   Analyze the association between sex and party affiliation for each of the categories of the *agecat* variable. What do you find? Does the nature or the strength of the association change from what we saw in Table 8.1? You will see the answer in the discussion that follows. (*For extra practice at computing lambda,* compute lambda for each of the tables by hand. Then check your answer against the lambda statistic that SPSS produces.)

Now compare the values of lambda in the tables controlling for age as compared to the value of lambda for the association between *sex* and *partyaf* without the control variable (Table 8.2). Lambda for the association between sex and party affiliation without the control variable is .04, whereas Goodman and Kruskal's tau is .007. What happens to these statistics when the control variable is introduced?

TABLE 8.7 Partial Tables for the Association Between Sex and Party Affiliation Controlling for Age (With the *agecat* Variable) in the gss96subset File

PARTYAF recoded party identification * SEX RESPONDENTS SEX * AGECAT recoded age - four categories Crosstabulation

AGECAT recoded age - four categories				1 MALE	2 FEMALE	Total
				SEX RESPONDENTS SEX		
1 18 thru 25	PARTYAF recoded party identification	1 Democrat	Count	28	68	96
			% within SEX RESPONDENTS SEX	18.2%	34.3%	27.3%
		2 Independent	Count	90	86	176
			% within SEX RESPONDENTS SEX	58.4%	43.4%	50.0%
		3 Republican	Count	34	43	77
			% within SEX RESPONDENTS SEX	22.1%	21.7%	21.9%
		4 Other	Count	2	1	3
			% within SEX RESPONDENTS SEX	1.3%	.5%	.9%
	Total		Count	154	198	352
			% within SEX RESPONDENTS SEX	100.0%	100.0%	100.0%
2 26 thru 39	PARTYAF recoded party identification	1 Democrat	Count	97	175	272
			% within SEX RESPONDENTS SEX	23.7%	33.5%	29.2%
		2 Independent	Count	159	208	367
			% within SEX RESPONDENTS SEX	38.8%	39.8%	39.4%
		3 Republican	Count	144	128	272
			% within SEX RESPONDENTS SEX	35.1%	24.5%	29.2%
		4 Other	Count	10	11	21
			% within SEX RESPONDENTS SEX	2.4%	2.1%	2.3%
	Total		Count	410	522	932
			% within SEX RESPONDENTS SEX	100.0%	100.0%	100.0%
3 40 thru 64	PARTYAF recoded party identification	1 Democrat	Count	155	253	408
			% within SEX RESPONDENTS SEX	28.1%	41.3%	35.0%
		2 Independent	Count	220	197	417
			% within SEX RESPONDENTS SEX	39.9%	32.1%	35.8%
		3 Republican	Count	173	156	329
			% within SEX RESPONDENTS SEX	31.3%	25.4%	28.2%
		4 Other	Count	4	7	11
			% within SEX RESPONDENTS SEX	.7%	1.1%	.9%
	Total		Count	552	613	1165
			% within SEX RESPONDENTS SEX	100.0%	100.0%	100.0%
4 65 thru 89	PARTYAF recoded party identification	1 Democrat	Count	70	128	198
			% within SEX RESPONDENTS SEX	41.9%	46.4%	44.7%
		2 Independent	Count	45	63	108
			% within SEX RESPONDENTS SEX	26.9%	22.8%	24.4%
		3 Republican	Count	49	80	129
			% within SEX RESPONDENTS SEX	29.3%	29.0%	29.1%
		4 Other	Count	3	5	8
			% within SEX RESPONDENTS SEX	1.8%	1.8%	1.8%
	Total		Count	167	276	443
			% within SEX RESPONDENTS SEX	100.0%	100.0%	100.0%

TABLE 8.8 Measures of Association for the Variables Sex and Party Affiliation Controlling for Age (*agecat*) in the gss96subset File

Directional Measures

AGECAT recoded age - four categories				Value	Asymp. Std. Error[a]	Approx. T[b]	Approx Sig.
1 18 thru 25	Nominal by Nominal	Lambda	Symmetric	.015	.040	.374	.709
			PARTYAF recoded party identification Dependent	.000	.000	[c]	[c]
			SEX RESPONDENTS SEX Dependent	.032	.085	.374	.709
		Goodman and Kruskal tau	PARTYAF recoded party identification Dependent	.019	.011		.000[d]
			SEX RESPONDENTS SEX Dependent	.036	.019		.005[d]
2 26 thru 39	Nominal by Nominal	Lambda	Symmetric	.016	.017	.971	.332
			PARTYAF recoded party identification Dependent	.000	.000	[c]	[c]
			SEX RESPONDENTS SEX Dependent	.039	.039	.971	.332
		Goodman and Kruskal tau	PARTYAF recoded party identification Dependent	.008	.004		.000[d]
			SEX RESPONDENTS SEX Dependent	.018	.009		.001[d]
3 40 thru 64	Nominal by Nominal	Lambda	Symmetric	.074	.030	2.414	.016
			PARTYAF recoded party identification Dependent	.075	.027	2.648	.008
			SEX RESPONDENTS SEX Dependent	.072	.048	1.466	.143
		Goodman and Kruskal tau	PARTYAF recoded party identification Dependent	.010	.004		.000[d]
			SEX RESPONDENTS SEX Dependent	.020	.008		.000[d]
4 65 thru 89	Nominal by Nominal	Lambda	Symmetric	.000	.000	[c]	[c]
			PARTYAF recoded party identification Dependent	.000	.000	[c]	[c]
			SEX RESPONDENTS SEX Dependent	.000	.000	[c]	[c]
		Goodman and Kruskal tau	PARTYAF recoded party identification Dependent	.001	.002		.624[d]
			SEX RESPONDENTS SEX Dependent	.003	.005		.756[d]

a. Not assuming the null hypothesis.

b. Using the asymptotic standard error assuming the null hypothesis.

c. Cannot be computed because the asymptotic standard error equals zero.

d. Based on chi-square approximation

Age category 18 through 25 Notice that lambda (with *partyaf* dependent) is zero but Goodman and Kruskal's tau is larger, indicating that the association between sex and party affiliation is a little stronger than it is for the relationship without the control variable. (Remember that lambda can be zero even when there is an association between two variables.) The nature of the relationship has changed a little. For respondents who are young adults, women are more likely than men to say they are Democrats, whereas men are more likely than women to say they are Independents. There is almost no gap at all between the percentages of men and women who say they are Republicans or Other.

Age category 26 through 39 Lambda is zero, but Goodman and Kruskal's tau is only slightly larger than for the association without the control variable. However, the nature of the association has changed—women are more likely than men to be Democrats, whereas men are more likely than women to be Republicans. Women are as likely as men to be Independents or Other.

Age category 40 through 64   Lambda is a little larger. The nature of the association between sex and party affiliation for respondents in the age 40 through 64 category is about the same as it is for respondents as a whole, but it is a little stronger in this age group. Women are more likely than men to be Democrats, whereas men are more likely than women to be Independents or Republicans. The differences in the percentages across the rows are not large, so the association is still fairly weak, as indicated by Goodman and Kruskal's tau, which is .01.

Age category 65 through 89   Among respondents of retirement age, the association is weaker than it is among respondents as a whole, and weaker than it is in the other age categories. Lambda is zero, whereas Goodman and Kruskal's tau is .001. The nature of the association is nearly the same, though. Women are more likely than men to say they are Democrats, whereas men are more likely than women to say they are Independents. However, men are as likely as women to say they are Republicans or Other.

Effect of the Control Variable

Age seems to be a factor influencing the association between sex and party affiliation. The nature of the gender gap doesn't change much across age categories. It is strongest among those who are young adults and weakest among those of retirement age.

In all age categories, women are more likely than men to say they are Democrats. In some of the age categories, men are more likely than women to say they are Republicans (the middle-age categories, ages 26 through 64), whereas in other age categories men are as likely as women to say they are Republicans (the young adult and retirement age categories). Where men are as likely as women to say they are Republicans (age categories 18 through 25 and 65 through 89), men are more likely than women to say they are Independents.

The gender gap is largest among those in the youngest age category, 18 through 25. 34.3% of female respondents say they are Democrats as compared to 18.2% of the male respondents—a gap of 16 percentage points. However, men in that age category are more likely to be Independents than Republicans, and they are somewhat more likely than women to say they are Independents—58.4% compared to 43.4%, a gap of 15 percentage points.

The gender gap is the narrowest among those in the retirement age category—ages 65 through 89. Women are only slightly more likely than men to say they are Democrats. As with the youngest age group, men and women are equally likely to say they are Republicans. Men are more likely than women to say they are Independents, but the difference is not a large one—less than 5 percentage points.

Another Example

Let's try another example, this time using two ordinal variables: satisfaction with one's financial situation (*satfin*) and political affiliation (*polaf*), controlling for *sex*. When we looked at the association between these variables earlier in this chapter, we found that the more satisfied the respondents are with their financial situations, the more likely they are to be conservative; the less satisfied, the more likely they are to be liberal. The association is positive, and gamma (.132) suggests it is fairly weak.

Produce a set of contingency tables for the association between *satfin* and *polaf*, controlling for *sex*. Don't forget to ask for percentages on the columns and for the gamma statistic. Your tables should look like the ones in Tables 8.9 and 8.10.

Interpretation   For males and females, the general pattern remains—the more satisfied the respondents are, the more likely they are to be conservative, but the association is weaker for males than for females. For males, those who are more or less satisfied are more likely to be either liberal or moderate than those who are satisfied or who are not at all satisfied. Those who are satisfied are more likely to be conservative than those who are more or less satisfied. The association is much stronger for females, and it looks more like the association among the respondents as a whole. The association is positive for both males and females.

Gamma is consistent with our analysis—weaker for males and a little stronger for females than the association for all respondents together. It is positive for both groups. In sum, satisfaction with one's financial situation has more of an effect on the political views of female than male respondents. Knowing the association between satisfaction with one's finances and political affiliation helps us reduce our errors in predicting male respondents' political affiliations by 11%, but it reduces errors in predicting female respondents' political affiliations by 15%.

TABLE 8.9 Contingency Table for the Association Between Satisfaction With One's Financial Situation and Political Affiliation, Controlling for Sex, in the gss96subset File

POLAF recoded political views * SATFIN SATISFACTION WITH FINANCIAL SITUATION * SEX RESPONDENTS SEX Crosstabulation

SEX RESPONDENTS SEX				SATFIN SATISFACTION WITH FINANCIAL SITUATION			Total
				1 NOT AT ALL SAT	2 MORE OR LESS	3 SATISFIED	
1 MALE	POLAF recoded political views	1 Liberal	Count	74	155	57	286
			% within SATFIN SATISFACTION WITH FINANCIAL SITUATION	25.1%	26.6%	16.7%	23.5%
		2 Moderate	Count	99	227	120	446
			% within SATFIN SATISFACTION WITH FINANCIAL SITUATION	33.6%	39.0%	35.2%	36.6%
		3 Conservative	Count	122	200	164	486
			% within SATFIN SATISFACTION WITH FINANCIAL SITUATION	41.4%	34.4%	48.1%	39.9%
	Total		Count	295	582	341	1218
			% within SATFIN SATISFACTION WITH FINANCIAL SITUATION	100.0%	100.0%	100.0%	100.0%
2 FEMALE	POLAF recoded political views	1 Liberal	Count	137	183	89	409
			% within SATFIN SATISFACTION WITH FINANCIAL SITUATION	30.3%	28.3%	21.2%	26.9%
		2 Moderate	Count	186	254	155	595
			% within SATFIN SATISFACTION WITH FINANCIAL SITUATION	41.2%	39.3%	37.0%	39.2%
		3 Conservative	Count	129	210	175	514
			% within SATFIN SATISFACTION WITH FINANCIAL SITUATION	28.5%	32.5%	41.8%	33.9%
	Total		Count	452	647	419	1518
			% within SATFIN SATISFACTION WITH FINANCIAL SITUATION	100.0%	100.0%	100.0%	100.0%

TABLE 8.10 Measures of Association for the Association Between Satisfaction With One's Financial Situation and Political Affiliation, Controlling for Sex, in the gss96ssubset File

Symmetric Measures

SEX RESPONDENTS SEX			Value	Asymp. Std. Error[a]	Approx. T[b]	Approx. Sig.
1 MALE	Ordinal by Ordinal	Gamma	.105	.040	2.632	.008
	N of Valid Cases		1218			
2 FEMALE	Ordinal by Ordinal	Gamma	.147	.034	4.259	.000
	N of Valid Cases		1518			

a. Not assuming the null hypothesis.

b. Using the asymptotic standard error assuming the null hypothesis.

Avoiding Common Pitfalls Problems students have with measures of association for control variables largely stem from questions about how to assess the level of measurement of the variables in order to apply the correct measure of association. This problem is easy to solve, because the level of measurement of the control variable has no bearing on the measure of association used. The measure of association is selected based solely on the level of measurement of the independent and dependent variables. Thus, if the independent and dependent variables are nominal, lambda can be used, even if the control variable is ordinal or numerical. Similarly, if the independent and dependent variables are ordinal, gamma can be applied, even if the control variable is nominal or numerical.

SUMMARY

In this chapter you were introduced to measures of association, statistics that allow us to assess the extent of an association between two variables. We focused on two primary measures: lambda for nominal variables and gamma for ordinal variables. You learned to compute both measures by hand and to find them using SPSS.

Measures of association are evaluated on a scale of 1 or −1 to 0. The closer to zero a measure is, the weaker is the association between an independent and dependent variable. The closer to either 1 or −1, the stronger is the association.

In addition to telling us about the strength of relationship, many of the measures introduced in this chapter have a proportional reduction in error (PRE) interpretation. By multiplying the association statistic by 100, you can read the statistic as a percentage. Doing so tells you how much your ability to predict the dependent variable is improved if you know the nature of the association between an independent and dependent variable.

Finally, you learned to apply measures of association to partial tables in order to assess changes in an independent–dependent variable relationship when a third, control variable is introduced.

In the next chapter you will learn some techniques for assessing the extent of an association between two numerical variables.

KEY CONCEPTS

Measures of association	Lambda	Gamma
Proportional reduction in error (PRE)	Symmetric value	Concordant pair
	Asymmetric value	Discordant pair
		Tied pair

ANSWERS TO SKILLS PRACTICES

1. You should get a contingency table for *rcregion* and *partyaf* like the one that follows.

PARTYAF recoded party identification * RCREGION recoded region variable Crosstabulation

				1 Northeast	2 Midwest	3 Southeast	4 West	Total
				RCREGION recoded region variable				
PARTYAF recoded party identification	1 Democrat	Count		202	227	345	203	977
		% within RCREGION recoded region variable		35.3%	32.6%	34.1%	32.9%	33.7%
	2 Independent	Count		231	278	339	223	1071
		% within RCREGION recoded region variable		40.4%	39.9%	33.5%	36.1%	37.0%
	3 Republican	Count		131	182	316	178	807
		% within RCREGION recoded region variable		22.9%	26.1%	31.2%	28.8%	27.8%
	4 Other	Count		8	10	12	13	43
		% within RCREGION recoded region variable		1.4%	1.4%	1.2%	2.1%	1.5%
Total		Count		572	697	1012	617	2898
		% within RCREGION recoded region variable		100.0%	100.0%	100.0%	100.0%	100.0%

What does this tell us about the association between these two variables? First, you may notice that respondents from the Northeast are more likely to say they are Democrats than respondents from any other region, and they are also more likely to say they are Independents (although only slightly more likely than respondents from the Midwest). Respondents from the Southeast are more likely than respondents from other regions to say they are Republicans, whereas respondents in the West are more likely to identify with some other party. In most cases, though, the differences are small—only a matter of a few percentage points. Exceptions are the differences between the percentages of respondents from the Northeast and Midwest who say they are Independents as compared to respondents from the Southeast, and there is a difference of nearly 10% between the respondents from the Southeast who say they are Republicans and the respondents from the Northeast who say they are Republicans. On the whole, however, this association doesn't appear to be very strong. On the face of it, knowing where a respondent is from probably wouldn't help to guess their party affiliation very much.

2. Your frequency distribution should look like the one that follows.

PARTYAF recoded party identification * RELIG RS RELIGIOUS PREFERENCE Crosstabulation

| | | | RELIG RS RELIGIOUS PREFERENCE | | | | | |
			1 PROTESTANT	2 CATHOLIC	3 JEWISH	4 NONE	5 OTHER	Total
PARTYAF recoded party identification	1 Democrat	Count	559	248	38	92	38	975
		% within RELIG RS RELIGIOUS PREFERENCE	33.6%	36.4%	55.9%	27.3%	26.6%	33.7%
	2 Independent	Count	535	252	19	180	82	1068
		% within RELIG RS RELIGIOUS PREFERENCE	32.2%	37.0%	27.9%	53.4%	57.3%	36.9%
	3 Republican	Count	548	172	7	60	20	807
		% within RELIG RS RELIGIOUS PREFERENCE	33.0%	25.2%	10.3%	17.8%	14.0%	27.9%
	4 Other	Count	21	10	4	5	3	43
		% within RELIG RS RELIGIOUS PREFERENCE	1.3%	1.5%	5.9%	1.5%	2.1%	1.5%
Total		Count	1663	682	68	337	143	2893
		% within RELIG RS RELIGIOUS PREFERENCE	100.0%	100.0%	100.0%	100.0%	100.0%	100.0%

Follow Formula 8.1 to find lambda.

Step 1. Look down the row marginal totals until you find the highest frequency of the dependent variable *partyaf*. The highest frequency is associated with the category Independent, so circle the frequency for that category, 1,068. Find E_1 by subtracting 1,068 from N. $E_1 = 2,893 - 1,068 = 1,825$.

Step 2. Find E_2 by looking down each column of the independent variable and circling the highest frequency in each column (excluding the column marginal totals): Protestant, 559; Catholic, 252; Jewish, 38; None, 180; Other, 82. Now add the circled frequencies: 559 ¦ 252 ¦ 38 ¦ 180 ¦ 82 = 1,111. Subtract 1,111 from N to get E_2. $E_2 = 2,893 - 1,111 = 1,782$.

Step 3. Apply Formula 8.1.

$$E_1 = 1{,}825 \qquad E_2 = 1{,}782$$

$$\lambda = \frac{E_1 - E_2}{E_1} = \frac{1{,}825 - 1{,}782}{1{,}825} = \frac{43}{1{,}825} = .02$$

What does lambda tell us? As we thought, the relationship isn't very strong. Knowing the association between the independent and dependent variables, *religion* and *party affiliation,* doesn't help us very much at guessing the dependent variable, *party affiliation.* Our ability to predict the dependent variable is improved only by about 2%.

3. A. Race and party affiliation: The correct lambda to use is the asymmetric lambda with *partyaf* dependent, .082. The relationship is fairly weak. Knowing the association between race and party affiliation improves our ability to predict the dependent variable, *party affiliation,* only by about 8%.

   B. Party affiliation and political affiliation: The lambda to use in this case is the asymmetric lambda with *partyaf* dependent, .156. This association appears to be a little stronger than most. Knowing the association between the political affiliation and party affiliation variables improves our ability to predict party affiliation by nearly 16%.

   C. Party affiliation and voting in 1992: In this relationship, the dependent variable is voting in 1992, so the lambda to use is the one with *vote92* dependent, .000. Is there really no relationship between the variables? No, because an analysis of the contingency table shows us that Democratic and Republican respondents were more likely to vote than Independents and those affiliated with some other party. Conversely, Independents and Others were more likely to say they did not vote in 1992, and Independents were more likely to say they weren't eligible to vote. Clearly there is a pattern here. An association between these variables is confirmed if you look down at Goodman and Kruskal's tau, with *vote92* as the dependent variable, .043. The measure indicates that the association is weak, but knowing the association between the independent and dependent variables improves our ability to predict the dependent variable by about 4%.

4. A compared to B is discordant. A compared to C is discordant. A compared to D is concordant. A compared to E is tied (on the party affiliation variable). A compared to F is concordant.

5. In general the more education respondents have, the more liberal they are likely to be. The association is negative (based on the *values* associated with the categories of the variable—a high value on the independent variable is associated with a low value on the dependent variable). The association appears to be fairly strong.

6. Concordant pairs for Table 8.5:

Concordant pairs in relation to cell A =
$4(8 + 2 + 0 + 1 + 8 + 0 + 2 + 1) = 4(22) = \qquad 88$

Concordant pairs in relation to cell B =
$6(2 + 0 + 1 + 0 + 2 + 1) = 6(6) = \qquad 36$

Concordant pairs in relation to cell C = $0(0 + 1 + 2 + 1) = 0(4) = \quad 0$

Concordant pairs in relation to cell D = $2(1 + 1) = 2(2) = \qquad 4$

Concordant pairs in relation to cell F = $2(8 + 0 + 2 + 1) = 2(11) = \quad 22$

Concordant pairs in relation to cell G = $8(0 + 2 + 1) = 8(3) = \qquad 24$

Concordant pairs in relation to cell H = $2(2 + 1) = 2(3) = \qquad 6$

Concordant pairs in relation to cell I = $0(1) = \qquad 0$

Total number of concordant pairs = $\qquad \overline{180}$

7. Discordant pairs for Table 8.5:

Discordant pairs in relation to cell E =
$2(2 + 8 + 2 + 0 + 9 + 8 + 0 + 2) = 2(31) = \qquad 62$

Discordant pairs in relation to cell D =
$2(2 + 8 + 2 + 9 + 8 + 0) = 2(29) = \qquad 58$

Discordant pairs in relation to cell C = $0(2 + 8 + 9 + 8) = \qquad 0$

Discordant pairs in relation to cell B = $6(2 + 9) = 6(11) = \qquad 66$

Discordant pairs in relation to cell J = $1(9 + 8 + 0 + 2) = 1(19) = \quad 19$

Discordant pairs in relation to cell I = $0(9 + 8 + 0) = \qquad 0$

Discordant pairs in relation to cell H = $2(9 + 8) = 2(17) = \qquad 34$

Discordant pairs in relation to cell G = $8(9) = \qquad \underline{72}$

Total number of discordant pairs = $\qquad 311$

8. Analyzing and computing gamma for the contingency table.

A. To see whether you are really paying attention, this table looks different from what you might expect to see. The association between the variables, generally, is that the more conservative respondents are in terms of religion, the more liberal they are politically. The association doesn't appear to be very strong, because it isn't consistent across the rows of the categories of the Liberal and Conservative categories of the dependent variable. In fact, religious moderates are the most likely to be both politically moderate *and* politically conservative. Religious conservatives are more likely to be politically liberal than religious moderates or religious liberals, but 29% of those who say they are religious liberals describe themselves as politically liberal. The association is negative—the higher the value on the independent variable (the more conservative a respondent is religiously), the lower the value on the dependent variable.

B. Computation of gamma:

Concordant pairs in relation to cell A:
$7(20 + 10 + 15 + 5) = 7(50) =$ 350

Concordant pairs in relation to cell B: $2(10 + 5) = 2(15) =$ 30

Concordant pairs in relation to cell D: $9(15 + 5) = 9(20) =$ 180

Concordant pairs in relation to cell E: $20(5) =$ 100

Total number of concordant pairs = 660

Discordant pairs in relation to cell C: $9(9 + 20 + 8 + 15) =$ 468

Discordant pairs in relation to cell B: $2(9 + 8) =$ 34

Discordant pairs in relation to cell F: $10(8 + 15) =$ 230

Discordant pairs in relation to cell E: $20(8) =$ 160

Total number of discordant pairs = 892

Apply the formula for gamma:

$$\text{Gamma} = \frac{C - D}{C + D}$$

$$= \frac{660 - 892}{660 + 892} = -\frac{232}{1,552}$$

$$\text{Gamma} = -.149$$

Interpretation: Gamma confirms our interpretation of the association. It is negative, indicating that the more conservative respondents are in terms of religion, the more liberal they are likely to be politically as well. Gamma is also somewhat weak (much closer to 0 than -1), as we thought it might be. Knowing the association between religious views and political views improves our ability to guess the dependent variable (political views) by 15%.

9. In interpreting the association between satisfaction with one's financial situation and one's political affiliation, you should get a set of statistics like the ones in the following table.

Symmetric Measures

		Value	Asymp. Std. Error[a]	Approx. T[b]	Approx. Sig.
Ordinal by Ordinal	Gamma	.132	.026	5.051	.000
N of Valid Cases		2736			

a. Not assuming the null hypothesis.

b. Using the asymptotic standard error assuming the null hypothesis.

Gamma is positive, but it is fairly weak. At .132 gamma suggests that the more satisfied respondents are, the more conservative they are likely to be. Knowing the association between the independent and dependent variables reduces errors in predicting the dependent variable by 13%, which is a substantial amount.

12. To begin, you should have tables like the ones that follow. Circle the highest percentages across the rows of each of the contingency tables to find the patterns in the associations. Then circle the appropriate statistics in the Directional Measures table. Your analysis should be along the following lines:

The only class for which the nature of the association between sex and party affiliation is different than it is for the respondents as a whole is lower class. Among lower-class respondents, women are more likely than men to be Democrats or Republicans, whereas men are more likely than women to be Independents. The association looks a little weaker than it does when all respondents are grouped together.

For all other classes, the nature of the association is about the same as it is for the respondents as a whole. Women are more likely than men to be Democrats, whereas men are more likely than women to be Independents or Republicans. Lower-class men are more likely than women to identify with some other party.

The gender gap is largest among the upper-class respondents, appears to be about the same for working-class and middle-class respondents, and looks smallest for the lower-class respondents. Lambda doesn't help us assess the strength of the association among upper-class respondents, because it is zero. For upper-class respondents, Goodman and Kruskal's tau is slightly larger (.021), suggesting a stronger association than that among all respondents, but a weak one nevertheless. Lambda for lower-class respondents is a little weaker (.032) than it is for all respondents.

PARTYAF recoded party identification * SEX RESPONDENTS SEX * CLASS SUBJECTIVE CLASS IDENTIFICATION Crosstabulation

CLASS SUBJECTIVE CLASS IDENTIFICATION				SEX RESPONDENTS SEX		Total
				1 MALE	2 FEMALE	
1 LOWER CLASS	PARTYAF recoded party identification	1 Democrat	Count	22	54	76
			% within SEX RESPONDENTS SEX	40.0%	47.4%	45.0%
		2 Independent	Count	25	45	70
			% within SEX RESPONDENTS SEX	45.5%	39.5%	41.4%
		3 Republican	Count	5	15	20
			% within SEX RESPONDENTS SEX	9.1%	13.2%	11.8%
		4 Other	Count	3		3
			% within SEX RESPONDENTS SEX	5.5%		1.8%
	Total		Count	55	114	169
			% within SEX RESPONDENTS SEX	100.0%	100.0%	100.0%
2 WORKING CLASS	PARTYAF recoded party identification	1 Democrat	Count	160	268	428
			% within SEX RESPONDENTS SEX	27.2%	37.7%	32.9%
		2 Independent	Count	265	271	536
			% within SEX RESPONDENTS SEX	45.0%	38.2%	41.3%
		3 Republican	Count	153	157	310
			% within SEX RESPONDENTS SEX	26.0%	22.1%	23.9%
		4 Other	Count	11	14	25
			% within SEX RESPONDENTS SEX	1.9%	2.0%	1.9%
	Total		Count	589	710	1299
			% within SEX RESPONDENTS SEX	100.0%	100.0%	100.0%
3 MIDDLE CLASS	PARTYAF recoded party identification	1 Democrat	Count	161	285	446
			% within SEX RESPONDENTS SEX	27.9%	39.6%	34.4%
		2 Independent	Count	202	215	417
			% within SEX RESPONDENTS SEX	34.9%	29.9%	32.1%
		3 Republican	Count	210	210	420
			% within SEX RESPONDENTS SEX	36.3%	29.2%	32.4%
		4 Other	Count	5	10	15
			% within SEX RESPONDENTS SEX	.9%	1.4%	1.2%
	Total		Count	578	720	1298
			% within SEX RESPONDENTS SEX	100.0%	100.0%	100.0%
4 UPPER CLASS	PARTYAF recoded party identification	1 Democrat	Count	7	19	26
			% within SEX RESPONDENTS SEX	13.2%	31.7%	23.0%
		2 Independent	Count	19	18	37
			% within SEX RESPONDENTS SEX	35.8%	30.0%	32.7%
		3 Republican	Count	27	23	50
			% within SEX RESPONDENTS SEX	50.9%	38.3%	44.2%
	Total		Count	53	60	113
			% within SEX RESPONDENTS SEX	100.0%	100.0%	100.0%

Directional Measures

CLASS SUBJECTIVE CLASS IDENTIFICATION				Value	Asymp. Std. Error[a]	Approx. T[b]	Approx. Sig.
1 LOWER CLASS	Nominal by Nominal	Lambda	Symmetric	.041	.047	.850	.395
			PARTYAF recoded party identification Dependent	.032	.073	.438	.662
			SEX RESPONDENTS SEX Dependent	.055	.031	1.748	.081
		Goodman and Kruskal tau	PARTYAF recoded party identification Dependent	.005	.007		.402[c]
			SEX RESPONDENTS SEX Dependent	.044	.014		.059[c]
2 WORKING CLASS	Nominal by Nominal	Lambda	Symmetric	.000	.000	[d]	[d]
			PARTYAF recoded party identification Dependent	.000	.000	[d]	[d]
			SEX RESPONDENTS SEX Dependent	.000	.000	[d]	[d]
		Goodman and Kruskal tau	PARTYAF recoded party identification Dependent	.006	.003		.000[c]
			SEX RESPONDENTS SEX Dependent	.013	.006		.001[c]
3 MIDDLE CLASS	Nominal by Nominal	Lambda	Symmetric	.034	.024	1.409	.159
			PARTYAF recoded party identification Dependent	.058	.022	2.550	.011
			SEX RESPONDENTS SEX Dependent	.000	.035	.000	1.000
		Goodman and Kruskal tau	PARTYAF recoded party identification Dependent	.008	.003		.000[c]
			SEX RESPONDENTS SEX Dependent	.016	.007		.000[c]
4 UPPER CLASS	Nominal by Nominal	Lambda	Symmetric	.043	.079	.537	.591
			PARTYAF recoded party identification Dependent	.000	.000	[d]	[d]
			SEX RESPONDENTS SEX Dependent	.094	.167	.537	.591
		Goodman and Kruskal tau	PARTYAF recoded party identification Dependent	.021	.017		.099[c]
			SEX RESPONDENTS SEX Dependent	.048	.038		.066[c]

a. Not assuming the null hypothesis.

b. Using the asymptotic standard error assuming the null hypothesis.

c. Based on chi-square approximation

d. Cannot be computed because the asymptotic standard error equals zero.

Overall, the respondents' class position does seem to have a bearing on the gender gap. It doesn't affect the nature of the association very much, but the strength of the association changes, particularly for lower-class and upper-class respondents.

13. In analyzing the association between *satfin* and *polaf,* controlling for *race,* your tables should look like the ones that follow, and your analysis should be along these lines:

For White and Other respondents, the association is similar to the one we see among the respondents as a whole: the more satisfied the respondents, the more conservative they are likely to be. However, it is

POLAF recoded political views * SATFIN SATISFACTION WITH FINANCIAL SITUATION * RACE RACE OF RESPONDENT Crosstabulation

RACE RACE OF RESPONDENT					SATFIN SATISFACTION WITH FINANCIAL SITUATION			
					1 NOT AT ALL SAT	2 MORE OR LESS	3 SATISFIED	Total
1 WHITE	POLAF recoded political views	1 Liberal		Count	155	265	125	545
				% within SATFIN SATISFACTION WITH FINANCIAL SITUATION	27.6%	26.0%	19.0%	24.4%
		2 Moderate		Count	210	403	237	850
				% within SATFIN SATISFACTION WITH FINANCIAL SITUATION	37.4%	39.6%	36.0%	38.0%
		3 Conservative		Count	196	350	296	842
				% within SATFIN SATISFACTION WITH FINANCIAL SITUATION	34.9%	34.4%	45.0%	37.6%
	Total			Count	561	1018	658	2237
				% within SATFIN SATISFACTION WITH FINANCIAL SITUATION	100.0%	100.0%	100.0%	100.0%
2 BLACK	POLAF recoded political views	1 Liberal		Count	40	57	15	112
				% within SATFIN SATISFACTION WITH FINANCIAL SITUATION	29.4%	35.8%	22.4%	30.9%
		2 Moderate		Count	55	51	25	131
				% within SATFIN SATISFACTION WITH FINANCIAL SITUATION	40.4%	32.1%	37.3%	36.2%
		3 Conservative		Count	41	51	27	119
				% within SATFIN SATISFACTION WITH FINANCIAL SITUATION	30.1%	32.1%	40.3%	32.9%
	Total			Count	136	159	67	362
				% within SATFIN SATISFACTION WITH FINANCIAL SITUATION	100.0%	100.0%	100.0%	100.0%
3 OTHER	POLAF recoded political views	1 Liberal		Count	16	16	6	38
				% within SATFIN SATISFACTION WITH FINANCIAL SITUATION	32.0%	30.8%	17.1%	27.7%
		2 Moderate		Count	20	27	13	60
				% within SATFIN SATISFACTION WITH FINANCIAL SITUATION	40.0%	51.9%	37.1%	43.8%
		3 Conservative		Count	14	9	16	39
				% within SATFIN SATISFACTION WITH FINANCIAL SITUATION	28.0%	17.3%	45.7%	28.5%
	Total			Count	50	52	35	137
				% within SATFIN SATISFACTION WITH FINANCIAL SITUATION	100.0%	100.0%	100.0%	100.0%

Symmetric Measures

RACE RACE OF RESPONDENT			Value	Asymp. Std. Error[a]	Approx. T[b]	Approx. Sig.
1 WHITE	Ordinal by Ordinal	Gamma	.127	.029	4.383	.000
	N of Valid Cases		2237			
2 BLACK	Ordinal by Ordinal	Gamma	.071	.070	1.007	.314
	N of Valid Cases		362			
3 OTHER	Ordinal by Ordinal	Gamma	.195	.118	1.622	.105
	N of Valid Cases		137			

a. Not assuming the null hypothesis.

b. Using the asymptotic standard error assuming the null hypothesis.

clear that the association is stronger among respondents who identify themselves as Other than among White respondents.

For Black respondents, the nature of association changes. Black respondents who are satisfied are more likely to be conservative than those who are more or less satisfied or not at all satisfied, but respondents who are not at all satisfied are more likely to be moderate than those who are satisfied or more or less satisfied. Those who are more or less satisfied are more likely to be liberal than those who are not at all satisfied or satisfied.

Gamma bears out this analysis—it is about the same for Whites as it is for all respondents and a little stronger for those who say they are Other. For Blacks, it is somewhat weaker. Knowing the association between the independent and dependent variables reduces errors in predicting political affiliation among Black respondents by about 7%, whereas knowing the association between the variables reduces errors among White respondents by 13% and for Others by about 20%.

Overall, race does have an impact on the association between satisfaction with one's financial situation and one's political views. It is more important as a factor in the association for Whites and Others than it is for Blacks.

GENERAL EXERCISES

For Exercises 1–4, evaluate the nature and strength of the associations in the given contingency table. Then compute and interpret lambda for the table, which is drawn from the 1996 GSS for respondents ages 18 through 21.

1.

POLAF recoded political views * RELIG RS RELIGIOUS PREFERENCE Crosstabulation

| | | | RELIG RS RELIGIOUS PREFERENCE | | | | | |
			1 PROTESTANT	2 CATHOLIC	3 JEWISH	4 NONE	5 OTHER	Total
POLAF recoded political views	1 Liberal	Count	6	5	1	10		22
		% within RELIG RS RELIGIOUS PREFERENCE	14.0%	16.7%	50.0%	40.0%		20.4%
	2 Moderate	Count	22	15	1	6	7	51
		% within RELIG RS RELIGIOUS PREFERENCE	51.2%	50.0%	50.0%	24.0%	87.5%	47.2%
	3 Conservative	Count	15	10		9	1	35
		% within RELIG RS RELIGIOUS PREFERENCE	34.9%	33.3%		36.0%	12.5%	32.4%
Total		Count	43	30	2	25	8	108
		% within RELIG RS RELIGIOUS PREFERENCE	100.0%	100.0%	100.0%	100.0%	100.0%	100.0%

2.

POLAF recoded political views * RCREGION recoded region variable Crosstabulation

			RCREGION recoded region variable				Total
			1 Northeast	2 Midwest	3 Southeast	4 West	
POLAF recoded political views	1 Liberal	Count	9	1	3	9	22
		% within RCREGION recoded region variable	39.1%	4.3%	9.1%	31.0%	20.4%
	2 Moderate	Count	10	12	16	13	51
		% within RCREGION recoded region variable	43.5%	52.2%	48.5%	44.8%	47.2%
	3 Conservative	Count	4	10	14	7	35
		% within RCREGION recoded region variable	17.4%	43.5%	42.4%	24.1%	32.4%
Total		Count	23	23	33	29	108
		% within RCREGION recoded region variable	100.0%	100.0%	100.0%	100.0%	100.0%

3.

POLAF recoded political views * SEX RESPONDENTS SEX Crosstabulation

			SEX RESPONDENTS SEX		Total
			1 MALE	2 FEMALE	
POLAF recoded political views	1 Liberal	Count	13	9	22
		% within SEX RESPONDENTS SEX	24.5%	16.4%	20.4%
	2 Moderate	Count	26	25	51
		% within SEX RESPONDENTS SEX	49.1%	45.5%	47.2%
	3 Conservative	Count	14	21	35
		% within SEX RESPONDENTS SEX	26.4%	38.2%	32.4%
Total		Count	53	55	108
		% within SEX RESPONDENTS SEX	100.0%	100.0%	100.0%

4.

POLAF recoded political views * RACE RACE OF RESPONDENT Crosstabulation

			RACE RACE OF RESPONDENT			Total
			1 WHITE	2 BLACK	3 OTHER	
POLAF recoded political views	1 Liberal	Count	18	2	2	22
		% within RACE RACE OF RESPONDENT	22.8%	10.0%	22.2%	20.4%
	2 Moderate	Count	35	11	5	51
		% within RACE RACE OF RESPONDENT	44.3%	55.0%	55.6%	47.2%
	3 Conservative	Count	26	7	2	35
		% within RACE RACE OF RESPONDENT	32.9%	35.0%	22.2%	32.4%
Total		Count	79	20	9	108
		% within RACE RACE OF RESPONDENT	100.0%	100.0%	100.0%	100.0%

For Exercises 5–8, evaluate the nature and strength of the associations in the given contingency table. Then compute and interpret gamma for the table, which is drawn from the 1996 GSS for respondents ages 18 through 21.

5.

POLAF recoded political views * SATFIN SATISFACTION WITH FINANCIAL SITUATION Crosstabulation

| | | | SATFIN SATISFACTION WITH FINANCIAL SITUATION | | | |
			1 NOT AT ALL SAT	2 MORE OR LESS	3 SATISFIED	Total
POLAF recoded political views	1 Liberal	Count	7	12	3	22
		% within SATFIN SATISFACTION WITH FINANCIAL SITUATION	24.1%	26.1%	9.1%	20.4%
	2 Moderate	Count	17	18	16	51
		% within SATFIN SATISFACTION WITH FINANCIAL SITUATION	58.6%	39.1%	48.5%	47.2%
	3 Conservative	Count	5	16	14	35
		% within SATFIN SATISFACTION WITH FINANCIAL SITUATION	17.2%	34.8%	42.4%	32.4%
Total		Count	29	46	33	108
		% within SATFIN SATISFACTION WITH FINANCIAL SITUATION	100.0%	100.0%	100.0%	100.0%

6.

POLAF recoded political views * DEGREE RS HIGHEST DEGREE Crosstabulation

| | | | DEGREE RS HIGHEST DEGREE | | | |
			0 LT HIGH SCHOOL	1 HIGH SCHOOL	2 JUNIOR COLLEGE	Total
POLAF recoded political views	1 Liberal	Count	6	16		22
		% within DEGREE RS HIGHEST DEGREE	18.8%	22.5%		20.6%
	2 Moderate	Count	15	33	2	50
		% within DEGREE RS HIGHEST DEGREE	46.9%	46.5%	50.0%	46.7%
	3 Conservative	Count	11	22	2	35
		% within DEGREE RS HIGHEST DEGREE	34.4%	31.0%	50.0%	32.7%
Total		Count	32	71	4	107
		% within DEGREE RS HIGHEST DEGREE	100.0%	100.0%	100.0%	100.0%

7.

POLAF recoded political views * CLASS SUBJECTIVE CLASS IDENTIFICATION Crosstabulation

			CLASS SUBJECTIVE CLASS IDENTIFICATION				
			1 LOWER CLASS	2 WORKING CLASS	3 MIDDLE CLASS	4 UPPER CLASS	Total
POLAF recoded political views	1 Liberal	Count	1	15	6		22
		% within CLASS SUBJECTIVE CLASS IDENTIFICATION	14.3%	30.0%	12.8%		20.6%
	2 Moderate	Count	5	22	22	2	51
		% within CLASS SUBJECTIVE CLASS IDENTIFICATION	71.4%	44.0%	46.8%	66.7%	47.7%
	3 Conservative	Count	1	13	19	1	34
		% within CLASS SUBJECTIVE CLASS IDENTIFICATION	14.3%	26.0%	40.4%	33.3%	31.8%
Total		Count	7	50	47	3	107
		% within CLASS SUBJECTIVE CLASS IDENTIFICATION	100.0%	100.0%	100.0%	100.0%	100.0%

8.

CONLEGIS CONFIDENCE IN CONGRESS * POLAF recoded political views Crosstabulation

			POLAF recoded political views			
			1 Liberal	2 Moderate	3 Conservative	Total
CONLEGIS CONFIDENCE IN CONGRESS	1 HARDLY ANY	Count	6	9	6	21
		% within POLAF recoded political views	46.2%	26.5%	26.1%	30.0%
	2 ONLY SOME	Count	6	19	12	37
		% within POLAF recoded political views	46.2%	55.9%	52.2%	52.9%
	3 A GREAT DEAL	Count	1	6	5	12
		% within POLAF recoded political views	7.7%	17.6%	21.7%	17.1%
Total		Count	13	34	23	70
		% within POLAF recoded political views	100.0%	100.0%	100.0%	100.0%

SPSS EXERCISES

1. In SPSS Exercise 1 in Chapter 7, you used SPSS to examine the association (nature and strength of the relationship) between *rcregion* and *vote92*. Now supplement your analysis by obtaining and interpreting lambda and Goodman and Kruskal's tau.

2. In SPSS Exercise 2 in Chapter 7, you used SPSS to examine the association (nature and strength of the relationship) between *race* and *vote92*. Now supplement your analysis by obtaining and interpreting lambda and Goodman and Kruskal's tau.

3. In SPSS Exercise 3 in Chapter 7, you used SPSS to examine the association (nature and strength of the relationship) between *relig* and *vote92*. Now supplement your analysis by obtaining and interpreting lambda and Goodman and Kruskal's tau.

4. In SPSS Exercise 4 in Chapter 7, you used SPSS to examine the association (nature and strength of the relationship) between *agecat* and *vote92*. Now supplement your analysis by obtaining and interpreting lambda and Goodman and Kruskal's tau.

5. Use SPSS and an appropriate measure of association to analyze the relationship between *class* and *polaf*.

6. Use SPSS and an appropriate measure of association to analyze the relationship between *cappun* and *polaf*.

7. Use SPSS and an appropriate measure of association to analyze the relationship between *finrela* and *polaf*.

8. Use SPSS and an appropriate measure of association to analyze the relationship between *life* and *polaf*.

9. Use SPSS to obtain contingency tables for the association between *satfin* and *vote92*. Interpret the table (nature, strength, and, if appropriate, the direction of the relationship) and supplement your analysis with an appropriate measure of association. Control for the variable *sex*. Describe the changes in the association between *satfin* and *vote92* in the partial tables when you introduce the control variable.

10. Use SPSS to obtain contingency tables for the association between *degree* and *satfin*. Interpret the table (nature, strength, and, if appropriate, the direction of the relationship) and supplement your analysis with an appropriate measure of association. Control for the variable *race*. Describe the changes in the association between *degree* and *satfin* in the partial tables when you introduce the control variable.

11. Use SPSS to obtain contingency tables for the association between *finrela* and *satfin*. Interpret the table (nature, strength, and, if appropriate, the direction of the relationship) and supplement your analysis with an appropriate measure of association. Control for the variable *agecat*. Describe the changes in the association between *finrela* and *satfin* in the partial tables when you introduce the control variable.

Measures of Association for Numerical Variables

INTRODUCTION

By now you should have a sense of how measures of association work to help us make predictions. These numbers can help us make more accurate guesses about important characteristics of individuals. For example, we learned that if you know a person's sex, you can make a better guess about his or her political affiliation. You may not always guess correctly, but your chances of making an accurate prediction are improved.

In this chapter we will look at some measures of association for numerical variables—statistics that will do for numerical variables what lambda, phi, Cramer's V, and gamma can do for categorical variables. You will be learning about two techniques in this chapter. The first technique, comparison of means, is a simple way to look at the relationship between categorical variables and numerical variables. The second technique is called regression analysis and it is used with pairs of numerical variables.

We will use these techniques to answer questions such as, Are there differences in educational achievement among the respondents to the General Social Survey? Does educational achievement vary by sex, race, age, or region of residence? To what extent do fathers' or mothers' educational achievements account for their offsprings' achievements? Do people tend to have spouses with educational backgrounds similar to their own?

In the "News to Use" section there is a report from the U.S. Bureau of the Census that addresses a number of these questions. You will notice as you read the article that a variety of techniques are employed to address these issues, including the analysis of frequency distributions, contingency tables, and the comparison of means. (See Table 9.1 at the end of the article.)

Educational Attainment in the United States: March 1997[1]

JENNIFER DAY AND ANDREA CURRY

Educational attainment is one of the most important influences on economic well-being. More education tends to be reflected in greater socioeconomic success for individuals and the country. Although the United States' overall trend reflects a more educated population, significant differences in educational attainment remain with regard to age, gender, race, and origin. Nevertheless, the educational attainment of the young adults (ages 25 to 29), who provide a glimpse of our Nation's future, indicates a dramatic improvement in educational attainment by those groups who have historically been less educated.

This report provides information on basic educational trends and attainment levels across many segments of the U.S. population. The findings are based on data collected in the Current Population Survey (CPS) conducted by the Bureau of the Census in March 1997 and refer to the population 25 years and over unless otherwise specified.

Americans Are More Educated than Ever

The high school educational attainment level of the adult population continued to rise in 1997, following a general trend that has been noted in the Current Population Survey since educational attainment was first measured in 1947. . . .

DEFINING EDUCATIONAL ATTAINMENT

A single question on the Current Population Survey which asks for the highest grade or degree completed is used to determine educational attainment. Prior to 1992, educational attainment

was measured only as years of completed schooling. In March 1997, over four-fifths (82.1%) of all adults age 25 or older reported completing at least high school, a record high, and over 1 in 5 adults (23.9%) had attained at least a Bachelor's degree.

The Increase in Young Adults' Educational Attainment May Be Leveling Off

Almost 9 in 10 young adults ages 25 to 29 (87.4%) had completed high school by 1997; this percentage was not different from that recorded in 1996 and 1995. Over the last 20 years, annual point estimates of high school completion among young adults have been in the range of 85–87%. The percentage of young adults who had completed a Bachelor's degree in 1997 (27.8%) was statistically equivalent to the record high level recorded in 1996. During the past two decades, the proportion of the young adult population with a Bachelor's degree has changed only modestly, with the proportion remaining above 20%.

The Younger Population Is More Educated than the Older Population

[H]igh school educational attainment levels were substantially higher for younger age groups and decreased successively for each older age group—just over half (60.4%) of those age 75 and older had completed high school compared with 87.4% for ages 25 to 29. Only the 40 to 44 age group deviates from this pattern. Similarly, for postsecondary schooling, one-eighth (12.7%) of the population age 75 and older had a Bachelor's degree compared with 27.8% of the 25 to 29 population. Given the very large differences in education between younger and older age groups, the attainment level

[1]U.S. Bureau of the Census *Current Population Reports,* May 1998, <http://www.census.gov/prod/3/98pubs/p20-505.pdf>.

of the total adult population will continue to rise for some time, as younger, more educated, age groups replace older, less educated, ones, even if attainment levels for young adults remain constant.

Educational Attainment Differs by Socioeconomic Factors

Gender Overall, educational attainment levels were higher for men than women. . . . Statistically, men and women had the same rate of high school completion (82.0 vs. 82.2%, which were not statistically different).

In fact, the last time a statistical difference existed was in 1989. However, for postsecondary schooling, men had higher college attainment levels than women, with 26.2% of men but only 21.7% of women with a Bachelor's degree or more, and 49.9% of men and 46.9% of women having completed some college or more.

However, for the population ages 25 to 29, educational attainment levels for women exceeded those of men. At the high school level, 88.9% of these young women had completed high school, compared with 85.8% of young men. At the college level, 29.3% of women and 26.3% of men had earned a Bachelor's degree or more. The last time young women and men had equal rates of high school and college attainment was in 1995.

Race The percentages of Whites and Blacks with a high school education both maintained a record level in 1997. Among Whites, 83.0% were high school graduates or more, statistically different from the 74.9% recorded for Blacks and the 84.9% for Asians.[2] The high school graduation rates of Blacks and Asians were also statistically different.

The Black/White high school attainment gap has narrowed for all adults, as the proportion of Black students obtaining a high school degree has

increased considerably during the past decade. For the population 25 and over, the Black/White differential in the proportion of high school graduates decreased from 13.6 percentage points in 1987 (63.4% of Blacks and 77.0% of Whites) to about 8 percentage points in 1997.

For young adults (ages 25 to 29), the Black/White high school attainment gap has disappeared. In 1987, the young White high school educational attainment level exceeded that of the young Blacks (83.3% for Black to 86.3% for White). Even though the educational attainment levels of both the young Blacks and young Whites have increased over the past decade, there is no statistical difference between their 1997 values. . . .

Asians have the greatest proportion of college graduates. At the college completion level, differences by race for ages 25 and over were evident— with the highest levels reported by Asians: 42.2% have a Bachelor's degree or more, compared with 24.6% of Whites, and 13.3% of Blacks. Even among young adults, Asians had significantly higher college completion levels. One-half of the young Asian population (50.5%) had attained a Bachelor's degree. In comparison, almost 1 in 3 Whites (28.9%) and 1 in 7 Blacks (14.4%) in the 25 to 29 age group had a Bachelor's degree.

. . .

Marital status Differences in educational attainment across marital statuses reflect, to a large extent, differences in the age composition of marital status groups. For example, the high level of high school completion among the never married population (83.6%) reflects the fact that this group is relatively young. Conversely, the low level among the widowed population (60.3%) is in part because this group consists primarily of an older population. A similar pattern is seen in college completion levels.

Labor force Educational attainment is higher for the employed than for the unemployed population, who in turn generally have higher attainment than those who are not in the labor force. Among em-

---

[2]Includes Pacific Islanders

ployed people, educational attainment is quite high, with 89.3% of them reporting completing high school, and 29.2% completing a Bachelor's degree. . . .

Occupation Educational attainment also varied across occupational categories. While 99.3% of the workers in professional specialty occupations have completed high school, only 63.4% of private household workers have achieved this level of education. With respect to higher education, 75.5% of people in professional specialty occupations have completed a Bachelor's degree or more, the highest level across the major occupational groups. For many occupations, however, fewer than 10% of the workers had completed college, including categories such as precision production workers and machine operators.

Earnings Earnings for the population 18 years and over were higher at each progressively higher level of education (Table 9.1). This relationship holds true not only for the entire population, but across each subgroup defined by gender, race, and Hispanic origin. Within each specific educational level, earnings differ by gender and race. This variation may result from a variety of

factors, such as occupation, age, or labor force experience.

Regions and states Educational attainment levels were lowest in the South. Among the four Census regions (Northeast, Midwest, South and West) the proportion of people who completed high school ranged from 79.3 in the South to 85.2 in the Midwest. In terms of college attainment, the West was highest in the completion of some college or more (55.6%), and the Northeast and West were highest in the completion of a Bachelor's degree or more (26.6% and 25.9%, which were not statistically different). The data also show that attainment levels were higher in metropolitan areas than in non-metropolitan areas.

. . .

SOURCE OF THE DATA

Most estimates in this report come from data obtained in March 1997 from the Current Population Survey (CPS). Some estimates are based on data obtained from the CPS in earlier years and from decennial censuses. The Bureau of the Census conducts the survey every month, although this report uses only March data for its estimates.

TABLE 9.1 Average 1996 Earnings by Educational Attainment, and Gender, Race, and Hispanic Origin, for the Population Ages 18 and Over

Characteristic	Total	Not a High School Graduate	High School Graduate	Some College or Associate Degree	Bachelor's Degree	Advanced Degree
Total	$28,106	$15,011	$22,154	$25,181	$38,112	$61,317
Male	34,705	17,826	27,642	31,426	46,702	74,406
Female	20,570	10,421	16,161	18,933	28,701	42,625
White	28,844	15,358	22,782	25,511	38,936	61,779
Black	21,978	13,110	18,722	23,628	31,955	48,731
Hispanic Origin	19,439	13,287	18,528	22,209	32,955	49,873

Note: Hispanics may be of any race.
Source: U.S. Bureau of the Census, Current Population Survey, March 1997.

COMPARING MEANS

Some of the questions we want to answer require us to examine a numerical variable (like educational achievement—*educ* in the General Social Survey) in concert with one or more categorical variables (*sex, race, age, region of residence,* and *labor force status*). As you may recall from Chapter 7, trying to produce a contingency table with a numerical variable can create an enormous table that runs over several pages. You may also recall that the larger the contingency table, the more difficult it is to see the patterns in the data. **Comparing means** is an easy way to see patterns in numerical variables when they are paired with categorical variables.

You have already had some exposure to this technique. In Chapter 5 you did a comparison of means when you split the data file by whether or not the respondents have children and then found the mean for the variable *wage earners.* You learned that respondents with children had the same number of wage earners in their households, on average, as respondents without children. Let's try the Split File procedure again.

Skills Practice 1   Split your file by the variable *sex* (use the command path Data ➙ Split File, click on Organize Output by Groups, and select the variable *sex*) and then find the mean for *educ.* An easy way to find the mean is to use the command path Analyze ➙ Descriptive Statistics ➙ Descriptives, select the variable *educ,* and then click on OK. You automatically get the number of valid cases, the minimum and maximum values of the variable, the mean, and the standard deviation. What do you learn about the association between the variables *sex* and *educ*? (You'll find the answer as you work through the next section on comparing means using SPSS.)

Now let's learn how to perform the same function without having to go through the trouble of first splitting the data file by one variable and then finding the mean for another variable. (Before you go through the next section, be sure to clear the Split File feature.)

SPSS Guide: Comparing Means

Open the SPSS program and your gss96subset data file, then click on the Analyze menu item.

❶ Click on Compare Means.

❷ When the Compare Means menu opens, click on Means to open the Means dialog box.

❸ At the Means dialog box, scroll down to your categorical (independent) variable, *sex,* and put it in the Independent List box.

❹ Scroll down to your numerical (dependent) variable, *educ,* and put it in the Dependent List box.

❺ Click on OK.

In your Output window, you will get a table labeled Report, like the one in Table 9.2.

As with the Split File procedure, comparing the means allows us to see whether there is a difference, on average, in the educational achievements of male respondents compared to female respondents.

TABLE 9.2 Comparison of Means for the Variables *sex* and *educ* in the gss96subset File

Report

EDUC HIGHEST YEAR OF SCHOOL COMPLETED

SEX RESPONDENTS SEX	Mean	N	Std. Deviation
1 MALE	13.56	1283	2.95
2 FEMALE	13.21	1612	2.91
Total	13.36	2895	2.93

What do we look for in this table of information and how do we interpret it?

- First, look at the differences in the means. Which group has the higher average years of education? The answer is males (an average of 13.56 years). Female respondents have an average of 13.21 years.

- Second, notice the size of the difference—is it a large one or a small one? The difference in this case is about a third of a year.

- Third, notice the size of the standard deviations and the differences in the standard deviations between the two groups. You may remember from Chapter 6 that, in general, the larger the standard deviation is in relation to the range, the more variability there is. In both of these groups, the standard deviation is relatively small in relation to the range. The distributions are more homogeneous than heterogeneous. The distribution of female responses is the most homogeneous, because it has a smaller standard deviation than the distribution of responses for males.

Why is it important to pay attention to the standard deviation? First, it will help us later on as we start to understand whether or not we can generalize from the sample of General Social Survey respondents to the larger population these respondents represent. Second, it can help us describe the two groups. Remember that we can subtract 1 standard deviation from the mean, and we can add 1 standard deviation to the mean to describe the middle 68% of the respondents. We can say something like, *assuming a normally distributed set of responses,* about 68% of the male respondents can be assumed to have between 10.61 years of education (the mean minus 1 standard deviation, or 13.56 − 2.95) and 16.51 years of education (the mean plus 1 standard deviation, or 13.56 + 2.95). About 68% of the female respondents have between 10.30 years of education (13.21 − 2.91) and 16.12 years of education (13.21 + 2.91). Looking at the range of values 1 standard deviation below the mean to 1 standard deviation above it reinforces our conclusion that the distribution for males is more heterogeneous than the distribution for females.

Skills Practice 2 Follow the command path Analyze ➥ Compare Means ➥ Means to open the Means dialog box. Analyze the association between race (using the variable *race*) and educational achievement (using *educ*). Is race associated with educational achievement? What makes you think so?

Now let's turn our attention to techniques for examining the association between two numerical variables—regression analysis.

REGRESSION ANALYSIS

Regression analysis involves the application of a set of statistics to evaluate the association between two numerical variables. Just as the analysis of associations between nominal or ordinal variables begins by using contingency tables to assess a relationship, regression analysis begins with a visual display of data called a scatterplot. To the visual display, we can add a line, called the regression line, which provides additional information about the association. Finally, we can supplement what we learn visually with a set of statistics— Pearson's *r* (a measure of association), the coefficient of determination (or *r*-squared), and statistics about the characteristics of the line through the data—that allow us to make predictions about the relationship.

The Scatterplot

The visual display of the association between two numerical variables is called a scatterplot. A **scatterplot** is simply the graphic representation of the responses to two variables plotted along a horizontal *x*-axis (for the independent variable) and a vertical *y*-axis (for the dependent variable). The scatterplot shows us how changes in the values of one variable are related to changes in the values of a second.

Let's start by seeing whether the respondents' educational achievements influence their earning power. For this example, I am using some made-up data—for an association between years of education and annual income—so you can see how a scatterplot illustrates associations (Figure 9.1). Notice that the points on the scatterplot rise from the lower left to the upper right corners of the diagram. This pattern suggests that changes (increases) in the values of the first variable, *years of education,* are associated with or related to changes (increases) in the values of the second variable, *annual income.* Responses to the two variables change together. **Covariation** is the term we use to describe situations in which responses to the values or categories of

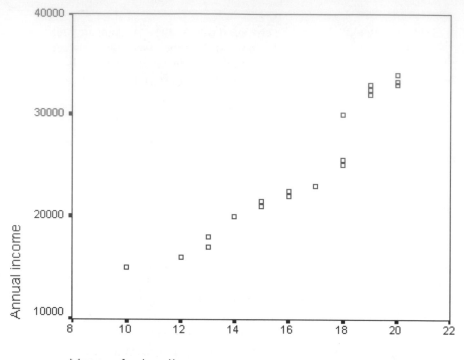

Figure 9.1 Scatterplot for the association between years of education and annual income for a set of hypothetical data.

one variable are related to responses to the values or categories of a second variable.

The association between the variables is very clear in Figure 9.1. If we drew a line through the middle of the points on the scatterplot (Figure 9.2) it would be a fairly steep line, and most of the points in the scatterplot would fall very close to the line. Taken together, these features of the scatterplot suggest a very strong and positive association between these two variables. As the respondents' education rises, their level of income increases correspondingly.

We rarely see associations this clear when we are using real-world data, but we do see some fairly strong associations. We can use the variables *paeduc* (father's education) and *educ* (respondent's education) to see how scatterplots are a little more likely to look. If we were to start by looking at the association between the respondents' educational achievements and their fathers' education, we could obtain a scatterplot diagram like the one in Figure 9.3, which would represent the association. Notice the features of the scatterplot:

- The independent variable, *father's education,* is on the horizontal axis (the *x*-axis).

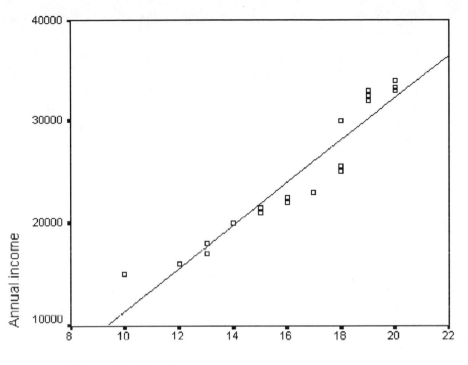

Figure 9.2 Scatterplot with a regression line for the association between years of education and annual income for a set of hypothetical data.

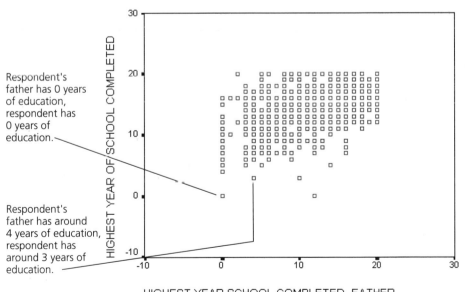

Respondent's father has 0 years of education, respondent has 0 years of education.

Respondent's father has around 4 years of education, respondent has around 3 years of education.

Figure 9.3 Scatterplot for the variables *paeduc* and *educ* in the gss96subset file.

- The dependent variable, *respondent's education,* is on the vertical axis (the *y*-axis).

- Each of the squares within the scatterplot represents the characteristics of a respondent. Starting in the bottom left corner of the scatterplot, we can see that at least one respondent has 0 years of education with a father who also has 0 years of education. Moving up and to the right, the next square represents a respondent who has 3 years of education with a father who has about 4 years of education. Note that a scatterplot may not have as many squares as there are respondents, because there may be more than one respondent sharing a particular set of characteristics. (Many respondents may have the same level of education, for example.)

What does the scatterplot tell us? First, we can see whether the general pattern of the association between two variables is positive or negative. How? By looking at the shape of the distribution. In Figure 9.3, we can see that the points tend to spread out across the graph starting in the lower left corner and moving upward toward the right corner. Low values of the independent variable, *father's education,* are associated with low values of the dependent variable, *respondent's education,* and vice versa. In short, there is a positive association between the two variables. The more education the respondents' fathers have, the more education the respondents are likely to have.

Second, we can assess the strength of the association by drawing a line around the points. Then

1. See whether the resulting shape looks more like a pencil (strong association), a cigar (weaker association), an oval (still weaker), or a circle (almost no association).

2. Look at the steepness of the slope of the shape we have drawn—as a rule of thumb, the steeper the slope the stronger the association. However, the steepness of the slope has to be interpreted in conjunction with the shape of the line drawn around the plot points.

Practice with Figure 9.3. Draw a line that encompasses most of the points (you can exclude for the time being those points that fall outside what appears to be the general pattern of the data). You should get a shape like the one in Figure 9.4.

Note that the shape extends from the lower left corner of the graph to the upper right corner, a positive association. It looks somewhat like an oval, but it is fairly steeply sloped. Taken together, the shape and slope indicate an association somewhere in the moderate range.

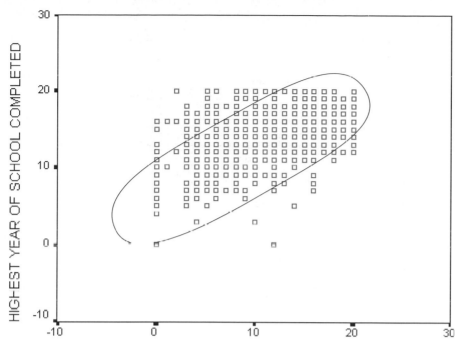

Figure 9.4 Using a scatterplot to determine the direction of an association for the variables *paeduc* and *educ* in the gss96subset file.

The Regression Line

Now, let's add one more feature to the graph—a straight line. Try drawing a straight line through the middle of the points to indicate the general direction and the slope of the association. Try to draw your line in such a way that the distance between the line and each of the points is minimized; the line should come as close to as many of the points as possible, while at the same time halving the distance between the points that aren't close to the line. I realize these instructions may be a little abstract, but do the best you can. You will probably come up with a line somewhat like the one in Figure 9.5.

The line you came up with is conceptually similar to a regression line. A **regression line,** like the one in Figure 9.5, is a mathematically derived line drawn through the points in a set of data so as to minimize the average of the squared distances between each point and the line itself—but more about that in a minute. Like the general shape of the distribution, the line itself can indicate the direction of an association. It's positive if the line slopes from the bottom left corner of the graph up toward the top right corner (Figure 9.6), and negative if the line slopes from the top left corner of the diagram toward the bottom right corner (Figure 9.7).

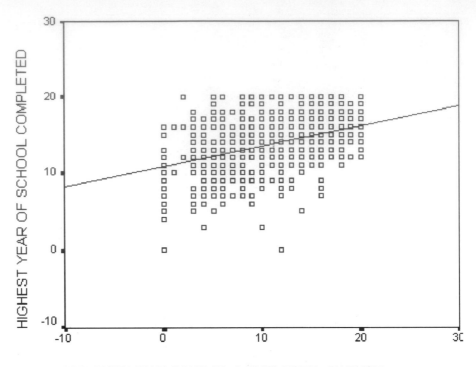

Figure 9.5   Scatterplot for the variables *paeduc* and *educ* with a regression line, using the gss96subset file.

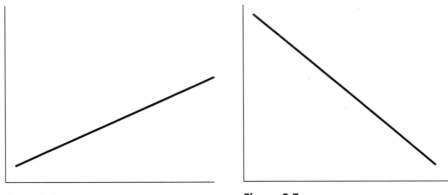

Figure 9.6   **Figure 9.7**

The strength of the regression line can be estimated by looking at the steepness of the slope and the relationship between the points and the line—the closer the points are to the line, the stronger the association is (Figure 9.8); the more spread out the points are in relation to the line, the weaker the association is (Figure 9.9).

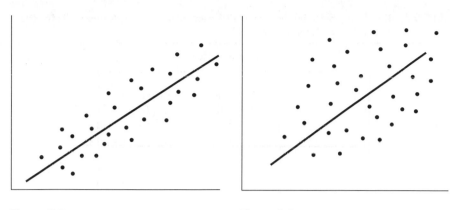

Figure 9.8

Figure 9.9

Skills Practice 3 Look at the scatterplot shown here for the association between the respondents' mothers' education (*maeduc*) and respondents' education (*educ*). Is the association between the variables positive or negative? How strong do you think it is?

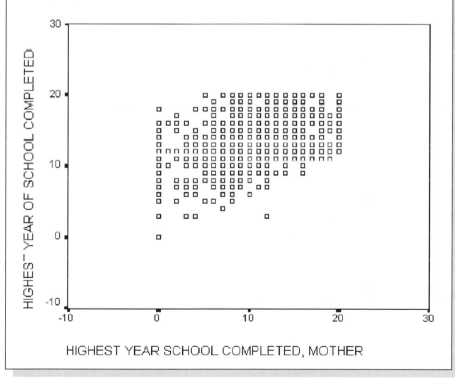

TABLE 9.3 Randomly Selected Sample of 17 Cases From the gss96subset File for the Variables *paeduc* and *educ*

Case Summaries

	HIGHEST YEAR OF SCHOOL COMPLETED, FATHER	HIGHEST YEAR OF SCHOOL COMPLETED
1	16	15
2	20	12
3	16	18
4	6	18
5	10	15
6	16	16
7	8	12
8	12	17
9	19	19
10	18	13
11	11	16
12	12	16
13	16	16
14	8	12
15	14	15
16	8	12
17	12	12
Total N	17	17

Constructing a Scatterplot by Hand

A scatterplot is fairly easy to produce. Let's use the data in Table 9.3 to make one.

Start by drawing the *x*-axis and *y*-axis for your scatterplot. (See Figure 9.10.) Label the independent and dependent variables, and mark off the values of each variable. Use as many of the values of each variable as there are in the data. (See Figure 9.11.) Now place a dot on your diagram to represent each of the cases. For example, starting with case 1, you should have a mark at the point where the father's education (16 years) intersects the respondent's education (15 years). (See Figure 9.12.) Continue on until all 17 cases have been plotted.

What if there is more than one case at a particular point? Add a number next to your plot point or dot indicating how many cases there are at a single plot point. (SPSS will count the cases at a particular point and show you the

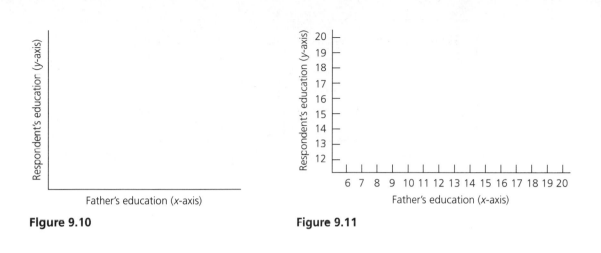

Figure 9.10   Figure 9.11

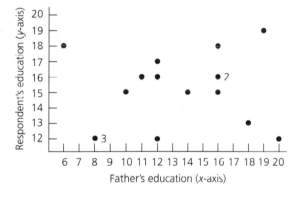

Figure 9.12

result with a "sunflower," a circle with a "petal" extending from it—one petal per case. If you have two cases at a single point, the sunflower will look like a circle with two petals on it, ♾. If you have three cases at a single point, the sunflower will look like a dot with three petals on it, ♾, and so on.)

Skills Practice 4   What does Figure 9.12 tell you about the direction and the strength of the association between the two variables, *father's education* and *respondent's education,* for this random sample of respondents from the gss96subset file?

Construct a scatterplot for the hypothetical cases in the following table. Describe the association between the two variables, *hrswrk* and *freetime*.

Case Summaries

	HRSWRK Hours worked last week	FREETIME Hours of free time last week
1	55	16
2	52	17
3	50	18
4	50	20
5	48	20
6	48	21
7	46	23
8	43	25
9	43	25
10	42	26
11	40	28
12	40	28
13	40	28
14	38	30
15	38	31
16	37	33
17	36	33
18	36	35
19	35	35
20	35	37
Total N	20	20

Distinguishing Between Linear and Nonlinear Associations

Scatterplot analysis is very important because we have to know what the general pattern of an association is before we can apply the appropriate statistics to it. Like measures of association for categorical variables, many statistics for use with numerical variables are best at detecting patterns in which the association between two variables is linear. A **linear association** is one in which the responses to the categories of one variable rise or fall as the responses to the categories of a second variable rise or fall (as illustrated in Figure 9.1). The pattern of the scatterplot points forms a line that rises from the bottom left corner to the top right, or falls from the top left to the bottom right. If you draw a line around the greatest concentration of the points, you end up with a pencil-shaped (or at least a cigar-shaped) object.

Associations can take other forms, though—they can be nonlinear. In **nonlinear associations,** variables are associated in ways that can't be captured by straight lines or by simple statements such as the more education the

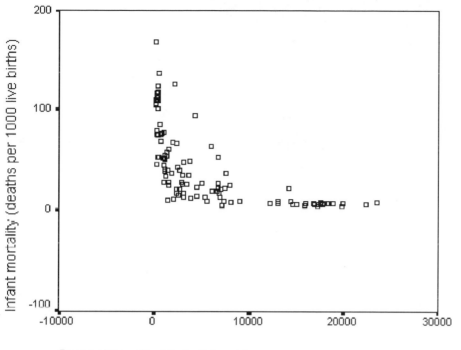

Figure 9.13

respondents' mothers have, the more education the respondents are likely to have. A nonlinear association can take the shape of a curve. When it does so, it is called a **curvilinear association.** How do you know when an association is curvilinear rather than linear? By drawing a line around the points and seeing what shape the pattern takes. Figures 9.13 through 9.15 show you several of the different forms that nonlinear associations can take. These examples are drawn from a set of national-level data that comes with the SPSS program in a file labeled WORLD95. In each of these illustrations, there appears to be an association between the independent and dependent variable that is not a linear association. As with contingency tables, we have to be open to the many possible shapes that an association can take; otherwise, we might over look associations that are very strong but not linear.

Obtaining Scatterplots Using SPSS

Having learned how to construct scatterplots by hand, let's see how to do them using SPSS.

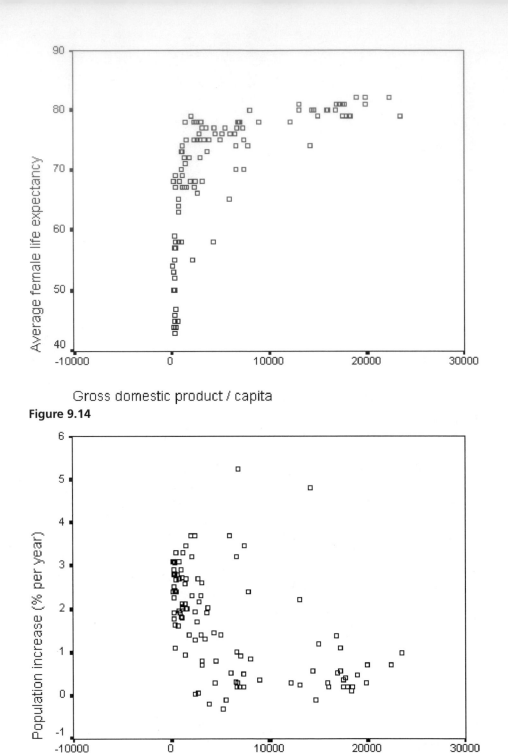

Figure 9.14

Gross domestic product / capita

Figure 9.15

SPSS Guide: Obtaining a Scatterplot

Open your SPSS program and the gss96subset file. At the SPSS Data Editor window:

❶ Click on Graphs.

❷ Click on Scatter to open the Scatterplot window.

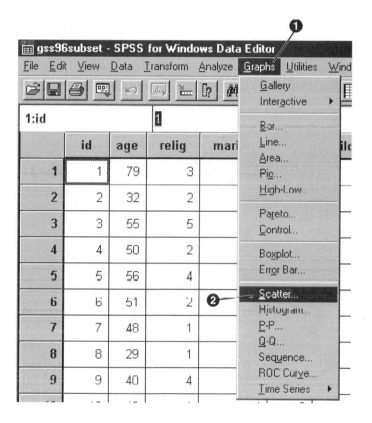

When the Scatterplot window opens:

❶ Click on Simple.

❷ Click on Define to open the Simple Scatterplot dialog box.

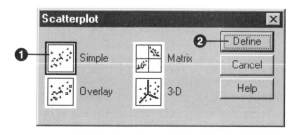

The Simple Scatterplot dialog box opens.

❶ Select your dependent variable (let's use *educ,* respondent's education), and click on the ▶ to put it in the Y Axis (dependent variable) box.

❷ Follow the same procedure to select your independent variable, *paeduc,* for the X Axis (independent variable) box.

❸ Click on OK. A graph like the one in Figure 9.3 will appear in your Output window.

Now let's add sunflowers and a regression line to our scatterplot.

SPSS Guide: Adding Sunflowers and a Regression Line to a Scatterplot

Place your cursor on your scatterplot in the SPSS Output window, and double click. The SPSS Chart Editor window opens.

❶ Click on Chart.

❷ When the menu opens under Chart, click on Options. . . .

The Scatterplot Options window opens.

❶ Under Fit Line, click on the box next to Total to make the $\sqrt{}$ appear.

❷ Under Sunflowers, click on the box next to Show Sunflowers.

③ Click on OK. When you return to the Chart Editor window, click on the X (exit) button in the upper right corner of the window. Your scatterplot should now look like the one in Figure 9.16.

What can we tell about the association? First, notice the sunflowers. Some have very few petals, whereas others look more like dandelions. The more petals, the more cases there are at a particular point on the diagram. The density of the petals tells us where most of the cases are clustered. As might be expected, we can see that the respondents tend to be clustered around the 12 years of education category, for both the respondents themselves and their fathers. Second, we can tell that the association is positive by looking at the direction in which the line slopes (from lower left to upper right). The more education the respondents' fathers have, the more education the respondents have. Third, we can tell that the association seems to be in the moderate range—the slope of the line is fairly steep, and most cases fall close to the line.

> **Skills Practice 6**   Produce a scatterplot with sunflowers and the regression line for the variables respondent's education (*educ*) and mother's education (*maeduc*). What is its direction and strength?

Assessing the Direction and Strength of an Association Using Regression Statistics

In addition to using visual representations of numerical variables, we can assess the direction and strength of associations between variables using statistics—numbers that, like the measures for categorical variables, function as indexes to the association.

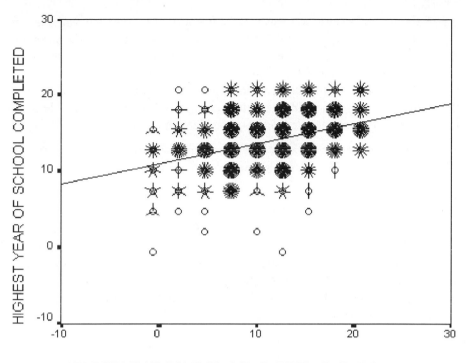

Figure 9.16 Scatterplot for the variables *paeduc* and *educ* from the gss96subset file with sunflowers and the regression line.

Pearson's *r* One very commonly used statistic for assessing the strength and direction of an association between two variables is called Pearson's *r* or Pearson's correlation. **Pearson's *r*** evaluates the extent to which the responses to two variables tend to vary together. For example, it answers the question, Do respondents whose fathers are highly educated tend to be more highly educated themselves (a positive association), or do respondents whose fathers have a lot of education tend to have less education (a negative association)?

Pearson's *r* ranges in value between −1 and +1. Like the measures for categorical variables, the closer the value is to −1 or +1, the stronger is the association. The closer Pearson's *r* is to zero, the weaker the association is. The sign on the variable—negative or positive (which is indicated by the absence of any sign at all)—tells us the direction of an association.

***r*-squared, the coefficient of determination** If you square Pearson's *r*, the result is a statistic called ***r*-squared** (represented symbolically as r^2) or the coefficient of determination. Unlike Pearson's *r*, the **coefficient of determination** doesn't indicate the direction of an association, but it does have a proportional reduction in error (PRE) interpretation.

The value of r^2 tells us how much of the variation in a dependent variable can be explained by the variation in the independent variable. It answers the question, *How much* of the variation in the respondents' educational achievements can be explained by the variation in their fathers' educational achievements? In the terms we used for describing the measures in Chapter 8, we can express r-squared as the degree of improvement in our ability to guess the dependent variable from knowledge of the general independent–dependent variable relationship.

The Computation of Pearson's *r* and *r*-squared

The computation of Pearson's r (and subsequently, r-squared) is similar to the computation of the deviations from the mean. The one twist is that you will have to find the mean, and the deviations from the mean, for two variables—the independent and the dependent variables. In addition, you will have to find the squares of the deviations (as you did to find the variance) for both variables as well as the products of the deviations. The formulas presented first are the conceptual formulas, which I am using largely to promote understanding of how the regression statistics work.

> **FORMULA 9.1(A):** Conceptual formula for Pearson's r

$$\text{Pearson's r} = \frac{\Sigma(X - \overline{X})(Y - \overline{Y})}{\sqrt{[\Sigma(X - \overline{X})^2][(\Sigma Y - \overline{Y})^2]}}$$

where X represents a value of the independent variable, Y represents a value of the dependent variable, $\overline{X}$ is the mean of the independent variable, and $\overline{Y}$ is the mean of the dependent variable.

This formula looks more difficult than it really is. The process of solving it involves the following steps:

Step 1. Find the mean for each of your two variables—the independent, or X, variable and the dependent, or Y, variable.

Step 2. Find the deviations from the mean for each value of your variables X and Y.

Step 3. Multiply the deviations from the mean—the deviation for X and the deviation for Y—by each other, and then add up the result (the numerator for Formula 9.1a).

Step 4. Square each of the deviations from the mean—first for X and then for Y, add them up, multiply the sum of the deviations squared for X and Y against each other, and take their square root (the denominator for Formula 9.1a).

Step 5. Divide the result you obtained in Step 3 by the result you obtained in Step 4.

TABLE 9.4 A Set of Hypothetical Data for the Association Between a Father's Education and a Respondent's Education

Father's Education, X	Respondent's Education, Y
10	10
10	11
12	12
14	13
14	14

Example: Let's work with the small set of data in Table 9.4. The variables are *father's education* (the independent, or *X,* variable) and *respondent's education* (the dependent, or *Y,* variable).

Step 1. Begin by finding the means for each of these variables. (Use the raw scores formula for the mean, Formula 5.2a). You should obtain a mean for the independent variable (X) of 12, and a mean of the dependent variable (Y) of 12.

Step 2. Find the deviations from the mean for each of these variables (see the figure on p. 217 of Chapter 6 for an illustration of the process). Start by subtracting the mean for the independent variable from each of the values of the independent variable. Then do the same for the dependent variable—subtract the mean for Y from each of the values of Y). You should get these answers:

Father's Education, $X - \overline{X}$	Respondent's Education, $Y - \overline{Y}$
$10 - 12 = -2$	$10 - 12 = -2$
$10 \quad 12 = 2$	$11 \quad 12 = 1$
$12 - 12 = 0$	$12 - 12 = 0$
$14 - 12 = 2$	$13 - 12 = 1$
$14 - 12 = 2$	$14 - 12 = 2$

Step 3. Multiply each of the deviations from the means—the deviation for each value of X times the deviation for each value of Y.

Father's Education, $X - \bar{X}$	Respondent's Education, $Y - \bar{Y}$	$(X - \bar{X})(Y - \bar{Y})$
$10 - 12 = -2$	$10 - 12 = -2$	$(-2)(-2) = 4$
$10 - 12 = -2$	$11 - 12 = -1$	$(-2)(-1) = 2$
$12 - 12 = 0$	$12 - 12 = 0$	$(0)(0) = 0$
$14 - 12 = 2$	$13 - 12 = 1$	$(2)(1) = 2$
$14 - 12 = 2$	$14 - 12 = 2$	$(2)(2) = 4$
		$\Sigma(X - \bar{X})(Y - \bar{Y}) = 12$

Then add up the results to get the sum of the deviations of the mean for X times the deviations from the mean for Y. The result is the numerator for the formula for Pearson's r.

Step 4. Square each of the deviations from the mean, first for each value of the X variable and then for each value of the Y variable.

Father's Education, $X - \bar{X}$	$(X - \bar{X})^2$	Respondent's Education, $Y - \bar{Y}$	$(Y - \bar{Y})^2$
$10 - 12 = -2$	4	$10 - 12 = -2$	4
$10 - 12 = -2$	4	$11 - 12 = -1$	1
$12 - 12 = 0$	0	$12 - 12 = 0$	0
$14 - 12 = 2$	4	$13 - 12 = 1$	1
$14 - 12 = 2$	4	$14 - 12 = 2$	4
	$\Sigma(X - \bar{X})^2 = 16$		$\Sigma(Y - \bar{Y})^2 = 10$

Add up the squared deviations from the mean—first for the X variable, then for the Y variable. Multiply the sum of the squared deviations of X times the sum of the squared deviations of Y:

$$[\Sigma(X - \bar{X})^2][\Sigma(Y - \bar{Y})^2] = (16)(10) = 160$$

Take the square root of the product:

$$\sqrt{160} = 12.6491$$

The result is the denominator of the formula for Pearson's r.

Step 5. Finally, plug these values into your formula for Pearson's r:

$$\text{Pearson's } r = \frac{\Sigma(X - \overline{X})(Y - \overline{Y})}{\sqrt{[\Sigma(X - \overline{X})^2][\Sigma(Y - \overline{Y})^2]}} = \frac{12}{12.6491} = .95$$

Computational formula for Pearson's r   As with the formula for standard deviation, there is a computational version of the formula for Pearson's r. The computational formula is easier to use because it avoids the process of subtraction, should you need to find Pearson's r by hand.

FORMULA 9.1(B): Computational formula for Pearson's r

$$r = \frac{\Sigma XY - (N\overline{X}\overline{Y})}{\sqrt{(\Sigma X^2 - N\overline{X}^2)(\Sigma X^2 - N\overline{Y}^2)}}$$

where X represents a value of the independent variable, Y represents a value of the dependent variable, $\overline{X}$ is the mean of the independent variable, and $\overline{Y}$ is the mean of the dependent variable.

To work this formula, follow these steps:

Step 1. Multiply each value of X by each value of Y, and add up the products (the result of each multiplication of X times Y) to get ΣXY.

Step 2. Find the mean for each of your two variables: the independent, or X, variable and the dependent, or Y, variable.

Step 3. Multiply N by the mean of X by the mean of Y to get $N\overline{X}\overline{Y}$.

Step 4. Square each value of X and add up the results to get ΣX^2, and square each value of Y and add up the results to get ΣY^2.

Step 5. Square the mean of X and multiply it by N to get $N\overline{X}^2$ and square the mean of Y and multiply it by N to get $N\overline{Y}^2$.

Step 6. Plug the results of these computations into your formula for Pearson's r (Formula 9.1b).

Example: Let's work with the data in Table 9.4.

Step 1. Begin by multiplying each value of X by each value of Y and adding up the products.

Father's Education, X	Mother's Education, Y	XY
10	10	100
10	11	110
12	12	144
14	13	182
14	14	196
		$\Sigma XY = 732$

Step 2. Find the mean for each of the variables X and Y.

Father's Education, X	Mother's Education, Y
10	10
10	11
12	12
14	13
14	14
$\Sigma X = 60$	$\Sigma Y = 60$

$$\overline{X} = \frac{\Sigma X}{N} = \frac{60}{5} = 12$$

$$\overline{Y} = \frac{\Sigma Y}{N} = \frac{60}{5} = 12$$

Step 3. Multiply N by $\overline{X}$ by $\overline{Y}$ to get $N\overline{X}\,\overline{Y}$:

$$N\overline{X}\,\overline{Y} = 5 \times 12 \times 12 = 720$$

Step 4. Square each value of X and add up the results. Do the same for each value of Y.

Father's Education, X	Mother's Education, Y	X^2	Y^2
10	10	100	100
10	11	100	121
12	12	144	144
14	13	196	169
14	14	196	196
		$\Sigma X^2 = 736$	$\Sigma Y^2 = 730$

Step 5. Square the mean of X and multiply by N to get $N\bar{X}^2$:

$$\bar{X}^2 = 12 \times 12 = 144$$

$$N\bar{X}^2 = 5 \times 144 = 720$$

Do the same for the mean of Y:

$$\bar{Y}^2 = 12 \times 12 = 144$$

$$N\bar{Y}^2 = 5 \times 144 = 720$$

Step 6: Plug the results into the computation formula for Pearson's r (Formula 9.1b):

$\Sigma XY = 732$ $N\bar{X}\bar{Y} = 720$ $\Sigma X^2 = 736$ $\Sigma Y^2 = 730$ $N\bar{X}^2 = 720$ $N\bar{Y}^2 = 720$

$$r = \frac{\Sigma XY - (N\bar{X}\bar{Y})}{\sqrt{(\Sigma X^2 - N\bar{X}^2)(\Sigma Y^2 - N\bar{Y}^2)}}$$

$$= \frac{732 - 720}{\sqrt{(736 - 720)(730 - 720)}} = \frac{12}{\sqrt{16 \times 10}} = \frac{12}{12.6491}$$

$$r = .95$$

Note that the answer is the same as the one you obtained using the conceptual formula for Pearson's r (Formula 9.1a).

Interpreting Pearson's r and r-squared   Pearson's r, at .95, suggests a very strong association between the variables *father's education* and *respondent's education,* and it is a positive association. The more education respondents' fathers have, the more education the respondents are likely to have.

To find r-squared, simply square the value of Pearson's r (multiply .95 by .95). We get an r-squared of .90, suggesting that 90% of the variation in the respondents' years of education can be accounted for by variations in their fathers' years of education. In PRE terms, knowing the association between fathers' educational achievements and respondents' educational achievements improves our ability to predict respondents' educational levels by about 90% in this hypothetical case.

Skills Practice 7   Use the computational formula to calculate and interpret Pearson's r and r-squared for the following set of data:

Mother's Education, X	Respondent's Education, Y
13	12
13	14
14	15
15	16
15	13

Calculating the regression line Once you have found Pearson's *r*, doing the computations for the regression line becomes easy. You may recall from algebra or geometry that a line can be represented by an equation, shown here as Formula 9.2.

FORMULA 9.2: The regression line

$$Y = a + (b)(X)$$

where *Y* is a value of the dependent variable; *X* is a value of the independent variable; *a* is the *y-intercept* or constant, the value of the dependent variable when the value of the independent variable is 0; and *b* is the **slope** of the line, or the amount by which the dependent variable changes for each unit change in the independent variable. (For example, the slope of the line for the association between father's education and respondent's education represents the increase in the number of years of education of the respondent for each year of education the father has.)

One of the most interesting aspects of this equation is that we can use it to make predictions. Suppose we want to know the predicted value of the dependent variable (*Y*) for any given value of the dependent variable (*X*). We can figure it out if we also know *a* (the constant) and *b* (the slope of the line). How do we get *a* and *b*?

Step 1. Start by finding *b*, the slope of the line. The formula for the slope is:

FORMULA 9.2(A) Conceptual formula for the slope of a line

$$b = \frac{\Sigma(X - \bar{X})(Y - \bar{Y})}{\Sigma(X - \bar{X})^2}$$

You may recognize this formula. It has the same numerator as the formula for Pearson's *r*. The denominator is different, but when you do the computations for Pearson's *r*, you have to find the denominator for the slope, which is the sum of the squared deviations from the mean for the independent variable.

Example: To find the slope of the regression line for the data in Table 9.4, plug in the numerator for Pearson's *r* and divide it by the sum of the squared deviations from the mean for the independent variable. For the previous example, we found the numerator for Pearson's *r*, 12, in Step 3. We found the sum of the squared deviations from the mean for the independent variable, 16, in Step 4 [see the column labeled $(X - \bar{X})^2$].

To find the slope of the regression line, divide 12 by 16.

$$b = \frac{\Sigma(X - \bar{X})(Y - \bar{Y})}{\Sigma(X - \bar{X})^2} = \frac{12}{16} = .75$$

As there is for Pearson's r, there is a computational formula for the slope of a regression line.

FORMULA 9.2(B): Computational formula for the slope of a line

$$b = \frac{\Sigma XY - (NXY)}{\Sigma X^2 - N\overline{X}^2}$$

Like the conceptual formula, the computational formula uses the numerator for Pearson's r. The computations for the denominator are similar, too. You find ΣX^2 and $N\overline{X}^2$ when you compute Pearson's r (in Steps 4 and 5).

Example: To find the slope of the regression line for the data in Table 9.4, plug the numerator for Pearson's r into the formula for the slope along with ΣX^2 and $N\overline{X}^2$.

$$\Sigma XY - N\overline{X}\,\overline{Y} = 12 \qquad \Sigma X^2 = 736 \qquad N\overline{X}^2 = 720$$

$$b = \frac{\Sigma XY - (N\overline{XY})}{\Sigma X^2 - N\overline{X}^2}$$

$$= \frac{12}{736 - 720} - \frac{12}{16}$$

$$b = .75$$

Again, the answer is the same as the one you obtained with the conceptual formula.

Step 2. Next find the value for a, the constant—the value of the dependent variable when the value of the independent variable is 0.

FORMULA 9.2(C): The constant for a regression line

$$a = \overline{Y} - (b)(\overline{X})$$

where $\overline{Y}$ is the mean of the dependent variable and $\overline{X}$ is the mean of the independent variable; and b is the slope of the regression line.

Example: For the data in Table 9.4, the mean of the independent variable is 12, and the mean of the independent variable is 12. (How do we know? We calculated the means as the first step toward finding Pearson's r.) We found that the slope of the regression line is .75. Insert these numbers into the formula.

$\overline{Y}$ (mean of the dependent variable) $= 12$ b (slope of the regression line) $= .75$
$\overline{X}$ (mean of the independent variable) $= 12$

$$a = \overline{Y} - (b)(\overline{X})$$

$$= 12 - (.75)(12) - 12 - 9$$

$$a = 3$$

Using the regression line   We can use the values for the slope and the constant in the formula for the regression line to predict the dependent variable. For example, we can use these values to ask, What would we predict a respondent's education to be if we know the father has 13 years of education? To answer this question, we solve the formula for the regression line, $Y = a + (b)(X)$, using the values for the slope (b) and the constant (a) along with the given, the value of the independent variable (13, in this case).

a (constant) = 3 b (slope) = .75 X (given value of independent variable) = 13

$$Y = a + (b)(X)$$
$$= 3 + (.75)(13) = 3 + 9.75$$
$$Y = 12.75$$

This tells us that a respondent whose father has 13 years of education can be expected to have 12.75 years of education.

Does this answer make sense? Check it out. Construct a scatterplot for the values in Table 9.4. It should look like the scatterplot in Figure 9.17. How can you add the regression line? First, find the constant—the value of the dependent variable (*respondent's education*) when the independent variable (*father's education*) is zero. For the data in Table 9.4, the constant is 3. Draw a plot point in which the father's education is zero and the respondent's education is 3. Now add a plot point for the predicted value of the respondent's education (12.75) when the father's education is 13. Finally, connect these two plot points with a line. Now your scatterplot should look like Figure 9.18.

Skills Practice 8   Find the slope, using the computational formula, and the constant for the set of data in Skills Practice 7. What is the predicted value of a respondent's education when the mother's education is 15? Draw the scatterplot and the regression line.

Let's see how we can use SPSS to find Pearson's r and r-squared along with the slope and constant of the regression line.

Finding Pearson's r and r-squared Using SPSS

There are several avenues to finding Pearson's r and r-squared. You will most often use these statistics in conjunction with a scatterplot, so it may be easiest to call them up while you are at the Output window looking at your scatterplot for the association between *paeduc* and *educ*.

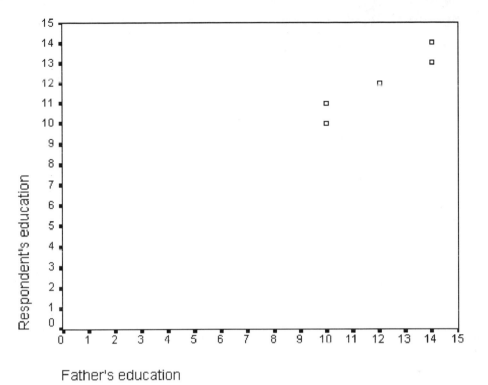

Father's education

Figure 9.17 Scatterplot of set of hypothetical data in Table 9.4 for the variables *father's education* and *respondent's education.*

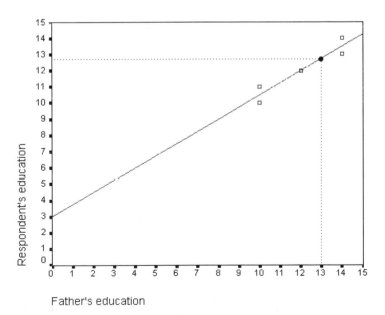

Father's education

Figure 9.18 Scatterplot with regression line for set of hypothetical data for the variables *father's education* and *respondent's education.*

SPSS Guide: Finding Pearson's *r* and *r*-squared From a Scatterplot

With your cursor on the scatterplot, double-click to open the Chart Editor window.

❶ Click on Analyze.

❷ Look under Analyze for Regression and click on it.

❸ Then click on Linear.

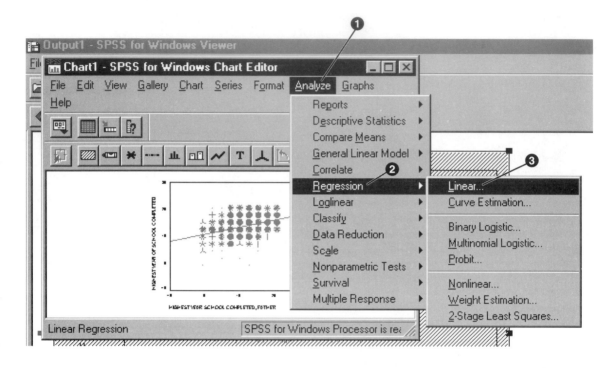

The Linear Regression dialog box opens.

❶ Select the dependent variable (*educ*) and put it in the Dependent box.

❷ Select the independent variable, *paeduc,* and put it in the Independent(s) box.

❸ Click on OK.

You will get a set of statistics like the ones in Table 9.5. Don't worry—we'll cut through the mass of information you get in your Output window to focus on a few of the most important statistics. (The rest will have to wait for an advanced course.)

Interpreting Pearson's *r* and *r*-squared   What do we focus on in the output from the regression command? First, notice Pearson's *r*. It appears in two places—under Model Summary *without* the sign as R, and then *with its sign* under Coefficients as the Standardized Coefficient.[3] Without the sign, Pearson's *r* at .391 confirms what we thought about the association—it is in the moderate (or even moderately weak) range. The sign (remember the absence of sign indicates a positive association) tells us that the more education the respondents' fathers have, the more education the respondents are likely to have.

---

[3]The correlation statistic under the Model Summary agrees with the statistic under the Standardized Coefficient because we are doing regression involving only two variables. When you increase the number of variables in the regression model, these statistics will no longer be identical.

TABLE 9.5   Regression Statistics for *paeduc* and *educ* in the gss96subset File.

Variables Entered/Removed[b]

Model	Variables Entered	Variables Removed	Method
1	PAEDUC HIGHEST YEAR SCHOOL COMPLETED, FATHER[a]		Enter

— The independent variable

a. All requested variables entered.

b. Dependent Variable: EDUC HIGHEST YEAR OF SCHOOL COMPLETED

Pearson's *r* reported without the sign

Model Summary

Model	R	R Square	Adjusted R Square	Std. Error of the Estimate
1	.391[a]	.153	.152	2.56

r-squared

a. Predictors: (Constant), PAEDUC HIGHEST YEAR SCHOOL COMPLETED, FATHER

ANOVA[b]

Model		Sum of Squares	df	Mean Square	F	Sig.
1	Regression	2429.575	1	2429.575	371.232	.000[a]
	Residual	13501.556	2063	6.545		
	Total	15931.130	2064			

a. Predictors: (Constant), PAEDUC HIGHEST YEAR SCHOOL COMPLETED, FATHER

b. Dependent Variable: EDUC HIGHEST YEAR OF SCHOOL COMPLETED

Pearson's *r* reported with the sign (the beta coefficient)

Coefficients[a]

Model		Unstandardized Coefficients		Standardized Coefficients	t	Sig.
		B	Std. Error	Beta		
1	(Constant)	10.802	.167		64.840	.000
	PAEDUC HIGHEST YEAR SCHOOL COMPLETED, FATHER	.264	.014	.391	19.267	.000

a. Dependent Variable: EDUC HIGHEST YEAR OF SCHOOL COMPLETED

The value for *r*-squared, which appears under the Model Summary, is .153. It tells us that 15% of the variation in a respondent's level of educational achievement can be accounted for by variations in the father's educational achievement. Using the PRE interpretation, we can also say that, knowing the association between fathers' educational achievements and respondents' educational achievements improves our ability to predict respondents' educational achievements by about 15%.

Skills Practice 9   Find and interpret Pearson's *r* and *r*-squared for the association between *maeduc* and *educ*.

Predicting the Dependent Variable Using the Regression Line

Statistics that we get with the regression command in SPSS do more than allow us to assess the strength and direction of an association; they also enable us to make predictions about a dependent variable based on the value of an independent variable, as we did earlier using the data in Table 9.4 and Skills Practice 7. We can use regression statistics to predict a respondent's level of education if we know the father's level of education. Putting it another way, we can answer a question like, How much education can a respondent be expected to have whose father has 16 years of education?

We can make these kinds of predictions by using the slope and constant of the regression line for *paeduc* and *educ*—statistics produced whenever we perform the linear regression function in SPSS.

We find the *y*-intercept (the constant) and the slope among the regression statistics. They are in the box labeled Coefficients. See Table 9.6. How do we find out how many years of education a respondent has whose father has 16 years? We plug the statistics for the *y*-intercept and the slope into our formula:

a (the constant or *y*-intercept) = 10.802 b (the slope) = .264

X (the given value of the independent variable) = 16

$$Y = a + (b)(X)$$

$$= 10.802 + (.264)(16) = 10.802 + 4.224$$

$$Y = 15.026$$

TABLE 9.6 Coefficients From the Regression Output for the Relationship Between *paeduc* and *educ* in the gss96subset File

Coefficients[a]

Model		Unstandardized Coefficients		Standardized Coefficients	t	Sig.
		B	Std. Error	Beta		
1	(Constant)	10.802	.167		64.840	.000
	PAEDUC HIGHEST YEAR SCHOOL COMPLETED, FATHER	.264	.014	.391	19.267	.000

Constant or y-intercept (*a*) — 10.802

Slope (*b*) — .264

a. Dependent Variable: EDUC HIGHEST YEAR OF SCHOOL COMPLETED

✔️ **Checking Your Work**   It's easy to see whether our answer is in the ballpark by looking at the scatterplot with the regression line for the variables *paeduc* and *educ* (Figure 9.19). Look up the value of the independent variable on the *x*-axis. Find where it intersects with the regression line, and then look across the scatterplot to see which value of the dependent variable on the *y*-axis is associated with the point at which the given value of the independent variable hits the regression line. The figure demonstrates the process.

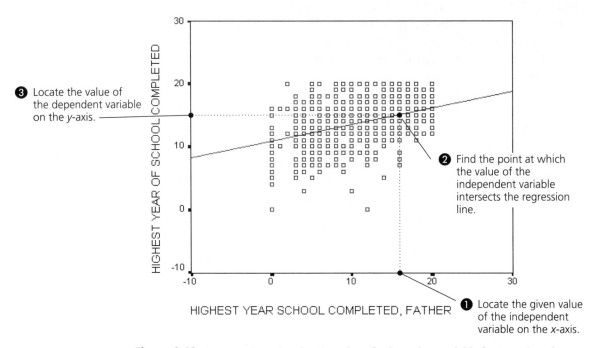

❸ Locate the value of the dependent variable on the *y*-axis.

❷ Find the point at which the value of the independent variable intersects the regression line.

❶ Locate the given value of the independent variable on the *x*-axis.

HIGHEST YEAR OF SCHOOL COMPLETED

HIGHEST YEAR SCHOOL COMPLETED, FATHER

Figure 9.19   Process for estimating the value of a dependent variable from a value of an independent variable using the regression line for the variables *paeduc* and *educ* in the gss96subset file.

CONTROLLING FOR THIRD VARIABLES

Controlling for Third Variables Using the Compare Means Command

We learned in the first part of this chapter that men, on average, have more
years of education than women. Does this association hold up for women and
men in all age categories? We can use the Compare Means command and control
for the variable *agecat* to find out.

SPSS Guide: Using the Compare Means Command With a
Third Variable

Use the Analyze ➥ Means ➥ Compare Means command path to open the
Means dialog box.

① Enter your dependent and independent variables (*educ* and *sex*, respectively).

② Click on the Next button.

③ Notice that the label on the Independent List box is now Layer 2 of 2. Enter the variable *agecat* as an independent variable. *agecat* shows up in the Layer 2 of 2: Independent List as a control variable.

④ Click on OK.

TABLE 9.7 **A Comparison of Means for the Variables *sex* and *educ*, Controlling for *agecat*, in the gss96subset File**

Report

EDUC HIGHEST YEAR OF SCHOOL COMPLETED

SEX RESPONDENTS SEX	AGECAT recoded age - four categories	Mean	N	Std. Deviation	
1 MALE	1 18 thru 25	12.80	153	2.03	
	2 26 thru 39	13.89	409	2.58	
	3 40 thru 64	13.93	553	3.07	
	4 65 thru 89	12.19	168	3.53	← Average years of education for all male respondents
	Total	13.56	1283	2.95	
2 FEMALE	1 18 thru 25	13.07	198	2.08	
	2 26 thru 39	13.64	523	2.65	
	3 40 thru 64	13.69	612	2.98	
	4 65 thru 89	11.44	274	3.06	← Average years of education for all female respondents
	Total	13.21	1607	2.91	
Total	1 18 thru 25	12.95	351	2.06	
	2 26 thru 39	13.75	932	2.62	
	3 40 thru 64	13.80	1165	3.02	
	4 65 thru 09	11.72	442	3.26	
	Total	13.37	2890	2.93	

Included in your output will be a report like the one in Table 9.7. You will get a mean for the years of education broken down by sex, and within each of the categories of sex, the mean will be displayed by categories of the control variable.

Interpretation   How do we read this? First, compare each of the means for males with the corresponding means for females for each category of age. Is the relationship between sex and education the same for each category of age as it is for all respondents together? Start with the first of the means for males. Notice that, unlike the respondents as a whole, males in the 18 through 25 age category have less education, on average, than females in the same age group.

Second, look at the size of the difference in the means: Is it larger or smaller for each age category than it is among respondents as a whole? You can see that, for all respondents, men had only .35 of a year more education than women. (You can find the means for males as a whole and females as a whole by looking at the Total mean for the category Male and the Total mean for the category Female.) Among respondents in the 18 through 25 age category, the difference in average years of education is a little smaller, with female respondents reporting only .27 of a year more education, on average, than males.

As you make these comparisons for the rest of the age categories, you should see the following patterns.

For every age category except 18 through 25, men have more education, on average, than women. The largest difference is in the age category 65 through 89. Men in the 65 through 89 age category have about three quarters of a year more education than do women. The smallest difference in the average years of education is in the 40 through 64 age category (in which the difference is less than one quarter of a year).

Skills Practice 11   Analyze the association between sex and education, this time controlling for social class (using the *class* variable).

Using Regression Statistics With Third Variables

To examine an association between two numerical variables in light of a third variable, you can use the Selection box in the Linear Regression dialog box. For example, if you want to see whether the association between a father's education and a respondent's education is as strong for men as for women, use the command path Analyze ➡ Regression ➡ Linear to open the dialog box. Then follow these instructions.

SPSS Guide: Using Linear Regression With Control Variables

❶ Enter the variables *paeduc* (the independent variable) and *educ* (the dependent variable).

❷ Click on the variable *sex* and put it in the Selection variable box. Note that the selection variable, *sex,* now has a question mark next to it; SPSS wants to know which category of the variable to use as the control category. Let's begin with Males or category 1.

❸ Click on the Rule button to open the Linear Regression: Set Rule box.

4 Place your cursor under Value: and enter 1 (for the category Male of the *sex* variable). Then click on Continue.

5 At the Linear Regression dialog box, click on OK.

Model Summary

Model	R SEX RESPONDENTS SEX= 1 MALE (Selected)	R Square	Adjusted R Square	Std. Error of the Estimate
1	.378[a]	.143	.142	2.59

a. Predictors: (Constant), PAEDUC HIGHEST YEAR SCHOOL COMPLETED, FATHER

Model Summary

Model	R SEX RESPONDENTS SEX= 2 FEMALE (Selected)	R Square	Adjusted R Square	Std. Error of the Estimate
1	.398[a]	.159	.158	2.53

a. Predictors: (Constant), PAEDUC HIGHEST YEAR SCHOOL COMPLETED, FATHER

You will get a set of regression statistics for the association between *paeduc* and *educ* for the male respondents. This is the first part of Table 9.8.

Now repeat the process, but this time when you enter your selection variable, *sex,* click on Rule and enter Value: 2 for the female respondents. You will get a table like the second part of Table 9.8. Remember that the goal of third-variable analysis is to examine the extent to which the nature (direction) and strength of an association changes when a third variable is introduced. For the respondents as a whole, the Pearson's r for the association between fathers' education and respondents' education is positive (indicating that the more education a father has, the more education a respondent has) and (at .391) moderate to moderately weak. The r-squared is .153. About 15% of the variation in respondents' educational levels can be explained by their fathers' educational achievements.

Does anything change when a third variable is introduced? To find out, look at the Model Summary for males and females. (They are reproduced in Table 9.8, but you won't see them this close together on your screen. You'll have to locate them among the many tables in your output.) Notice that for males, the direction of the association is unchanged, but it is slightly weaker (with Pearson's $r = .378$ and r-squared $= .143$). For females, however, the association is stronger than it is for males (with Pearson's $r - .398$ and r-squared $= .159$). For both groups, the strength of the association is moderate to moderately weak.

Interpretation   Once again, be sure to note any changes in the direction or strength of an association. In this case, you could point out that

> for males, the association between fathers' educational achievements and respondents' educational achievements is slightly weaker than it is for respondents as a whole, but there is no change in direction. Among females, though, the association is stronger than it is for males, and it is a little stronger than for all respondents together. The direction is unchanged—the more education the respondents' fathers have, the more education the respondents are likely to have. The variable *sex* appears to have some influence on the association between a father's education and the respondent's education. The association is weaker for males than for females. Fathers' educational achievements explain more of the variations in respondents' educational achievements among females than among males.

Skills Practice 12   Analyze the association between respondents' mothers' educational levels (*maeduc*) and the respondents' educational levels (*educ*), controlling for *sex*.

At this point, you should have a number of tools at your disposal for describing associations between variables in a set of data—lambda, gamma, and Pearson's r, to name a few. To review what you've learned so far, refer to the chart on the next page. It's a guide to the application of measures of association.

In the next chapter, I will introduce concepts for understanding inferential statistics—statistics that help us assess the likelihood that what we have been learning about the sample of GSS respondents is true of the larger population the sample is supposed to represent.

USING MEASURES OF ASSOCIATION

Use the following chart as a guide to the correct application of measures of association. How you will use these statistics depends on the level of measurement of the variables you are analyzing. This guide will help you decide when and how to use each of the measures. For example, if you are wondering how to approach measuring associations involving categorical variables, look down the flow chart to the box Categorical Variables. Notice you have two choices—one for associations involving nominal variables and one for associations between ordinal variables. Under each of those boxes are the appropriate measures of associations, references to the formulas for the manual computations of the measure, and abbreviated SPSS instructions.

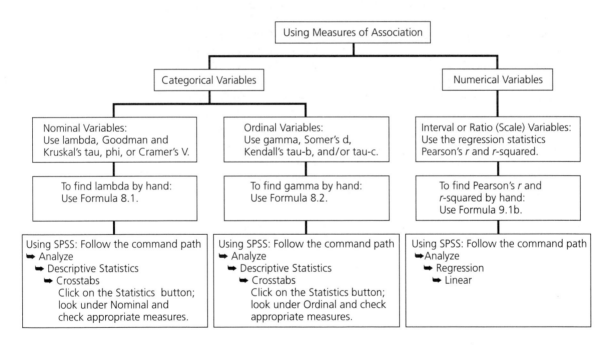

SUMMARY

This chapter focused on two techniques for evaluating associations involving numerical variables: comparing means and linear regression. Comparing means is useful for associations between numerical variables and categorical variables. For example, you can see whether there are any differences in average years of education between men and women. Linear regression, on the other hand, is applied to associations involving two numerical variables, like the one between the respondents' educational levels and their parents' (mothers' or fathers') educational levels.

Although not explicitly covered in this chapter, the comparison of means can be calculated by hand simply by dividing a set of data by the values of a categorical variable (like males or females) and then computing means for each group. Pencil-and-paper computations for linear regression were covered, but largely for conceptual understanding. It is unlikely you would attempt computations of this sort without the help of a computer.

Consequently, greater attention was paid to using SPSS to obtain a comparison of means for a numerical variable and to interpret the statistical output. In addition, you learned to use SPSS to obtain and interpret a scatterplot with a regression line and sunflowers for two numerical variables, Pearson's r (the correlation coefficient) and r^2 (r-squared, the coefficient of determination), and regression line statistics (the slope and the y-intercept or constant). Finally, you should be able to use regression line statistics to make predictions about the value of a dependent variable based on values of some independent variable.

In the concluding sections, you learned to use the Analyze ➡ Compare Means ➡ Means command path and the Selection Variable box of the Linear Regression dialog box to control for third variables.

KEY CONCEPTS

Comparison of means	Linear association	r-squared (coefficient
Scatterplot	Nonlinear association	of determination)
Covariation	Curvilinear association	y-intercept (constant)
Regression line	Pearson's r	Slope

2. Respondents who are classified as Other have completed more years of education, on average, than White or Black respondents. White respondents have completed more years of education, on average, than Black respondents. The differences in the averages are not large, though. The difference between those who say they are Other and White respondents is only .18, less than one fifth of a year, whereas the difference between Other and Black respondents is over a year. The difference between White and Black respondents is not quite a year.

3. The scatterplot appears positive, much like the scatterplot for father's education and respondent's education. The association appears to be moderate.

4. The association appears to be positive, as the points flow generally from the lower left corner of the graph to the upper right corner. The association looks fairly weak, because the points are spread out rather than clustered near a single line.

5. A scatterplot would look like the one that follows:

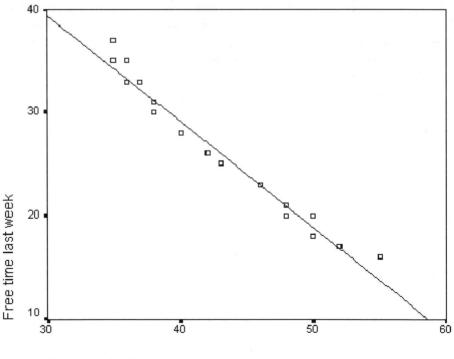

Hours worked last week

The association appears negative and strong. The more hours respondents work, the less free time they have.

6. A scatterplot with the regression line and sunflowers for *maeduc* and *educ* should look like the one you see here.

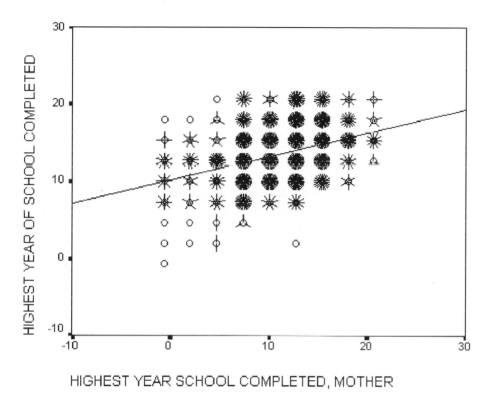

Like the association with father's education, the association between a respondent's education and his or her mother's education is positive. The more education respondents' mothers have, the more education respondents are likely to have. The association looks to be at least moderate, given the steepness of the slope of the line along with the concentration of data near the line.

7. The variables are *mother's education* (the independent, or X, variable) and *respondent's education* (the dependent, or Y, variable).

Step 1. Begin by multiplying each value of X by each value of Y and adding up the products.

Mother's Education, X	Respondent's Education, Y	XY
13	12	156
13	14	182
14	15	210
15	16	240
15	13	195
		$\Sigma XY = 983$

Step 2. Find the mean for each of the variables, X and Y.

Mother's Education, X	Respondent's Education, Y
13	12
13	14
14	15
15	16
15	13
$\Sigma X = 70$	$\Sigma Y = 70$

$$\bar{X} = \frac{\Sigma X}{N} = \frac{70}{5} = 14$$

$$\bar{Y} = \frac{\Sigma Y}{N} = \frac{70}{5} = 14$$

Step 3. Multiply N by $\bar{X}$ by $\bar{Y}$ to get $N\bar{X}\bar{Y}$.

$$N\bar{X}\bar{Y} = 5 \times 14 \times 14 = 980$$

Step 4. Square each value of X and add up the results. Do the same for each value of Y.

Mother's Education, X	Respondent's Education, Y	X^2	Y^2
13	12	169	144
13	14	169	196
14	15	196	225
15	16	225	256
15	13	225	169
		$\Sigma X^2 = 984$	$\Sigma Y^2 = 990$

Step 5. Square the mean of X and multiply by N to get $N\bar{X}^2$.

$$\bar{X}^2 = 14 \times 14 = 196$$

$$N\bar{X}^2 = 5 \times 196 = 980$$

Do the same for the mean of Y:

$$\bar{Y}^2 = 14 \times 14 = 196$$

$$N\bar{Y}^2 = 5 \times 196 = 980$$

Step 6. Plug the results into the computational formula for Pearson's r (Formula 9.1b):

$$\Sigma XY = 983 \qquad N\bar{X}\,\bar{Y} = 980 \qquad \Sigma X^2 = 984 \qquad \Sigma Y^2 = 990$$

$$N\bar{X}^2 = 980 \qquad N\bar{Y}^2 = 980$$

$$r = \frac{\Sigma XY - (N\bar{X}\bar{Y})}{\sqrt{(\Sigma X^2 - N\bar{X}^2)(\Sigma Y^2 - N\bar{Y}^2)}}$$

$$= \frac{983 - 980}{\sqrt{(984 - 980)(990 - 980)}} = \frac{3}{\sqrt{4 \times 10}}$$

$$= \frac{3}{\sqrt{40}} = \frac{3}{6.3246}$$

$$r = .47$$

Interpreting Pearson's and r-squared: Pearson's r, at .47, suggests a moderate association between the variables *mother's education* and *respondent's education,* and it is a positive association. The more education a respondent's mother has, the more education the respondent is likely to have.

To find r-squared, simply square the value of Pearson's r (multiply .47 by .47). The r-squared is .22, suggesting that 22% of the variation in the respondents' years of education can be accounted for by variations in their mothers' years of education. In PRE terms, knowing the association between mothers' educational achievements and respondents' educational achievements improves our ability to predict respondents' educational levels by about 22%.

8. To find the slope of the regression, use Formula 9.2(b):

numerator for Pearson's $r = 3$ sum of the squared values of X minus $\overline{X}^2$ times $N = 4$

$$b = \frac{\Sigma XY - (N\overline{X}\overline{Y})}{\Sigma X^2 - N\overline{X}^2}$$

$$= \frac{3}{4}$$

$$b = .75$$

The numerator, 3, was calculated in the process of finding Pearson's r for the previous exercise. The denominator, 4, is simply the sum of each of the squared values of the independent variable, *mother's education,* from which we subtracted the squared value of its mean times N. To work the formula, divide 3 by 4. To find the constant, use the formula:

$$a = \overline{Y} - (b)(\overline{X})$$

$$= 14 - (.75)(14)$$

$$= 14 - 10.5$$

$$a = 3.5$$

The predicted value of a respondent's education when the mother's education is 15 can be computed by plugging the relevant values into the formula for a line:

$$Y = a + (b)(X)$$
$$= 3.50 + (.75)(15) = 3.50 + 11.25$$
$$Y = 14.75$$

A respondent whose mother has 15 years of education can be expected to have almost that much: 14.75 years of education.

Your scatterplot should look somewhat like the one that follows:

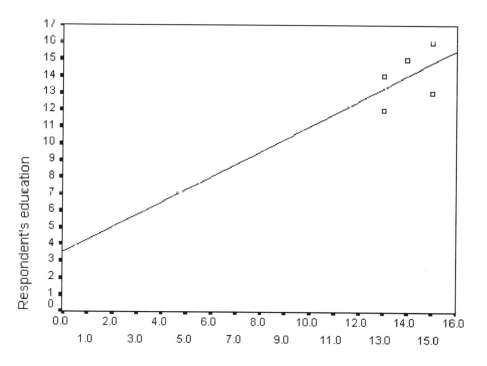

9. You should get regression statistics like the ones you see here:

Model Summary

Model	R	R Square	Adjusted R Square	Std. Error of the Estimate
1	.373[a]	.139	.138	2.59

a. Predictors: (Constant), MAEDUC HIGHEST YEAR SCHOOL COMPLETED, MOTHER

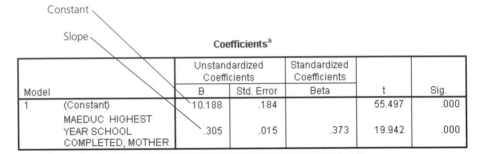

Coefficients[a]

Model		Unstandardized Coefficients		Standardized Coefficients	t	Sig.
		B	Std. Error	Beta		
1	(Constant)	10.188	.184		55.497	.000
	MAEDUC HIGHEST YEAR SCHOOL COMPLETED, MOTHER	.305	.015	.373	19.942	.000

a. Dependent Variable: EDUC HIGHEST YEAR OF SCHOOL COMPLETED

The association between mother's education and respondent's education is, at best, moderate with Pearson's *r* at .373. The absence of a sign on the Standardized Coefficient suggests that the association is positive. The more education respondents' mothers have, the more education the respondents have. The *r*-squared tells us that about 14% of the variation in the respondents' educational achievements can be explained by their mothers' educational achievements. The PRE interpretation suggests that knowing the relationship between mothers' educational levels and respondents' educational levels improves our ability to predict the respondents' educational levels by about 14%.

10. A. The predicted value of a respondent's educational level when the father has 12 years is:

$$Y = a + (b)(X)$$
$$= 10.802 + (.264)(12) = 10.802 + 3.168$$
$$Y = 13.97$$

The predicted value of a respondent's educational level when the father has 18 years is:

$$Y = a + (b)(X)$$
$$= 10.802 + (.264)(18)$$
$$= 10.802 + 4.752$$
$$Y = 15.554$$

B. Look for the constant and the slope of the regression line for the association between *maeduc* and *educ* in the coefficients table in the answer to Skills Practice 9.

The constant is 10.188 and the slope is .305. To predict a respondent's education when the mother's education is 16, use the following formula:

$$Y = a + (b)(X)$$
$$= 10.188 + (.305)(16)$$
$$- 10.188 + 4.880$$
$$Y = 15.068$$

11. You should get a table like the following:

Report

EDUC HIGHEST YEAR OF SCHOOL COMPLETED

SEX RESPONDENTS SEX	CLASS SUBJECTIVE CLASS IDENTIFICATION	Mean	N	Std. Deviation
1 MALE	1 LOWER CLASS	12.35	55	2.79
	2 WORKING CLASS	12.62	588	2.54
	3 MIDDLE CLASS	14.39	578	2.91
	4 UPPER CLASS	15.89	53	3.24
	Total	13.55	1274	2.93
2 FEMALE	1 LOWER CLASS	11.18	114	3.49
	2 WORKING CLASS	12.70	709	2.38
	3 MIDDLE CLASS	13.86	718	2.97
	4 UPPER CLASS	15.32	60	2.85
	Total	13.21	1601	2.90
Total	1 LOWER CLASS	11.56	169	3.32
	2 WORKING CLASS	12.67	1297	2.45
	3 MIDDLE CLASS	14.10	1296	2.96
	4 UPPER CLASS	15.58	113	3.04
	Total	13.36	2875	2.92

There doesn't seem to be much of an effect of class on the association between sex and education. Across all class levels except working class, men have more education than women. The size of the difference changes somewhat. For example, among lower-class respondents the difference is more than a year, with men having more education, on average, than women.

12. Here are the statistics you should focus on for the analysis (although they won't be this close together in your Output window):

Model Summary

Model	R SEX RESPONDENTS SEX = 1 MALE (Selected)	R Square	Adjusted R Square	Std. Error of the Estimate
1	.312[a]	.097	.097	2.75

a. Predictors: (Constant), MAEDUC HIGHEST YEAR SCHOOL COMPLETED, MOTHER

Model Summary

Model	R SEX RESPONDENTS SEX = 2 FEMALE (Selected)	R Square	Adjusted R Square	Std. Error of the Estimate
1	.423[a]	.179	.178	2.45

a. Predictors: (Constant), MAEDUC HIGHEST YEAR SCHOOL COMPLETED, MOTHER

There does seem to be an effect of sex on the association between the respondents' education and their mothers' education. For men, the association is weaker ($r = .312$) than it is for women ($r = .423$). In addition, the association is weaker for men than among respondents as a whole, and it is stronger for women than it is among respondents as a whole. The r-squared tells us that about 10% of the variation in male respondents' educational achievements can be explained by their mothers' educational achievements. For women, their mothers' educational achievements account for 18% of the variation in the respondents' educational achievements—somewhat more than for men.

GENERAL EXERCISES

For Exercises 1 and 2, use the sets of data (drawn at random from the 1996 GSS) to construct and interpret (describing the nature, strength, and direction of the association) scatterplots. Think about how to set up each scatterplot—which variables should be independent and which should be dependent.

1.

Case Summaries

	HIGHEST YEAR OF SCHOOL COMPLETED	HIGHEST YEAR SCHOOL COMPLETED, SPOUSE
1	12	12
2	16	14
3	5	5
4	20	15
5	12	12
6	12	12
7	16	16
8	16	16
9	8	11
10	12	12
11	18	16
12	12	12
13	14	12
14	17	14
15	12	13
16	16	16
Total N	16	16

2.

Case Summaries

		HIGHEST YEAR OF SCHOOL COMPLETED	NUMBER OF HOURS WORKED LAST WEEK
1		10	15
2		16	40
3		5	40
4		12	40
5		13	4
6		12	40
7		14	20
8		16	55
9		16	40
10		16	50
11		8	35
12		12	40
13		18	40
14		12	57
15		14	40
16		17	40
17		12	19
18		12	50
19		16	40
Total	N	19	19

3. Use the following hypothetical data to compute and interpret Pearson's *r* and *r*-squared for the variables *years of education* and *spouse's education*.

Years of Education	Spouse's Education
10	11
11	12
13	14
15	15
16	18

4. Use the following hypothetical data to compute and interpret Pearson's *r* and *r*-squared for the variables *years of education* and *hours worked per week*.

Years of Education	Hours Worked per Week
10	40
11	50
13	40
15	45
16	50

5. Use the following hypothetical data to compute and interpret Pearson's *r* and *r*-squared for the variables *years of education* and *age*.

Years of Education	Age
10	45
11	50
13	35
15	40
16	55

6. Use the following hypothetical data to compute and interpret Pearson's *r* and *r*-squared for the variables *spouse's education* and *hours worked per week*.

Spouse's Education	Hours Worked per Week
11	40
12	50
14	40
15	45
18	50

7. Use the following hypothetical data to compute and interpret Pearson's *r* and *r*-squared for the variables *hours worked per week* and *age*.

Hours Worked per Week	Age
40	45
50	50
40	35
45	40
50	55

8. Use the following hypothetical data to compute and interpret Pearson's *r* and *r*-squared for the variables *spouse's education* and *age.*

Spouse's Education	Age
11	45
12	50
14	35
15	40
18	55

9. Use the data in General Exercise 3 to compute the slope and the constant for the regression line for the association between *years of education* and *spouse's education.*

10. Use the data in General Exercise 4 to compute the slope and the constant for the regression line for the association between *years of education* and *hours worked per week.*

11. Use the data in General Exercise 5 to compute the slope and the constant for the regression line for the association between *years of education* and *age.*

12. Use the data in General Exercise 6 to compute the slope and the constant for the regression line for the association between *spouse's education* and *hours worked per week.*

SPSS EXERCISES

1. Is there any difference in educational achievement (*educ*) based on marital status (*marital*)?

2. Is there any difference in educational achievement (*educ*) based on employment status (*wrkstat*)?

3. Is there any difference in educational achievement (*educ*) based on region of the country in which one resides (*rcregion*)?

4. Is there any difference in educational achievement (*educ*) based on age (*agecat*)?

For Exercises 5–8, use SPSS to obtain and interpret (describe the nature, strength, and direction of the association) scatterplots with sunflowers and the regression line for the association between the given variables. Think about how to set up each scatterplot—which variable should be independent, which should be dependent.

5. *speduc* (spouse's education) and *educ.*

6. *educ* and *age.*

7. *educ* and *earnrs.*

8. *childs* and *educ.*

9. Find and interpret Pearson's *r* and *r*-squared for the association between *educ* and *speduc.* Use the slope and constant (*y*-intercept) to answer this question: How many years of education will a respondent's spouse have if the respondent has 16 years of education?

10. Find and interpret Pearson's *r* and *r*-squared for the association between *educ* and *age.* Use the slope and constant (*y*-intercept) to answer this question: How many years of education can we expect a respondent who is 21 years old to have?

11. Find and interpret Pearson's *r* and *r*-squared for the association between *educ* and *childs.* Use the slope and constant (*y*-intercept) to answer this question: How many children would we predict a respondent with 18 years of education to have?

12. Find and interpret Pearson's *r* and *r*-squared for the association between *educ* and *earnrs.* Use the slope and constant (*y*-intercept) to answer this question: How many wage earners would we expect to find in the household of a respondent with 14 years of education?

13. For Skills Practice 2, you looked at the association between education (*educ*) and race. Now see what happens to the nature and strength of the association when control variables are introduced. Use the Compare Means command to analyze the association between *educ* and *race* and control for *sex.*

14. What happens to the association between *educ* and *class* when you introduce the control variable *agecat?*

15. In Exercise 9, you used Pearson's *r* and *r*-squared to examine the association between a respondent's education and their spouse's education (using *educ* and *speduc*). Now control the association for the variable *sex.* Does the control variable affect the nature or strength of the association between *educ* and *speduc?*

16. Reexamine the association between *educ* and *speduc* using the control variable *race.* Does the control variable affect the nature or strength of the association between *educ* and *speduc?*

17. Look at the association between *educ* and *speduc* one more time. This time control for the variable *class.* Does the control variable affect the nature or strength of the association between *educ* and *speduc?*

An Introduction to Making Inferences

INTRODUCTION

In 1998 a hotly contested race for the U.S. Senate took place in the state of New York between the incumbent, Republican Alfonse D'Amato, and the challenger, Democratic Congressman Charles Schumer. There were charges and countercharges of all sorts: in short, a negative campaign on both sides. Were the voters paying attention, or were the allegations that flew from both sides falling on deaf ears? A *New York Times*/CBS poll tried to find the answer.

Not only are the answers interesting, in part because they bear on the issue of how jaded we are becoming in response to campaigns like these, but the methodology—the way researchers come to their conclusions—is interesting, too. In the "News to Use" section, you will see an excerpt from the article reporting the results of the poll and a description of how the poll participants were selected and the results analyzed. In the section "How the Poll Was Conducted," pay particular attention to the explanation of how to use the results of the sample to generalize, or draw conclusions about, the views of all adult New Yorkers and the views of those adults who are likely to vote. These are inferential statistics in action.

In Poll, New York Voters See Senate Race as Too Negative[1]

Adam Nagourney With Marjorie Connelly

New York voters are growing increasingly critical of the caustic tone of the campaign for Senate, but the daily rounds of attacks between Senator Alfonse M. D'Amato and Representative Charles E. Schumer have yet to sway significant numbers of them, according to the latest *New York Times*/CBS News poll.

The Republican Senator and his Democratic challenger are each favored by 44% of likely voters, according to the poll, which was taken from Oct. 21 through Oct. 25. . . .

Political analysts from both parties said Mr. D'Amato and Mr. Schumer were equally responsible for the harsh tone of this race. Mr. Schumer, for example, ends his television advertisements with the tag line, "Too many lies for too long."

But voters clearly see Mr. D'Amato as running the more negative campaign. 73% of those polled said he was spending more time attacking his opponent than explaining what he would do in Congress, an extraordinarily high figure. Only 12% said he was spending more time explaining. By contrast, 54% said Mr. Schumer was spending more time attacking, compared with 21% explaining. . . .

By a slight margin, 49% to 43%, voters agreed with another central contention of Mr. Schumer, that Mr. D'Amato has been in office too long. . . . Mr. D'Amato was elected in 1980. . . .

HOW THE POLL WAS CONDUCTED

The latest *New York Times*/CBS News Poll of New York State was based on telephone interviews conducted October 21 to 25 with 1,791 adults throughout the state. Of these, 1,235 said they were registered to vote. Interviews were conducted in either English or Spanish.

The sample of telephone exchanges called was randomly selected by a computer from a complete list of 2,500 active residential exchanges across the state.

Within each exchange, random digits were added to form a complete telephone number, thus permitting access to both listed and unlisted numbers. Within each household one adult was designated by a random procedure to be the respondent for the survey.

The results have been weighted to take account of household size and number of telephone lines into the residence, as well as to adjust for variations relating to region of the state, race, sex, age, Hispanic origin, and education.

In addition, results about registered voters' intended vote in November have been weighted by the statewide distribution of ballots in recent comparable elections from New York City (29%), its suburbs (24%), and the rest of the state (47%).

According to statistical theory, in 19 out of 20 cases, the results based on such samples will differ by no more than 3 percentage points in either direction from those that would have been obtained by seeking out all adults in New York State.

The potential sampling error for smaller subgroups is larger. For example, for results based only on "likely voters" it would be plus or minus 4 percentage points. Registered voters were judged as likely to vote based on their stated intentions, attention to the campaign, and past voting behavior.

In addition to sampling error, the practical difficulties of conducting any survey of public opinion may introduce other sources of error into the poll. Differences in the wording and order of questions, for instance, can lead to somewhat varying results.

---

[1]The *New York Times,* 10 October 1998, pp. A1 and B4.

What are **inferential statistics**? They are numbers that help us assess the likelihood that patterns we observe in randomly drawn samples will be found in the populations from which those samples were drawn. A very important part of this definition is the idea that inferential statistics should be used only with randomly drawn samples. Examples of inferential statistics in the article's section "How the Poll Was Conducted" include the statement that "in 19 out of 20 cases, the results based on . . . samples will differ by no more than 3 percentage points in either direction from those that would have been obtained by seeking out all adults in New York State." In statistical terminology, the *New York Times* writers are discussing confidence limits and confidence intervals, tools to which you'll be exposed as you learn about inferential statistics.

In this chapter I will lay the groundwork for understanding inferential statistics by introducing the assumptions on which inferential statistics are based, beginning with the difference between a sample and a population. Then I will cover the properties of randomly drawn samples that allow us to make inferences from samples to populations. In the next chapter you will learn how to apply these principles to the computation of confidence intervals at specified confidence levels, like the one in the *New York Times* "News to Use" article.

Samples and Populations

As you may recall from Chapter 1, **samples** are subsets of populations. **Populations** are sets of elements that researchers are interested in knowing something about. Populations can be sets of individuals, organizations, states, or even nations. In the "News to Use" at the beginning of this chapter, the population of interest is the set of New York State adults. Samples are those subsets of populations about which researchers gather data, usually to make generalizations about the populations from which the samples are drawn. To make generalizations from samples to populations, researchers must draw their samples at random from frames (lists—as complete as researchers can make them—of all elements in a population). The sample in the *New York Times*/CBS poll consists of the 1,791 adults who were interviewed by telephone about the Senate race. Was the sample drawn randomly? It apparently was, because telephone numbers were selected at random from a frame of all possible telephone numbers in New York State.

Sampling Statistics

The question then becomes, How likely is it that the sample selected by the pollsters is representative of the population? You will probably argue that if the sample has been drawn randomly, it's logical to assume it will be representative, and you may be right—most of the time. However, if you have had any experience drawing random samples, you have seen that sometimes you can draw a sample not at all representative of the population from which the sample was drawn.

To illustrate this point, look at Table 10.2 on p. 416. You will see the means for the variable *age* in five different randomly drawn samples from the 1996 General Social Survey. How close are these sample means to the actual average age (44.78 years old) of the respondents? In a couple of cases they are extremely close, but in one case, not very close at all—nearly 7 years off.

How can researchers know whether their sample is one of the representative ones or one of the samples that doesn't represent the population at all? The frustrating answer is, they can't. They can never know with 100% certainty whether their sample is representative or not. All they can do is assess the likelihood—the probability—that their sample *is* representative. They can never guarantee that it is.

It's somewhat like buying a new car. You do a lot of research on the different makes and models. You find one you like—it looks nice, drives well, and has an excellent repair record. The odds are that you've got a good car. However, you won't know for sure until you own it whether you've got a car that acts like most cars or is a "lemon." The proof is in the outcome—and so it is with social science research. We can never know for sure. Sometimes pollsters see the proof in the outcome. Who wins the election? The candidate the pollsters said would win, or the opponent? Often, researchers don't know for sure how accurate their samples are as representations of populations. Look at some of the General Social Survey questions. We can never know for certain whether the percentage of respondents who oppose abortion, or say they attend church regularly, or graduate from high school is identical (or even close) to the percentage of people in the population who share those characteristics.

How then can we know the likelihood that our sample represents the population? We can use inferential statistics—statistics that assess the probability or likelihood. To begin understanding how these statistics work, we need to revisit the normal distribution and get a handle on the related concept of Z scores.

THE NORMAL DISTRIBUTION REVISITED: Z SCORES

Do you remember the normal distribution, commonly known as the bell-shaped curve? It is a symmetrically distributed set of scores for which there is only one mode and the mean, median, and mode are identical. If you were to graph the distribution, it would look somewhat like a bell, although not necessarily like the Liberty Bell. In Chapter 6 you learned how to use the properties of the normal distribution to evaluate the distribution or dispersion of responses to a variable in relation to the mean. As a rule of thumb, the smaller a standard deviation is in relation to the range of responses to a variable, the more homogeneous are the responses. The larger the standard deviation is in relation to the range, the more heterogeneous are the responses. Moreover, we can assume that, in a normally distributed set of responses to a variable, about 68% of the responses will fall within a range of values 1 standard deviation below the mean to 1 standard deviation above the mean. About 95% of the responses will fall within a range of values 2 standard deviations below the mean to 2 standard deviations above it.

Skills Practice 1   Compare the means, medians, and standard deviations for the educational levels of male and female respondents to the 1996 General Social Survey (see the tables below).

A. Could any of these distributions be normal? How can you tell?

B. Which distribution is the most homogeneous?

C. Use the standard deviation for males to find out the range of values 1 standard deviation below the mean and 1 standard deviation above the mean, and the range of values 2 standard deviations below the mean to 2 standard deviations above it.

Statistics[a]

EDUC HIGHEST YEAR OF SCHOOL COMPLETED

N	Valid	1283
	Missing	2
Mean		13.56
Median		13.00
Mode		12
Std. Deviation		2.95
Range		17

a. SEX RESPONDENTS SEX = 1 MALE

Statistics[a]

EDUC HIGHEST YEAR OF SCHOOL COMPLETED

N	Valid	1612
	Missing	7
Mean		13.21
Median		13.00
Mode		12
Std. Deviation		2.91
Range		20

a. SEX RESPONDENTS SEX = 2 FEMALE

As this exercise demonstrates, you can use the properties of the normal distribution to find out the value of 1 or more standard deviations from the mean (by adding 1 or more standard deviations to the mean, or subtracting 1 or more standard deviations from the mean).

Besides using the characteristics of the normal distribution to describe the dispersion of responses to a variable, we can use it to tell where in the distribution a particular value might fall. For example, if we want to describe the educational achievements of the male respondents to the General Social Survey, we can find the value of 1 standard deviation below the mean by subtracting 1 standard deviation from the mean, and we can find 1 standard deviation above the mean by adding 1 standard deviation to the mean. Then we can make the statement that about 68% of the male respondents have between 10.61 and 16.51 years of education. If we subtract 2 standard deviations from the mean and then add 2 standard deviations to the mean, we can say that about 95% of the male respondents have between 7.66 and 19.46 years of education.

We can also use the properties of the normal distribution to find out how many standard deviations from the mean a particular respondent or group of respondents might fall. Suppose we want to know where in the distribution we would find respondents with 10 years of education. We can find the answer by finding the Z score for the value, 10 years of education.

A **Z score** expresses the relationship between a particular value in a distribution and the mean in units of the standard deviation. Using the example in Skills Practice 1, you found that for males, the value 10.61 is 1 standard deviation below the mean. Another way of expressing this same idea is to say that the value 10.61 has a Z score of -1. In other words, the value 10.61 is 1 standard deviation below the mean. On the other hand, the value 16.51 has a Z score of $+1$. It is 1 standard deviation above the mean.

Suppose we want to work the relationship the other way. Instead of finding out what the value is at a certain Z score 1 or 2 units above or below the mean, we want to know, given a certain value, what its Z score is. How far is it from the mean? The solution is fairly simple: we can use a formula for finding a Z score.

FORMULA 10.1: Z scores for samples

$$Z = \frac{X_i - \overline{X}}{s}$$

where X_i is a given score within the range of values for a variable, $\overline{X}$ is the mean for the distribution of scores, and s is the standard deviation.

Example: Where in the distribution of scores does a male respondent with 10 years of education fall? Use the formula for Z scores:

X_i (the given) = 10 years of education $\overline{X}$ (the mean for *educ*) = 13.56

s (the standard deviation for *educ*) = 2.95

$$Z = \frac{X_i - \overline{X}}{s}$$

$$= \frac{10 - 13.56}{2.95} = -\frac{3.56}{2.95}$$

$$Z = -1.2068$$

Interpretation

What does the Z score tell us? Fundamentally, a Z score is nothing more than a deviation from the mean divided by a standard deviation. Remember that the formula for finding a deviation from the mean is $X - \overline{X}$, the numerator of the formula for the Z score. In essence then, the Z score is a proportion, and a Z score of -1.21 for a respondent with 10 years of education tells us that a respondent with 10 years of education falls 1.21 standard deviations *below* the mean. We know the respondent is below the mean and not above it because the sign on the Z score is negative.

> **Skills Practice 2**   What is the Z score for a male respondent with 14 years of education? What does the Z score tell us about where that respondent falls in relation to the mean?

Besides learning that a respondent with 10 years of education falls 1.21 standard deviations below the mean, we can find out where the other respondents fall in relation to those who have 10 years of education. We can use the Z score to answer the question, What percentage of the respondents fall between someone who has 10 years of education and the mean of 13.56 years of education? We answer this question by looking up the Z score on a table of scores, called "Area Under the Normal Curve" (Appendix A), which tells us the area that falls between a given Z score and the mean.

Go to Appendix A now and find the Z score, 1.21, in the (a) column labeled Z. Look to the (b) column immediately to the right, and you will see the number .3869. You can read this number as a percentage. It tells us that about 39% of the male respondents have between 10 and 13.56 (the mean) years of education. You can also read it as a probability—there are 39 chances out of a hundred that a male respondent has between 10 and nearly 13 years of education.

Finally, you can find out what percentage of the respondents have less than 10 years of education by reading across to column (c) on the right, where you find the number .1131. The number tells us that about 11% of the respondents have less than 10 years of education. See Figure 10.1 for an illustration of the relationship between Z scores and the area under the normal curve.

> **Skills Practice 3**   Use the Z score you computed for Skills Practice 2 and Appendix A to answer these questions:
>
> **A.** What percentage of male respondents have between 13.56 and 14 years of education?
>
> **B.** What percentage have more than 14 years of education?

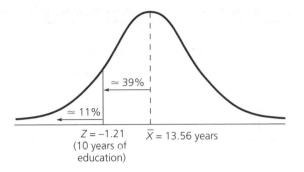

Figure 10.1 Relationship of $Z = -1.21$ to the mean of 13.56 for the variable *educ* in the gss96subset file.

Now, let's see how to find Z scores using SPSS.

SPSS Guide: Finding Z Scores

Finding Z scores is a fairly simple process. Follow the command path Analyze ➡ Descriptive Statistics ➡ Descriptives to open the Descriptives window.

❶ Select the variable for which you want Z scores. Scroll down to *educ* and click on it. Place it in the Variable selection box.

❷ Click on Save Standardized Values as Variables.

❸ Click on OK.

TABLE 10.1   Descriptive Statistics for the Variable *educ* in the gss96subset File

Descriptive Statistics

	N	Minimum	Maximum	Mean	Std. Deviation
EDUC HIGHEST YEAR OF SCHOOL COMPLETED	2895	0	20	13.36	2.93
Valid N (listwise)	2895				

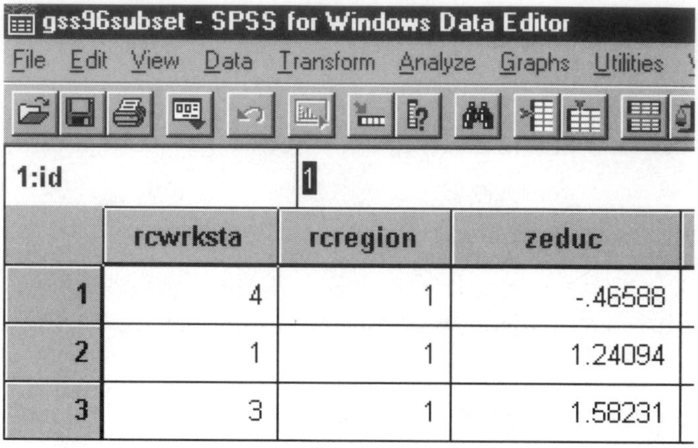

Figure 10.2

In the Output window, you will see a set of Descriptive statistics like the one in Table 10.1. For the variable *educ,* you will see the total number of valid responses, the minimum and maximum values of the variable, the mean, and the standard deviation.

Where are the Z scores? They show up in your Data Editor window as a new variable. Switch back to the Data Editor window, and scroll to the end of the variables list on the screen, as shown in Figure 10.2. You will see a new variable, *zeduc.* (SPSS automatically assigns this variable name—the name of your original variable preceded by the letter Z.) The values of *zeduc* are the Z scores for each of the values of the *educ* variable. You can read these values (find their associated value for *educ*) by scrolling back across the screen until you find the corresponding *educ* value for a particular Z score.

The Properties of Z Scores

We can use SPSS to explore some of the properties of Z scores. You can follow along on your computer as I go through this next section, or you can simply use the figures included in this portion of the text to understand the concepts.

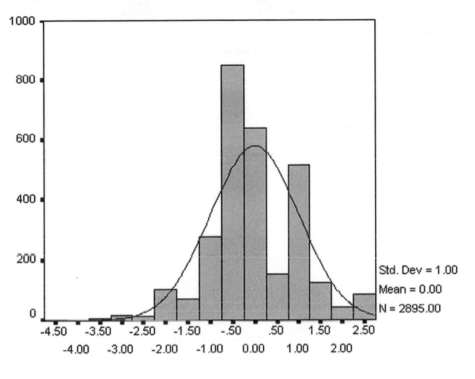

Zscore: HIGHEST YEAR OF SCHOOL COMPLETED

Figure 10.3 Histogram with normal curve for the Z scores variable *zeduc* in the gss96subset file.

As for any other variable, you can produce a histogram along with measures of central tendency and dispersion for the distribution of Z scores, *zeduc*. If you use the command path Graphs ➥ Histogram to obtain the mean and standard deviation for the distribution of the variable *zeduc*, you get a histogram and a set of statistics like the ones in Figure 10.3.

Notice that the mean for a set of Z scores is zero and that the standard deviation of the Z scores is 1. Given what we know about a normal distribution, we can assume that about 68% of all Z scores fall within the range of Z scores 1 standard deviation below the mean of zero and 1 standard deviation above the mean. Ninety-five percent of all Z scores fall between 2 standard deviations below the mean and 2 standard deviations above it. Where exactly a particular score falls, however, can be found using the table in Appendix A.

Soon you will see the importance of Z scores for making generalizations about populations from samples. However, before I can get to that, I need to introduce a few more of the concepts central to understanding inferential statistics, beginning with the concept of sampling statistics.

SAMPLING STATISTICS

Z scores are a type of sampling statistic. A **sampling statistic** is any statistic that describes the distribution of values for a variable, or relationships between variables, in a sample. Sampling statistics apply only to the samples they are designed to describe. Examples of sampling statistics, besides Z scores, include measures of central tendency, such as the mean, median, and mode; measures of dispersion, like the interquartile range and the standard deviation; and measures of association, including lambda and gamma.

You have already seen how useful sampling statistics are for describing the characteristics of respondents. Sampling statistics serve another important function—they can be used to estimate **population parameters.** Population parameters are the estimated characteristics of a population derived from sampling statistics.

The concept of population parameters is an abstract idea. The true characteristics of a population are usually not knowable. For example, it would be impossible to know for sure the average age of American adults, because there are too many adults to account for. We can only estimate the average age of all adults based on the average age of the adults we might include in a random sample designed to represent everyone. This estimate of the age of a population based on what we learn from a sample is an example of a population parameter.

How can estimates of populations be made with any degree of accuracy from samples alone? To find out, let's explore the characteristics of sampling distributions.

The Sampling Distribution

For any particular population, we can draw any one of a number of possible samples of a given sample size. The General Social Survey for 1996 is one possible sample of about 3,000 individuals drawn to represent all English-speaking, noninstitutionalized American adults (18 years old or older). In actuality, there are a tremendous number of different samples that could *possibly* be drawn. It's hard to imagine how many there could be—so many that it would be impossible to draw them all. Even among a small group of people, there are many possible samples of a given size that could be drawn. Look around your classroom. Suppose you wanted to draw a random sample of only 10 people to represent your class. Think about how many possible configurations there are of 10 people in your class. In a class of only 20 people there are 184,756 possible combinations of 10!

For each of the samples we might draw, we can compute sampling statistics—a mean, a median, a mode, a standard deviation for specific variables in the sample. We have already done this for many of the GSS variables. The key to understanding inferential statistics is this next point—these sampling statistics themselves have a distribution. Think about this for a second.

- For any population, we can draw a large number of different samples of a certain sample size. From a population of 20 students, we can draw 184,756 different samples of 10.

- For each of the samples we might draw, we can compute one or more sampling statistics. Let's say we find the average age of the students in each of our samples.

- For these means of ages, we can construct a distribution, and this distribution will have its own mean, median, standard deviation, and so on.

This distribution of sampling statistics from all possible samples of a given size drawn from the same population is called the **sampling distribution.** Unfortunately this distribution is hypothetical—imaginary. We couldn't ever draw all possible samples of a given size from a particular population, especially if the population is a large one. However, understanding the idea is key to understanding inferential statistics.

Let's make this more concrete by going back to an example I used in Chapter 5 when I discussed the stability of the mean. For this example, let's treat our respondents to the 1996 GSS as a population—a population of respondents. In Chapter 5 I showed you five samples drawn at random from the 1996 GSS. For each of these samples, I computed a mean, median, and mode for the variable *age*. I came up with the set of figures you see in Table 10.2.

TABLE 10.2 Measures of Central Tendency for the Variable *age* in Five Randomly Drawn Samples From the General Social Survey

	Mean	Median	Mode
Sample 1	44.68	40.00	29
Sample 2	51.17	49.00	49
Sample 3	37.46	35.00	22
Sample 4	50.39	46.50	25
Sample 5	43.69	43.00	43

Although these five samples are far from every conceivable sample I could draw, they can be used to illustrate the concept of the sampling distribution. First, think about how each of the measures of central tendency—the mean, median, and mode—could be treated as separate variables. For each of them, I could compute descriptive statistics, like an average of the means and an average of the medians, and I could compute the standard deviation of the means and the standard deviation of the medians.

Now picture what would happen if I had hundreds of samples from the General Social Survey for 1996 and, therefore, hundreds of sampling statistics—means, medians, and modes. For each of these sets of sampling statistics, I could come up with a sampling distribution. Let's explore just one of the possibilities—coming up with a distribution for all of the means in a sampling distribution, also called the sampling distribution of sample means.

The Sampling Distribution of Sample Means

The **sampling distribution of sample means** is the hypothetical distribution of all possible sample means of a given sample size from a particular population. Whereas the term *sampling distribution* refers generally to the distribution of all sampling statistics for a particular set of samples drawn from a population, the sampling distribution of sample means refers specifically to the distribution of just one sampling statistic, the mean. For the five samples in Table 10.2, the sampling distribution of sample means could be displayed as a frequency distribution of the means.

As I mentioned earlier, it is not only possible to construct a frequency distribution for all of the sample means in a sampling distribution, I can also compute descriptive statistics for the sample means. To find the average of all of the sample means in Table 10.2, I would sum the means from each of the five samples and divide the total by the number of samples I have. The result is called the mean of the sampling distribution of sample means. It is the average of the sample means. The computation of the mean of the sampling distribution of sample means can be expressed as follows:

FORMULA 10.2: The mean of the sampling distribution of sample means

$$\mu_{\overline{X}} = \frac{\Sigma \overline{X}}{N}$$

where the Greek symbol μ (or mu, pronounced "mew") represents the sampling distribution, and the subscript $\overline{X}$ represents the mean (read it as "the mean of the sampling distribution of sample means"); $\Sigma \overline{X}$ represents the sum of the means from a sampling distribution; and N equals the number of samples drawn from a population.

Example: For Table 10.2, the mean of the sampling distribution of sample means is equal to the sum of the means in the table (227.39) divided by the number of samples drawn (5). Applied to Formula 10.2, the sampling distribution of sample means is computed as follows:

$$\mu_{\overline{X}} = \frac{\Sigma \overline{X}}{N}$$

$$= \frac{227.39}{5}$$

$$\mu_{\overline{X}} = 45.48$$

Skills Practice 5 Compute the mean for the sampling distribution of sample means for the two variables in the 10 randomly drawn samples of 30 respondents from the gss96subset file given here.

Sample	*Sample Means for* age	*Sample Means for* educ
1	44.10	13.63
2	51.10	13.47
3	41.23	13.67
4	47.57	13.07
5	47.00	14.47
6	42.77	12.67
7	47.03	13.73
8	42.27	13.60
9	41.27	13.73
10	44.37	13.17

In addition to finding the mean for a sampling distribution, we can compute any other statistic that might help us characterize the distribution of the samples. For example, we could find the standard deviation of the sample means. The standard deviation of the means of the samples would tell us how homogeneous or heterogeneous the distribution is or how much variation we would expect to find in the sample means. The significance of this concept will be discussed later in this chapter.

To find the standard deviation of the means, we can use a variation of Formula 6.3a (in Chapter 6) for computing the standard deviation from raw scores:

FORMULA 10.3: The standard deviation of the sampling distribution of sample means

$$\sigma_{\bar{X}} = \sqrt{\left(\frac{\Sigma X^2}{N-1}\right) - \left(\frac{N}{N-1}\right)(\bar{X})^2}$$

where the Greek symbol σ (or sigma) represents the standard deviation, and the subscript $\bar{X}$ represents the mean (read it as the standard deviation of the sampling distribution of sample means); X represents the scores (the means) in the sampling distribution; ΣX^2 means to add up the squared scores (means) in the sampling distribution; $(\bar{X})^2$ is the mean for the sampling distribution squared; and N is the number of samples in the sampling distribution.

Example: Let's use the data in Table 10.2—the means of the ages of respondents in five randomly drawn samples from the 1996 General Social Survey. Follow these steps to get the standard deviation of the sampling distribution of sample means:

Step 1. Square each of the means in Table 10.2 and add them up to get the sum of the squared means ($\Sigma X^2 = 10,465.8911$).

Step 2. Square the mean for the sampling distribution of sample means, which we already calculated (45.48), to get $\bar{X}^2$ (2,068.4304).

Step 3. Use these values to solve the formula for the standard deviation for the sampling distribution.

ΣX^2 (sum of squared means) $= 10,465.8911$ $\qquad$ N (number of samples) $= 5$

$\bar{X}^2$ (square of the mean of the sampling distribution) $= 2,068.4304$

$$\sigma_{\bar{X}} = \sqrt{\left(\frac{\Sigma X^2}{N-1}\right) - \left(\frac{N}{N-1}\right)(\bar{X})^2}$$

$$= \sqrt{\left(\frac{10,465.8911}{5-1}\right) - \left[\left(\frac{5}{5-1}\right)(2,068.4304)\right]}$$

$$\sigma_{\bar{X}} = 5.56$$

The standard deviation of the sampling distribution is 5.56, which indicates a fairly homogeneous distribution (with relatively little variation among the means), given the range of values in the sampling distribution of sample means ($51.17 - 37.46 = 13.71$).

Skills Practice 6   Compute the standard deviation for each of the distributions in Skills Practice 5. How would you describe the distribution of the means for the variable *age* as compared to the distribution of the means for the variable *educ*?

Bringing It All Back Home

Finally, we can tie these two ideas together—the mean of the sampling distribution of sample means and the standard deviation of the sampling distribution of sample means—with our concept of Z scores introduced at the beginning of this chapter. In addition to learning about the average of the means and their distribution (using standard deviation), we can use Z scores to find out where each of the individual sample means falls in relation to the rest of the distribution of sample means. Remember the Z score formula applied to a sample:

$$Z = \frac{X_i - \overline{X}}{s}$$

When applied to a population, the Z score formula changes somewhat.

FORMULA 10.4:   Computing Z scores for a population

$$Z = \frac{\overline{X} - \mu_{\overline{X}}}{\sigma_{\overline{X}}}$$

where $\overline{X}$ is the mean for a sample drawn from a population, $\mu_{\overline{X}}$ is the mean of the sampling distribution of sample means, and $\sigma_{\overline{X}}$ is the standard deviation of the sampling distribution of sample means.

To find the Z score for any individual sample mean, we simply insert it into the formula as $\overline{X}$. The mean of the sampling distribution of sample means is $\sigma_{\overline{X}}$. The standard deviation for the sampling distribution of sample means (computed previously) is $\sigma_{\overline{X}}$ in the denominator.

Example: To find the Z score for the first of the sample means, 44.68, in Table 10.2, apply the Z score formula:

$$Z = \frac{\overline{X} - \mu_{\overline{X}}}{\sigma_{\overline{X}}}$$

$$= \frac{44.68 - 45.48}{5.56} = \frac{-.80}{5.56}$$

$$Z = -.14$$

The mean, 44.68, is about one tenth of a standard deviation *below* the mean of the sampling distribution. If you look up the number .14 in the table in Appendix A, you can find out what percentage of the sampling distribution of sample means fall between 44.68 and the mean of the sampling distribution and what percentage of the sampling distribution of sample means fall below 44.68. Do that now. You should see that only about 6% of the means of the sampling distribution of sample means fall between the mean of 44.68 and the mean for the sampling distribution of sample means of 45.48, whereas over 44% of the sampling distribution means of sample means fall below the mean of 44.68. Figure 10.4 illustrates this distribution.

> **Skills Practice 7**   Compute the Z score for the mean from Sample 2 in Table 10.2. What percentage of the sampling distribution means fall between the Sample 2 mean and the mean of the sampling distribution of sample means? What percentage of means fall above it?

The Standard Error of the Mean

The standard deviation of the sampling distribution of sample means is also called the **standard error of the mean.** To illustrate the concept, I had you calculate the standard deviation for a set of 10 samples in Skills Practice 6. In actuality the sampling distribution is a theoretical idea. It doesn't actually exist, because the sampling distribution is the distribution of all possible samples of a certain size that could be drawn from a particular population, not just 10 of them.

The few samples I drew to illustrate the concept don't constitute the entire realm of all possible samples of 30 respondents. If we were to treat the respondents to the General Social Survey as a population, and we drew a series of random samples of 30 respondents each to estimate the age of the population, then the sampling distribution would be composed of all possible samples of 30 respondents that could be drawn from the population of 2,904 General Social Survey respondents—a huge number.

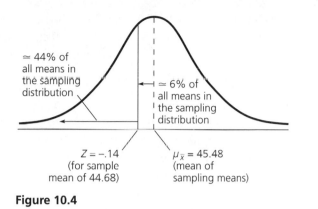

≈ 44% of all means in the sampling distribution

≈ 6% of all means in the sampling distribution

$Z = -.14$
(for sample
mean of 44.68)

$\mu_{\bar{x}} = 45.48$
(mean of
sampling means)

Figure 10.4

The formula for the standard error of the mean allows us to *estimate* the standard deviation of the sampling distribution of sample means that would be included in the sampling distribution. To use the formula, though, we have to know the standard deviation of the population. In this case, we can use the Analyze ➥ Descriptive Statistics ➥ Descriptives command path to find the standard deviations of the variables in the gss96subset file—our population for the purposes of this example. Find the standard deviation for the variable *age*. You should get 16.87. Let's use it to find the standard error of the mean.

FORMULA 10.5: The standard error of the mean

$$\sigma_{\bar{X}} = \frac{\sigma}{\sqrt{N}}$$

where $\sigma_{\bar{X}}$ is the standard deviation of the sampling distribution of sample means; σ, the standard deviation of the scores, is the standard deviation of the population for a particular variable; and N is the sample size.

Example: Let's find the standard error of the mean for the variable *age,* assuming a sample size of 30. We know that the standard deviation for the variable *age* in the population (the 1996 General Social Survey respondents) is 16.87, and we know N (the sample size) is 30. Insert these values into the formula for the standard error of the mean

$$\sigma_{\bar{X}} = \frac{\sigma}{\sqrt{N}}$$

$$= \frac{16.87}{\sqrt{30}} = \frac{16.87}{5.4772255}$$

$$\sigma_{\bar{X}} = 3.08$$

Interpretation   What does this tell us? Think about the meaning of the standard deviation in any normal distribution. The smaller the standard deviation is in relation to the range of values, the more homogeneous is the distribution. In this case, the distribution of values is the dispersion of sample means in a set of randomly drawn samples from a population. More specifically, the standard error of 3.08 is the standard deviation of the average ages that could be computed for all possible samples of 30 respondents from the 1996 General Social Survey. It tells us that about 68% of the means could be expected to fall within a range of only a little more than 6 years (extending slightly more than 3 years below the mean to 3 years above the mean), a fairly narrow range (given the range of the *age* variable) indicating a somewhat homogeneous distribution of means. Another way to put it is that the standard error of the mean indicates little variation in the means of the sampling distribution.

Avoiding Common Pitfalls   The terminology at this point is probably getting confusing: population parameters, sampling statistics, sampling means, the sampling distribution of sample means, and the mean of the sampling distribution of sample means. To help sort all of this out, notice that population parameters (estimates of population characteristics based on sample statistics) are designated by Greek letters (like μ and σ), whereas sample statistics (the characteristics of samples) are represented by phonetic symbols (like $\overline{X}$ and s).

You're probably wondering why this concept of the standard error of the mean is important. The reason is that when there is little variation in the sampling distribution of sample means, we can have more confidence that our predictions about populations will be accurate. The more homogeneous the characteristics of the sampling distribution (the mean, for example) are, the more likely it is that any single sample we draw from a population will be representative of the population as a whole. We can't guarantee that the sample is an accurate reflection of the population, but the likelihood of the sample reflecting the population is improved.

Skills Practice 8   Use SPSS to find the standard deviation for the variable *educ* (using the command path Analyze ➡ Descriptive Statistics ➡ Descriptives). Assuming samples of 30 respondents each are drawn from the population, the 1996 General Social Survey, what is the standard error of the mean? Write a sentence explaining what the standard error tells you.

The Central Limit Theorem

The **Central Limit Theorem** is a theory about the characteristics of the sampling distribution. It tells us that the larger the size of a sample from a population is, the more likely it is that the mean of a single sample will be close to (or approximate) the mean of the population from which the sample was drawn. If you are a researcher interested in learning about the characteristics of a population, the more people you include in your sample, the more likely it is that any mean you compute for the sample will be close to the actual mean in the population as a whole.

Think about this for a second and you will see how intuitively simple this is. Suppose you have a bag of 100 balls of different colors. Someone asks you to draw one out and guess the characteristics of all of the balls in the bag. If you draw out one red ball, you would have to guess that the balls are red. Then you get to draw out another ball. It's green. Now you know there are some green balls and some red balls. You would probably guess that half the balls in the bag are red and the other half are green. You may not be right, but by doubling the size of the sample (from one ball to two balls) your accuracy at guessing the characteristics of all the balls has improved. The more balls you draw out, the more accurate you can be at predicting what all of the balls look like.

Let's apply this to the General Social Survey. The more individuals the researchers include in their sample, the more likely it is that any average computed for any particular numerical variable (like *age, years of education, number of siblings*) will be representative of the average for that variable in the population of American adults. In addition, the larger the size of the samples in a sampling distribution, the more likely it is that the sampling distribution of sample means will itself be normal. This means that if you were to compute the mean and the median for all possible samples in a sampling distribution,

- The mean and the median for the sampling distribution of sample means should be identical (one of the properties of a normal distribution) or pretty close to it.
- There should be only one mode.
- The distribution of means should be symmetrical.

A frequency distribution of the means from the sampling distribution would look like the normal curve.

This is important because if all of this is so, then you can find out where the population mean falls in relation to the array of all possible means in the sampling distribution. How can you do this? Isn't the population mean a theoretical number, a number that we can't ever really know? How can we figure out, for example, where the actual average age of the population for the General Social

Survey falls in relation to the distribution of all possible sampling means? We can do this by using some of the concepts we have discussed to construct *confidence intervals* at specified *confidence limits* around *point estimates* to approximate the parameters of a population, skills you will learn in the next chapter.

SUMMARY

This chapter introduced you to some of the fundamental concepts of inferential statistics. You should understand the relation of Z scores to a normal distribution, and you should be able to calculate a Z score by hand and use SPSS to find Z scores. More important, you should be able to interpret a Z score.

It is also important to be able to distinguish between sampling statistics (the characteristics of samples) and population parameters (the estimated characteristics of populations).

The concepts you should understand at this point include the sampling distribution, a hypothetical distribution of the characteristics of all possible samples of a certain size drawn from the same population. The distribution of sample means is the distribution of means in the sampling distribution, and the mean of the sampling distribution of sample means is the average of the sample means in the sampling distribution. The standard error of the mean is the standard deviation of the sampling distribution of sample means. These concepts will be used more extensively in the next chapter as we compute confidence limits and levels for point estimates in samples.

KEY CONCEPTS

Inferential statistics
Sample
Population
Sampling statistics
Z score

Properties of Z scores
Population parameter
Sampling distribution
Sampling distribution
   of sample means

Standard error of the
   mean
Central Limit Theorem

ANSWERS TO SKILLS PRACTICES

1. A. Neither of the distributions is normal, because the mean, median, and mode are not equal for either distribution.

   B. The distribution for females is the most homogeneous, because the standard deviation is smaller for females than for males.

   C. The answer follows the Skills Practice.

2. To compute Z scores for the male respondents to the variable *educ,* use the formula for the Z score.

X_i (the given) = 14 years of education

X (the mean for *educ*) = 13.56

s (the standard deviation for the variable *educ*) = 2.95

$$Z - \frac{X_i - \overline{X}}{s}$$

$$= \frac{14 - 13.56}{2.95} = \frac{.44}{2.95}$$

$$Z = .15$$

A respondent with 13 years of education falls more than a tenth of a standard deviation (or .15 standard deviation) above the mean.

3. Use the table in Appendix A to show that

   A. About 6% of the male respondents have between 13.56 and 14 years of education.

   B. About 44% of the male respondents have more than 14 years of education.

4. A. To compute Z scores using the variable *speduc,* use the mean (13.45) and the standard deviation (2.85) for the variable *speduc.* Apply the Z scores formula:

$$Z = \frac{X_i - \overline{X}}{s}$$

X_i is the value for which you are trying to find the Z score.

The Z score for 12 years of education	*The Z score for 14 years of education*	*The Z score for 16 years of education*
$Z = \dfrac{12 - 13.45}{2.85}$	$Z = \dfrac{14 - 13.45}{2.85}$	$Z = \dfrac{16 - 13.45}{2.85}$
$= \dfrac{-1.45}{2.85}$	$= \dfrac{.55}{2.85}$	$= \dfrac{2.55}{2.85}$
$Z = -.509$	$Z = .193$	$Z = .895$

You can check your work as follows. First, get the Z scores for the variable *speduc* using SPSS. Then find the years of education under the *speduc* variable and scroll across the screen to match it with its corresponding Z score. For example, locate a respondent with 12 years of education under the *speduc* variable. Then, scroll across the screen until you get to the *zspeduc* variable, where you can see the Z score associated with 12 years of education. The SPSS answers won't be exactly the same as the ones you compute by hand, because SPSS uses more exact computations of the mean and standard deviation, but your answers will be close.

B. The histogram you will get for the *zspeduc* variable will look like this:

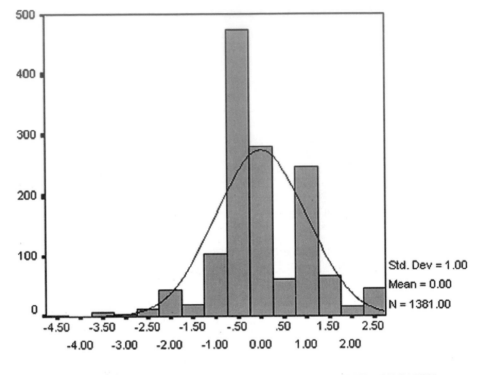

Std. Dev = 1.00
Mean = 0.00
N = 1381.00

Zscore: HIGHEST YEAR SCHOOL COMPLETED, SPOUSE

Note that the mean is zero, and the standard deviation is 1.

5. To find the sampling distribution of the mean for the variable *age,* add up the means of the 10 samples to get the sum of the means ($\Sigma \bar{X}$). You should get 448.71. Then use this number in the formula for the sampling distribution of sample means:

$$\mu_{\bar{X}} = \frac{\Sigma \bar{X}}{N}$$

$$= \frac{448.71}{10}$$

$$\mu_{\bar{X}} = 44.87$$

For the variable *education,* the sum of the means is 135.21, so the mean of the sampling distribution of sample means is:

$$\mu_{\bar{X}} = \frac{\Sigma \bar{X}}{N}$$

$$= \frac{135.21}{10}$$

$$\mu_{\bar{X}} = 13.52$$

6. To find the standard deviation of the sampling distribution for the variable *age,* note that the mean of the sampling distribution is 44.87, and the sum of the squared means is 20,227.5943. Use these values in the formula for the standard deviation:

$$\sigma_{\bar{X}} = \sqrt{\left(\frac{\Sigma \bar{X}^2}{N-1}\right) - \left[\left(\frac{N}{N-1}\right)(\bar{X})^2\right]}$$

$$= \sqrt{\left(\frac{20,227.5943}{10-1}\right) - \left[\left(\frac{10}{10-1}\right)(2,013.3169)\right]}$$

$$\sigma_{\bar{X}} = 3.24$$

For the variable *educ,* the mean of the sampling distribution is 13.52, and the sum of the squared means is 1,830.2561. Use these values in the formula for the standard deviation:

$$\sigma_{\bar{X}} = \sqrt{\left(\frac{\Sigma \bar{X}^2}{N-1}\right) - \left[\left(\frac{N}{N-1}\right)(\bar{X})^2\right]}$$

$$= \sqrt{\left(\frac{1,830.2561}{10-1}\right) - \left[\left(\frac{10}{10-1}\right)(182.7904)\right]}$$

$$\sigma_{\bar{X}} = .51$$

Based on a comparison of the standard deviations, the distribution of means for the variable *educ* appears to be more homogeneous (shows less variability) than the distribution of the means for the variable *age*. We reach this conclusion by assessing the standard deviation for each variable in relation to its range. The standard deviation for the variable *age* is 3.24, but the range of the sampling means is 9.87. About 68% of the sample means fall within about two thirds of the values in the range of means. On the other hand, the standard deviation for the variable *educ* is .51. In relation to its range, 1.80, about 68% of the means fall within a little more than one half of the values in the range.

7. To find the Z score for Sample 2 in Table 10.2, use the formula for Z scores.

$$Z = \frac{\overline{X} - \mu_{\overline{X}}}{\sigma_{\overline{X}}}$$

$$= \frac{51.17 - 45.48}{5.56} = \frac{5.69}{5.56}$$

$$Z = 1.02$$

The mean of 51.17 is a little more than 1 standard deviation above the mean of the sampling distribution (45.48). Using the table in Appendix A, we can see that about 35% of the means in the sampling distribution of sample means fall between the mean of 51.17 and the mean of the sampling distribution of 45.48, and about 15% of the means fall above the Sample 2 mean of 51.17.

8. To find the standard error of the mean, note that the standard deviation for *educ* is 2.93. Use this value, along with the sample size of 30, in the formula for the standard error of the mean.

$$\sigma_{\overline{X}} = \frac{\sigma}{\sqrt{N}}$$

$$= \frac{2.93}{\sqrt{30}} = \frac{2.93}{5.4772}$$

$$\sigma_{\overline{X}} = .53$$

The standard deviation of the sampling distribution of sample means for the variable *educ* in which the samples are composed of 30 respondents each is .53. About 68% of the means would fall within a range of about 1 year. Given the range of values for this variable, this is a very homogeneous distribution of sample means.

GENERAL EXERCISES

Use the statistics for female respondents to the *educ* variable (in Skills Practice 1) to answer questions 1–4:

1. Find and interpret the Z scores for respondents with 12 years of education. What percentage of the female respondents have between 13.21 (the mean) and 12 years of education? What percentage of the female respondents have less than 12 years of education?

2. Find and interpret the Z scores for respondents with 14 years of education. What percentage of the female respondents have between 13.21 (the mean) and 14 years of education? What percentage of the female respondents have more than 14 years of education?

3. Find and interpret the Z scores for respondents with 16 years of education. What percentage of the female respondents have between 13.21 (the mean) and 16 years of education? What percentage of the female respondents have more than 16 years of education?

4. Find and interpret the Z scores for respondents with 18 years of education. What percentage of the female respondents have between 13.21 (the mean) and 18 years of education? What percentage of the female respondents have more than 18 years of education?

5. Compute the mean of the sampling distribution of sample means for the variable *educ* in this set of 10 randomly drawn samples of 30 respondents from the gss96subset file:

Sample	educ	Sample	educ
1	13.60	6	13.66
2	13.86	7	13.10
3	14.38	8	13.86
4	12.69	9	13.57
5	13.96	10	13.64

6. Compute the mean of the sampling distribution of sample means for the variable *speduc* in this set of 10 randomly drawn samples of 30 respondents from the gss96subset file:

Sample	speduc	Sample	speduc
1	14.53	6	13.67
2	14.22	7	13.26
3	14.36	8	14.75
4	13.69	9	14.15
5	12.67	10	14.33

7. Compute the standard deviation of the sampling distribution of sample means for the variable *educ* in the sampling distributions in General Exercise 5.

8. Compute the standard deviation of the sampling distribution of sample means for the variable *speduc* in the sampling distributions in General Exercise 6.

9. Compute the *Z* score for the mean from Sample 1 for the variable *educ* in General Exercise 5. What percentage of the sampling distribution of sample means fall between the mean for the sample and the mean of the sampling distribution? What percentage of sampling means fall below it?

10. Compute the *Z* score for the mean from Sample 1 for the variable *speduc* in General Exercise 6. What percentage of the sampling distribution of sample means fall between the mean for the sample and the mean of the sampling distribution? What percentage of sampling means fall above it?

11. Compute the *Z* score for the mean from Sample 5 for the variable *educ* in General Exercise 5. What percentage of the sampling distribution of sample means fall between the mean for the sample and the mean of the sampling distribution? What percentage of sampling means fall below it?

12. Compute the *Z* score for the mean from Sample 5 for the variable *speduc* in General Exercise 6. What percentage of the sampling distribution of sample means fall between the mean for the sample and the mean of the sampling distribution? What percentage of sampling means fall below it?

13. Find the standard error of the mean for the variable *speduc,* assuming we were to draw random samples from the GSS of 30 respondents each to represent all respondents to the variable. The standard deviation for the population (the GSS, in this case) is 2.85.

14. Find the standard error of the mean for the variable *paeduc,* assuming we were to draw random samples from the GSS of 30 respondents each to represent all respondents to the variable. The standard deviation for the population (the GSS, in this case) is 4.10.

15. Find the standard error of the mean for the variable *maeduc,* assuming we were to draw random samples from the GSS of 30 respondents each to represent all respondents to the variable. The standard deviation for the population (the GSS, in this case) is 3.40.

16. Find the standard error of the mean for the variable *educ,* assuming we were to draw random samples from the GSS of 50 respondents each to represent all respondents to the variable. The standard deviation for the population (the GSS, in this case) is 2.93.

17. Find the standard error of the mean for the variable *age,* assuming we were to draw random samples from the GSS of 50 respondents each to represent all respondents to the variable. The standard deviation for the population (the GSS, in this case) is 16.87.

18. Find the standard error of the mean for the variable *paeduc,* assuming we were to draw random samples from the GSS of 50 respondents each to represent all respondents to the variable. The standard deviation for the population (the GSS, in this case) is 4.10.

19. Find the standard error of the mean for the variable *maeduc,* assuming we were to draw random samples from the GSS of 50 respondents each to represent all respondents to the variable. The standard deviation for the population (the GSS, in this case) is 3.40.

20. Compare the standard errors of the mean for sample sizes of $N = 30$ (in General Exercises 14 and 15) and sample sizes of $N = 50$ (computed for General Exercises 18 and 19). For which of the sample sizes is the standard error smaller? Why?

SPSS EXERCISES

1. Use SPSS to compute the Z scores for the variable *paeduc.* Then answer these questions:

   a. What is the Z score for a respondent with 12 years of education?

   b. What is the Z score for a respondent with 14 years of education?

   c. What is the Z score for a respondent with 16 years of education?

   d. What is the Z score for a respondent with 18 years of education?

2. Use SPSS to compute the Z scores for the variable *hrs1.* Then answer these questions:

   a. What is the Z score for a respondent who worked 20 hours?

   b. What is the Z score for a respondent who worked 35 hours?

   c. What is the Z score for a respondent who worked 40 hours?

   d. What is the Z score for a respondent who worked 50 hours?

3. Produce a histogram with a normal curve for your Z scores variable for *paeduc* (*zpaeduc*). What are its mean and standard deviation?

4. Produce a histogram with a normal curve for your Z scores variable for *hrs1* (*zhrs1*). What are its mean and standard deviation?

Making Inferences for Single Variables

The "News to Use" article in the previous chapter tried to estimate how all adult New Yorkers felt about a Senate race based on the responses of a relatively small sample of 1,791 adults. The researchers can't guarantee that what they are learning from their sample is true of all adult New Yorkers. However, they can tell us there is a 95% chance that what they learned from their sample—the percentage of respondents who feel one way or another about the race—would differ from the population by no more than 6% (3% more or 3% less). How did they determine that? In this chapter you will learn the skills to construct confidence intervals at specified confidence levels in relation to point estimates such as sampling means and percentages, just like the pollsters who conducted the "News to Use" survey you read about in Chapter 10.

A **point estimate** is simply a characteristic of a sample that we are using as an estimate of a population parameter.[1] For example, when we use the average age of the respondents in the General Social Survey (44.78) to estimate or represent the age of all American adults, the average age of GSS respondents is being used as a point estimate. In the Chapter 10 "News to Use" article, there are many examples of point estimates. When the authors say that 44% of likely voters favor D'Amato and 44% favor Schumer, they are using point estimates in the sample to represent a characteristic of the population (likelihood of voting for one candidate or other).

A **confidence interval** is the range of values within which a given point estimate (like the mean or a proportion) is likely to fall, and a **confidence level** specifies how likely or probable it is that a point estimate will fall within that range. Confidence intervals with their associated levels are constructed around or in relation to point estimates. Confidence intervals and confidence

---

[1]Recall that a population parameter is a statistical characteristic of a population, like the mean, median, mode, or a percentage.

levels are often used in newspapers and magazines, most commonly when poll results are reported. For example, in the "News to Use" article at the beginning of Chapter 10, you read the statement, "According to statistical theory, in 19 out of 20 cases, the results [from a random sample] will differ by no more than 3 percentage points in either direction from those that would have been obtained by seeking out all adults in New York State." This sentence is an expression of a confidence interval (the 3-percentage-point range) and a confidence level (the 19 times out of 20).

We can translate this into plain English by looking at the confidence interval and level in relation to one of the point estimates. According to the *New York Times*/CBS News poll, 73% of the respondents in the *sample* believe that D'Amato is spending most of his time attacking his opponent rather than explaining what he would do if he were elected. Now, let's apply the confidence interval and the confidence level to this point estimate. The confidence *level* tells us that in 19 out of 20 samples (or 95 times out of 100), the percentage of individuals who feel D'Amato is spending most of his time attacking his opponent will fall between 70% and 76% (the confidence *interval*). We use the point estimate in the *sample,* 73%, to construct the interval. Because 73% of the respondents in the sample feel D'Amato is spending most of his time attacking his opponent, we can use the interval—3% in either direction—to conclude that it is highly likely that between 70% (73% minus 3%) and 76% (73% plus 3%) of all New Yorkers feel that way. Note this does *not* mean we can be absolutely certain that somewhere between 70% and 76% of all New York voters feel D'Amato is spending most of his time attacking his opponent. It does mean that it's highly *probable* 70% to 76% of all New Yorkers feel this way.

Confidence intervals and confidence levels can be constructed around many different estimates of population parameters, including means and proportions. This chapter focuses on confidence intervals and levels for means and proportions, beginning with confidence intervals and levels for means.

POINT ESTIMATES, CONFIDENCE INTERVALS, AND CONFIDENCE LEVELS FOR MEANS

We come up with these intervals and levels by (1) applying many of the concepts we learned in Chapter 10 about the characteristics of a sampling distribution and (2) employing the assumptions of the Central Limit Theorem, which tells us that the sampling distribution of sample means is normal.

Finding the Standard Error of the Mean

To begin, let's understand how we can apply the concept of the sampling distribution of sample means by revisiting the standard error of the mean. Remember that the **standard error of the mean** is the standard deviation of the sampling distribution of sample means for a particular population. We calculate this standard error of the mean with the formula you learned in Chapter 10:

$$\sigma_{\bar{X}} = \frac{\sigma}{\sqrt{N}}$$

In Chapter 10 I illustrated the concept of the standard error of the mean by treating the 1996 General Social Survey respondents as a population. However, as you know, the GSS is itself a sample designed to represent the population of American adults. The standard deviation of the ages in the population of American adults is not knowable. How do we compute the standard error of the mean for a variable when its standard deviation in a population is not known? We substitute the standard deviation of a sample to estimate or represent the standard deviation of the population. We make the assumption that the standard deviation of a sample drawn from a population is a reliable estimate of the standard deviation in the population itself. Later on in this chapter, we will find the relationship between a specific, *knowable* sample mean (the mean we calculate for a sample drawn from a population) and the *theoretical* sampling distribution of sample means.

To illustrate, let's find the standard error of the mean for the variable *age*. Use SPSS to find the standard deviation for *age* in the GSS sample (by following the command path Analyze ➡ Descriptive Statistics ➡ Descriptives). You should get 16.87. What is the size of the sample? Look at the Statistics box in your Output window. You should see an *N* of 2,898. Use these values in your formula for the standard error of the mean.

$\sigma_{\bar{X}}$ (standard deviation for the variable *age* in the gss96subset file) = 16.87

N (number of valid responses to the variable *age* in the gss96subset file) = 2,898

$$\sigma_{\bar{X}} = \frac{\sigma}{\sqrt{N}}$$

$$= \frac{16.87}{\sqrt{2{,}898}} = \frac{16.87}{53.8331}$$

$$\sigma_{\bar{X}} = .31$$

Interpretation   The standard deviation of the sampling distribution of sample means is .31, and it tells us that the sampling means are fairly homogeneously distributed. Ninety-five percent of all sample means (calculated for the set of all possible random samples of 2,898 respondents from the population of American adults) would fall within a range of only a few values. The exact values between which the mean is likely to fall will be explored later when we learn to compute confidence intervals.

You can check your work by using SPSS to find the standard error of the mean. See the next SPSS Guide for instructions.

SPSS Guide: Finding the Standard Error of the Mean

Follow the command path Analyze ➡ Descriptive Statistics ➡ Frequencies. At the Frequencies dialog box, select the variable for which you want to find the standard error of the mean. Let's use *age*. Now click on the Statistics button, as you did when you found the standard deviation.

❶ Under the list of commands labeled Dispersion, click on Std. Deviation and S.E. mean.

❷ Click on Continue to return to the Frequencies dialog box.

❸ At the Frequencies dialog box, click on OK.

TABLE 11.1 Statistics Output Including the Standard Error of the Mean and the Standard Deviation for the Variable *age* in the gss96subset File

Statistics

AGE AGE OF RESPONDENT

N	Valid	2898
	Missing	6
Std. Error of Mean		.31
Std. Deviation		16.87

TABLE 11.2 Statistics Output for the Variable *educ* in the gss96subset File

Statistics

EDUC HIGHEST YEAR OF SCHOOL COMPLETED

N	Valid	2895
	Missing	9
Std. Error of Mean		5.44E-02

Your Statistics output should now include the standard error of the mean, as in Table 11.1. Note that it is the same value, .31, we computed by hand.

Skills Practice 2 Use SPSS to find the standard error of the mean for the variable *educ*. Note: You should get Table 11.2. If your output looks a little strange, see the next "Avoiding Common Pitfalls."

Avoiding Common Pitfalls Sometimes SPSS produces some strange-looking output. For example, when you try to find the standard error of the mean for *educ*, you may get the answer in scientific notation, illustrated in Table 11.2. The E-02 following 5.44 tells you to move the decimal point two places to the left, so you can read 5.44E-02 as equal to .0544. (If the scientific notation indicated E+.02, you would move two decimal places to the right.)

To see the standard error of the mean without scientific notation, place your cursor on the output and double-click. Then place your cursor on the number 5.44E-02 and double-click again. Your table should now look like Figure 11.1.

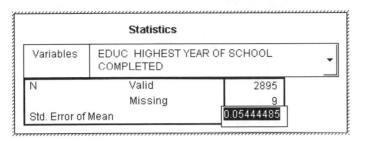

Figure 11.1 The statistics output for the variable *educ*, showing the standard error of the mean without scientific notation.

Using the Standard Error of the Mean to Specify Confidence Intervals and Levels

What does knowing the standard error of the mean allow us to do? In conjunction with what we know about a normal distribution (and remember that the Central Limit Theorem allows us to assume that the sampling distribution of sample means *is* normal), we can find out how likely it is (confidence level) that the population mean is included within a particular range of means (confidence interval).

We know that in any normally distributed set of scores (means, in this case), about 68% of all scores fall within the range of values from 1 standard deviation below the mean to 1 standard deviation above it, and about 95% of all scores fall within the range of values from 2 standard deviations below the mean to 2 standard deviations above it. (See the illustration on p. 220 in Chapter 6.)

With this information, we can use our sampling mean as an estimate of the mean of the sampling distribution of sample means to build a normal distribution around the sampling mean of 44.78 (the mean for the variable *age*), using the standard error of the mean, .31, which is the standard deviation of sample means in a sampling distribution. Our distribution of means would look like the one in Figure 11.2.

Where is the population mean? We can't know for sure, but we *can* narrow the range of possibilities if we make two assumptions:

1. The sampling distribution of sample means is normal.

2. At least one of the means in the sampling distribution of sample means is identical to the population mean.

If we accept these assumptions, the properties of the normal distribution allow us to infer that about 95% of *all* possible sampling means in the sampling distribution fall within the range of 44.16 to 45.40 (the range of values 2 standard deviations below the mean to 2 standard deviations above the mean).

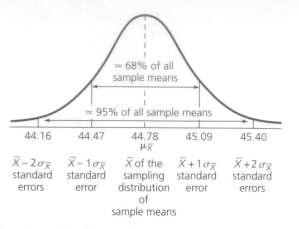

Figure 11.2 The estimated distribution of sampling means for the variable *age,* using the mean and the standard error of the mean.

Therefore, there are 95 chances out of 100 that the mean of the population falls somewhere within that range of values. This range of values—from 44.16 to 44.50—is the confidence interval, whereas the 95% likelihood that the population mean lies between these values is the confidence level.

These are somewhat abstract concepts, so let's make them a little more concrete by returning to the example of the 10 samples drawn at random from the General Social Survey (reproduced as Table 11.3). The means for the variables *age* and *educational level* for these 10 samples are displayed. Remember that when we treat the GSS as a population, we *can* know the population parameters. We do know, for example, that the average age of the GSS respondents is 44.78. Using a population for which the parameters are known, let's see how accurately our samples in Table 11.3 represent the population mean of ages.

If you look down the list of sampling means for the variable *age,* you see that a couple of the sampling means are pretty close to the population mean—the means for Sample 1 and Sample 10. None of the sampling means is exactly right but they don't have to be. We only need to use them to construct confidence intervals that are *likely* to contain the population mean.

Thus, the important questions are: Do the confidence intervals and levels we might create for each of the samples contain the population mean, and how do we find out? First, think about the information we need to construct a confidence interval for a particular sample. We need to know

- The standard error of the mean (the standard deviation of the sampling distribution of sample means).

- The mean for a particular sample (to represent the mean of the sampling distribution of sample means).

TABLE 11.3 Means for the Variables *age* and *educ* in 10 Randomly Drawn Samples of 30 Respondents Each From the gss96subset File

Sample	Mean for *age*	Mean for *educ*
1	44.10	13.63
2	51.10	13.47
3	41.23	13.67
4	47.57	13.07
5	47.00	14.47
6	42.77	12.67
7	47.03	13.73
8	42.27	13.60
9	41.27	13.73
10	44.37	13.17

You may recall from Chapter 10 that we found the standard error of the mean for the variable *age* with a sample size of 30 to be 3.08. Now let's use the standard error of the mean to construct a confidence interval for the first sample in Table 11.3. We know that

- The sampling mean for Sample 1 is 44.10 (we get it from Table 11.3).
- 44.10 *minus* 2 standard errors is 37.94.
- 44.10 *plus* 2 standard errors is 50.26.

Consequently, our confidence interval is 37.94 to 50.26. What percentage of all possible means from samples in the sampling distribution are included in this interval? The answer is about 95%. We know this because approximately 95% of all values in a normal distribution fall between the range of scores that is 2 standard errors below the mean to 2 standard errors above the mean. This confidence interval, therefore, encompasses around 95% of all possible sampling means for sample sizes of 30 respondents each. Is the population mean (44.78) within this range? Yes, it is. Figure 11.3 shows the relationship between the mean and the confidence interval for this example.

It's important to remember, though, that we are dealing only in likelihoods, not certainties. If 95% of all possible sampling means in a sampling distribution are likely to fall within a specified range of values, we have to remember that 5% of the sampling values still fall outside of that range. It is possible for the population mean to be one of the values outside of the range of the confidence interval. To see an example of the conditions under which this could be so, construct a confidence interval for the sampling

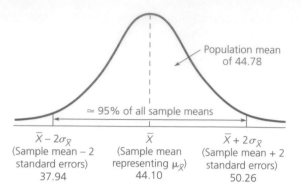

Figure 11.3 A population mean in relation to a confidence interval.

mean of Sample 2, 51.10. Use the standard error of the mean, 3.08, to construct it.

- Subtract 2 standard errors (3.08 + 3.08 = 6.16) from the mean of 51.10 (51.10 − 6.16 = 44.94).
- Add 2 standard errors to the mean of 51.10 (51.10 + 6.16 = 57.26).

The confidence interval for a sample with a mean of 51.10 is 44.94 to 57.26. About 95% of all sampling means in a sampling distribution are expected to fall within this range. However, we know that the population mean of 44.78 falls short of this range. Although not *likely,* it is *possible* to draw at random a sample that is not representative of the population from which it was selected.

Skills Practice 3   Using the education variable in Table 11.3,

   A. Construct a confidence interval at the 95% level of confidence for the sampling means in Samples 1 and 5. Use the standard error of the mean for the education variable you computed for Skills Practice 8 in Chapter 10. (Keep in mind that this standard error is for random samples drawn from the General Social Survey of 30 respondents each.)

   B. Write a sentence describing what the confidence interval and the confidence level tell you about the population mean.

   C. For which of the two samples does the population mean of 13.36 fall within the confidence intervals you established?

Although it's fairly simple to construct confidence intervals for specified confidence levels by hand, SPSS will find confidence intervals, too, as you can see in the following SPSS Guide.

SPSS Guide: Finding Confidence Intervals

Click on Analyze, then Descriptive Statistics, and look on the menu list for Explore. Click on Explore to open that dialog box.

❶ Select the variable for which you want confidence intervals. Try *age*. Click on the arrow (▶) pointing to the Dependent List box.

❷ Click on Statistics in the Display box.

❸ Click on the Statistics button to open the Explore: Statistics window.

At the Explore: Statistics window,

❶ Make sure there is a check (√) in the Descriptives box.

❷ Click on Continue to return to the Explore window. At the Explore dialog box, click on OK.

TABLE 11.4 Descriptive Statistics for the Variable *age* Using the Explore Command with the gss96subset File

Descriptives

			Statistic	Std. Error
AGE AGE OF RESPONDENT	Mean		44.78	.31
	95% Confidence Interval for Mean	Lower Bound	44.16	
		Upper Bound	45.39	
	5% Trimmed Mean		44.04	
	Median		42.00	
	Variance		284.519	
	Std. Deviation		16.87	
	Minimum		18	
	Maximum		89	
	Range		71	
	Interquartile Range		23.00	
	Skewness		.604	.045
	Kurtosis		-.417	.091

You will get a set of Descriptive statistics in the Output window like those in Table 11.4. In addition to the mean and the confidence interval, you will see many other statistics you recognize: the median, the variance, standard deviation, the minimum and maximum values of the variable, the range, and the interquartile range.

To interpret the confidence interval, focus on the first three statistics in the Statistics column and the standard error of the mean (.31) in the Std. Error column. The first of the statistics in the Statistics column is the mean for the variable *age*. The second statistic is the lower limit of the confidence interval (the mean minus 2 standard errors of the mean). The third statistic, the upper limit of the confidence interval, is equal to the mean plus 2 standard errors of the mean.

The confidence level is given in the table at 95%. (Even if it weren't specified, we could tell what it was because the lower limit is 2 standard errors below the mean, whereas the upper limit is 2 standard errors above the mean. Remember that a standard error of the mean is the standard deviation of the sampling distribution of the means, and we know that, in a normally distributed set of values, approximately 95% of the values will fall within the range of values that are within 2 standard deviations of the mean—2 above and 2 below.)

Interpretation   What do the confidence intervals and the confidence level tell us? Very simply put:

> There are 95 chances out of 100 that the population mean—the average age of American adults—is between 44.16 and 45.39.

Another way to put this (and the way you often see confidence intervals expressed in newspaper articles and magazines) is that

> there are 19 chances out of 20 [which is another way of saying 95 chances out of 100] that the average age of the adults in the population is 44.78, plus or minus .62 year [2 standard errors of the mean].

Sometimes, you see only the confidence interval, and the confidence level isn't mentioned at all. Notice, for example, how the authors of the report "Parents of Teens and Teens Discuss Sex, Love, and Relationships" discuss their methodology in the "News to Use" section of Chapter 2. Generally speaking, when no confidence level is specified, we can assume that it is at least 95%.

What If We Want to Be More or Less Confident? The Return of the Z Score

From understanding how we can use the standard error of the mean to develop confidence intervals around sampling means, it's a fairly small step to understanding how we can specify confidence intervals of almost any size. Taking this step brings us full circle to the concept of the Z score. Let's see how Z scores tie in to the concept of confidence intervals.

Remember that the *Z score* tells us the distance from the mean, expressed in standard deviations, of a particular value in a set of data. Thus, if we have a sampling distribution[2] for which we are going to assume the mean is 44.78, we can find out how far from that mean any other mean in the distribution might be.

For example, let's use the sample mean for *age* of 44.78 as an estimate of the mean of the sampling distribution of sample means. Where, in relation to that mean, would a sample mean of 44.16 be found? Let's use the Z scores formula for a population to find out. Remember to use the standard error of the mean (.31) for the variable *age* in the denominator.

$$Z = \frac{X - \mu_{\overline{X}}}{\sigma_{\overline{X}}}$$

$$= \frac{44.16 - 44.78}{.31} = \frac{-.62}{.31}$$

$$Z = -2$$

The mean of 44.16 is 2 standard deviations below the mean of the sampling distribution of sample means of 44.78. What is the Z score for the sample mean, 45.40? You have probably guessed that the Z score for 45.40 is +2, but you can use the Z scores formula to confirm your hunch. If you look up

---

[2]Keep in mind that the sampling distribution is the *theoretical* set of all possible means for samples of a given sample size drawn from the same population.

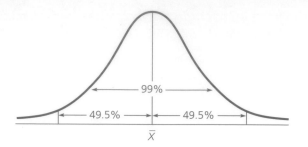

Figure 11.4 Area under normal curve for a 99% confidence level.

the Z score in the table in Appendix A, you will see that about 47.7% of all values fall within the range of values 2 standard deviations below or above the mean in a normal distribution—close to 95%, the confidence level.

We can work this process in reverse to produce confidence levels of any size. For example, suppose we create a confidence interval that will include our population mean 99 times out of 100 rather than just 95 times—a confidence interval with a level of 99%. Let's find out what the Z score for such an interval would be.

First, realize that for a confidence level of 99% we have to find the range of means within which 99% of the means in the sampling distribution are likely to fall. Half of this range will fall below the sampling distribution of the sample means, and half will fall above it. Thus, we divide 99 by 2 to find the Z score, or the distance in standard deviation units from the mean, for the half of the means that will fall below the sampling distribution of the mean and the half that will fall above it. The result of $99 \div 2$ is 49.5. Figure 11.4 shows the distribution of the area under a normal curve for a 99% confidence interval.

Turn the percentage, 49.5, into a proportion by dividing it by 100, and look up the result, .495, on the table in Appendix A. To look up a proportion, use the *second* column (b) of the table (the area between the mean and Z). The first proportion you come to that is closest to .495 is .4949. The Z score associated with .4949 is 2.57. This tells us that the portion of the normal distribution that contains about 49.5% of the values or scores falls about 2½ standard deviations below the mean (Figure 11.5).

Now let's find the mean that is 2.57 standard deviations below the sampling mean we are using as our point estimate. To locate the lower limit of our confidence interval, we assign a negative value to the Z score of 2.57 and solve the Z score formula for the mean that falls at that score.

$$Z = \frac{\overline{X} - \mu_{\overline{X}}}{\sigma_{\overline{X}}}$$

$$-2.57 = \frac{? - 44.78}{.31}$$

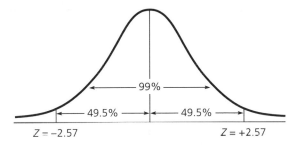

Figure 11.5 Z scores associated with a 99% confidence level.

Another expression of this same formula, one that makes clearer how to solve for the missing sample mean, is the following set of formulas for finding confidence intervals:

FORMULA 11.1: The confidence interval formulas

$$CI_u = \overline{X} + (Z)(\sigma_{\overline{X}})$$

$$CI_l = \overline{X} + (Z)(\sigma_{\overline{X}})$$

where CI is the upper (CI_u) or lower (CI_l) limit of the confidence interval, $\overline{X}$ is the sample mean (used to estimate the mean of the sampling distribution of sample means), Z represents the Z score at the lower or upper limit, and $\sigma_{\overline{X}}$ represents the standard error of the mean.

Example: Let's find the upper limit of the interval with a confidence level of .99 for the variable *age*. We know it has a Z score of 2.57. We know because we divided .99 by 2 to get .495, and we looked up .495 in column (b) of the table for the area under the normal curve (Appendix A). Then we matched .495 with its associated Z score of 2.57 in column (a). We also know the standard error of the mean for *age* is .31 (computed earlier by hand and using SPSS).

$\overline{X}$ (sample mean) = 44.78 Z (Z score) = 2.57 $\sigma_{\overline{X}}$ (standard error of the mean) = .31

$$CI_u = \overline{X} + (Z)(\sigma_{\overline{X}})$$
$$= 44.78 + (2.57)(.31) = 44.78 + (.7967)$$
$$CI_u = 45.58$$

Now, let's find the lower limit of the confidence interval.

$\overline{X}$ (sample mean) = 44.78 Z (Z score) = 2.57 $\sigma_{\overline{X}}$ (standard error of the mean) = .31

$$CI_u = \overline{X} + (Z)(\sigma_{\overline{X}})$$
$$= 44.78 - (2.57)(.31) = 44.78 - (.7967)$$
$$CI_l = 43.98$$

Interpretation   What do these confidence limits at the 99% confidence level tell us? There are 99 chances out of 100 that the population mean (the average age of adult Americans) is between 43.98 and 45.58 years; or, as we see more often, we can be 99% sure that the average age of adult Americans is 44.78, give or take about .80 year (2.57 standard errors of the mean).

Skills Practice 4   Find the confidence interval with a confidence level of 99% for the variable *educ.* (You will probably figure out right away that the Z score is identical to that for *age,* but what changes is the mean for the sample and the standard error of the mean for *educ.*)

Specifying Confidence Levels Using SPSS

You can specify different confidence levels using SPSS simply by changing the confidence level in the Explore: Statistics window.

SPSS Guide: Specifying Confidence Levels

Follow the command path Analyze ➥ Descriptive Statistics ➥ Explore.

❶ Scroll down the variable list to find your variable. Let's use *educ.* Click on the variable to highlight it, then click on the ▶ pointing at the Dependent List box to select it.

❷ Under Display, click on Statistics.

❸ Click on the Statistics button to open the Explore: Statistics window.

Explore

conpress
consci
contv
courts
degree
diconfed
diconleg
earnmore
earnrs
evstray

Dependent List:
❶ educ

OK
Paste
Reset
Cancel
Help

Factor List:

Label Cases by:

Display ❷
○ Both ● Statistics ○ Plots

❸
Statistics... Plots... Options...

When the Explore: Statistics window opens,

❶ Place your cursor in the box next to Confidence Interval for Mean, and backspace over 95 to remove it. Then type in the confidence level you want to specify. Let's try 99.

❷ Click on Continue to return to the Explore dialog box.

Explore: Statistics

☑ Descriptives
   Confidence Interval for Mean: ❶ 99 %
☐ M-estimators
☐ Outliers
☐ Percentiles ❷

Continue Cancel Help

At the Explore dialog box, click on OK. You will get a report in your Output window like the one you see in Table 11.5.

TABLE 11.5 Descriptive Statistics for the Variable *educ* in the gss96subset File, Using a 99% Confidence Level

Descriptives

			Statistic	Std. Error
EDUC HIGHEST YEAR OF SCHOOL COMPLETED	Mean		13.36	.05
	99% Confidence Interval for Mean	Lower Bound	13.22	
		Upper Bound	13.51	
	5% Trimmed Mean		13.39	
	Median		13.00	
	Variance		8.581	
	Std. Deviation		2.93	
	Minimum		0	
	Maximum		20	
	Range		20	
	Interquartile Range		4.00	
	Skewness		-.147	.046
	Kurtosis		.904	.091

If your output reports the standard error in scientific notation as 5.44E-02, you can double-click on the report, then double-click on Std. Error to see the nonscientific notation version of the standard error.

Notice that the answers you obtained using SPSS are only slightly different than the confidence levels you computed by hand. The reason they are different is because we rounded the mean to two decimals when we did our hand computations. SPSS doesn't do that.

So far, we have concentrated on how to establish confidence intervals for means. However, you may have noticed that the article about the New York Senate race in the "News to Use" at the beginning of Chapter 10 doesn't use means, it uses percentages. What do we do when we want to know how likely it is that a sampling percentage represents the population? You'll be happy to know that the process is substantially the same.

CONFIDENCE INTERVALS AND LEVELS FOR PERCENTAGES

Let's look at a few of the variables in the General Social Survey that explore attitudes of the respondents toward various issues. The heated contest between Alfonse D'Amato and Charles Schumer, and the impeachment by the House of Representatives and subsequent trial of President Clinton in the Senate, made me wonder about the general perceptions of the public toward their governing institutions. The General Social Survey contains a series of variables asking respondents how much confidence they have in various in-

TABLE 11.6 Frequency Distribution for the Variable *conlegis* in the gss96subset File

CONLEGIS CONFIDENCE IN CONGRESS

		Frequency	Percent	Valid Percent	Cumulative Percent
Valid	1 HARDLY ANY	820	28.2	44.1	44.1
	2 ONLY SOME	893	30.8	48.0	92.1
	3 A GREAT DEAL	146	5.0	7.9	100.0
	Total	1859	64.0	100.0	
Missing	0 NAP	979	33.7		
	8 DK	61	2.1		
	9 NA	5	.2		
	Total	1045	36.0		
Total		2904	100.0		

stitutions, like the Congress (*conlegis*), the Presidency (*confed*), and the Supreme Court (*conjudge*). Look these variables over before you go further to familiarize yourself with them.

A very easy way to see how much confidence people have in one of these institutions is to look at a frequency distribution. Follow the command path Analyze ➡ Descriptive Statistics ➡ Frequencies to see a frequency distribution for the variable *conlegis*. You should be looking at a frequency distribution like the one in Table 11.6.

How much confidence would you say the GSS respondents have in Congress as an institution? On the whole, not much. Only a little more than half of the respondents have at least some confidence. About 44% have hardly any confidence at all. Is it likely that the proportion of respondents who say they have hardly any confidence is representative of the population the GSS is designed to represent? We can construct a confidence interval around the proportion to find out. The first step is to find the sampling error of proportions.

Standard Error of Proportions

Just as there are sampling distributions of sample means, there are sampling distributions of sample proportions. We can assume that for a sampling distribution of a given size, the sampling distribution of sample proportions will be normal. Moreover, we can calculate descriptive statistics for the sampling distribution of sample proportions, just as we can for the sampling distribution of sample means. We can find the standard deviation of the sampling distribution of sample proportions, for example, called the standard error of the proportions. We can compute it using the following formula.

$$\sigma_P = \sqrt{\frac{(\pi)(1 - \pi)}{N}}$$

where σ_P is the standard error of proportions (the standard deviation of the sample proportions in the sampling distribution), π (called pi) is the population proportion of the category of a particular variable, and N is the size of the population.

Of course, we don't know the population proportion. If we did, we would not need a random sample to try to estimate it. Thus, when we solve the formula, we use the sample proportion as a point estimate in place of pi to represent the population proportion. The formula then can be expressed as follows.

FORMULA 11.2: The standard error of proportions

$$\sigma_P = \sqrt{\frac{(P)(1 - P)}{N}}$$

where σ_P is the standard error of proportions, P is the sample proportion, and N is the number of valid cases in a sample.

Example: To find the standard error of the proportion for the variable *conlegis,* we need to know the proportion of respondents who said they hardly have any confidence in the legislature, and we need to know how many respondents there are for this variable. Both of these numbers can be found in the frequency distribution. Use the number of valid cases, 1,859, for N. For the proportion, divide the percentage who answered "Hardly Any" by 100 to get .441. Then use these values in Formula 11.2.

P (proportion of respondents to the GSS for 1996 who have hardly any confidence in Congress) = .441

N (number of valid responses to the variable *conlegis*) = 1,859

$$\sigma_P = \sqrt{\frac{(P)(1 - P)}{N}}$$

$$= \sqrt{\frac{(.441)(1 - .441)}{1,859}} = \sqrt{\frac{(.441)(.559)}{1,859}}$$

$$= \sqrt{\frac{.2465}{1,859}} = \sqrt{.0001325}$$

$$\sigma_P = .01$$

Interpretation The standard error of proportions is .01, which tells us that the standard deviation among the sample proportions in the sampling distribution is very small. It isn't likely that there is much variance among the proportions in the sampling distribution of sample proportions.

Once we find the standard error of proportions we can find confidence intervals for a proportion.

Constructing Confidence Intervals at Specified Levels for Proportions

Remember the formula for finding confidence intervals for means? With a slight modification, we can also use it to find confidence intervals for proportions.

FORMULA 11.3:   Confidence intervals for proportions

$$CI_u = P + (Z)(\sigma_P)$$

$$CI_l = P \quad (Z)(\sigma_P)$$

where CI is the confidence interval at the upper (CI_u) or lower (CI_l) limit of the confidence interval, P is the sample proportion, Z is the Z score associated with the confidence level for which you are trying to find the interval, and σ_P is the estimated standard error of proportions.

Example: Let's find the confidence interval associated with a confidence level of 95%. We already know that the sample proportion, or point estimate, around which we want to construct an interval is .441. We know that the Z score associated with a 95% level of confidence is 2. (Why? Because the range of scores 2 standard deviations below the mean to 2 standard deviations above the mean encompasses about 95% of all scores in a normal distribution of scores.) We also found that the sampling error of proportions is .01. With these values we can find our confidence interval, starting with the upper limit—the value of the interval that falls above the sample proportion.

P (sample proportion) = .441 Z (Z score) = 2 σ_P (standard error of proportions) = .01

$$CI_u = P + (Z)(\sigma_P)$$

$$= .441 + (2)(.01) = .441 + (.02)$$

$$CI_u - .461$$

Next, find the confidence interval for the lower limit of the interval.

P (sample proportion) $= .441$ Z (Z score) $= 2$ σ_P (standard error of proportions) $= .01$

$$CI_l = P - (Z)(\sigma_P)$$
$$= .441 - (2)(.01) = .441 - (.02)$$
$$CI_l = .421$$

Interpretation   There are 95 chances out of 100 that the proportion of those in the population who have hardly any confidence in Congress falls within the range of .421 to .461. The way you see this expressed in the media is that there are 19 chances out of 20 that 44.1% of adult Americans have hardly any confidence in Congress (give or take 2%).

Skills Practice 5   Use the variable about confidence in the executive branch, *confed,* to do the following:

   A.   Find the standard error of proportions for those who have hardly any confidence in the executive branch.

   B.   Find the confidence interval with a confidence level of 95% for those who have hardly any confidence in the executive branch.

Constructing Confidence Intervals for Any Category

Although I picked the proportion Hardly Any in the frequency distribution for the variable *conlegis* as my point estimate for constructing a confidence interval at the 95% level, you can construct a confidence interval around any of the proportions in the distribution. For example, you can use the category Hardly Any Confidence as your point estimate, as I did. You can also use any of the other proportions in the frequency distribution.

Skills Practice 6   Try constructing a confidence interval at the 95% level using the category of A Great Deal for the *conlegis* variable as your point estimate. Begin by finding the standard error of proportions for the category A Great Deal, and then use the result in the formula for finding confidence intervals. What do you come up with?

You are not limited to a confidence level of 95%. You can construct confidence intervals for any level of confidence.

Skills Practice 7 Having found the confidence interval for a 95% level of confidence for the category A Great Deal, now construct a confidence interval at the 99% level of confidence. You will not have to recompute the standard error of proportions, but you will have to find the Z score for the 99% confidence level.

How can we find these sorts of confidence intervals for proportions using SPSS? Unfortunately, SPSS doesn't have the capability to find confidence intervals for the various categories of ordinal and nominal variables. However, if we dichotomize a variable, we can use the Explore command to find the confidence intervals for a specified level.

Using SPSS to Find Confidence Intervals and Levels for Proportions

SPSS can be used to find confidence intervals and levels for proportions with dichotomized variables. As you learned in Chapter 2, a dichotomy is any variable with only two categories. However, for the purpose of using SPSS to find confidence intervals, we will employ a specific type of dichotomy called a dummy variable. A **dummy variable** is any variable for which the categories indicate either the presence or the absence of a characteristic. For example, we can think of the variable *sex* as a dichotomy—males and females—or we can think of it as two categories, one that is the absence of the characteristic of maleness and the other that is the presence of the characteristic. When we create dichotomies to reflect the presence or absence of a characteristic, a dichotomy is coded to reflect this definition. Rather than coding the categories 1 for Male and 2 for Female, we code them 0 for Not Male and 1 for Male. We could also code them 0 for Not Female and 1 for Female. It doesn't really matter for our purposes.

Almost any variable can be dichotomized. We could turn the religion variable into Not Christian and Christian, or the race variable into Not White and White. To see how we can specify confidence levels and intervals using SPSS, let's turn the variable *conlegis* into Hardly Any and At Least Some.

Old Values of *conlegis*	Old Labels of *conlegis*	New Labels	New Values
0	NAP	NAP	7
1	Hardly any	Hardly any	0
2	Only some	At least some	1
3	A great deal		
8	DK	DK	8
9	NA	NA	9

New variable name: *diconleg*
New variable label: DICHOTOMIZED CONFIDENCE IN LEGISLATURE
Level of measurement: Ordinal

Figure 11.6 Recode diagram for the variable *conlegis,* confidence in Congress, in the gss96subset file.

To dichotomize the *conlegis* variable, use the Recode command. Start the process by looking at the frequency distribution for the variable and deciding how to recode it. Create a recode diagram on paper.

- Take the category Hardly Any and make it category 0 (the absence of the characteristic Confidence).

- Take the next two categories, A Great Deal and Only Some, and group them together to make the new category At Least Some Confidence with a code of 1 (the presence of the characteristic Confidence).

- Turn the NAP category (currently category 0) into category 7.

- Make the new category 7, along with the categories DK (8) and NAP (9), your missing value categories.

- Call the new variable *diconleg* and label it DICHOTOMIZED CONFIDENCE IN LEGISLATURE.

Use Figure 11.6 to check your recode diagram for the variable *conlegis.*

In the SPSS Data Editor window, use the command path Data ➡ Recode ➡ Into Different Variables to enter your old and new values. After you create your new variable, don't forget to give your variable new values and new value labels, define the missing values, and specify the level of measurement. (If you need help with recoding or defining your values and labels, see the SPSS Guide, "Recoding Variables," in Chapter 4.) Finally, check your new, recoded variable against the frequency distribution in Table 11.7.

Now you can use the Analyze ➡ Descriptive Statistics ➡ Explore command path to find the confidence intervals for the variable *diconleg*. Notice that the confidence interval is expressed as the interval around the proportion

TABLE 11.7   Recoded *conlegis* Variable, *diconleg*

DICONLEG dichotomized confidence in legislature

		Frequency	Percent	Valid Percent	Cumulative Percent
Valid	0 hardly any confidence	820	28.2	44.1	44.1
	1 at least some	1039	35.8	55.9	100.0
	Total	1859	64.0	100.0	
Missing	7 NAP	979	33.7		
	8 DK	61	2.1		
	9 NA	5	.2		
	Total	1045	36.0		
Total		2904	100.0		

TABLE 11.8   Statistics for the Variable *diconleg* (a Recoded Confidence in the Legislative Branch Variable) in the gss96subset File

Descriptives

			Statistic	Std. Error
DICONLEG dichotomized confidence in legislature	Mean		.56	.01
	95% Confidence Interval for Mean	Lower Bound	.54	
		Upper Bound	.58	
	5% Trimmed Mean		.57	
	Median		1.00	
	Variance		.247	
	Std. Deviation		.50	
	Minimum		0	
	Maximum		1	
	Range		1	
	Interquartile Range		1.00	
	Skewness		-.237	.057
	Kurtosis		-1.946	.113

with the value of 1, or At Least Some Confidence, in this case. You will get a Descriptives report like the one in Table 11.8.

The Descriptives report shows us that there is a 95% likelihood that the proportion of American adults who have at least some confidence in the legislature is between 54% and 58%.

Skills Practice 8   Recode the variable *confed* to dichotomize it (as we did with *conleg*). Then find the confidence interval for the proportion of respondents who said they have at least some confidence at the 95% level.

In the next two chapters you will learn to make inferences about associations between variables.

SUMMARY

With this chapter we began our application of the principles of making inferences from samples to populations. Our first application involved drawing inferences from sampling characteristics involving single variables, such as the mean for a distribution of responses to a variable and the proportion of responses to a category of a variable.

The sampling characteristic about which we want to make an inference is called a point estimate. A point estimate can be a mean or a proportion. Using the point estimate, we can construct a confidence interval for a specified confidence level. For example, we can determine the likelihood that a population mean falls within a particular range of means. We can never be sure that the population mean falls within the specified range, but we can assess the probability that it does. We can also construct confidence limits at specified levels for proportions.

You should be able to perform these functions—finding confidence limits at specified levels—by hand and using SPSS. In the next chapter we'll apply the principles of inferential statistics to associations between variables.

KEY CONCEPTS

Point estimate
Confidence interval
Confidence level

Standard error of the
  mean

Dummy variable

ANSWERS TO SKILLS PRACTICES

1. The standard deviation for the variable *educ* is 2.93, and *N* is equal to 2,895. Use these values in the formula for the standard error of the mean.

$$\sigma_{\overline{X}} = \frac{\sigma}{\sqrt{N}}$$

$$= \frac{2.93}{\sqrt{2,895}} = \frac{2.93}{53.8052}$$

$$\sigma_{\overline{X}} = .054$$

3. For the education variable,

    A. The standard error of the mean for the variable *educational level* with sample sizes of $N = 30$ is .53 (which you computed for Skills Practice 8). For Sample 1 in Table 11.3, the confidence interval would be constructed as follows:

    Mean (13.63) minus 2 standard errors [(.53)(2) = 1.06], or $13.63 - 1.06 = 12.57$

    Mean (13.63) plus 2 standard errors (1.06), or $13.63 + 1.06 = 14.69$

    The confidence interval would range from 12.57 years of education to 14.69 years of education.

  For Sample 5, the confidence interval would be constructed as follows:

    Mean (14.47) minus 2 standard errors (1.06) = 13.41

    Mean (14.47) plus 2 standard errors (1.06) = 15.53

    The confidence interval would range from 13.41 years of education to 15.53 years of education.

    B. For Sample 1, a sample of 30 respondents drawn at random from the General Social Survey, there are about 95 chances out of 100 that the population mean falls between 12.57 and 14.69 years of education. For Sample 5, another sample of 30 respondents, there are around 95 chances out of 100 that the population mean falls between 13.41 and 15.53 years of education.

    C. The population mean of 13.36 falls within the confidence interval for Sample 1, but not for Sample 5.

4. To construct a confidence interval with a level of 99%, begin by finding the lower limit of the interval, using Formula 11.1. The Z score at the lower limit for an interval that will include 99% of the means in the sampling distribution of the mean is 2.57. For the variable *educ,* the mean is 13.36 and the standard error of the mean is .054. Use these values in the formula for the confidence interval to find the lower and upper limits of the interval.

$$CI_l = \bar{X} - (Z)(\sigma_{\bar{X}})$$

$$= 13.36 - (2.57)(.054) = 13.36 - (.1388)$$

$$CI_l = 13.22$$

$$CI_u = \bar{X} + (Z)(\sigma_{\bar{X}})$$

$$= 13.36 + (2.57)(.054) = 13.36 + (.1388)$$

$$CI_u = 13.50$$

We can interpret the result as follows: There are 99 chances out of 100 that the population mean for the variable *education* will fall between 13.22 and 13.50. Another way to put it is that there is a 99% chance the population represented by the General Social Survey has an average of 13.36 years of education, give or take .14 year.

5.

A. To find the standard error of proportions, use Formula 11.2. Notice the formula asks for a proportion and the N for the variable. With SPSS (and the command path Analyze ➥ Descriptive Statistics ➥ Frequencies), you can produce a frequency distribution for the variable *confed* that will contain the values you need to work the formula. The proportion of those who have hardly any confidence in the executive branch is .431, and the N (number of valid cases) is 1,856. Use these values to work the formula for the standard error of proportions.

$$\sigma_P = \sqrt{\frac{(P)(1-P)}{N}}$$

$$= \sqrt{\frac{(.431)(1-.431)}{1,856}} = \sqrt{\frac{(.431)(.569)}{1,856}}$$

$$= \sqrt{\frac{.2452}{1,856}} = \sqrt{.0001321}$$

$$\sigma_P = .01$$

B. To find the confidence interval with a confidence level of 95%, use Formula 11.3. Start by finding the value at the upper limit of the confidence interval.

$$CI_u = P + (Z)(\sigma_P)$$

$$= .431 + (2)(.01) = .431 + (.02)$$

$$CI_u = .451$$

Then find the value of the lower limit of the confidence interval.

$$CI_l = P + (Z)(\sigma_P)$$

$$= .431 - (2)(.01) = .431 - (.02)$$

$$CI_l = .411$$

There are 95 chances out of 100 that the percentage of American adults represented by the GSS who have hardly any confidence in the executive branch falls between 41% and 45%.

6. First, find the standard error of proportions. For the proportion of responses to the category A Great Deal of confidence, the proportion in Table 11.6 is .079 (7.9 ÷ 100), and the N is 1,859, the number of valid responses to the variable *conlegis*.

$$\sigma_P = \sqrt{\frac{(P)(1 - P)}{N}}$$

$$= \sqrt{\frac{(.079)(1 - .079)}{1,859}} = \sqrt{\frac{(.079)(.921)}{1,859}}$$

$$= \sqrt{\frac{.0728}{1,859}} = \sqrt{.0000391}$$

$$\sigma_P = .01$$

Second, use the standard error of proportions in the formula for the confidence interval. The Z score at the 95% confidence level is 2.

Lower limit	Upper limit
$CI_l = P - (Z)(\sigma_P)$	$CI_u = P + (Z)(\sigma_P)$
$= .079 - (2)(.01)$	$= .079 + (2)(.01)$
$= .079 - (.02)$	$= .079 + (.02)$
$CI_l = .059$	$CI_u = .099$

There are 95 chances out of 100 that the proportion of American adults who have a great deal of confidence in Congress falls in the range of 5.9% to 9.9%.

7. To find the confidence interval at the 99% level, it is only necessary to change the Z score. The Z score at the 99% level is 2.57. Use this Z score, the standard error of proportions (.01), and the proportion .079 in the formula for the confidence interval.

Lower limit	Upper limit
$CI_l = P - (Z)(\sigma_P)$	$CI_u = P + (Z)(\sigma_P)$
$= .079 - (2.57)(.01)$	$= .079 + (2.57)(.01)$
$= .079 - (.0257)$	$= .079 + (.0257)$
$CI_l = .0533$	$CI_u = .1047$

There are 99 chances out of 100 that the proportion of American adults who have a great deal of confidence in Congress falls between 5.33% and 10.47%.

8. You should get a frequency distribution for the dichotomized *confed* variable like the one that follows.

DICONFED dichotomized confidence in executive

		Frequency	Percent	Valid Percent	Cumulative Percent
Valid	0 hardly any confidence	800	27.5	43.1	43.1
	1 at least some	1056	36.4	56.9	100.0
	Total	1856	63.9	100.0	
Missing	7 NAP	979	33.7		
	8 DK	68	2.3		
	9 NA	1	.0		
	Total	1048	36.1		
Total		2904	100.0		

Your confidence intervals will be contained within the descriptive statistics you produce with the Analyze ➡ Descriptive Statistics ➡ Explore command path, as you see in the following table.

Descriptives

			Statistic	Std. Error
DICONFED dichotomized confidence in executive	Mean		.57	.01
	95% Confidence Interval for Mean	Lower Bound	.55	
		Upper Bound	.59	
	5% Trimmed Mean		.58	
	Median		1.00	
	Variance		.245	
	Std. Deviation		.50	
	Minimum		0	
	Maximum		1	
	Range		1	
	Interquartile Range		1.00	
	Skewness		-.279	.057
	Kurtosis		-1.924	.114

There are 95 chances out of 100 that between 55% and 59% of American adults have at least some confidence in the executive branch of government.

GENERAL EXERCISES

Use the standard deviation and N for the following variables to compute the standard error of the mean for each variable.

1. *Variable*   *Standard Deviation* N

 paeduc   4.10   2,066

2. *Variable*   *Standard Deviation* N

 maeduc   3.40   2,472

3. *Variable*   *Standard Deviation* N

 speduc   2.85   1,381

For General Exercises 4–7, use the sample means for the two variables, *respondent's education* and *spouse's education,* in General Exercises 5 and 6 in Chapter 10.

4. Construct and interpret a confidence interval at the 95% level for the mean in Sample 9 (in General Exercise 5, Chapter 10) for the respondent's education variable ($\sigma_{\bar{X}} = .53$). The population mean is 13.36. Does it fall within the confidence interval?

5. Construct and interpret a confidence interval at the 95% level for the mean in Sample 1 (in General Exercise 6, Chapter 10) for the spouse's education variable ($\sigma_X - .52$). The population mean is 13.45. Does it fall within the confidence interval?

6. Construct and interpret a confidence interval at the 99% level for the mean in Sample 9 (in General Exercise 5, Chapter 10) of the respondent's education variable ($\sigma_X - .53$). Does the population mean fall within the confidence interval?

7. Construct and interpret a confidence interval at the 99% level for the mean in Sample 1 (in General Exercise 6, Chapter 10) of the spouse's education variable ($\sigma_{\bar{X}} = .52$). Does the population mean fall within the confidence interval?

Use the frequency distribution in the following table to answer General Exercises 8–14.

CONBUS CONFIDENCE IN MAJOR COMPANIES

		Frequency	Percent	Valid Percent	Cumulative Percent
Valid	1 HARDLY ANY	260	9.0	14.1	14.1
	2 ONLY SOME	1137	39.2	61.7	75.8
	3 A GREAT DEAL	447	15.4	24.2	100.0
	Total	1844	63.5	100.0	
Missing	0 NAP	979	33.7		
	8 DK	80	2.8		
	9 NA	1	.0		
	Total	1060	36.5		
Total		2904	100.0		

8. Compute the standard error of proportions for the category A Great Deal.

9. Compute the standard error of proportions for the category Only Some.

10. Compute the standard error of proportions for the category Hardly Any.

11. Construct a confidence interval with a confidence level of 95% for the category Only Some.

12. Construct a confidence interval with a confidence level of 95% for the category A Great Deal.

13. Construct a confidence interval at the 99% level for the category Only Some.

14. Construct a confidence interval at the 99% level for the category Hardly Any.

SPSS EXERCISES

1. Use the gss96subset file to find the standard error of the mean for the variables *paeduc, maeduc,* and *speduc.* Check your SPSS answers against your computations in General Exercises 1, 2, and 3.

2. Dichotomize the variable *conbus.* Give the value 1 (at least some) to those who have a great deal and only some confidence, and give the value 0 (hardly any confidence) to those who have hardly any confidence. Set up missing values for the NAP, DK, and NA categories. Then use SPSS to find the standard error of the proportion and the lower and upper limits of a confidence interval at the 95% level for the proportion.

3. Use SPSS and your dichotomized *conbus* variable to find the standard error of the proportion and the lower and upper limits of a confidence interval at the 99% level for the proportion.

12 Making Inferences for Associations Between Categorical Variables: Chi-Square

Like inferential statistics for single variables, inferential statistics for measures of association allow us to answer the question, How likely is it that what we are learning from a sample is true of the population from which the sample was drawn? Finding out whether we can generalize about an association from a sample to a population involves a process of analysis called *hypothesis testing*.

The process of hypothesis testing, which occurs in the next-to-last step of the research process (described in Chapter 1), is outlined as follows:

Step 1. Specify a research hypothesis and the null hypothesis.

Step 2. Compute the value of a test statistic for the relationship.

Step 3. Calculate the degrees of freedom for the variables involved.

Step 4. Look up the distribution of the test statistic to find its critical value at a specified level of probability (to determine the likelihood that a test statistic of a particular value could have occurred by chance alone).

Step 5. Decide whether to reject the null hypothesis.

In this chapter and the next, you will be learning to do hypothesis testing for associations involving two variables. We will begin with hypothesis testing for categorical variables using chi-square. In the next chapter you will learn about hypothesis testing for associations involving numerical variables. To get started we'll review what a hypothesis is, and then I will introduce some of the concepts important to hypothesis testing.

As defined in Chapter 1, a hypothesis is simply a statement that describes a relationship between at least two variables. So far, we have analyzed all sorts of relationships, including that between sex and political affiliation, and the effect of parents' educational levels on the educational achievements of their offspring. In the "News to Use" article in this chapter, the headline describes another relationship: the one between age and happiness. The hypothesis suggested by the headline is that the older a person is, the happier he or she is likely to be.

> **Skills Practice 1** Let's see whether the pattern reported in the "News to Use" article holds up for the General Social Survey respondents. Use *agecat* and *happy* to find out whether one's general level of happiness seems to increase with age. Open your gss96subset file in SPSS and produce a contingency table for these two variables. Write an analysis of what you find and compare what you learn with the "News to Use" article.

NEWS TO USE: Statistics in the "Real" World

Happiness May Grow With Aging, Study Finds[1]

ERICA GOODE

Aging brings predictable travails: The body starts to crumble, memory decays, old friends begin to fall ill and die. But a new study indicates the passage of years may also bestow a heightened sense of well-being, at least for the generation of Americans now well into their retirement years.

Dr. Daniel Mroczek of Fordham University and his colleague, Christian Kolarz, analyzed the responses of more than 2,700 adults between the ages of 25 and 74 to questions designed to assess happiness and life satisfaction. They found that the older the respondents, the more frequently they reported feeling positive emotions like cheerfulness, good spirits, and happiness within the past 30 days. The relationship held even when the researchers took into account education, marital status, health, stress, personality and other factors that might affect the results.

The link between well-being and age was strongest for men, who showed both an increase in positive emotions and a decrease in negative emotions—feeling sad, nervous, hopeless or worthless—with advancing years, Dr. Mroczek said. Older women also reported more positive emotions, but the researchers found no difference for women in negative emotions across age categories. The happiest subjects were not only older and male, but also married and high scorers on a measure of extroversion.

The scientists, whose report will appear in the November issue of the *Journal of Personality and Social Psychology,* analyzed data collected as part of a large national telephone and mail survey by the John D. and Catherine T. MacArthur Foundation Research Network on Successful Midlife Development.

What the Fordham results mean is still being debated. It could be that the study, which surveyed a cross-section of Americans rather than following the same individuals over decades, simply demonstrates that adults raised before the advent of Oprah Winfrey are less willing to reveal unhappiness or dissatisfaction. Or it could be that a generation of people who survived the Great Depression and World War II are happy because they are aware that life could get much worse.

---

[1]*The New York Times on the Web,* <http://www.nytimes.com>, Oct. 26, 1998.

But previous research suggests that whether someone reports being happy is surprisingly independent of factors like income, age and level of education. And at least some other studies have yielded findings supporting the notion that happiness actually increases with age.

Dr. Laura Carstensen, a Stanford University psychologist whose work has also shown a relationship between age and well-being, theorizes that older people may feel happier because they have more practice regulating their emotions, and because they are more likely to live in the moment. "It's not that old people are happy-go-lucky," Carstensen said, "but that there is an appreciation of life that is associated with a sense of well-being and satisfaction."

How can we tell if it is likely that the association we found in our sample of GSS respondents—the older respondents are, the happier they are likely to be—is true of all American adults, 18 years old or older, noninstitutionalized, and English-speaking? The answer is, by engaging in hypothesis testing. Before we can do that, we have to develop an understanding of a set of core concepts related to making inferences, or generalizations, from samples to populations.

CORE CONCEPTS FOR HYPOTHESIS TESTING

The Research Hypothesis and the Null Hypothesis

The first concept to understand involves the difference between a research hypothesis and the null hypothesis. A **research hypothesis,** symbolized by H_1, involves specifying the nature of the relationship between two variables. We have been exploring research hypotheses throughout this text. For example, a research hypothesis might state one of the following:

H_1: Men are more likely to be Republicans than are women.

H_1: The more education a GSS respondent's parents have, the more education the respondent is likely to have.

H_1: The older people are, the happier they are likely to be.

The **null hypothesis,** on the other hand, speculates that there is no association between two variables. Null hypotheses are symbolized with H_0. The following are some examples of null hypotheses:

H_0: Men are no different from women in their political affiliations.

H_0: There is no relationship between a respondent's educational level and his or her parents' achievements.

H_0: Older people are no more likely to be happy than younger people.

The null hypothesis has a specific purpose in hypothesis testing; it is the only hypothesis that can be tested. We often assume that if we reject the null hypothesis, the research hypothesis is confirmed. Technically, however, we can only reject or fail to reject the null hypothesis—nothing more.

Let's illustrate this with an example. The null hypothesis related to happiness and age says that

H_0: There is no association between age and happiness among American adults.

To test this hypothesis—to see whether it is true or not—we draw a random sample from the population. When we examine the association between the two variables in our sample, we find that there is an association between them. In fact, you learned from the contingency table you produced for the first Skills Practice in this chapter (Table 12.1 on p. 469) that the older the respondents, the more likely they are to say they are happy.

However, there's a problem. You may recall from our work in Chapters 10 and 11 that randomly drawn samples are *likely* to represent the populations from which they are drawn, but they don't always. The question we have to ask ourselves now is, How likely is it that the association we are seeing in our sample reflects real differences in happiness based on age in the population? Is what we are seeing merely a chance occurrence, the result of the sample we were unlucky enough to draw? More to the point, what is the likelihood that we could have drawn a sample at random for which there appears to be an association *even when* there is no association in the population as a whole?

If it is likely that the association we find is *not* a chance occurrence, then the null hypothesis can be rejected. In other words, we would be on fairly firm ground in rejecting the idea that we have drawn a sample showing an association between age and happiness from a population in which there is no such association. Where does that leave us? Generally, most researchers argue for the relationship observed in the sample. If we reject the null hypothesis, then it is assumed there is a relationship in the population like the one in the sample—the older people are, the happier they tend to be.

On the other hand, what happens if we find that there is a good chance that the association between age and happiness *is* an accident, and we simply happened to have selected a sample for which age is related to happiness? Then we cannot reject the null hypothesis. We conclude, at least for the time being, that there is not enough evidence to reject the idea that there is no association between the variables. In failing to reject the null hypothesis, we are not saying for certain that there is no association. All we are saying is that we don't have enough evidence to reject that idea.

In the absence of rejecting the null hypothesis, researchers often say that they are "accepting" the null hypothesis. I don't think it's because they don't know better. Saying that they are "failing to reject" the null hypothesis is too convoluted for the lay person to understand. I will sometimes discuss hypothesis testing in these terms—rejecting the null hypothesis or accepting the null hypothesis. I hope you will keep in mind that using the term "accepting" the null hypothesis is a substitute for the more accurate phrase, "failing to reject" the null hypothesis.

Statistical Independence

The concept of statistical independence provides us with another way to look at the difference between a research hypothesis and the null hypothesis. When two variables are **statistically independent,** changes in one variable (*age of respondents*) have nothing to do with changes in a second (*happiness*). They vary *independently* of one another. Conversely, when two variables are statistically dependent on one another, changes in one variable are associated with changes in a second variable. For example, changes in age (older respondents) are associated with changes in levels of happiness (more happiness).

We can use this concept of statistical independence in framing a null hypothesis. For instance, we can hypothesize that age is statistically independent of happiness. We are saying that differences among respondents on the variable *age* are unrelated to any differences we may see in their levels of reported happiness. With hypothesis testing, we can assess the likelihood that the degree of statistical independence we see in a sample is due to chance. If we find that the degree of statistical independence found in the sample is not likely to be due to chance, the null hypothesis is rejected. If we find that it is likely to be due to chance, the null hypothesis is accepted. Either way, we always run the risk of making mistakes.

Type I and Type II Errors

The mistakes we can make are of two types. Both arise from the fact that any given sample may or may not be representative of a population. We can only assess the likelihood that it is, never the certainty.

Type I errors   We can reject a null hypothesis, even when there really is no association between two variables. Based on what we learn from a sample, it is possible to reject the idea that there is no association between age and happiness *even though* the null hypothesis is correct—there is no association between age and happiness in the population. This type of mistake or error, rejecting a null hypothesis when there really is no association between two variables, is called a **Type I error.**

Type II errors   We can do the opposite; that is, we can accept the null hypothesis—the idea that there is no association between two variables— even though there is one. We could, for example, accept the idea that there is no association between age and happiness even though, in reality, there is an association between these variables in the population at large. This kind of mistake—accepting the null hypothesis when there really is an association between two variables—is called a **Type II error.**

The real kicker is that the more you do to avoid Type I errors, the more likely you are to make a Type II error. Taking steps to limit Type II errors increases the likelihood of Type I errors. In this chapter, we will focus on how to avoid Type I errors. If you move on to higher level courses in research methods, you will learn about techniques for reducing Type II errors.

To assess whether or not we can reject a null hypothesis, we must first compute an appropriate test statistic (given the levels of measurement of the variables involved in our association and other assumptions that I will go into as the various test statistics are introduced). One such test statistic, chi-square, can be computed from contingency tables.

CALCULATING AND INTERPRETING THE TEST STATISTIC FOR CONTINGENCY TABLES: CHI-SQUARE (χ^2)

A measure of inference appropriate for use with contingency tables (and therefore any pair of variables for which contingency table analysis is appropriate) is called **chi** (pronounced "ki" with a long i)-**square** and indicated by the symbol χ^2. Like many measures of inference, chi-square has two components: a test statistic, called the **obtained value** of chi-square, and a **critical value** of the statistic, which is the value the test statistic must reach to reject the null hypothesis. We will examine this later.

The Test Statistic for Chi-Square

The first component of chi-square is a test statistic. Most measures of inference start off with the computation of a statistic called a **test statistic.** It assesses the degree of statistical independence, or the extent to which two variables change together (are dependent) or are acting independently of one another. Chi-square can assess the extent to which happiness changes as a function of age, for example, or if happiness varies independently—without regard to the age of the respondents. The formula for the obtained value of chi-square is fairly straightforward.

FORMULA 12.1: Obtained chi-square

$$\chi^2 = \sum\left[\frac{(f_o - f_e)^2}{f_e}\right]$$

where f_o represents the observed frequencies in a contingency table, and f_e represents the expected frequencies in a contingency table.

TABLE 12.1   A Contingency Table for *agecat* and *happy* in the gss96subset File

HAPPY GENERAL HAPPINESS * AGECAT recoded age - four categories Crosstabulation

| | | | AGECAT recoded age - four categories | | | | |
			1 18 thru 25	2 26 thru 39	3 40 thru 64	4 65 thru 89	Total
HAPPY GENERAL HAPPINESS	1 NOT TOO HAPPY	Count	43	102	148	55	348
		% within AGECAT recoded age - four categories	12.3%	11.0%	12.8%	12.4%	12.1%
	2 PRETTY HAPPY	Count	219	556	652	228	1655
		% within AGECAT recoded age - four categories	62.4%	60.0%	56.2%	51.6%	57.5%
	3 VERY HAPPY	Count	89	268	360	159	876
		% within AGECAT recoded age - four categories	25.4%	28.9%	31.0%	36.0%	30.4%
Total		Count	351	926	1160	442	2079
		% within AGECAT recoded age - four categories	100.0%	100.0%	100.0%	100.0%	100.0%

The observed frequency

To understand how to work this formula, we have to learn the difference between observed and expected frequencies.

Expected and observed frequencies   The concept of chi-square is based on the difference between expected and observed frequencies in a distribution involving two variables (a contingency table). If we use the association between age and happiness as an example, we can construct a contingency table in which there is no association between two variables—the contingency table we would *expect* to see if the two variables had nothing to do with, or no effect upon, one another.

We know from Skills Practice 1 that a contingency table showing the relationship between *agecat* and *happy* looks like the one in Table 12.1. The frequencies in each cell are called the **observed frequencies**, the actual frequencies we found for the association between *agecat* and *happy* in our sample of GSS respondents.

We find the **expected frequencies,** the frequencies in a contingency table for which there is no association between two variables, by reconstructing the table. Let's assume there is no association between *agecat* and *happy*. What would the cell frequencies look like? To answer this question you have to understand that a table with no association between two variables would show no differences in percentages across the categories (rows) of the dependent variable. They would be identical all the way across. To reconstruct our contingency table so that it shows no association between the variables, we have to recalculate the cell frequencies. How can we do this?

Start by imagining the contingency table with the cells empty, as in Table 12.2.

TABLE 12.2   Contingency Table for *agecat* and *happy* in the gss96subset File With the Cells Empty

Row marginal percentage
(row proportion = row marginal % ÷ 100)

HAPPY GENERAL HAPPINESS * AGECAT recoded age - four categories Crosstabulation

| | | | AGECAT recoded age - four categories | | | | |
			1 18 thru 25	2 26 thru 39	3 40 thru 64	4 65 thru 89	Total
HAPPY GENERAL HAPPINESS	1 NOT TOO HAPPY	Count					348
		% within AGECAT recoded age - four categories					12.1%
	2 PRETTY HAPPY	Count					1655
		% within AGECAT recoded age - four categories					57.5%
	3 VERY HAPPY	Count					876
		% within AGECAT recoded age - four categories					30.4%
Total		Count	351	926	1160	442	2879
		% within AGECAT recoded age - four categories	100.0%	100.0%	100.0%	100.0%	100.0%

Column marginal total

To find the expected frequencies, we work with the column *marginal totals* for each category of the independent variable and the row *marginal percentages* for each category of the dependent variable. To find the expected cell frequency for those who are 18 through 25 and not too happy, multiply the column marginal total for 18 through 25 (351) by the row marginal proportion[2] for those who are not too happy (.121). Round to the nearest whole number.

$351 \times .121 = 42$, so the expected cell frequency for the categories 18 through 25 and not too happy is 42. Record the expected cell frequency in the contingency table in Table 12.3.

Move down to the next cell, the 18 through 25-year-olds who are pretty happy. To find the expected cell frequency, multiply the column marginal (351) by the row marginal proportion for those who are pretty happy. The row marginal proportion = 57.5% ÷ 100, or .575. We see that $351 \times .575 = 202$, so the expected cell frequency for those who are 18 through 25 years old and pretty happy is 202.

Skills Practice 2   Fill in the rest of the expected cell frequencies for the contingency table. The answers are in Table 12.3. (The expected cell frequencies in Table 12.3 were computed using SPSS, which rounds off to the first decimal. Your answers rounded off to the nearest whole number should be close.) You can also check your work using the SPSS Guide, "Finding Expected Cell Frequencies."

---

[2]To find the row marginal proportion, divide the row marginal percentage (12.1%) by 100 to get .121.

TABLE 12.3 Expected Cell Frequencies for *agecat* and *happy* in the gss96subset File

HAPPY GENERAL HAPPINESS * AGECAT recoded age - four categories Crosstabulation

| | | | AGECAT recoded age - four categories | | | | |
			1 18 thru 25	2 26 thru 39	3 40 thru 64	4 65 thru 89	Total
HAPPY GENERAL HAPPINESS	1 NOT TOO HAPPY	Expected Count	42.4	111.9	140.2	53.4	348.0
		% within AGECAT recoded age - four categories					12.1%
	2 PRETTY HAPPY	Expected Count	201.8	532.3	666.8	254.1	1655.0
		% within AGECAT recoded age - four categories					57.5%
	3 VERY HAPPY	Expected Count	106.8	281.8	353.0	134.5	876.0
		% within AGECAT recoded age - four categories					30.4%
Total		Expected Count	351.0	926.0	1160.0	442.0	2879.0
		% within AGECAT recoded age - four categories	100.0%	100.0%	100.0%	100.0%	100.0%

SPSS Guide: Finding Expected Cell Frequencies

At the SPSS Data Editor window, go to the Crosstabs dialog box using the command path Analyze ➡ Descriptive Statistics ➡ Crosstabs. Select the variables *agecat* and *happy*. At the Crosstabs dialog box, click on the Cells button to open the Crosstabs: Cell Display window.

❶ Look under Counts and click on the box next to Expected.

❷ Click on Continue to return to the Crosstabs window.

❸ At the Crosstabs dialog box, click on OK.

TABLE 12.4 Contingency Table With Observed and Expected Cell Frequencies for *agecat* and *happy* in the gss96subset File

Observed frequency   Expected frequency

HAPPY GENERAL HAPPINESS * AGECAT recoded age - four categories Crosstabulation

			AGECAT recoded age - four categories				
			1 18 thru 25	2 26 thru 39	3 40 thru 64	4 65 thru 89	Total
HAPPY GENERAL HAPPINESS	1 NOT TOO HAPPY	Count	43	102	148	55	348
		Expected Count	42.4	111.9	140.2	53.4	348.0
		% within AGECAT recoded age - four categories	12.3%	11.0%	12.8%	12.4%	12.1%
	2 PRETTY HAPPY	Count	219	556	652	228	1655
		Expected Count	201.8	532.3	666.8	254.1	1655.0
		% within AGECAT recoded age - four categories	62.4%	60.0%	56.2%	51.6%	57.5%
	3 VERY HAPPY	Count	89	268	360	159	876
		Expected Count	106.8	281.8	353.0	134.5	876.0
		% within AGECAT recoded age - four categories	25.4%	28.9%	31.0%	36.0%	30.4%
Total		Count	351	926	1160	442	2879
		Expected Count	351.0	926.0	1160.0	442.0	2879.0
		% within AGECAT recoded age - four categories	100.0%	100.0%	100.0%	100.0%	100.0%

Your contingency table will look like Table 12.4.

What do we do with the expected frequencies? First, we can recalculate the cell column percentages to demonstrate that there is no association between the independent (*age*) and dependent (*happiness*) variables. Do that now.

Skills Practice 3   Use the expected cell frequencies to recalculate the column percentages in Table 12.4. Round to the second decimal. Your table should look like Table 12.5.

What's the association between age and happiness? If you read across the first row of the dependent variable, Not Too Happy, you will see there is no association at all—the percentages are identical. The same is true of the second and third rows.

TABLE 12.5 Contingency Table with Expected Frequencies for *agecat* and *happy* in the gss96subset File Showing Column Percentages Computed From the Expected Frequencies

HAPPY GENERAL HAPPINESS * AGECAT recoded age - four categories Crosstabulation

			AGECAT recoded age - four categories				
			1 10 thru 25	2 26 thru 39	3 40 thru 64	4 65 thru 89	Total
HAPPY GENERAL HAPPINESS	1 NOT TOO HAPPY	Expected Count	42.4	111.9	140.2	53.4	348.0
		% within AGECAT recoded age - four categories	12.1%	12.1%	12.1%	12.1%	12.1%
	2 PRETTY HAPPY	Expected Count	201.8	532.3	666.8	254.1	1655.0
		% within AGECAT recoded age - four categories	57.5%	57.5%	57.5%	57.5%	57.5%
	3 VERY HAPPY	Expected Count	106.8	281.8	353.0	134.5	876.0
		% within AGECAT recoded age - four categories	30.4%	30.4%	30.4%	30.4%	30.4%
Total		Expected Count	351.0	926.0	1160.0	442.0	2879.0
		% within AGECAT recoded age - four categories	100.0%	100.0%	100.0%	100.0%	100.0%

You should now be able to see how the computation of expected frequencies produces a contingency table in which there is no association between two variables. The next step is to use the differences between these expected frequencies and the observed frequencies to assess the degree of statistical independence between two variables. Remember that the observed cell frequencies are those we obtained for the variables *agecat* and *happy* in our sample of 1996 GSS respondents (see Table 12.1). We need to know how much difference there is between the expected frequencies and the observed ones. The *smaller* the difference, the *greater* the statistical independence (the more one variable changes irrespective of the other).

Think about this for a second. In a table of *expected* frequencies, there is no association between two variables. How old one is has no effect on how happy one is. There is no change in happiness across the categories of the variable *age*. The variable *happy* has nothing to do with the variable *age;* they vary independently of one another. If the frequencies we obtain through observation of a sample (the 1996 GSS respondents, in this case) are substantially the same as the expected ones, then there is no association between the two variables. If the expected and observed frequencies are different, there is more statistical dependence—more effect of one variable on the other.

We rarely see either no association whatsoever between two variables or only perfect associations between two variables. Instead, we see something in between, and in the social sciences we tend to see smaller associations rather than larger ones. Consequently, what we have to measure is not the presence or absence of statistical independence, but the extent. We do that with the obtained chi-square formula, Formula 12.1.

$$\chi^2 = \sum \left[\frac{(f_o - f_e)^2}{f_e} \right]$$

The chi-square formula requires us to go through the contingency table cell by cell, as follows:

Step 1. Find the observed (f_o) and expected (f_e) frequency.

Step 2. Subtract the expected from the observed frequency ($f_o - f_e$).

Step 3. Square the result: $(f_o - f_e)^2$.

Step 4. Divide the result by the expected frequency (f_e).

Step 5. Add up the computations for each of the cells.

Example: To find chi-square for Table 12.4, go through the cells in the table one by one. Start with the first cell, the respondents who are 18 through 25 and not too happy.

Step 1. Find the observed frequency ($f_o = 43$) and the expected frequency, rounded to the nearest whole number ($f_e = 42$).

Step 2. Subtract the expected from the observed frequencies: $43 - 42 = 1$.

Step 3. Square the result: $1^2 = 1$.

Step 4. Divide by the expected frequency ($f_e = 42$): $1 \div 42 = .024$ (rounded to the nearest thousandth).

Move down to the next cell in the column 18 through 25, the youngest respondents who are pretty happy, and repeat the process:

Step 1. Find the observed frequency ($f_o = 219$) and the expected frequency, rounded to the nearest whole number ($f_e = 202$).

Step 2. Subtract the expected from the observed frequencies: $219 - 202 = 17$.

Step 3. Square the result: $17^2 = 289$.

Step 4. Divide by the expected frequency ($f_e = 202$): $289 \div 202 = 1.431$ (rounded to the nearest thousandth).

TABLE 12.6 Contingency Table for *agecat* and *happy* Showing the Computations for Chi-Square: $(f_o - f_e)^2/f_e$

HAPPY GENERAL HAPPINESS * AGECAT recoded age - four categories Crosstabulation

		AGECAT recoded age - four categories			
		1 18 thru 25	2 26 thru 39	3 40 thru 64	4 65 thru 89
HAPPY GENERAL HAPPINESS	1 NOT TOO HAPPY	.024	.893	.457	.075
	2 PRETTY HAPPY	1.431	1.083	.337	2.661
	3 VERY HAPPY	3.028	.695	.139	4.664

Skills Practice 4   Complete the process for each cell in the table:

Step 1. Record the observed frequency and expected frequency.

Step 2. Find the difference between the observed and expected frequencies.

Step 3. Square the difference.

Step 4. Divide the result by the expected frequency.

Check your answers against Table 12.6.

Finally, the formula for chi-square calls for us to sum the proportion computed for each cell:

$$\chi^2 = \sum \left[\frac{(f_o - f_e)^2}{f_e} \right]$$

$$= .024 + .893 + .457 + .075 + 1.431 + 1.083 +$$

$$.337 + 2.661 + 3.028 + .695 + .139 + 4.664$$

$$= 15.487$$

The result is an obtained chi-square of 15.487. Generally, the greater the chi-square, the more statistical dependence between two variables. However, the value of chi-square has no absolute meaning by itself. We have to interpret it in the context of its associated degrees of freedom and the likelihood of obtaining it by chance.

TABLE 12.7 Understanding Degrees of Freedom Using a Hypothetical Set of Data

Age		18 through 39	40 and Up	Row Totals
Happiness	Not too happy	13		22
	Happy			3
	Column Totals	15	10	$N = 25$

Degrees of freedom   Having found the test statistic for chi-square, the next question to ask is, What is the likelihood that we could obtain a chi-square of this magnitude in a contingency table of this size strictly by chance? Put another way, What is the probability that we could find this much statistical dependence in a sample drawn from a population in which the two variables are statistically independent?

To find the answer, we have to consider the size of the contingency table. The size of the table is measured in degrees of freedom. The concept of degrees of freedom derives from the idea that once you know the values of a certain number of cells, the values in the rest of the cells are determined. Let's illustrate this point with a simple example. Suppose we construct a contingency table with only four cells, like the one in Table 12.7, to examine the association between age and happiness. We select 25 respondents at random from the 1996 GSS and classify them according to how old they are and how happy they are. Of the 25 respondents, we notice right away that 15 are ages 18 to 39 and 10 are 40 and up. We enter those values in our contingency table as the column marginal totals for the two categories of the independent variable. Then we discover that 22 are not too happy and 3 are happy. We enter those numbers as the row marginal totals for the two categories of the dependent variable. Next we start to fill in the cells of the table. We begin by finding out how many belong in the first cell, young and not too happy. We learn that 13 belong in the first cell, so we enter the number 13.

Once we have done that, notice that all of the values in the rest of the cells are determined by the row and column marginal totals—we don't even have to count the respondents cell by cell. We know that there are 2 respondents in the 18 through 39 and happy cell. (How? Because 13 + 2 = the column marginal total, 15.) We know there are 9 respondents in the 40 and up and not too happy cell (because 13 + 9 = the row marginal total, 22). There is one respondent who is 40 and up and happy.

When we know the row and column marginal totals, we only have to know the contents of one of the cells in the table to complete the whole contingency table. Only one cell, therefore, is free to vary. Consequently, this table is one in which there is only one degree of freedom. The concept **degrees of freedom** tells us how many cells in a table are free to vary, once the row and column marginal totals are known.

TABLE 12.8 Contingency Table With Row and Column Totals for a Random Sample of 48 1996 GSS Respondents for the Variables *agecat* and *happy*

HAPPY GENERAL HAPPINESS * AGECAT recoded age - four categories Crosstabulation

		AGECAT recoded age - four categories				
		1 18 thru 25	2 26 thru 39	3 40 thru 64	4 65 thru 89	Total
HAPPY GENERAL HAPPINESS	1 NOT TOO HAPPY					19
	2 PRETTY HAPPY					26
	3 VERY HAPPY					3
Total		7	13	15	13	48

Skills Practice 5   See whether you can figure out how many degrees of freedom there are in Table 12.8, a table of 48 respondents selected at random from the 1996 GSS. How many cell frequencies do you have to fill in before the values in the rest of the cells are determined? You will see the answer when you get to Example 2 in the next section. (Hint: Try filling in the cells with hypothetical frequencies to see how many you have to fill in before the rest are determined.)

Although it's important to understand how degrees of freedom are determined, the degrees of freedom in a table can be found more easily using a formula.

FORMULA 12.2:   Degrees of freedom for chi-square

$$df = (r - 1)(c - 1)$$

where r represents the number of rows in a contingency table, and c represents the number of columns.

Example 1:   For Table 12.7, we can compute the degrees of freedom with the formula by counting the number of rows and number of columns and entering them in the formula.

$$df = (r - 1)(c - 1) = (2 - 1)(2 - 1) = (1)(1) = 1$$

There is only one degree of freedom in Table 12.7. The frequency for only one cell is free to vary. Once that frequency has been determined, the row and column marginal totals dictate the contents of the rest of the cells.

Example 2:   For Table 12.8, we can compute the degrees of freedom as follows:

$$df = (r - 1)(c - 1) = (4 - 1)(3 - 1) = (3)(2) = 6$$

> **Skills Practice 6** How many degrees of freedom are there in the contingency tables in General Exercises 1–6 from Chapter 8? (See whether you can figure it out without applying the formula. Then check yourself by using the formula for degrees of freedom.)

Interpreting Chi-Square Values

We use chi-square to decide whether to accept or reject the null hypothesis by using it, and its associated degrees of freedom, in conjunction with a statistic called a probability or p value. You see these often in scholarly articles. Researchers may write something like, "We learned that the older a respondent, the more likely he or she is to report being happy ($p < .05$)."

To understand how chi-square works with probability values, you have to look at chi-square as a sampling statistic—a characteristic of the observed relationship between two variables in a sample. Just like other sampling statistics (the sampling mean, for example), chi-square has its own distribution for tables of different sizes. I will not go into the mechanics of the construction of chi-square distributions. Suffice it to say that the likelihood of chi-square values of a specific magnitude occurring by chance in tables of different sizes have been computed and made available to us in statistical charts of critical values of chi-square and their associated p values.

Probability values and alpha values Generally, the **p or probability value** indicates the likelihood that a test statistic of a particular magnitude computed from a sample is simply a chance or random occurrence rather than a consequence of real associations between the variables in a population. For chi-square, it tells us the likelihood that the degree of statistical dependence observed in a sample is simply due to the luck of the random draw.

The lower the p value is, the *less* likely it is that the statistical dependence observed in a sample is due to chance. A p value of .05, for instance, tells us that there are no more than 5 chances in 100 that the statistical dependence observed in a sample is due to chance. There are, therefore, 95 chances in 100 that the statistical dependence found in the sample is *not* due to chance. We can conclude, therefore, that we have enough evidence to reject the null hypothesis, the hypothesis of no association between two variables. However, it is often assumed to be more likely than not that the specific association we find in the sample is present in the population.

If the likelihood is not high that the degree of statistical dependence found in a sample is a chance occurrence, the null hypothesis—that there is no association between two variables—is rejected. On the other hand, if we find that the likelihood is high, the null hypothesis cannot be rejected. We have to

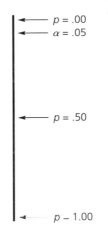

p = .00
α = .05

p = .50

p – 1.00

Figure 12.1   Relationship between probability values and alpha levels.

accept the fact that we cannot rule out the possibility of no association between two variables.

Note that, the higher the p or probability value is, the less likely we are to make Type I errors. With a p value of .95 or .99, we are less likely to reject the null hypothesis when there truly is no association between two variables than if we used lower p values.

The concept of the alpha value (indicated by the symbol α) is closely related to the probability value. The **alpha value** is the level at or below which we would expect a particular probability value to fall before we decide to reject the null hypothesis. The alpha value is not computed so much as it is set. I think of the alpha value as a bar the probability has to jump over before we can reject the null hypothesis.

Perhaps Figure 12.1 will help you to understand this concept. Probability values range from .00 to 1.00. The lower the probability value, the less likely you are to find that an association in a sample is a chance occurrence. By extension, the higher the probability value, the more likely it is that an association in a sample is due only to the specific elements you happened to draw into the sample. If you have a sample of individuals, a low p value tells you it is highly unlikely that the degree of statistical dependence found in the sample is an accident. A high p value tells you the opposite—that the degree of statistical dependence you observe is probably due to chance.

Anything with a p value of .50 or more indicates the likelihood that an association in a sample will not be found in the population. At .50, the p value is telling us that the likelihood is 50–50 that an association we see in a sample is due to nothing more than chance. But at p values higher than .50—let's pick .70 as an example—the odds are greater that associations we find in samples are due to dumb luck, and are not real associations between variables in populations. We can't base decisions on dumb luck, so we don't draw conclusions from associations in samples that are far more likely than not due to chance.

However, what happens when p values fall below .50? Are we willing to conclude that the older one is, the happier he or she is likely to be if the odds of an association being due to chance are only 1 in 4 ($p = .25$)? (By extension, can we say the odds are 3 in 4 that the association is reflective of a real association in the population?) Some would say yes—go ahead and reject the null hypothesis. However, in the social sciences, alpha levels—hurdles that p values have to jump over before the null hypothesis can be rejected—have been set fairly low, usually at .05 or less. Consequently, as a rule of thumb (and there is considerable debate about this) alpha levels of .05 have been established as the "bar" that p values have to clear. Before we can reject the null hypothesis that the associations we see in samples are due to chance and are not real associations between variables in populations, we must have p values at .05 or less. I will follow this practice in this chapter and the next as we test various null hypotheses.

Testing the null hypothesis Table 12.4 has a chi-square value of 15.487 (which we computed earlier) and 6 degrees of freedom. What is the likelihood of obtaining a chi-square of 15.487 in a table with 6 degrees of freedom constructed for a sample drawn from a population in which there is no association between the variables *age* and *happiness*? Is it probable that we would get a chi-square this large in a table with 6 degrees of freedom simply by chance? We can use a statistical table of critical chi-square values to find out. There is an excerpt from such a statistical table in Table 12.9. (A more complete table is found in Appendix B.)

Tables of critical chi-square values are formatted like the segment in Table 12.9. The degrees of freedom are listed down the side (the rows) of the table. Alpha values are listed across the top (the columns of the table). The critical values of chi-square make up the body of the table.

For a chi-square value of 15.487 in a table with 6 degrees of freedom, the likelihood is low that the association we see in our table is simply due to chance. How do we know? Note first that the higher the chi-square value, the less likely it is that the value obtained is due to chance. Look at the last column in the table. It tells us that for a chi-square value of 22.457 or more in a table with 6 degrees of freedom, there is no more than 1 chance in 1,000 that the result is due to chance. On the other hand, look at the first column in the table. It tells us that for a chi-square value of 5.348 or less, there are at least 50 chances in 100 that the association is due to mere chance. Our chi-square value is 15.487, more than the critical value 15.033, so there are no more than 2 chances in 100 that our association is due to chance.

TABLE 12.9 Section of a Statistical Table of Values of Chi-Square for Contingency Tables With 6 Degrees of Freedom

df				p Values				
	.50	.30	.20	.10	.05	.02	.01	.001
6	5.348	7.231	8.558	10.645	12.592	15.033	16.812	22.457

As a rule of thumb, to reject the null hypothesis we have to reach the critical value of chi-square associated with the .05 alpha level. Why? Because with an alpha level of .05 we can say that there are only 5 chances in 100 that the statistical dependence we find in the sample is due to chance. For a table with 6 degrees of freedom, the critical chi-square for the .05 level is 12.592. Our value is more. We can reject the null hypothesis and make the assumption that age and happiness are more likely than not statistically dependent in the population from which we drew our sample.

How do you put all of this together to write about your analysis of chi-square? Here's an example:

> For the association between age and happiness in the 1996 GSS, we can reject the null hypothesis. We have enough evidence to rule out the idea that the association we observed in our sample is due to chance. As a result, we can conclude that the association between age and happiness in the sample reflects a connection between these variables in the population of American adults from which the sample was drawn.

In the next example, the following Skills Practice, we'll see what happens when we get a different value of chi-square.

Skills Practice 7 Let's explore the research hypothesis that the higher a person's subjective identification of his or her social class status, the happier the person is. State the null hypothesis for this association. Then describe the association between class and happiness in the contingency table in Table 12.10. Analyze the table first. Next compute chi-square for the table. How many degrees of freedom does the table have? What is the likelihood that any association you observe between these variables is due to chance? (Use Table 12.9 to find out.)

When we find that a chi-square value (or any measure of inference) is more than likely a consequence of real associations between variables (and not merely chance), then we say that the association is "statistically significant."

TABLE 12.10   Contingency Table for *class* and *happy* From the gss96subset File

HAPPY GENERAL HAPPINESS * CLASS SUBJECTIVE CLASS IDENTIFICATION Crosstabulation

			CLASS SUBJECTIVE CLASS IDENTIFICATION				
			1 LOWER CLASS	2 WORKING CLASS	3 MIDDLE CLASS	4 UPPER CLASS	Total
HAPPY GENERAL HAPPINESS	1 NOT TOO HAPPY	Count	51	157	131	7	346
		% within CLASS SUBJECTIVE CLASS IDENTIFICATION	30.5%	12.2%	10.1%	6.2%	12.1%
	2 PRETTY HAPPY	Count	84	810	704	50	1648
		% within CLASS SUBJECTIVE CLASS IDENTIFICATION	50.3%	62.7%	54.4%	44.2%	57.5%
	3 VERY HAPPY	Count	32	325	458	56	871
		% within CLASS SUBJECTIVE CLASS IDENTIFICATION	19.2%	25.2%	35.4%	49.6%	30.4%
Total		Count	167	1292	1293	113	2865
		% within CLASS SUBJECTIVE CLASS IDENTIFICATION	100.0%	100.0%	100.0%	100.0%	100.0%

Often, you will see something like, "the association between self-identified social class and happiness is significant at the .001 level." This means simply that there is no more than 1 chance in 1,000 that the association found in the sample is due to the luck of the draw. We infer that it is more likely than not due to real associations between the variables in the population from which the sample was drawn.

Statistical significance refers to the likelihood of any pattern in a sample being no more than a chance occurrence. It is distinct from the concept of strength or the concept of practical significance. Whether a pattern we observe in a sample is important or not, or whether an association between two variables is strong or weak, is another matter, independent of statistical significance. We'll explore this point further in the last section of this chapter.

Limitations of Chi-Square

Chi-square, like measures of association, has its limits or conditions under which the chi-square value may be misleading in its assessment of statistical independence.

First, chi-square assumes that you are working with samples drawn using a probability design. It is not appropriate to use chi-square, or any other measure of inference, for samples that are not selected using probability techniques.

Second, chi-square shouldn't be used with contingency tables for which the expected frequency for one or more cells is less than 5. When expected frequencies are less than 5, it is possible for the difference between expected and observed frequencies in a single cell to have an inordinate impact on the chi-square value. There are situations in which the difference in a single cell can result in a chi-square value high enough to reject the null hypothesis. Consequently, when we see expected values less than 5, we should be cautious in our use of the chi-square statistic.

What can you do to overcome these limitations? Sometimes it is possible to collapse some of the categories of one or both variables in the contingency table to create larger observed and expected frequencies within the cells. You can use the recoding procedure to accomplish this. However, you can only combine categories of variables when the categories are logically related to one another. In general, you can only combine adjacent categories of ordinal variables. For example, you can take a variable like *happy* and combine the very happy respondents with the pretty happy respondents, but it wouldn't make any sense to combine the very happy and the not too happy respondents merely to get larger observed and expected frequencies.

For small contingency tables, those with only two categories of the independent and dependent variables (also called 2-by-2 tables) and only 1 degree of freedom, you cannot use chi-square if any of the expected cell frequencies fall below 5. If cell frequencies are 5 or more, but less than 10, you must use a slight variation on the chi-square formula, called **Yates' correction.**

FORMULA 12.3: Yates' correction for chi-square

$$\chi^2 = \sum \left\{ \frac{[(f_o - f_e) - .5]^2}{f_e} \right\}$$

Note that you are simply subtracting .5 from the difference between the observed and expected cell frequencies before squaring the result. The effect of this adjustment is to reduce the impact on the chi-square value of the difference in a single cell.

The third limitation is that chi-square can be affected by large sample sizes. When you compute chi-square in a contingency table showing a weak association between two variables in a small sample, chi-square will probably indicate that the association you are observing is due to chance. However, when an association of the same strength is observed in a larger sample, chi-square gets much larger. Consequently, for an association observed in a small sample, you may be more likely to reject the null hypothesis. In an association observed in a larger sample, you will be more likely to fail to reject the null hypothesis, even though the strength of the association is the same.

Some researchers believe that this limitation of chi-square causes us to fail to reject null hypotheses for fairly minor associations. As a result, you will see reports of "statistically significant" associations that are very weak. Even though the association is weak, we find that it is not likely due to mere chance.

Other researchers believe that this is not a limitation of chi-square at all. As sample sizes grow larger, we *should* be more confident that associations we find in samples are representative of the populations from which the samples are drawn. These researchers separate the issues of practical significance from the issue of statistical significance, which is a skill you will work on later in this chapter.

In the next section you will practice finding and interpreting chi-square using SPSS.

FINDING AND INTERPRETING CHI-SQUARE STATISTICS USING SPSS

SPSS Guide: Finding Chi-Square

Finding chi-square is fairly simple. At the SPSS Data Editor window, open the Crosstabs dialog box by following the command path Analyze ➡ Descriptive Statistics ➡ Crosstabs.

- At the Crosstabs window, select the variables for your contingency table. (Let's try *agecat* and *happy* again.)

- Click on Cells, look under Percentages, and click on Column. Then click on Continue to go to back to the Crosstabs dialog box.

- Click on Statistics to open the Statistics window. Look for Chi-Square in the upper left corner and click on it.

Click on Continue to go back to the Crosstabs dialog box. Then click on OK. You will get a contingency table for the variables *agecat* and *happy* along with a set of chi-square statistics like the ones in Table 12.11.

The chi-square you learned to calculate by hand is the Pearson chi-square.

TABLE 12.11 Chi-Square Values for *agecat* and *happy* in the gss96subset File

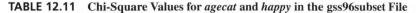

Chi-square value   Degrees of freedom   *p* value
                        for your contingency
                        table

Chi-Square Tests

	Value	df	Asymp. Sig. (2-sided)
Pearson Chi-Square	15.146[a]	6	.019
Likelihood Ratio	15.150	6	.019
Linear-by-Linear Association	4.510	1	.034
N of Valid Cases	2879		

a. 0 cells (.0%) have expected count less than 5. The minimum expected count is 42.43.

Interpretation   The *p* value, .019, tells us that there are only 19 chances in 1,000 that the association we see in our contingency table is a chance occurrence and does not reflect real associations between age and happiness in the population. Notice that you get a more precise reading of the probability here than you get in the tables of critical values of chi-square. The bottom line is the same—we reject the null hypothesis that there is no association between age and happiness.

Avoiding Common Pitfalls   You may wonder why the chi-square value computed by SPSS for *agecat* and *happy* doesn't match the one we computed by hand. The difference is due to rounding. When we computed expected cell frequencies by hand, we rounded to the nearest whole number. SPSS doesn't do that. Similarly, when we computed the difference between observed and expected frequencies, we rounded to the nearest thousandth. SPSS doesn't do that, either. SPSS computations will be more precise than those we can do by hand, but the answers you get for chi-square computations will be very close to those obtained using SPSS.

Skills Practice 8   Let's test the research hypothesis that there is a relationship between financial satisfaction and happiness. State the null hypothesis for this association. Then use SPSS to produce a contingency table with column percentages for the association between *satfin* (satisfaction with one's financial situation) and *happy*. Describe the association between these two variables (nature, direction, and strength). Use chi-square to assess the likelihood that a table showing this degree of statistical independence between the two variables could have been produced by chance.

USING CHI-SQUARE WITH MEASURES OF ASSOCIATION

Earlier in this chapter I said that the issues of statistical and practical significance are distinct. Chi-square is a measure of statistical significance, not a measure of practical significance. It can't tell you how strong an association is or (in the case of ordinal variables) anything about its direction. You may notice that chi-square does tend to be higher in tables with strong associations between variables, and smaller in tables with weaker associations. This is not always the case. Chi-square has to be used in conjunction with some other, appropriate (given the level of measurement of variables in the table) measure of association.

For the example we have been following so far, the association between *agecat* and *happy,* the appropriate measure of association is gamma or Somer's d. As you should recall from Chapters 8 and 9, measures of association allow us to evaluate the nature (including direction for ordinal and numerical variables) and strength of an association.

> **Skills Practice 9**   Use SPSS to find Somer's d (because the association is asymmetric) for *agecat* and *happy.* What do you learn about the association (its nature, direction, and strength)? You will find the answer next.

Let's put what you just learned about the relationship between *agecat* and *happy* using an appropriate measure of association with what you learned about the likelihood that the association is simply due to chance.

There appears to be an association between age and happiness. The older the respondents are, the happier they say they are. The relationship is weak. With a Somer's d of .034 (the asymmetric computation of Somer's d with *happy* dependent), we can confirm that the association is positive. Knowing the association between age and happiness improves our ability to predict how happy respondents are from their ages by only about 3%. It is not likely that a chi-square value of 15.146 in a table with 6 degrees of freedom is a chance occurrence ($p = .019$). The null hypothesis, that there is no association between age and happiness in the population from which this sample was drawn, is rejected.

> **Skills Practice 10**   Use SPSS to find an appropriate measure of association to examine the relationship between *satfin* and *happy.* Write an analysis of the contingency table for these variables. Describe the nature, direction, and strength of the association. Use chi-square statistics to determine how likely it is that the association you observe in the table is due to chance.

In the next chapter you will learn about measures of inference for associations involving numerical variables.

SUMMARY

This chapter introduced you to measures of inference for variables in contingency tables. Measures of inference allow us to decide whether or not to reject the null hypothesis, the hypothesis that there is no association between two variables in the population from which a random sample is drawn. Testing a null hypothesis involves computing a test statistic, chi-square in this case, and then seeing whether the test statistic reaches the values of the statistic that are critical for rejecting the null hypothesis.

For computing chi-square, it is necessary to understand the difference between expected frequencies in a frequency table (those frequencies we would expect to see in a table in which there is no association between two variables), and the observed frequencies in a table (those frequencies we find when we do some sort of observation of a sample drawn using probability techniques). The chi-square statistic is based on the degree of difference between the expected and observed frequencies. The difference between the two allows us to assess the degree of statistical independence—the extent to which the values (or responses to the values) of one variable change independently of the values (or responses to the values) of a second variable.

Once we compute a test statistic, we can compare it to a table of critical values of the test statistic. This comparison allows us to see whether our test value is likely to have occurred by chance, or whether it represents associations in samples that are likely to be representative of the populations from which the samples were drawn. If it is likely that the test value of chi-square is simply due to a chance occurrence, then we cannot reject the null hypothesis. We cannot give up the idea that the sample does not represent real associations between variables in a population. If the value of chi-square isn't likely to be due merely to chance, then we can reject the null hypothesis.

KEY CONCEPTS

Research hypothesis	Obtained value of a test statistic	Degrees of freedom
Null hypothesis		Probability value
Statistical independence	Critical value of a test statistic	(p value)
Type I error	Chi-square	Alpha value, alpha level
Type II error	Observed frequencies	Statistical significance
Test statistic	Expected frequencies	Yates' correction

ANSWERS TO SKILLS PRACTICES

1. Like the association in the "News to Use" article, there is a relationship between age and happiness among the respondents to the 1996 General Social Survey. The older respondents are, the happier they are likely to be. The association is positive, but it appears to be weak. The association is consistent across the Pretty Happy and Very Happy categories of the dependent variable, but much less so across the Not Too Happy category. Even in the Pretty Happy and Very Happy categories, the differences in the percentages across the rows are not very large. Unlike the respondents in the "News to Use" article who are between 25 and 74 years old, the GSS respondents cover a wider range of ages (18 to 89). We are dealing with a more heterogeneous set of respondents to the GSS than in the study reported in the article. The contingency table for *agecat* and *happy* is shown in Table 12.1.

6. The tables in General Exercises 1–6 at the end of Chapter 8:

   1. *polaf* and *relig:* $df = 8$ 4. *polaf* and *race:* $df = 4$
   2. *polaf* and *rcregion:* $df = 6$ 5. *polaf* and *satfin:* $df = 4$
   3. *polaf* and *sex:* $df = 2$ 6. *polaf* and *degree:* $df = 4$

7. The null hypothesis is that there is no association between subjective social class identification and happiness, or that social class and happiness are statistically independent. The association between class and happiness in Table 12.10 is one in which the higher the respondents' self-identified class position is, the happier they say they are. It is a positive association. To find out whether it is likely that the statistical dependence found in the sample could come from a population in which there is no association between the two variables, we compute chi-square.

   The following table gives the observed (count) and expected cell frequencies (expected count) for Table 12.10.

Observed frequency   Expected frequency

HAPPY GENERAL HAPPINESS * CLASS SUBJECTIVE CLASS IDENTIFICATION Crosstabulation

			CLASS SUBJECTIVE CLASS IDENTIFICATION				
			1 LOWER CLASS	2 WORKING CLASS	3 MIDDLE CLASS	4 UPPER CLASS	Total
HAPPY GENERAL HAPPINESS	1 NOT TOO HAPPY	Count	51	157	131	7	346
		Expected Count	20.2	156.0	156.2	13.6	346.0
	2 PRETTY HAPPY	Count	84	810	704	50	1648
		Expected Count	96.1	743.2	743.8	65.0	1648.0
	3 VERY HAPPY	Count	32	325	458	56	871
		Expected Count	50.8	392.8	393.1	34.4	871.0
Total		Count	167	1292	1293	113	2865
		Expected Count	167.0	1292.0	1293.0	113.0	2865.0

Next are given the computations for each cell for the chi-square formula

$$\frac{(f_o - f_e)^2}{f_e}.$$

For the first cell (Lower Class and Not Too Happy), the computations are as follows:

$$\frac{(f_o - f_e)^2}{f_e} = \frac{(51 - 20)^2}{20} = \frac{(31)^2}{20} = \frac{961}{20} = 48.050$$

See the following table. (Note: The computations assume expected cell frequencies are rounded to the nearest whole numbers.)

HAPPY GENERAL HAPPINESS * CLASS SUBJECTIVE CLASS IDENTIFICATION Crosstabulation

		CLASS SUBJECTIVE CLASS IDENTIFICATION			
		1 LOWER CLASS	2 WORKING CLASS	3 MIDDLE CLASS	4 UPPER CLASS
HAPPY GENERAL HAPPINESS	1 NOT TOO HAPPY	48.050	.006	4.006	3.500
	2 PRETTY HAPPY	1.500	6.042	2.151	3.462
	3 VERY HAPPY	7.078	11.766	10.751	14.235

Add up the contents of each cell to get the chi-square statistic:

48.050 + .006 + 4.006 + 3.500 + 1.500 + 6.042 + 2.151 + 3.462 + 7.078 + 11.766 + 10.751 + 14.235 = 112.547

Interpretation The likelihood of obtaining a chi-square value of 112.547 in a contingency table with six degrees of freedom by chance is less than 1 in 1,000 ($p < .001$). The null hypothesis—that social class and happiness are statistically independent—is rejected. By extension, then, we accept the premise that there is an association between social class and happiness in the population—the higher the respondents' subjective social class status is, the happier they say they are.

8. The null hypothesis is that there is no association between financial satisfaction and happiness (or that financial satisfaction and happiness are statistically independent).

Your contingency table should look like the one that follows.

HAPPY GENERAL HAPPINESS * SATFIN SATISFACTION WITH FINANCIAL SITUATION Crosstabulation

| | | | SATFIN SATISFACTION WITH FINANCIAL SITUATION | | | |
			1 NOT AT ALL SAT	2 MORE OR LESS	3 SATISFIED	Total
HAPPY GENERAL HAPPINESS	1 NOT TOO HAPPY	Count	186	117	44	347
		% within SATFIN SATISFACTION WITH FINANCIAL SITUATION	23.3%	9.1%	5.5%	12.1%
	2 PRETTY HAPPY	Count	484	801	372	1657
		% within SATFIN SATISFACTION WITH FINANCIAL SITUATION	60.7%	62.6%	46.4%	57.6%
	3 VERY HAPPY	Count	127	361	385	873
		% within SATFIN SATISFACTION WITH FINANCIAL SITUATION	15.9%	28.2%	48.1%	30.3%
Total		Count	797	1279	801	2877
		% within SATFIN SATISFACTION WITH FINANCIAL SITUATION	100.0%	100.0%	100.0%	100.0%

What's the association? The more satisfied respondents are with their financial situations, the happier they are. The association is positive, and it looks fairly strong because the highest percentages in each row are lined up on a diagonal, and the differences between the percentages are somewhat large.

Your chi-square statistics should look like the ones in the following table.

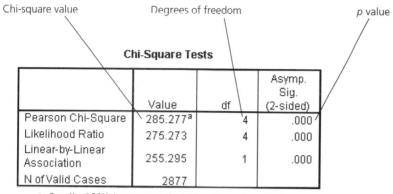

Chi-square value   Degrees of freedom   *p* value

Chi-Square Tests

	Value	df	Asymp. Sig. (2-sided)
Pearson Chi-Square	285.277[a]	4	.000
Likelihood Ratio	275.273	4	.000
Linear-by-Linear Association	255.295	1	.000
N of Valid Cases	2877		

a. 0 cells (.0%) have expected count less than 5. The minimum expected count is 96.13.

The probability of obtaining a specific chi-square value by chance is computed to only three decimal places. We can conclude that there are less than 5 chances in 10,000 that the association we see in the table is a chance occurrence.[3] As a result, the null hypothesis is rejected. More likely than not, the association between financial satisfaction and happiness is the result of a real relationship between these variables in the population from which the sample was drawn.

10. Using Somer's d (because an asymmetric measure is appropriate for these two variables), we see that the association is weak to moderate (.254) and positive. The more satisfied with their financial situations respondents are, the happier they are likely to be. Knowing the association between the independent and dependent variables improves our ability to predict the dependent variable by 25%—a fairly good improvement.

The likelihood of obtaining a chi-square of over 285 in a table with 6 degrees of freedom by chance is less than .0005. We can reject the null hypothesis that there is no association between one's happiness and one's level of satisfaction with finances in the population the sample represents.

---

[3]We know that we can assign the value $p < .0005$, because if the fourth digit of the p value were 5 or greater, then it would be rounded up to the nearest thousand ($p = .001$).

TABLE 12.12   Section of a Statistical Table of Values of Chi-Square for Contingency Tables with 6, 7, and 8 Degrees of Freedom

				p Values				
df	.50	.30	.20	.10	.05	.02	.01	.001
6	5.348	7.231	8.558	10.645	12.592	15.033	16.812	22.457
7	6.346	8.383	9.803	12.017	14.067	16.622	18.475	24.322
8	7.344	9.524	11.030	13.362	15.507	18.168	20.090	26.125

GENERAL EXERCISES

For the contingency tables in Exercises 1–3, find the obtained chi-square for the 1996 GSS respondents who are 25 to 74 years old. Calculate degrees of freedom. Compare your obtained chi-square values with the critical values of chi-square in Table 12.12. Interpret what you find.

1.

HAPPY GENERAL HAPPINESS * AGE25_74 respondents ages 25 thru 74 Crosstabulation

			AGE25_74 respondents ages 25 thru 74				Total
			1 25 thru 30	2 31 thru 49	3 50 thru 65	4 66 thru 74	
HAPPY GENERAL HAPPINESS	1 NOT TOO HAPPY	Count	34	156	67	24	281
		% within AGE25_74 respondents ages 25 thru 74	9.1%	12.6%	11.9%	10.8%	11.7%
	2 PRETTY HAPPY	Count	230	727	308	110	1375
		% within AGE25_74 respondents ages 25 thru 74	61.5%	58.7%	54.6%	49.3%	57.3%
	3 VERY HAPPY	Count	110	356	189	89	744
		% within AGE25_74 respondents ages 25 thru 74	29.4%	28.7%	33.5%	39.9%	31.0%
Total		Count	374	1239	564	223	2400
		% within AGE25_74 respondents ages 25 thru 74	100.0%	100.0%	100.0%	100.0%	100.0%

2.

HAPPY GENERAL HAPPINESS * DEGREE RS HIGHEST DEGREE Crosstabulation

			DEGREE RS HIGHEST DEGREE					
			0 LT HIGH SCHOOL	1 HIGH SCHOOL	2 JUNIOR COLLEGE	3 BACHELOR	4 GRADUATE	Total
HAPPY GENERAL HAPPINESS	1 NOT TOO HAPPY	Count	58	145	22	36	20	281
		% within DEGREE RS HIGHEST DEGREE	18.3%	11.5%	13.1%	8.2%	9.3%	11.7%
	2 PRETTY HAPPY	Count	165	746	106	246	112	1375
		% within DEGREE RS HIGHEST DEGREE	52.1%	59.2%	63.1%	56.3%	52.1%	57.3%
	3 VERY HAPPY	Count	94	370	40	155	83	742
		% within DEGREE RS HIGHEST DEGREE	29.7%	29.3%	23.8%	35.5%	38.6%	30.9%
Total		Count	317	1261	168	437	215	2398
		% within DEGREE RS HIGHEST DEGREE	100.0%	100.0%	100.0%	100.0%	100.0%	100.0%

3.

HAPPY GENERAL HAPPINESS * CLASS SUBJECTIVE CLASS IDENTIFICATION Crosstabulation

			CLASS SUBJECTIVE CLASS IDENTIFICATION				
			1 LOWER CLASS	2 WORKING CLASS	3 MIDDLE CLASS	4 UPPER CLASS	Total
HAPPY GENERAL HAPPINESS	1 NOT TOO HAPPY	Count	42	122	108	6	278
		% within CLASS SUBJECTIVE CLASS IDENTIFICATION	32.1%	11.3%	10.0%	6.3%	11.7%
	2 PRETTY HAPPY	Count	63	676	588	41	1360
		% within CLASS SUBJECTIVE CLASS IDENTIFICATION	48.1%	62.9%	54.2%	43.2%	57.4%
	3 VERY HAPPY	Count	26	277	388	48	739
		% within CLASS SUBJECTIVE CLASS IDENTIFICATION	19.8%	25.8%	35.8%	50.5%	31.0%
Total		Count	131	1075	1084	95	2385
		% within CLASS SUBJECTIVE CLASS IDENTIFICATION	100.0%	100.0%	100.0%	100.0%	100.0%

SPSS EXERCISES

For the variables in Exercises 1–3, write an appropriate null hypothesis, then use SPSS to test it. Produce a contingency table. Analyze it, and find and interpret an appropriate measure of association and chi-square.

1. *sex* and *happy*

2. *marital* and *happy*

3. *rcattend* and *happy*

4. Use what you learned about the association between *agecat, class, satfin,* and *happy* in this chapter along with what you learned about the associations between *happy* and *sex, marital,* and *rcattend* in the previous exercises to write a paragraph that answers the question, What are the characteristics of people who tend to be happy?

Making Inferences Involving Numerical Variables

Do Americans watch too much television? That question has been a hot topic of discussion, particularly as it concerns the viewing habits of children. How much TV adults watch doesn't seem to be considered a problem like children's viewing often is. The reason may be that children are looked on as a more malleable audience, more easily swayed by what they see, whereas adults are assumed to be more discerning and less influenced by what they watch. Exactly how much *are* adults watching, and are there differences in how much adults watch by sex, age, and educational level? In the "News to Use" article you will find a summary of various studies that have examined the viewing habits of Americans—adults and children.

NEWS TO USE: Statistics in the "Real" World

Excerpts From The Media Awareness Network's "Statistics on Media Usage"[1]

U.S. FAMILY VIEWING HABITS

- Four of five (78%) adults in the United States consider watching TV with their children to be a family activity.

- More than a quarter (26%) watch television every night during dinner.

- 19% say they could not survive without television.

- 47% of households have a TV in a child's room.

[1]From the Media Awareness Center's website: <www.media-awareness.ca/eng/issues/stats/statuse.htm> (July 1998).

Source: The USSB Telescoop Survey, November 1995, conducted by United States Satellite Broadcasting (USSB).

GENDER TRENDS IN U.S. TV VIEWING PATTERNS

- Women outnumber men in the population, and generally watch more TV. Nielsen Media Research estimates that women in the U.S. number 100.6 million and tune in 4.5 hours daily. Men number 92.3 million and watch 40 minutes less a day.

- A Sept. 97 poll by the Los Angeles *Times* found that 40% of men change channels when a commercial comes on; only 28% of women do.

- Only 7% of men claim never to flip channels during a program, as opposed to 17% of women. But since (according to Nielsen) three quarters of U.S. households have two or more TV sets, women and men can coexist by watching separately.

Source: The Ottawa Citizen, April 14, 1998.

T.V. VIEWING TIME FOR CHILDREN

- Children average 2.55 hours of TV viewing per day, compared to an average of one hour for homework.

- Preschoolers watch an average of 2.6 hours a day, elementary school children average about 2.4 hours of TV viewing daily, and teenagers watch about 2.63 hours per day.

Source: "Television in the Home 1998: 3rd Annual National Survey of Parents and Children," by Annenberg Public Policy Center, June 22, 1998.

CHILDREN'S VIEWING HABITS

- 58% of children watch at least 2 hours of television a day.

- 66% live in a household with three or more television sets.

- 54% have a television set in their own room.

- 55% usually watch television alone or with friends, but not with their family.

- 44% watch different shows when alone than when they're with their parents (25% choose MTV).

Source: Sending Signals: Kids Speak Out About Values in the Media, 1995. A Children Now Poll, conducted by Fairbank, Maslin Maullin & Associates (USA).

TELEVISION USE AND LITERACY

- Those most likely to watch TV for significant periods of time are those at lower literacy levels. Over 10% of those in the lowest [level] watch more than 5 hours a day; over 20% of those at the highest level watch less than an hour a day.

Source: International Adult Literacy Survey (IALS), a collaboration between seven governments and three intergovernmental organizations, December 1995.

Let's start our exploration of this topic by finding out how much TV Americans are watching.

> **Skills Practice 1** Use SPSS to find the mean for the variable *tvhours*. What is the confidence interval for the mean at the 95% level? (Hint: Follow the command path Analyze ➡ Descriptive Statistics ➡ Explore to find out.)

Now let's look at some of the variables that may be associated with TV watching. Then we'll see whether any of these associations are likely to be found in the population of American adults that the General Social Survey represents. Like making inferences for associations involving categorical variables, making inferences for numerical variables involves the same hypothesis testing process introduced in Chapter 12 (p. 463). What is different when we are dealing with numerical variables is the test statistic. In addition, our assumptions about the null hypothesis change a little, and there are a few more concepts related to hypothesis testing you need to have a handle on.

CORE CONCEPTS FOR HYPOTHESIS TESTING WITH NUMERICAL VARIABLES

Directional and Nondirectional Hypotheses

To test hypotheses involving numerical variables, we have to understand the difference between two possible forms of the research hypothesis. Most commonly, research hypotheses specify the nature of an association. For example, we can hypothesize that men watch TV *more often* than do women. A hypothesis in this form is **directional,** because it tells us which category of the independent variable—males or females—is likely to score higher on the dependent variable, TV watching, than the other.

Another form of the research hypothesis states that there is a difference between groups of respondents in a sample, but we don't know the nature of the difference. For example, we can hypothesize that the average hours of television watching reported by men is different from the average hours reported by women. A research hypothesis in this form doesn't speculate about which group spends more time watching TV than the other. It is **nondirectional,** because it doesn't say anything about the nature of the association between the variables.

One- and Two-Tailed Tests of Significance

Whether a hypothesis is directional or nondirectional plays a role in how we determine if the null hypothesis can be rejected. Directional hypotheses require **one-tailed tests of significance,** whereas nondirectional hypotheses require **two-tailed tests of significance.**[2]

What do we mean by "tails"? To understand the concept of one-tailed and two-tailed tests, we have to go back to the concept of the normal distribution.

---

[2]Regardless of whether a hypothesis is directional or not, we test it using some sort of test statistic—a number, like chi-square, that is a sampling characteristic (or a characteristic of differences between samples) and whose sampling distribution is known.

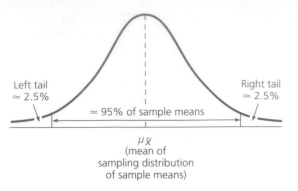

Left tail
≈ 2.5%

Right tail
≈ 2.5%

≈ 95% of sample means

$\mu_{\bar{X}}$
(mean of
sampling distribution
of sample means)

Figure 13.1 The tails of a normal distribution.

Recall from the discussion of inferential statistics in Chapters 10 and 11 that sampling statistics have distributions of their own. When samples are large enough, we can assume that these distributions are normal or close to normal. Using this assumption, we can assess the likelihood that a particular sampling statistic, the test statistic, has occurred in a particular sample due to chance. When we rule out the likelihood that a sampling statistic is nothing more than a chance occurrence, we assume that the pattern we observe in our sample is representative of the population from which the sample was drawn.

Let's go back to the way we tested the sampling mean as an example of the process. When we are assessing how likely it is that a particular sampling mean is representative of a particular population, we looked at where the sampling mean fell in a distribution of sampling statistics. When the sampling mean fell far away from the mean of the sampling distribution of sample means—in one of the tails of the normal distribution—we concluded that the sampling mean was less likely to be representative of the population. When the sampling mean was included in the 95% of sampling means that fell near the mean of the sampling distribution, we concluded that the sampling mean was more likely to be representative of the population. Figure 13.1 diagrams a normal distribution, the tails of the distribution, and a hypothetical sampling mean in relation to the mean of the sampling distribution of sample means.

Using a process like this one, we can assess whether test statistics for numerical variables are more or less likely to have occurred by chance. Keep in mind that we are always testing the null hypothesis—the hypothesis of no association. With research hypotheses that are directional, we can reject the null hypothesis if we can establish the probability of the test statistic being in one of the tails of the distribution—the one above or below the test statistic, depending on the specific research hypothesis.

With hypotheses that are nondirectional, we can reject the null hypothesis if we can establish the probability of the test statistic falling in either of the two tails. This process will be made clearer as we encounter some examples. We'll begin with testing Pearson's *r* for statistical significance.

TESTING PEARSON'S *r* FOR SIGNIFICANCE

Calculating and Interpreting the *t* Statistic for Pearson's *r*

In Chapter 9 you learned to use Pearson's *r* as a measure of association for numerical variables. Like the measures of association for categorical variables, Pearson's *r* tells us about the strength and direction of an association. Like the other measures of association, it can be used in conjunction with an inferential statistic to tell us whether or not any association we observe in a sample is just a chance occurrence.

The test statistic associated with Pearson's *r* is one of a group of statistics that can be tested with a particular distribution, called the distribution of Student's *t*. It is more commonly called the *t* statistic or the *t* test. It can be positive or negative in value (like *Z* scores), and its computation is fairly simple. Like chi-square, the *t* statistic has both an obtained and a critical value. The obtained value is the value of *t* we compute. The critical value is the value we must obtain in order to reject the null hypothesis for a set of data with a particular number of degrees of freedom.

FORMULA 13.1(A):   The *t* statistic for use with Pearson's *r*

$$t_o = r\sqrt{\frac{(N-2)}{1-r^2}}$$

where t_o is the obtained or computed value of the *t* statistic, *r* is Pearson's *r*, and *N* is the number of valid responses to the two variables being analyzed.

Example: Bearing in mind that Pearson's *r* is an assessment of the extent of the linear relationship between two variables, let's hypothesize that there is a linear relationship between age and the number of hours of television watched (a nondirectional hypothesis, because we aren't speculating about whether TV watching increases or decreases with age). The null hypothesis, the one we can test, is that there is no linear association between age and the number of hours spent watching television.

To evaluate our hypothesis, we can calculate the value of a test statistic, the obtained *t,* for the association between age and hours of television watched. To do so, we have to know the values of *r* and *N*. Let's find them using SPSS. The easiest way to do that is by producing Pearson's *r* using the correlation command. Follow the command path Analyze ➡ Correlate ➡ Bivariate. Enter the variables *age* and *tvhours* (the order doesn't matter). You will get a set of statistics, called a correlation matrix, like the one in Table 13.1.

In a correlation matrix, each variable you enter will be correlated against every other variable you enter: *age* will be correlated with *tvhours,* and *tvhours* with *age*. In addition, the matrix correlates *age* with itself and *tvhours* with itself.

TABLE 13.1   Correlation Matrix (With Pearson's *r*) for *age* and *tvhours* in the gss96subset File

Correlations

		AGE AGE OF RESPONDENT	TVHOURS HOURS PER DAY WATCHING TV
AGE AGE OF RESPONDENT	Pearson Correlation	1.000	.117**
	Sig. (2-tailed)	.	.000
	N	2898	1943
TVHOURS HOURS PER DAY WATCHING TV	Pearson Correlation	.117**	1.000
	Sig. (2-tailed)	.000	.
	N	1943	1947

**. Correlation is significant at the 0.01 level (2-tailed).

Note: Pearson's *r* and *N* for age and *tvhours* appear in two places.

Take a second to analyze the association between hours spent watching TV and age. What do you find? Based on Pearson's *r*, we know the association is positive—the older the respondents, the more time they spend watching TV. However, the relationship is fairly weak, at $r = .117$. Is this association one that is more likely due to chance or to a real relationship between age and TV watching in the population from which the GSS respondents were selected? As the first step toward finding out, we compute the test statistic, the *t* statistic, for Pearson's *r*.

Use Pearson's *r* and *N* in Formula 13.1(a):

$$N = 1{,}943 \qquad \text{Pearson's } r = .117$$

$$t_o = r\sqrt{\frac{(N - 2)}{1 - r^2}}$$

$$= .117\sqrt{\left(\frac{1{,}943 - 2}{1 - .117^2}\right)} = .117\sqrt{\frac{1{,}941}{1 - .014}}$$

$$= .117\sqrt{\frac{1{,}941}{.986}} = .117\sqrt{1{,}968.560}$$

$$= .117 \times 44.368$$

$$t_o = 5.191$$

Degrees of freedom   Like chi-square, the test statistic has to be interpreted in the context of the degrees of freedom for the variables involved. Degrees of freedom for Pearson's *r* are computed using the following formula.

FORMULA 13.1(B):   Degrees of freedom for Pearson's r

$$df = N - 2$$

Example: For the correlation matrix in Table 13.1, $df = N - 2 = 1{,}943 - 2 = 1{,}941$.

Interpretation   Generally, the t statistic for a specified number of degrees of freedom allows us to determine whether the association we see in a sample is more likely than not a chance occurrence. Keep in mind that, technically, we are always assessing the null hypothesis. In this case, the null hypothesis is that there is no linear association between *age* and *tvhours*. Expressed in terms of Pearson's r, the null hypothesis can be represented symbolically as:

$$H_0: r = 0$$

Alternatively, the research hypothesis is that age is associated with the self-reported number of hours spent watching television, or:

$$H_1: r \neq 0$$

We can answer the question, Is a t statistic as large as 5.196 for 1941 degrees of freedom likely to have occurred by chance in a sample drawn from a population in which there is no association between these variables?

As with chi-square, an obtained value of the t statistic has to be compared with a critical value for a given alpha level. With an obtained value of 5.196, what is the critical value of t we need to reject the null hypothesis at an alpha level of .05 (a likelihood of only 5 chances in 100 that our association occurred by chance)? To find out, we have to use a table of the distribution of the critical values of t (like the table of critical values of chi-square). The table itself is huge; there is an abbreviated version of the t distribution table in Appendix C.

For 1941 degrees of freedom, we have to have reached at least a t statistic of 1.960 (two-tailed) in order to reject the null hypothesis. (Notice that for all associations with more than 120 degrees of freedom the t statistics are substantially alike, so no breakdown is given for $df > 120$.) Our value of t is higher than 1.960, so we can reject the null hypothesis.

Let's explore the idea of two-tailed versus one-tailed tests a little more, beginning with the logic of the two-tailed test. To do so, we need to return to the normal distribution. The t statistic is a sampling characteristic, and as such, it has its own sampling distribution. For large samples (sample sizes larger than 120), it approximates the normal distribution. We can chart the distribution of t values on a normal curve, like the one in Figure 13.2.

In a distribution of t values for which no association between two variables exists, we would expect the mean and median of the distribution to be zero. Ninety-five percent of all t values would fall in the range of values 2 standard deviations below the mean to 2 standard deviations above it. If our sample was drawn from a population in which there was no linear association

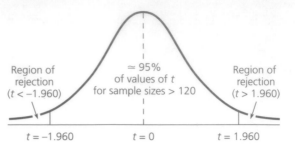

Figure 13.2   Normal distribution of *t* values for *df* > 120 and *p* = .05.

between *age* and *tvhours,* then we would expect that 95 times out of 100, an obtained *t* would fall in the range of *t* values between −1.960 and +1.960. Our *t* value clearly falls outside this range.

Our *t* statistic, 5.191, is above +1.960, so it falls in one of the tails of the distribution, also called the **region of rejection.** If a test statistic falls within this area, we can reject the null hypothesis. Remember that the region of rejection for a two-tailed test can include positive or negative values of the *t* statistic, and when we do the computations for *t* you will see that you can get positive or negative *t* statistics. We can reject the null hypothesis if *t* exceeds the critical value in either tail of the distribution—the positive or the negative. When a test statistic falls within the region of rejection, there are less than 5 chances in 100 that our sample could have been drawn from a population in which there was no linear association between the variables of interest. It would therefore be more likely than not that our sample was drawn from a population in which age was related to hours spent watching television.

For the one-tailed test, using a directional hypothesis, we make the same assumptions about the normal distribution. However, the region of rejection changes. Let's assume we hypothesized that older respondents watched more television than younger respondents, a positive association between the variables *age* and *tvhours.* To reject the null hypothesis, we would, first of all, have to come up with a positive value of *t.* Consequently, the region of rejection must include all negative values of the *t* statistic. (Why? Because we hypothesized a positive, not a negative association.) Remember that 50% of the area under the normal curve falls below the mean. Forty-five percent of the remaining possible values of *t* will fall between the mean and the critical value of *t* of 1.646. The other 5% will be in the positive tail of the distribution (more than 1.645). Consequently, to reject the null hypothesis, we would have to have a *t* statistic greater than 1.645 to conclude that there are less than 5 chances in 100 that our sample came from a population in which there is no association between age and TV watching. Figure 13.3 shows the distribution of *t* for a one-tailed test.

Like chi-square, the *t* statistic is a measure of inference rather than of strength or direction. When we use it, it has to be in conjunction with appropriate measures of association (Pearson's *r* and *r*-squared in this case). A more

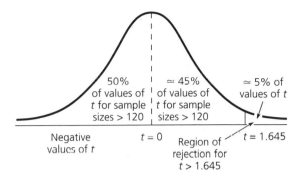

Figure 13.3 Distribution of the *t* statistic for a one-tailed test with *df* > 120 and *p* = .05.

complete interpretation of the association between *age* and *tvhours* would be something along these lines:

> A Pearson's *r* of .117 indicates a fairly weak association between a respondent's age and the number of hours he or she watches television. Moreover, the *r*-squared of .014 tells us that only a little over 1% of the variation in hours of TV watching among the respondents can be explained by how old the respondents are. However, with a value of *t* equal to 5.191 and 1941 degrees of freedom, we have enough evidence to reject the null hypothesis at the .05 level. Consequently, it is more likely than not that the association we observed in our sample—the older the respondents are, the more hours they report watching television—will be found in the population of American adults represented by the General Social Survey.

Skills Practice 2   Let's explore another research hypothesis: one's level of educational achievement is related to the number of hours one watches TV. Find the *t* statistic for the association between *educ* and *tvhours*. Follow the command path Analyze ➡ Correlate ➡ Bivariate to obtain Pearson's *r* and *N*, then use them in Formula 13.1(a). Interpret the results. Assume that the critical value of *t* that you need to reject the null hypothesis at the .05 level is 1.960.

Limitations of Pearson's *r*

Pearson's *r* can be used to analyze variables

1. for which we can assume a normal distribution of values for both variables in the population from which the sample was drawn.

2. that appear to have a linear association with one another (as observed in a scatterplot).

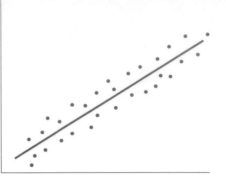

Figure 13.4 A homoscedastic association.

3. that are **homoscedastic** in relation to one another. This means that the values of the dependent variable need to be distributed evenly along a line drawn through the data, with about as many values of the dependent variable falling above the line as below it. Figure 13.4 shows how a homoscedastic association would look on a scatterplot.

When you are deciding whether Pearson's *r* is appropriate or not, you can look at a scatterplot for the association between two variables. If it looks more cigar-shaped than circular, then you can test Pearson's *r* with the *t* statistic.

FINDING THE *t* STATISTIC USING SPSS

SPSS Guide: Finding the *t* Statistic for Pearson's *r*

Getting the *t* statistic is easy. You don't have to do anything more than request a linear regression. With your gss96subset file open, follow the command path Analyze ➥ Regression ➥ Linear. Select your dependent and independent variables. Let's use *age* and *tvhours*. Then click on OK.

You should get a set of output like the one in Table 13.2. (It will be familiar to you from your work in Chapter 9. There will be more output on your screen than is displayed in Table 13.2, so look for the charts that match the ones in the table). You should know how to find and interpret Pearson's *r* and *r*-squared. You should also know where to locate the slope and the *y*-intercept and how to use them to predict values of the dependent variable given values of the independent variable. What we will add is an understanding of the *t* statistic for Pearson's *r*.

TABLE 13.2 Regression Statistics, With the *t* Statistic and Its *p* Value, for *age* and *tvhours* in the gss96subset File

Model Summary

Model	R	R Square	Adjusted R Square	Std. Error of the Estimate
1	.117[a]	.014	.013	2.37

a. Predictors: (Constant), AGE AGE OF RESPONDENT

t statistic for Pearson's *r*

p value

Coefficients[a]

Model		Unstandardized Coefficients		Standardized Coefficients	t	Sig.
		B	Std. Error	Beta		
1	(Constant)	2.218	.152		14.555	.000
	AGE AGE OF RESPONDENT	.017	.003	.117	5.207	.000

a. Dependent Variable: TVHOURS HOURS PER DAY WATCHING TV

The value of the *t* statistic (5.207) is listed next to the Standardized Coefficients—Beta (which we learned in Chapter 9 is the same as Pearson's *r*). Next to the value of the *t* statistic is the *p* value of .000 ($p < .0005$, two-tailed) associated with a statistic of that magnitude for the specified degrees of freedom. These numbers tell us that there are less than 5 chances in 10,000 that a *t* statistic of 5.207 with 1941 degrees of freedom could have been obtained by chance in a sample drawn from a population in which there is no linear association between age and number of hours spent watching TV. We can reject the null hypothesis.

We can use the *p* value for the two-tailed test to make an assessment of the directional research hypothesis that the older respondents are, the more television they watch. All you have to do is divide the *p* value for the two-tailed test in half. Thus, the likelihood that we could have obtained a *t* statistic of 5.207 with 1941 degrees of freedom from a population with no linear association between *age* and *tvhours* is still very small, because the *p* of .0005 ÷ 2 = .00025). The null hypothesis is rejected.

Skills Practice 3 Use SPSS to find and interpret the *t* statistic and its *p* value for the association between *educ* and *tvhours*. Assume your research hypothesis is that there is an association between respondents' educational achievements and the number of hours they watch television.

In addition to testing the relationships between numerical variables to see whether patterns in samples are likely to be found in populations, we can test differences in means, like the difference between the sample and population means and the differences between means for groups within a sample (like men and women). In the next section you will learn to apply inferential statistics to examine individual sampling means (like the average number of hours spent watching TV) and associations between means (like the difference between the average number of hours men spend watching TV as compared to the average number of hours women spend).

TESTING DIFFERENCES IN MEANS FOR STATISTICAL SIGNIFICANCE

You have already learned to compute means for samples (in Chapter 5), and you learned to compare means (in Chapter 9). Now we will find out the likelihood that a mean for a single variable is representative of the population from which it was drawn. Then we will do the same thing for differences in means. Who watches more TV—men or women? Is the difference we find in our sample likely to be a reflection of differences in the population of American adults from which the sample was drawn?

The One-Sample *t* Test

In Chapters 10 and 11 you learned about one way to test the representativeness of sampling statistics when you learned to compute confidence intervals around means and proportions. There are other ways to test for the representativeness of means. One of them is a test statistic called the one-sample *t* test.

Avoiding Common Pitfalls   A word about terminology: The use of the word "sample" may be confusing. In the one-sample *t* test, we are making the assumption that the respondents to a single variable constitute one sample. Consequently, the one-sample *t* test refers to a test performed on the respondents to a single variable. It may make more sense for you to think of the test as the "one-*variable t* test."

The **one-sample** *t* test allows us to answer the question, How likely is it that the mean for our sample is different from the mean for the population from which the sample was drawn? In terms of the null hypothesis, we can test the proposition that the sample mean is *no different from* the population mean. The *t* statistic for one sample is fairly easy to find.

FORMULA 13.2(A): t statistic for the one-sample t test

$$\text{one-sample } t \text{ statistic} = \frac{\overline{X}}{\sigma_{\overline{X}}}$$

where $\overline{X}$ is the sample mean, and $\sigma_{\overline{X}}$ is the standard error of the mean.

We know (from Chapter 10, Formula 10.5) that the standard error of the mean is:

$$\sigma_{\overline{X}} = \frac{\sigma}{\sqrt{N}}$$

For the purpose of computing the one-sample t statistic, we can read Formula 13.2(a) as:

$$\text{one-sample } t \text{ statistic} = \frac{\overline{X}}{\dfrac{s}{\sqrt{N}}}$$

where $\overline{X}$ is the mean for the sample; s is the standard deviation for the sample, representing the standard deviation of the population (σ) from which the sample was drawn; and N is the number of respondents in the sample.

Example: Let's find the t statistic for one sample—the GSS respondents to the variable *tvhours*. Follow the command path Analyze ➡ Descriptive Statistics ➡ Descriptives to find N, the mean, and the standard deviation for the variable *tvhours*. You should get a table of statistics like Table 13.3. Use these values in your formula for the one-sample t statistic.

$\overline{X}$ (sample mean for *tvhours*) = 2.96 s (sample standard deviation) = 2.38

$$N = 1{,}947$$

$$\text{one-sample } t \text{ statistic} = \frac{\overline{X}}{\dfrac{s}{\sqrt{N}}}$$

$$= \frac{2.96}{\dfrac{2.38}{\sqrt{1{,}947}}} = \frac{2.96}{\dfrac{2.38}{44.1248}}$$

$$= \frac{2.96}{.0539} = 54.92$$

TABLE 13.3 Descriptive Statistics for *tvhours*

Descriptive Statistics

	N	Minimum	Maximum	Mean	Std. Deviation
TVHOURS HOURS PER DAY WATCHING TV	1947	0	24	2.96	2.38
Valid N (listwise)	1947				

Degrees of freedom   Like other test statistics, the one-sample *t* test has to be interpreted along with its associated degrees of freedom. The computation in this case is simple.

FORMULA 13.2(B):   Degrees of freedom for the one-sample *t* test

$$df = N - 1$$

Example: The degrees of freedom associated with the variable *tvhours* in the GSS sample is:

$$df = N - 1 = 1{,}947 - 1 = 1{,}946$$

Interpretation   What do we do with the one-sample *t* statistic and its degrees of freedom? Keep in mind what we are testing: the research hypothesis that the sample mean represents the population mean, a nondirectional hypothesis. The null hypothesis is that the sample mean is no different from the population mean.

In this case, our sample is the set of respondents to the variable *tvhours*. The mean is the average number of hours of television watched per day by these respondents, 2.96. What is the likelihood we would obtain a *t* statistic of 54.92 with 1946 degrees of freedom for this mean in a sample drawn from a population in which the mean is substantially *different* from the sample mean? To put it another way, how likely is it that we would obtain by chance a sampling mean different from the population mean? If it is highly likely, then we can reject the null hypothesis, that the sample and population means are equivalent. If it is not very likely, we accept the null hypothesis that the sample and population means are equivalent.

To find this likelihood, we have to arrive at a critical value of *t*—the value *t* must reach to establish that, at a given level of alpha, the null hypothesis can be rejected. As with other tests, we normally use .05 as our alpha value. The critical value of the *t* statistic for 1946 degrees of freedom at the .05 level is ±1.960. Our *t* value is much higher than 1.960. Consequently, we can conclude that there are less than 5 chances in 100 that we would get a *t* statistic of 54.92 with 1946 degrees of freedom when the population mean is substantially different from the sample mean. The odds are fairly low that our sample mean is not representative of the population mean, so the null hypothesis—that the sample mean and the population mean are equal—is accepted.

> **Skills Practice 4**   Use SPSS to get the descriptive statistics (follow the command path Analyze ➥ Descriptive Statistics ➥ Descriptives) for *age*. Calculate the one-sample *t* statistic for the variable *age*. If the critical *t* for 2897 degrees of freedom at an alpha level of .05 is ±1.960, can we reject the null hypothesis that the sample mean and the population mean are equal?

Let's use SPSS to check our work and see how we did.

SPSS Guide: The One-Sample *t* Test

With your gss96subset file open, follow the command path Analyze ➥ Compare Means ➥ One-Sample T Test to open the One Sample T Test dialog box. Select the variable *tvhours*. Click on OK.

You will find a set of statistics like the ones in Table 13.4 in your Output window.

Interpretation   This table tells us that the *t* statistic is 54.79 (slightly lower than the one we computed by hand, because we rounded off the mean and standard deviation and SPSS doesn't). We see that the degrees of freedom are 1946, as we thought. For a *t* statistic of this magnitude and these degrees of freedom, the likelihood that we would have drawn by chance a sample with a mean substantially different from the population mean is less than 5 chances

TABLE 13.4 One-Sample *t* Test for *tvhours* in the gss96subset File

One-Sample Statistics

	N	Mean	Std. Deviation	Std. Error Mean
TVHOURS HOURS PER DAY WATCHING TV	1947	2.96	2.38	.0540

One-Sample Test

	Test Value = 0					
					95% Confidence Interval of the Difference	
	t	df	Sig. (2-tailed)	Mean Difference	Lower	Upper
TVHOURS HOURS PER DAY WATCHING TV	54.789	1946	.000	2.96	2.85	3.07

t statistic   Degrees of freedom   *p* value   Mean   Confidence limits at 95% level

in 10,000 (because *p* < .0005). These are fairly good odds, so we do accept the null hypothesis (that the sample mean and the population mean are equivalent). We can be fairly confident that our sample mean is an accurate indication of the population mean.

Skills Practice 5   Use SPSS to perform the one-sample *t* test for the variable *age.* How do the results compare with your computation by hand?

Differences in Means for Two Samples: The Independent Samples *t* Test

The "News to Use" article says that women watch more TV than men (surprising considering the stereotype of men glued to the TV watching sports while their houses burn down around them). Does this pattern show up among the GSS respondents? If so, is it generalizable to the larger population of American adults? To see whether this pattern exists and to make sure it's not accidental, we will employ a statistic called the independent samples *t* test.

The **independent samples *t* test** assesses the differences between the means—or averages—of one dependent, numerical variable, which we will call the **test variable,** when it is grouped by a second, independent variable that we will call the **grouping variable.** This idea of grouping should be familiar to you—it's what we did when we used the Split File command to divide the GSS into groups based on variables like *sex,* and it is what we did when we used the Compare Means command. When we group our GSS respondents by the categories of a variable like *sex,* we can look at differences in average hours of TV watching between males and females. Then we can assess the sampling distribution of the difference in the sampling means for each group.

Avoiding Common Pitfalls   Another word about terminology: The independent samples *t* test treats the respondents to each of the categories of the independent or grouping variables involved in the test as separate samples. For example, if you are examining the test variable *tvhours* to see who watches more television, males or females, you are treating the variable *sex* as an independent, grouping variable. You are, in effect, dividing the respondents into two groups—males and females—to see who watches more TV. For the independent samples *t* test, we make the assumption that each of these groups, males and females, is an independently selected sample of respondents. With the independent samples *t* test, you might want to think of the separate samples as categories of a variable.

Like other sampling statistics, the difference in two means has a sampling distribution. The sampling distribution of differences in means is assumed to be normal for sample sizes over 100. This means that there have to be at least 100 respondents, combined, to the categories of the variable for which we are finding means. In this case, we need at least 100 males and females to assume that the sampling distribution of the differences in means is normal.

With this in mind, let's begin by being clear about our research hypothesis. Suppose we speculate that men and women differ in the number of hours they watch television (a nondirectional hypothesis). Our null hypothesis is that there is no difference for men and women in the number of hours spent watching television. The *t* test allows us to assess the likelihood that any difference in average hours spent watching TV in our sample is representative of real differences in our population (American adults).

The formulas for understanding the *t* test look a little more complicated than they really are. They begin with the assumption that the sampling distribution of differences in sample means can be tested with a *Z* score, like the one we used to analyze the distribution of means in Chapter 11.

FORMULA 13.3(A):   *Z* scores for the sampling distribution of the differences in sample means

$$Z = \frac{\overline{X}_1 - \overline{X}_2}{\sigma_{\overline{X}_1 - \overline{X}_2}}$$

where $\overline{X}_1$ is the mean of the first sample (or group), $\overline{X}_2$ is the mean of the second sample (or group), and $\sigma_{\overline{X}_1 - \overline{X}_2}$ is the standard error of the sampling distribution of differences in sample means.

The problem is that we don't know the standard error of the sampling distribution of the differences in means. (Remember that the sampling distribution of anything is theoretical, consisting of the distribution of a statistic in all possible samples of a certain size that could conceivably be drawn from a single population.) We must estimate the standard deviation of the sampling distribution of the differences in sample means with one of two formulas. When we do so, we change the nature of the statistic. In essence, its distribution changes, from one that can be represented by the distribution of Z scores, to one that is better represented by the distribution of Student's t.

If we can assume that the two samples (or groups) with which we are dealing have similar variances on the variable of interest (TV watching, in this case), then we use a formula to estimate the standard error of the sampling distribution of the differences in means that assumes equality of variances. (You can look to see whether the variances in two groups are similar. I will show you how to do that later in this chapter.)

FORMULA 13.3(B): Standard deviation of the sampling distribution of the differences in sample means for samples in which the variances are assumed to be equal

$$\sigma_{\overline{X}-\overline{X}} = \sqrt{\frac{s_p^2}{N_1} + \frac{s_p^2}{N_2}}$$

where s_p^2 is the weighted average of the variances in each sample or group, N_1 is the number of respondents in the first sample (or group), and N_2 is the number of respondents in the second sample (or group).

To find the weighted averages of the variances (s_p^2), we use the following formula:

FORMULA 13.3(C): The weighted average of variances

$$s_p^2 = \frac{(N_1 - 1)s_1^2 + (N_2 - 1)s_2^2}{(N_1 + N_2) - 2}$$

where N_1 is the number of cases in the first sample or group, s_1 is the standard deviation of the variable of interest in the first sample or group, N_2 is the number of cases in the second sample or group, and s_2 is the standard deviation of the variable of interest in the second sample or group.

Substitute Formula 13.3(b) for the denominator in the formula for the Z scores of the distribution of the differences in sample means (Formula 13.3a). With this modification, it becomes Formula 13.3(d), which we use to find the t statistic, assuming equality of variances between the two samples (or groups) being compared. Formula 13.3(d) (also called the **pooled variance t test**) is Formula 13.3(a) with Formula 13.3(b) replacing its denominator.

FORMULA 13.3(D): Pooled variance *t* test for independent samples

$$\text{obtained pooled } t = \frac{\overline{X}_1 - \overline{X}_2}{\sqrt{\dfrac{s_p^2}{N_1} + \dfrac{s_p^2}{N_2}}}$$

Example: Your head may be swimming at this point, as you try to figure out where to begin to approach calculation of the *t* test statistic. Let's try to simplify the process. All you need to work the formula are the following pieces of information:

   Two categories of a grouping variable for which the means on a dependent, test variable are known

   The number of respondents in each category of the grouping variable

   The standard deviations of the distributions of the test variable in each category of the grouping variable

If we want to know whether there is a difference between men and women on the variable hours spent watching TV, we need to have the following:

   The average number of hours spent watching TV for men and women

   The number of men and women in the sample

   The standard deviations for the distributions of hours spent watching TV for men and for women

These pieces of information are easily obtained using SPSS by following the command path Analyze ➡ Compare Means ➡ Means.

Skills Practice 6 Use the command path Analyze ➡ Compare Means ➡ Means to find the means and standard deviation for males and females in the General Social Survey (gss96subset) file. Your independent variable is *sex* and your dependent variable is *tvhours*. You should be looking at a set of statistics like the following.

Report

TVHOURS HOURS PER DAY WATCHING TV

SEX RESPONDENTS SEX	Mean	N	Std. Deviation
1 MALE	2.78	856	2.13
2 FEMALE	3.11	1091	2.56
Total	2.96	1947	2.38

Plug these numbers into the formula for the obtained t statistic. You will have to first find s_p^2. This isn't nearly as difficult as it appears. Use Formula 13.3(c):

$$N_1 \text{ (males)} = 856 \qquad s_1 \text{ (standard deviation, males)} = 2.13$$
$$N_2 \text{ (females)} = 1{,}091 \qquad s_2 \text{ (standard deviation, females)} = 2.56$$

$$s_p^2 = \frac{(N_1 - 1)s_1^2 + (N_2 - 1)s_2^2}{(N_1 + N_2) - 2}$$

$$= \frac{(856 - 1)2.13^2 + (1{,}091 - 1)2.56^2}{(856 + 1{,}091) - 2}$$

$$= \frac{(856 - 1)4.5369 + (1{,}091 - 1)6.5536}{(856 + 1{,}091) - 2}$$

$$= \frac{(855)4.5369 + (1{,}090)6.5536}{(1{,}947) - 2}$$

$$= \frac{3{,}879.0495 + 7{,}143.4240}{1{,}945}$$

$$= \frac{11{,}022.473}{1{,}945}$$

$$s_p^2 = 5.67$$

Use s_p^2 in Formula 13.3(d) for the pooled t test, along with the means from the table in Skills Practice 6.

$$\overline{X}_1 \text{ (males)} = 2.78 \qquad \overline{X}_2 \text{ (females)} = 3.11$$
$$s_p^2 \text{ from Formula 13.3(c)} = 5.67$$
$$N_1 \text{ (males)} = 856 \qquad N_2 \text{ (females)} = 1{,}091$$

$$\text{obtained pooled } t = \frac{\overline{X}_1 - \overline{X}_2}{\sqrt{\dfrac{s_p^2}{N_1} + \dfrac{s_p^2}{N_2}}}$$

$$= \frac{2.78 - 3.11}{\sqrt{\dfrac{5.67}{856} + \dfrac{5.67}{1{,}091}}} = \frac{-.33}{\sqrt{.0066 + .0052}}$$

$$= \frac{-.33}{\sqrt{.0118}} = \frac{-.33}{.1086}$$

$$\text{obtained pooled } t = -3.04$$

We cannot interpret the t statistic without the degrees of freedom that accompany it.

Degrees of freedom   Finding degrees of freedom for the independent samples t test is easy.

FORMULA 13.3(E):   Degrees of freedom for the t statistic for independent samples

$$df = N_1 + N_2 - 2$$

Example: For the relationship between sex and TV watching,

$$df = 856 + 1,091 - 2 = 1,945$$

You may recognize the result from the denominator in Formula 13.3(c).

Interpretation   The independent samples t test answers the question, How likely is it that we would obtain a t statistic of -3.04 (with 1945 degrees of freedom) in samples drawn from a population in which there is really no difference between the means for men and women on the variable *hours spent watching television*? To answer the question, we need to decide the following:

1.   Will we apply the one- or two-tailed test of significance?

2.   What will our acceptable alpha level be?

Remember that our research hypothesis—there is a difference between men and women in the average number of hours of television watched—is nondirectional. Consequently, we use the two-tailed test of significance.

The most commonly used cut-off is an alpha level of .05. This means that we want there to be no more than 5 chances in 100 that a test statistic of this size could be found by chance in samples drawn from a population in which there are no differences in means. To reach an alpha level of .05, a two-tailed test of significance requires that we reach a critical t value of at least ± 1.960. Our t statistic is somewhat larger than -1.960. Consequently, there is sufficient evidence to reject the null hypothesis. Alternatively, we assume that there is a difference between men and women on the variable *hours spent watching TV*—men watch fewer hours of TV than women, similar to the "News to Use" statistics.

Remember that the t statistic is a measure of inference only. We have to ask ourselves whether the difference between men and women is of any practical significance. Men watch an average of 2.78 hours of television, whereas women watch an average of 3.11 hours, a difference of one third of an hour (20 minutes)—not a very large difference.

Skills Practice 7   Use SPSS to compare the means for the dependent variable *tvhours* for the independent variable *rchilds* (a variable you created for a Skills Practice in Chapter 5). With the statistics you obtain, compute the t statistic. Assume your research hypothesis is that there are differences in how many hours people who have no children watch TV compared to those who do have children. If the critical t statistic for the appropriate degrees of freedom is ± 1.960 at alpha level .05 (for the two-tailed test), should we reject or accept the null hypothesis?

What if the variances aren't equal? In the preceding computations, we have assumed that the variances are equal between men and women for hours spent watching TV. What if they aren't? Then you use a different formula for the t statistic that assumes the variances are not equal, the t **test for unequal variances.**

FORMULA 13.3(F): t statistic assuming unequal variances

$$t \text{ (unequal variances)} = \frac{\bar{X}_1 - \bar{X}_2}{\sqrt{\dfrac{s_1^2}{N_1} + \dfrac{s_2^2}{N_2}}}$$

where s_1 is the standard deviation of the first sample (or group), N_1 is the number of respondents in the first sample (or group), s_2 is the standard deviation of a second sample (or group), and N_1 is the number of respondents in the second sample (or group).

Example: Let's use the statistics in the report in Skills Practice 6 to find obtained t with Formula 13.3(f), the formula for samples with unequal variances.

$$\bar{X}_1 \text{ (males)} = 2.78 \qquad\qquad \bar{X}_2 \text{ (females)} = 3.11$$

s_1 (standard deviation, males) $= 2.13$ $\quad$ s_2 (standard deviation, females) $= 2.56$

$$N_1 \text{ (males)} = 856 \qquad\qquad N_2 \text{ (females)} = 1,091$$

$$t \text{ (unequal variances)} = \frac{\bar{X}_1 - \bar{X}_2}{\sqrt{\dfrac{s_1^2}{N_1} + \dfrac{s_2^2}{N_2}}}$$

$$= \frac{2.78 - 3.11}{\sqrt{\dfrac{2.13^2}{856} + \dfrac{2.56^2}{1,091}}}$$

$$= \frac{-.33}{\sqrt{\dfrac{4.5369}{856} + \dfrac{6.5536}{1,091}}}$$

$$= \frac{-.33}{\sqrt{.0053 + .0060}}$$

$$= \frac{-.33}{\sqrt{.0113}}$$

$$= \frac{-.33}{.1063}$$

$$t \text{ (unequal variances)} = -3.10$$

Now let's have a look at how SPSS computes the independent samples t test. We'll use the variables *sex* and *age* to see whether SPSS confirms our computations of the t values for pooled variances and for unequal variances.

SPSS Guide: Conducting the Independent Samples t Test

With your gss96subset file open, follow the command path Analyze ➡ Compare Means ➡ Independent Samples T Test.

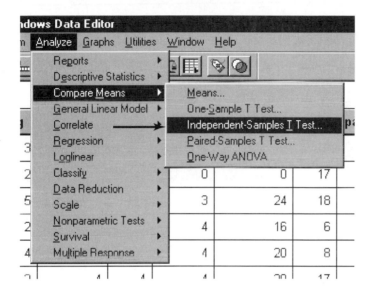

The Independent Samples T Test dialog box opens.

❶ Select a test variable, the numerical variable *tvhours.*

❷ Select a grouping variable (the independent samples, usually a categorical variable). Use *sex* in this example. Note that you get two question marks in the Grouping Variables box when you select your grouping variable. SPSS wants to know the values of the categories by which you want to group the variable *sex.*

③ Click on Define Groups and open the Define Groups window to enter the values.

④ Type in 1 for the value of the category Male.

⑤ Type in 2 for the value of the category Female.

⑥ Click on Continue.

⑦ At the Independent Samples T Test dialog box, click on OK.

You will get a set of statistics like the ones in Table 13.5.

You get a great deal of information. In the first box, labeled Group Statistics, you get the means, the standard deviations, and the standard errors of the means for both groups or samples—one for males, one for females. You can

TABLE 13.5 Independent Samples *t* test for Grouping Variable *sex* and Test Variable *tvhours* From the gss96subset File

Group Statistics

	SEX RESPONDENTS SEX	N	Mean	Std. Deviation	Std. Error Mean
TVHOURS HOURS PER DAY WATCHING TV	1 MALE	856	2.78	2.13	.07
	2 FEMALE	1091	3.11	2.56	.08

Independent Samples Test

		Levene's Test for Equality of Variances		t-test for Equality of Means						95% Confidence Interval of the Difference	
		F	Sig.	t	df	Sig. (2-tailed)	Mean Difference	Std. Error Difference	Lower	Upper
TVHOURS HOURS PER DAY WATCHING TV	Equal variances assumed	6.855	.009	-3.035	1945	.002	-.33	.11	-.54	-.12
	Equal variances not assumed			-3.101	1937.647	.002	-.33	.11	-.54	-.12

Test statistic for equality of variances (*F* statistic)   *p* value for the *F* statistic   *t* statistic assuming equality of variances   *t* statistic if equality of variances cannot be assumed   Degrees of freedom   *p* values for *t* statistics

see whether there is any difference between the means for the two groups on the variable of interest, *tvhours,* and how large the difference is.

In the second box, labeled Independent Samples Test, you get the *t* statistic, degrees of freedom, and associated *p* values for the *t* statistics computed for pooled variances (top line) and unequal variances (bottom line).

Interpretation What do we learn from all of this information? First, note the size of the difference between the average hours of TV watching for males as compared to females. We can say that, based on a comparison of means, females tend to watch a little more TV than do males. The size of the difference is small, a third of an hour, or a little more than 20 minutes. Assuming equal variances in the hours of TV watched for males and females, a *t* statistic of −3.035 with 1945 degrees of freedom is likely to occur by chance less than 2 times in 1,000 ($p = .002$). Consequently, we have sufficient evidence to reject the null hypothesis that there are no differences in the average hours of TV watching for males and females in the population from which the sample was drawn.

Determining whether the variances are really equal Based on what we observed in our sample, we assumed an equality of variances among male and female respondents to the variable of hours spent watching TV. Moreover, we assumed that the equality of variances observed in the sample is representative of the population. Are we safe in making these assumptions? We can find out by using a statistic to test the null hypothesis that variances in TV hours watched for men and women are equal. To test this null hypothesis, we need a test statistic (**Levene's test for equality of variances**), its degrees of freedom, and p value.

The first line of the Independent Samples Test output shows us the test statistic, F. With Levene's test statistic and its associated probability value, we can answer the question, How likely is it that we would obtain a sample with unequal variances by chance from a population in which the variances are equal? The smaller the p value that is associated with the test statistic, the less likely it is that differences in variances found in a sample are due to chance. The larger the p value is, the more likely it is that differences in variances are due to chance. In this case, we have an F statistic of 6.855 with a p value of .009, suggesting that it is unlikely that chance alone could produce a sample of unequal variances from a population in which the variances are equal. Consequently, we are not allowed to assume that the variances in TV watching are equal for males and females in the population of American adults. As a result, the t statistic in the second line of the Independent Samples Test output, the t statistic for equal variances not assumed, is the most appropriate one to use for analyzing the association between *sex* and *tvhours*.

Had the p value been large—more than an alpha level of .05—then it would be more likely than not that the variances in the population are equal. We would use the first line of the Independent Samples Test output in our analysis of the association between *sex* and *tvhours*.

Skills Practice 8   Test the null hypothesis that there are no differences in average number of hours of TV watched between those who have children and those who don't. Use *rchilds* and *tvhours* to perform the independent samples t test using SPSS. Can we assume equality of variances?

ANALYSIS OF VARIANCE

So far, you've learned how to use measures of inference with two numerical variables, with single numerical variables, and with numerical variables that are grouped by two categories of some other variable. What do you do when you want to analyze a variable by a categorical variable that has more than two categories? You use the **one-way analysis of variance** (sometimes called by its acronym, ANOVA).

Analysis of variance is based on assumptions similar to those of the *t* test for independent samples. It explores the likelihood that you could obtain a set of different means for an independent (test) variable in a sample when there is no difference in those means in a population. For example, suppose we want to know whether TV watching is related to social class. We could conduct an analysis of variance to see whether the average hours of TV watched is different for those who identify themselves as members of the lower class, the working class, the middle class, and the upper class. If we found that, in fact, the means for the variable *tvhours* differed from one social class to another, we next want to know whether these differences are more likely due to chance or are the result of real differences in the average number of hours of TV watching among members of different social classes in the population. Analysis of variance helps us to find the answers.

How Analysis of Variance Works

Analysis of variance, like the *t* test, involves the computation of a test statistic that has a known distribution. The test statistic for analysis of variance is called an *F* ratio. It assesses the ratio of variance in an independent, test variable *between* categories of a second grouping variable as compared to the variance *within* categories of the grouping variable. For example, in pursuing the issue of class differences in average hours spent watching TV, we would assess the variances in hours spent watching TV between categories of the variable *class* as compared to variances in hours spent watching TV within each category of the variable *class*. If there is greater variance between categories than there is within categories, we will get an *F* ratio greater than 1.00.

FORMULA 13.4: *F* ratio

$$F \text{ ratio} = \frac{\text{mean square estimates between categories}}{\text{mean square estimates within categories}}$$

Variations between and within categories are assessed using differences in mean squares. I will show you what this means as we go through the process of how the *F* ratio is computed. Although some of the computations are fairly straightforward, some are very complex. I am presenting the formulas and examples in this section for conceptual, rather than computational, understanding. The computation of the *F* ratio begins with the differences in mean squares between categories.

Differences in mean squares between categories   The differences in means between categories of a variable are assessed with the formula

$$\Sigma[N_k(\overline{X}_k - \overline{X})^2]$$

where N_k is the number of cases in a particular category (number of upper-class respondents, for example), $\overline{X}_k$ is the mean of the responses to a variable for a single category (average hours spent watching TV of upper-class respondents), and $\overline{X}$ is the mean across all categories of a given variable (mean for the variable *tvhours* for all respondents).

The formula requires that the difference between each category mean and the mean for all respondents be squared. Then each of the squared differences for each of the categories is multiplied by the number of respondents in the category. Finally, the results are added up to get the sum of the squares of the weighted differences in means between categories.

For example, to get the "between" category means for *tvhours* and *class,* you would need to know the number of respondents in each category, the mean for each category, and the mean for all respondents, regardless of class. You can find these easily with the Analyze ➡ Compare Means ➡ Means command path in SPSS, which produces a set of statistics like those in Table 13.6. To find the "between" category differences in means, start with the category Lower Class.

Step 1.   Subtract the mean for all categories from the mean for the lower-class respondents:

$$3.95 - 2.96 = .99$$

Step 2.   Square the result:

$$.99 \times .99 = .9801$$

Step 3.   Multiply the result by the number of lower-class respondents:

$$.9801 \times 112 = 109.7712$$

Repeat the process for each of the categories, then add up the results for each of the categories. As you soon will see, SPSS computes this number for you when it calculates the F ratio.

Differences in mean squares within categories   Differences in means within categories are computed using the formula

$$\Sigma(N_k - 1)s_k^2$$

where N_k is the number of respondents in a single category of the grouping variable, and s_k^2 is the variance (the standard deviation squared) for the distribution of the independent (test) variable in a single category of the grouping variable.

TABLE 13.6 Comparison of Means for the Variables *class* and *tvhours* in the gss96subset File

Report

TVHOURS HOURS PER DAY WATCHING TV

CLASS SUBJECTIVE CLASS IDENTIFICATION	Mean	N	Std. Deviation	
1 LOWER CLASS	3.95	112	2.80	N_k
2 WORKING CLASS	3.06	875	2.42	$\bar{X}_k$
3 MIDDLE CLASS	2.80	869	2.28	
4 UPPER CLASS	2.23	78	2.00	$\bar{X}$
Total	2.96	1934	2.38	

The formula requires us to find the variance (square the standard deviation) for a given category of the grouping variable and multiply the result by the number of respondents to the category minus 1. Repeat the process for each category of the grouping variable. Then add up the results.

Using the descriptive statistics in Table 13.6, start the process with the category Lower Class.

Step 1. Find the variance for *tvhours* among the lower-class respondents:

$$s^2 = 2.80^2 = 7.84$$

Step 2. Find $N_k - 1$:

$$112 - 1 = 111$$

Step 3. Multiply the variance times $N_k - 1$:

$$7.84 \times 111 = 870.24$$

Repeat the process for each category of the grouping variable, *class,* and add up the results. As you will see shortly, SPSS computes this value, too.

Degrees of Freedom

Like other test statistics, the *F* ratio has to be interpreted in light of the degrees of freedom involved. Unlike other test statistics, the *F* ratio uses two different computations of the degrees of freedom: one for the "between" category means and one for the "within" category means.

Degrees of freedom between categories   The degrees of freedom between categories is very simple to find. It is the number of categories (4, in this case) minus 1. The formula is

$$\text{degrees of freedom between categories} = k - 1$$

where k is the number of categories.

Degrees of freedom within categories   The degrees of freedom within categories is found by subtracting the number of categories from N. The formula is

$$\text{degrees of freedom within categories} = N - k$$

where N is the number of respondents, and k is the number of categories. For the relationship between *tvhours* and *class,* the degrees of freedom within categories is $1,934 - 4 = 1,930$.

Computing the *F* Ratio From the Mean Square Estimates

To get the mean square estimates between categories and within categories, the mean squares are divided by their associated degrees of freedom. For example, to get the mean square estimates for the mean squares differences between categories, you divide the mean square differences by the degrees of freedom for between category differences. The between category mean square differences for the association between *tvhours* and *class* is 181.419 with 3 degrees of freedom, so the mean estimate of between square differences is 60.473 ($181.419 \div 3 = 60.473$). The within category mean square differences is 10,799.594 with 1930 degrees of freedom, so the mean square estimate of the within category differences is 5.596 ($10,799.594 \div 1,930 = 5.596$).

The mean square estimates are plugged into the *F* ratio formula to find the *F* ratio:

$$F \text{ ratio} = \frac{\text{mean square estimates between categories}}{\text{mean square estimates within categories}}$$

$$= 60.473 \div 5.596$$

$$= 10.81$$

The *F* ratio is interpreted in relation to a critical value or *p* value of *F*. I will show you how to interpret the *F* ratio when I introduce the SPSS computations of the statistic.

A Limitation of One-Way Analysis of Variance

Unlike the *t* test, one-way analysis of variance assumes equality of variances. Consequently, the application of analysis of variance must include an evaluation of this assumption. Are we safe in assuming that the variances in the distribution of a variable among groups in a population are equal? In this case, can we assume that the variances in hours spent watching TV are the same among social classes, or do some groups show more (or less) heterogeneity than others? I will show you how to make this assessment when we examine the one-way analysis of variance statistics using SPSS.

Using SPSS for Analysis of Variance

Like other inferential statistics, analysis of variance begins with a research hypothesis and a null hypothesis. Let's explore the research hypothesis that there are differences among members of the lower, working, middle, and upper classes in the average number of hours of TV they watch. Our null hypothesis, by way of contrast, is that there are no differences among social classes in the mean hours of TV watched. Because the computations involved in the analysis of variance are complex, it is highly unlikely you would attempt them by hand. It is far more likely that you will turn to a computer for help, as we will do now.

SPSS Guide: Analysis of Variance

Follow the command path Analyze ➡ Compare Means ➡ One-Way ANOVA.

The One-Way ANOVA dialog box opens.

① Select your dependent (numerical) variable, *tvhours*.

② Select your grouping variable, *class*.

③ Click on Options to open the One-Way ANOVA: Options window.

④ Click on Descriptive.

⑤ Click on Homogeneity-of-Variance.

⑥ Click on Continue to return to the One-Way ANOVA dialog box.

At the One-Way ANOVA dialog box, click on OK. You will see a set of output like that in Table 13.7.

TABLE 13.7   Analysis of Variance for *class* and *tvhours* in the gss96subset File

Descriptives

TVHOURS HOURS PER DAY WATCHING TV

	N	Mean	Std. Deviation	Std. Error	95% Confidence Interval for Mean		Minimum	Maximum
					Lower Bound	Upper Bound		
1 LOWER CLASS	112	3.95	2.80	.26	3.42	4.47	0	18
2 WORKING CLASS	875	3.06	2.42	.08	2.90	3.22	0	24
3 MIDDLE CLASS	869	2.80	2.28	.08	2.65	2.95	0	20
4 UPPER CLASS	78	2.23	2.00	.23	1.78	2.68	0	12
Total	1934	2.96	2.38	.05	2.85	3.07	0	24

Test of Homogeneity of Variances

TVHOURS HOURS PER DAY WATCHING TV   — Test statistic for equality of variances

Levene Statistic	df1	df2	Sig.
2.623	3	1930	.049

p value for test for equality of variances

Between category mean squares   Degrees of freedom   Mean square estimate

ANOVA

TVHOURS HOURS PER DAY WATCHING TV   — F statistic for ANOVA

	Sum of Squares	df	Mean Square	F	Sig.
Between Groups	181.419	3	60.473	10.807	.000
Within Groups	10799.594	1930	5.596		
Total	10981.013	1933			

p value for F statistic

Within category mean squares   Degrees of freedom   Mean square estimate

Interpretation   What do we learn from all of this output? First, note the differences in the means for each category of the variable *class*. To see them, look in the chart labeled Descriptives and find the column for Mean. What do you see? The means vary from one class to another, generally decreasing. As social class increases, the average number of hours TV is watched decreases. Respondents who identify themselves as lower class watch the most TV with an average of 3.95 hours. Members of the middle class watch the least, at 2.23 hours. The difference is nearly two hours. The differences by social class are fairly large ones.

Can we assume that the variances among the social classes in the number of hours TV is watched come from a population in which the variances are equal or unequal? To answer this question, we move down to the next chart, Test of

Homogeneity of Variances. Using Levene's statistic and its associated p value (and interpreting them as we did for equality of variances in the independent samples t test), we can answer the question, How likely is it that we would obtain unequal variances by chance in a sample from a population in which the variances are equal? In this case, we see that the odds are low that we could get unequal variances by chance alone. Therefore, we cannot assume that the sample we have drawn comes from a population in which the variances in the number of hours of TV watching are equal among the social classes.

Nevertheless, let's see how likely it is that the differences in the means we are finding in our sample come from a population in which there is no difference in means. In terms of the null hypothesis, how likely is it that we could draw a sample by chance showing the differences in means we see here from a population in which there is no difference in mean hours of TV watched from one social class to another? The test statistic we use to assess the null hypothesis—the F ratio—is reported in the ANOVA chart, the third chart on your screen. In addition, you see the p value associated with the reported F ratio, .000. There are less than 5 chances in 10,000 that the differences we are finding in our sample could occur by chance. If we establish an alpha of .05 as our critical value, then we have more than met the standard for rejecting the null hypothesis. It is highly unlikely that we have by chance drawn a sample that shows differences in mean hours of TV watched, even when there are no differences in the population.

Skills Practice 9 Test the research hypothesis that there are differences in the average number of hours spent watching TV by educational achievement. Specify the null hypothesis. Then test it using *tvhours* and *degree* with the one-way analysis of variance feature in SPSS. Can we assume equality of variances? Assuming you can make that assumption, what does the F ratio tell you?

SUMMARY

In this chapter you learned to compute, by hand and using SPSS, measures of inference for numerical variables. As with measures of association for categorical variables, the process begins by computing a test statistic, Student's t (the t statistic), for most of the measures. Student's t has a distribution, like chi-square. We can compare the obtained or computed value of the t statistic against the critical values of the t statistic to assess the likelihood of obtaining a computed t strictly by chance.

We performed this procedure for single variables (using the one-sample t test) and for several measures of association: Pearson's r; the independent samples t test, and the one-way analysis of variance.

KEY CONCEPTS

Directional research hypothesis

Nondirectional research hypothesis

One-tailed test of significance

Two-tailed test of significance

Region of rejection

Homoscedastic

One-sample *t* test

Independent samples *t* test

Test variable

Grouping variable

Pooled variance *t* test

t test for unequal variances

Levene's test for equality of variances

One-way analysis of variance (ANOVA)

ANSWERS TO SKILLS PRACTICES

1. The statistics you get with the Explore command should look like these:

Descriptives

			Statistic	Std. Error
TVHOURS HOURS PER DAY WATCHING TV	Mean		2.96	.05
	95% Confidence Interval for Mean	Lower Bound	2.85	
		Upper Bound	3.07	
	5% Trimmed Mean		2.70	
	Median		2.00	
	Variance		5.684	
	Std. Deviation		2.38	
	Minimum		0	
	Maximum		24	
	Range		24	
	Interquartile Range		2.00	
	Skewness		2.787	.055
	Kurtosis		13.658	.111

The respondents watch an average of nearly 3 hours of television a day (which is about the same amount as their kids, as reported in the "News to Use" article). There are 95 chances in 100 that the population mean—the number of television hours watched by all adult Americans, 18 or older, who are English-speaking and noninstitutionalized—falls somewhere between 2.85 and 3.07.

2. Your correlation matrix for *tvhours* and *educ* should look like this:

Correlations

		EDUC HIGHEST YEAR OF SCHOOL COMPLETED	TVHOURS HOURS PER DAY WATCHING TV
EDUC HIGHEST YEAR OF SCHOOL COMPLETED	Pearson Correlation	1.000	-.244**
	Sig. (2-tailed)	.	.000
	N	2895	1942
TVHOURS HOURS PER DAY WATCHING TV	Pearson Correlation	-.244**	1.000
	Sig. (2-tailed)	.000	.
	N	1942	1947

**. Correlation is significant at the 0.01 level (2-tailed).

Use the statistics in Formula 13.1(a):

$$t_o = r\sqrt{\frac{(N-2)}{1-r^2}}$$

$$= -.244\sqrt{\frac{(1,942-2)}{1-.244^2}} = -.244\sqrt{\frac{1,940}{1-.060}}$$

$$= -.244\sqrt{\frac{1,940}{.94}} = -.244\sqrt{2,063.8297}$$

$$= -.244 \times 45.4294$$

$$t_o = -11.08$$

The more education a respondent has, the less TV the respondent watches. The association is weak to moderate (Pearson's $r = -.244$). Variations among respondents' years of education account for about 6% of the variations in hours of TV watched. With a t statistic of -11.08 and 1940 degrees of freedom, the critical value of t, ± 1.960, is exceeded. Consequently, the null hypothesis (that there is no linear association between education and hours spent watching television) is rejected. We can assume, therefore, that the association we see in the sample is more likely than not present in the population of American adults.

3. You should get regression statistics for *educ* and *tvhours* like these:

Model Summary

Model	R	R Square	Adjusted R Square	Std. Error of the Estimate
1	.244ª	.060	.059	2.31

a. Predictors: (Constant), EDUC HIGHEST YEAR OF
SCHOOL COMPLETED

Coefficients[a]

Model		Unstandardized Coefficients		Standardized Coefficients	t	Sig.
		B	Std. Error	Beta		
1	(Constant)	5.647	.248		22.800	.000
	EDUC HIGHEST YEAR OF SCHOOL COMPLETED	-.201	.018	-.244	-11.095	.000

a. Dependent Variable: TVHOURS HOURS PER DAY WATCHING TV

The *t* statistic of −11.095 (a little higher than the one we computed by hand) with a *p* value of .000 tells us that the likelihood of finding the *t* statistic of −11.905 in a sample drawn from a population in which there is no linear association between education and TV watching is less than .0005 (5 chances in 10,000). Consequently, we have sufficient evidence to reject the null hypothesis.

4. The descriptive statistics you obtain with SPSS should look like these:

Descriptive Statistics

	N	Minimum	Maximum	Mean	Std. Deviation
AGE AGE OF RESPONDENT	2898	18	89	44.78	16.87
Valid N (listwise)	2898				

Use the formula for the one-sample *t* statistic:

$$\text{one-sample } t\text{-statistic} = \frac{\overline{X}}{\dfrac{s}{\sqrt{N}}}$$

$$= \frac{44.78}{\dfrac{16.87}{\sqrt{2{,}898}}} = \frac{44.78}{\dfrac{16.87}{53.8331}}$$

$$= \frac{44.78}{.3134} = 142.88$$

The degrees of freedom = $N - 1 = 2{,}898 - 1 = 2{,}897$. Our value of t far exceeds the critical value. We can be very confident that it is not likely we would obtain a t statistic of this magnitude at 2897 degrees of freedom by chance from a sample drawn from a population with a substantially different mean. The null hypothesis, that the sample mean and population mean are equal, is accepted. We assume, therefore, that our sample mean is representative of the population mean.

5. You should get a set of statistics like these:

One-Sample Statistics

	N	Mean	Std. Deviation	Std. Error Mean
AGE AGE OF RESPONDENT	2898	44.78	16.87	.31

One-Sample Test

	Test Value = 0					
					95% Confidence Interval of the Difference	
	t	df	Sig. (2-tailed)	Mean Difference	Lower	Upper
AGE AGE OF RESPONDENT	142.906	2897	.000	44.78	44.16	45.39

What do we learn? The chances are less than 5 in 10,000 ($p < .0005$) that a sample with a t statistic of 142.906 and 2897 degrees of freedom could have been selected by chance from a population with a different mean than the one we see in our sample. The null hypothesis, that the sample and population means are equal, is accepted. We can assume that the sampling mean, the average age of 44.78, is an accurate representation of the adult population from which the sample was drawn.

7. With the Compare Means command, you should get a set of statistics like these:

Report

TVHOURS HOURS PER DAY WATCHING TV

RCHILDS recoded childs variable	Mean	N	Std. Deviation
0 Has no children	2.70	540	2.15
1 Has children	3.06	1397	2.46
Total	2.96	1937	2.39

To compute the t statistic, start with the formula (assuming equality of variances) for the t statistic for pooled variances:

$$\text{obtained pooled } t = \frac{\overline{X}_1 - \overline{X}_2}{\sqrt{\dfrac{s_p^2}{N_1} + \dfrac{s_p^2}{N_2}}}$$

The means and the N for each sample are in the set of statistics you obtained with the Compare Means procedure. You need to compute s_p^2 using the following formula:

$$s_p^2 = \frac{(N_1 - 1)s_1^2 + (N_2 - 1)s_2^2}{(N_1 + N_2) - 2}$$

$$= \frac{(540 - 1)2.15^2 + (1,397 - 1)2.46^2}{(540 + 1,397) - 2}$$

$$= \frac{(539)4.6225 + (1,397)6.0516}{(1,937) - 2} = \frac{2,491.5275 + 8,454.0852}{1,935}$$

$$= \frac{10,945.612}{1,935}$$

$$s_p^2 = 5.66$$

Use s_p^2 in the formula for the pooled t test:

$$\text{obtained pooled } t = \frac{\overline{X}_1 - \overline{X}_2}{\sqrt{\dfrac{s_p^2}{N_1} + \dfrac{s_p^2}{N_2}}}$$

$$= \frac{2.70 - 3.06}{\sqrt{\dfrac{5.66}{540} + \dfrac{5.66}{1,397}}} = \frac{-.36}{\sqrt{.0105 + .0041}}$$

$$= \frac{-.36}{\sqrt{.0146}} = \frac{-.36}{.1208}$$

$$\text{obtained pooled } t = -2.98$$

The degrees of freedom are computed as follows:

$$df = N_1 + N_2 - 2 = 540 + 1,397 - 2 = 1,935$$

Interpretation First, we should note that the differences in the means is small. Respondents with children watch a little more television (one third of an hour more) than those without children. However, it is likely that this is not merely a chance difference. With a t value of -2.73 and

1935 degrees of freedom, we exceed the critical *t* value of ±1.960 (two-tailed) needed to reject the null hypothesis at the .05 level. There are no more than 5 chances in 100 that the difference in the means we see in our sample is an accident of sampling. In short, we have enough evidence to rule out the possibility that the differences in the means we find in our samples is simply a chance occurrence. It is more likely than not a result of real differences in TV watching between those with no children and those with children in the population of American adults from which the sample was drawn.

8. Your output from the independent samples *t* test should look like this:

Group Statistics

	RCHILDS recoded childs variable	N	Mean	Std. Deviation	Std. Error Mean
TVHOURS HOURS PER DAY WATCHING TV	0 Has no children	540	2.70	2.15	.09
	1 Has children	1397	3.06	2.46	.07

Independent Samples Test

		Levene's Test for Equality of Variances		t-test for Equality of Means							
										95% Confidence Interval of the Difference	
		F	Sig.	t	df	Sig. (2-tailed)	Mean Difference	Std. Error Difference	Lower	Upper
TVHOURS HOURS PER DAY WATCHING TV	Equal variances assumed	2.553	.110	-2.942	1935	.003	-.35	.12	-.59	-.12
	Equal variances not assumed			-3.122	1112.881	.002	-.35	.11	-.58	-.13

Interpretation There is a difference in the average number of hours spent watching TV between those respondents with children and those with no children, but it's small—only about .36 hour. The appropriate *t* statistic assumes equal variances. There are 11 chances in 100 that we could obtain a sample with unequal variances by chance from a population in which the variances are equal. Consequently, we may assume the variances are equal. The *t* statistic for equal variances is −2.942, and the likelihood of obtaining samples with differing means purely by chance from a population in which the means are equal is low: $p = .003$. The null hypothesis is rejected. Those with children watch more TV as compared to those with no children.

9. Our null hypothesis is that there are no differences in average number of hours spent watching TV based on levels of education. Your output should include the following.

Descriptives

TVHOURS HOURS PER DAY WATCHING TV

	N	Mean	Std. Deviation	Std. Error	95% Confidence Interval for Mean		Minimum	Maximum
					Lower Bound	Upper Bound		
0 LT HIGH SCHOOL	293	3.88	2.91	.17	3.55	4.22	0	22
1 HIGH SCHOOL	1068	3.10	2.43	.07	2.95	3.24	0	24
2 JUNIOR COLLEGE	117	2.57	1.68	.16	2.27	2.88	0	10
3 BACHELOR	314	2.23	1.77	.10	2.03	2.42	0	13
4 GRADUATE	154	2.03	1.62	.13	1.77	2.28	0	12
Total	1946	2.96	2.38	.05	2.85	3.07	0	24

Test of Homogeneity of Variances

TVHOURS HOURS PER DAY WATCHING TV

Levene Statistic	df1	df2	Sig.
14.092	4	1941	.000

ANOVA

TVHOURS HOURS PER DAY WATCHING TV

	Sum of Squares	df	Mean Square	F	Sig.
Between Groups	591.587	4	147.897	27.428	.000
Within Groups	10466.206	1941	5.392		
Total	11057.793	1945			

Interpretation There seems to be a clear pattern among the differences in means. The more education respondents have, the fewer hours they spend watching television. The difference is fairly large between the respondents with the least and most education, over an hour and a half per day. Can we assume the equality of variances necessary to conduct an analysis of variance? No, we cannot, because the odds are low ($p < .0005$ for Levene's statistic) that we could have obtained unequal variances by chance from a population in which variances in the number of hours of TV watching are equal among those with different levels of education. Had we been able to assume equality of variances, the F ratio would tell us about the likelihood that we could have obtained differences in means in a sample by chance even though there are no differences in means in the population. The chances are less than 5 in 10,000 ($p < .0005$). The null hypothesis, that there are no differences in means by levels of education in the population, would have been rejected.

GENERAL EXERCISES

1. For the following correlation matrix, state the null hypothesis. Interpret Pearson's *r*. Then compute the *t* statistic and its associated degrees of freedom. Assume that the critical value of the *t* statistic at the .05 level is ±1.960, and interpret your results. Can the null hypothesis be rejected?

Correlations

		TVHOURS HOURS PER DAY WATCHING TV	HRS1 NUMBER OF HOURS WORKED LAST WEEK
TVHOURS HOURS PER DAY WATCHING TV	Pearson Correlation	1.000	-.119**
	Sig. (2-tailed)	.	.000
	N	1947	1320
HRS1 NUMBER OF HOURS WORKED LAST WEEK	Pearson Correlation	-.119**	1.000
	Sig. (2-tailed)	.000	.
	N	1320	1935

**. Correlation is significant at the 0.01 level (2-tailed).

2. For the following correlation matrix, state the null hypothesis. Interpret Pearson's *r*. Then compute the *t* statistic and its associated degrees of freedom. Assume that the critical value of the *t* statistic at the .05 level is ±1.960, and interpret your results. Can the null hypothesis be rejected?

Correlations

		TVHOURS HOURS PER DAY WATCHING TV	PAEDUC HIGHEST YEAR SCHOOL COMPLETED, FATHER
TVHOURS HOURS PER DAY WATCHING TV	Pearson Correlation	1.000	-.139**
	Sig. (2-tailed)	.	.000
	N	1947	1392
PAEDUC HIGHEST YEAR SCHOOL COMPLETED, FATHER	Pearson Correlation	-.139**	1.000
	Sig. (2-tailed)	.000	.
	N	1392	2066

**. Correlation is significant at the 0.01 level (2-tailed).

Use the following table to do the computations in General Exercises 3–5. For each variable, compute the *t* statistic and its associated degrees of freedom. Assuming that the critical value of *t* at the .05 level is ±1.960, interpret the *t* statistic. Can the null hypothesis be rejected?

Descriptive Statistics

	N	Minimum	Maximum	Mean	Std. Deviation
CHILDS NUMBER OF CHILDREN	2889	0	8	1.83	1.68
EDUC HIGHEST YEAR OF SCHOOL COMPLETED	2895	0	20	13.36	2.93
HRS1 NUMBER OF HOURS WORKED LAST WEEK	1935	2	89	42.35	14.14
Valid N (listwise)	1921				

3. *Number of children.*

4. *Highest year of school completed.*

5. *Number of hours worked last week.*

For the reports in Exercises 6 and 7, state the null hypothesis for the association between the variables. Use the statistics in the report to calculate the independent samples *t* statistic (assuming equality of variances) and its associated degrees of freedom. Next, assume that the critical value of *t* at the .05 level is ±1.960, and interpret the *t* statistics. Can you reject the null hypothesis?

6.

Report

TVHOURS HOURS PER DAY WATCHING TV

DICONFED dichotomized confidence in executive	Mean	N	Std. Deviation
0 hardly any confidence	3.16	427	2.68
1 at least some	2.95	510	2.25
Total	3.05	937	2.46

7.

Report

TVHOURS HOURS PER DAY WATCHING TV

DICONLEG dichotomized confidence in legislature	Mean	N	Std. Deviation
0 hardly any confidence	3.22	447	2.45
1 at least some	2.91	500	2.44
Total	3.06	947	2.45

SPSS EXERCISES

For the variables in Exercises 1 and 2, state the null hypothesis. Use the command path Analyze ➡ Regression ➡ Linear to find Pearson's r and the associated t statistics. Then interpret your results. Can the null hypothesis be rejected?

1. *tvhours* and *sphrs1*

2. *tvhours* and *maeduc*

Use SPSS to conduct and interpret the one-sample t test for the variables in Exercises 3–5.

3. *childs*

4. *educ*

5. *hrs1*

6. Conduct and interpret the independent samples t test for the association between *diconfed* (your dichotomized variable created in Chapter 11) and *tvhours*. Can we assume equality of variances? Can the null hypothesis be rejected?

7. Conduct and interpret the independent samples t test for the association between *diconleg* (your dichotomized variable created in Chapter 11) and *tvhours*. Can we assume equality of variances? Can the null hypothesis be rejected?

For Exercises 8–11, use SPSS to perform a one-way analysis of variance for the given variables. Begin by stating the null hypothesis for each pair. Then use SPSS to obtain and interpret the relevant statistics (descriptives, test for equality of variance, and ANOVA).

8. *tvhours* and *race*

9. *tvhours* and *wrkstat*

10. *tvhours* and *marital*

11. *tvhours* and *vote92*

12. Use what you have learned in this chapter and the exercises to write a profile of those who seem to spend the most time watching television.

A Area Under the Normal Curve

Column (a) lists Z scores from 0.00 to 4.00. Only positive scores are displayed, but, because the normal curve is symmetrical, the areas for negative scores will be exactly the same as areas for positive scores. Column (b) lists the proportion of the total area between the Z score and the mean. Figure A.1 displays areas of this type. Column (c) lists the proportion of the area beyond the Z score, and Figure A.2 displays this type of area.

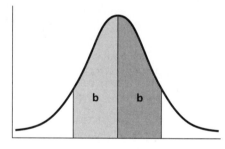

Figure A.1 Area between mean and Z.

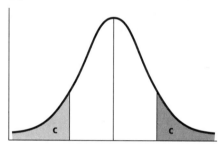

Figure A.2 Area beyond Z.

(a)	(b) Area Between Mean and Z	(c) Area Beyond Z	(a)	(b) Area Between Mean and Z	(c) Area Beyond Z
Z			Z		
0.00	0.0000	0.5000	0.11	0.0438	0.4562
0.01	0.0040	0.4960	0.12	0.0478	0.4522
0.02	0.0080	0.4920	0.13	0.0517	0.4483
0.03	0.0120	0.4880	0.14	0.0557	0.4443
0.04	0.0160	0.4840	0.15	0.0596	0.4404
0.05	0.0199	0.4801	0.16	0.0636	0.4364
0.06	0.0239	0.4761	0.17	0.0675	0.4325
0.07	0.0279	0.4721	0.18	0.0714	0.4286
0.08	0.0319	0.4681	0.19	0.0753	0.4247
0.09	0.0359	0.4641	0.20	0.0793	0.4207
0.10	0.0398	0.4602			

(a)	(b) Area Between Mean and Z	(c) Area Beyond Z	(a)	(b) Area Between Mean and Z	(c) Area Beyond Z
Z			Z		
0.21	0.0832	0.4168	0.71	0.2611	0.2389
0.22	0.0871	0.4129	0.72	0.2642	0.2358
0.23	0.0910	0.4090	0.73	0.2673	0.2327
0.24	0.0948	0.4052	0.74	0.2703	0.2297
0.25	0.0987	0.4013	0.75	0.2734	0.2266
0.26	0.1026	0.3974	0.76	0.2764	0.2236
0.27	0.1064	0.3936	0.77	0.2794	0.2206
0.28	0.1103	0.3897	0.78	0.2823	0.2177
0.29	0.1141	0.3859	0.79	0.2852	0.2148
0.30	0.1179	0.3821	0.80	0.2881	0.2119
0.31	0.1217	0.3783	0.81	0.2910	0.2090
0.32	0.1255	0.3745	0.82	0.2939	0.2061
0.33	0.1293	0.3707	0.83	0.2967	0.2033
0.34	0.1331	0.3669	0.84	0.2995	0.2005
0.35	0.1368	0.3632	0.85	0.3023	0.1977
0.36	0.1406	0.3594	0.86	0.3051	0.1949
0.37	0.1443	0.3557	0.87	0.3078	0.1922
0.38	0.1480	0.3520	0.88	0.3106	0.1894
0.39	0.1517	0.3483	0.89	0.3133	0.1867
0.40	0.1554	0.3446	0.90	0.3159	0.1841
0.41	0.1591	0.3409	0.91	0.3186	0.1814
0.42	0.1628	0.3372	0.92	0.3212	0.1788
0.43	0.1664	0.3336	0.93	0.3238	0.1762
0.44	0.1700	0.3300	0.94	0.3264	0.1736
0.45	0.1736	0.3264	0.95	0.3289	0.1711
0.46	0.1772	0.3228	0.96	0.3315	0.1685
0.47	0.1808	0.3192	0.97	0.3340	0.1660
0.48	0.1844	0.3156	0.98	0.3365	0.1635
0.49	0.1879	0.3121	0.99	0.3389	0.1611
0.50	0.1915	0.3085	1.00	0.3413	0.1587
0.51	0.1950	0.3050	1.01	0.3438	0.1562
0.52	0.1985	0.3015	1.02	0.3461	0.1539
0.53	0.2019	0.2981	1.03	0.3485	0.1515
0.54	0.2054	0.2946	1.04	0.3508	0.1492
0.55	0.2088	0.2912	1.05	0.3531	0.1469
0.56	0.2123	0.2877	1.06	0.3554	0.1446
0.57	0.2157	0.2843	1.07	0.3577	0.1423
0.58	0.2190	0.2810	1.08	0.3599	0.1401
0.59	0.2224	0.2776	1.09	0.3621	0.1379
0.60	0.2257	0.2743	1.10	0.3643	0.1357
0.61	0.2291	0.2709	1.11	0.3665	0.1335
0.62	0.2324	0.2676	1.12	0.3686	0.1314
0.63	0.2357	0.2643	1.13	0.3708	0.1292
0.64	0.2389	0.2611	1.14	0.3729	0.1271
0.65	0.2422	0.2578	1.15	0.3749	0.1251
0.66	0.2454	0.2546	1.16	0.3770	0.1230
0.67	0.2486	0.2514	1.17	0.3790	0.1210
0.68	0.2517	0.2483	1.18	0.3810	0.1190
0.69	0.2549	0.2451	1.19	0.3830	0.1170
0.70	0.2580	0.2420	1.20	0.3849	0.1151

(b) Z	(c) Area Between Mean and Z	(a) Area Beyond Z	(b) Z	(c) Area Between Mean and Z	(a) Area Beyond Z
1.21	0.3869	0.1131	1.71	0.4564	0.0436
1.22	0.3888	0.1112	1.72	0.4573	0.0427
1.23	0.3907	0.1093	1.73	0.4582	0.0418
1.24	0.3925	0.1075	1.74	0.4591	0.0409
1.25	0.3944	0.1056	1.75	0.4599	0.0401
1.26	0.3962	0.1038	1.76	0.4608	0.0392
1.27	0.3980	0.1020	1.77	0.4616	0.0384
1.28	0.3997	0.1003	1.78	0.4625	0.0375
1.29	0.4015	0.0985	1.79	0.4633	0.0367
1.30	0.4032	0.0968	1.80	0.4641	0.0359
1.31	0.4049	0.0951	1.81	0.4649	0.0351
1.32	0.4066	0.0934	1.82	0.4656	0.0344
1.33	0.4082	0.0918	1.83	0.4664	0.0336
1.34	0.4099	0.0901	1.84	0.4671	0.0329
1.35	0.4115	0.0885	1.85	0.4678	0.0322
1.36	0.4131	0.0869	1.86	0.4686	0.0314
1.37	0.4147	0.0853	1.87	0.4693	0.0307
1.38	0.4162	0.0838	1.88	0.4699	0.0301
1.39	0.4177	0.0823	1.89	0.4706	0.0294
1.40	0.4192	0.0808	1.90	0.4713	0.0287
1.41	0.4207	0.0793	1.91	0.4719	0.0281
1.42	0.4222	0.0778	1.92	0.4726	0.0274
1.43	0.4236	0.0764	1.93	0.4732	0.0268
1.44	0.4251	0.0749	1.94	0.4738	0.0262
1.45	0.4265	0.0735	1.95	0.4744	0.0256
1.46	0.4279	0.0721	1.96	0.4750	0.0250
1.47	0.4292	0.0708	1.97	0.4756	0.0244
1.48	0.4306	0.0694	1.98	0.4761	0.0239
1.49	0.4319	0.0681	1.99	0.4767	0.0233
1.50	0.4332	0.0668	2.00	0.4772	0.0228
1.51	0.4345	0.0655	2.01	0.4778	0.0222
1.52	0.4357	0.0643	2.02	0.4783	0.0217
1.53	0.4370	0.0630	2.03	0.4788	0.0212
1.54	0.4382	0.0618	2.04	0.4793	0.0207
1.55	0.4394	0.0606	2.05	0.4798	0.0202
1.56	0.4406	0.0594	2.06	0.4803	0.0197
1.57	0.4418	0.0582	2.07	0.4808	0.0192
1.58	0.4429	0.0571	2.08	0.4812	0.0188
1.59	0.4441	0.0559	2.09	0.4817	0.0183
1.60	0.4452	0.0548	2.10	0.4821	0.0179
1.61	0.4463	0.0537	2.11	0.4826	0.0174
1.62	0.4474	0.0526	2.12	0.4830	0.0170
1.63	0.4484	0.0516	2.13	0.4834	0.0166
1.64	0.4495	0.0505	2.14	0.4838	0.0162
1.65	0.4505	0.0495	2.15	0.4842	0.0158
1.66	0.4515	0.0485	2.16	0.4846	0.0154
1.67	0.4525	0.0475	2.17	0.4850	0.0150
1.68	0.4535	0.0465	2.18	0.4854	0.0146
1.69	0.4545	0.0455	2.19	0.4857	0.0143
1.70	0.4554	0.0446	2.20	0.4861	0.0139

(b)	(c)	(a)		(b)	(c)	(a)
	Area	Area			Area	Area
	Between	Beyond			Between	Beyond
Z	Mean and Z	Z		Z	Mean and Z	Z
2.21	0.4864	0.0136		2.71	0.4966	0.0034
2.22	0.4868	0.0132		2.72	0.4967	0.0033
2.23	0.4871	0.0129		2.73	0.4968	0.0032
2.24	0.4875	0.0125		2.74	0.4969	0.0031
2.25	0.4878	0.0122		2.75	0.4970	0.0030
2.26	0.4881	0.0119		2.76	0.4971	0.0029
2.27	0.4884	0.0116		2.77	0.4972	0.0028
2.28	0.4887	0.0113		2.78	0.4973	0.0027
2.29	0.4890	0.0110		2.79	0.4974	0.0026
2.30	0.4893	0.0107		2.80	0.4974	0.0026
2.31	0.4896	0.0104		2.81	0.4975	0.0025
2.32	0.4898	0.0102		2.82	0.4976	0.0024
2.33	0.4901	0.0099		2.83	0.4977	0.0023
2.34	0.4904	0.0096		2.84	0.4977	0.0023
2.35	0.4906	0.0094		2.85	0.4978	0.0022
2.36	0.4909	0.0091		2.86	0.4979	0.0021
2.37	0.4911	0.0089		2.87	0.4979	0.0021
2.38	0.4913	0.0087		2.88	0.4980	0.0020
2.39	0.4916	0.0084		2.89	0.4981	0.0019
2.40	0.4918	0.0082		2.90	0.4981	0.0019
2.41	0.4920	0.0080		2.91	0.4982	0.0018
2.42	0.4922	0.0078		2.92	0.4982	0.0018
2.43	0.4925	0.0075		2.93	0.4983	0.0017
2.44	0.4927	0.0073		2.94	0.4984	0.0016
2.45	0.4929	0.0071		2.95	0.4984	0.0016
2.46	0.4931	0.0069		2.96	0.4985	0.0015
2.47	0.4932	0.0068		2.97	0.4985	0.0015
2.48	0.4934	0.0066		2.98	0.4986	0.0014
2.49	0.4936	0.0064		2.99	0.4986	0.0014
2.50	0.4938	0.0062		3.00	0.4986	0.0014
2.51	0.4940	0.0060		3.01	0.4987	0.0013
2.52	0.4941	0.0059		3.02	0.4987	0.0013
2.53	0.4943	0.0057		3.03	0.4988	0.0012
2.54	0.4945	0.0055		3.04	0.4988	0.0012
2.55	0.4946	0.0054		3.05	0.4989	0.0011
2.56	0.4948	0.0052		3.06	0.4989	0.0011
2.57	0.4949	0.0051		3.07	0.4989	0.0011
2.58	0.4951	0.0049		3.08	0.4990	0.0010
2.59	0.4952	0.0048		3.09	0.4990	0.0010
2.60	0.4953	0.0047		3.10	0.4990	0.0010
2.61	0.4955	0.0045		3.11	0.4991	0.0009
2.62	0.4956	0.0044		3.12	0.4991	0.0009
2.63	0.4957	0.0043		3.13	0.4991	0.0009
2.64	0.4959	0.0041		3.14	0.4992	0.0008
2.65	0.4960	0.0040		3.15	0.4992	0.0008
2.66	0.4961	0.0039		3.16	0.4992	0.0008
2.67	0.4962	0.0038		3.17	0.4992	0.0008
2.68	0.4963	0.0037		3.18	0.4993	0.0007
2.69	0.4964	0.0036		3.19	0.4993	0.0007
2.70	0.4965	0.0035		3.20	0.4993	0.0007

(b) Z	(c) Area Between Mean and Z	(a) Area Beyond Z	(b) Z	(c) Area Between Mean and Z	Area Beyond Z
3.21	0.4993	0.0007	3.41	0.4997	0.0003
3.22	0.4994	0.0006	3.42	0.4997	0.0003
3.23	0.4994	0.0006	3.43	0.4997	0.0003
3.24	0.4994	0.0006	3.44	0.4997	0.0003
3.25	0.4994	0.0006	3.45	0.4997	0.0003
3.26	0.4994	0.0006	3.46	0.4997	0.0003
3.27	0.4995	0.0005	3.47	0.4997	0.0003
3.28	0.4995	0.0005	3.48	0.4997	0.0003
3.29	0.4995	0.0005	3.49	0.4998	0.0002
3.30	0.4995	0.0005	3.50	0.4998	0.0002
3.31	0.4995	0.0005	3.60	0.4998	0.0002
3.32	0.4995	0.0005	3.70	0.4999	0.0001
3.33	0.4996	0.0004			
3.34	0.4996	0.0004	3.80	0.4999	0.0001
3.35	0.4996	0.0004			
3.36	0.4996	0.0004	3.90	0.4999	<0.0001
3.37	0.4996	0.0004	4.00	0.4999	<0.0001
3.38	0.4996	0.0004			
3.39	0.4997	0.0003			
3.40	0.4997	0.0003			

B

Distribution of the Critical Values of Chi-Square

df	.99	.98	.95	.90	.80	.70	.50	.30	.20	.10	.05	.02	.01	.001
1	$.0^3157$	$.0^3628$	.00393	.0158	.0642	.148	.455	1.074	1.642	2.706	3.841	5.412	6.635	10.827
2	.0201	.0404	.103	.211	.446	.713	1.386	2.408	3.219	4.605	5.991	7.824	9.210	13.815
3	.115	.185	.352	.584	1.005	1.424	2.366	3.665	4.642	6.251	7.815	9.837	11.341	16.268
4	.297	.429	.711	1.064	1.649	2.195	3.357	4.878	5.989	7.779	9.488	11.668	13.277	18.465
5	.554	.752	1.145	1.610	2.343	3.000	4.351	6.064	7.289	9.236	11.070	13.388	15.086	20.517
6	.872	1.134	1.635	2.204	3.070	3.828	5.348	7.231	8.558	10.645	12.592	15.033	16.812	22.457
7	1.239	1.564	2.167	2.833	3.822	4.671	6.346	8.383	9.803	12.017	14.067	16.622	18.475	24.322
8	1.646	2.032	2.733	3.490	4.594	5.527	7.344	9.524	11.030	13.362	15.507	18.168	20.090	26.125
9	2.088	2.532	3.325	4.168	5.380	6.393	8.343	10.656	12.242	14.684	16.919	19.679	21.666	27.877
10	2.558	3.059	3.940	4.865	6.179	7.267	9.342	11.781	13.442	15.987	18.307	21.161	23.209	29.588
11	3.053	3.609	4.575	5.578	6.989	8.148	10.341	12.899	14.631	17.275	19.675	22.618	24.725	31.264
12	3.571	4.178	5.226	6.304	7.807	9.034	11.340	14.011	15.812	18.549	21.026	24.054	26.217	32.909
13	4.107	4.765	5.892	7.042	8.634	9.926	12.340	15.119	16.985	19.812	22.362	25.472	27.688	34.528
14	4.660	5.368	6.571	7.790	9.467	10.821	13.339	16.222	18.151	21.064	23.685	26.873	29.141	36.123
15	5.229	5.985	7.261	8.547	10.307	11.721	14.339	17.322	19.311	22.307	24.996	28.259	30.578	37.697
16	5.812	6.614	7.962	9.312	11.152	12.624	15.338	18.418	20.465	23.542	26.296	29.633	32.000	39.252
17	6.408	7.255	8.672	10.085	12.002	13.531	16.338	19.511	21.615	24.769	27.587	30.995	33.409	40.790
18	7.015	7.906	9.390	10.865	12.857	14.440	17.338	20.601	22.760	25.989	28.869	32.346	34.805	42.312
19	7.633	8.567	10.117	11.651	13.716	15.352	18.338	21.689	23.900	27.204	30.144	33.687	36.191	43.820
20	8.260	9.237	10.851	12.443	14.578	16.266	19.337	22.775	25.038	28.412	31.410	35.020	37.566	45.315
21	8.897	9.915	11.591	13.240	15.445	17.182	20.337	23.858	26.171	29.615	32.671	36.343	38.932	46.797
22	9.542	10.600	12.338	14.041	16.314	18.101	21.337	24.939	27.301	30.813	33.924	37.659	40.289	48.268
23	10.196	11.293	13.091	14.848	17.187	19.021	22.337	26.018	28.429	32.007	35.172	38.968	41.638	49.728
24	10.856	11.992	13.848	15.659	18.062	19.943	23.337	27.096	29.553	33.196	36.415	40.270	42.980	51.179
25	11.524	12.697	14.611	16.473	18.940	20.867	24.337	28.172	30.675	34.382	37.652	41.566	44.314	52.620
26	12.198	13.409	15.379	17.292	19.820	21.792	25.336	29.246	31.795	35.563	38.885	42.856	45.642	54.052
27	12.879	14.125	16.151	18.114	20.703	22.719	26.336	30.319	32.912	36.741	40.113	44.140	46.963	55.476
28	13.565	14.847	16.928	18.939	21.588	23.647	27.336	31.391	34.027	37.916	41.337	45.419	48.278	56.893
29	14.256	15.574	17.708	19.768	22.475	24.577	28.336	32.461	35.139	39.087	42.557	46.693	49.588	58.302
30	14.953	16.306	18.493	20.599	23.364	25.508	29.336	33.530	36.250	40.256	43.773	47.962	50.892	59.703

Source: Table IV from *Statistical Tables for Biological, Agricultural and Medical Research* (6th ed.), by Fisher and Yates, 1974, London: Longman Group Ltd. (previously published by Oliver & Boyd Ltd., Edinburgh). Reprinted by permission of Addison Wesley Longman Ltd.

C

Distribution of the Critical Values of Student's *t*

Degrees of Freedom (*df*)	Level of Significance for One-Tailed Test					
	.10	.05	.025	.01	.005	.0005
	Level of Significance for Two-Tailed Test					
	.20	.10	.05	.02	.01	.001
1	3.078	6.314	12.706	31.821	63.657	636.619
2	1.886	2.920	4.303	6.965	9.925	31.598
3	1.638	2.353	3.182	4.541	5.841	12.941
4	1.533	2.132	2.776	3.747	4.604	8.610
5	1.476	2.015	2.571	3.365	4.032	6.859
6	1.440	1.943	2.447	3.143	3.707	5.959
7	1.415	1.895	2.365	2.998	3.499	5.405
8	1.397	1.860	2.306	2.896	3.355	5.041
9	1.383	1.833	2.262	2.821	3.250	4.781
10	1.372	1.812	2.228	2.764	3.169	4.587
11	1.363	1.796	2.201	2.718	3.106	4.437
12	1.356	1.782	2.179	2.681	3.055	4.318
13	1.350	1.771	2.160	2.650	3.012	4.221
14	1.345	1.761	2.145	2.624	2.977	4.140
15	1.341	1.753	2.131	2.602	2.947	4.073
16	1.337	1.746	2.120	2.583	2.921	4.015
17	1.333	1.740	2.110	2.567	2.898	3.965
18	1.330	1.734	2.101	2.552	2.878	3.922
19	1.328	1.729	2.093	2.539	2.861	3.883
20	1.325	1.725	2.086	2.528	2.845	3.850
21	1.323	1.721	2.080	2.518	2.831	3.819
22	1.321	1.717	2.074	2.508	2.819	3.792
23	1.319	1.714	2.069	2.500	2.807	3.767
24	1.318	1.711	2.064	2.492	2.797	3.745
25	1.316	1.708	2.060	2.485	2.787	3.725
26	1.315	1.706	2.056	2.479	2.779	3.707
27	1.314	1.703	2.052	2.473	2.771	3.690
28	1.313	1.701	2.048	2.467	2.763	3.674
29	1.311	1.699	2.045	2.462	2.756	3.659
30	1.310	1.697	2.042	2.457	2.750	3.646
40	1.303	1.684	2.021	2.423	2.704	3.551
60	1.296	1.671	2.000	2.390	2.660	3.460
120	1.289	1.658	1.980	2.358	2.617	3.373
∞	1.282	1.645	1.960	2.326	2.576	3.291

Source: Table III from *Statistical Tables for Biological, Agricultural and Medical Research* (6th ed.), by Fisher and Yates, 1974, London: Longman Group Ltd. (previously published by Oliver & Boyd Ltd., Edinburgh).

D Distribution of the Critical Values of F

$p = .05$

n_1 n_2	1	2	3	4	5	6	8	12	24	∞
1	161.4	199.5	215.7	224.6	230.2	234.0	238.9	243.9	249.0	254.3
2	18.51	19.00	19.16	19.25	19.30	19.33	19.37	19.41	19.45	19.50
3	10.13	9.55	9.28	9.12	9.01	8.94	8.84	8.74	8.64	8.53
4	7.71	6.94	6.59	6.39	6.26	6.16	6.04	5.91	5.77	5.63
5	6.61	5.79	5.41	5.19	5.05	4.95	4.82	4.68	4.53	4.36
6	5.99	5.14	4.76	4.53	4.39	4.28	4.15	4.00	3.84	3.67
7	5.59	4.74	4.35	4.12	3.97	3.87	3.73	3.57	3.41	3.23
8	5.32	4.46	4.07	3.84	3.69	3.58	3.44	3.28	3.12	2.93
9	5.12	4.26	3.86	3.63	3.48	3.37	3.23	3.07	2.90	2.71
10	4.96	4.10	3.71	3.48	3.33	3.22	3.07	2.91	2.74	2.54
11	4.84	3.98	3.59	3.36	3.20	3.09	2.95	2.79	2.61	2.40
12	4.75	3.88	3.49	3.26	3.11	3.00	2.85	2.69	2.50	2.30
13	4.67	3.80	3.41	3.18	3.02	2.92	2.77	2.60	2.42	2.21
14	4.60	3.74	3.34	3.11	2.96	2.85	2.70	2.53	2.35	2.13
15	4.54	3.68	3.29	3.06	2.90	2.79	2.64	2.48	2.29	2.07
16	4.49	3.63	3.24	3.01	2.85	2.74	2.59	2.42	2.24	2.01
17	4.45	3.59	3.20	2.96	2.81	2.70	2.55	2.38	2.19	1.96
18	4.41	3.55	3.16	2.93	2.77	2.66	2.51	2.34	2.15	1.92
19	4.38	3.52	3.13	2.90	2.74	2.63	2.48	2.31	2.11	1.88
20	4.35	3.49	3.10	2.87	2.71	2.60	2.45	2.28	2.08	1.84
21	4.32	3.47	3.07	2.84	2.68	2.57	2.42	2.25	2.05	1.81
22	4.30	3.44	3.05	2.82	2.66	2.55	2.40	2.23	2.03	1.78
23	4.28	3.42	3.03	2.80	2.64	2.53	2.38	2.20	2.00	1.76
24	4.26	3.40	3.01	2.78	2.62	2.51	2.36	2.18	1.98	1.73
25	4.24	3.38	2.99	2.76	2.60	2.49	2.34	2.16	1.96	1.71
26	4.22	3.37	2.98	2.74	2.59	2.47	2.32	2.15	1.95	1.69
27	4.21	3.35	2.96	2.73	2.57	2.46	2.30	2.13	1.93	1.67
28	4.20	3.34	2.95	2.71	2.56	2.44	2.29	2.12	1.91	1.65
29	4.18	3.33	2.93	2.70	2.54	2.43	2.28	2.10	1.90	1.64
30	4.17	3.32	2.92	2.69	2.53	2.42	2.27	2.09	1.89	1.62
40	4.08	3.23	2.84	2.61	2.45	2.34	2.18	2.00	1.79	1.51
60	4.00	3.15	2.76	2.52	2.37	2.25	2.10	1.92	1.70	1.39
120	3.92	3.07	2.68	2.45	2.29	2.17	2.02	1.83	1.61	1.25
∞	3.84	2.99	2.60	2.37	2.21	2.09	1.94	1.75	1.52	1.00

Values of n_1 and n_2 represent the degrees of freedom associated with the between and within estimates of variance, respectively.
Source: Table V from *Statistical Tables for Biological, Agricultural and Medical Research* (6th ed.), by Fisher and Yates, 1974, London: Longman Group Ltd. (previously published by Oliver and Boyd Ltd., Edinburgh). Reprinted by permission of Addison Wesley Longman Ltd.

n_1 n_2	1	2	3	4	5	6	8	12	24	∞
1	4052	4999	5403	5625	5764	5859	5981	6106	6234	6366
2	98.49	99.01	99.17	99.25	99.30	99.33	99.36	99.42	99.46	99.50
3	34.12	30.81	29.46	28.71	28.24	27.91	27.49	27.05	26.60	26.12
4	21.20	18.00	16.69	15.98	15.52	15.21	14.80	14.37	13.93	13.46
5	16.26	13.27	12.06	11.39	10.97	10.67	10.27	9.89	9.47	9.02
6	13.74	10.92	9.78	9.15	8.75	8.47	8.10	7.72	7.31	6.88
7	12.25	9.55	8.45	7.85	7.46	7.19	6.84	6.47	6.07	5.65
8	11.26	8.65	7.59	7.01	6.63	6.37	6.03	5.67	5.28	4.86
9	10.56	8.02	6.99	6.42	6.06	5.80	5.47	5.11	4.73	4.31
10	10.04	7.56	6.55	5.99	5.64	5.39	5.06	4.71	4.33	3.91
11	9.65	7.20	6.22	5.67	5.32	5.07	4.74	4.40	4.02	3.60
12	9.33	6.93	5.95	5.41	5.06	4.82	4.50	4.16	3.78	3.36
13	9.07	6.70	5.74	5.20	4.86	4.62	4.30	3.96	3.59	3.16
14	8.86	6.51	5.56	5.03	4.69	4.46	4.14	3.80	3.43	3.00
15	8.68	6.36	5.42	4.89	4.56	4.32	4.00	3.67	3.29	2.87
16	8.53	6.23	5.29	4.77	4.44	4.20	3.89	3.55	3.18	2.75
17	8.40	6.11	5.18	4.67	4.34	4.10	3.79	3.45	3.08	2.65
18	8.28	6.01	5.09	4.58	4.25	4.01	3.71	3.37	3.00	2.57
19	8.18	5.93	5.01	4.50	4.17	3.94	3.63	3.30	2.92	2.49
20	8.10	5.85	4.94	4.43	4.10	3.87	3.56	3.23	2.86	2.42
21	8.02	5.78	4.87	4.37	4.04	3.81	3.51	3.17	2.80	2.36
22	7.94	5.72	4.82	4.31	3.99	3.76	3.45	3.12	2.75	2.31
23	7.88	5.66	4.76	4.26	3.94	3.71	3.41	3.07	2.70	2.26
24	7.82	5.61	4.72	4.22	3.90	3.67	3.36	3.03	2.66	2.21
25	7.77	5.57	4.68	4.18	3.86	3.63	3.32	2.99	2.62	2.17
26	7.72	5.53	4.64	4.14	3.82	3.59	3.29	2.96	2.58	2.13
27	7.68	5.49	4.60	4.11	3.78	3.56	3.26	2.93	2.55	2.10
28	7.64	5.45	4.57	4.07	3.75	3.53	3.23	2.90	2.52	2.06
29	7.60	5.42	4.54	4.04	3.73	3.50	3.20	2.87	2.49	2.03
30	7.56	5.39	4.51	4.02	3.70	3.47	3.17	2.84	2.47	2.01
40	7.31	5.18	4.31	3.83	3.51	3.29	2.99	2.66	2.29	1.80
60	7.08	4.98	4.13	3.65	3.34	3.12	2.82	2.50	2.12	1.60
120	6.85	4.79	3.95	3.48	3.17	2.96	2.66	2.34	1.95	1.38
∞	6.64	4.60	3.78	3.32	3.02	2.80	2.51	2.18	1.79	1.00

Values of n_1 and n_2 represent the degrees of freedom associated with the between and within estimates of variance respectively.

E

Codebook for the gss96subset File

These questions correspond to each of the variables in the General Social Survey. Keep in mind that these questions are asked in face-to-face interviews with the respondents, with the interviewers recording the answers given by the respondents. The category (value) labels NA, NAP, and DK are used to record nonresponses. NA = no answer; NAP = question is not applicable to the respondent (and, therefore, not asked); DK = don't know. Responses in these categories are treated as missing data, and these categories, along with the category REFUSED, are not used to assess the level at which a variable is being measured.[1]

1. **age**   AGE OF RESPONDENT

   What is your date of birth?

   VALUE LABELS
   98 DK
   99 NA

2. **relig**   RS RELIGIOUS PREFERENCE

   What is your religious preference? Is it Protestant, Catholic, Jewish, some other religion, or no religion?

   VALUE LABELS
   1 PROTESTANT   5 OTHER
   2 CATHOLIC   8 DK
   3 JEWISH   9 NA
   4 NONE

---

[1]*Sources: General Social Surveys, 1972–1996: Cumulative Codebook* by James Allan Davis and Tom W. Smith, 1996, Chicago: National Opinion Research Center, and the General Social Survey Data Information and Retrieval System website at <http://www.icpsr.umich.edu/gss/codebook.htm>. A number of variables have been recoded to change the order of the response categories. The codebook has been modified to include these changes.

3. **marital**   MARITAL STATUS

Are you currently—married, widowed, divorced, separated, or have you never been married?

VALUE LABELS

1	MARRIED	4	SEPARATED
2	WIDOWED	5	NEVER MARRIED
3	DIVORCED	9	NA

4. **sibs**   NUMBER OF BROTHERS AND SISTERS

How many brothers and sisters did you have? Please count those born alive, but no longer living, as well as those alive now. Also include stepbrothers and stepsisters, and children adopted by your parents.

VALUE LABELS
98 DK
99 NA

5. **childs**   NUMBER OF CHILDREN

How many children have you ever had? Please count all that were born alive at any time (including any you had from a previous marriage).

VALUE LABELS
8 EIGHT OR MORE   9 NA

6. **agekdbrn**   R's AGE WHEN 1ST CHILD BORN

VALUE LABELS
0 NAP
98 DK
99 NA

7. **educ**   HIGHEST YEAR OF SCHOOL COMPLETED

What is the highest grade in elementary school or high school that [you] finished and got credit for? _____ [A] Did [you] ever complete one or more years of college for credit—not including schooling such as business college, technical or vocational school? If yes, how many years did [you] complete? _____ [B] [Add [A] and [B] to get highest year of school completed: _____ (educ)]

VALUE LABELS
97 NAP   98 DK   99 NA

8. **paeduc**   HIGHEST YEAR SCHOOL COMPLETED, FATHER

What is the highest grade in elementary school or high school that your father finished and got credit for? Did he complete one or more years of college for credit—not including schooling such as business college, technical, or vocational school? IF YES: How many years did he complete?

VALUE LABELS
97 NAP
98 DK
99 NA

9. **maeduc**   Highest Year School Completed, Mother

What is the highest grade in elementary school or high school that your mother finished and got credit for? Did she complete one or more years of college for credit—not including schooling such as business college, technical, or vocational school? IF YES: How many years did she complete?

VALUE LABELS
97 NAP
98 DK
99 NA

10. **speduc**   Highest Year School Completed, Spouse

What is the highest grade in elementary school or high school that your [husband/wife] finished and got credit for? Did he/she complete one or more years of college for credit—not including schooling such as business college, technical, or vocational school? IF YES: How many years did he/she complete?

VALUE LABELS
97 NAP
98 DK
99 NA

11. **degree**   RS Highest Degree

IF FINISHED 9TH–12TH GRADE OR DK: Did you ever get a high school diploma or a GED certificate? Did you complete one or more years of college for credit—not including schooling such as business college, technical or vocational school? IF YES: How many years did you complete? Do you have any college degrees? (IF YES: What degree or degrees?) CODE HIGHEST DEGREE EARNED.

VALUE LABELS

0	LT HIGH SCHOOL	4	GRADUATE
1	HIGH SCHOOL	7	NAP
2	JUNIOR COLLEGE	8	DK
3	BACHELOR	9	NA

12. **padeg** FATHER'S HIGHEST DEGREE

IF FINISHED 9TH–12TH GRADE OR DK: Did your father ever get a high school diploma or a GED certificate? Did he complete one or more years of college for credit—not including schooling such as business college, technical or vocational school? IF YES: How many years did he complete? Does he have any college degrees? (IF YES: What degree or degrees?) CODE HIGHEST DEGREE EARNED.

VALUE LABELS

0	LT HIGH SCHOOL	4	GRADUATE
1	HIGH SCHOOL	7	NAP
2	JUNIOR COLLEGE	8	DK
3	BACHELOR	9	NA

13. **madeg** MOTHER'S HIGHEST DEGREE

IF FINISHED 9TH–12TH GRADE OR DK: Did your mother ever get a high school diploma or a GED certificate? Did she complete one or more years of college for credit—not including schooling such as business college, technical or vocational school? IF YES: How many years did she complete? Does she have any college degrees? (IF YES: What degree or degrees?) CODE HIGHEST DEGREE EARNED.

VALUE LABELS

0	LT HIGH SCHOOL	4	GRADUATE
1	HIGH SCHOOL	7	NAP
2	JUNIOR COLLEGE	8	DK
3	BACHELOR	9	NA

14. **sex** RESPONDENT'S SEX

VALUE LABELS
1 MALE
2 FEMALE

15. **race** RACE OF RESPONDENT

CODE WITHOUT ASKING ONLY IF THERE IS NO DOUBT IN YOUR MIND. What race do you consider yourself? RECORD VERBATIM AND CODE.

VALUE LABELS
1 WHITE
2 BLACK
3 OTHER

16. **region**   REGION OF INTERVIEW

VALUE LABELS

0	NOT ASSIGNED	5	SOUTH ATLANTIC
1	NEW ENGLAND	6	E. SOU. CENTRAL
2	MIDDLE ATLANTIC	7	W. SOU. CENTRAL
3	E. NOR. CENTRAL	8	MOUNTAIN
4	W. NOR. CENTRAL	9	PACIFIC

17. **hompop**   NUMBER OF PERSONS IN HOUSEHOLD

Now I would like you to think about the people who live in this household. Please include any persons who usually live here but are away temporarily—on business, on vacation, or in a general hospital—and include all babies and small children. Do not include college students who are living away at college, persons stationed away from here in the Armed Forces, or persons away in institutions.
Total persons _____

VALUE LABELS
98   DK
99   NA

18. **earnrs**   HOW MANY IN FAMILY EARNED MONEY

Just thinking about your family now—those people in the household who are related to you . . . How many persons in the family, including yourself, earned any money last year [1995] from any job or employment?

VALUE LABELS
8   EIGHT OR MORE
9   NA

19. **class**   SUBJECTIVE CLASS IDENTIFICATION

If you were asked to use one of four names for your social class, which would you say you belong in: the lower class, the working class, the middle class, or the upper class?

VALUE LABELS

0	NAP		
1	LOWER CLASS	5	NO CLASS
2	WORKING CLASS	8	DK
3	MIDDLE CLASS	9	NA
4	UPPER CLASS		

20. **income**   TOTAL FAMILY INCOME

In which of these groups did your total family income from all sources
fall, last year before taxes, that is? Just tell me the letter. [Note: The
letter selected by the respondent was turned into one of the categories
listed below.]

VALUE LABELS

0	NAP		
1	LT $1000	9	$10000–14999
2	$1000–2999	10	$15000–19999
3	$3000–3999	11	$20000–24999
4	$4000–4999	12	$25000 OR MORE
5	$5000–5999	13	REFUSED
6	$6000–6999	98	DK
7	$7000–7999	99	NA
8	$8000–9999		

21. **rincome**   RESPONDENT'S INCOME

Did you earn any income from [the occupation you described earlier] in
[1995]? IF YES: In which of these groups did your earnings from [your
occupation] for last year [1995] fall? That is, before taxes or other
deductions. Just tell me the letter. [Note: The letter selected by the
respondent was turned into one of the categories listed below.]

VALUE LABELS

0	NAP	8	$8000–9999
1	LT $1000	9	$10000–14999
2	$1000–2999	10	$15000–19999
3	$3000–3999	11	$20000–24999
4	$4000–4999	12	$25000 OR MORE
5	$5000–5999	13	REFUSED
6	$6000–6999	99	DK/NA
7	$7000–7999		

22. **income91**   TOTAL FAMILY INCOME ON 1991–1996 SURVEYS

In which of these groups did your total family income from all sources
fall, last year before taxes, that is? Just tell me the letter. [Note: The
letter selected by the respondent was turned into one of the categories
listed below.]

VALUE LABELS

0	NAP	4	$4000–4999
1	LT $1000	5	$5000–5999
2	$1000–2999	6	$6000–6999
3	$3000–3999	7	$7000–7999

8	$8000–9999	17	$35000–39999
9	$10000–12499	18	$40000–49999
10	$12500–14999	19	$50000–59999
11	$15000–17499	20	$60000–74999
12	$17500–19999	21	$75,000+
13	$20000–22499	22	REFUSED
14	$22500–24999	98	DK
15	$25000–29999	99	NA
16	$30000–34999		

23. **rincom91**   RESPONDENT'S INCOME ON 1991–1996 SURVEYS

Did you earn any income from [the occupation you described earlier] in [1995]? IF YES: In which of these groups did your earnings from [your occupation] for last year [1995] fall? That is, before taxes or other deductions. Just tell me the letter. [Note: The letter selected by the respondent was turned into one of the categories listed below.]

VALUE LABELS

0	NAP	13	$20000–22499
1	LT $1000	14	$22500–24999
2	$1000–2999	15	$25000–29999
3	$3000–3999	16	$30000–34999
4	$4000–4999	17	$35000–39999
5	$5000–5999	18	$40000–49999
6	$6000–6999	19	$50000–59999
7	$7000–7999	20	$60000–74999
8	$8000–9999	21	$75000+
9	$10000–12499	22	REFUSED
10	$12500–14999	99	DK/NA
11	$15000–17499		
12	$17500–19999		

24. **earnmore**   WHO EARNS MORE MONEY

Who earns more money?

VALUE LABELS

0 NAP
1 I EARN MUCH MORE THAN MY SPOUSE/PARTNER
2 I EARN SOMEWHAT MORE THAN MY SPOUSE/PARTNER
3 WE EARN ABOUT THE SAME AMOUNT
4 MY SPOUSE/PARTNER EARNS SOMEWHAT MORE
5 MY SPOUSE/PARTNER EARNS MUCH MORE
8 DK
9 NA

25. **wrkstat**   LABOR FORCE STATUS

Last week were you working full time, part time, going to school, keeping house, or what?

VALUE LABELS
0   NAP
1   WORKING FULL-TIME
2   WORKING PART-TIME
3   TEMPORARILY NOT WORKING
4   UNEMPLOYED, LAID OFF
5   RETIRED
6   SCHOOL
7   KEEPING HOUSE
8   OTHER
9   NA

26. **hrs1**   NUMBER OF HOURS WORKED LAST WEEK

IF WORKING, FULL OR PART TIME: How many hours did you work last week, at all jobs?

VALUE LABELS
−1   NAP
98   DK
99   NA

27. **sphrs1**   NUMBER OF HRS SPOUSE WORKED LAST WEEK

IF WORKING, FULL OR PART TIME: How many hours did (he/she) work last week, at all jobs?

VALUE LABELS
−1   NAP
98   DK
99   NA

28. **satfin**   SATISFACTION WITH FINANCIAL SITUATION

We are interested in how people are getting along financially these days. So far as you and your family are concerned, would you say that you are pretty well satisfied with your present financial situation, more or less satisfied, or not satisfied at all?

VALUE LABELS
1   NOT SATISFIED AT ALL
2   MORE OR LESS SATISFIED
3   SATISFIED (recoded from "Pretty Well Satisfied" in 1996 GSS)
8   DK
9   NA

29. **finalter**   CHANGE IN FINANCIAL SITUATION

During the last few years, has your financial situation been getting better, worse, or has it stayed the same?

VALUE LABELS
1   GETTING WORSE
2   STAYED THE SAME
3   GETTING BETTER
8   DK
9   NA

30. **finrela**   OPINION OF FAMILY INCOME

Compared with American families in general, would you say your family income is far below average, below average, average, above average, or far above average?

VALUE LABELS
1   FAR BELOW AVERAGE   5   FAR ABOVE AVERAGE
2   BELOW AVERAGE   8   DK
3   AVERAGE   9   NA
4   ABOVE AVERAGE

31. **partyid**   POLITICAL PARTY AFFILIATION

Generally speaking, do you usually think of yourself as a Republican, Democrat, Independent, or what?

VALUE LABELS
0   STRONG DEMOCRAT   5   NOT STR REPUBLICAN
1   NOT STR DEMOCRAT   6   STRONG REPUBLICAN
2   IND, NEAR DEM   7   OTHER PARTY
3   INDEPENDENT   8   DK
4   IND, NEAR REP   9   NA

32. **vote92**   DID R VOTE IN 1992 ELECTION

In 1992, you remember that Clinton ran for President on the Democratic ticket against Bush for the Republicans and Perot as an Independent. Do you remember for sure whether or not you voted in that election?

VALUE LABELS
0   NAP   4   REFUSED
1   VOTED   8   DK
2   DID NOT VOTE   9   NA
3   NOT ELIGIBLE

33. **pres92** VOTE FOR CLINTON, BUSH, PEROT

IF VOTED: Did you vote for Clinton, Bush, or Perot?

VALUE LABELS

0	NAP	4	OTHER
1	CLINTON	6	NO PRES. VOTE
2	BUSH	8	DK
3	PEROT	9	NA

34. **if92who** WHO WOULD R HAVE VOTED FOR–1992 ELECTION

IF DID NOT VOTE OR INELIGIBLE: Who would you have voted for, for President, had you voted?

VALUE LABELS

0	NAP	4	OTHER
1	CLINTON	5	WOULDNT VOTE
2	BUSH	8	DK
3	PEROT	9	NA

35. **polviews** THINK OF SELF AS LIBERAL OR CONSERVATIVE

We hear a lot of talk these days about liberals and conservatives. I'm going to show you a seven-point scale on which the political views that people might hold are arranged from extremely liberal—point 1—to extremely conservative—point 7. Where would you place yourself on this scale?

VALUE LABELS

0	NAP	5	SLIGHTLY CONSERVATIVE
1	EXTREMELY LIBERAL	6	CONSERVATIVE
2	LIBERAL	7	EXTREMELY CONSERVATIVE
3	SLIGHTLY LIBERAL	8	DK
4	MODERATE	9	NA

The next three variables, *attend, fund,* and *reliten,* are follow-up questions to question 2, *relig.*

36. **attend** HOW OFTEN R ATTENDS RELIGIOUS SERVICES

How often do you attend religious services?

VALUE LABELS

0	NEVER	5	2–3 TIMES A MONTH
1	LESS THAN ONCE A YEAR	6	NEARLY EVERY WEEK
2	ABOUT ONCE OR TWICE A YEAR	7	EVERY WEEK
3	SEVERAL TIMES A YEAR	8	SEVERAL TIMES A WEEK
4	ABOUT ONCE A MONTH	9	DK, NA

37. **fund**   How Fundamentalist Is R Currently

VALUE LABELS

0	NAP	3	LIBERAL
1	FUNDAMENTALIST	8	DK
2	MODERATE	9	NA-EXCLUDED

38. **reliten**   Strength of Affiliation

ASK EVERYONE WITH ANY RELIGIOUS PREFERENCE NAMED IN [question 2], Would you call yourself a strong (PREFERENCE NAMED IN QUESTION 2) or a not very strong (PREFERENCE NAMED IN QUESTION 2)?

VALUE LABELS

0	NAP	4	STRONG
1	NO RELIGION	8	DK
2	NOT VERY STRONG	9	NA
3	SOMEWHAT STRONG		

39. **life**   Is Life Exciting or Dull

In general, do you find life exciting, pretty routine, or dull?

VALUE LABELS

0	NAP	3	EXCITING
1	DULL	8	DK
2	ROUTINE	9	NA

40. **happy**   General Happiness

Taken all together, how would you say things are these days—would you say that you are very happy, pretty happy, or not too happy?

VALUE LABELS

1	NOT TOO HAPPY	8	DK
2	PRETTY HAPPY	9	NA
3	VERY HAPPY		

41. **hapmar**   Happiness of Marriage

Taking all things together, how would you describe your marriage? Would you say that your marriage is very happy, pretty happy, or not too happy?

VALUE LABELS

1	NOT TOO HAPPY	8	DK
2	PRETTY HAPPY	9	NA
3	VERY HAPPY		

42. **grass**   SHOULD MARIJUANA BE MADE LEGAL

Do you think the use of marijuana should be made legal or not?

VALUE LABELS
0 NAP
1 LEGAL
2 NOT LEGAL
8 DK
9 NA

43. **abdefect**   STRONG CHANCE OF SERIOUS DEFECT

Please tell me whether or not you think it should be possible for a pregnant woman to obtain a legal abortion if: there is a strong chance of a serious defect in the baby?

VALUE LABELS
0 NAP
1 YES
2 NO
8 DK
9 NA

44. **abnomore**   MARRIED—WANTS NO MORE CHILDREN

Please tell me whether or not you think it should be possible for a pregnant woman to obtain a legal abortion if: she is married and does not want any more children?

VALUE LABELS
0 NAP
1 YES
2 NO
8 DK
9 NA

45. **abhlth**   WOMAN'S HEALTH SERIOUSLY ENDANGERED

Please tell me whether or not you think it should be possible for a pregnant woman to obtain a legal abortion if: the woman's own health is seriously endangered by the pregnancy?

VALUE LABELS
0 NAP
1 YES
2 NO
8 DK
9 NA

46. **abpoor**   Low Income—Can't Afford More Children

Please tell me whether or not you think it should be possible for a pregnant woman to obtain a legal abortion if: the family has a very low income and cannot afford any more children?

VALUE LABELS
0 NAP
1 YES
2 NO
8 DK
9 NA

47. **abrape**   Pregnant as Result of Rape

Please tell me whether or not you think it should be possible for a pregnant woman to obtain a legal abortion if: she became pregnant as a result of rape?

VALUE LABELS
0 NAP
1 YES
2 NO
8 DK
9 NA

48. **absingle**   Not Married

Please tell me whether or not you think it should be possible for a pregnant woman to obtain a legal abortion if: she is not married and does not want to marry the man?

VALUE LABELS
0 NAP
1 YES
2 NO
8 DK
9 NA

49. **abany**   Abortion if Woman Wants for Any Reason

Please tell me whether or not you think it should be possible for a pregnant woman to obtain a legal abortion if: the woman wants it for any reason?

VALUE LABELS
0 NAP
1 YES
2 NO
8 DK
9 NA

50. **cappun**   FAVOR OR OPPOSE DEATH PENALTY FOR MURDER

Do you favor or oppose the death penalty for persons convicted of murder?

VALUE LABELS
0   NAP
1   FAVOR
2   OPPOSE
8   DK
9   NA

51. **gunlaw**   FAVOR OR OPPOSE GUN PERMITS

Would you favor or oppose a law which would require a person to obtain a police permit before he or she could buy a gun?

VALUE LABELS
0   NAP
1   FAVOR
2   OPPOSE
8   DK
9   NA

52. **courts**   COURTS DEALING WITH CRIMINALS

In general, do you think the courts in this area deal too harshly or not harshly enough with criminals?

VALUE LABELS
0	NAP	3	NOT HARSH ENOUGH
1	TOO HARSH	8	DK
2	ABOUT RIGHT	9	NA

53. **premarsx**   SEX BEFORE MARRIAGE

There's been a lot of discussion about the way morals and attitudes about sex are changing in this country. If a man and woman have sex relations before marriage, do you think it is always wrong, almost always wrong, wrong, wrong only sometimes, or not wrong at all?

VALUE LABELS
0	NAP	4	NOT WRONG AT ALL
1	ALWAYS WRONG	8	DK
2	ALMOST ALWAYS WRONG	9	NA
3	SOMETIMES WRONG		

54. **teensex**   SEX BEFORE MARRIAGE—TEENS 14–16

What if they are in their early teens, say 14 to 16 years old? In that case, do you think sex relations before marriage are always wrong, almost always wrong, wrong only sometimes, or not wrong at all?

VALUE LABELS

0	NAP	4	NOT WRONG AT ALL
1	ALWAYS WRONG	8	DK
2	ALMOST ALWAYS WRONG	9	NA
3	SOMETIMES WRONG		

55. **xmarsex**   SEX WITH PERSON OTHER THAN SPOUSE

What is your opinion about a married person having sexual relations with someone other than the marriage partner—is it always wrong, almost always wrong, wrong only sometimes, or not wrong at all?

VALUE LABELS

0	NAP	4	NOT WRONG AT ALL
1	ALWAYS WRONG	8	DK
2	ALMOST ALWAYS WRONG	9	NA
3	SOMETIMES WRONG		

56. **sexeduc**   SEX EDUCATION IN PUBLIC SCHOOLS

Would you be for or against sex education in the public schools?

VALUE LABELS

1   FOR
2   AGAINST
8   DK
9   NA

57. **pillok**   BIRTH CONTROL TO TEENAGERS 14–16

Do you strongly agree, agree, disagree, or strongly disagree that methods of birth control should be available to teenagers between the ages of 14 and 16 if their parents do not approve?

VALUE LABELS

0	NAP	4	STRONGLY DISAGREE
1	STRONGLY AGREE	8	DK
2	AGREE	9	NA
3	DISAGREE		

58. **partners**   HOW MANY SEX PARTNERS R HAD IN LAST YEAR

How many sex partners have you had in the last twelve months?

VALUE LABELS
- −1 NAP
- 0 NO PARTNERS
- 1 1 PARTNER
- 2 2 PARTNERS
- 3 3 PARTNERS
- 4 4 PARTNERS
- 5 5–10 PARTNERS
- 6 11–20 PARTNERS
- 7 21–100 PARTNERS
- 8 MORE THAN 100 PARTNERS
- 9 1+ PARTNERS, DON'T KNOW NUMBER
- 95 SEVERAL
- 98 DK
- 99 NA

59. **evstray**   HAVE SEX OTHER THAN SPOUSE WHILE MARRIED

Have you ever had sex with someone other than your husband or wife while you were married?

VALUE LABELS
0	NAP	3	NEVER MARRIED
1	YES	8	DK
2	NO	9	NA

The next 10 variables are responses to the question, "I am going to name some institutions in this country. As far as the people running these institutions are concerned, would you say you have a great deal of confidence, only some confidence, or hardly any confidence at all in them?"

60. **conbus**   CONFIDENCE IN MAJOR COMPANIES

VALUE LABELS
0	NAP	3	A GREAT DEAL
1	HARDLY ANY	8	DK
2	ONLY SOME	9	NA

61. **conclerg**   CONFIDENCE IN ORGANIZED RELIGION

VALUE LABELS
0	NAP	3	A GREAT DEAL
1	HARDLY ANY	8	DK
2	ONLY SOME	9	NA

62. **coneduc**   CONFIDENCE IN EDUCATION

VALUE LABELS
0	NAP	3	A GREAT DEAL
1	HARDLY ANY	8	DK
2	ONLY SOME	9	NA

63. **confed**   CONFIDENCE IN EXEC BRANCH OF FED GOVT

VALUE LABELS
0	NAP	3	A GREAT DEAL
1	HARDLY ANY	8	DK
2	ONLY SOME	9	NA

64. **conlabor**   CONFIDENCE IN ORGANIZED LABOR

VALUE LABELS
0	NAP	3	A GREAT DEAL
1	HARDLY ANY	8	DK
2	ONLY SOME	9	NA

65. **conpress**   CONFIDENCE IN PRESS

VALUE LABELS
0	NAP	3	A GREAT DEAL
1	HARDLY ANY	8	DK
2	ONLY SOME	9	NA

66. **conmedic**   CONFIDENCE IN MEDICINE

VALUE LABELS
0	NAP	3	A GREAT DEAL
1	HARDLY ANY	8	DK
2	ONLY SOME	9	NA

67. **contv**   CONFIDENCE IN TELEVISION

VALUE LABELS
0	NAP	3	A GREAT DEAL
1	HARDLY ANY	8	DK
2	ONLY SOME	9	NA

68. **conjudge**   CONFIDENCE IN UNITED STATES SUPREME COURT

VALUE LABELS
0	NAP	3	A GREAT DEAL
1	HARDLY ANY	8	DK
2	ONLY SOME	9	NA

69. **consci**   CONFIDENCE IN SCIENTIFIC COMMUNITY

VALUE LABELS
0	NAP	3	A GREAT DEAL
1	HARDLY ANY	8	DK
2	ONLY SOME	9	NA

70. **conlegis**   CONFIDENCE IN CONGRESS

VALUE LABELS
0	NAP	3	A GREAT DEAL
1	HARDLY ANY	8	DK
2	ONLY SOME	9	NA

71. **tvhours**   HOURS PER DAY WATCHING TV

On the average day, about how many hours do you personally watch television?

VALUE LABELS
-1	NAP
98	DK
99	NA

Bells and Whistles: Advanced Features of SPSS

THE EDIT-OPTIONS FEATURES OF SPSS

One of the SPSS menu items, Edit-Options, tells SPSS how to display variables, tables, and charts. You may need to access this feature at the beginning of each SPSS session so that your screens will look like the ones in the text. First, click on the Edit menu item. A list of options like these will appear:

Untitled - SPSS for Windows Data Editor				
File Edit View Data Transform Analyze Graphs Utilities Window Help				

	Undo	Ctrl+Z				
	Cut	Ctrl+X				
	Copy	Ctrl+C				
	Paste	Ctrl+V	var	var	var	var
	Clear	Del				
	Find...	Ctrl+F				
	Options...					

Then click on Options. The Options window opens. It looks like a set of file folders. Each folder has its own tab, like General, Viewer, and so on.

Point to one of the items, like Display Labels, and click using the right-most click key on the mouse. A box will open up describing the item. To close the box, move your cursor off the item, and click again with the right-most key. Try this with a few of the other items on the screen.

Some of the options have circles next to them. The circles with the black dots in the center (called radio buttons) show you which options are active. Make sure the options selected under Variable Lists in the General folder are Display Names and Alphabetical. Those options should be the ones with the black dots in the radio buttons next to them, like on the following screen. (If they aren't, then point to the button next to the option and click with the left-most click key on the mouse.)

❶ Under Variable Lists, click on Display Names.

❷ Click on Alphabetical.

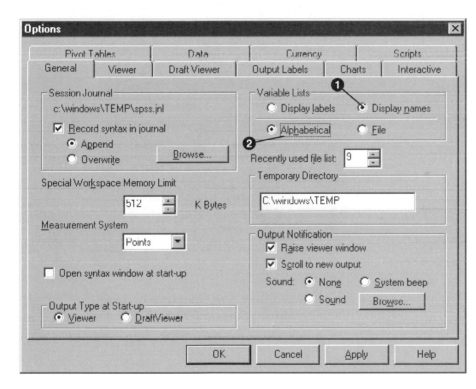

If you make a mistake and click on the wrong button, click again, and the black dot will disappear. When you're finished, put your cursor on the

Output Labels tab and click. When you click on the Output Labels tab in the Options window, you will see a folder like the following:

Note that the choices are Outline Labeling and Pivot Table Labeling. Under each choice, look at the options. Point your cursor at each of the options, like Variables in Item Labels Shown As, and click the right-most click key to see a description of it. A box will open showing a brief description of the option. To close the description box, move your cursor away from it and click again with the right-most click key.

Look at the choices under each of the Labeling options by clicking on the down arrows ▼ (in the box under each of the options). You will see choices like the ones following. To select one of the choices, place your cursor on it and click. Try it.

Use this feature to set the options under Outline Labeling and Pivot Table Labeling to look like the screen you see here:

Click on the Draft Viewer tab. Make sure the following items have been selected (that is, have a ✔ in the box next to them).

If the item isn't checked off (like it is in the preceding screen), click on the box next to the item. If it is checked off (but shouldn't be), click on the box next to the item and the ✔ will disappear. Click on OK to go back to the SPSS Data Editor. (If you get a Warning, like this one, click on OK.)

This warning tells you that your option changes take effect the next time you open a data file. (If you have a data file open already, close it and reopen it to cause your option changes to go into effect.)

THE VIEW FEATURE

Another way to display the values of variables is to use the menu item, View. Click on View. A drop-down menu appears. Click on Value Labels. A ✔ will appear next to it.

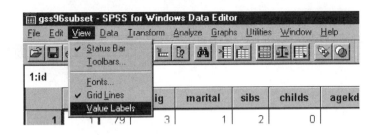

The SPSS Data Editor now shows you all of the value labels for each variable so you can see the data for each respondent in a way that makes more sense, but you may still need to use the Variables window to help interpret some of the variables. To turn off the Value Labels and return to showing all of your data as numbers, click on View and then click on Value Labels again.

	id	age	relig	marital	sibs	childs	agekdbrn	educ	paeduc	maeduc
1	1	79	JEWIS	MARRIED	2	0	NAP	12	DK	NAP
2	2	32	CATHO	NEVER M	1	0	NAP	17	16	14
3	3	55	OTHER	DIVORCE	2	3	24	18	NAP	12
4	4	50	CATHO	MARRIED	DK	4	16	6	NAP	NAP

PRINTING SPSS OUTPUT

Sometimes it's helpful to be able to print out tables and charts that appear in your SPSS Output window. At the SPSS Output window, place your cursor on the chart or table that you would like to print. Then click once with your mouse key. You will notice that the chart or table is highlighted with a black border, like the following example.

Output1 - SPSS for Windows Viewer

File   Edit   View   Insert   Format   Analyze   Graphs   Utilities   Window   Help

Frequencies

Statistics

RACE RACE OF RESPONDENT

N	Valid	2904
	Missing	0

RACE RACE OF RESPONDENT

		Frequency	Percent	Valid Percent	Cumulative Percent
Valid	1 WHITE	2349	80.9	80.9	80.9
	2 BLACK	402	13.8	13.8	94.7
	3 OTHER	153	5.3	5.3	100.0
	Total	2904	100.0	100.0	

Now click on the printer icon (the one with the printer on it) to open the Print window. When the Print window opens, look under Print Range. Note that the option, Selection, is highlighted. This means that only the chart or table with the black border around it will be printed. (If you want to print everything in the Output window, you can change this option to All Visible Output. Be warned that *everything* in the Output window will be printed, so scroll up and down in the Output window before you choose this option to make sure you really want it all.) Once you have made your choice—either Selection or All

Visible Output—click on OK. The item(s) you requested should begin to print (provided the printer is turned on, there is paper in it, and so on).

USING CASE SUMMARIES TO CHECK DATA

When you are entering data, you can check it against its source using Case Summaries. The Case Summaries feature produces a list of each value of each variable for each case. With a data file open, follow the command path Analyze ➥ Reports ➥ Case Summaries.

At the Summarize Cases dialog box,

❶ Select the variables for which you want to check the values. You should always include the respondent identification variable (*id*) as the first variable on your list.

❷ If you have a large file of data, turn off the Limit Cases feature.

❸ Turn off the Show Only Valid Cases Option.

❹ Click on OK.

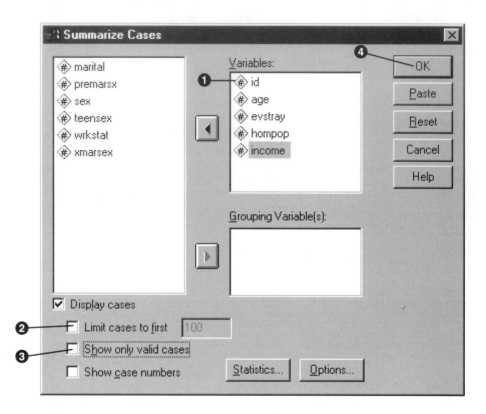

You'll get a report like the one that follows. You can use this report to check your data against its original source to make sure you entered it correctly. Note that you have your *id* variable, the values of numerical values (like *age* and *hompop*), and the values and labels for categorical variables (*evstray* and *income*).

Case Summaries

	ID Respondent's id number	AGE Respondent's age	EVSTRAY Ever stray from marriage	HOMPOP Number in household	INCOME Total family income
1	1	79	2 NO	2	17 $35000-39999
2	2	61	3 NEVER MARRIED	1	17 $35000-39999
3	3	63	1 YES	2	18 $40000-49999
4	4	53	9 NO ANSWER	1	1 LT $1000
5	5	76	2 NO	2	12 $17500-19999
6	6	43	2 NO	2	99 NO ANSWER
7	7	41	9 NO ANSWER	1	99 NO ANSWER
8	8	77	3 NEVER MARRIED	1	10 $12500-14999
9	9	70	2 NO	2	15 $25000-29999
10	10	68	1 YES	1	19 $50000-59999
11	11	53	3 NEVER MARRIED	2	15 $25000-29999
12	12	39	2 NO	4	99 NO ANSWER
13	13	42	3 NEVER MARRIED	2	21 $75000+
14	14	43	1 YES	4	21 $75000+
15	15	47	3 NEVER MARRIED	2	15 $25000-29999
16	16	48	1 YES	3	19 $50000-59999
17	17	38	3 NEVER MARRIED	2	17 $35000-39999
18	18	36	2 NO	4	17 $35000-39999
19	19	46	2 NO	4	18 $40000-49999
20	20	40	2 NO	3	16 $30000-34999
Total N	20	20	18	20	17

USING THE OUTLINE FEATURE IN THE OUTPUT WINDOW

When you create SPSS output by running one of the SPSS commands (a frequency distribution, for example), you create an outline of the work you are doing. For example, if you produce a frequency distribution for the variable *sex*, you will get

❶ The frequency distribution.

❷ An outline of the output on the left-hand side of the Output window.

You can use the outline to move around in the Output window. For example, if you click on one of the items in the outline, the corresponding item in the Output window is highlighted with a black box.

❶ Click on the outline item Statistics.

❷ Note that the Statistics output is highlighted.

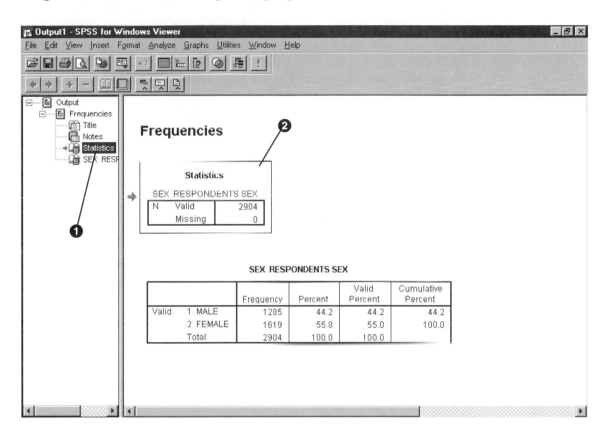

The Notes item in the outline is the only item that doesn't have corresponding output. When we used the Edit-Options feature to select the Draft Viewer option, we did not select the Notes feature, so the notes remain hidden. You can change the outline default settings by clicking on Edit then Options and selecting the Draft Viewer tab.

If you click on the main outline heading, Frequencies, all of the output associated with the heading is highlighted. You can delete the highlighted items by pressing the Delete key, or you can print all of the highlighted output by clicking on the printer icon and following the instructions for printing output in the "Bells and Whistles" section, "Printing SPSS Output."

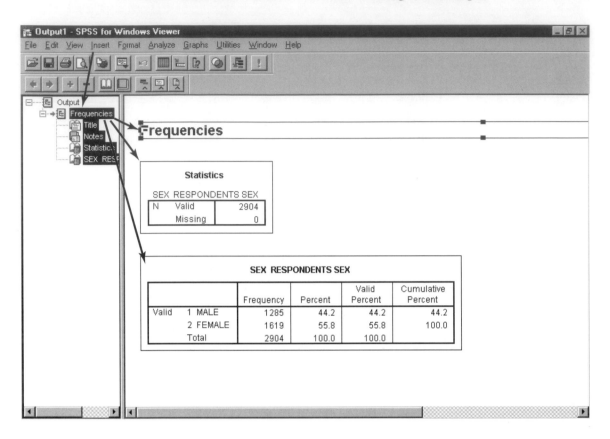

As you do more work in an SPSS session, the outline will become longer and longer. You can click on the Outline items to move back and forth in the Output window, to select items to print, or to delete output you no longer need.

USING THE CHART EDITOR TO CUSTOMIZE CHARTS

Whenever you create a chart with SPSS, it's a simple matter to customize it using the SPSS Chart Editor. To access the Chart Editor, just place your cursor on the chart in the SPSS Output window you want to customize. Let's illustrate this with a pie chart for the variable *sex* in the gss96subset file. Use the SPSS Guide, "Creating a Pie Chart," in Chapter 4 to obtain a pie chart like the following.

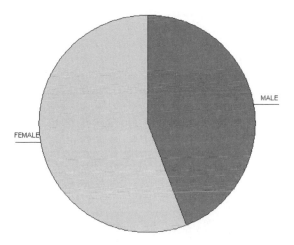

To customize the pie chart, put your cursor on it and double-click. The Chart Editor opens.

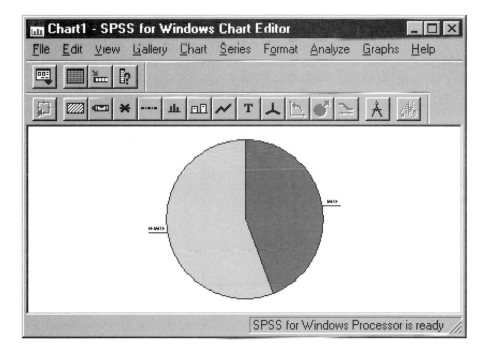

There are dozens of things you can do to a chart with the SPSS Chart Editor. (Don't be afraid to explore these features.) One of the features allows you to add percentages to a pie chart.

1 Click on Chart.

2 Click on Options.

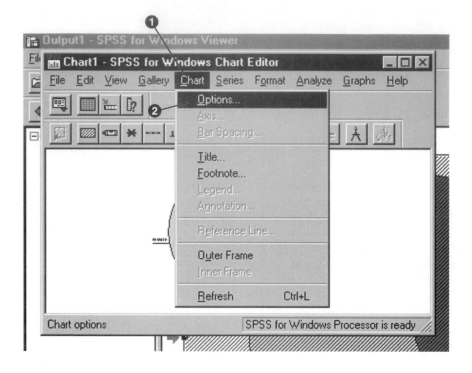

3 When the Pie Options box opens, click on Percents.

4 Click on OK.

❺ At the Chart Editor, click on the X in the upper right corner to exit from the editor. Your pie chart will look like the one here.

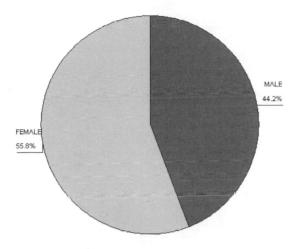

You can open the Chart Editor for any chart: bar charts, pie charts, histograms, and so on. Experiment with some of the features that allow you to customize your charts.

SAVING YOUR SPSS RECODES

When you recode a variable, it is often helpful to save the recode commands. If you make a mistake—or you want to change something about the recode—you can retrieve the recode commands and correct them. To save your recode commands, you need to add one step to the recode process. After you have completed recoding your variable (entered a new variable name, a new variable label, and the old and new values for your recoded variable) at the Recode into Different Variables window, click on the command button Paste before you execute the recode.

For example, when you are creating a new variable, like *rcattend,* click on Paste before you click on OK to execute the recode command. When you click on Paste, the SPSS Syntax Editor opens. The Syntax Editor keeps track of the SPSS commands used to execute various functions, like recodes.

You can save these commands. Click on File. Then click on Save As. Click on the down arrow next to Save In and then click on 3½ Floppy [A:].

Give your set of syntax commands a file name, like rcattend. Then click on Save.

At the SPSS Syntax Editor window, click on the X in the upper right-hand corner. Your commands for creating the new *rcattend* variable are now stored in a file with the name rcattend.sps. It is an SPSS syntax file, and you can open it if you ever need to recall or change a recoded variable.

To open a syntax file, click on the File menu item in the SPSS Data Editor. Then click on the down arrow (▼) next to Files of Type. Find Syntax [*.sps] and click on it.

Your syntax file, rcattend, appears in the directory. Click on rcattend and then click on Open (or simply double-click on rcattend).

Open File

Look in: 3½ Floppy (A:)

rcattend

File name: rcattend

Files of type: Syntax(*.sps)

Open

Paste

Cancel

The SPSS Syntax Editor opens. To rerun the recode commands, click on Run and click on All. Then click on the X in the upper right corner of the screen.

rcattend - SPSS for Windows Syntax Editor

File Edit View Analyze Graphs Utilities Run Window Help

Run menu:
All
Selection
Current   Ctrl+R
To End

```
RECODE
  attend
  (0=0) (9=9) (1 thru 3=1) (4 thru 6=2) (7 thru 8=3) INTO RCATTEND .
VARIABLE LABELS RCATTEND 'recoded church attendance'.
EXECUTE .
```

Run All   SPSS for Windows Processor is ready

You can also modify the recode itself. Place your cursor inside the window with the commands, and correct anything that is in error (using the insert, delete, backspace, character, and number keys on the keyboard). Be sure to save your changes by clicking on the Diskette (Save File) icon. To execute the changes, click on Run then All.

G   Answers to Odd-Numbered Exercises

CHAPTER 1

General Exercise 1:

a. Students at SUNY Cortland, or first-year students at SUNY Cortland.

b. Students.

c. Students.

d. Independent variable: type of Introduction to Sociology course (service learning or traditional); dependent variable: student achievement (grades in the courses, attendance, and attitudes toward social justice, social responsibility, and ability to make change).

e. Age, sex, race, high school grade point average, SAT scores.

General Exercise 3:

Females are more likely than males to support making birth control pills available to teenagers. Control variables could include age (older females and older males may be less likely to support making birth control pills available to teenagers); religious fundamentalism (with those who are more conservative less likely to support making birth control pills available to teenagers); political affiliation (with liberals more likely to support making birth control pills available to teenagers). Other possible control variables: race, class, degree.

General Exercise 5:

The older the respondents are, the more likely they are to believe that it is wrong for teenagers to be having sex. Control variables could include sex (with male respondents less likely to believe teenagers having sex is wrong than female respondents), religious fundamentalism, political affiliation, race, class, and degree.

CHAPTER 2

General Exercise 1:

Own or rent home: categorical and nominal

Marital status: categorical and nominal

Head of household: categorical and ordinal; dichotomous

Employment status: categorical and nominal

Political party affiliation: categorical and nominal

Number of adults 18 or older: numerical

Level of education: categorical and nominal

Total number living in household: categorical and ordinal (may be treated as numerical)

Age of respondent: numerical

Attitudes toward teenage sexual activity with precautions: categorical and ordinal

Attitudes toward teenage sexual activity with birth control: categorical and nominal

General Exercise 3:

Total number living in household: discrete

Age of respondent: continuous

Attitudes toward teenage sexual activity with precautions: continuous

Attitudes toward teenage sexual activity with birth control: continuous

SPSS Exercise 1:

Open your gss96subset file. Click on the Variables icon (the one with the blue question mark on it). Check the level of measurement of each variable—nominal, ordinal, or scale (numerical)—against your own classification of the variables for General Exercise 2.

CHAPTER 3

General Exercise 1:

Suggested codes for the variables in General Exercise 1, Chapter 2. The levels of measurement for each of the variables are in the answers to General Exercise 1.

Adult Demographic Variables

1. **Own or rent home?** Variable Name: ownrent (or any other 8-character name that follows the SPSS rules for naming variables)

   1 Own
   2 Rent
   7 Don't know
   8 Refused [to answer]
   9 Missing data

2. **Marital status** Variable Name: marital

   1 Single
   2 Single, living with a partner
   3 Married
   4 Separated
   5 Widowed
   6 Divorced
   9 Missing data

3. **Are you the head of the household?** Variable Name: headhous

   1 Yes
   2 No
   9 Missing data

4. **Employment status** Variable Name: wrkstat

   1 Full-time
   2 Part-time
   3 Retired
   4 Housewife
   5 Student
   6 Temporarily unemployed
   7 Disabled/Handicapped
   8 Other
   9 Missing data

5. **Political party affiliation** Variable Name: partyaf

   1 Republican
   2 Democrat
   3 Independent
   4 Other
   9 Missing data

6. **Total number of adults 18 or older living in household**
Variable Name: adultpop

   9 Missing data

7. **Level of education**   Variable Name: edlevel

   1 Less than high school graduate
   2 High school graduate
   3 Some college
   4 College graduate
   5 Postgraduate school or more
   6 Technical school/other (unspecified)
   9 Missing data

8. **Total number living in household**   Variable Name: hompop

   8 Eight or more
   9 Missing data

Teen Demographics

9. **Age of Respondent**   Variable Name: age

   99 Missing data

Teen and Adult Attitude Variables

10. Some people think it is basically acceptable for high school teenagers to be sexually active, as long as they take steps to prevent pregnancy and sexually transmitted diseases including AIDS. Others do not think it is acceptable for high school teenagers to be sexually active whether they take precautions or not. Which comes closer to your view, the first statement or the second one?

    1 Teen sexual activity acceptable as long as teens take precautions; OR
    2 Teen sexual activity not acceptable even if they take precautions.
    9 Missing data

    Variable Name: teensex

11. I'm going to read you three statements about teens and sex. Please tell me which one comes closest to your view:

    1 Teens should NOT be sexually active and should not have access to birth control;
    2 Teens should NOT be sexually active, but teens who ARE should have access to birth control, OR

3 It's OKAY for teens to be sexually active, AS LONG AS they have access to birth control.

9 Missing data

Variable Name: pillok

12. Respondent identification number   Variable Name: ID

Level of measurement: nominal

SPSS Exercise 1:

Check your work by using the Variables icon to see each of the variables you created. Compare what you see for your variables with the variable names and labels and value names and labels you prepared for the variables. Make sure that

1. The variable names and labels appear as you entered them.
2. Each categorical variable has values and value labels, including values and labels for missing data.
3. Each numerical variable has at least one missing data value and label.
4. The level of measurement for each variable corresponds to the answers to General Exercise 1, Chapter 2.
5. There is an identification code variable.

CHAPTER 4

General Exercise 1:

Sex (X)	f	Percent	Cumulative Percent
Male	10	50	50
Female	10	50	100
Total	$N = 20$	100	

The respondents are equally divided between male and female. The distribution is as heterogeneous as you can get for this variable.

General Exercise 3:

Highest Year of School Completed (X)	f	Percent	Cumulative Percent
8	2	7	7
10	4	14	21
12	4	14	36
13	4	14	50
14	5	18	68
15	1	4	71
16	3	11	82
17	1	4	86
18	4	14	100
Total	N = 28	100	

Most respondents have completed at least 12 years of education. Only 21% of the respondents have less than 12 years. 79% have at least 12 years. A little less than one third of the respondents (29%) have completed at least 16 years—the equivalent of a college degree. Only 14% have 18 years of education. The distribution is fairly heterogeneous with the respondents distributed somewhat evenly across the categories of the variable.

General Exercise 5:

Sex Before Marriage (X)	f	Percent	Cumulative Percent
Always wrong	2	15	15
Sometimes wrong	4	31	46
Not wrong at all	7	54	100
Total	N = 13	100	

The majority of the respondents in this random sample believe that sex before marriage is not wrong at all. Slightly over half (54%) hold that belief, whereas 46% believe that it is sometimes wrong or always wrong. Relatively few (15%) believe that sex before marriage is always wrong. The distribution is fairly homogeneous, if you look at the large percentage of respondents who answered in the Not Wrong at All category. The distribution is more heterogeneous if you divide it between those who think that sex before marriage is at least sometimes wrong (46%) and those who think it is not wrong at all (54%).

SPSS Exercise 1:

The respondents to the 1996 General Social Survey are fairly evenly divided between males and females. Slightly more than half of the respondents (55.8%) are female, whereas a little less than half (44.2%) are male.

SPSS Exercise 3:

Most of the GSS 1996 respondents—nearly 81%—identified themselves as White. Less than one fifth (14%) of the respondents said they are Black, and about 5% identified themselves as Other.

SPSS Exercise 5:

Respondents to the 1996 GSS are somewhat divided on the issue of making birth control available to teenagers 14- to 16-years-old. Nearly 61% say it's OK to do that, but over 39% say that they disagree or disagree strongly with giving birth control to teenagers.

SPSS Exercise 7:

There is almost no difference between male and female respondents to the 1996 GSS on the issue of making birth control available to teenagers. A slightly higher percentage of females than males (61.4% vs. 59.6%) either agree or strongly agree that it's OK to give birth control to teenagers. Conversely, a slightly lower percentage of females as compared to males (38.6% vs. 40.4%) either disagree or strongly disagree with making birth control available.

SPSS Exercise 9:

As with males and females, there is almost no difference in support for giving birth control to teenagers ages 14–16 based on race. A slightly smaller percentage of respondents who identified themselves as White (60.3%) said they strongly agree or agree with making birth control available to teenagers as compared to those who identified themselves as Black (61.8%) or Other (62.1%).

SPSS Exercise 11:

Either a pie chart or a bar chart could be used to examine the distribution of responses to the variable *sex*. The distribution of responses to the variable *sex* is fairly heterogeneous. In the pie chart, the pie "slices" for males and females are about the same size, and in the bar chart, the bars for males and females are about the same height.

SPSS Exercise 13:

Either a pie chart or a bar chart could be used to examine the distribution of responses to the variable *pillok*. The distribution of responses to the variable *pillok* is fairly heterogeneous. In the pie chart, the pie "slices" for those who strongly agree, agree, disagree, or strongly disagree are about the same size, and in the bar chart, the bars are about the same height.

SPSS Exercise 15:

The frequency distribution for your recoded variable should look like this one:

RCTEENSX recoded teensex

		Frequency	Percent	Valid Percent	Cumulative Percent
Valid	1 Acceptable	83	2.9	4.3	4.3
	2 Not acceptable	1851	63.7	95.7	100.0
	Total	1934	66.6	100.0	
Missing	0 NAP	944	32.5		
	8 DK	23	.8		
	9 NA	3	.1		
	Total	970	33.4		
Total		2904	100.0		

Respondents to the 1996 GSS overwhelmingly believe that sex among teenagers is not acceptable. Nearly all (95.7%) say that teen sex isn't acceptable, whereas only 4.3% believe that it is acceptable. The distribution of responses to the recoded variable are very homogeneous. In contrast, respondents to the NCPTP study are less disapproving of sex among teens. Whereas nearly two thirds (63%) say that it isn't acceptable, over one third (35%) believe that it is acceptable as long as teens take precautions. Although still fairly homogeneous, the distribution of responses in the NCPTP is more heterogeneous than the distribution of responses in the 1996 GSS.

The differences in response to the variables in the two studies may be due to the wording of the questions. The GSS asks respondents whether sex among teenagers 14–16 is always wrong, almost always wrong, sometimes wrong, or not wrong at all. No conditions for teen sexual activity are specified, and the age group is specific. In the NCPTP study, the age group is high school teenagers (presumably 14–18 years old) and the conditions under which sexual activity might take place (with or without precautions) are specified.

SPSS Exercise 17:

The frequency distribution for your new *agecat* variable should look like this one:

AGECAT recoded age - four categories

		Frequency	Percent	Valid Percent	Cumulative Percent
Valid	1 18 thru 25	353	12.2	12.2	12.2
	2 26 thru 39	934	32.2	32.2	44.4
	3 40 thru 64	1167	40.2	40.3	84.7
	4 65 thru 89	444	15.3	15.3	100.0
	Total	2898	99.8	100.0	
Missing	99 NA	6	.2		
Total		2904	100.0		

SPSS Exercise 19:

The frequency distribution for your new *polaf* variable should look like this:

POLAF recoded political views

		Frequency	Percent	Valid Percent	Cumulative Percent
Valid	1 Liberal	696	24.0	25.4	25.4
	2 Moderate	1045	36.0	38.1	63.5
	3 Conservative	1002	34.5	36.5	100.0
	Total	2743	94.5	100.0	
Missing	8 DK	155	5.3		
	9 NA	6	.2		
	Total	161	5.5		
Total		2904	100.0		

CHAPTER 5

General Exercise 1:

The mode is Never Married. The most frequently occurring response to the *marital status* variable is Never Married. It is also the case that most respondents (85.6%) 18–21 years of age have never married.

General Exercise 3:

The mode is High School. The most commonly occurring response to the question about the respondents' highest degree obtained is High School. Slightly more than two thirds of the respondents ages 18–21 have high school degrees.

General Exercise 5:

The median is High School. (The median case is 58.5. $N + 1 = 116 + 1 = 117$. $117 \times .50 = 58.5$. The value associated with case 58.5 is 1, High School, and the value at the 50th percentile is value 1, High School.) Half of the respondents ages 18–21 have at least finished high school, whereas half either have completed high school or have less than high school educations.

General Exercise 7:

The median is More or Less Satisfied. (The median case is 59.5. $N + 1 = 118 + 1 = 119$. $119 \times .50 = 59.5$. The value associated with case 59.5 is 2, More or Less Satisfied, and the value at the 50th percentile is 2, More or Less Satisfied.) Half of the respondents ages 18–21 are satisfied or more or less satisfied with their financial situations, whereas half are more or less satisfied or not at all satisfied.

General Exercise 9:

The median is 2 Earners. (The median case is 58. The value associated with the 58th case is 2, and the value at the 50th percentile is 2.) Half of the respondents ages 18–21 have from 0 to 2 earners in their families, whereas half have 2 to 6 earners in their families.

General Exercise 11:

Use the formula for the mean of an ungrouped frequency distribution:

$$\overline{X} = \frac{\Sigma(fX)}{N} = \frac{249}{115} = 2.1652$$

The average number of earners in the families of respondents ages 18–21 is 2.17.

General Exercise 13:

Use the formula for the mean of an ungrouped frequency distribution:

$$\overline{X} = \frac{\Sigma(fX)}{N} = \frac{1,399}{118} = 11.8559$$

Respondents ages 18–21 have completed an average of 11.86 years of education.

General Exercise 15:

The distribution is positively skewed. The mean (2.17) is higher than the median (2).

General Exercise 17:

The distribution is negatively skewed. The mean (11.86) is lower than the median (12).

SPSS Exercise 1:

hrs1, the number of hours respondents worked last week, is a numerical variable. The mean, median, and mode are appropriate measures of central tendency.

The 40-hour work week seems to be alive and well among 1996 GSS respondents. The most frequently occurring response to the question "How many hours did you work last week?" is 40 hours. One third of the respondents said they worked 40 hours. Respondents said they worked an average of 42.35 hours per week. Half worked 40 hours or less and half worked 40 hours to 89 hours. Nearly three quarters of the respondents (74.2%) worked at least 40 hours. Only about 20% worked 50 hours or more in one week, and slightly less than 8% worked 60 hours or more. Similarly, slightly more than 8% worked 20 hours a week or less, and only 12.6% worked less than 30 hours.

SPSS Exercise 3:

hompop, the number of persons in the respondents' households, is a numerical variable. The mean, median, and mode are appropriate measures of central tendency.

Respondents to the 1996 GSS live in fairly small households. The most frequently occurring response to the question pertaining to the number of persons living in a household is 2. Over one third (34%) of the respondents live in households of 2 people. The average size of the respondents' households is 2.55 members. Half of the respondents are living in households of 1 to 2 members, and half are living in households of from 2 to 10 members. About one quarter live alone—households of 1 person—and less than 10% live in households of more than 4 people.

SPSS Exercise 5:

There is almost no difference at all in the number of hours worked in a week for respondents who have children compared to respondents who have no children. The most frequently occurring response for both groups is 40 hours per week, although 30% of those without children reported working 40 hours as compared to 34.6% of those with children. A larger percentage of respondents without children (44.2% vs. 39.6%) worked more than 40 hours. The median for each group is 40 hours—half work more than 40 hours and half work less, and the average of the hours worked each week is nearly identical—42.38 for those with no children compared to 42.29 hours per week for those with children. By all measures, the number of hours worked each week as reported by the 1996 respondents is about the same, regardless of whether the respondents have children or not.

SPSS Exercise 7:

satfin, satisfaction with one's financial situation, is ordinal. The mode and the median are appropriate measures of central tendency. Males and females are about equally satisfied with their financial situations. The percentage of males and females who said they are satisfied is nearly identical. The most frequently occurring response among both groups to the question in the 1996 GSS about satisfaction with one's financial situation is More or Less Satisfied. Half of the males said they are satisfied or more or less satisfied, and half said they are more or less satisfied or not at all satisfied. The same is true for the female respondents. However, a larger percentage of female respondents (30.3%) are not at all satisfied as compared to male respondents (24.6%).

SPSS Exercise 9:

finrela, opinion of family income, is an ordinal variable. The mode and median are appropriate measures of central tendency. Females are about as likely as males to perceive their family incomes to be average. However, females are a little more likely to say their incomes are below average. For both males and females, the most frequently occurring response to the 1996 GSS question about family incomes is that respondents perceive their incomes as average. Half of the female respondents believe their incomes to be average to far below average, and half perceive their incomes to be average to far above average. The same is true for males. However, 33.6% of female respondents believe their family incomes are below average or far below average, whereas 26.8% of male respondents believe their incomes are in the below average or far below average range. On the other hand, 24.9% of male respondents (compared to 18.1% of female respondents) believe their incomes are above average or far above average.

CHAPTER 6

General Exercise 1:

The formula for the IQV is:

$$IQV = \frac{\text{total observed differences}}{\text{maximum possible differences}}$$

To find the numerator, use the formula for observed differences:

$$\text{observed differences} = \Sigma f_i f_j$$

$$= 16(1 + 101) = 16(102) = 1{,}632$$

$$1(101) = \underline{\qquad\qquad 101}$$

$$1{,}733$$

To find the denominator, use the formula for maximum possible differences:

$$\text{possible differences} = \frac{K(K-1)}{2}\left(\frac{N}{K}\right)^2$$

$$= \frac{3(3-1)}{2}\left(\frac{118}{3}\right)^2$$

$$= \frac{3(2)}{2}(39.3333)^2$$

$$= \frac{6}{2}(1{,}547.1084) = 3(1{,}547.1084)$$

$$= 4{,}641.3252$$

Return to the formula for the IQV and insert the results for the total observed differences and the maximum number of possible differences:

$$IQV = \frac{\text{total observed differences}}{\text{maximum possible differences}}$$

$$= \frac{1{,}733}{4{,}641.3252}$$

$$= .37$$

The distribution of responses is more homogeneous than heterogeneous (or you could say the distribution of responses is fairly homogeneous). This interpretation of the IQV is supported by an analysis of the frequency distribution. Most respondents (85.6%) are concentrated in one category of the variable, Never Married.

General Exercise 3:

The mode is working full-time. The formula for the IQV is:

$$IQV = \frac{\text{total observed differences}}{\text{maximum possible differences}}$$

To find the numerator, use the formula for observed differences:

$$\text{observed differences} = \Sigma f_i f_j$$

$$= 79(3 + 3 + 2) = 79(8) = 632$$

$$3(3 + 2) = 3(5) = \qquad 15$$

$$3(2) = \qquad\qquad \underline{\quad 6}$$

$$\qquad\qquad\qquad\qquad 653$$

To find the denominator, use the formula for maximum possible differences:

$$\text{possible differences} = \frac{K(K-1)}{2}\left(\frac{N}{K}\right)^2$$

$$= \frac{4(4-1)}{2}\left(\frac{87}{4}\right)^2 = \frac{4(3)}{2}(21.75)^2$$

$$= \frac{12}{2}(473.0625) = 6(473.0625)$$

$$= 2{,}838.375$$

Return to the formula for the IQV and insert the results for the total observed differences and the maximum number of possible differences:

$$\text{IQV} = \frac{\text{total observed differences}}{\text{maximum possible differences}}$$

$$= \frac{653}{2{,}838.375}$$

$$= .23$$

The distribution of responses is somewhat homogeneous. This interpretation of the IQV is supported by an analysis of the frequency distribution. The vast majority of respondents (90.8%) are concentrated in one category of the variable, Working Full-Time.

General Exercise 5:

The mode and the median are high school (value 1). The formula for the interquartile range is $Q_3 - Q_1$. First, find the value at Q_1:

Locate the case at Q_1 with the formula $(N + 1)(.25) = (116 + 1)(.25) = 29.25$.

Locate the value at Q_1. The case at Q_1 is associated with the value 0 (less than high school).

Second, find the value at Q_3:

Locate the case at Q_3 with the formula $(N + 1)(.75) = (116 + 1)(.75) = 87.75$.

Locate the value at Q_3. The case at Q_3 is associated with the value 1 (high school).

Find the interquartile range: $Q_3 - Q_1 = 1 - 0 = 1$. In relation to the range $(2 - 0 = 2)$, the distribution is fairly heterogeneous. Half of the respondents have either a less than high school or a high school education. One quarter have less than high school, and another quarter have high school or junior college degrees.

General Exercise 7:

The formula for the interquartile range is $Q_3 - Q_1$. First, find the value at Q_1:

Locate the case at Q_1 with the formula $(N + 1)(.25) = (118 + 1)(.25) = 29.75$.

Locate the value at Q_1. The case at Q_1 is associated with the value 1 (not at all satisfied).

Second, find the value at Q_3:

Locate the case at Q_3 with the formula $(N + 1)(.75) = (118 + 1)(.75) = 89.25$.

Locate the value at Q_3. The case at Q_3 is associated with the value 3 (satisfied).

Find the interquartile range: $Q_3 - Q_1 = 3 - 1 = 2$. In relation to the range $(3 - 1 = 2)$, the distribution is heterogeneous. Half of the respondents are satisfied, more or less satisfied, or not at all satisfied. One quarter are satisfied and another quarter are not at all satisfied.

General Exercise 9:

The measures of central tendency appropriate for this variable are the mode and the median. The most frequently occurring response to the question "Who earns more money?" among respondents who earn $75,000 or more is "I earn much more than my spouse." The median is the same. The formula for the interquartile range is $Q_3 - Q_1$. First, find the value at Q_1:

Locate the case at Q_1 with the formula $(N + 1)(.25) = (41 + 1)(.25) = 10.5$.

Locate the value at Q_1. The case at Q_1 is associated with the value 1 (I earn much more than my spouse).

Second, find the value at Q_3:

Locate the case at Q_3 with the formula $(N + 1)(.75) = (41 + 1)(.75) = 31.5$.

Locate the value at Q_3. The case at Q_3 is associated with the value 1 (I earn much more than my spouse).

Find the interquartile range: $Q_3 - Q_1 = 1 - 1 = 0$. In relation to the range $(4 - 1 = 3)$, the distribution is very homogeneous. Over 80% of the respondents say they earn much more than their spouses. This category includes the middle 50% of the respondents who all earn much more than their spouses. Less than one quarter of the respondents earn somewhat more or the same amount or have spouses who earn somewhat more.

General Exercise 11:

The formula for a standard deviation from an ungrouped frequency distribution is:

$$\overline{X} = 2.1652 \qquad N = 115 \qquad \Sigma fX^2 = 721$$

$$s = \sqrt{\left(\frac{\Sigma fX^2}{N-1}\right) - \left[\left(\frac{N}{N-1}\right)(\overline{X})^2\right]}$$

$$= \sqrt{\left(\frac{721}{115-1}\right) - \left[\left(\frac{115}{115-1}\right)(2.1652)^2\right]}$$

$$s = 1.26$$

Assuming a normal distribution of responses to the question "How many in your family earned money?" about 68% of the responses fall in the range of .91 to 3.42, or from about 1 earner to between 3 and 4 earners. Given the range of responses to the variable $(6 - 0 = 1)$, this is a more homogeneous than heterogeneous distribution. Most respondents are concentrated in the categories of 1 to 3 earners.

General Exercise 13:

Apply the formula for the standard deviation from an ungrouped frequency distribution.

$$\overline{X} = 11.8559 \qquad N = 118 \qquad \Sigma fX^2 = 16,793$$

$$s = \sqrt{\left(\frac{\Sigma fX^2}{N-1}\right) - \left[\left(\frac{N}{N-1}\right)(\overline{X})^2\right]}$$

$$= \sqrt{\left(\frac{16,793}{118-1}\right) - \left[\left(\frac{118}{118-1}\right)(11.8559)^2\right]}$$

$$s = 1.33$$

Assuming a normal distribution of scores for the variable years of education, we can estimate that about 68% of the respondents to the 1996 GSS in the 18 to 21 age bracket have between 10.53 and 13.19 years of education. The distribution is fairly homogeneous. Sixty-eight percent of the respondents are concentrated in less than three of the eight categories of the variable in the range.

General Exercise 15:

Appropriate measures of central tendency are the mode (16 years of education), the median (16 years of education), and the mean (16.5632 years of education). The most frequently occurring response to the question about how many years of school have been completed among 1996 GSS respondents who earn more than $75,000 a year is 16 years of education. Half have 11 to 16 years of education, and half have 16 to 20 years. Respondents completed an average of 16.56 years of education. The formula for a standard deviation from an ungrouped frequency distribution is:

$$\overline{X} = 16.5632 \qquad N = 87 \qquad \Sigma f X^2 = 24{,}475$$

$$s = \sqrt{\left(\frac{\Sigma f X^2}{N-1}\right) - \left[\left(\frac{N}{N-1}\right)(\overline{X})^2\right]}$$

$$= \sqrt{\left(\frac{24{,}475}{87-1}\right) - \left[\left(\frac{87}{87-1}\right)(16.5632)^2\right]}$$

$$s = 2.66$$

Assuming a normal distribution of responses to the variable, about 68% of the responses fall in the range of 13.90 to 19.22, or about 14 years to about 19 years of education. Given the range of responses to the variable ($20 - 11 = 9$), this is a somewhat heterogeneous response, although there are concentrations of responses in the categories 12 Years of Education, 16 Years of Education, and 20 Years of Education, perhaps because these categories represent the completion of high school, bachelor's, and graduate degrees.

SPSS Exercise 1:

Respondents' incomes seem to be fairly modest. The interquartile range for the responses to the variable *respondent's income* runs from $10,000 to $39,999. Half of the respondents to the 1996 GSS have incomes in that somewhat low to moderate range of individual incomes. The IQR is 8 ($17 - 9 = 8$), and the range is 20 ($21 - 1$). Consequently, the distribution is a little more homogeneous than heterogeneous, although the frequency distribution indicates a fairly heterogeneous distribution. One quarter of the respondents have incomes in the $10,000 to $12,499 range or less, and one quarter have incomes in the $35,000 to $39,999 range or more.

SPSS Exercise 3:

Family incomes for those 1996 GSS respondents with children seem a little lower when compared to those for respondents with no children. The interquartile range among respondents who have children is 8 ($19 - 11 = 8$), whereas the interquartile range for those with no children is 7 ($19 - 12 = 7$). The range for both distributions is 20, so both distributions are slightly more homogeneous than heterogeneous, although the frequency distributions for both variables show fairly heterogeneous responses.

Half of the respondents with children have family incomes from $15,000 to $59,999, whereas half of the respondents with no children have family incomes within a narrower and slightly higher range of $17,500 to $59,999. On the other hand, a higher percentage of respondents with children have family incomes of $75,000 or more (14%) as compared to those respondents with no children (9.8%).

The boxplots for those who have children and those who don't confirm this analysis. The boxplot for those with no children shows a more homogeneous distribution of responses to the variable *respondent's family income*.

SPSS Exercise 5:

Men who responded to the 1996 GSS are more satisfied with their financial situations than women. Responses to the variable, *satisfaction with one's finances,* indicate that men are on the whole more satisfied than women. The interquartile ranges (1 for men compared to 2 for women) show a more homogeneous set of responses among men as compared to women. Half of the male respondents are either satisfied or more or less satisfied with their financial situations, whereas the middle 50% of female responses range from satisfied to not at all satisfied.

The boxplots for these distributions confirm our analysis. The boxplot for male respondents shows that half of the male respondents are at the median (more or less satisfied) or higher (satisfied), whereas the female responses are more evenly dispersed on either side of the median (more or less satisfied), including not at all satisfied and satisfied.

CHAPTER 7

General Exercise 1:

Whereas males and females are about equally likely to say they are Republicans, males are somewhat more likely to say they are Independents than are females. Females are more likely to say they are Democrats than are males. The association appears to be fairly strong, with 26% more men than women saying they are Independent, whereas 37% more women than men say they are Democrats. Men are more likely than women to say they have some other party affiliation.

	Sex		
Party Affiliation	Male	Female	Row Totals
Democrat	2 20%	8 57%	10 42%
Independent	4 40%	2 14%	6 25%
Republican	3 30%	4 29%	7 29%
Other	1 10%	0 0%	1 4%
Column Totals	10 100%	14 100%	N = 24

General Exercise 3:

There is not much effect of satisfaction with respondents' finances on their likelihood of voting in the 1992 elections. Slightly higher percentages of those who are satisfied with their finances voted as compared to those who are more or less satisfied or not at all satisfied. Those who are more or less satisfied are a little less likely to have voted as compared to those who are not at all satisfied.

Did Respondent Vote in 1992?	Satisfaction With Financial Situation			
	Not at All Satisfied	More or Less Satisfied	Satisfied	Row Totals
Voted	9 82%	9 90%	8 100%	26 90%
Did not vote	2 8%	1 10%	0 0%	3 10%
Column Totals	11 100%	10 100%	8 100%	N = 29

SPSS Exercise 1:

a. The Southeast; the Southeast

b. The Midwest; the Southeast; the Northeast

c. 66.8%; 26.7%

d. 2,854

SPSS Exercise 3:

a. Protestant; Protestant

b. Jewish; Other; Other

c. 66.8%; 26.7%

d. 2,850

SPSS Exercise 5:

1996 GSS respondents in the western half of the United States were a little more likely to vote than were voters in the eastern half of the United States. A slightly higher percentage of respondents in the Midwest (70.2%) and West (67.4%) voted as compared to respondents in the Northeast and the Southeast (about 65% in each region). A higher percentage of respondents from the Southeast did not vote (29%) as compared to respondents from the other regions (in the vicinity of 25%). Respondents in the West and the Northeast were a little more likely to say they were not eligible to vote. The association between region of residence and voting isn't very strong, though, because the differences in the percentages across the rows are not large.

SPSS Exercise 7:

Jewish respondents to the 1996 GSS were somewhat more likely to vote than respondents of other religions. 87.9% of Jewish respondents said they voted compared to the Protestant and Catholic respondents (69% and 66.6%, respectively).

In general, respondents who identified themselves as Protestant, Catholic, or Jewish were more likely to say they voted compared to respondents who said their religion is Other or who said they have no religious affiliation.

Conversely, Jewish respondents were the least likely to say they did not vote (9%) compared to Protestants and Catholics. Those whose religion is Other or who have no affiliation were the most likely to say they did not vote (31.1% and 32.6%). They are also the respondents most likely to say they are not eligible to vote.

The relationship seems like it could be weak to moderate. Nearly 20% more Jewish respondents voted as compared to those in the next highest category of voters, the Protestant respondents. Except for the responses of those who said they are Jewish, the differences in voting between respondents in the remaining categories of the variable are not as large.

SPSS Exercise 9:

As might be expected, respondents to the 1996 GSS who attend church frequently are more likely to say they are conservative. Those who attend church less frequently are more likely to identify themselves as liberals. Whereas 32.4% of those who never attend church say they are liberal, only 16% of those who attend church at least once a week say they are liberal. On the other hand, those who attend church at least once a week are more likely to say they are conservative (nearly 50%) as compared to those who never go (about 30%).

The direction of the association is positive, and the association looks like it could be in the moderate to moderately weak range. The differences in the percentages across the rows range from a maximum of nearly 16% among those who are liberal to 20% among those who are conservative. Moreover, the association appears to be fairly consistent for each category of the dependent variable.

SPSS Exercise 11:

a.   The nature of the association is nearly the same for males and females. Respondents in the Midwest and West are more likely to say they voted in the 1992 elections. However, in the Did Not Vote category, the association changes a little. Male voters in the Midwest and Northeast were the ones most likely to say they did not vote, but it was female voters in the Southeast and Northeast who were most likely not to vote.

b.   Although still not very strong, the association is somewhat stronger for females than for males. The association between region of residence and voting in the 1992 elections is almost nonexistent for males. At the most, only a few percentage points separate the respondents across the categories of the dependent variable.

c.   Sex seems to have an effect on the association between region of residence and voting. For males, the association weakens, whereas for females it becomes a little stronger than it is among respondents as a whole.

SPSS Exercise 13:

a. For both males and females, the nature of the association is the same. Older respondents are more likely to say they voted. Younger respondents are more likely to say they did not vote, and they are much more likely to say they were not eligible to vote.

b. The association is stronger for males than for females. As an illustration of the differences in strength, 87% of the male respondents in the age category 65 through 89 said they voted as compared to 27% of the respondents in the 18 through 25 category—a difference of 60%. By way of contrast, 81% of the female respondents in the age category 65 through 89 voted as compared to 35% of the respondents in the age category 18 through 25—a difference of 46%.

c. The general association between age and voting in 1992 seems fairly strong. However, sex seems to affect the association. Age matters somewhat more for males than it does for respondents as a whole (and a little less for females) when it comes to voting.

CHAPTER 8

General Exercise 1:

Among the 1996 GSS respondents between the ages of 18 and 21, those who identify themselves as Jewish or having no religion are more likely to also identify themselves as liberal than are Protestants, Catholics, or those who say they are Other. Fifty percent of those who say they are Jewish and 40% of those with no religious affiliation say they are liberal as compared to Protestants (14%), Catholics (17%), and Others (0%). Those with some other religious identity are the most likely to say they are moderates. Eighty eight percent of them said they are moderates compared to about half of the Protestant, Catholic, and Jewish respondents and about a quarter of those with no religious affiliation. About a third of the Protestants, Catholics, and respondents with no affiliation say they are conservative, compared with the Other respondents (13%) and Jewish respondents (0%).

The association looks moderate to moderately weak. Some of the differences in the percentages across the rows are fairly large, but others are not.

Lambda can be computed with the formula:

$$\lambda = \frac{E_1 - E_2}{E_1} = \frac{57 - 53}{57} = \frac{4}{57} = .07$$

Lambda is fairly weak, when interpreted on the number line scale from 0 to 1. Knowing the respondents' religious preference (and knowing the general association between religious preference and political affiliation) improves our ability to predict their political affiliation by 7%.

General Exercise 3:

Among the 1996 GSS respondents between the ages of 18 and 21, male respondents are more likely than females to identify themselves as liberal or moderate, whereas female respondents are more likely than males to call themselves conservatives. Nearly 25% of the male respondents say they are liberal compared to 16% of female respondents, whereas 38% of female respondents say they are conservative compared to 26% of the male respondents. The percentages of male and female moderates are about the same: 49% for males and 46% for females.

Lambda can be computed using the formula:

$$\lambda = \frac{E_1 - E_2}{E_1} = \frac{57 - 57}{57} = \frac{0}{57} = 0$$

What does lambda tell us? Not much in this case, because the lambda of zero is misleading. The lambda of zero does not mean there is no association. There is an association between sex and political affiliation as previously described.

General Exercise 5:

In general, among 1996 GSS respondents between the ages of 18 and 21, the more satisfied the respondents are with their financial situations, the more likely they are to identify themselves as conservatives. Forty-two percent of those who are satisfied say they are conservatives, whereas 17% of those who are not at all satisfied say they are conservatives. In contrast, 24% of those who are not at all satisfied with their finances and 26% of those who are more or less satisfied say they are liberal, as compared to only 9% of those who are satisfied. The direction of the association is positive. The association looks like it might be fairly weak. Although there are clear differences, they aren't large ones, and the pattern isn't consistent across all categories of the dependent variable. For example, those who are not at all satisfied are more likely to be moderate as compared to those who are more or less satisfied, but those who are satisfied are also more likely to be moderate than those who are more or less satisfied.

To compute gamma, use the formula:

$$\text{gamma} = \frac{C - D}{C + D}$$

The number of concordant pairs $(C) = 1,570$. The number of discordant pairs $(D) = 858$. Inserted into the formula for gamma:

$$\frac{C - D}{C + D} = \frac{1,570 - 858}{1,570 + 858} = .29$$

The value of gamma suggests that the relationship between satisfaction with the respondents' financial situation and political affiliation is somewhat weak (in the context of the number line). It is positive, indicating that the more satisfied respondents are, the more conservative they are likely to be. Knowing the respondents' level of satisfaction with their financial situations improves our ability to predict their political affiliation by 29% (if we also know the general association between the two variables), and that's a fairly good level of improvement.

General Exercise 7:

The association between class and political affiliation among the 1996 GSS respondents ages 18 through 21 is not very clear. In general, it looks as though the higher the respondents' self-reported social class position, the more likely they are to say they are conservative. Working-class respondents are more likely to say they are liberal than are lower-, middle-, or upper-class respondents. Middle-class respondents are more likely to say they are conservative than are lower-, working-, or upper-class respondents. However, the lower-class respondents are more likely to say they are moderate than are working- or middle-class respondents. This is also true of the upper-class respondents, who are more likely to say they are moderate than the working- or middle-class respondents. The direction of the association appears to be positive.

The association looks like it might be weak. It is not consistent across the rows of the dependent variable, and the differences in the percentages are sometimes large, but mostly not very large at all.

To compute gamma, use the formula:

$$\text{gamma} = \frac{C - D}{C + D}$$

The number of concordant pairs $(C) = 1,384$. The number of discordant pairs $(D) = 732$. Inserted into the formula for gamma:

$$\frac{C - D}{C + D} = \frac{1,384 - 732}{1,384 + 732} = .31$$

The value of gamma suggests that the relationship between self-reported social class and political affiliation is somewhat weak (in the context of the number line). It is positive, indicating that the higher the respondents' self-reported social class is, the more conservative they are likely to be. Knowing the respondents' social class improves our ability to predict their political affiliation by 31% (if we also know the general association between the two variables), and that's a fairly good level of improvement.

SPSS Exercise 1:

Symmetric lambda (with *vote92* dependent) is zero. However, this is misleading. There is an association, as described earlier. Tau is weak at .002.

SPSS Exercise 3:

Symmetric lambda (with *vote92* dependent) is zero. However, this is misleading. There is an association, as described earlier. Tau is weak at .012.

SPSS Exercise 5:

The lower the respondents' self-reported social class, the more likely the respondents are to say they are liberal. Twenty-eight percent of the respondents to the 1996 GSS who identified themselves as lower class also identified themselves as liberal, as compared to close to a quarter of the working-, middle-, and upper-class respondents. Conversely, over half of the upper-class respondents identified themselves as conservative, compared with around one third of the lower-, working-, and upper-class respondents. The association is positive, and it appears to be fairly consistent (although not entirely consistent) across the categories of the dependent variable. Except for the category Conservative, the differences in percentages across the categories of the dependent variable are small.

Gamma is fairly weak at .085. Knowing the respondents' social class only improves our ability to predict their political affiliation (if we know the general association between social class and political affiliation) by 8.5%.

SPSS Exercise 7:

There isn't much of an association between respondents' assessments of their family income and their political affiliation. In general, it appears that the better the respondents' perceptions of their family incomes are, the more likely they are to be conservatives. Forty-three percent of the respondents who say their income is far above average are conservative, as compared to 38.7% of those who say their income is far below average. However, respondents whose incomes are far above average are also more likely than others to be liberal. Nearly 36% of those who say their income is far above average are liberal, whereas 28% of those whose income is far below average say they are liberal. The direction of the association looks positive, but it is a weak association. The differences in the percentages across the rows are small and the pattern is inconsistent.

Gamma, at .041, confirms that the association is positive—the better the respondents think their family income is, the more conservative they are likely to say they are—but it is weak. Knowing the respondents' opinions of their family incomes improves our ability to predict their political views only by 4% (assuming we know the general pattern of association between the two variables).

SPSS Exercise 9:

1996 GSS respondents who are satisfied with their financial situations are more likely to have voted in 1992, whereas those who are not satisfied are more likely to have not voted or to have been ineligible to vote. Seventy-four percent of the respondents satisfied with their financial situations voted, compared to 66% of those who were more or less satisfied and 61% of those who were not at all satisfied. On the other hand, 32% of those who were not at all satisfied did not vote (compared to 28% of those who were more or less satisfied and 19% of those who were satisfied). The association is fairly consistent across the categories of the dependent variable, but the differences in the percentages across the rows are moderate at best. Consequently, the association appears to be on the weaker side. The lambda of zero (with *vote92* dependent) is not very helpful in determining the strength of the association, because the modes of the categories of the independent variable are in the same row. Goodman and Kruskal's tau at .01 indicates a weak association, though.

Controlling for the variable *sex* reveals only a small effect of sex on the association between the respondents' satisfaction with their finances and their likelihood of voting in 1992. For males, the association appears to be a little stronger than it is among respondents as a whole. For women, it appears to be slightly weaker. The nature of the association is also slightly different for men than for women. Males who are satisfied with their financial situations are more likely to have been ineligible to vote than those who are more or less satisfied or not at all satisfied. Lambda isn't helpful at all in assessing strength, for the same reason as it wasn't helpful for assessing strength among respondents as a whole—the highest frequencies of the categories of the independent variable are in the same row. Goodman and Kruskal's tau confirms that the association is slightly stronger for men (.018) and weaker for women (.007).

SPSS Exercise 11:

Among respondents to the 1996 GSS, the better the respondents' perceptions of their family incomes are, the more satisfied they are with their financial situations. This is a positive association. The farther above average respondents perceive their income to be, the more satisfied they are. For example, 51% of those who say their family incomes are far above average say that they are satisfied with their financial situations, whereas only 14% of those whose incomes are perceived to be far below average are satisfied. On the other hand, 64% of those who say their incomes are far below average are not at all satisfied with their financial situations, whereas one quarter of those who think their incomes are far above average are not satisfied.

The association looks fairly strong—the differences in percentages across the rows are substantial—especially in the Satisfied and Not at All Satisfied categories of the dependent variable. The pattern of the association is fairly consistent, too.

Gamma is at least moderate at .478, and it is positive. Knowing respondents' opinions of their family incomes improves our ability to predict their satisfaction with their financial situations (assuming we know the general association between the two variables) by nearly 48%. That's a very good improvement.

Age does have an effect on the association between respondents' opinions of family income and their satisfaction with their financial situations.

The nature of the association doesn't change across the categories of the *age* variable, but the strength does. Analysis of gamma reveals that the association is strongest (.626) among the youngest (ages 18 through 25) respondents. This amounts to a nearly 15% improvement in the ability to predict the dependent variable from the independent variable as compared to respondents as a whole. It is a little stronger than it is among respondents as a whole for those respondents who are 26 through 39 (gamma = .527) and 65 through 89 (gamma = .514). It is weaker for those in the age category 40 through 64.

CHAPTER 9

General Exercise 1:

Your scatterplot should look like this one (with numbers instead of sunflower petals).

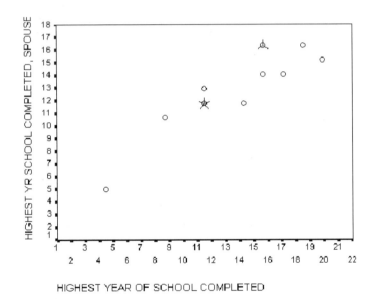

HIGHEST YEAR OF SCHOOL COMPLETED

The more education the respondents have, the more education their spouses are likely to have. The association is positive, and it appears to be fairly strong.

General Exercise 3:

The computational formula for Pearson's r is:

$$r = \frac{\Sigma XY - (N\bar{X}\bar{Y})}{\sqrt{(\Sigma X^2 - N\bar{X}^2)(\Sigma Y^2 - N\bar{Y}^2)}}$$

$\Sigma XY = 937$ $N\bar{X}\bar{Y} = 910$ $\Sigma X^2 = 871$

$\Sigma Y^2 = 1{,}010$ $N\bar{X}^2 = 845$ $N\bar{Y}^2 = 980$

$$r = \frac{937 - 910}{\sqrt{(871 - 845)(1{,}010 - 980)}}$$

$$r = .97$$

Pearson's r indicates a very strong positive association between the respondents' years of education and their spouses' years of education. The more education the respondents have, the more education their spouses are likely to have. The r-squared (.94) tells us that 94% of the variation in the respondents' spouses' years of education can be accounted for by the respondents' years of education. Another way to express it is that knowing the respondents' years of education improves our ability to predict their spouses' years of education by 94% (assuming we know the general association between respondents' years of education and spouses' years of education).

General Exercise 5:

Use the computational formula for Pearson's r (see the answer to General Exercise 3).

$\Sigma XY = 2{,}935$ $N\bar{X}\bar{Y} = 2{,}925$ $\Sigma X^2 - 10{,}375$

$\Sigma Y^2 = 871$ $N\bar{X}^2 = 10{,}125$ $N\bar{Y}^2 = 845$

$$r = \frac{2{,}935 - 2{,}925}{\sqrt{(10{,}375 - 10{,}125)(871 - 845)}}$$

$$r = .12$$

Pearson's r indicates a fairly weak but positive association between the respondents' ages and their years of education. The older the respondents are, the more years of education they are likely to have. The r squared (.01) tells us that 1% of the variation in the respondents' years of education can be accounted for by their ages. Another way to express it is that knowing the respondents' ages improves our ability to predict their years of education by 1% (assuming we know the general association between age and years of education).

General Exercise 7:

Use the formula for Pearson's r (see the answer to General Exercise 3).

$$\Sigma XY = 10{,}250 \qquad N\bar{X}\,\bar{Y} = 10{,}125 \qquad \Sigma X^2 = 10{,}375$$

$$\Sigma Y^2 = 10{,}225 \qquad N\bar{X}^2 = 10{,}125 \qquad N\bar{Y}^2 = 10{,}125$$

$$r = \frac{10{,}250 - 10{,}125}{\sqrt{(10{,}375 - 10{,}125)(10{,}225 - 10{,}125)}}$$

$$r = .79$$

Pearson's r indicates a strong positive association between the respondents' ages and the hours they work each week. The older the respondents are, the more hours they work each week. The r-squared (.62) tells us that 62% of the variation in the hours the respondents work each week can be accounted for by their ages. Another way to express it is that knowing the respondents' ages improves our ability to predict their hours worked by 62% (assuming we know the general association between age and hours worked per week).

General Exercise 9:

The computational formula for the slope of the regression line is:

$$r = \frac{\Sigma XY - (N\bar{X}\,\bar{Y})}{\Sigma X^2 - N\bar{X}^2}$$

numerator from Pearson's $r = 27$ $\qquad\qquad \Sigma X^2 - N\bar{X}^2 = 26$

$$b = \frac{27}{26}$$

$$b = 1.0385$$

The constant for the regression line is equal to:

$$a = \bar{Y} - (b)(\bar{X}) = 14 - (1.0385)(13) = .50$$

General Exercise 11:

Use the computational formula for the slope of the regression line (see the answer to General Exercise 9).

numerator for Pearson's $r = 10$ $\qquad\qquad \Sigma X^2 - N\bar{X}^2 = 250$

$$b = \frac{10}{250} = .04$$

The constant for the regression line is equal to:

$$a = \bar{Y} - (b)(\bar{X}) = 13 - (.04)(45) = 11.2$$

SPSS Exercise 1:

There is a little difference in the years of school completed among 1996 GSS respondents when the sample is divided by marital status. The most notable difference is that respondents who are widowed have nearly 2 years less education (11.42 years) than the average for all respondents (13.36 years). Those who have never been married have the highest average years of education (13.78). The difference may have more to do with age than marital status.

SPSS Exercise 3:

There is not much difference in average years of education among 1996 GSS respondents based on region of the country. Those in the Southeast have the lowest average, 13.03, whereas those in the West have the highest average, 13.91. The difference between the lowest and highest averages is less than 1 year, not a very big difference.

SPSS Exercise 5:

With respondents' education (*educ*) on the *x*-axis (the independent variable) and spouses' education (*speduc*) on the *y*-axis (the dependent variable), the association is positive. The more education respondents have, the more education their spouses are likely to have. The association looks fairly strong—with the line sloping fairly steeply and the sunflowers being somewhat close to the line, although forming a shape more like an oval than a cigar.

SPSS Exercise 7:

With respondents' education (*educ*) on the *x*-axis (the independent variable) and number of wage earners (*earnrs*) on the *y*-axis (the dependent variable), the association is positive. The more education respondents have, the more earners there are likely to be in their households. The association appears to be fairly weak, however. The slope of the line is slight, and the sunflowers are spread out around the line more like a shapeless cloud than an oval or a cigar.

SPSS Exercise 9:

The more education respondents have, the more education their spouses tend to have. Among respondents to the 1996 GSS, the correlation between respondents' years of education and their spouses' years of education is more than moderate at .573 and it is positive. The *r*-squared of .328 indicates that about 32% of the variation in the respondents' spouses' years of education can be accounted for by variations in the respondents' years of education.

We can insert the constant (*a*) for the regression line (5.79) and its slope (*b,* or .56) into the formula for a line, $y = a + bx$, to find the predicted value of the dependent variable when the independent variable is 16. A respondent's spouse can be expected to have 14.75 years of education when the respondent has 16 years of education.

SPSS Exercise 11:

The more education respondents have, the fewer children they are likely to have. Among 1996 GSS respondents the association is a somewhat weak, negative one, with Pearson's r equal to $-.234$. The r-squared, at .05, indicates that about 5% of the variation in the number of children respondents have can be accounted for by differences in their years of education. A respondent with 18 years of education can be expected to have 1.29 children.

SPSS Exercise 13:

When the relationship between education and race is reexamined controlling for sex, it is clear that sex influences the association somewhat. Although the differences in average years of education are not large for the categories of the *race* variable, they become larger for females and smaller for males when the control variable is introduced. For example, the gap between Whites and Blacks is almost a year for all respondents together. The gap between male Whites and male Blacks is a little smaller, .81 of a year, whereas the gap between female Whites and female Blacks is a little wider—a little over one year. On the other hand, when you look at the relationship between Whites and Others, the nature of the association changes. The gap between male Whites and male Others is larger than it is among females of those two groups. The same can be said of the differences between male Blacks and male Others, and female Blacks and female Others.

SPSS Exercise 15:

Sex has an effect on the strength of the association between respondents' years of education and their spouses' years of education, but it doesn't affect the nature of the association. When controlling for sex, the nature of the association between respondents' education and their spouses' education does not change. For both groups it is positive: the more education the respondents have, the more education their spouses are likely to have. The association is a little stronger for males than for females, however. Pearson's r for males is .601 as compared to .559 for females. The correlation for males is also a little stronger than it is for respondents as a whole, whereas the correlation for females is a little weaker than it is among respondents as a whole.

SPSS Exercise 17:

Class has almost no effect on the association between respondents' years of education and spouses' years of education. There is no effect at all on the nature of the association. It remains positive across class lines; the more education respondents have, the more education their spouses are likely to have. The strength of the association as measured by Pearson's r varies a little from one class to another, but the difference is negligible. There is very little difference between the weakest and the strongest associations. The strength of all of the associations is less than it is for respondents as a whole, however.

CHAPTER 10

General Exercise 1:

Use the formula for computation of a Z score.

$$X_i = 12 \qquad \overline{X} = 13.21 \qquad s = 2.91$$

$$Z = \frac{X_i - \overline{X}}{s}$$

$$= \frac{12 - 13.21}{2.91}$$

$$Z = -.42$$

The Z score of $-.42$ is almost one half of a standard deviation below the mean of 13.21. Assuming a normal distribution of scores, 16% of all respondents have between 12 and 13.21 years of education, whereas about 34% of the respondents have less than 12 years of education.

General Exercise 3:

Use the formula for computation of a Z score.

$$X_i = 16 \qquad \overline{X} = 13.21 \qquad s = 2.91$$

$$Z = \frac{X_i - \overline{X}}{s}$$

$$= \frac{16 - 13.21}{2.91}$$

$$Z = .96$$

The Z score of .96 is almost 1 standard deviation above the mean of 13.21. Assuming a normal distribution of scores, 33% of all respondents have between 13.21 and 16 years of education, whereas about 17% of the respondents have more than 16 years of education.

General Exercise 5:

The mean of the sampling distribution of sample means is 13.63. (Add up the means, and divide by 10.)

General Exercise 7:

The standard deviation of the sampling distribution of sample means is .47. Use the following formula:

$$\Sigma X^2 = 1{,}860.2614 \qquad N = 10 \qquad \overline{X} = 13.632$$

$$\sigma_{\overline{X}} = \sqrt{\left(\frac{\Sigma X^2}{N-1}\right) - \left[\left(\frac{N}{N-1}\right)(\overline{X})^2\right]}$$

$$= \sqrt{\left(\frac{1{,}860.2614}{10-1}\right) - \left[\left(\frac{10}{10-1}\right)(13.632)^2\right]}$$

$$\sigma_{\overline{X}} = .47$$

General Exercise 9:

Use the formula for computation of a Z score for population.

$$\overline{X} = 13.60 \qquad \mu_{\overline{X}} = 13.63 \qquad \sigma_{\overline{X}} = .47$$

$$Z = \frac{\overline{X} - \mu_{\overline{X}}}{\sigma_{\overline{X}}}$$

$$= \frac{13.60 - 13.63}{.47}$$

$$Z = -.06$$

Assuming a normal distribution of means, about 2% of all means in the sampling distribution will fall between 13.60 and the mean of the sampling distribution of sample means of 13.63. Another 48% of all means will fall below the sample mean of 13.60.

General Exercise 11:

Use the formula for computation of a Z score for population.

$$\overline{X} = 13.96 \qquad \mu_{\overline{X}} = 13.63 \qquad \sigma_{\overline{X}} = .47$$

$$Z = \frac{\overline{X} - \mu_{\overline{X}}}{\sigma_{\overline{X}}}$$

$$= \frac{13.96 - 13.63}{.47}$$

$$Z = .70$$

Assuming a normal distribution of means, about 26% of all means in the sampling distribution will fall between the mean of the sampling distribution of sample means of 13.63 and the sample mean of 13.96. Another 24% of all means will fall above the sample mean of 13.96.

General Exercise 13:

The standard error of the mean for the variable *speduc* is simply the standard deviation for the variable (2.85) divided by the square root of N (30), so the standard error is .52.

General Exercise 15:

The standard error of the mean for the variable *maeduc* with $N = 30$ is .62.

General Exercise 17:

The standard error of the mean for the variable *age* with $N = 50$ is 2.39.

General Exercise 19:

The standard error of the mean for the variable *maeduc* with $N = 50$ is .48.

SPSS Exercise 1:

a. .13832

b. .62556

c. 1.11280

d. 1.60004

SPSS Exercise 3:

The mean for the distribution of Z scores for the variable *paeduc* is 0.00 and its standard deviation is 1.00.

CHAPTER 11

General Exercise 1:

To find the standard error of the mean, use the following formula:

$$\sigma_{\bar{X}} = \frac{\sigma}{\sqrt{N}} = \frac{4.10}{\sqrt{2,066}} = .090$$

General Exercise 3:

$$\sigma_{\bar{X}} = \frac{\sigma}{\sqrt{N}} = \frac{2.85}{\sqrt{1,381}} = .077$$

General Exercise 5:

Use the confidence interval formulas:

$$CI_u = \bar{X} + (Z)(\sigma_{\bar{X}})$$

$$CI_l = \bar{X} + (Z)(\sigma_{\bar{X}})$$

To work the formulas we need the sample mean, the Z score for the confidence level specified, and the standard error of the mean.

$$\overline{X} = 14.53 \text{ (for Sample 1, General Exercise 6, Chapter 10)} \qquad Z = 2.00$$

$$\sigma_{\overline{X}} = .52 \text{ (computed for General Exercise 13 in Chapter 10)}$$

$$CI_u = 14.53 + (2.00)(.52)$$

$$CI_u = 15.57$$

$$CI_l = 14.53 - (2.00)(.52)$$

$$CI_l = 13.49$$

Ninety-five times out of 100 the population mean will fall between 13.49 years of education and 15.57 years of education. In this case, it does not.

General Exercise 7:

To work the formulas we need the sample mean, the Z score for the confidence level specified, and the standard error of the mean.

$$\overline{X} = 14.53 \text{ (for Sample 1, General Exercise 6, Chapter 10)} \qquad Z = 2.57$$

$$\sigma_{\overline{X}} = .52 \text{ (computed for General Exercise 13 in Chapter 10)}$$

$$CI_u = 14.53 + (2.57)(.52)$$

$$CI_u = 15.87$$

$$CI_l = 14.53 - (2.57)(.52)$$

$$CI_l = 13.19$$

Ninety-nine times out of 100 the population mean will fall between 13.19 years of education and 15.87 years of education. In this case, it does.

General Exercise 9:

Use the formula:

$$\sigma_P \sqrt{\frac{(P)(1 - P)}{N}}$$

$$P = .617 \text{ (from the frequency distribution on p. 462)} \qquad N = 1,844$$

$$\sigma_P = \sqrt{\frac{(.617)(1 - .617)}{1,844}} = .01$$

General Exercise 11:

Use the formulas for confidence intervals for proportions:

$$CI_u = P + (Z)(\sigma_P)$$

$$CI_l = P - (Z)(\sigma_P)$$

$P = .617$ $Z = 2.00$ $\sigma_P = .01$

$$CI_u = .617 + (2.00)(.01)$$

$$CI_u = .64$$

$$CI_l = .617 - (2.00)(.01)$$

$$CI_l = .60$$

There are 95 chances out of 100 that the proportion of people who have only some confidence in our major companies is between 60% and 64%.

General Exercise 13:

To construct a confidence interval at the 99% level, only the Z score changes (from 2.00 to 2.57).

$$CI_u = .617 + (2.57)(.01)$$

$$CI_u = .64$$

$$CI_l = .617 - (2.57)(.01)$$

$$CI_l = .59$$

There are 99 chances out of 100 that the proportion of people in the population who have only some confidence in our major companies is between 59% and 64%. You may notice that, in this case, increasing the confidence level does not expand the confidence limits by very much.

SPSS Exercise 1:

Use the following table to see whether you obtained the correct standard error of the mean for each variable, *paeduc, maeduc,* and *speduc,* and to check your work for General Exercises 1–3.

Descriptive Statistics

	N	Minimum	Maximum	Mean		Std.
	Statistic	Statistic	Statistic	Statistic	Std. Error	Statistic
PAEDUC HIGHEST YEAR SCHOOL COMPLETED, FATHER	2066	0	20	11.43	.090	4.10
MAEDUC HIGHEST YEAR SCHOOL COMPLETED, MOTHER	2472	0	20	11.50	.068	3.40
SPEDUC HIGHEST YEAR SCHOOL COMPLETED, SPOUSE	1381	1	20	13.45	.077	2.85
Valid N (listwise)	994					

The standard error of the proportion for the category At Least Some is .008. There are 99 chances out of 100 that the proportion of people in the population who have at least some confidence in our major companies is between 84% and 88%.

CHAPTER 12

General Exercise 1:

The following table shows the observed frequencies, the expected frequencies, and the ratio between the differences squared divided by the expected cell frequency for each cell.

HAPPY GENERAL HAPPINESS * AGE25_74 respondents ages 25 thru 74 Crosstabulation

			AGE25_74 respondents ages 25 thru 74			
			1 25 thru 30	2 31 thru 49	3 50 thru 65	4 66 thru 74
HAPPY GENERAL HAPPINESS	1 NOT TOO HAPPY	Count	34	156	67	24
		Expected Count	44	145	66	26
		observed - expected frequencies squared/ expected frequencies	2.273	.834	.015	.154
	2 PRETTY HAPPY	Count	230	727	308	110
		Expected Count	214	710	323	128
		observed - expected frequencies squared/ expected frequencies	1.196	.407	.697	2.531
	3 VERY HAPPY	Count	110	356	189	89
		Expected Count	116	384	175	69
		observed - expected frequencies squared/ expected frequencies	.310	2.042	1.120	5.797

The observed chi-square is 17.376. The table has 6 degrees of freedom. At 6 degrees of freedom, the observed value of chi-square exceeds the critical value (16.812) for $p = .01$. Consequently, the null hypothesis—that age and happiness are statistically independent—is rejected. It is not likely we could obtain a chi-square of this size in a table with 6 degrees of freedom by accident. The older the respondents are, the happier they say they are.

General Exercise 3:

The following table shows the observed frequencies, the expected frequencies, and the ratio between the differences squared divided by the expected cell frequency for each cell.

HAPPY GENERAL HAPPINESS * CLASS SUBJECTIVE CLASS IDENTIFICATION Crosstabulation

			CLASS SUBJECTIVE CLASS IDENTIFICATION			
			1 LOWER CLASS	2 WORKING CLASS	3 MIDDLE CLASS	4 UPPER CLASS
HAPPY GENERAL HAPPINESS	1 NOT TOO HAPPY	Count	42	122	108	6
		Expected Count	15	126	127	11
		observed - expected frequencies squared / expected frequencies	48.600	.127	2.843	2.273
	2 PRETTY HAPPY	Count	63	676	588	41
		Expected Count	75	617	622	55
		observed - expected frequencies squared / expected frequencies	1.920	5.642	1.859	3.564
	3 VERY HAPPY	Count	26	277	388	48
		Expected Count	41	333	336	29
		observed - expected frequencies squared / expected frequencies	5.488	9.417	8.048	12.448

The observed chi-square is 102.229. The table has 6 degrees of freedom. At 6 degrees of freedom, the observed value of chi-square far exceeds the critical value (22.457) for $p - .001$. Consequently, the null hypothesis—that social class and happiness are statistically independent—is rejected. It is not likely we could obtain a chi-square of this size in a table with 6 degrees of freedom by accident. The higher the self-reported social class of the respondents is, the happier they say they are.

SPSS Exercise 1:

The null hypothesis (H_0) is that there is no association between the respondents' sex and their happiness. Men and women are equally likely to say they are very happy, pretty happy, or not too happy. The contingency table for the variables *sex* and *happy* shows that there is very little difference between males and females in their self-reported levels of happiness, although a slightly higher percentage of men say they are very happy as compared to women. On the other hand, slightly higher percentages of women say they are pretty happy or not too happy. The association between sex and happiness is weak.

Lambda is equal to zero, but that is because the modes of the independent variable are all in the same row. Goodman and Kruskal's tau is very weak at .001. A chi-square of 3.304 does not exceed the critical value needed to reject the null hypothesis at the .05 level. Consequently, we cannot rule out the possibility that the degree of statistical dependence we observe in our sample is more likely than not due to chance instead of a real association between the variables in the population.

SPSS Exercise 3:

The null hypothesis (H_0) is that there is no association between the respondents' frequency of church attendance and their happiness. Those who attend frequently or infrequently are equally likely to say they are very happy, pretty happy, or not too happy. The contingency table for the recoded church attendance variable (*rcattend*) and *happy* shows that, in general, the more frequently respondents attend church, the happier they say they are. Nearly 40% of those who go to church at least once a week say they are very happy compared with about 27% of those who never go or go once a year or less. On the other hand, nearly 18% of those who never go say they are not too happy, whereas 10% of those who go at least once a week say the same. The association between church attendance and happiness looks like it might be in the weak to moderate range. The pattern of the association is fairly consistent across the rows of the dependent variable, but the differences in the percentages across the rows are not very large.

Gamma is .153, indicating a fairly weak, positive association. Knowing the respondents' frequency of church attendance improves our ability to predict their self-reported level of happiness by 15% (if we also know the general pattern of the association between the variables). The obtained value of chi-square, 52.553, far exceeds the critical value of chi-square needed to reject the null hypothesis at the .001 level. Consequently, we can conclude that a chi-square of this size in a table with 6 degrees of freedom is not likely to be a chance occurrence. More likely than not the association we see in the table—the more frequently people attend church, the happier they are—is true of the population.

CHAPTER 13

General Exercise 1:

The null hypothesis is that for the association between the number of hours respondents said they worked in a week and the number of hours they said they watched TV, Pearson's r would be expected to equal zero. There is no association between the number of hours worked and the numbers of hours spent watching television.

Pearson's r at $-.119$ tells us the association is a fairly weak, negative one. As might be expected, the more hours the respondents said they worked in a week, the less the number of hours they reported watching television. An r-squared of .01 indicates that only about 1% of the variation in hours spent watching TV can be accounted for by differences in the number of hours worked in a week. Knowing how many hours respondents worked in a week doesn't help us very much in predicting the number of hours they say they watch television.

Use the formula for finding the observed value of the t statistic for Pearson's r:

$$t \text{ (obtained)} = r\sqrt{\frac{(N-2)}{1-r^2}} = -.119\sqrt{\frac{(1,320-2)}{1-.119^2}} = -4.35$$

Even though the relationship is weak, the t statistic of -4.35 exceeds the critical value of t at the .05 level. Consequently, the null hypothesis can be rejected. It is not likely that we would obtain a t statistic of this magnitude at 1318 degrees of freedom by chance. More likely than not the association we find in our sample—the more hours respondents work in a week, the less they watch television—is true of the population.

General Exercise 3:

Use the formula for the one-sample t statistic:

$$\text{one-sample } t \text{ statistic} = \frac{X}{\dfrac{s}{\sqrt{N}}} = \frac{1.83}{\dfrac{1.68}{\sqrt{2,889}}} = 58.47$$

The observed value of t at 2888 degrees of freedom far exceeds the critical value of t for $p = .05$. The likelihood is remote that a t of this magnitude with 2888 degrees of freedom could be found by chance in a sample for which the mean is *not* representative of the population. Consequently, we accept the proposition that the average number of children reported by respondents, 1.83, is representative of the population from which the sample was drawn.

General Exercise 5:

Use the formula for the one-sample t statistic:

$$\text{one-sample } t \text{ statistic} = \frac{\overline{X}}{\dfrac{s}{\sqrt{N}}} = \frac{42.35}{\dfrac{14.14}{\sqrt{1,935}}} = 131.77$$

The observed value of t at 1934 degrees of freedom far exceeds the critical value of t for $p = .05$. The likelihood is remote that a t of this magnitude with 1934 degrees of freedom could be found by chance in a sample for which the mean is *not* representative of the population. Consequently, we accept the proposition that the average number of hours spent working in one week reported by respondents, 42.35, is representative of the population from which the sample was drawn.

General Exercise 7:

The null hypothesis is that the average number of self-reported hours spent watching TV will be the same for respondents who have at least some confidence in the legislative branch as it is for those respondents who say they have hardly any confidence.

To test the null hypothesis, start with the formula for the pooled t test:

$$\text{obtained pooled } t = \frac{\overline{X}_1 - \overline{X}_2}{\sqrt{\dfrac{s_p^2}{N_1} + \dfrac{s_p^2}{N_2}}}$$

From the table given in the exercise, you can find the following statistics you need to work the formula:

$\overline{X}_1$ (hardly any confidence) = 3.22　　$\overline{X}_2$ (at least some confidence) = 2.91

N_1 (hardly any confidence) = 447　　N_2 (at least some confidence) = 500

You will need to compute s_p^2 with the formula:

N_1 (hardly any confidence) = 447　　s_1 (standard deviation, hardly any) = 2.45

N_2 (at least some confidence) = 500　　s_2 (standard deviation, some confidence) = 2.44

$$s_p^2 = \frac{(N_1 - 1)s_1^2 + (N_2 - 1)s_2^2}{(N_1 + N_2) - 2}$$

$$= \frac{(447 - 1)2.45^2 + (500 - 1)2.44^2}{(447 + 500) - 2}$$

$$s_p^2 = 5.9767$$

Returning to the formula for the pooled t test:

$$\text{obtained pooled } t = \frac{\overline{X}_1 - \overline{X}_2}{\sqrt{\dfrac{s_p^2}{N_1} + \dfrac{s_p^2}{N_2}}} = \frac{3.22 - 2.91}{\sqrt{\dfrac{5.9767}{447} + \dfrac{5.9767}{500}}} = 1.94$$

The obtained t statistic of 1.94 with 945 degrees of freedom doesn't exceed the critical value of t of ± 1.960. Consequently, we cannot rule out that chance, and not an actual association between the number of hours spent watching television and confidence in the legislative branch of government, produced a t statistic of this magnitude. The null hypothesis, that there is no association between these two variables, cannot be rejected.

SPSS Exercise 1:

The null hypothesis is that $r = 0$ for the association between the number of hours the respondents' spouses worked in a week and the number of hours the respondents say they spent watching television. Another way to state the null hypothesis is that there is no association between the number of hours respondents' spouses work and the number of hours the respondents say they watch television.

At −.007, Pearson's *r* is very weak. The association between the number of hours the respondents' spouses worked in a week and the number of hours the respondents say they spent watching television is negligible. At −.169 the *t* statistic does not come close to reaching the critical value necessary for rejecting the null hypothesis at the .05 level. In fact, there are 866 chances in 1,000 that the *t* statistic of −.169 could be found by chance. Consequently, the null hypothesis cannot be rejected.

SPSS Exercise 3:

The *t* statistic for the variable *number of children* at 58.598 with 2888 degrees of freedom exceeds the critical value of *t* at $p < .0005$. It is unlikely that a *t* statistic of this magnitude would be obtained by chance in a sample drawn from a population with a mean different from the one in the sample. More likely than not, the mean of 1.83 children is representative of the population from which the GSS sample was drawn.

SPSS Exercise 5:

The *t* statistic for the variable *hours GSS respondents said they worked in a week* at 131.757 with 1934 degrees of freedom exceeds the critical value of *t* at $p < .0005$. It is unlikely that a *t* statistic of this magnitude would be obtained by chance in a sample drawn from a population with a mean different from the one in the sample. More likely than not, the mean of 42.35 hours worked in a week is representative of the population from which the GSS sample was drawn.

SPSS Exercise 7:

1996 GSS respondents who report having hardly any confidence in the legislative branch of the federal government have a higher average number of hours spent watching television than respondents who have at least some confidence, but the difference is small—about one half of an hour. The null hypothesis, that there is no association between time spent watching TV and confidence in the legislative branch, can be tested with the independent samples *t* test.

At 1.930 (assuming equality of variances) the *t* statistic falls just short of exceeding the critical value needed to reject the null hypothesis at the .05 level. As a result, we cannot rule out the possibility that a *t* statistic of this magnitude with 945 degrees of freedom could be obtained by chance.

Can we assume equality of variances? The *F* statistic is .306. It tests the likelihood of drawing a sample in which variances of the groups being compared are relatively unequal by chance from a population in which the variances are equal. (The null hypothesis is that the variances observed in the groups in a sample are drawn from a population in which the variances of the groups being compared are equal.) The *F* statistic, with its associated *p* value, indicates that there are 580 chances in 1,000 that an *F* statistic of this magnitude can occur as an artifact of sampling. The null hypothesis cannot be rejected. (Although technically an oversimplification, it might help to think of *accepting* the null hypothesis—that the relatively unequal variances observed in the groups being compared are not representative of variances in the population.)

SPSS Exercise 9:

Among respondents to the 1996 GSS, there are differences in the average number of self-reported hours spent watching television based on work status. Respondents who are retired, keeping house, or in some other work status, have the highest averages of time spent watching TV—around 4 hours to 4¼ hours per day. Those who are working full-time, part-time, or in school have the lowest averages of time spent watching TV—about 2½ to 2¾ hours per day.

The F ratio of 23.974 exceeds the critical value of F at $p < .0005$. Consequently, we can reject the null hypothesis—that there is no association between hours spent watching TV and work status. More specifically, it is unlikely that an F ratio of 23.974 would be found by chance in a sample drawn from a population in which there are no differences in the means for TV watching for the categories of work status.

Can we assume equality of variances? In terms of the null hypothesis, must we reject the proposition that the variances for the categories of work status are equal? Levene's statistic exceeds the critical value at $p < .0005$ needed to reject the null hypothesis. In rejecting the null hypothesis, we are saying it is unlikely that the variances among the groups are equal. Therefore, the equality of variances necessary for the one-way analysis of variance cannot be assumed.

SPSS Exercise 11:

Among respondents to the 1996 GSS, those who voted in 1992 or were not eligible to vote average less hours of self-reported TV watching than those who did not vote. The difference between those who voted and those who did not vote isn't very large—only six tenths of an hour. The difference between those who were not eligible to vote and those who didn't vote is slightly larger.

The F ratio of 13.310 exceeds the critical value of F at $p < .0005$. Consequently, we can reject the null hypothesis—that there is no association between hours spent watching TV and respondents' voting. More specifically, it is unlikely that an F ratio of 13.310 would be found by chance in a sample drawn from a population in which there are no differences in the average number of self-reported hours spent watching television between those who voted, did not vote, or were not eligible to vote.

Can we assume equality of variances? In terms of the null hypothesis, can we reject the proposition that the variances for the categories of work status are equal? Levene's statistic exceeds the critical value at $p < .0005$ needed to reject the null hypothesis. In rejecting the null hypothesis, we are saying it is unlikely that the variances among the groups are equal. Therefore, the equality of variances necessary for the one-way analysis of variance cannot be assumed.

Credits

Glossary/Index

Page numbers in **boldface** type denote the primary use of key terms.

median: The category of response that divides the respondents to a variable in half, **164**–172, 179–180
  computation of, 164–172
  interpreting, 172
  normal distribution and, 182–185
median case: In an ordered set of responses to a variable, the respondent in the middle, **165**
median value: The value associated with the median case, **165**
missing values: Variable categories—like NA, NAP, and DK in the General Social Survey—that capture instances in which respondents do not answer survey questions, **26**, 58–59
  SPSS define variable and, 70
mnemonics: Aids to remembering; the 8-character variable names in SPSS designed to remind us of the lengthier variable labels, **23**
  SPSS variable names and, 56–57
mode: The category or categories of response to a variable most frequently chosen by respondents; the category or categories of a variable with the largest frequencies, **160**–164, 179–180
  computation of, 160–163
  interpreting, 163
  normal distribution and, 182–185
multistage sampling process: A sampling technique in which there are several steps in the process of drawing a probability sample, involving the stratification of a sampling frame and/or clustering prior to the selection of a random sample of population elements, **12**

N: The total number of responses to a variable, **100**, 123–124
  in contingency tables, 253
nature of an association: In bivariate analysis, a description of how two variables are related to or associated with one another, **263**–264, 294–295
negative association: In bivariate analysis of ordinal or numerical variables, an association

in which an increase in the value of one variable is associated with a decrease in the value of a second variable or vice versa, **267**
negative skew: A distribution of responses to a variable in which there are more cases above the mean than below it, **184**
new label and value: In the SPSS recoding process, the values and labels of a new variable created by recoding an existing, old variable in a data file, **130**–131
new variable: In the SPSS recoding process, the variable created by recoding an existing, old variable in a data file, **129**
nominal variable: A categorical variable being measured in such a way that the categories indicate differences among respondents, with no hierarchy or rank order implied in those differences, **43**
nondirectional research hypothesis: A research hypothesis stating that an association exists between two variables in a population but not specifying its nature, **497**
nonlinear association: In bivariate analysis of ordinal or numerical variables, an association in which the pattern of the relationship cannot be summarized by a straight line, 268, **358**–359
normal distribution: A theoretical distribution of responses to a variable that is bell-shaped, unimodal, and symmetrical, and for which the mean, median, and mode have the same value, **183**, 407–408
null hypothesis (H_0): A hypothesis specifying that there is no relationship between two variables in a population, **465**
  testing with chi-square, 480–481
numerical (scale) variable: A variable for which data are gathered as inherently meaningful numbers, **39**

observed frequencies: The cell frequencies in a contingency table representing the number of respondents that meet the criteria of the cells, **469**
obtained value of a test statistic: The value of a test statistic computed from a sample, **468**
  See also chi-square, one-sample *t* test, independent samples *t* test, one-way analysis of variance
old label and value: In the SPSS recoding process, the values and value labels of the variable a researcher wants to recombine to create a new variable, **130**–131
old variable: In the SPSS recoding process, the variable for which a researcher wants to recombine categories to create a new variable, **129**
one-sample *t* test: A measure of inference appropriate for assessing a characteristic of a single sample, **506**–510
  computation of, 506–509
  degrees of freedom for, 508
  interpreting, 508–509, 510
  SPSS guide for, 509
one-tailed test of significance: A test of statistical significance for analyzing associations between two variables for which the research hypothesis is directional, **497**–498
one-way analysis of variance (ANOVA): A measure of inference appropriate for assessing the association between a dependent numerical variable and the categories of another, independent variable, **520**–528
  computation of, 522–523
  degrees of freedom for, 523–524
  F ratio and, 524
  interpreting, 527–528
  limitations of, 524–525
  SPSS guide for, 525–526
ordinal variable: A categorical variable being measured in such a way that the categories have some inherent rank, hierarchy, or order, **43**

outlier: An unusually high or low value of a variable in relation to the interquartile range, **214**–216

partial table: Contingency table showing an association between two variables for the categories of a third, control variable, **273**–275

Pearson's *r*: A measure of association for numerical variables assessing the extent to which two variables covary, **365**, 366–379

computation of, 366–371
control variables and, 384–387
interpreting, 371, 377–379
significance testing for, 499–504
SPSS guides for, 374–377, 504–505

percent column: The column in a frequency distribution showing the percentage of responses to the categories of a variable, **101**

percentage: The proportion of respondents to a category of a variable multiplied by 100, **124**–125

computation of, 124–125
cumulative, 101
valid, 101

percentile: The point at or below which a specified percentage of responses to a variable fall, **127**

phi and Cramer's *v*, 305

pie chart: A graphic representation of data in which the frequencies or percentages of response to the categories of a variable are depicted as slices of a pie, **119**–121

interpreting, 121
SPSS guide for, 119–121

point estimate: A characteristic of a sample being used as an estimate of a population parameter, **432**

pooled variance *t* test: In the independent samples *t* test, the *t* statistic that is appropriate when we can assume equality of variances in the distributions of responses to the test variable by the categories of the grouping variable, **512**–513

See also independent samples *t* test

population: The set of those elements a researcher wants to know something about, **9**, 10, 406

population parameters: Statistics that estimate the characteristics of populations, **414**

positive association: In bivariate analysis of ordinal or numerical variables, an association in which an increase in the value of one variable is associated with an increase in the value of a second variable, **266**

positive skew: A distribution of responses to a variable in which there are more cases below the mean than above, **184**

probability sample: A sample selected in such a way that each element in a population has the same chance of being drawn into the sample as every other element in the population, **11**

probability value: A statistic used to assess the likelihood that a test statistic of a particular magnitude would be found by chance in a sample drawn randomly from a population, **478**–480

proportion: The frequency of response to the category of a variable divided by the total number of responses to the variable, **124**

proportional reduction in error (PRE): The extent to which knowledge of the categories of an independent variable reduces one's errors in predicting the categories of a dependent variable, **294**

quartile: In an ordered distribution of responses to a variable, the value associated with the respondents who are at the 25th, 50th, or 75th percentiles, **204**
See also interquartile range

r-squared (coefficient of determination): A measure of association for numerical variables, it is the square of Pearson's *r*

and it has a proportional reduction in error interpretation, **365**, 371, 374–378

computation of, 371
control variables and, 384–387
interpreting, 371, 377–378
SPSS guide for, 374–377

range: A measure of dispersion for ordinal and numerical variables, it is the highest value minus the lowest value in a distribution of responses to a variable, **202**–203

computation of, 202–203
interpreting, 203

ratio variable: A numerical variable for which zero means the absence of the characteristic being measured. The distances between each of the units on a numerical scale are the same and proportional, **40**

raw data: Data that have not been processed in any way, **92**

raw scores: Scores in a set of data that have not been summarized in any way, **92**

recode diagram: The pencil-and-paper chart created prior to recoding a variable showing how the categories of an existing variable are to be recombined to create a new variable, **130**

recoding: In SPSS, a technique for data analysis that allows a researcher to change how the responses to the categories of a variable are classified by recombining variable categories, **129**–144

analysis of, 143
checking, 142–143
saving, 143
steps for, 129
SPSS define variable and, 138–142
SPSS guide for, 131–138

region of rejection: The area under the normal curve for the sampling distribution of a test statistic in which the test statistic computed for a specific sample must fall for the null hypothesis to be rejected, **502**

regression line: A mathematically derived line drawn through the points in a scatterplot in such a way as to minimize the average of the squared distances between the line and each of the points, **353**–355, 363–364, 372–374, 379–381

computation of, 372–374

predicting values of a dependent variable with, 379–381

SPSS guide for, 361–365

research hypothesis (H₁): A hypothesis that specifies there is a relationship between two variables, **465**

research process: The steps followed by social scientists for performing research, 6–9

row marginals: In a contingency table, the total number of responses to a single category of the dependent variable, **252**

sample: A subset of the elements of a population, 11, 406

sampling, 11–12

sampling distribution: The theoretical distribution of sampling statistics from all possible samples of a given size that could be drawn from the same population, 416

sampling distribution of sample means: The theoretical distribution of the means for all possible samples of a given size that could be drawn from the same population, **416**

sampling frame: A list of the elements in a population, **11**

sampling statistics: Statistics that describe the distribution of values for a variable, or relationships between variables, in a sample, 406–407, **414**

scale variable, 39

scatterplot: Visual display of the association between two numerical variables, **349**–352

constructing, 356–357

regression line on, 353–356, 363–365

SPSS guide for, 361–364

sunflowers on, 363–365

simple random sample: A sample in which each element selected for the sample is chosen at random, like drawing names out of a hat, **11**

skew: The extent to which a distribution of responses departs from normal, **183**–185

slope: In the computation of the regression line, the amount by which the dependent variable changes for each unit change in the independent variable, **372**

Somer's d: A measure of association with asymmetrical and symmetrical values used with ordinal variables and computed from contingency tables, **320**

splitting a data file, 105–108

spurious association: An association between an independent and a dependent variable that disappears when a third variable is included in the analysis, **274**–275

SPSS: A software program for the analysis of quantitative data produced by Statistical Product and Service Solutions, Inc., **6**, 17

data editor, 19

defaults, 65

dialog box, 96

exiting from, 29

menu, 19

output window, 98

switching screens, 99

tool bar, 19

variables icon, 25

standard deviation: A measure of dispersion for numerical variables, it is the square root of the variance, **219**–233

computation of, 220–222

interpreting, 223–224, 229–231

normal curve and, 231–233

SPSS guide for, 227–229

standard deviation of the sampling distribution of sample means, 418–419

standard error of the mean: The standard deviation of the sampling distribution of sample means, **420**–422, 433–437

computation of, 421

confidence intervals and limits and, 437–440

interpreting, 422, 434

SPSS guide for, 435–437

standard error of proportions, 449–453

computation of, 449–450

confidence intervals and limits and, 451–453

interpreting, 450

SPSS guide for, 453–455

statistical independence: A condition in which the changes in the values of one variable are unrelated to changes in the values of another, **467**

statistical significance: The likelihood that any pattern observed in a sample is not merely a chance occurrence, **482**

statistics: Numbers that help describe patterns in data or assess whether patterns we find in samples are likely to be representative of the populations from which the samples were drawn, **1**

stratification: A sampling technique in which the elements in a sampling frame are grouped according to one or more characteristics prior to being selected for a sample, **12**

strength of an association: In bivariate analysis, the extent to which two variables are related to or associated with one another, **265**–266

string variable, 65

student's t, 499

distribution of critical values of, 546

symmetric value: A value of a measure of association that assumes neither variable in an association is independent or dependent in relation to the other, **303**

symmetrical association: A relationship between variables in which neither variable is independent or dependent in relation to the other, **257**

symmetrical distribution, 183
See also normal distribution

systematic sampling with a random start: A variation on the simple random sampling technique in which only the first element in the sample is chosen at random and then each *n*th element is selected after that, **11**

t **test for unequal variances:** In the independent samples *t* test, the *t* statistic appropriate when we cannot assume equality of variances in the distributions of responses to the test variable by the categories of the grouping variable, **516**–517, 519–520

test statistic: A sampling statistic used in hypothesis testing— like chi-square and the *t* test—with its own sampling distribution, **468**
See also chi-square, Pearson's *r*, one-sample *t* test, independent samples *t* test, one-way analysis of variance

test variable: In the independent samples *t* test, the dependent, numerical variable being evaluated in relation to the categories of another variable, **510**

tied pair: In the bivariate analysis of ordinal variables, a relationship in which the value of the independent or dependent variable in one case is identical to one or both of the corresponding values in another, comparison case, **307**

two-tailed test of significance: A test of statistical significance for analyzing associations be-

tween two variables for which the research hypothesis is non-directional, **497**–498

Type I error: An error made by rejecting the null hypothesis when there is no association between two variables, **467**

Type II error: An error made by accepting the null hypothesis when there is an association between two variables, 467–**468**

unimodal distribution: A distribution of responses to a variable in which there is only one mode, **183**

unit of analysis: The specific entity that a researcher is trying to learn something about, **10**

univariate analysis: The analysis of variables, one at a time, **89**

valid cases: Cases for which respondents provided a meaningful answer to a question, **100**

Valid Percent column: The column in an SPSS frequency distribution showing the percentage of responses to the categories of a variable for which the computations exclude missing cases, **101**

value labels: The labels attached to category values, **24**

values of a variable: The numbers assigned to the categories of a variable, **13**

variability: The degree of variation, or the extent of the dispersion, in the responses to the categories of a variable, **197**

variable: Any aspect or characteristic of a unit of analysis that can vary from one unit to the next, **12**–13, 15–16

variable categories: The response categories researchers assign to variables, 13, **57**

variable label: In SPSS, the lengthier label assigned to a variable to describe it, 23, **67**

variable name: In SPSS, the 8-character mnemonic assigned to a variable, 23, **56**–57, 64

variance: A measure of dispersion for numerical variables calculated by averaging the squared deviations from the mean, **218**
computation of, 218
interpreting, 223
SPSS guide for, 227–229

***x*-axis and *y*-axis:** The *x*-axis is the horizontal axis on a bar chart, histogram, or scatterplot and the *y*-axis is the vertical axis, **116**
bar chart and histogram and, 116, 118
scatterplot and, 349

***y*-intercept (constant):** In the computation of the regression line, the value of the dependent variable when the independent variable is zero, **372**

Yates' correction: A mathematical adjustment to the formula for chi-square used whenever any of the expected cell frequencies in a contingency table is greater than 5 but less than 10, **483**

Z score: A number expressing the relationship between a particular value in a distribution of numerical variables and the mean in units of the standard deviation, **409**
computation of, for samples, 409
computation of, for populations, 419–420
confidence intervals and, 443–446
interpreting, 410–411
properties of, 412–414
SPSS guide for, 411–412